CONSTITUTIONAL THEORY

Carl Schmitt

CONSTITUTIONAL THEORY

Translated and edited by Jeffrey Seitzer

Foreword by Ellen Kennedy

Duke University Press   Durham and London 2008

Designed by C. H. Westmoreland
Typeset in Warnock Pro by Tseng Information Systems, Inc.

Library of Congress Cataloging-in-Publication Data
Schmitt, Carl, 1888–1985.
[Verfassungslehre. English]
Constitutional theory / translated and edited by Jeffrey Seitzer;
foreword by Ellen Kennedy.
p. cm.
Includes bibliographical references and index.
ISBN-13: 978-0-8223-4011-9 (cloth : alk. paper)
ISBN-13: 978-0-8223-4070-6 (pbk. : alk. paper)
1. Constitutional law—Germany. 2. Constitutional law.
I. Seitzer, Jeffrey. II. Title.
KK4450.S3613 2007
342.43—dc22   2007026690

FOR

Bob and Sherry Seitzer

Rob and Aleta Smith

Contents

Contents　　　　　　　　　　　　　　　ix

Contents xi

Foreword

Ellen Kennedy

The publication of Carl Schmitt's *Constitutional Theory* (1928) fills a significant gap in the available English translations of this important political thinker. The text is remarkable for two things: its rigorous conception of a constitution and its concepts and the mastery of historical evidence and usage that informed and for long shaped the central ideas of law and political theory in the West. *Constitutional Theory* has never been out of print in German, and has long been available in the other major European languages. It now appears here in a felicitous and scholarly translation by Jeffrey Seitzer at an especially appropriate time.

Written simultaneously with his most famous text, *The Concept of the Political*, Schmitt's *Constitutional Theory* addressed the boundary of the political. The first text makes the radical claim that the distinction between friend and enemy is a criterion by which all political actions and motives can be judged—a claim that appears to reduce our conception of politics to struggle, suggesting in a remarkable reversal of Clausewitz that politics is the extension of war by other means. The apparent imbalance is redressed by this book. The topic here is the political association of friends that is possible in the modern world and within the legal structure of the modern state.

Constitutional Theory differed importantly from other contemporary works on the "liberal rule of law state" (*bürgerliche Rechtsstaat*) and from standard texts on constitutional law then and now. In the first place, it is not a case book and not a commentary but the theory of a particular type of state "which is dominant today" and of which the Weimar constitution was one example. Although there is an extensive register of articles of the Weimar constitution discussed herein, the reader will not find an account comparable to those of Gerhard Anschütz and others that were the standard texts of university teaching in Germany and crucial to informed judicial opinion. Schmitt offers, instead, a system that demonstrates the relationship of law and politics to each other, not just in this one German constitution, but in all constitutional states of the "liberal rule of law" type. The result is a brilliant attempt at what we today call comparative constitutionalism, and the following pages are replete with examples from across modern political history. More than that, it is an as yet unsurpassed political theory of the modern state in an age of world wars fought by arms and ideas that transformed the original foundations of the state.

Here, as in Schmitt's other works, the tension between the democratic elements of the political constitution and liberal forms of the rule of law comes under scrutiny. In contrast to the polemics and pessimism of *The Crisis of Parliamentary Democracy* (1923), *Constitutional Theory* assumes that the mixed form of modern constitutions does not necessarily conflict with its democratic foundation, even though the task of balancing them, as Schmitt's many historical examples demonstrate, is a constant demand.

It is, finally, an appropriate moment in the history of the liberal-democratic state and its rule of law for the appearance of *Constitutional Theory* in a translation that makes it available to a wide readership. The vulnerability of the constitution is never absent from the discussion. Behind controversies over particular articles, Schmitt argues, is the larger question of the constitution as a whole. This insistence on the constitution as a positive choice for political unity (pt. 1, sect.3) was Schmitt's great contribution to the constitutional debates of the Weimar period. Read with *The Concept of the Political,* the present text captures the seriousness of constituting *this* people in *this* time, not as a set of technical issues in law and electoral strategy, but as a boundary that secures the existential survival of a particular way of life.

Constitutional Theory was a product of Weimar's best years, a period of relative calm that soon gave way to intense crisis in which constitutional defense and constitutional treason were the bywords, as evidenced in Schmitt's *Legality and Legitimacy* (1932), also translated for Duke University Press by Jeffrey Seitzer. In the present controversy over executive power and representation in the United States, the schematic of constitutional change at the end of part one of *Constitutional Theory* is an important perspective on normal constitutional disagreements. These need not become a cycle of "constitutional violation" and "constitutional suspension" as they did in Weimar.

Only a few paragraphs, less than a page, were ever added to the 1928 text. In 1954 Schmitt added a new preface, remarking that a systematic work such as the *Constitutional Theory* did not need to rush to compete with the many constitutional texts that emerge over time "as long as the type remains." The American constitution of 1789 is one example of this type. It is scarcely mentioned here, but in Schmitt's discussion of "apocryphal acts of sovereignty" the observant reader will find much to ponder in our current circumstances.

Translator's Preface

There is considerable disagreement about Carl Schmitt's contribution to political theory and his place in German history. Few dispute, however, that he was a gifted German stylist and a master essayist. *Constitutional Theory* is remarkable for the clarity and elegance of its prose, as are many of Schmitt's essays from the Weimar period, such as *Political Theology*, *The Crisis of Parliamentary Democracy*, and *Concept of the Political.* Stylistically, however, it differs significantly from his essays. Cast in the form of a traditional treatise, the work is divided into elaborate sets of narrowly defined treatments of specific concepts, with each of these sections building on one another in a way that can become repetitive. Moreover, the work is replete with rather technical qualifying phrases, often inserted into the middle of already long sentences, meant to ensure the systematic development of the concepts in question.

Nonetheless, Schmitt presents his "systematic" treatment of constitutional theory in a highly readable form. This is because his deft use of the German language's structural variability, along with his extensive use of the passive voice, enables him to compensate for the inherent repetitiveness of such a lengthy, intricate, and highly technical argument.

The English language, however, is more limited in terms of sentence structure than German, and the frequent use of the passive voice poses significant stylistic problems for English prose. To maintain the clarity and flow of the original, therefore, I believe it necessary to diverge from a literal rendering. First, I use synonyms for key terms, such as *Macht* (power) and *Gewalt* (authority), when they do not introduce shades of meaning that might confuse the reader and suggest inconsistencies in Schmitt's argument not present in the original. I have also broken up and rearranged long sentences, particularly when the original German contained elaborate or repetitive qualifying phrases. Finally, I have changed the passive to the active voice where a subject is clearly identifiable and where the active voice does not change the meaning of the sentence.

I discuss potentially contentious renderings, along with unfamiliar features of German law and controversial aspects of Schmitt's argument, in explanatory notes to the main text. These notes are placed in brackets to distinguish them from Schmitt's. Because of their prominence in the argument, however, certain matters merit discussion at the outset.

First, a number of terms remain in the original German. The most prominent of these, *Rechtsstaat*, has no clear English equivalent. Much of

German legal and political theory concerns the meaning of this term and its significance for law, politics, and society in Germany. I decided not to offer an awkward locution, such as "legal state," because doing so might distract the reader from Schmitt's effort to define the term.

Some of the names for levels and systems of government are also not translated. *Reich* (national level of government from 1870 to 1933), *Reichstag* (federal parliament from 1870 to 1945), *Bundesrat* (federal chamber from 1870 to 1919 and again in the post–World War II period), *Reichsrat* (federal chamber in the Weimar period), *Staatsgerichtshof* (high court for federalism and separation of powers questions during the Weimar era), and *Reichsgericht* (federal high court for civil and criminal cases from 1877 to 1945) appear frequently throughout the work. Leaving them in the original German ensures that references to levels and institutions of government remain clear without long and awkward phrases that would make the text much less readable.

The German word *Land* remains in the original as well, though for somewhat different reasons. Land might be rendered "state," as in the fifty American states, and yet it also means "country" in the sense of a nation-state. The fact that the German word *Staat* means "state" complicates matters even more. I believe the best response is not translating Land when it refers to state-level governments in Germany and rendering it as country or an appropriate synonym if it refers to a nation-state. Staat, however, will always be state. The plural form for Land, *Länder*, while elegant, is rather unfamiliar, so I have adopted the English plural "Lands." With both Land and Lands, though, I retained the capitalization to keep these specific usages distinct from general references to non-German states.

I translate the other primary institutions of the national government, *Reichspräsident*, *Reichskanzler*, and *Reichsregierung* as President, Chancellor, and Reich government, respectively. This is because there are commonly used English words for them, which are neither confusing nor awkward.

There is one more general point on terminology. Schmitt includes many foreign words and phrases. He often defines them; and when he does not, their meaning is almost always clear from the context. I translate these foreign terms and phrases only in the rare instances when their meaning is not readily apparent.

The reader should note that the translation is of the original 1928 edition. In later editions, the publisher made some changes, most notably the inclusion of italics. I have incorporated only some of these. Specifically, instead of italicizing all proper names and place references, as the German publisher does, I have included italics only where they are clearly meant to emphasize the importance of a concept or statement.

Translator's Preface

Finally, to aid those readers interested in consulting the original text, I have indicated the original page breaks in brackets. With the exception of a few pages in the index, the pagination of the original edition is identical with the most recent paperback one. So those without access to the original 1928 edition may easily consult this one as well, using the bracketed page numbers. Schmitt's cross-references are to the page numbers in the original 1928 edition, but cross-reference page numbers are not enclosed in brackets.

I incurred many debts during the completion of this work. Miriam Angress, Valerie Millholland, and Pam Morrison patiently guided the work through the intricate publication process. George Schwab, two anonymous reviewers, and an exceptional copyeditor, Paul Betz, shared their thoughts on the entire manuscript. Rainer Forst, Oliver Lepsius, John McCormick, Magnus Ryan, Christopher Thornhill, and Eric Warshaw advised me on a number of important issues, while the Holcombe Academic Translation Trust provided much-needed financial assistance. Finally, Janet Smith and Ethan McGinnis Seitzer made me finish it or else!

An Introduction to Carl Schmitt's
Constitutional Theory: Issues and Context

Jeffrey Seitzer and Christopher Thornhill

The scholarly interest in the German legal and political theorist Carl Schmitt continues to grow,[1] and the reception of his ideas, whether it is positive or negative, now shapes constitutional debate in many different contexts and countries.[2] Schmitt's place within the intellectual and political culture of the Weimar Republic alone would generate considerable interest in his works.[3] Through a number of essays, such as *Political Theology*, *The Crisis of Parliamentary Democracy*, *The Concept of the Political*, and *Legality and Legitimacy*, he exerted considerable influence on thinkers across the political spectrum in this era. He was also an active participant in the politics of the Republic. His work on the possibility of instituting a constitutional dictatorship, under Art. 48 of the Weimar Constitution, found the ear of conservative politicians, who then made him an adviser during the final crisis of the Republic in the period 1930–33.[4]

Moreover, Schmitt's role in the early Nazi regime has rendered him arguably the most controversial German thinker of the last century. For much of the Weimar period, Schmitt criticized liberal parliamentary government because he considered it too weak to respond adequately to challenges presented by radical groups from both the right and the left, and he argued that presidential government, subject to few, if any, limitations, was the only institutional means of preserving the Republic against these radical opponents. In this limited respect, most of Schmitt's Weimar works were designed to contribute to the defense of the constitutional order. Though he never explicitly called for the banning of the Nazi Party late in the Republic, he implied in his last major work before the Nazi ascension to power, *Legality and Legitimacy*, that such an action would fall within the purview of presidential authority under Art. 48. Yet to the surprise and consternation of many, Schmitt collaborated with the Nazis between 1933 and 1936, authoring several essays in support of the new regime's most brutal policies, such as the so-called Night of the Long Knives, and serving on the Prussian State Council under Hermann Goering.[5]

After 1936, Schmitt was no longer actively involved with the regime of the NSDAP (Nationalsozialistische Deutsche Arbeitspartei). But after the war he refused to submit to the denazification process or to admit any guilt concerning the regime's actions. Barred from returning to his university post, Schmitt retired to his native Plettenberg and continued to publish essays on politics and culture. There he exerted a considerable influence on young conservative legal thinkers, a large number of whom visited Schmitt in his home,[6] and his work on constitutional theory from the Weimar era continued to find an international audience.[7]

Schmitt's political activity is unavoidably an issue that must be considered in any treatment of his works, and this one is no exception. To gain an understanding of this work, however, it is not necessary to scrutinize it for traces of political contamination or to address the question of whether, as is often suggested, there exists a cleft (*Zäsur*) between his writings and political activities of the Weimar era and those of the Nazi era.[8] *Constitutional Theory* elaborates with considerable richness many of the themes developed in previous works, and it anticipates some of the positions of later ones. But this work is methodologically distinct from his other works, and it also contains some substantive changes in key positions. So it is imperative that *Constitutional Theory* not be treated merely as a historical fleshing out of Schmitt's other, more polemical works. In *Constitutional Theory*, more specifically, the intellectual-historical approach employed in works like *The Crisis of Parliamentary Democracy*, where Schmitt evaluates contemporary political practice in reference to exaggeratedly ideal standards, gives way to a comparative history of the theory and practice of constitutional government. This comparative historical methodology is especially noteworthy, not merely because it is more complete and subtler than the earlier approach, but also because it constitutes a deconstruction of the ideal standards used in works like *Crisis*. Schmitt's historical reconstruction of the liberal constitutional tradition in this work thus signals a limited, though significant, rapprochement with liberalism, which distinguishes *Constitutional Theory* from his other important works from the period in substantive as well as methodological terms.[9]

In what follows, we will sketch the context in which Schmitt wrote *Constitutional Theory* and consider the work's claim on the attention of contemporary readers. The first part addresses the cultural and intellectual context; then the second part considers Schmitt and the politics of the Weimar Republic. The third part points out what is methodologically distinctive about the work, and the fourth and fifth parts examine, respectively, how *Constitutional Theory* has been received in the postwar era and its larger theoretical ramifications.

The Weimar Republic:
Cultural and Intellectual Background

Schmitt's most important and influential works were written during the Weimar Republic (1919–33). The Weimar era was not only a time of rapid and volatile political change; it was also marked by far-reaching processes of intellectual and ideological transformation, in which, across all spheres of inquiry, theoretical and philosophical positions enjoying official sanction or status were fundamentally questioned, reconfigured, and, in many cases, abandoned for more radical alternatives. This process of intellectual reorientation was due, in part, to the unstable practical reality of governance in the aftermath of 1918, a period that, in Germany especially, saw the abolition of many previous institutions of monarchical rule, the full and immediate enfranchisement of previously marginalized sociopolitical groups, and, of course, the palpable threat of further revolution from the Bolshevik left. At the same time, the intellectual horizon throughout the Weimar was also shaped in fundamental manner by a critical dialogue with the outlooks that had propped up the intellectual establishment of Imperial Germany (1871–1918), and by a repudiation of the formalistic philosophical ideas and the liberal political doctrines that had given foundation to the quasi-democratic *Rechtsstaat*[10] of the Imperial period. The rapid collapse of the civilized and legally pacified European states into World War I, it was widely perceived, had thoroughly discredited the orthodoxies of the late *Kaiserreich*. Consequently, at all points of the political spectrum and in all fields of discourse, intellectual life in Weimar focused on a rejection of the paradigms, especially those contaminated by the suspicion of formalism or liberalism, around which pre-1914 debate had tended to organize itself. Schmitt's own work stands at the very core of these processes of denial and reorientation, and his work both reflected and initiated wider intellectual patterns of reconsolidation.

The Decline of Neo-Kantianism   At the outbreak of World War I, the dominant philosophical orthodoxy in Germany was neo-Kantianism, which was divided into two schools, the Marburg School that was centered on the thinking of Hermann Cohen and the South West German School based on the views of Heinrich Rickert. Other highly influential neo-Kantian philosophers included Rudolf Stammler, Franz Staudinger, Karl Vorländer, Paul Natorp, and Emil Lask. The philosophy of the Marburg School, as represented chiefly by Cohen, but also by Natorp and, more debatably, by Stammler,[11] was based on a reconstruction of Kantian philosophy that argued that Kantian thinking should be construed most essentially as a practical doctrine of personal autonomy.[12] Kant's philosophy, Cohen claimed, is in essence an account of the conditions under which human reason, in the form of the pure will, can independently deduce universally binding moral or even natural-legal principles to justify and explain its actions. Neo-Kantian philosophy viewed the highest accomplishment of reason as its ability to reflect and stipulate pure laws with consistency, which then form a realm of norms distinct from the realm of social facts, and thus regulate human action and guide it toward universal validity. Cohen extended this theory of practical moral consciousness to argue that the legitimate political order is one that gives universal and concrete form to the principles of law deduced by autonomous consciousness. The political aspect of his philosophy culminated in an ethical concept of the Rechtsstaat, which asserted that the state can only obtain legitimacy where it represents and enacts the founding universal principles by which human reason sustains its own moral autonomy and universal validity.[13] The realized moral person of Kantian practical reason, Cohen concluded, is the foundation of the legal personality of the Rechtsstaat.

The philosophers in the South West German School were less directly political in their theoretical ambitions, although Emil Lask wrote an important work on the philosophy of law. Nonetheless, the philosophies of this school were also held together by a reading of Kant stressing the greater importance of practical reason over pure reason, and so viewed Kantian thinking mainly as a means of deriving abstract universal principles, or values, to guide human judgment, human action, and human politics.[14]

It is difficult to find any intellectual of note in Germany or Austria in the first decades of the twentieth century who was not deeply marked, either critically or positively, by neo-Kantianism. Its influence extended beyond practical philosophy into epistemology, political theory, theology, and aesthetics. Apart from Schmitt himself, thinkers as diverse as Martin Heidegger, Max Weber, Eugen Ehrlich, Hermann Kantorowicz, Georg Lukács, Karl Barth, Franz Rosenzweig, Max Adler, Otto Bauer, Walter Benjamin, Theodor W. Adorno, and Hans Kelsen would surely have followed very different theoretical trajectories if they had not encountered and been challenged by neo-Kantian philosophy.

Of equal importance to their purely theoretical contributions, moreover, was the fact that some major proponents of neo-Kantianism declared an open enthusiasm for the SPD (German Social Democratic Party). This, in itself, was very unusual in Imperial Germany around 1900, where the SPD had not yet been fully assimilated into mainstream politics, and where intellectual mandarins tended to align themselves either to the diffuse left-liberal parties or to the right-of-center National Liberals. However, neo-Kantian conceptions of the state as a universal moral person gradually came to feed directly into the programmatic foundation of the SPD, or at least into the doctrines of its more liberal components, as the party emerged from the period of its political ghettoization following the repeal of the Anti-Socialist Laws in 1890. Some leading neo-Kantians, especially Cohen, became semiofficial philosophers of the revisionist wing of the SPD, led by Eduard Bernstein, which abandoned the party's earlier ideological emphasis on revolutionary combat as the motor of social change and instead advocated peaceful progression toward socialism within the parameters of the parliamentary Rechtsstaat. These neo-Kantians endorsed a gradualist and morally inflected doctrine of evolution toward a common economy, and they also opposed the determinist line of dialectical materialism that had been the initial orthodoxy of the SPD. Above all, they argued that the evolution of society toward a condition of greater justice and equality should not be viewed merely as a social or material process; instead, they claimed that social development could not be separated from legal evolution, and all wider social progress must be steered by moral law.[15] Underlying the moral socialism of the neo-Kantians was an intensely *juridical* understanding of how people and societies operate, claiming that the telos of all social formation is to constitute *legal communities*, that social and political existence invariably becomes more and more susceptible to legal regulation and formalization, and that all social problems are ultimately open to legal resolution. This view concluded that the emergence of the modern Rechtsstaat and constitutional states represents a full realization of essential human capacities for self-legislation, and that the state regulated by prior laws marks the most adequate collective form for self-realized human life.

Even during the decline of neo-Kantianism after 1918, the distinctive vision of moral socialism, based on the legal regulation of economic production, remained very pervasive among the Austro-Marxists, and neo-Kantian ideas were central to many political projects of the early period of the First Republic in Austria. The major neo-Kantian whose influence survived into the Weimar era was Hans Kelsen, who wrote the first drafts for the Austrian democratic constitution of 1920. Kelsen's constitutional thought was guided, first, by the quasi-Kantian claim that the state cannot be defined as a state if it does not act as a bearer of legal order, or as a "system of norms."[16] He ascribed to the state an irreducibly normative character, which has no reality independently of law, and no voluntaristic force or personal identity beyond its unity with the law.[17] He thus saw the *depoliticization* of the state and its construction as a neutral objective legal order as a guarantee that it would operate as a Rechtsstaat, in procedural compliance with the objective norms embedded in its own constitution. Second, he argued that the normative form of the state is derived from an exclusively ideal realm of norms, which are distinct from and unaffected by natural or sociological facts.[18] The state, he claimed, validates its power and legitimacy through reference to a pure realm of objective legal norms and to the processes through which these norms are applied,[19] not to any material, historical, or sociological processes that lead to or influence its constitution. The state is always positioned over and against the modes of conflict and association that determine society more generally, and it applies laws as pure objective norms that have no foundation in determinately volitional, personal, or social interests, and that construct the social phenomena to which they are applied as purely objective legal facts.[20] Third, and most important, he elaborated these arguments to enunciate a thorough critique of all personalistic or voluntaristic attempts to found a doctrine of political sovereignty, claiming that the tendency to separate sovereignty from the law and to imagine the power of the state as evolving from a particular or collective will, to which the supralegal attribute of sovereignty might be imputed, is the result of a corruption of legal analysis by juridically inadmissible, "meta-legal," or even covertly metaphysical prescriptions.[21] In each of these preconditions, Kelsen's constitutional thinking formed perhaps the most important critical background for Schmitt's work.

Despite this survival of neo-Kantian ideas, many aspects of the Weimar Republic's intellectual life were determined, across most lines of intellectual inquiry, by an increasingly intense aversion to neo-Kantianism, and especially toward its formalizing account of human consciousness and its apparent reduction of social being to questions of legal necessity and evolution. In purely philosophical debate, Georg Lukács's early contributions to the emergence of a Western Marxist tradition, in *History and Class Consciousness* (1923), are the theoretical outcome of his lengthy reflections on the neo-Kantian philosophy to which he was exposed in Heidelberg. Equally, Martin Heidegger's writings of the 1920s focus primarily on the attempt to overcome neo-Kantian paradigms for explaining consciousness, ethics, and law.[22] Much of Max Scheler's work was driven similarly by hostility toward Kantian moral formalism,[23] and the early existentialism of Karl Jaspers revolves around a reconstruction of Kant that was designed to rescue Kant from the neo-Kantians.[24] Even Paul Natorp, earlier an important exponent of the neo-Kantian doctrine of the formal autonomy of reason, began after 1918 to entertain more vitalist and metaphysical notions in his political thought.[25] In legal and political thought, the Free Law Movement, around Kantorowicz, Ehrlich, and the young Gustav Radbruch, had already declared war on moral-positivist legal ideas before 1918, seeking to abandon the formal-normative construction of the law in favor of a free and creative approach to legal interpretation and to the conditions of legal validity.[26] The resulting climate of anti-Kantian debate was reinforced, however, by

Erich Kaufmann's postwar demolition of neo-Kantian legal philosophy.[27] Around the same time, the conservative Hegelianism of Julius Binder,[28] the left-leaning distributive corporatism of Hugo Sinzheimer,[29] the left-liberal organic theory of Hermann Heller, and the value-based integration theory of Rudolf Smend all proceeded from the belief that the more positivist outgrowths of neo-Kantianism provide only a highly impoverished account of political and ethical life.[30] Primarily, though, all major theorists of politics and law in the 1920s concurred in arguing that neo-Kantianism reduces legitimate politics to the application of either formal-subjective or formal-objective laws, and it can only imagine political legitimacy in the weakest or most illusory terms, by evacuating all social, cultural, and historical determinacy from political coexistence and experience.

Schmitt's earliest writings were strongly influenced by neo-Kantian claims about legal universality, however vehemently anti-Kantian sentiments were at the heart of his work of the Weimar era. Indeed, if an attempt were made schematically to reduce Schmitt's political theory to its basic elements, it might easily be argued that each of these elements turns on an antagonism toward neo-Kantian political conceptions. First, for instance, in purely party-political terms Schmitt is obviously opposed to the Social Democratic movement, and he views Marxist materialism as absolutely incompatible with any type of political ethic or any substantial explanation of political legitimacy. At different junctures in his oeuvre he indicates that Marxism is an outlook that is tantamount to the death of politics and that leads to the replacement of representative modes of governance by technical or naturalized accounts of social life and political necessity. The neo-Kantian claim that Marxism should be reconstructed as a theory of common ethical self-realization is therefore a perspective to which Schmitt is deeply hostile.

Second, Schmitt's approach to political, legal, and constitutional analysis possesses a pronounced sociological dimension that opposes the neo-Kantian tendency to interpret social processes in normative or universal categories and that rejects the Kantian suggestion that all legal phenomena only exist as facts of law, detached from processes of social formation. To describe Schmitt's method as "sociological" naturally does not mean that we can see his work as containing a distinctive sociological system or an overarching account of how all spheres of modern society work. However, Schmitt analyses institutions, and especially legal institutions, as historically and socially produced forms.[31] These institutions, for Schmitt, originate in complex expressions of social conflict, antagonism, and unity. They cannot be interpreted as manifestations of universal moral orientations or deductions, nor can they be adequately interpreted by purely legal or ethical analysis. There are also no formal legal or moral standards that allow us to assess the validity or legitimacy of institutions. Above all, Schmitt's thinking is profoundly critical of Kantian perspectives that view legitimate law as a system of formal or invariable moral norms and that assume that the application of such law serves to reconcile deep-lying social antagonisms and to confer legitimacy on historically formed institutions.

Third, then, Schmitt also differs fundamentally from neo-Kantianism in his conception of the constitutional personality of the state. Neo-Kantians argue that the state becomes legitimate when it gives to itself a constitution, through which it represents the essential attributes of the human person and refers to the anthropological origins of legitimate political power. In this, the essential condition of the human being is defined as one of *realized autonomy*: that is, as a capacity for deducing and implementing universal laws. The personality of the legitimate state consequently evolves as the state gives itself the constitutional form of universal moral law, and as it then accepts, through the constitution, the necessity of its own compliance with this law. Schmitt at times moves close to neo-Kantian thought in that he too imputes an anthropological-representative substructure to the state, and he insists that the state derives legitimacy from its foundation in essential human qualities. For Schmitt, however, the constitutional personality of the state is not in any way external to the state. The legitimate state has a constitution that represents either the concretely unified will of its constituents or some higher quasi-existential idea of true politics that the state itself embodies and enacts. The constitution does not, however, represent norms deduced independently of the state. Schmitt thus firmly rejects the suggestion that the state is bound by any measurable legal standards or by any obligations that might be imposed on it, independently or externally, through the medium of law. The constitutional personality of the state, for Schmitt, is merely the state's own foundation of identity, and this constitution has no reality apart from the state itself.

Fourth, consequently, Schmitt also focuses his political theory and his concept of representation on a highly voluntaristic or decisionistic model of legitimacy, which directly opposes Kantian ideas about the legal origins of legitimate power. In fact, Schmitt's thought directly inverts the Kantian claim that the constitution of the state becomes more legitimate as it is detached from any particular will, and as it represents a hypothetical pure will or a pure set of universalizable human interests. Against this, he claims that constitutional legitimacy is rooted in a concrete and substantial will. At different points in his trajectory, this is envisioned either as a personal will, expressed in personal decisions and in personal principles of order, or in the common underlying will of the historically formed people. But for Schmitt, in any case, neo-Kantian thinking thoroughly undervalues the voluntaristic elements of constitutional formation, and, by reducing all law to formal law, it contributes to the creation of weak states, chronically vulnerable to destabilization.

The major point of opposition between Schmitt and Kantian political thought, though, resides in the particular way in which Schmitt addresses the relation between legality and legitimacy. The first political principle of Kantian thinking about politics is that politics is the technical or executive component of the political apparatus, and that this component is justified only if determined by pure and universalizable laws, which are enshrined in the constitution. Hence, legality is the constitutional determinant and precondition of all legitimacy. The constitution determines legitimacy by placing legal-moral limits on the authority of the state and the exercise of its power, or even by referring to natural-legal norms as it checks the operations of the state. Schmitt argues, however, that this relation between law and power is badly misconceived in Kantian philosophy. Legality, for Schmitt, is a formal condition that must be given meaning and content by a prior structure of legitimacy: legitimacy is obtained only through the representation of the unified will or the historical existence of the people, and this must be presupposed as the origin of the constitution, and indeed of all law. On Schmitt's account, politics is *before the law*, and the necessary content of law cannot be stipulated in abstraction from the particular political system in which it originates. Law, in short, cannot constitute legitimacy on its own, and law that is not informed by a particular political will is always likely to undermine the legitimacy of a political order. The result of this is that, unlike Kantian thinkers, Schmitt does not see the constitution of a state as a legal order possessing priority or distinct dignity over the state. Rather, he sees the constitution as united with the state, representing a uniform political will that cannot be reduced to formal or autonomous legal principles. Indeed, at the heart of Schmitt's work is a direct inversion of Kantian ideas about the state and the law. The constitutional law of the state, based in the will of the state, must prevail over all other laws. States that are bound to compliance with technical or external laws, he concludes, are always likely to be fragile and susceptible to crisis.

Like other examples of the post-1918 anti-Kantian literature, Schmitt's hostility to Kant reflects the belief that the Kantian tendency to exclude vital, historical, and metaphysical contents from its account of necessary order impoverishes human freedom by defining it merely as a formal capacity for obtaining and validating laws. Consequently, Schmitt believes that underlying Kantian thought is always a debilitating misinterpretation of what it means—or might mean—to be a free political being in a free political order, and this restricts political life to a condition of obedience to thinly abstracted norms and values. Against such conceptions, he argues that the constitution of legitimacy cannot be distilled from any set of prior legal principles; the constitution must express the political will of the people, or of *a* people, and this will might accommodate notions of freedom and identity that cannot be transposed into universal norms. The constitution of a state, in short, must therefore firstly be political, not legal.

Positivism: Its Survival and Critique If neo-Kantianism was the dominant outlook in debates in practical and political philosophy before 1914, the dominant outlook in pure legal debate was still positivism. Positivism originally developed in the early years of the nineteenth century as a school of legal analysis devoted to clarifying the juridical preconditions for the emerging capitalist economy in the German states, and for setting out a systematic account of private law on the foundation of the pandects of Roman law. The early positivist theorists, such as Georg Friedrich Puchta, the young Rudolf Jhering, and Carl Friedrich von Gerber, focused to a large extent on clarifying the legal conditions of economic autonomy outside the state, and on providing a contemporary account of the rights and entitlements imputable to legal subjects in the system of private law. Although broadly socially progressive and insistent that private-legal order could only be obtained if the political apparatus took the form of some kind of Rechtsstaat, the positivists were, to a large extent, rather conservative political thinkers. They had little express conception of law as a potent political force, and they were content to see the early capitalist economy, with guarantees of property rights, unrestricted circulation of capital and mobility of labor, coexisting with the remnants of the absolutist political orders in Prussia and the other smaller German states. Some thinkers close to the early development of positivism, most notably Anton F. J. Thibaut, did surely use their analysis of private law to propose a conception of the person under law as a model of public order, on the grounds of which they argued for the imposition of legal constraints on the state apparatus.[32] More generally, though, the positivists tended to emphasize the close relation between legal analysis and the natural sciences. They argued that the evolution of law should be viewed as following purely positive patterns, and that law should be constructed as an internally and systematically consistent unity of principles and norms, relatively closed against normative, purposive, or directly politicized external input.[33] Legal prescriptions, in consequence, should be viewed as nothing more than inner-juridical facts, constructs formed by the law itself to facilitate its own application. On these grounds, they concluded that the validity of law depended on its status as an internally consistent set of rules, and it could not be reconstructed or interpreted on the basis of moral prescriptions. These doctrines culminated in the conceptual jurisprudence of Bernhard Windscheid, who defined legal

Introduction

science exclusively as a discipline for the production of formal concepts to assist in judicial and legislative procedures.[34]

Importantly for Schmitt, however, during the later decades of the nineteenth century the original private-legal ideas of positivism were gradually transformed into a more determinate analysis of the necessities of political form, and eventually rearticulated as principles of public law. Perhaps the most significant political development in the history of positivism occurred in the works of Paul Laband,[35] who reoriented the early-positivist account of the individual legal person as a subject of private law to propose an account of the state itself as a legal person. The early positivists had placed at the heart of modern law a concept of the legal person that saw the rights and obligations of the person under private law as simple and necessary constructs of the law itself, not as the result of moral deductions or political consensus. Laband, then, took this paradigm of private law as the grounding for a conception of the state as a legal person of public or constitutional law, and he argued that the state could be best understood if it too were interpreted essentially as a pure legal construct, or as a formal legal person, whose rights and entitlements were defined in accordance with a system of pure legal rules: legal rules, that is, which form the state's constitution. The state, Laband thus explained, has the power to make the law, and to exercise certain legal entitlements and authorities. Indeed, the state has the specific legal attribute that it makes and authorizes laws. Yet, like other legal persons, the state is not above the law. As a person of public law, it must also comply with certain legal and procedural obligations, determined in its own constitutional form. As much as any intellectual, Laband's thought offered a blueprint for the institutional reality of Imperial Germany in the era of Bismarck (1870–1890) and in the aftermath of this era. His positivist doctrine set out the most perfect endorsement of the limited Rechtsstaat emerging at this time: that is, of a Rechtsstaat defined as democratic and legitimate by its responsibility to follow certain formal procedures in its legislative and executive functions, not by any overarching democratic consensus or popular will formation. Underlying this analysis was the paradoxical conviction that law exists as a formal system of constitutional rules and procedures independent of the state yet that the state is the ultimate origin of the law, and legal validity relies lastly on the ability of the state to produce and to implement both constitutional laws and general statutes.

Through the latter part of the nineteenth century, the principles of positivism increasingly came under fire from the corporatist perspectives of the Germanic School of law, firstly expressed by Georg Beseler, then by Johann Caspar Bluntschli and Otto von Gierke, and later by Hugo Preuß. Indeed, the defining legal-political controversy of late nineteenth-century Germany was the debate between the positivists, on one hand, and the theorists of the Germanic School, on the other. The theorists of the Germanic School opposed the positivist conception of the political apparatus as a formal legal person, and they rejected the transporting of private-legal and Roman-legal terms into the account of the political system. Such privatist and atomistic tendencies, they argued, were incapable of understanding the genuinely *political* content of statehood, and they provided only a thoroughly insubstantial description of the origins of the state's power. The Germanists argued instead that the legitimate political system is one that expresses and consolidates the associative life of the national community and that forms a substantial legal person, integrating into itself all the associational and organic constituents of civil society.[36] The state, they thus concluded, is not a formal legal person or a formal construct of the law. It is a corporation, overlying and guiding all of society, but comprising and evolving from a great number of legal agreements formed between distinct smaller corporations. The antagonism between these schools was manifest through all the periods of legal codification and foundation between the unification of Germany in 1870–71 and the establishment of the Weimar Republic. Indeed, the major legal documents of the time, especially the Civil Code of 1900 and the Weimar Constitution of 1918–19, might all be seen, in their technical elements, to revolve around uneasy and fluctuating compromises between positivist and organic ideas about the social origins of the state, about its legal construction, and about the validity of law. Nowhere is this more clearly seen than in the works of Max Weber, who in some respects might be viewed as the dominant political-theoretical influence on Schmitt, and whose ideas directly influenced the early drafts of the Weimar Constitution, especially those aspects of the document that Schmitt viewed most favorably. Weber rejected the positivist rule-theoretical grounding for law, and he evidently sought to provide sociological and integrative explanations of the origins of the law and the state. However, in his attachment to the belief that the strong executive is the origin of law and in his argument that law can be validated only by the state, he also obviously still subscribed to basic positivist preconditions.

The immediate horizon for Schmitt's work, in short, was generally marked by a deep polarization of legal thinking in its attitude toward positivism. On the one hand, the organic ideas of Preuß and Sinzheimer had a deep influence on the Weimar Constitution. On the other hand, positivist accounts of legal validity remained influential throughout the 1920s, often with a neo-Kantian inflection. As was discussed above, Kelsen's drafts for the Austrian constitution, anchored in the assumption that the constitution forms a closed system of norms applied by a constitutional court and that these norms provide a basis for the regulation of all political activity and all social conflict, clearly took positivist conceptions of purity in law to a new degree of refinement.

Like Weber, Schmitt might be viewed as a theorist who was determined to break with positivism, but who nonetheless remained attached to some of its defining claims. His opposition to positivism has several quite distinct motives. First, he rejects the Labandian and Kelsenian idea of law as a politically neutral sequence of norms, and he turns against all formal-legalist approaches to law. Second, he clearly thinks that the Labandian notion that the state makes the law, only then to have its authority limited by the law, is rather absurd. Indeed, as we have seen, he views the dualist belief that the laws of the constitution are somehow external or prior to the state as one of the supremely paradoxical delusions of the tradition of liberal legal-state thinking. In this respect, he repeatedly takes issue with the claim that the state can be interpreted as a legal construct, resulting from the law's own explanations of legal personality and obligation, and he also rejects the belief that the legal personality of the state depends on its negative compliance with legal or procedural terms set down in the constitution. In fact, the dualist elements in Labandian positivism must appear to Schmitt almost as a theoretically devalued expression of Kantian legal politics, which, like Kantianism, serves only to undermine the voluntaristic essence of state-hood. Third, he sets himself against all legal theories that place private-law models of the person at the center of their account of the law of state; such approaches, he suggests, are incapable of interpreting the essentially political or collective character of the processes through which a state obtains legitimacy. Fourth, methodologically, his sociological examination of the origins of law and his critique of the reduction of legal analysis to a purely exegetic science also speak emphatically against positivist ideas.

Underlying all these criticisms of positivism is the claim that positivism misconceives the importance of the state, as a historical and sociological center of human existence, and, perhaps more important, that it misconceives the essential relation between the constitution of the state and the state itself. Constitutional law, Schmitt argues simply, cannot be treated as distinct from politics and the state, and all descriptions of law as a constitutionally countervailing check on politics, as a formal or procedural precondition of political legitimacy, or as a binding system of moral values, simply reflect the self-deceiving and weak-spirited tendencies inherent in Rechtsstaat liberalism. As we have noted, Schmitt sees constitutional law as both the form and the will of the state, and all other law must be subordinate to it. Indeed, for Schmitt, positivism perfectly demonstrates the fallacies of liberalism, at least in the context of modern Germany. He sees positivism as a doctrine that aims to provide an analysis of law in order to restrict the arbitrary use of state power, but that cannot avoid positing the state as the origin of all law, and so results merely in a conception of the constitution of the state as a minimal set of procedural norms, which have no actual constitutive or political importance in forming the state. Schmitt, of course, distinguishes strictly between politics and law. Indeed, much of his work is devoted to demonstrating that what is usually considered to be politics is in fact only a technical manipulation of the law. However, he also argues that at a constitutional level law cannot be separated out from the state: the constitution of the state is always the inner political will of the state. Positivism marks the most paradoxical and self-undermining attempt to obscure and deny this basic fact of political order.

Despite these critical points, however, it might also be argued that Schmitt retains strong ties to the positivist tradition. Most obviously, his argument that the strong state is the sole origin of law, and that legal order is always contingent on the state, does not wholly contradict the positivist view of the state. More fundamentally, though, the anti-normative position in Schmitt's work, claiming that law cannot be made transparent to moral foundations or ethical imperatives, also places him in the terrain of positivist thinking. In fact, in his argument that law is secondary to politics and that the political constitution cannot be determined in universal-ethical categories, Schmitt shares the widespread positivist claim that law should be taken to reflect the "normativity of the factual": in other words, that law obtains legitimacy simply because of the fact that it has evolved into a certain positive form and that, supported by a state apparatus, it provides a concrete order of norms that shape and structure social expectations. In this respect, the sociological element in Schmitt's account of legitimate law places him in proximity to late-positivist views on the relation between power and norms. Georg Jellinek's argument that the state has both a sociological aspect and a normative aspect, and that the normative quality of law is always inseparable from the factual form of the state, is especially close to Schmitt's thought.[37] Consequently, although he sets himself against the positivist mainstream of political liberalism in Imperial Germany, Schmitt shares certain arguments with the more cautious versions of liberalism at this time, and his thought reflects some theoretical perspectives that were quite widespread on the more conservative fringes of liberal thinking before 1914.

Schmitt in Weimar Politics

Like many of his generation, Schmitt shared the prevailing view toward the end of the Wilhelmine Reich that the state and its institutions represented national unity and purpose, while partisan political struggles taking place in the popularly elected legislature, the Reichstag, pitted narrow self-interests against one another in a struggle that resulted in disunity. The aftermath of World War I, however, caused Schmitt to reconsider his understanding of the relation of law and the state to politics. In the power vacuum caused by the sudden collapse of the monarchical regime, there were a number of attempts by groups on the radical left to seize state authority at a local and regional level and institute revolutionary change. Though the regular army, in conjunction with rightist paramilitary groups, the Free Corps, were able to suppress these threats to the existing order, Schmitt and the bourgeoisie generally felt personally threatened. Schmitt became convinced that political theory should not merely provide appropriate principles to guide state action, but must also consider the actual conditions for the exercise of state authority, so that the state can effectively discharge its mission of producing and upholding moral principles and national unity. A primary issue in *Political Theology*, for example, was whether legal standards are actually enforced, not merely articulated or defined, and in *The Crisis of Parliamentary Democracy* Schmitt warned of the threat to parliamentary democracy from groups radically opposed to liberal government. One may rightly take issue with some of Schmitt's analysis in these and other works, such as *Hüter der Verfassung* (*Guardian of the Constitution*). But it is undeniable that Schmitt viewed the consideration of the actual exercise of state authority as a central component of political theory.

This concern is reflected quite clearly in *Constitutional Theory*, where Schmitt examines the actual functioning of contrasting systems of government in order to address problems in Weimar Germany. Before turning to these features of the work in the next section, however, we need to review some of the practical problems of the Republic. No attempt will be made to explain the collapse of the Weimar Republic. Instead, we provide a brief overview of the problems it faced and Schmitt's role in its politics, which might aid the reader in evaluating Schmitt's argument.

While historians disagree about the role played by representatives of social and political elites, such as Schmitt, in the demise of the Weimar Republic, it is generally agreed that the Republic did not enjoy widespread popular support. In other words, there is some truth to the claim that the Weimar Republic was a democracy without democrats. To be sure, there were some people who were fully committed to the Republic and the democratic political and social order it sought to institute. These were greatly outnumbered, however, first by those who supported the Republic only reluctantly and for pragmatic reasons, the so-called republicans of reason (*Vernunftrepublikaner*). These lukewarm supporters of the Republic often had a preferred alternative to it, whether they expressed it or not, such as a return to the monarchy or the establishment of a full-fledged socialist republic, but they did not believe their preferred option was a viable one at the time. This group also included those who supported the Republic, simply because it was the legally constituted authority, and who feared the possibility of political and social chaos if this authority was undermined.

Worse still, there was no shortage of persons opposed to the Republic in principle. The radical right sought either a return to the monarchy or the establishment of some vaguely conceived nationalist alternative. Their resentment of the Republic was intense and remained unabated throughout the period. A reliable source of hostility toward the Republic was the mistaken view that it was responsible for the defeat in World War I. In late 1918, the Army Supreme Command, sensing though not acknowledging imminent defeat, had turned authority over to a civilian provisional government, compelling the latter to accept peace terms from the victorious allies. At the time, however, German troops were still in enemy territory, fueling claims that the leaders of the new Republic had "stabbed" the soldiers "in the back" by agreeing to surrender unnecessarily. This bitterness toward the Republic was intensified once the new republican leaders were compelled to accept the humiliating terms of the Versailles Treaty, which set the final conditions of the peace, and it escalated still further during the Ruhr crisis several years later, when the government was forced to admit defeat in its campaign of resistance to the French occupation of the important industrial area to ensure the fulfillment of the reparations payments imposed under the Versailles Treaty.

The Republic found supporters on the left, but the left in Weimar was highly divided. The first governmental coalition of the Republic, known as the Weimar coalition, the main party of which was the Social Democrats, had some success in integrating potential radical-leftist opposition to the Republic. For example, even the leaders of the Workers and Soldiers Councils (*Räte*), who had been instrumental in bringing down the imperial system and who controlled considerable territory after the war, accepted the cross-party compromises that formed the basis of the coalition government in the first years of the Republic.[38] Moreover, some of the major changes in industrial relations and labor law swept in by the revolution initially satisfied many leftists, who might otherwise have pushed for a more far-ranging socialist revolution. Trade union officials and Social Democrats thought that along with the expansion of social welfare programs, these corporatist mediating devices were the best means of achieving socialist goals within the established system. But the Social Democrats' participation in the Weimar coalition diminished its capacity to speak for the left. A major factor in this was the government's use of rightist paramilitary groups to put down a number of leftist attempts to seize control of local and Land-level governments. The excessive violence of these rightist groups, bolstered by the scaled-down military, caused intense resentment on the far left, compelling many to turn their backs on the Social Democrats and to support more radical alternatives, such as the Independent Social Democrats and the Communists.

Another factor in the widening divisions on the left was growing dissatisfaction felt by workers with the merely modest gains they had obtained through the revolution and under the new constitution. In order to avoid a genuine socialist revolution, during the early years of the Weimar Republic business leaders felt compelled to agree to a number of changes, such as the eight-hour day, enhanced social welfare programs, and various corporatist mechanisms for resolving labor disputes (tribunals, shop councils, etc.). However, after 1923 the international competitive advantage of industry diminished owing to the stabilization of the currency, and the successful suppression of both right- and left-wing attempts to overthrow the Republic suggested that the possibility of more radical socialist experiments seemed to have passed. For both reasons, industry became ever less cooperative with plans for economic reform, though not with all redistribution programs that continued through the 1920s.[39] With the onset of the Great Depression after the Wall Street crash in 1929, however, business leaders began to work toward the complete dismantling of the welfare state, and they found considerable support for this from the governments that, after early 1930, relied on presidential emergency decrees to govern during the final crisis of the Republic. Many on the left were greatly disappointed. Unable to counteract this right-wing retrenchment, from 1930 onward the Social Democrats lost more support to the Communists, who, like the Nazis, were willing to undermine the Republic to clear the way for an anticipated revolution and could exploit the despair felt by many workers without offering a positive governmental program in the context of the existing state. Overall, therefore, the factionalism of the left meant that the natural support of Weimar democracy was never fully secure and, in fact, contributed to its instability and eventual overthrow. The infirm support for the Republic greatly complicated the task of governing. The Weimar coalition of Social Democrats, Democrats, and Catholic Center Party leaders, who founded the Republic, faltered quite early. In the election of 1920, the coalition lost its majority in parliament and never regained it, although the coalition was sporadically revived after 1920. For the remainder of the Republic, the possibilities for a majority government were quite limited. One option was to form a minority government, which required the toleration of parties, such as the German National People's Party or the German People's Party, both of which, but especially the former, had a tense and, after 1928, openly hostile relationship with the Republic. An alternative to this was to form a Grand Coalition, which at times included parties, such as the Social Democrats and the

German People's Party, whose programs were diametrically opposed to one another in some key respects, especially taxation and welfare. Either way, the resulting coalitions were chronically unstable.[40]

Many have claimed that the system of proportional representation was a primary reason why the Reichstag had difficulty forming effective governments, because it led to the fragmentation of the Reichstag. But the significant continuity between the party structure in the Imperial era and the early Weimar period suggests that the proportional representation system was not alone responsible for the fragmentation of the party system in Weimar.[41] Also, the fragmentation of the party system did not become a serious problem until 1928, when splinter parties first appeared with 17.1 percent of the vote. Moreover, splinter parties were a significant feature of the electoral landscape for only two elections, and this was mostly on the right end of the spectrum.[42]

Whatever the cause, the fragmented party system meant that the structural inducements to compromise were relatively weak. Parties sought to retain core constituencies in tightly contested elections, as the ever more splintered party system encouraged supporters to jump ship in favor of parties more attuned to their narrowly defined interests. The moderates were constantly forced to look over their shoulders at the radical right and left when contemplating cooperation with other moderate parties.[43]

Moreover, even if the Reichstag could have agreed on a program of action, it is not clear what policies it might have been able to implement, as the chronically weak economy provided it with very little room to maneuver.[44] Though the German economy had enormous productive potential after the war, it remained weak throughout the Weimar period. Only by 1927 did it return to 1913 production levels.[45]

With such a tenuous political base, the early governments were forced to rely on extraordinary means to govern. Art. 48 of the Constitution permitted the President to exercise emergency powers, for example, to restore order or compel Land governments to implement federal dictates. In the Republic's first extended crisis, from 1918 to 1923, however, the President not only made frequent recourse to emergency powers to suppress rebellion and restore order; the first President, the Social Democrat Friedrich Ebert, also used emergency powers to institute significant policy changes and budgetary packages. Also in this period, the Reichstag passed enabling acts that empowered the President to undertake extraordinary measures and enact policy.[46]

With the passing of the currency crisis in 1923, the Republic enjoyed five years of relative stability and some prosperity. Though the governments in this period could not rely on a broad base of support and were not able to institute major reforms, such as reform of the federal system,[47] they were not targets of coup attempts, and the government did not need presidential emergency powers in order to govern. The political situation deteriorated drastically with the onset of the Great Depression of 1929. With rising unemployment, the Republic's capacity to govern through parliament was again put to the test. Early in the decade the Great Inflation had ironically allowed the government to soften the common experience of recession by funding expansive social welfare programs and compensating striking workers in the Ruhr crisis. With the inflation over and the overall economy still weak in the late 1920s, the government was unable to fully fund existing programs and provisions. In consequence, a major breach between the governing parties developed over the issue of unemployment compensation, which had been fixed at a level highly advantageous for the workforce in 1927, and commitment to which was a key factor in the cohesion of the subsequent cross-party governmental cabinets. Fearing loss of support to the Communists, the Social Democrats, who had already compromised their positions on numerous occasions to shore up governing coalitions, were unwilling to alter the insurance law and to allow an increase in the burden of contribution placed on workers. The Grand Coalition government (formed in 1928) collapsed in early 1930, and the Republic entered its final crisis, which lasted until 1933.

This crisis differed from the initial one in several very important respects. First, economic conditions were much worse. Besides the ending of inflation, which, as noted, had some perversely positive benefits early in the decade, the global character of the depression had particularly deleterious effects on Germany. The Americans were no longer willing to provide its allies relief on their debt, which, in turn, made it difficult to grant further relief to the Germans, though at this point reparations had mostly become a moot issue. More important, however, American banks were no longer willing to extend credits to local governments in Germany, which were burdened with the need to meet the rising demand for welfare benefits. There was also diminished demand for German goods and services, and less interest in direct investment. Together with long-term structural changes in the German economy, which had caused significant increases in unemployment apart from the global depression, these more acute economic problems with an international dimension restricted the already limited range of options open to the government.

Second, the electorate had begun to splinter even more. Besides the fragmentation of the left, which occurred ten years earlier, now the bourgeois parties were losing support to more radical parties, such as the Nazis. The potential range of governing coalitions, always limited, was becoming smaller. Moreover, groups committed to the destruction of the Republic now held significant numbers of seats, so even a minority government might not count on parties supportive of the Republic, such as the Social Democrats, to tolerate their government, in order to prevent further deterioration of the political situation.

The final difference between the crisis in the late Weimar era and that of the early 1920s was the outlook of upper-echelon government officials. As noted, during the first crisis of the Republic, the government relied extensively on presidential emergency decrees under Art. 48 and even enabling acts not merely to reestablish order in response to radical attempts to overthrow the current system. The government also instituted wide-ranging economic reforms using these extraordinary means. As Schmitt pointed out in *Guardian of the Constitution* (1931) and *Legality and Legitimacy*, the use of presidential emergency powers was already a well-established practice by the time of the second crisis of the Republic. The point of contention, however, is the purpose and ultimate effect of these two instances of extraordinary government authority. The first President, Friedrich Ebert, was a Social Democrat firmly committed to the Republic and the extensive economic, social, and political compromises that served as its foundation. The use of extraordinary means of governance in the first crisis of the Republic, therefore, was never meant to subvert or replace parliamentary government. It was, rather, seen as a means of responding to a temporary crisis, which would return parliamentary government to a firm footing once the crisis was resolved. The second President, by contrast, was former general Paul von Hindenburg, whose attitude toward the Republic and its liberal and social democratic foundation was ambivalent at best. Though he was committed to upholding the Constitution and ensuring the maintenance of strict legality, Hindenburg sought to place existing institutions on a more rightist foundation. The cabinets that Hindenburg established after 1930 reflected this different orientation in that, to varying degrees, they utilized presidential emergency powers less as a means of reestablishing parliamentary government than of reconstituting core principles and institutions of the Republic.

In the Republic's first decade, Schmitt produced a number of influential works on parliamentary democracy, political romanticism, and political Catholicism, among other topics. He also addressed the issue of presidential emergency powers with varying degrees of explicitness.[48] Though his works on emergency powers garnered considerable attention, they did not exercise significant influence on governmental policy until the final crisis of the Republic. An especially important turning point in this regard was his move to Berlin in 1928, when he left the University of Bonn to take a position at the Handelshochschule (Business College), in order to be part of the capital's intellectual and political life. Schmitt felt quite at home in the mostly Catholic Rhineland. But residing in the capital, though in a less prestigious post, brought him into contact with leading governmental officials, giving him an opportunity for direct political influence. While in Berlin, for example, he became friends with Johannes Popitz, a state secretary for finance, and General Kurt von Schleicher, whose behind-the-scenes machinations greatly influenced government policy in the Republic's final crisis. Through these contacts in Berlin, Schmitt became directly influential, as his earlier writings on emergency powers and constitutional dictatorship appealed strongly to politicians seeking to reorganize the Republic as a prerogative or presidential regime.

The onset of the Great Depression provided the impetus for Schleicher to realize his plans for a presidential regime with limited parliamentary foundation. Under considerably strained finances, the Grand Coalition led by the Social Democrat Heinrich Mueller in March 1930 resigned after reaching an impasse over the issue of unemployment compensation. Following Schleicher's suggestion, President von Hindenburg appointed Heinrich Brüning as Chancellor and charged him with forming a government above parties. When the Reichstag rejected his economic policies, Brüning instituted them through a presidential emergency decree under Art. 48. The Reichstag rescinded the decrees two days later, prompting Brüning to dissolve parliament and call new elections, which were scheduled for two months later, on 14 September 1930.

In the interim, the question arose whether the government could govern through emergency decrees while the Reichstag was not in session. The pressing nature of this question brought Schmitt into true prominence. Seeking a theoretical foundation for the new presidential regime, the Brüning government requested a *Gutachten* (consultant's report) from Schmitt on the legality of the disputed presidential emergency decrees. Schmitt argued that this use of presidential emergency powers was appropriate. Because the decrees aimed to reestablish and maintain the existing constitutional order, they constituted a "commissarial," not a "sovereign," dictatorship, which would replace the existing order. Schmitt also argued that the government could institute the decrees while the Reichstag was not in session and continue to govern without a majority until after the next elections. The President had democratic legitimacy and could exercise sovereign authority like the Reichstag. Once in session again, the Reichstag would reject the decrees. Until then, they were legitimate state acts. Moreover, though they were decrees, not statutes, they could substitute for statutes (*Gesetzvertretendeverordnungen*) and thus carried the authority of formal laws.

The election proved a serious miscalculation. The Social Democrats lost a few seats. The Nazis, however, made significant gains, increasing their share of the vote from twelve to 107 seats, drawing mostly from the bourgeois block of parties, while the extreme left went from fifty-four to seventy-seven seats. This meant that no workable governing majority could be formed and that parties opposed to the current system could combine to form so-called negative majorities. Not composed with a view to instituting a positive governmental program, such majorities aimed only at undermining the current system. Parliamentary government was effectively dead. For the next two years, the government continued to rule by decree due to the toleration of the Social Democrats, who opposed no-confidence motions in order to prevent further electoral gains by radical parties opposed to the Republic.

The next major turning point for the Republic and Schmitt's career came in 1932. General von Schleicher proposed seeking a non-Nazi rightist government that would be tolerated by the Nazis. To gain the cooperation of the Nazis, he offered to call new elections and to lift the ban on the political activity of the SA and SS. In addition, he convinced President von Hindenburg to dismiss Brüning in favor of Franz von Papen, who then, in July 1932, used a presidential emergency decree under Art. 48 to initiate the infamous Preußenschlag: the federal takeover of the SPD-led Prussian Land government by the Reich, under the pretext that this would help restore order in Prussia. This latter move was also intended to draw support from the Nazis by showing conservatives that the new government was an effective bulwark against the left.

Like Brüning, Schleicher seriously miscalculated in calling new elections. The non-Nazi right did not make any electoral gains at the expense of the Nazis, as Schleicher had hoped. In fact, the Nazis doubled their share in the Reichstag, now having 37.8 percent of the seats. The Communists improved their standing as well, holding now 14.6 percent. Together with the Communists, they formed the sort of negative majority Schmitt warned about that could block any positive governmental action by parliament and rescind any action taken by the President under Art. 48.[49]

The ostensible reason for removing the Prussian caretaker government was to restore order in Prussia, but the Prussian government had been a fairly effective bulwark against radical threats to the Republic. For example, though the Weimar coalition lost its majority status at the national level in 1920, it remained in the majority in the Prussian Land parliament until the election of April 1932. Prussia was the largest Land by far, comprising over 66 percent of German territory and 60 percent of its overall population, and its police force was equivalent in size to the Reich army. The Land government had used its sizable police force to control radical activity of both right- and left-wing extremists with some success until the Reich ban on political activity by the right was lifted. Moreover, the Prussian government had used its majority in the Land parliament to pass a provision requiring an absolute majority for the election of the next Minister President. This provision prevented the Nazis from taking control of the Prussian government after its electoral victory in 1932, and it permitted the anti-Nazi caretaker government of the Social Democrat Otto Braun to stay in power after the election.

While the takeover of the Prussian government was of questionable value in terms of maintaining the order and security of the Reich, it was an important part of the Papen government's plan for constitutional reform. Specifically, the Papen government wanted to establish an aristocratic upper house as a counterweight to the Reichstag and institute changes in voting law in order to limit popular sovereignty. Bringing the Prussian province under central control would eliminate a potential source of opposition to its plans.

Schmitt had long advocated greater centralization as a hedge against German particularism. But he opposed any constitutional changes in the near term, particularly those undertaken by the presidential regime. The presidential government, in his view, was legitimate as a commissarial, not a sovereign, dictatorship. In other words, the government could not institute fundamental changes in the basic constitutional order via presidential emergency decrees. It could only institute temporary changes meant to bolster the existing constitutional order.

Schmitt defended the takeover of the Prussian government in these terms once he was commissioned to represent the Reich government in the trial before the Supreme Court when it was considering the legality of the government's action. Schmitt argued that the Reich government's actions were an appropriate exercise of Art. 48, because the Land government's policies threatened to push Prussia into a state of civil war. The preelection provision stipulating an absolute majority for the election of a Minister President, Schmitt argued, was an instance of one political party utilizing governmental power to exclude another from an "equal chance" at political power. Schmitt's opponents pointed out that the Prussian government's action was an attempt to realize Schmitt's position in *Legality and Legitimacy*, published in the summer of 1932, in which he argued that parties opposed to the current system should not be granted an equal chance to fundamentally alter the system via legal means. Schmitt considered such use of governmental power illegitimate, because in his view only the President, standing above political parties as a neutral third, could legitimately make such a determination.[50] Leaving such a decision to political parties in power, he argued, might prompt parties fearing exclusion in this way to engage in civil war as a means of self-defense.

The Staatsgerichtshof ruled that the Reich takeover of the Prussian government was a legitimate exercise of state authority, in order to ensure the order and security of the Reich. However, the Reich government could not entirely displace Land institutions. The Prussian government could continue to represent Prussia in the Prussian parliament, in the Reichsrat, and in relations with other Land governments.

Though the Reich government could not legally subsume Prussian governmental institutions, it was now effectively the governmental authority in Prussia. Despite this considerable legal victory, Papen's more general plans for constitutional reform were not as successful. President von Hindenburg refused to agree to the establishment of a state of emergency, which would permit the Papen regime to institute its reform plans without parliamentary support. Moreover, Hindenburg had lost confidence in Papen and agreed to permit Schleicher to attempt a rightist-led popular front government as an alternative to the Nazis. A key component of this plan was to seek to detach the left wing of the Nazi party and join its support with that of the Trade Unions and Social Democrats by proposing extensive public works programs, among other measures. Both intended partners in this popular front government, the business community and trade unions, continued to mistrust one another and the Schleicher government. Without the necessary parliamentary support, the Schleicher government failed as an alternative to Papen's cabinet of barons.

With new elections looming, the question of whether President von Hindenburg should continue to govern by emergency decree without parliamentary support became increasingly pressing and contested. The President had always favored rightist cabinets and was willing to govern by decree for extended periods without parliamentary support. But the law stipulated that elections had to be called within a specified period. Deferring elections beyond this point would be a strict violation of the law. Schmitt did not support Papen's idea of using a state of emergency to institute constitutional reform, first because this would constitute a sovereign, not a commissarial, dictatorship, but also because it might spark outright civil war. Nonetheless, in his opinion, a violation of strict legality in the form of continuing government by decree without new elections was preferable to a Nazi-led government. Hindenburg, however, declined to pursue either alternative, opting instead to request that Hitler, as leader of the largest parliamentary party, form a cabinet that included traditional nationalists, such as Papen, who believed that his presence would serve to moderate Hitler. This belief, obviously, proved illusory. Within relatively short order, the Hitler government used legal means and political intimidation to consolidate its hold on power and eventually establish a totalitarian dictatorship.

There is no easy explanation for the failure of the Weimar Republic. It is hard to imagine more difficult circumstances for the establishment of a republic. A chronically weak economy, domestic and foreign hostility, rapid social and cultural change together left the leaders of the Republic limited options in responding to pressing problems of the day. A long-standing democratic regime would have been placed under considerable strain under these circumstances. Such strain proved too much for a fledgling republic like Weimar, established in a nation with a short history of national unity and with little experience of successful democratic rule. Perhaps given more time, the Republic might have reached workable compromises on divisive issues, which, in turn, might have provided it sufficient support to weather periodic storms of discontent.

Given these circumstances, it might be too much to say that the Republic's collapse was due to the failure of elites. By 1930, the Republic was in a state of paralysis, and its options for governing by parliament were quite limited. At the same time, it is clear that the Republic's elites did not serve it well at key points. The governments under President von Hindenburg in the final crisis of the Republic (those of Brüning and Schleicher) were at best not committed to exploring options for governing with parliament, if they existed. And at worst, these governments were intent on undermining the Republic and replacing it with their preferred alternative (Papen). In either case, government officials displayed considerable naïveté in believing that the governmental crises they at least helped accentuate, if not orchestrate, would in the end work to their political advantage and that they could control implacable opponents of the Republic, like the Nazis.

Nonetheless, in view of the horrendous consequences of the Nazi regime, it is understandable that any action that seemed to contribute to the Republic's demise and establishment of the Nazi regime would spark outrage. This was certainly true of Schmitt's role in the presidential governments between 1930 and 1933. The potential for presidential government via Art. 48 had been amply demonstrated during the first crisis of the Republic. While the move toward presidential government had already been made by Brüning and Schleicher, Schmitt certainly rendered the institutional implications of Art. 48 more explicit and provided these implications with a theoretical foundation more congenial to the minds of authoritarian politicians and to some degree the interested public as well. The same applies to his collaboration with the Nazis between 1933 and 1936. Whatever one's position on the underlying rationale and practical import of Schmitt's support of the regime, it is understandable that a cloud of suspicion rests over Schmitt and his work generally.

It is not our aim to dispel this cloud of suspicion, nor do we mean to offer a defense of Schmitt's role in interwar Germany. In the following section, however, we hope to show that *Constitutional Theory* is distinctive among Schmitt's works from the period. As a sophisticated work in comparative constitutionalism, more specifically, it is deserving of careful attention by contemporary and future readers concerned not just with the problems of the Weimar Constitution and German constitutionalism in particular, but with the enduring problems of constitutional government more generally.

Methodology in the Weimar-Era Works

Few thinkers have played as central a role in politics as Schmitt did from 1930 to 1936. Born into a devoutly Catholic family midway through the Reich period,[51] it seemed likely that Schmitt would lead an intellectual life quite detached from politics. He chose law as a subject almost on a whim, but he pursued its study in a way typical of the time in that his early scholarly work on law reflected the reigning neo-Kantianism, which sought to avoid political considerations in jurisprudence. The revolutionary tumult of 1918–19, however, convinced Schmitt of the importance of politics, so he turned his attention first to a serious study of political theory and then to a consideration of the actual functioning of contrasting systems of government.

Earlier works like *Political Theology* and *The Crisis of Parliamentary Democracy* stressed, respectively, the need to consider the actual enforcement of legal norms and the tangible threats to parliamentary democracy. But these works mostly made reference to these issues as central to normative theory without supplying extensive analysis or much evidence to support their claims, and they reach quite immoderate conclusions about the nature of sovereignty and the viability of parliamentary government. Subsequent works also made reference to the need to examine how institutions actually function. *The Guardian of the Constitution*, for example, emphasized the institutional limitations of the judiciary in defending the constitution against radical opponents, while *Legality and Legitimacy* reiterated Schmitt's claim from *Guardian* that only the President was institutionally suited to fulfill this role. Of these two later works, however, only the latter provided extensive analysis and supporting evidence for its conclusions. *Legality and Legitimacy* was primarily conceptual in methodological and substantive terms. But in both works, Schmitt does not fully acknowledge the limitations of his own position or conscientiously consider alternatives to his preferred institutional solution, presidential government, which tended to collapse the system of separation of powers and provide few tangible limitations on executive action.

While one can raise objections to Schmitt's conclusions on particular issues, *Constitutional Theory* is his most successful effort at linking theory and practice in political theory. First, *Constitutional Theory* is not only the most moderate of his works in terms of its substantive conclusions with regard to democratic government. These conclusions are also tempered by a recognition of their limitations. This is clear, for example, in his discussion of the role of the President in the Weimar constitutional system. On Schmitt's account in *Constitutional Theory*, the President is ultimately the central point of the system, but Schmitt's portrayal of the supremacy of the President recognizes limitations of the office and its position within a larger constitutional system. The directly elected President can exert considerable leverage over a parliament organized by political parties, but the parliament, in this case the Reichstag, retains important checks on presidential authority, such as the power to rescind presidential emergency decrees. Also, the President's ability to escape the political polarization hindering the Reichstag depends to a great extent on the personal characteristics of the particular occupant. In the context of *Constitutional Theory* as a whole, however, the President gains the upper hand. Because the President is directly elected, the office bears democratic legitimacy not accorded an unelected head of state or even the representative parliament. Moreover, while the President retains many of the competencies exercised by the Kaiser under the Imperial system, such as command of the armed forces (192), he can also make recourse to expansive emergency powers. These emergency powers do not include setting aside the entire constitution, promulgating a new constitution, or even nullifying particular provisions. But the President can suspend seven important constitutional rights enumerated in Art. 48(2).[52] And Schmitt's insistence in this context that the constitution as a whole is superior to any particular provision suggests that he believes the President can suspend any individual provision, not merely those mentioned in Art. 48(2), if he deems this necessary to save the constitutional system as a whole (26–27 and 109–12).[53] That the Reichstag can repeal emergency decrees is of little consequence in view of its chronic ineffectiveness. Besides, Schmitt argues that the President can dissolve the Reichstag, even if this exceeds narrow legal limits, if he deems a no-confidence vote is merely an attempt at obstruction (357–58). This means that the President can effectively circumvent parliamentary control, as Schmitt urged late in the Republic.[54]

Constitutional Theory is also the most concrete-historical of Schmitt's Weimar-era works. In addition to developing more fully some of Schmitt's positions from earlier essays, it offers an impressive schematic treatment of the important lines of development and of the actual functioning of major systems of government, particularly as these bear on central normative issues in contemporary government. The work is divided into four major parts, and each part examines, in order, the concept of constitutions (2–121), the legal (125–220) and the political (223–359) components of constitutions, and the constitutional theory of federations (363–91). Each of these parts is divided into sections examining topics such as the absolute (3–11) and relative (11–20) concepts of constitutions. Although within these topics Schmitt discusses major developments, there is no overarching narrative or chronology. His aim is to identify essential continuities and discontinuities in the development of key concepts and consider their relevance for major features of the Weimar Constitution. He accomplishes this by examining the principal features of the Weimar Constitution in reference to major developments in constitutional government in other countries, principally France and, to a lesser degree, both the United Kingdom and the United States, but other countries as well. In this way, he intends to identify the peculiar challenges facing the Weimar Constitution and to consider the question of what might be done to make it more viable as a constitutional system.

Along the way, Schmitt discusses 103 of the Constitution's 181 provisions, though only to illustrate larger issues. Art. 153 (concerning the right to property), for example, is considered under the headings of the "positive concept of a constitution" (27), constitutional amendments (101 and 111), the concept of statutes in the *Rechtsstaat* (152), and constitutional rights (160, 165, 166, 171, and 172). Schmitt's more general concern in addressing constitutional provisions in reference to a number of different issues is to provide a "systematic framework" for considering the problems of the "*bourgeois Rechtsstaat*" (XL). In this way, Schmitt seeks to shift the center of gravity of legal theory debates away from the analysis of individual provisions of the Weimar Constitution by examining the Constitution in a much broader comparative historical framework, one in which the issue of practical relevance of the resulting normative concepts is addressed directly through the process of concept formation.

Schmitt's comparative-historical approach in *Constitutional Theory* distinguishes the work from constitutional commentaries at the time. Gerhard Anschütz's classic commentary on the Weimar Constitution is an illuminating point of comparison in this respect. In the introduction to this work,[55] Anschütz addresses a few general issues, such as whether revolutions are legitimate sources of new laws and whether, if at all, there is legal continuity with the prewar system.[56] The remainder of the work, however, is organized around the particular provisions of the Constitution, treated in chronological order. In regard to each article, Anschütz lists the relevant literature, analyzes its scope and substance, and discusses the political-legal practice relating to it. Throughout, Anschütz does not engage in a significant degree of comparative-historical analysis, nor does he address the practical efficacy of particular provisions, let alone of the Constitution as a whole.

Moreover, Schmitt's use of comparative history is a significant departure from his methodology in earlier works, which, when historical, was centered on intellectual history. A useful point of comparison is one of Schmitt's most influential works, the short polemical tract titled *The Crisis of Parliamentary Democracy*. This controversial work appeared originally in 1923, the high point of the first extended crisis of the Republic, and it was reprinted with a new preface in 1926 at approximately the middle point of a period of relative stability. Schmitt's primary claim in *Crisis* is that parliamentary democracy is facing a challenge to its very foundations, because important social changes, summarized under the heading "modern mass democracy," render problematical the open discussion essential to this form of government. Universal suffrage has given rise to "mass parties," which demand total loyalty from their members and which are expert at the manipulation of the rapidly changing communications media. Parliamentary representatives are no longer "independent" of particular interests and constituencies, willing to concede the force of the better argument. They are the instruments of various political-social groups that determine their position in closed session outside parliament or in its back chambers and that are unwilling to compromise their positions once they are determined. Parliament has become a "showplace," controlled by groups, many of which were irresponsible in that they have no genuine commitment to the system other than to use it for their own purposes.

Among the many critical responses at the time, one deserving special mention is that by Richard Thoma, who questioned why Schmitt sought out the "moral underpinnings" of parliamentary government in works written long ago in response to significantly different problems. Thoma suggested that, to discern the "purpose" of parliamentary government, Schmitt would do better to examine the works of those actually involved in the establishment of the current system, such as Hugo Preuß, Friedrich Naumann, and Max Weber, because they were responding directly to current conditions.[57] Thoma's criticisms obviously struck a nerve. For not only does Schmitt formally respond to Thoma in the preface to the second edition of *Crisis*, but in *Constitutional Theory* Schmitt bitterly recounts Thoma's charge that he wrongly focuses on the "moldy greats" of political theory in addressing the problems of parliament (e.g., 313).[58] Moreover, changes in Schmitt's method suggest he is responding to Thoma's insistence on the need for a more pragmatic, context-sensitive approach. In the preface to the second edition of *Crisis*, for example, Schmitt mostly only reiterates his claim that the present challenge to parliamentary democracy was a "spiritual" one rooted in fundamental social changes since the nineteenth century. Any approach to reform not focusing on the moral/intellectual foundations of parliamentary government will not get at the root of the problem. Parliaments might continue to function, in Schmitt's view, but only as hollow shells teetering on dangerously unstable axes. In *Constitutional Theory*, by contrast, Schmitt examines the actual history of parliamentary government in Europe in order to address the distinctive problems of the Weimar Republic. Reinhard Mehring and William Scheuerman are both right in claiming that there is a sense in which Schmitt's elaborate comparative history in *Constitutional Theory* constitutes a more empirical reworking of his argument in *Crisis.*[59] Schmitt reviews the "ideal foundations" of parliamentary government, though with much greater attention to the actual legal, political, and social developments that render parliamentary democracy obsolete in his view (307–19). Nonetheless, Schmitt's treatment of parliament in *Constitutional Theory* constitutes an important shift in emphasis from the interrelationships among normative theory, social change, and politics, on the one hand, to the structural determinants of the Weimar state crisis, on the other.

Note, for example, the treatment of the importance of social change for the ideal of government by discussion, which was so prominent in *Crisis*. While an examination of the ideal of government by discussion (307–19) is the first substantive section of Schmitt's treatment of parliament in *Constitutional Theory*, it is arguable that it forms the pivot point of his approach. In fact, this section is oddly out of place in the context of the entire discussion (303–59). It is preceded by a brief section (303–7), which effectively serves as an introduction to the subsequent problem-oriented history of the various structural means of organizing political leadership. In this introductory section, Schmitt sketches the four "parliamentary subsystems," which together form an "elastic, comprehensive system." Schmitt argues that it is "necessary to distinguish among these subsystems in order to understand parliamentary government in general, but *above all* to understand the exceptionally difficult and rather opaque system established by the Weimar Constitution" (306–7, our emphasis). With the aid of this conceptual framework, Schmitt examines how constitutional structures in Belgium, France, and Germany reflect and shape political practice in these countries (320–59).

This shift in emphasis toward a comparative-historical analysis of the structural determinants of political practice is also indicated by the fact that besides the section examining the ideal of government by discussion, the only other point at which analysis of social change figures prominently is the brief review of English parliamentary practice (320–26). These sections aim primarily at revealing the hollowness of German liberal visions of parliamentary government, which are based on the English model. Schmitt argues, for example, that the cabinet, not the allegedly sovereign parliament, provided political leadership in the nineteenth century. The parliament was at best the point of connection between the electorate that reached political decisions and the government, which provided political leadership. This partial deconstruction of Schmitt's own ideal standard is, indeed, peculiar, if his purpose is to lend more muscle to the rather sketchy narrative of *Crisis*.

These features of Schmitt's treatment of parliament in *Constitutional Theory* suggest that Schmitt seeks to engage critics like Thoma on the concrete institutional level as well. Through his comparative history of parliamentary government, Schmitt sets out to show the ways in which the peculiar constitutional structure of the Weimar Republic reflects more or less unique German developments and concerns (334–38 and340–41) and why Europe-wide trends in economics, law, politics, and society have been telescoped in a particularly disastrous way in Weimar. More important, Schmitt attempts to identify how the Republic's constitutional structure simultaneously limits and enhances the ability of particular institutions and that of the state generally to pursue coherent long-term policies (343–59).

Schmitt's enhanced concern in *Constitutional Theory* with institutional detail and his use of comparative history to address the practical problems of the contemporary system calls to mind Weber's political writings in the aftermath of World War I. Near the end of World War I, other systems were proposed as models for the reformation of the German system, raising the question of whether and to what extent these institutions were suitable for the German context with its unique characteristics. Comparative studies, Weber argued, indicate precise points of similarity and difference between the respective contexts, which aid in addressing this important question.[60] But in these political writings, Weber did not apply the ideal typical method, relying instead on more impressionistic contrasts between systems.[61] Weber's refusal to apply ideal types in his own normative arguments reflects his concern not to lend false scientific status to his claims. "The coming of age of science always implies the transcendence of the ideal type," in Weber's view.[62] Take, for example, "Benjamin Constant's theory of the ancient state," which, according to Weber, "serves as a harbor until one has learned to navigate safely in the vast sea of empirical facts." Weber argued that it "is still legitimate today to use the brilliant Constant hypothesis to demonstrate certain aspects and historically unique features of ancient political life, as long as one carefully bears in mind its ideal-typical character."[63] For viewing ideal types as empirically valid is tantamount to assuming an affirmative, decidedly one-sided answer to the important question of the cultural significance of the object of study.[64]

Schmitt's approach to comparative history in *Constitutional Theory* incorporates some aspects of Weber's ideal typical method.[65] Like Weber, for example, Schmitt develops guiding concepts through one-sided exaggerations of certain aspects of his object of study, in this case the Western constitutional tradition. As such, Schmitt's concepts may prove useful as heuristic devices, providing a means of comparison of actual instances of constitution making. As with Weber's *The Protestant Ethic and the Spirit of Capitalism* and other works utilizing ideal types,[66] the appropriateness for this purpose of concepts such as that of identity does not depend on whether they accurately portray historical individuals narrowly defined, since such artificial constructs necessarily obscure important features of events and developments in order to achieve conceptual clarity. The question is whether and to what extent the categories enable us to determine the concrete significance for a particular problem of certain works, events, and developments. In *Dictatorship*, for example, Schmitt uses the concepts of the sovereign and commissarial forms of dictatorship to identify and analyze changes in the theory and practice of constitutional dictatorship in the modern era. One can also say this of *Constitutional Theory* insofar as Schmitt uses the concept of identity to establish a spectrum of actual instances of constitution making. Schmitt's concept of identity resembles an ideal type in that it does not represent what is "common" to the myriad instances of constitution making before the founding of the Weimar Republic. In fact, according to Schmitt, the French Revolution was the first instance of a people reaching a decision regarding their political existence as a whole. Schmitt then argues that other instances of constitution making, such as the English Revolution of 1688 and the American Revolution of 1776, deviate in different respects from the French model. Using certain aspects of the French Revolution as a baseline, in other words, Schmitt executes a "systematic" study of constitution making.

The problem with Schmitt's use of concepts in *Constitutional Theory* is that he has not taken fully to heart Weber's admonition that for concepts to be used effectively in historical research they must be carefully calibrated to the range of phenomena under consideration. As the scope of the study increases, a point is reached beyond which one must break the concepts down into several, less general categories covering narrower sets of phenomena. In a subsequent work, *The Guardian of the Constitution*, Schmitt responds partly to this difficulty by using conceptual frameworks that more effectively capture dynamic relationships among diverse phenomena relevant for particular policy questions. At the center of *Guardian* is a relatively brief discussion of the Weimar state crisis,[67] the central premise of which is that one cannot adequately address the Republic's governability problems without a clear understanding of the concrete conditions under which its constitutional system operates. Schmitt seeks to determine how the economic, legal, political, and social trends summarized under three concepts—federalism, pluralism, and polycracy—intersect to limit the range of options available to the Weimar state. As concepts, these terms do not accurately portray the complex reality of politics and society. In fact, taken alone, they misrepresent actual conditions, for they typically appear in combination with one or the other factor. But the three concepts provide points of departure for examining the complex reality of state action in the Weimar Republic.[68]

At key points in *Constitutional Theory*, however, Schmitt's conceptual schema is not highly differentiated. On Schmitt's account, for example, the relevant differences between the two seminal instances of constitution making are attributable to the fact that the French state facilitated the development of a common identity among the French before the Revolution by centralizing political authority to a much greater degree than occurred in the United States prior to the American Revolution. There is, indeed, a striking difference between the French and American constitutional traditions regarding degrees of administrative centralization, as emphasized by Tocqueville in his classic accounts of the respective political traditions.[69] And it is true that the French came to understand themselves as a political community far earlier than the Americans, for whom a national consciousness emerged briefly during the Revolutionary War, only to be subordinated to the long-standing state loyalties until after the Civil War.[70] But it is not clear that the French national identity forged by the Old Regime carries the explanatory power Schmitt ascribes to it, for the national political consciousness that he sees as a prerequisite for a genuine act of constitution making was produced to a great extent by the Revolution itself, as illustrated by the so-called Municipal Revolution.[71] The fact that the communes tended to support revolutionary changes in Paris lends credence to Schmitt's claim about the importance of preexisting unity to French efforts at constitution making. However, the more important point in terms of Schmitt's argument is the fact that the committees did not tend to support the National Assembly and then the Convention because of a preexisting national identity. Rather, their support of central authorities stemmed from the perceived national dimension of local problems. When one attends to events on the ground, so to speak, one gets an entirely different image than that of the French nation acting in its collective capacity to provide itself a new political form. Instead, one sees a series of ad hoc responses to pressing circumstances, with the only common thread being the perceived need for some fundamental change in the existing system. In this crucial respect, the French and American Revolutions resemble one another a good deal more than Schmitt claims.[72] The connection Schmitt makes between degrees of centralization/decentralization, on the one hand, and national/subnational identities, on the other, is too crude to capture the complex dynamics of constitution making in France and the United States, let alone more generally. Instead of focusing on the degree of centralization of state authority generally as a possible factor in the formation of national identity, as does Schmitt, one might distinguish between centralization in terms of legislative and administrative authority to obtain a more fine-grained understanding of the development and character of national identity. For if one does not limit the scope of coverage of conceptual devices in this way, the concepts tend to obscure rather than help identify concrete points of similarity and difference that are potentially relevant to the question examined. As Weber puts it, "The more inclusive the relationships to be presented, and the more many-sided their cultural significance has been, the *more* their comprehensive systematic exposition in a conceptual system approximates the character of an ideal type, and the less is it possible to operate with *one* concept."[73]

While perhaps not insignificant, this criticism misses the point in an important sense. For Schmitt's conceptually driven comparative histories aim not at explicating important concepts and developments, though Schmitt's schematic histories are often illuminating in this regard. His point, rather, is to provide a politically efficacious form of constitutional theory. In other words, the most important consideration for Schmitt is not whether individual exaggerations or inaccuracies yield greater historical or sociological insight. What matters is whether the resulting constitutional theory responds effectively to the unique problems of the Weimar Republic.

In most other works from the Weimar period, Schmitt's desire for a politically efficacious legal and political theory led him to portray liberal theory and practice as outdated at best. *Constitutional Theory*, however, is quite different. Here, this desire leads him not to attempt to discredit liberal constitutionalism so much as to transform it from the inside out. More specifically, Schmitt's one-sided reading of Sieyès's concept of a radical break with the past, when combined with the aforementioned exaggeration of the differences between the French and American instances of constitution making in terms of national identity, enables Schmitt to obscure a very important commonality between the two seminal instances of constitution making: that central to these revolutions and the traditions of constitutional theory and practice they inspired is the idea that the legitimacy of constitutions is intimately bound up with the protection of individual liberty, however one understands it. In other words, in arguing that the central lesson of these classic instances of liberal constitution making, particularly that stemming from the French Revolution, is the idea that the legitimacy of constitutions depends on a sovereign decision of the people, and not whether the resulting constitution protects individual liberty, Schmitt effectively shifts the theoretical epicenter of the liberal constitutional tradition. By separating what he terms the legal and political components of the constitution in this way, Schmitt seeks to provide his understanding of a strong state, with its wide-ranging executive authority, a solid normative foundation in the liberal constitutional tradition.[74]

We will leave it to the reader to evaluate the legitimacy and effectiveness of Schmitt's project of theoretical reconstruction. Our aim is the more limited one of making clear the distinctive place Schmitt's *Constitutional Theory* holds within his Weimar-era work generally. We have also attempted to show that *Constitutional Theory* presents challenges to liberal theory and practice, which are quite different from those of his other, more polemical works of the period. With this in mind, it is now necessary to consider the wider theoretical ramifications of Schmitt's thought, particularly his insistence on a strict distinction between law and politics in the modern state.

Schmitt's Influence in Subsequent Debates

Schmitt's work sets out a series of far-reaching claims about the law and the state. The most important of these are that law on its own is not capable of solving social antagonism or of mediating social tensions, that political unity or a political will must preexist the law if law is to be accepted as legitimate, and that political legitimacy must have a determinate substantial content. Each of these claims leads to the conclusion that political legitimacy cannot necessarily or reliably be derived from technical, material, or formal-legal arrangements or contracts, or from majoritarian mandates or interparty bargains. They also entail seeing legitimacy as depending on the existence of prior common agreements on all issues possessing political relevance. In each of these respects, Schmitt's work encapsulates many defining political perspectives of interwar European conservatism, and his ideas form a trenchant critical commentary on the different experiments with democracy in Central Europe after 1918. Schmitt clearly implies that the new democracies of this period tended badly to miscomprehend the character of true democracy, and, by confusing democracy with pluralism, party-based majoritarianism, welfarism, and liberalism, they jeopardized their own stability, and so finally proved incapable of producing long-term principles for secure governance.

Naturally, Schmitt's ideas have been primarily received in the conservative fringes of mainstream political thought, and much subsequent right-leaning debate has been deeply marked by the antinomical structure of the arguments and concepts that underpin *Constitutional Theory*. This is especially evident in Schmitt's views on the antinomy between law and constitutional legitimacy, the treatment of which is fundamental to this work. As discussed above, these ideas gained particular purchase during the period

1930–33. Clearly, Schmitt's tendency to view the main features of the liberal Rechtsstaat, especially the separation of the legislature and the executive, the commitment to representative pluralism, and the formal catalogues of rights, as signs that the will of the state has been subject to destabilizing and delegitimizing compromises was open to a positive reception by politicians, such as Papen, Schleicher, and Hindenburg, who viewed the strong unified executive as the bastion of political stability. Similarly, it is also not difficult to discern the abiding influence of these ideas in certain tendencies in the reemergence of conservative political theory in post-1945 Germany. Even after the foundation of the Federal Republic of Germany in 1949, a number of political and sociological theorists reappeared who were prepared to use Schmittian ideas to argue against the restitution of pure-parliamentary democracy under Konrad Adenauer and, above all, to protest the linkage of democracy and social provision in the nascent post-1949 welfare state. Such theorists tended to use Schmitt's earlier analyses of constitutional law to argue that the political system of the Federal Republic replicated the structural weaknesses of the Weimar state by conflating the pure political order of the constitution with inferior laws relating to material and economic provision. The post-1949 German right, therefore, saw the redistributive state of the Federal Republic, like that of the Weimar Republic, as a state that obstructed the evolution of a genuinely legitimized constitutional order, which was founded in an overarching popular will. Examples of this can be seen in the constitutional writings of Werner Weber and Ernst Forsthoff.[75]

However, the major arguments in *Constitutional Theory* also contain implications that hold a theoretical appeal for political reflection at a number of very different points in the political spectrum and that cannot be restricted to obviously reactionary perspectives. For example, the outstanding political theorists of the first generation of the Frankfurt School, Franz Neumann and Otto Kirchheimer, elaborated a strongly Schmittian analysis of majoritarian and liberal democracy. This analysis employed Schmitt's distinction between constitutional law and subsidiary legal adjuncts, and it linked Schmitt's insights to a political-Marxist account of the legitimating processes in modern democracies and of the role of modern law in such democracies. Kirchheimer especially argued that the basis of legitimacy in modern capitalist democracies is always undermined by the fact that the fundamental decisions regarding the constitutional form of the state are forced to coexist with more technical legal principles, especially in the sphere of private law.[76] As a consequence, Kirchheimer asserted that the principles of capitalist private law always obtain a certain primacy over constitutional law, and the founding conditions of political existence expressed in the constitution are eroded or even invalidated by the fact that the applicability of

constitutional law is limited by legal principles not subject to direct political control. Capitalist democracies, Kirchheimer concluded, always lack
legitimate foundations, struggle to generate laws that are universally recognized as consistent and legitimate, and tend to employ law as a medium for
balancing distinct social and economic interests, without a genuine consensual basis. In this argument, Kirchheimer extended Schmitt's theory of
constitutional law to assert that authentic constitutional legitimacy is only
possible where one volitional decision informs and gives structure to all the
areas of society that can be legally regulated, and where a total political and
economic will suffuses all spheres of social interaction and exchange.[77] This
programmatic Marxist type of constitutional voluntarism is quite expressly
at odds with Schmitt's own political intentions. However, it is not difficult
to see how Schmitt's constitutional analysis could be taken as the basis for
a radical critique of the relation between democratic constitutional law and
capitalist private law and hence for a political program that accentuates the
necessary economic and legal-political unity of all society.

After 1949, similar claims about the relation between legality, legitimacy,
and the nature of the democratic constitution began once more to assume
central importance for left-oriented theory in Germany, especially in debates about the constitutional form and legitimacy of the Federal Republic.
In his writings of the early 1950s, for example, Franz Neumann critically
reconstructed Schmittian ideas about constitutional law to suggest that the
process of constitutional foundation should be defined as the existential
horizon of political life, providing a framework for the active-democratic
reconciliation of social freedom and political power.[78] Underlying Neumann's account of constitutional life was the claim, clearly derived from
Schmitt, that the political resource of legitimacy is always prior to the law,
and that law obtains validity as it communicates elements of a publicly and
interactively established political will. At different times in his early trajectory, Jürgen Habermas also engaged in a reception of Schmitt's arguments,
though clearly harnessing these views to a radical-democratic conception
of legitimate political order. Most obviously, in *Structural Transformation
of the Public Sphere* (1962), Habermas joined Neumann and Kirchheimer
in asserting that modern capitalist democracies are invariably marked by a
tension between the factual conditions of legal application and the democratic principles that support the legitimacy of the constitution. In political
systems commonly viewed as democratic, he explained, the unitary political will of the people is undermined by corporate techniques of economic
management and by compromises between political parties.[79] As a result,
laws do not reflect commonly formed interests or agreements, but they are
utilized primarily for administering material goods in order to maintain
basic conditions of social harmony, and they always manifest weaknesses

at the heart of the polity, both structurally and in terms of legitimacy. In modern corporate democracies, Habermas therefore argued, law does not and cannot represent a clear political will, and the original principles and rights anchored in democratic constitutions are invariably sacrificed and materialized by technical, socially palliative, and regulatory strategies. For Habermas, only a democratic polity that is based in universal agreements that are obtained in communicative interaction in a free public sphere and that communicates these agreements in the form of constitutional law can be authentically legitimate.[80]

Later in his career, Schmittian ideas continued critically to inform Habermas's reflections on the role of the welfare state in modern democracy, culminating in his anti-welfarist strictures in the early 1970s. He claimed that the welfare states of capitalist democracies tie their legitimacy to the fulfillment of economic prerogatives unlikely to find universal-rational agreement among their citizens. These states integrate their citizens through falsely materialized compromises between rival interest groups and rival political wills, and the conditions of these compromises prevent the foundation of a constitutional order that is universalizable and thus integrally legitimate.[81] Modern welfare states use the law as a technical or prerogative medium for securing material consensus between antagonistic social formations in order to engineer chimerical or fragile forms of stability. Such use of the law, however, merely reflects a weakness or a communicative deficiency in the law, and it can never fully obscure the fact that these states do not possess genuine constitutional legitimacy. Further to the party-political left than Habermas, in the 1970s Ulrich K. Preuß also applied Schmittian arguments about constitutional law categories at different critical junctures in the history of the Federal Republic of Germany. This can be seen first in his critique of the use of subsidiary laws in the late 1960s and 1970s to move constitutional reality away from the original social decisions of the Basic Law.[82] More recently, in the wake of 1989, Preuß also reconfigured Schmittian ideas in his radical-democratic account of the constitution as the basis for post-reunification political integration.[83]

In addition to its observations on the relation between law and the constitution, the second great antinomy underlying *Constitutional Theory* is apparent in Schmitt's discussion of the terms *identity* and *representation*, which he defines as the two fundamental principles of political form. This also becomes a central problem in subsequent political discourse. Most important, Schmitt argues that modern democratic states, in societies with complexly structured populations and franchises, can never obtain fully democratic legitimacy, for democracy in the strict sense means that government is conducted on the basis of a self-identical will, formed and shared by all constituents of the state, and legitimacy arises as the concrete expression of such an identical will. Modern political systems, he claims, cannot be based in immediate identity, because in complex societies it is impossible for all members of the people to be actively involved in making decisions and to participate fully in the political process. In fact, it is precisely characteristic of modern mass democracies that the people are not engaged in political decision making and that the constitutive role of political interaction in the public sphere, which characterized early democracies, has been forfeited.[84] Political systems that attempt to overcome this problematic lack of legitimating identity by proposing *representation* as the basic principle of democracy do not, however, successfully generate legitimacy for themselves. Indeed, Schmitt sees the idea of representative democracy, in the common sense of democratic rule by parliamentary representation or by other modes of deputation, as little more than a contradictory device, which was originally employed as a strategy for limiting monarchical authority (219), but is unable to create conditions of truly democratic legitimacy. Where democratic governments seek to be representative—for instance, by putting up delegates, by organizing political parties as deputations of social interests, or by establishing chambers of parliamentarians—they in fact cease to be democratic. Representative governments actually serve only to particularize and atomize society into plural spheres of interest, and thus undermine the united will of the people and fragment the identity that properly founds democracy and democratic legitimacy. In consequence, when governments attempt to be more democratic and representative—perhaps, for instance, by linking their representative claims to specific issues or mandates, or by seeking to represent the particular concerns of public opinion, of corporate groups, or of political parties—they are always likely to erode their representative basis and to degenerate into a roughly pluralistic fusion of representative and democratic elements. Governments seeking to be more democratic by means of pluralistic or material representation, in short, always become less democratic. Democracy, Schmitt concludes, cannot be representative, because democracy presupposes identity, and representation (as it is usually understood) is always in contradiction with the identity that democracy posits as its foundation (218). Government, in consequence, can either be democratic or it can be representative, but *representative democracy*—in the pluralistic sense of this concept—is always a contradiction in terms.

In modern complex societies, Schmitt then asserts, the identical will of the people is most effectively reflected in the political process through public *acclamation*: that is, through the direct affirmation given by a substantially homogeneous people, assembled in public,[85] in response to precisely and "authoritatively formulated" questions.[86] Under such conditions, the political will is not manufactured and distorted by the delegatory functions of parliaments or of political parties; it is communicated directly from the public sphere to the executive, and the executive can refer immediately to this will as the justification for its exercise of power. In other words, Schmitt indicates that modern democracy is most truly democratic when it abandons the idea that it can found itself in constant and invariable identity, and when it simply *re-presents* the basis of identity that it requires in the symbolic form of leaders and powerful politicians, who either do or do not receive acclamation for their decisions.[87] Analogously, he argues that modern democracy is most democratic when it renounces the intention to represent all particular or pluralized interests in society or to integrate all people into all aspects of policy making, and when it simply represents what it constructs—for itself—as the irreducible united will of all members of society. This idea then provides Schmitt with a solution to the antinomy between democracy and representation. Governments that found their legitimacy in acclamation are, he claims, both democratic and representative. They are democratic because they are founded in substantial identity, and they maintain their legitimacy by re-presenting this identity to the publicly assembled and unified people, in which they have their legitimating origin and justification. Such representative systems, Schmitt concludes, are in fact always likely to be more truly democratic than systems based in liberal-democratic, parliamentary-democratic, or social-democratic modes of representation. This is because their processes of representation—via acclamation—consolidate the identity of the people as a symbolic resource, whereas more common models of representative democracy, organized around political parties, parliaments and interest groups, only serve to fragment and particularize the identical will of the people before it has even been fully formed. The key to understanding the relation between identity and representation is thus to detach representation from individual material concerns and to construe representation as a process that itself instigates and articulates identity throughout all society.

It is on these grounds that Schmitt outlines one of the greatest and most controversial challenges to modern political theory: that is, his claim that the conditions of legitimate democratic governance are in fact best maintained by systems that do not conform to standard conceptions of democracy. Most especially, he argues that in modern societies democracy must necessarily be *executive democracy*. Democracy, he concludes, is best secured by systems with strong executives, concentrated around symbolic leaders and figureheads, and that systems with strong parliamentary legislatures tend to undermine their democratic content and organization. One of the main reasons for this argument is that Schmitt sees the legislatures of modern democracies as being excessively dependent on political parties as organs of will formation and decision making. Political parties, Schmitt argues, only succeed in dividing up the identity of the people and so directly impede the establishment of a united political—or "democratic"—will. Political parties are also to a large extent responsible for the fragmentation of the constitution in modern societies. This is because they recruit support from very diverse factions in society, and they sustain their institutional power and influence by forming compromises with other parties and interest groups; as a result, they tend to use law to appease or—however temporarily—to reconcile their own naturally antagonistic memberships, and they introduce irreducibly pluralist, concessionary or technical principles into the original terms of the constitution. Constitutional legitimacy, in short, expresses unity in society, whereas party-political attempts to obtain legitimacy can only express a corrosive pluralization of social interests.

Many major theorists and practitioners of politics after Schmitt have responded directly to these arguments. Most obviously, as discussed, these ideas were enthusiastically received by the non-Nazi conservatives of the late-Weimar era, who took them as the theoretical basis for a new conception of democracy based in an extremely powerful executive, with limited independent legislative competence and with minimal powers of will formation granted to elected political parties. However, after the end of the National Socialist regime, these ideas began once again to filter into broader discussions, and especially into more critical reflections on the role of the political parties in the newly formed Federal Republic of Germany under Adenauer. At this time, many political and constitutional theorists, on both the left and the right, openly echoed Schmitt in suggesting that the party system of the Federal Republic possessed only the most technically devalued mechanisms for manifesting the popular will, and that it relied on the manipulation of public opinion by corporate bodies, powerful lobbies, and political parties. The newly founded democratic system, it was widely concluded, was already beginning to exhibit features usually associated with purely representative or even issue-based plebiscitary governance, and the role of the parties was now restricted to the technical fabrication of consensus. These ideas found perhaps their most exemplary articulation in the constitutional-theoretical writings of Gerhard Leibholz, but these were widespread arguments in the 1950s and 1960s.[88]

Most important, however, the works of the early Habermas might also be seen as a highly critical response to Schmitt's claim that democratic unity cannot be fully represented in modern democracies. The younger Habermas shared Schmitt's intense hostility to democratic systems revolving around corporate techniques of consensus-maintenance, and he too viewed the tendency toward the corporate balancing of interests as a major structural weakness in modern democracies. Likewise, he was prepared to concede Schmitt's point that parties serve merely to stabilize sections of the public will in interest blocs or pragmatically motivated groups, and that these then destroy both the unity of popular will and the genuinely representative function of the public system. However, rather than seconding Schmitt's willingness to relinquish the ideal of popular democracy, Habermas took Schmitt's critical theory of democracy as a productive irritant, and he developed his own radical-democratic theory around a constructive correction of Schmitt's model of executive democracy. The central theoretical objective of the young Habermas was to explain that, even in the most complex and materially divided democracies, the united and identical will of the people can indeed be represented, and to show how the dissolution of this will by delegation procedures might be overcome. On these grounds, Habermas rejected Schmitt's claim that the people must necessarily be defined as those who are not involved in the political process, and he sought to account for a possible reconfiguration of mass democracy in which meaningful participation in will formation would not be restricted to privileged representatives. This, he claimed, could only be accomplished through a thorough and far-reaching reconception of the role Schmitt ascribed to the public sphere. The public sphere, for Habermas, should not be viewed as a space for the relatively passive manifestation of enthusiasm or acclamation, but as a potential arena of communicative interaction and radical-republican discourse, in which one can obtain agreements that might ultimately form a basis of legitimacy for the political system. At the heart of this refiguring of the public sphere is the claim that identity and representation should not be viewed as antinomies that can only be reconciled via authoritarian techniques of symbolic governance, but rather that a vibrant public sphere, neither regulated from above by steering techniques nor determined from below by material interests, might connect the popular-democratic will with the representative institutions of the state. Habermas concurred with Schmitt in the claim that the people is a concept that "becomes present only in the public sphere" (243). But his entire work is determined by the attempt to explain how the public sphere might assume a far greater constitutive role in the production of legitimacy than Schmitt might be willing to countenance. Indeed, Habermas implicitly views Schmitt's denial that the public sphere has a constitutive function as the reason why he sees the relation between representation and identity in such problematic terms.

A further theoretically resonant set of antinomies that have central importance in this work are the terms *freedom* and *equality*. In his discussion of these terms, Schmitt echoes earlier conservative and historicist arguments. He indicates, first, that the organization of a political system around programmatic principles of equality (around, for example, prescribed material entitlements, or restrictions of status) must inevitably restrict the degree of freedom that this political system guarantees. Second, then, a political system which seeks constitutionally to enshrine individual freedoms (as inviolable rights or formal-subjective attributes) necessarily limits the extent of possible political equality, and it founds political order in an underlying condition of atomized pluralism and distinction. As a consequence of this, he argues that the liberal-democratic assumption that freedom is a precondition of political equality and the Marxist or social-democratic assertion that political or material equality is constitutive of freedom are both naïve and conceptually flawed. The relation between freedom and equality, he concludes, is always one of contradiction and ex-clusion. The tension between equality and freedom can only be overcome, he states, if freedom is not viewed as a condition of individual liberty, but rather as one of identity with a unified common will, and if equality is not to be viewed as a condition of material or legal entitlement, but rather as a state of *national* equality or homogeneity. In his reflections on freedom and equality, Schmitt thus repeats his conviction that in modern societies fac-tual equality is impossible, and that the distinction between those who gov-ern and those who are governed is a structural feature of political systems now characterized as democracies. However, where those who govern and those who are governed share similar national and ethnic characteristics the factual difference between them need not be construed as a qualitative difference. In fact, it is fundamental to genuine democracies that there is no such qualitative difference (235–37), and the most stable democracies are those that do not contain a difference of this type. All democracy must therefore presuppose a substantial (not material, legal or moral) equality between its members. Where equality is construed in such terms, in fact, Schmitt concludes, the otherwise insoluble contradiction between equality and freedom can be resolved. Where equality is reconceived as substantial equality, it provides a horizon for the substantial freedom of the constitu-ents of a democracy, for members of such a democracy know their freedom as shaped and underpinned by deep-rooted common habits and identities: equality and freedom thus become corollaries of one another. Democracy, therefore, cannot presuppose formally enshrined equality; indeed, where it does so it forfeits the component of freedom in democratic life. Likewise, democracy cannot seek to guarantee particular or plural freedoms; where it does so it endangers the necessary component of equality in democratic life. But democracy, strictly defined as a freely unified will, evolves precisely from a substantive refiguring of what equality and freedom mean and how they relate to each other.

In these respects, Schmitt once again provides a crucial stimulus for subsequent political theory. His indication that equality and freedom can only be taken as the substructure for democracy where freedom is not construed individually and where equality is not conceived formally or materially drives the later influential attempts of Neumann and Habermas to illuminate the conditions under which modern democracies might construe equality and freedom—like identity and representation—as reciprocally constitutive, not exclusive, terms. Neumann, for instance, responds critically to Schmitt's substantialism by indicating that the genuine and active exercise of political freedom must lead to agreement on the necessity of the formal (and probably also material) equality of all citizens, and that only the universal enjoyment of equality can create conditions for the exercise of authentic freedom.[89] Analogously, Habermas's work is motivated, even at its deepest level, by the impulse to show that freedom and equality are not true antinomies, but are in fact co-original elements of democratic existence, such that the full exercise of individual freedom requires the recognition of other people as equally entitled participants in democratic dialogue. For all their animosity toward Schmitt, however, it is notable that Neumann and Habermas—two of the most important representatives of the post-1945 democratic left in Europe—accept Schmitt's denial that rights and freedoms can be conceptualized in purely pluralistic terms, and both claim that rights and freedoms are only validated where they are politically articulated or expressed as elements of a common democratic will. Both therefore follow in Schmitt's steps in attempting to account for democratic legitimacy as a condition that can only evolve through a substantial reconciliation of the demand for social equality and the insistence on personal liberty.

The End of High-Modern Politics?

On one level, *Constitutional Theory* clearly questions whether classical ideas of democracy are sustainable in modern societies. Indeed, the central claim in this work could not be more straightforward. It is, namely, that classical conceptions of democracy, residing in the identity of those who govern with those who are governed, cannot be transposed onto modern political systems, and that liberal-parliamentary systems that seek to emulate the classical conditions of democratic legitimacy are forced to deploy technical and ideological devices to obscure the fact that this is impossible. As we have discussed, this perspective is of seminal importance for the evolution of modern reactionary political theory, but it also acts as a powerful critical stimulus for political thinking on the democratic left.

On a rather more nuanced level, however, Schmitt's work also declares a profound attachment to classical definitions of politics, and to classical or state-centered models of the institutional fabric of the polity. One further fundamental implication of this work is that political legitimacy can only ever be expressed through the constitution of the state, and that the possession—or loss—of constitutional legitimacy by the state, defined as a representative institution situated above and against all nonpolitical associations, is the most pressing concern for all sectors of society. Deficiencies in the legitimacy of the state, in short, undermine the cohesiveness of all society, and all operations of law and politics must be viewed as deeply relevant for the preservation of legitimacy. In this respect, Schmitt is emphatic that the state is the guarantor of stability, and that all attempts to undermine or divide the classical authority of the state threaten the well-being of all society.

Here, once again, Schmitt's thought is rather awkwardly and dialectically positioned between the perspectives of the left and the right. By insisting on the constitution of state as the sole focus of legitimacy, he asserts that it is still possible (indeed necessary) to imagine a society held together in its entirety by one political will and by one declared set of principles and macropolitical orientations or directives. Indeed, for Schmitt, it is only where the interactions and concerns belonging to politics can be made transparent to a foundation of uniform volition that a society, as a whole, is likely to obtain stability and durability. Schmitt's assertion that the cohesive will of all society must be represented in the state obviously identifies him, most immediately, as a theorist of the strong executive, as an antipluralist, and so, clearly, as an authoritarian statist. Yet his related intimation that the resources of legitimacy in modern society are intensely fragile and conflictual, that all social and legal problems are, potentially at least, political problems, which involve conflict over the monopoly of power, also places him in a certain involuntary proximity to left-oriented theory.

[margin annotation: AUTHORTARIAN STATIST]

Of the greatest import in this respect is the fact that Schmitt sets out a very expansive conception of what can be properly construed as *political*. He argues that no single aspect of the governmental use of power or law can be separated from politics (125), that all expressions of rights and freedom that might deflect from the unity of political volition in the state are always relevant to questions of legitimacy, and that the application of law can always be assessed as either reinforcing or undermining the integrity of the legitimate political will. This extended conception of politics moves Schmitt toward an intensely politicized conception of society. To be sure, we might accept Renato Cristi's argument that at times Schmitt replicates aspects of early-liberal thinking in his sporadic attempt to restrict the extent to which the private economy should be subject to politicization through state regulation.[90] Nonetheless, informing the broad trajectory of Schmitt's work is a very expansive notion of politics, which insists that all social agency and all legal claims must be viewed under the stringent perspective of their relation to the will of the state, and which thus implies that the state cannot allow itself to perceive any area of social communication as neutral or, at least potentially, without political significance. This argument, although deeply hostile to all elements of left-leaning pluralism, leads him away from perspectives that have come to be associated with political theory on the right, and it marks a last attempt to salvage a full conception of political legitimacy, which construes legitimacy in the state as a site of critical contestation, possessing the most profound relevance for all members of society.

As we have seen, Schmitt's doctrine of the constitution was positively appropriated by the radical conservatives during the dissolution of the Weimar Republic, and it clearly provided a model for governments inclined to restrict civil or public participation in the exercise of power. However, his relation with contemporary thinkers and politicians on the right was not always straightforward, and there are also elements of this doctrine that sit uneasily with the more widespread conservative arguments that evolved in the political climate of the 1930s and that, in any case, are clearly incompatible with the ideologies supporting the regime of the NSDAP after the end of the Weimar Republic. First, Schmitt's simple indication that government conducted by political parties tends to fragment the popular will and weaken political legitimacy is sufficient to place him outside the immediate theoretical orbit of the NSDAP. In fact, Schmitt's argument that the constitution is the primary manifestation of political will, and is as such distinct from all technical-administrative functions, appears almost as an anticipatory rejection of the NSDAP, which assigned to itself a coordinating role between society and the state, and so expressly devalued the structural dignity of the state. Second, Schmitt's hierarchical claim that the representative powers of the state are the final and exclusive source of legitimacy in modern societies also marks him in many respects as an opponent of the lines of reactionary thought that culminated in the ideology of the NSDAP. His insistence that a state obtains legitimacy only insofar as it remains politically distinct from the plurality of interests in society can clearly not be seen as conforming to a construction of political authority that sees all society as united in one political party, and this view is not easy to harmonize with the party-based, technocratic and quasi-corporate ideas of the Nazis. Indeed, the party-based apparatus of the NSDAP must necessarily have appeared to Schmitt as a terrible confirmation of his own darkest warnings in the 1920s: namely, that the unbridled pluralism of modern liberalism must ultimately threaten the overthrow of the institutions of modern liberalism that foster and sanction it. On both these counts, therefore, his belief that legitimacy is political and that politics is focused on the will of the state meant that Schmitt's work could not easily be reconciled to the orthodoxy of the NSDAP.

Viewed in a broader context, the intense state-centered political character of Schmitt's vision of society and the centrality of the constitution in this vision might also be seen as reasons why the lines of conservative discourse emerging after 1945 also, at times, found Schmitt rather problematic and controversial. In the early years of the Federal Republic of Germany, for example, the major conservative theorists, including Arnold Gehlen, Helmut Schelsky, Hans Freyer, and Ernst Forsthoff, generally favored highly technocratic models of government that construed legitimacy in politics, at most, as the result of adequate administrative competence. These models directly limited the steering role of the state in modern societies, and they openly questioned the extent to which society could still be structured around individual political decisions, around an integral political will—or around any determinate foundation of human interest.[91] In diverse ways, these theorists were content enough to muse wistfully on the demise of politics as a key development in modern social experience; they were happy to assign political decisions to subsidiary administrative locations; and they generally accepted that modern democracies are marked by a high degree of political dispersal or polycracy. Most important, the major perspectives of post-1945 conservatism tended to deprecate, or at least to problematize, the belief that political legitimacy acts as a central structural or personal focus of modern societies, and that the attenuation of legitimacy necessarily has chronic consequences for all society. For these reasons, the theories of the post-1945 conservatives ascribed only peripheral importance to the constitution itself. As all were skeptical about the idea that society might be centered on the resources of legitimacy in the state, all suggested that societies operate quite effectively with only a minimum of substantial legitimacy, and all were prepared to accept the constitution as a mere functional or technocratic document, lacking any fundamental representative qualities. Unlike Schmitt, all these theorists expressly recognized corporate groups (including parties) as playing a major role in the maintenance of social stability and political legitimacy. Gehlen, perhaps the most influential of these thinkers, openly endorsed a polyarchical system of governance or regulation, and he denied that institutional forms could be made transparent to categorical or determinate decisions.[92] Likewise, Ernst Forsthoff, the major conservative constitutionalist of post-1945 Germany, viewed the constitution, albeit in partly Schmittian terms, as an essentially technical arrangement of rules, designed for the adequate organization of the functions of the state, not for the consolidation of a uniform will.[93]

In general, therefore, political conservatives after 1945 tended to move toward a deeply depoliticized view of modern society and its institutions. Attempts to politicize society again, they indicated, fail to recognize the decentered nature of modern social order and cling to rather Romantic notions of legitimacy as resulting from a substantial and omnipresent will. In fact, most conservatives of this time pleaded for an unburdening of the state, and for an abandonment of the classical state-centered belief that the state should be seen as the final addressee for all social problems or that all social problems have relevance for politics. This willingness to impute only secondary importance to the political system and to the constitution was ultimately taken up by Niklas Luhmann.[94] Indeed, Luhmann was only prepared to see the state itself as a minimal organ of regulation and decision making; all claims that society is centered on the state or on resources of legitimacy generated by the state, he argued, simply reflect the fact that society is unable to understand its own essential plurality and clings to counterfactual and simplistically personalized accounts of its operations.[95] Through Luhmann's influence, this view has become a pervasive argument in more recent sociological reflections on legitimacy and on its functional transformation in late-capitalist democracies.

In certain respects, Schmitt himself also moved close to minimally democratic or even technocratic perspectives in the very last years of the Weimar Republic, and he too might conceivably have felt a degree of sympathy for these theoretical positions after 1945. However, in *Constitutional Theory* Schmitt clearly insists that political institutions must be correlated with a distinct and deeply politicized will, that the validity of these institutions depends on their relation to this will, and that the well-being of all society relies on the extent to which it has a center in a decisively legitimate order of the state. On these grounds, whatever his own political intentions and affiliations, Schmitt's insistence on the necessarily *political* nature of legitimacy and his refusal to accept legitimacy as a technical, administrative, or marginal problem clearly places him out of line with the subsequent contours of German and European conservatism. Although his notion of the state clearly has its origins in earlier traditions of conservative thought, his conviction that the maintenance of legitimacy must involve the representation, in politics, of substantial social agreements cannot be exclusively aligned to the right, and, in fact, it stands against many key positions in recent and current conservative debate.

The problem in positioning Schmitt's thinking among other lines of reactionary thought, either of the movement parties of the 1920s and 1930s, or of the less compact traditions of post-1945 Germany and Europe, is that his politicized conception of society at times appears to speak from a historical epoch that has already passed, and whose passing was clearly recognized and reflected by the NSDAP. Indeed, we might say that what characterizes the ideology of the National Socialists is that it constructed a radical reactionary outlook that abandoned what had previously been the central concept of radical reactionary thought: namely, the state. Instead of focusing its account of political order on the state, this ideology opted to found its model of order on party-based, corporate, and even quasi-liberal principles of diffuse power, and it rejected the notion that the representative—or strictly *political*—legitimacy of the state was of crucial importance for upholding social stability and cohesion. This denigration of politics and the state is very clear in the pronouncements of the more orthodox theorists of the NSDAP with whom Schmitt engaged in debate, most especially in those of Otto Koellreutter, who resolutely rejected the state-centered tradition of O. K. constitutional thought exemplified by Schmitt.[96] Underlying the appeal of National Socialists, then, was the fact that it fused its authoritarian stance to an implicitly postpolitical acceptance that the state alone could not act as an organ of political representation,[97] and that the central apparatus of state was merely an adjunct of more complex and socially dispersed mechanisms for communicating and enforcing power. The refusal of the Nazis to view state legitimacy as a central category of social administration in fact, arguably, marked a peculiar element of modernity in their outlook, and the technocratic political thinkers who defined German and European reactionary theory after 1945 gave new expression to these ideas. Far from making a theoretical break with the Nazi era, therefore, much conservative theory after 1945 was fundamentally determined by the same tendency toward a functionalist or technocratic depoliticization of political questions that had marked the 1930s.

In this respect, therefore, the simultaneous approval and rejection of Schmitt's political ideas in reactionary thought has much to do with the fact that his works appear as a last attempt to construct or preserve a high-modern model of the political system, in which politics is a decisive arena that transmits guiding principles through all society. For this model, the question of legitimacy is naturally the paramount issue for all society, as all social communications are relevant to legitimacy and legal and political decisions gain validity only where they represent and communicate substantial resources of legitimacy. Since the high point of Schmitt's greatest influence in the late 1920s and early 1930s, both liberal and reactionary thinkers, in distinct but parallel ways, have tended to move toward multifocal interpretations of society, and of the role of power and the state in society, and both liberals and reactionaries have tended to avoid the emphatic assumption that all society can be centered around political resources and political contests.[98] Indeed, in more recent debate both liberal and reactionary thinking have been bound by their willingness to accept that the economy is the bastion of social and cultural stability and that questions of wider economic orientation are outside the realm of what can be meaningfully integrated into political debate. It is mainly thinkers on the left who tend to look suspiciously at processes of political decentration, pluralization, and diffusion, who are skeptical about the granting of rights and freedoms where these are decoupled from participation in political will formation, who are prepared to see all social and economic problems as connected with power and its application, and who are therefore unwilling theoretically to accept that power and politics are secondary phenomena in modern societies. Moreover, it is usually thinkers on the left who impute a necessary unity to human nature and human interests, and a necessary centrality to the institutions designed to preserve and protect these interests and this nature. Such thinkers are thus often inclined to find important theoretical currency in Schmitt's work.

Perhaps, in short, we can describe Schmitt as the last great theorist of political high modernity, who rather desperately insists that the resources of power in a society should have their focus in a definite political location, and that society loses cohesiveness where it is not founded in constitutionally legitimized principles that are communicated as power. If this description is accurate, this stance has as much to offer to thinkers on the left as to those on the right or the center; the right and the center, for whatever ideological reasons, have become accustomed to imagining power as a diminishing resource and to viewing legitimacy as little more than a functional variable in the operations of the political system and other institutions. It is only the left that still utilizes modern or high-modern modes of political analysis, that still quantifies processes of social transformation as expressions of measurable power, and that still clings to the idea that all of society might be implicated in and affected by the production of legitimacy. Obviously, political thinking on the left is unlikely to feel any allegiance to Schmitt's aggressively nationalist construction of the foundation of legitimacy, but his reluctance to sacrifice the problem of legitimacy to the indifference of late modernity ensures that his work remains fully and critically contemporary, for all sides of the political spectrum.

CONSTITUTIONAL THEORY

Schmitt's Preface

The proffered work is neither a commentary nor a series of separate monographs. It is an attempt at a *system*. In Germany today, there are excellent commentaries and monographs on the Weimar Constitution, whose high value in theory and practice is recognized and requires no further praise. But it is also necessary to make an effort to construct a systematic constitutional theory and to treat the field of *constitutional theory* as a special branch of the theory of public law.[1]

This important and independent part of written commentary on public affairs in Germany has not been elaborated on during the last generation. In public law, its issues and materials have been lumped in with very different public law matters, or they have been more or less divided up and discussed in an incidental way in the general theory of the state.[2] This can be accounted for historically by the position of public law of the constitutional monarchy, perhaps also by the peculiarity of Bismarck's Reich Constitution, whose ingenious design combined elemental simplicity and complicated incompleteness. But it probably most of all stems from the political and social feeling of security of the prewar era.[3] A particular view of "positivism" serves to drive fundamental questions of public law from the realm of constitutional theory and into general state theory, where they occupy an unclear middle position between state theory generally and philosophical, historical, and sociological matters. It is necessary here to remind oneself that constitutional theory in France also developed late. In 1835, a professorship for constitutional law was established (for Rossi) in Paris, which, however, was once again eliminated in 1851 (after Napoleon the Third's coup d'état). The Republic established a new professorship in 1879, and yet in 1885 Boutmy still complained (in his *Etudes de Droit constitutionnel*) that the most important branch of public law in France was neglected and that no recognized authority had emerged in this field. Today, the characteristic property of this part of public law finds expression in famous names such as Esmein, Duguit, [XII] and Hauriou. It is predictable that the scholarly treatment of the Weimar Constitution also leads in Germany to the formation of a constitutional theory, when foreign or domestic disturbances do not hinder the calm and collective work toward this end. The public law events of recent years, especially the publications of the Association of German State Law Teachers, already exhibit this tendency. If the judicial review of the constitutionality of statutes develops further,[4] as is to be expected from the current position of the *Reichsgericht*, that will also lead to an engagement with the constitutional theory dimension of all legal questions.[5] Finally, permit me to mention that even the findings that I have been able to make since 1919, in lectures, exercises, and exams, confirm this view of constitutional theory as an independent area of public law meriting its own treatment. In fact, already now a large portion of university lectures on general state theory (politics) concern constitutional theory.

Because initially only a simple schematic should be outlined, it is not a question of exhausting monographically the individual questions of public law and of reviewing the literature. Incidentally, good compilations are found in the commentaries on the Weimar Constitution by Anschütz and by Giese as well as in the outline of the public law of the Reich and of individual Lands by Stier-Somlo, so that it is not necessary to repeat an inventory of book titles. In a scholarly exposition, quotations and debate are certainly unavoidable. In this context, however, they are above all thought of as examples and should clarify the position of specific individual questions in the system of constitutional theory. The issue here always is presenting clear, transparent, and systematic outlines. That must be emphasized, because a systematic consciousness seems to be lacking in Germany at present, and because already even in popular scholarly collections (which could still retain their justification only through the strictest systematic approach), the Weimar Constitution is considered "in the form of a free commentary," in other words, in the notes to the individual articles. My intention is to offer a systematic framework, which stands in contrast to the method of commentating on and glossing the constitution, but also in contrast to the breaking down of a unified subject into individual investigations. In such an approach, neither all the questions of public law nor all those of general state theory [XIII] will be answered. But in terms of both public law and general state theory, that should mean a clarification of the general principles as well as of some individual questions, if one succeeds in developing a constitutional theory in the sense intended here.

Most important, the constitutional theory of the bourgeois Rechtsstaat is presented.[6] In that regard, one can find no objection to the book, for today this type of state is still generally the dominant form, and the Weimar Constitution conforms thoroughly to its type. So it seemed appropriate to refer in the first instance to the classic exemplars of French constitutions. Nonetheless, these French constitutions should in no way be elevated to an absolute dogma, whose historically conditioned quality and political relativity must be ignored. On the contrary, it is among the tasks of constitutional theory to demonstrate how much some traditional formulas and concepts are entirely dependent on prior situations, so they are not at all old wine in new bottles, but instead only an outmoded and false etiquette. Numerous dogmatic ideas of contemporary public law are still entirely rooted in the mid-nineteenth century, with its long-forgotten sense of serving social "integration." I would like to use this concept, which Rudolf Smend made serviceable for public law, in order to refer to a simple factual situation. In the nineteenth century, when prominent definitions of statute and other important concepts originated, the concern was the integration of a certain social class, the educated and propertied bourgeoisie in particular, into a specific, then existing state, which was the monarchy that was more or less absolute. In a completely changed situation today, these formulations lose their substance. One will reply that even the concepts and distinctions of my work are conditioned by the circumstances of the period. But then it would already be an advantage if the concepts and distinctions were at least set in the present and did not presuppose a long past situation.

A special difficulty for the constitutional theory of the bourgeois Rechts-staat lies in the fact that even today the bourgeois Rechtsstaat component of the constitution is still confused with the entire constitution, although it cannot actually stand on its own. It serves, rather, only as a supplement to the political component. That one—falsely—casts the principles of the bourgeois Rechtsstaat as equivalent to the constitution in general has led to [XIV] the disregard of or failure to recognize essential processes of con-stitutional life. The treatment of the concept of sovereignty has suffered the most under this method of fictions and of disregarding specific circum-stances. In practice, then, the habit of apocryphal acts of sovereignty de-velops. It is characteristic of this practice that state authorities and offices, without being sovereign, nevertheless occasionally and under tacit accep-tance implement acts of sovereignty. The most important instances are dis-cussed at the appropriate point in the following exposition (pp. 108, 150, 177).[7] A detailed elaboration of this question would belong in the theory of sovereignty and, therefore, in general state theory. Also, the debate with H. Heller's theory of sovereignty (*Die Souveränität*, Berlin, 1927) concerns questions of state theory and must be addressed in another context. Only that which pertains to constitutional theory in its narrow sense is consid-ered here. The theory of state forms in general, like the theory of democ-racy, monarchy, and aristocracy in particular, is for the same reason lim-ited to that which is essential for constitutional theory (in contrast to state theory). And, by the way, the limitations of scope set by the publisher have already been exceeded.

While this work was in press, there appeared a series of writings and essays that are of particular interest for the theme of constitutional theory, and the great number of which demonstrate that the specific constitutional theory side of public law is emerging more emphatically. The proceedings of the conference of the German Teachers of State Law in 1927 are quoted according to the report of A. Hensel in the *Archiv des öffentlichen Rechts* (v. XIII, new series, 97ff.), because the complete publication (Heft 4 of the Publications of the Association of German Public Law Scholars, W. de Gruyter) first appeared in December of 1927. Also while the book was in press, I became aware of the following publications, which at least deserve mention: Adolf Merkl, *Allgemeines Verwaltungsrecht* (published by J. Springer); Walter Jellinek, *Verwaltungsrecht* (published by J. Springer); O. Koellreutter, the essay "State" in the *Handwörterbuch der Rechtswissenschaft*, edited by Stier-Somlo and A. Elster; the essays by G. Jèze, *L'entrée au service public* (Revue du droit public, XLIV); Carré de Malberg, *La constitutionalité des lois et al Constitution de 1875*; Berthélemy, *Les lois constitutionelles devant les juges* (*Revue politique et parlementaire* CXXX II/III); and W. Scheuner, "Über die verschiedenen Gestaltungen des parlamentarischen Regierungssystems" (*Archiv des öffentlichen Rechts*, XIII). A new edition of Poetzsch-Heffter's commentary on the Reich Constitution is announced for January 1928 (to be published by O. Liebmann). Unfortunately, it was not possible to take up the new work of these excellent jurists. Additionally, a book by Rudolf Smend on questions of constitutional theory has been announced. I have attempted in my present work to engage thoroughly his previous publications and have, in the process, for the first time experienced completely the richness and the deep fruitfulness of his thought. Therefore, I especially regret that I cannot become more acquainted with and make use of the anticipated constitutional theory essay.

BONN, DECEMBER 1927

Carl Schmitt

PART I

CONCEPT OF THE CONSTITUTION

§ 1.

Absolute Concept of the Constitution

(The Constitution as Unified Whole)

[3] The term "constitution" has various senses. In a general meaning of the word, everything, each man and thing, every business and association, is somehow included in a "constitution," and everything conceivable can have a "constitution." A distinctive concept does not derive from this. A proper understanding requires that the meaning of the term "constitution" be limited to the constitution of the *state*, that is to say, the political unity of the people. In this limited meaning, "constitution" can describe the state itself, and, indeed, an individual, concrete state as political unity or as a particular, concrete type and form of state existence. In this instance, it means the *complete condition* of political *unity* and *order.* Yet "constitution" can also mean a closed *system of norms* and, then, in the same way, can designate a unity, however, not a concrete existing unity, but instead a reflective, *ideal one.* In both cases, the concept of the constitution is *absolute* because it expresses a (real or reflective) *whole.* Moreover, a form of expression is dominant today, which calls any series of specially constituted *statutes* a constitution. In the process, constitution and constitutional law are treated as identical. Every *individual* constitutional law can appear as a constitution, so the concept becomes *relative.* It no longer concerns an entirety, an order and a unity. It involves, rather, a few, several, or many individual statutory provisions constituted in a particular way.

The usual textbook definition is a constitution = fundamental norm or basic law. What "fundamental" means here remains mostly unclear. It often means something especially politically important or inviolable, just as one also speaks ambiguously of "fundamental" rights, "anchorage," and so forth. The constitutional theoretical meaning of such turns of phrase result from the following conceptual investigation; compare the overview of the various meanings of "lex fundamentalis," "fundamental norm" or "fundamental law" below § 5, p. 42. [4]

I. *Constitution in the Absolute Sense* can mean, to begin with, the concrete manner of existence that is a given with every political unity.

1. The first meaning is constitution = the concrete, collective condition of political unity and social order of a particular state. Political unity and social order is part of every state. It is, in other words, some principle of unity and order, some decision-making authority that is definitive in critical cases of conflicts of interest and power. One can term this collective condition of political unity and social order a constitution. The word, then, designates not a system or a series of legal principles and norms, according to which the formation of the state will and the exercise of state activity

regulates itself, and in the following of which the order is evident. Rather, it actually only designates the concrete, individual state, such as German Reich, France, or England, in its concrete political existence. The state does not *have* a constitution, which forms itself and functions "according to" a state will. The state *is* constitution, in other words, an actually present condition, a *status* of unity and order. The state would cease to exist if this constitution, more specifically, this unity and order, ceased to exist. The constitution is its "soul," its concrete life, and its individual existence.

The word "constitution" often has this sense in Greek philosophy. According to Aristotle, the state (πολιτεία) is an order (τάξις) of the naturally occurring association of human beings of a city (πόλις) or area. The order involves governance in the state and how it is organized. By the virtue of this order, there is a ruler (κύριος). However, a component of this order is its living goal (τέλος), which is contained in the actually existing property of the concrete political formation (*Politics*, bk. IV, chap. I, 5). If this constitution is eliminated, the state is as well; if a new constitution is founded, a new state arises. Isocrates (*Areopag.* 14) calls the constitution the soul of the city (Φύχη πόλεως ἡ πολιτεία). It is perhaps best to clarify this idea of the constitution through a comparison. The song or musical piece of a choir remains the same if the people singing or performing change or if the place where they perform changes. The unity and order resides in the song and in the score, just as the unity and order of the state resides in its constitution.

When George Jellinek (*Allgemeine Staatslehre*, p. 491) describes the constitution as "an order that forms itself according to the state will," he confuses an actually existing order with a norm, which functions according to something lawlike and proper. All the ideas coming into consideration here, such as unity, order, aim (τέλος), life, soul, should denote something existing, not something merely normative, properly commanded.

2. The second meaning is constitution = a special type of political and social order. In this instance, constitution means the concrete type [5] of supremacy and subordination because there is in social reality no order without supremacy and subordination. The constitution is a special form of rule, which is part of every state and not detachable from its political existence, for example, monarchy, aristocracy, or democracy, or however one intends to divide up state forms. Constitution is the equivalent of *state form*. In this regard, the word "form" also denotes something already existing, a *status*, not something of the nature of a legal principle, rule, or normative command. Even in this sense of the term, every state obviously has a constitution, for the state always corresponds to one of the forms in which states exist. Even in this regard, it would be more exact to say that the state *is* a constitution. It *is* a monarchy, aristocracy, democracy, council republic, and does not *have* merely a monarchical or other type of constitution. The constitution is a *"form of forms,"* forma formarum.

In this sense, the word "status" (alongside other meanings of the ambiguous term, for example, condition in general, rank, etc.) is especially used in the medieval period and in the seventeenth century. Relying on Aristotle, Thomas Aquinas in his

[margin handwritten note:] ORDER RESULTS FROM SUPREMACY & SUBORDINATION

Absolute Concept of the Constitution

Summa theologica (I, II, 19, 10c) distinguished among state forms: 1. aristocratic state (status optimatum), in which a minority that is somehow distinguished and exceptional rules (in quo pauci virtuosi principantur); 2. oligarchy (status paucorum), in other words, the rule of a minority without regard to an especially distinguished quality; 3. democracy (the status popularis), in which the multitude of farmers, craftsmen, and workers rule. In terms of state forms, Bodin (*Les six livres de la République,* 1st edition 1577, especially in book VI) distinguishes the popular state (état populaire), monarchical state (état royal), and aristocratic state. In Grotius (*De iure belli ac pacis* 1625), status is, so far as the expression is of interest in this regard, the "forma civitatis," and, as such, also a constitution. In a similar way, Hobbes (for example, *De cive* 1642, chap. 10) speaks of status monarchicus, status democraticus, status mixtus etc.

A successful revolution directly establishes a new status and *eo ipso* a new constitution. Thus, in Germany after the transformation of November 1918, the Council of People's Deputies could speak of the "constitution established through the revolution" in its announcement of 9 December 1918 (W. Jellinek, "Revolution and Reichsverfassung," *Jahrbuch des öffentlichen Rechts* IX, 1920, p. 22).

3. The third meaning is constitution = the principle of the *dynamic emergence* of political unity, of the process of constantly renewed *formation* and *emergence* of this *unity* from a fundamental or ultimately effective *power* and *energy.* The state is understood not as something *existing,* resting statically, but as something emerging, as something always *arising* anew. [6] Political unity must form itself daily out of various opposing interests, opinions, and aspirations. According to the expression of Rudolf Smend, it must "integrate" itself.

This concept of constitution stands in opposition to previous ones, which speak of a *status* (in the sense of a static unity). Nevertheless, *Aristotle's* idea is there is also the dynamic element. The sharp separation of static and dynamic has something artificial and violent about it. In any case, this "dynamic" concept of constitution remains in the sphere of (emerging) being and of the existing. The constitution, therefore, does not yet become (as is the case with the constitutional concept to be handled below in section II a mere rule or norm, under which one subsumes something. The constitution is the active principle of a dynamic process of effective energies, an element of the becoming, though not actually a regulated procedure of "command" prescriptions and attributions.

Lorenz von Stein considered this constitutional concept in a large, systematic framework. He speaks, however, only of the French constitutions since 1789. Yet at the same time, he touches on a general dualistic principle of constitutional theory, which is recognized especially clearly in Thomas Aquinas (*Summa Theologica,* I, II, 105, art. 1), while two things are emphasized (duo sunt attendenda): first, the participation of all citizens in the formation of the state will (ut omnes aliquam partem habeant in principatu), and, second, the type of government and rule (species regriminis vel ordinationis principatum). It is the old opposition between freedom and order, which is related to the opposition of the principles of political form (identity and representation) developed below (§ 16, II). For Stein, the first constitutions of the revolution of 1789 (specifically, the constitutions of 1791, 1793, 1795) are state *constitutions* in the actual sense in contrast to the state *orders*), which begin with Napoleon (1799). The distinction is that the state *constitution* is that type of order which produces the agreement of the individual will with the collective state will and incorporates individuals into the living body of the state organism. All constitutional institutions and processes have the sense that the state "recognizes itself as the personal unity of the will of all free personalities that is determined through self-mastery." By contrast, the state *order* considers the individual and the authorities already as parts of the state and demands *obedience* from them. In the state constitution, state life rises from below to above; in the state order, it proceeds from above to below. The state constitution is the *free formation* of the state will; the state order is the organic execution of the will so formed (*Geschichte der sozialen Bewegung in Frankreich*, vol. I, *Der Begriff der Gesellschaft*, G. Salomon ed., Munich 1921, pp. 408/9; additionally, *Verwaltungslehre*, I., p. 25). The thought that the constitution is the effective fundamental principle of political unity found clear expression in the famous lecture of F. Lassalle, *Über Verfassungswesen*, 1862: "If, therefore, the constitution forms the basic law of a Land, then it would be an *effective power.*" Lassalle locates this effective power and the essence of the constitution in actual power relations.

Lorenz von Stein is the foundation for the nineteenth-century German thinking on constitutional theory (and, simultaneously, the conduit through which Hegel's philosophy of the state remains vital). Stein's thought is recognizable everywhere, in Robert Mohl, in the Rechtsstaat theory of Rudolf Gneist, in Albert Haenel. That stopped as soon as thought on constitutional theory ended. This means, specifically, it ceased with the ascendancy of Laband's method, which limits itself to exercising the art of literal interpretation of the text of constitutional provisions. That was called "positivism."[7]

Rudolf Smend first set the problem of constitutional theory again in its full scope in his essay "Die politische Gewalt im Verfassungsstaat und das Problem der Staatsform" (*Festgabe für W. Kahl*, Tübingen 1923). In the following, I will often revisit the ideas of this essay. Thus, the theory of "integration" of state unity, as it has until now—unfortunately only in the form of a sketch—been presented, seems to me to be a continuation of the theories of Lorenz von Stein.

II. A constitution in the absolute sense can mean a *fundamental legal regulation.* In other words, it can signify a unified, closed *system* of higher and ultimate *norms* (constitution equals norm of norms).

1. In this regard, constitution is not an actual existing condition, also not a dynamic becoming. It is, rather, something normative, a mere "command." Yet it is not a matter of individual laws or norms, perhaps even if they are very important or distinguished by external features. It involves the entire normative framework of state life in general, the basic law in the sense of a closed unity, and of the "law of laws." All other laws and norms must be traced back to this one norm. In one such meaning of the word, the state becomes a legal order that rests on the constitution as basic norm, in other words, on a unity of legal norms. In this instance, the word "constitution" denotes a unity and totality. Consequently, it is also possible to

identify state and constitution, not, however, as in the previous meaning of the term, in the manner of state = constitution, but the other way around. The constitution is the state, because the state is treated as something genuinely *imperative* that corresponds to norms, and one sees in the state only a system of norms, a "legal" order, which does not actually exist, though it is valid in normative terms. The legal order, nonetheless, establishes an absolute concept of the constitution because a closed, systematic unity of norms is implemented and rendered equivalent to the state. Therefore, it is also possible to designate the constitution as "sovereign" in this sense, although that is in itself an unclear form of expression. For only something existing in concrete terms can properly be sovereign. A merely valid norm cannot be sovereign.

The turn of phrase that norms and laws, not men, rule and, in this sense, should be "sovereign" is very old. For modern constitutional theory, the following historical development comes into consideration. In the time of the monarchical restoration in France and under the July Monarchy (therefore, from 1815 to 1848), the representatives of bourgeois liberalism in particular, the so-called "doctrinaires," designated the constitution (the Charte) as "sovereign." This remarkable [8] personification of a written law had the sense of elevating the statute, with its guarantees of bourgeois freedom and of private property,[1] over every political power. In this way, the actual political question whether the prince or the people are sovereign was evaded. The answer is simple. Neither the prince nor the people but rather "the constitution" is sovereign (cf. below § 6 II 7, p. 54). That is the typical answer of liberals under the bourgeois Rechtsstaat, for which the monarchy as well as democracy are restricted in the interest of bourgeois freedom and of private property (about this see below §16, p. 216). Thus a typical "doctrinaire" of the restoration and Louis-Philippe period, Royer-Collard, speaks of the sovereignty of the constitution (confirmation in J. Barthélemy, *Introduction du régime parlementaire en France*, 1904, p. 20ff.). Guizot, a classic representative of liberal commitment to the Rechtsstaat, speaks of the "sovereignty of reason," of justice, and of other abstractions, in the proper knowledge that a norm can be called "sovereign" only to the extent that it is not positive will and command but is the rationally correct will, reflects reason, and constitutes justice, and therefore has particular *qualities*; for otherwise only those who exercise will and command are sovereign. With regard to the French constitution of 1830, Tocqueville consistently advocated the inalterability of the constitution and emphasized that the collective powers of the people, of the king as well as of parliament, are derived from the constitution, and that outside of the constitution, all these political powers are nothing ("hors de la Constitution ils ne sont rien," n. 12 to vol. 1, chap. 6 of *Démocratie en Amérique*).

Hans Kelsen's state theory, reiterated in numerous books (*Hauptprobleme der Staatsrechtslehre, entwickelt aus der Lehre vom Rechtssatz*, 2d ed., 1923; *Das Problem der Souveränität und die Theorie des Völkerrechts*, 1920; *Der soziologische und der juristische Staatsbegriff*, 1922; *Allgemeine Staatslehre*, 1925), also portrays the state as a system and a unity of legal norms, however without the slightest effort to explain the substantive and logical principle of this "unity" and of this "system." Kelsen's state theory also does not fully consider how this unity occurs and according to what necessity it follows that the many positive legal provisions of a state and the various constitutional law norms form one such "system" or a "unity." The political *being* or *becoming* of the state unity and order is transformed into that which merely functions, the opposition of being and the normative is constantly mixed up with that of substantial *being* and legal *functioning*. However, the theory becomes understandable when one sees it as the final product of the previously discussed genuine theory of the bourgeois Rechtsstaat, which sought to make a legal order out of the state and perceives in it the essence of the Rechtsstaat. In its great epoch during the seventeenth and eighteenth centuries, the bourgeoisie mustered the strength to establish an effective system, in particular the individualistic law of reason and of nature, and formed norms valid in themselves out of concepts such as private property and personal freedom, [9] which should be valid prior to and above every political being, because they are *correct* and *reasonable* and can contain a genuine *command* without regard to the actually existing, that is, positive-legal reality. That was a logically consistent normative order. One was able to speak of system, order, and unity. With Kelsen, by contrast, only *positive* norms are valid, in other words, those which are *actually* valid. Norms are not valid because they *should* properly be valid. They are valid, rather, without regard to qualities like reasonableness, justice, etc., only, therefore, because they are *positive* norms. The imperative abruptly ends here, and the normative element breaks down. In its place appears the tautology of a raw factualness: something is valid when it is valid and because it is valid. That is "positivism." Whoever seriously insists that "the" constitution as "basic norm" is valid and that everything else that is valid should derive from it may not take any given, concrete provision as the foundation of a pure system of unadulterated norms, merely because it is set by a particular office, recognized, and designated as "positive." A normative unity or order is only derivable from systematic, *correct* principles, which are normatively consistent and, therefore, valid in themselves by virtue of reason and justice without regard for their "positive" validity.

2. The fact is a constitution is valid because it derives from a constitution-making capacity (power or authority)[2] and is established by the will of this constitution-making power. In contrast to mere norms, the word "will" denotes an actually existing power as the origin of a command. The will is existentially present; its power or authority lies in its being. A *norm* can be valid because it is *correct*. The logical conclusion, reached systematically, is natural law, not the positive constitution. The alternative is that a norm is valid because it is positively established, in other words, by virtue of an existing *will*. A norm never establishes itself (that is a fantastic manner of speaking). A norm is recognized as correct because it is derivable from principles whose character is also recognized as correct and not only as possessing a positive quality, which is understood to mean an actual establishment of a norm. Whoever says that the constitution is valid as basic *norm* (not as positive will) maintains, consequently, that the constitution is capable of bearing a closed system of correct principles by virtue of particular logical, moral, or other *substantive* qualities. It is a contradictory confusion to say that a constitution is valid not because of its normative correctness, but only because of its positive character, and that neverthe-

less the constitution as pure norm establishes a system or an order of pure norms. [10]

There is no closed constitutional system of pure norms, and it is arbitrary to treat a series of individual provisions, which one understands as constitutional laws, as a systematic unity and order, when the unity does not arise out of a preestablished, unified will. It is just as arbitrary to speak of legal order without further clarification. The concept of legal order contains two entirely different elements: the normative element of justice and the actually existing element of concrete order. The unity and order lies in the political existence of the state, not in statutes, rules, and just any instrument containing norms. The ideas and terms that speak of the constitution as "basic law" or a "basic norm" are for the most part unclear and imprecise. They attribute a systematic, normative, and logical unity to a series of highly diverse sets of norms, for example, the 181 articles of the Weimar Constitution. In view of the intellectual and substantive difference between the individual provisions, which are contained in most of the constitutional laws, that is nothing more than a crude fiction. The unity of the German Reich does not rest on these 181 articles and their validity, but rather on the political existence of the German people. The will of the German people, therefore something existential, establishes the unity in political and public law terms beyond all systematic contradictions, disconnectedness, and lack of clarity of the individual constitutional laws. The Weimar Constitution is valid because the German people "gave itself this constitution."

3. The images of the constitution as a normative unity and something absolute are explicable historically from the time in which one considered the constitution a complete codification. This rationalistic belief in the wisdom of the lawmaker dominated France during 1789, and one entrusted oneself with formulating a conscious and complete plan for the entire political and social life. Indeed, some even had doubts about moving the possibility of a change and revision into consideration. But there is no longer the belief in the possibility of a complete system of provisions that encompasses the state in its totality and is conclusively correct. Today, the contrary awareness is propagated: that the text of every constitution is dependent on the political and social situation of its time of origin. The reasons that certain legal determinations [11] are written into a "constitution" and not into a simple statute depend on political considerations and on the contingencies of party coalitions. But the purely normative concept of the constitution, as the liberal idea of an absolute Rechtsstaat presupposed, is eroding along with the belief in codification and systematic unity. This belief was only possible so long as the metaphysical assumptions of the bourgeois belief in natural law persisted. The constitution transformed itself now into a

series of individual positive constitutional laws. When today one nevertheless still speaks of fundamental norm, basic law, etc.—it is superfluous to
cite examples and evidence for this—one does so because of the aftereffect
of traditional formulas, which have long since become empty. It is just as
imprecise and confusing to always speak of "the" constitution. One actually
means an unsystematic majority or multitude of constitutional law provisions. The concept of the constitution is relativized as the concept of the
individual constitutional *law.*

§ 2.

Relative Concept of the Constitution

(The Constitution as a Multitude of Individual Laws)

Rendering relative the concept of constitution means that instead of a unified constitution in its entirety, there is only the *individual constitutional law*. The concept of constitutional law, however, is defined according to so-called *formal characteristics* that are external and peripheral.

I. Constitution in a relative sense, therefore, means the individual constitutional law. Every substantive and factual distinction is lost due to the dissolution of the unified constitution into a multitude of individual, formally equivalent constitutional laws. Whether the constitutional law regulates the organization of the state will or has any other content is a matter of indifference for this "formal" concept. It is no longer generally asked why a constitutional provision must be "fundamental." Moreover, this relative, so-called formal perspective, makes everything indistinguishable, renders equal whatever is in a "constitution." In other words, it makes everything equally relative. [12]

There are countless such provisions in the Weimar Constitution. From these provisions it is immediately evident that they are not fundamental in the sense of a "law of laws." Take, for example, Art. 123, 2, which provides that "open-air gatherings can be required to give prior notification by Reich statute and can be prohibited if there is a direct danger to public safety." Art. 129, 3, 3 stipulates that "the secrecy of his personal documents is guaranteed the civil servant." "Teachers in public schools," according to Art. 143, "have the rights and duties of civil servants." Art. 144, p. 2 provides that "supervision of schools will be exercised by expertly trained civil servants, who are acting in an official capacity." According to Art. 149, 3, "The theological faculties in universities are to be preserved." All these are *statutory* regulations, which became constitutional laws when incorporated into "the Constitution." The historical and political situation of the year 1919 explains their incorporation into "the Constitution." The parties, on whose mutual cooperation the majority of the Weimar National Assembly relied, placed value on giving just these provisions the character of constitutional law norms. A factual reason is not discernible for distinguishing, with legal-logical necessity, these individual provisions from other provisions, which are also very important. One could have just as well written into the constitution that civil law marriage and the indissolubility of marriage are guaranteed, that freedom of bequest exists, that those entitled to hunt must pay in full for damage to wilderness areas, or that rents may not be raised in the next ten years.

Such constitutional details are all equally "fundamental" for an approach to law that is indiscriminately formalistic and relativistic. The clause of Art. 1, 1 of the Weimar Constitution reading "The German Reich is a republic," and that of Art. 129 stating that "civil servants are secure in their personal effects," are both "basic norms," "law of laws," etc. However, it is self-evident that in such instances of formalization, these individual provisions in no way retain a fundamental character. On the contrary, the genuinely fundamental provisions are relegated to the level of constitutional law detail.

Now, the "formal" characteristics of the constitutional concept are at issue. Nevertheless, it is necessary to remind oneself that the confusion of manner of expression with concept formation, which is typical today, is very great. First, the constitution (as unity) and constitutional law (as detail) are tacitly rendered equivalent and confused with one another. Second, "constitution in the formal sense" and "constitutional law in the formal sense" are not distinguished. And, finally, for the determination of the "formal" character, two features are offered, which are drawn from entirely disparate perspectives. In one instance, only a *written* constitution is designated as a "constitution in the formal sense," and, in another, the formal element of constitutional law and the constitution that is implicitly rendered equivalent should consist in the *linkage of its alteration with qualified prerequisites and procedures.* [13]

II. *The Written Constitution.* Of course, the "formal component" of the written constitution cannot reside in the fact that someone sets some provisions or agreements down on paper, promulgates them or has them promulgated, hence meaning there is a written document. The character of the formal component is due to the fact that certain properties, whether of the person or office promulgating it or of its content, justify speaking of a constitution in a formal sense. Considered historically, the content and meaning of the written constitution can be very multifaceted and diverse.

In the nineteenth century, for example, up until the year 1848, the German bourgeoisie demanded a written constitution in its struggle with absolute monarchy. The concept of an ideal constitution became an ideal concept, in which the most diverse demands of the bourgeois Rechtsstaat were deposited. It is obvious that these demands of the liberal bourgeoisie for a written constitution were not fulfilled, merely because the king issued some order with any content whatsoever and prepared a proclamation for it. As a written constitution in the sense of this political demand, only that which corresponded substantively to these demands was valid. Cf. in this regard § 4, p. 39 below.

The reasons to designate a written constitution a constitution in the formal sense are also very diverse and derive from opposing perspectives, which must be distinguished from one another here. To begin with, it is the general idea that something that is fixed in writing can be demonstrated more effectively, that its content is stable and insulated against change. However, both perspectives, *demonstrability* and greater *stability*, do not suffice to enable one to speak of something as formal in a precise sense. More accurately, the act of putting something in written form must stem from an authoritative office. A process recognized as authoritative is presupposed before that which is put in writing can be validated as authentically written. The acts of writing down something and promulgating it only supplement a particular procedure and are not its definitive elements. The written constitution must come about in a special procedure, more specifically, one that is in accord with the demands of the nineteenth-century German bourgeoisie, or that which is *agreed upon* (cf. below § 6, p. 54). "If I pose this question (about the nature of the constitution) to a jurist, he will give me an answer like the following: A constitution is a pact, affirmed by oath, between king and people that establishes the fundamental principles of lawmaking and government in a country" (Lassalle, 1862). The constitution, therefore, would be a written *contract.* [14] Once the constitution is established, however, it is alterable via *legislation* and appears as a written *law.* In both cases, of course, it is only a matter of the popular assembly (the parliament) lending its consent. The concept "contract" and "statute" only have the political sense of guaranteeing the participation of the popular assembly. Like other formalities, such as the solemn act of oath taking, promulgation supplements popular consent. By themselves, such formal characteristics can never suffice.

The end result, however, is that the demand for a "written constitution" leads to the constitution being treated like a *statute.* Even if it comes about by way of an agreement between prince and the popular assembly, it should only be changed via legislation. Constitution becomes equivalent to a statute, even if a special type of statute, and as lex scripta it stands in opposition to customary law. Nonetheless, the principle, constitution = lex scripta, still need not mean the dissolution of the unified constitution into a series of individual constitutional laws. Historically, the practice of the modern written constitution begins as an opposition to English constitutional practice, which is principally based on custom and usage. The English colonies in North America, which declared themselves independent states on 4 June [*sic*] 1776, gave themselves written constitutions, which would be drafted and promulgated by the "constitution-making" assemblies as statutes (below § 4, II, 3, p. 40). These constitutions, however, were considered codifications, not individual constitutional laws. When the concept of the written constitution leads to the handling of the constitution as a statute, initially it is only in the sense of an absolute concept of the constitution, more specifically, as a *unity* and as an *entirety.* The English constitution, which rests on diverse acts, on agreements, contracts, individual statutes, customs, and precedents, is valid not as a constitution in the formal sense, because it is not complete. In other words, it is not written and issued as a closed codification in the form of a statute. There have been numerous individual constitutional laws issued in the form of statutes. To name only one example, there is the famous Act of Parliament of 1911, which limited the legislative consent of the upper house (below p. 295). This means England has constitutional laws in the sense of written individual constitutional laws. If [15] one nevertheless says that England has no constitution in the formal sense, one understands a constitution to be a closed codification, which regulates comprehensively the procedure of state will formation. The idea of a written constitution must consistently adhere to the broader idea of a closed constitutional codification and to an absolute concept of the constitution.

As noted, the belief in such codifications is absent today. The constitutions of different states appear as a series of diversely constituted sets of norms: organizational provisions regarding the most important state authorities, those regarding the legislative process and the government, programs and guidelines of a general type, guarantees of certain rights, and numerous individual provisions. These individual provisions are only written into the constitution because one intends to exempt them from shifting parliamentary majorities and because the parties, which determine the content of the "constitution," use the opportunity to confer the character of constitutional laws on their partisan demands. Even if such a series of constitutional laws is passed by a constitution-making assembly convened for this purpose, the unity of its provisions lies not in their substantive, systematic, and normative completeness. It lies, rather, in a political *will* external to these norms, which first makes all these norms into constitutional laws. And as the unified foundation of these norms, this political will itself generates its own unity. Among all countries with written constitutions today, only a majority of them actually have written constitutional *laws.*

So it is generally accepted that France has a written constitution, a constitution in the formal sense, and one speaks of "the" constitution of the year 1875 because in this and the following years several of the most important constitutional laws were issued. The constitutional laws of the year 1875, however, as Barthélemy-Duez, p. 39ff., rightly states, lacked any method, any dogmatic completeness, even the will to be complete and exhaustive. "Il n'y a pas de constitution; il y a des lois constitutionelles." Otherwise, everything rests on custom and tradition, and the state life of the French Republic would be entirely unrecognizable in the text of these constitutional laws. It would also be impossible to see in them the exhaustive establishment of norms for French public law, even in some only approximate sense.

Compared to these French constitutional laws, the Weimar Constitution is more systematic and complete in terms of its organizational part. But it also contains a series of individual laws and heterogeneous principles, so that even here one may not [16] speak of a codification in the substantive sense. The complete unity of a constitutional codification dissolves itself into a set containing numerous individual constitutional provisions.

Today, the so-called formal conceptual definition, constitution in the formal sense is a written constitution, means nothing more than the statement that a constitution is a series of written constitutional laws. The concept of *the* constitution is lost in the concept of individual constitutional *law*. Nothing distinctive is gained for the definition of the concept of the constitution. This so-called formal concept only makes the concept of the constitution relative, in other words, rendering the constitution in the sense of a closed unity into an assortment of outwardly distinct statutory provisions, which one then designates "constitutional laws." The additional question regarding the other formal characteristic of constitutional law, its qualified alterability, is thus raised.

III. *Qualified Alterability as a Formal Characteristic of the Constitutional Law.* The formal, defining marker of the constitution and (indiscriminately) of the constitutional law is found in the fact that constitutional *changes* are subjected to a special procedure with qualified conditions. Through the *qualified amendment conditions*, the duration and stability of constitutional law should be protected and the "legal status of the law" elevated.

Constitutional laws, according to Haenel (who otherwise falls victim to the typical confusion of constitution and constitutional law), are "exceptionally prominent laws, which are accorded a distinctive meaning under the given political circumstances, and which receive special guarantees of durability and inviolability through the fact that their amendments are bound to qualified forms and that their preservation is secured through special standards of accountability" (*Staatsrecht* I, p. 125). This conceptual definition of Haenel's is still remarkably substantive. G. Jellinek defines it simply. "The essential legal marker of constitutional laws," he argues, "lies exclusively in their heightened legality . . . consequently, the former states, which know no formal distinctions internal to their laws, are more consistent when they reject the summation of a series of legal provisions under the name of a constitutional promulgation" (*Allgemeine Staatslehre*, p. 520; *Gesetz und Verordnung*, p. 262). See also Laband, *Staatsrecht* II, p. 38ff.; Egon Zweig, *Die Lehre vom pouvoir constituant*, 1909, p. 5/6; and W. Hildesheimer, "Über die Revision moderner Staatsverfassungen" (*Abhandlungen aus dem Staats-, Verwaltungs- und Völkerrecht*, XV 1, Tübingen 1918), p. 5ff.

1. There are states where all legal provisions regardless of their content can be changed by a simple statute. Absent is any special protection against changes, and there is also no longer any difference between constitutional laws and simple statutes [17], so that one may not speak "formally" at all of constitutional laws. One speaks here of *elastic (flexible) constitutions,* a linguistic usage in which the question remains open what is generally still understood by "constitution" and "constitutional law."

England is the primary example of a country without a "constitution in the formal sense," because no distinction is made there between important organizational provisions, for example, those concerning the relationship of the upper and lower houses of Parliament and some other statute that is in comparative terms entirely unimportant, such as, for example, a statute regarding the practice of the dental profession. All statutes without exception can be established through parliamentary decision, so that formally the constitution would not be different from such a regulation regarding dentists. The inadequacy of such a type of "formalism" already reveals itself in the absurdity of this example.

In contrast to these "elastic constitutions," there are others that are *unyielding (rigid)*. An absolute, unbendable constitution must prohibit every change in any of its provisions. In this absolute sense, there may not be any more such constitutions today. Nevertheless, for *individual* constitutional provisions, one finds formal *constitutional* prohibitions against amendment. Thus, a French statute of 14 August 1884 *prohibits* proposals for constitutional amendments concerning the state form of the Republic. That is a special case, the actual meaning of which will be treated below. For the formal approach considered here, this statute otherwise does not yet make the French constitution an absolute, unyielding one.

However, there are also such constitutions described as unyielding or rigid that in terms of constitutional law provide for the possibility of constitutional changes or revisions, but this change or revision is linked to special, *qualified prerequisites* or *procedures.*

Art. 76, for example, provides that "the constitution can be amended via legislation. However, a decision of the Reichstag regarding the amendment of the constitution occurs when two-thirds of those present consent. Decisions of the Reichsrat regarding amendment of the constitution also require a two-thirds majority of the votes cast." "Changes of the constitution," according to Art. 78a of Bismarck's Reich Constitution, "are brought about by way of legislation. They are rejected when they receive 14 votes against them in the Reichsrat." Art. 8 of the French constitutional law of 25 February 1875 provides that constitutional amendments occur through the decision of a "national assembly," in other words, a decision reached in a joint assembly of both chambers, the House of Deputies and the Senate. See, additionally, Art. 118ff. of the Swiss Federal Constitution of 29 May 1874 (distinguishing between total and partial revision). On Art. V of the American federal constitution of 1787 etc., compare below § 11, p. 106.

When there are no constitutional provisions regarding constitutional amendments (for example, in the French constitutions [18] [Charten] of 1814 and 1830), it can be doubtful whether a flexible or an absolute, unyielding constitution is at issue. The issue, in other words, is whether constitutional changes come about via a simple statute or whether the silence of the constitution means that amendments are prohibited in general.

In this instance, the correct answer is that only the constitution as a *whole* can be eliminated through an act of the constitution-making power, while constitutional *law* changes are certainly prohibited. Hildesheimer is incorrect on this issue. See his *Über die Revision moderner Staatsverfassungen (Abhandlungen aus dem Staats-, Verwaltungs- und Völkerrecht*, XV 1, Tübingen 1918), p. 8, whose reasoning unfortunately cannot avoid becoming unclear because of the confusion of constitution and constitutional law.

2. In the requirement of qualified alterability lies a certain guarantee of duration and stability. Nevertheless, security and stability self-evidently erode when a party or party coalition has the necessary majorities at its

Relative Concept of the Constitution

disposal and somehow is in the position to satisfy the qualified prerequisites. Despite the great party fragmentation in Germany since 1919, there have been numerous statutes that correspond to the requirements of Art. 76 and, consequently, are designated as "constitution amending." The original sense of the guarantee of a *constitution* was lost when the constitution as a whole became relativized as a group of individual constitutional laws. According to its content and scope, the constitution is always something higher and more comprehensive than some individual statute. The content of the constitution was something special and distinctive not because of its qualified alterability. On the contrary, because of its fundamental significance, it should contain the guarantee of duration. This consideration lost importance when it no longer involved "the constitution" but instead concerned one or more individual constitutional laws. An entirely simple perspective in the form of partisan tactics became prominent. The qualified alterability lost its connection to the essential character of the constitution. Rather, the provision in question was made into a constitutional law in order to provide it protection from the legislature, that is, from shifting parliamentary majorities for some practical reasons (which have nothing to do with a basic norm). When in France during August 1926 a decision of the National Assembly forms a so-called "Caisse autonome" in order to constitutionally guarantee the use of certain income for the retirement of the public debt and to get around the budget law decisions of a transitory parliamentary majority, that is probably something [19] very important in practical terms. Yet it is not "fundamental" in the traditional sense. When the training of adult education teachers is to be regulated according to the principles of "higher education" (Art. 149, sec. 2), religious instruction is an established subject in schools (Art. 149, 1), and the personal papers of civil servants are protected (Art. 129), these are certainly very important provisions. They have the character of "constitutional laws," however, only insofar as they are protected from the amendment votes of shifting parliamentary majorities.

The substantive meaning of the constitution has completely receded because the constitution was rendered relative by its transformation into constitutional law and by the formalization of constitutional law. "The essential legal characteristic of constitutional laws lies exclusively in their enhanced formal legality" (G. Jellinek, *Allgemeine Staatslehre*, p. 520). The fact that a constitutional change requires satisfying the formalities of a constitutional article on constitutional amendments, Art. 76, actually reduces the duration and stability of the constitution. If that really were the definitive constitutional concept, then the provision on constitutional amendments for the Weimar Constitution, in other words Art. 76, would be the essential core and singular content of the constitution. The entire constitution would only be provisional and, in fact, an incomplete law, which must be filled out each time in line with the provisions on constitutional amendment. The following additional provision must be appended to every valid constitutional principle of current German constitutional law: excepting a change by way of Art. 76. "The German Reich is a Republic" (Art. 1), excepting a change via Art. 76; "marriage is the foundation of family life" (Art. 119), when something else is not determined in accord with Art. 76; "all inhabitants of the Reich enjoy full freedom of belief and conscience" (Art. 135), so far as these are not taken from them via Art. 76; etc. That would be the consequence of the "formal" constitutional concept, as it is apparently considered entirely self-evident in contemporary German state theory.

However, such a concept of a constitution is neither logically nor juristically possible. One cannot orient the conceptual definition of the constitution according to how a single constitutional law can be amended. It is also not permissible to define constitutional law as a statute amended through a certain procedure, for the qualified amendment conditions again ground [20] themselves on a constitutional legal provision and presuppose its concept. It would obviously be incorrect to say that Art. 76 is a constitutional law because it is subject to change under conditions it establishes, which, in turn, means Art. 76 can even eliminate itself. First, it is incorrect to assume that through Art. 76 any given constitutional legal regulation can be affected (cf. below § 11). And, second, the essence of a constitutional law does not reveal itself in the fact that it can be altered in a particular procedure. The essence of the object of change cannot in principle be defined in reference to the *amendment* procedure. A constitutional change conforming to the constitution is logically and temporally dependent on the constitution. Even without regard to Art. 76, the provisions of the Weimar Constitution are constitutional laws in the formal sense. Their legal force is not due to their eventual alterability. However, the provisions concerning amendment, as with other constitutional law provisions, owe their legal force to the constitution. If one wants to glean the formal concept of the constitution from the requirements for the amendment of a constitutional provision, then one confuses the constitution-making power of the German people with the authority that the Reichstag, the Reichsrat, or the electorate hold in Art. 76. The authority to undertake constitutional amendments resides in the framework of the constitution, is established through it, and does not extend beyond it. This authority does not include the power to establish a new constitution, and no power of the constitution can be gained in reference to this authority, neither a "formal" concept nor some other useful one. Consequently, another concept is needed besides this "formal" definition of the constitution.

§ 3.

The Positive Concept of the Constitution

(The Constitution as the Complete Decision over the Type and Form of the Political Unity)

A concept of the constitution is only possible when one distinguishes constitution and constitutional law. It is not acceptable to first dissolve the constitution into a multitude of individual constitutional laws [21] and then to define constitutional law in reference to some external characteristic or even according to the method of its alteration. An essential concept of state theory and the fundamental concept of constitutional theory are both lost in this way. It was a typical error when a famous public law teacher was able to claim that the transformation of the constitution into a "type of statute" is a "result of the present political culture." More precisely, the distinction of constitution and constitutional law is for constitutional theory the beginning of any further discussion.

The just cited expression, that the constitution is a "type of statute," stems from Bernatzik (*Grünhuts Zeitschrift für das Privat- und öffentliche Recht der Gegenwart*, vol. 26, 1899, p. 310). He is arguing against the opinion that the constitution is a *contract* (between prince and parliament) and would like to distinguish clearly the constitution as something lasting and irrefutable from the contract, which "creates a self-serving relationship" and is challengeable "under certain conditions, null, refutable, dissolvable." The confusion of constitution and constitutional law stems from the fact that the concept of the *law* above all should merely emphasize polemically the opposition to a *contract*, while today just the opposition to the law (in the sense of a decision of parliament) must be stressed, not in order to return to the contractual construction, but rather in order to protect the positive concept of a constitution against a formalistic dissolution and undermining.

I. The constitution in the positive sense originates from an *act of the constitution-making power*. The act of establishing a constitution as such involves not separate sets of norms. Instead, it determines the entirety of the political unity in regard to its peculiar form of existence through a single instance of decision. This act *constitutes* the form and type of the political unity, the existence of which is presupposed. It is not the case that the political unity first arises during the "establishment of a constitution." The constitution in the positive sense entails only the conscious determination of the particular complete form, for which the political unity decides. This external form can alter itself. Fundamentally new forms can be introduced without the state ceasing to exist, more specifically, without the political unity of the people ending. However, a subject capable of acting, one with the will to establish a constitution, is always a component of constitution making. Such a constitution is a conscious decision, which the political unity reaches *for itself* and provides *itself* through the bearer of the constitution-making power.

During the founding of new states (as in the year 1775 in the *United States of America* or in the year 1919 during the founding of *Czechoslovakia*) or during fundamental social transformations (*France* 1789, *Russia* 1918), this aspect of the constitution as a conscious [22] decision determining the political existence in its concrete form of being emerges especially clearly. Here can most easily arise the impression that a constitution must always found a new state, an error, moreover, which derives from the confusion of a "social contract" (founding the political unity) with the constitution. On this, cf. below § 7, p. 61. An additional, related error is viewing the constitution as an exhaustive codification. But the unity of the constitution lies not in the constitution itself, but rather in the political unity, the peculiar form of existence of which is determined through the act of constitution making.

The constitution, therefore, is nothing absolute insofar as it did not originate on its own. It is also not valid by virtue of its normative correctness or on the basis of its systematic completeness. The constitution does not establish itself. It is, rather, given to a concrete political unity. Linguistically, it is perhaps still possible to say that a constitution *"establishes itself"* without immediately noticing the odd character of this manner of speaking. However, that the constitution *establishes itself* is obviously nonsensical and absurd. The constitution is valid by virtue of the existing political will of that which establishes it. Every type of legal norm, even constitutional law, presupposes that such a *will* already exists.

On the contrary, *constitutional laws* are valid first on the basis of the constitution and presuppose a *constitution.* For its validity as a normative regulation, every statute, even constitutional law, ultimately needs a political *decision* that is prior to it, a decision that is reached by a power or authority that exists politically. Every existing political unity has its value and its "right to existence" not in the rightness or usefulness of norms, but rather in its existence. Considered juristically, what exists as *political* power has value because it exists. Consequently, its "right to self-preservation" is the prerequisite of all further discussions; it attempts, above all, to maintain itself in its existence, "in suo esse perseverare" (Spinoza); it protects "its *existence,* its *integrity,* its *security,* and its *constitution,*" which are all existential values.

The combination "existence, integrity, security, and constitution" is especially clear and correct. It is found in Art. 74a, which, in turn, had been adopted from the federal act of the German Federation of 18 August 1836. This federation act provided that any action against the existence, the integrity, the security, or the constitution of the German Federation in the individual states of the federation is judged and punished as high treason or treason against the individual Land. In its preamble, the Swiss federal constitution of 29 May 1874 declares the purpose of the covenant to be the strengthening of the federation as well as the preservation and advancement of the *unity, strength,* and *honor* of the Swiss nation. In its Art. 2, the federal constitution declares the goal of the Federation [23]: "The defense of the independence of the fatherland against those outside the Federation, enjoyment of peace and order internally," etc. There is no constitution without such existential concepts.

Because every being is a concrete and determined existence, some kind of constitution is part of every concrete political existence. But not every entity that exists politically decides in a conscious action the form of this political existence and reaches, through its own conscious determination, the decision regarding its concrete type, as did the American states in their Declaration of Independence and as did the French nation in the year 1789. Compared to this existential decision, all normative regulations are secondary. Even all concepts applied in legal norms, which presuppose political existence, concepts such as high treason, treason against a Land, etc., preserve their content and their sense not from a norm but rather from the concrete reality of something existing that is independent politically.

II. *The Constitution as Political Decision.* It is necessary to speak of the constitution as a unity and, in this regard, to adhere to an absolute sense of the constitution. At the same time, the relativity of the individual constitutional *laws* may not be misconstrued. The distinction between constitution and constitutional law, however, is only possible because the essence of the constitution is not contained in a statute or in a norm. Prior to the establishment of any norm, there is a fundamental *political decision by the bearer of the constitution-making power.* In a democracy, more specifically, this is a decision by the people; in a genuine monarchy, it is a decision by the monarch.

Thus, the 1791 French constitution contains the political decision by the French people for constitutional monarchy with two "representatives of the nation," the king and the legislative body. The Belgian constitution of 1831 contained the decision by the Belgian people for a (parliamentary-)monarchical government on a democratic foundation (constitution-making power of the people) in accordance with the form of the bourgeois Rechtsstaat. The Prussian constitution of 1850 contained a decision by the king (as the subject of the constitution-making power) for a constitutional monarchy in line with the bourgeois Rechtsstaat, whereby the monarchy as state form (not only as form of the executive) remains preserved. The 1852 French constitution contained the decision by the French people for the hereditary empire of Napoleon III. Etc.

These political decisions are fundamental for the Weimar Constitution. There is the decision for *democracy*, which the German people reached by virtue of its conscious political existence as a people. This decision finds expression in the preamble ("the German people provided itself this constitution") and in [24] Art. 1 sec. 2: "State authority derives from the people." Additionally, there is the decision for the *Republic* and against the monarchy in Art. 1 sec. 1: "The German Reich is a republic." There is also the decision for the retention of the Lands, therefore a *federal-state* (even if not a strictly federal) *structure for the Reich* (Art. 2). The Constitution also contains the decision for a fundamental *parliamentary-representative form of legislative authority and government*. Finally, there is the decision for the *bourgeois Rechtsstaat* with its principles, fundamental rights, and separation of powers (below § 12, p. 126). In this way, the German Reich of the Weimar Constitution characterizes itself as a constitutional democracy. In particular, it designates itself a bourgeois Rechtsstaat cast in the political form of a democratic republic with a federal-state structure. The Art. 17 provision prescribing a parliamentary democracy for all Land constitutions contains the strengthening of this fundamental, total decision for the parliamentary democracy.

1. These provisions are not constitutional laws. Clauses like "the German people provided itself this constitution," "state authority derives from the people," or "the German Reich is a republic," are not statutes at all and, consequently, are also not constitutional laws. They are not even framework laws or fundamental principles. As such, however, they are not something minor or not worthy of notice. They are *more* than statutes and sets of norms. They are, specifically, the concrete political decisions providing the German people's form of political existence and thus constitute the fundamental prerequisite for all subsequent norms, even those involving constitutional laws. Everything regarding legality and the normative order inside the German Reich is valid only on the basis and only in the context of these decisions. They constitute the substance of the constitution. The fact that the Weimar Constitution is actually a constitution and not a sum of disconnected individual provisions subject to change according to Art. 76, which the parties of the Weimar governmental coalition agreed to insert into the text on the basis of some "compromise," lies solely in the existential, comprehensive decision of the German people.

It is a typical error of prewar-era state theory to misconstrue the essence of such decisions and, from the [25] feeling that something other than a statutory norm is present, to speak "consequently" of "mere proclamations," "mere statements," or, indeed, "commonplaces." From both sides, the constitution dissolves itself into nothing: a few more or less tasteful modes of address, on the one side, a number of disconnected, externally distinguished statutes, on the other. These fundamental political decisions, when properly understood, are the defining and genuinely positive element for a positive jurisprudence. The additional norms, enumerations, and detailed delimitations of competencies, the statutes for which the form of constitutional law are chosen for whatever reason, are relative and secondary to the fundamental political decisions. The external distinctiveness of these relative and secondary provisions is that they may be changed or eliminated only through the qualified amendment procedure of Art. 76.

The 1871 and 1919 Reich Constitutions contain prefaces, "preambles," in which

Positive Concept of the Constitution

the political decisions are expressed especially clearly and emphatically. German constitutional law theory treated them mostly as "mere statements," cast as "historical utterance," "merely expressed, not dispositive" (thus Anschütz, *Kommentar*, p. 32; Meyer-Anschütz, p. 646n). Even the aforementioned writers, who display greater understanding for the legal meaning of these preambles and do not extend the meaning of such simple distinctions, claim only that the preambles should define "the spirit of the constitutional work," that it is a matter of "imponderables," etc. (Wittmayer, p. 40). E. Hubrich, *Das demokratische Verfassungsrecht des Deutschen Reiches*, Greifswald 1921, p. 13, has gone the furthest when he claims that the preamble of the Weimar Constitution has not merely an enumerative, but "a genuinely dispositive-juristic character." Why? Because it is promulgated according to § 6 of the statute of 10 February 1919! Additionally, however, he claims that it has this character because it contains binding rules, even if only "in entirely general outlines," which is an interesting linkage of helpless formalism with some sense for the substantive meaning of the preamble. In the proceedings of the Weimar National Assembly, prewar-era turns of phrase dominated (Kahl, *Protocol*, p. 490). One spoke of "mere determination," even of agitational effect and other psychologically interesting things. But the decisive point is that the preamble of the Weimar Constitution contains the authentic declaration of the German people that as the bearer of the constitution-making power, it will decide with full political consciousness. The distinctive democratic element of the constitution is that the people, not the king, exercise the constitutive power. In prewar jurisprudence certainly, there was no talk of this decisive opposition between the constitution-making power and any other derived authority and powers, and most jurists of the Weimar National Assembly spoke only in the vocabulary of monarchical public law.

2. The practical meaning of the difference between constitution and constitutional law makes itself evident in the following examples of its use.

(a) Constitutional *laws* can be changed by way of Art. 76. However, the constitution as a whole cannot be changed in this way. Art. 76 stipulates [26] that "the constitution" can be changed by legislation. Indeed, the wording of this article, which reflects the unclear linguistic usage that was typical until now, does not distinguish between constitution and constitutional law. Nevertheless, the sense is transparent and will emerge ever more clearly in later remarks (on the boundaries of the jurisdiction for constitutional amendments, [see] § 11, p. 102). That "the constitution" can be changed should not be taken to mean that the fundamental political decisions that constitute the substance of the constitution can be eliminated at any time by parliament and be replaced through some other decision. The German Reich cannot be transformed into an absolute monarchy or into a Soviet republic through a two-thirds majority decision of the Reichstag. The "legislature amending the constitution" according to Art. 76 is not omnipotent at all. The manner of speaking associated with the "all-powerful" English Parliament, which since de Lolme and Blackstone has been thoughtlessly repeated and applied to all other conceivable parliaments, has produced a great confusion. A majority decision of the English Parliament would not suffice to make England into a Soviet state. To maintain the opposite would not be a "formal way of thinking" at all. It would still be equally false whether taken politically and juristically. Only the direct, conscious will of the entire English people, not some parliamentary majority, would be able to institute such fundamental changes.

Consequently, constitution "*making*" and constitutional "*change*" (more accurately, revision of individual constitutional provisions) are *qualitatively* different, because in the first instance the word "constitution" denotes the constitution as complete, total decision, while in the other instance it denotes only the individual constitutional *law*. A "constitution-making" assembly is thus also qualitatively different from a conventional legislative body. In other words, it differs from a constitutionally sanctioned legislative body, such as a parliament. The text of the Weimar Constitution came about through the simple majority decision of a "constitution-making" assembly. Naturally, this constitution-making body cannot establish constitutional provisions by virtue of its own authority. It can do so, rather, on the basis of an unmediated special commission. If such a constitution-making assembly were not qualitatively different from a properly constituted parliament, one would be led to the nonsensical and unjust result that a parliament could bind all subsequent parliaments (selected by the same people according to democratic electoral methods) through simple majority decisions and could make a qualified majority necessary for the elimination of certain (not qualitatively different) laws, which came about through simple majority. On the distinction between constitution making and constitutional change in the broader sense, see below § 10, I, p. 92, and § 11, p. 101.

(b) *The constitution is inviolable.* Constitutional *laws,* by contrast, can be suspended during the state of exception and be violated by measures of the state of exception. [27] According to Art. 48, 2, the President is empowered to issue such measures, and the basic rights established in Articles 114, 115, 117, 118, 123, 124, and 153 can be set aside temporarily. All of this does not impinge on the fundamental political decisions and the substance of the constitution. It stands precisely in service of this constitution's preservation and creation. Therefore, it would be nonsensical to render every single constitutional law inviolable because the constitution is inviolable and to see in every single constitutional provision an insurmountable obstacle to the protection of the constitution in general. That meant in practice nothing other than placing the individual statute above the entirety of the political form of existence and to twist the meaning and purpose of the state of exception into its opposite.

For the interpretation of Art. 48, sec. 2 (dictatorship of the President), there is the theory that the President's measures may not "infringe" a single constitutional provision (except the seven Basic Rights that may be suspended), because "the constitution" is "inviolable." For example, the theory put forth by Richard Grau, which he himself dubbed the "theory of inviolability" (*Die Diktaturgewalt des Reichtspräsidenten und der Landesregierungen auf Grund des Artikels 48 der Reichsverfassung,* Berlin 1922; see also *Verhandlungen des 33. Deutschen Juristentags,* 1925, p. 81ff., and *Gedächtnisschrift für Emil Seckel,* 1927, p. 430ff.). This theory is only tenable as long as the constitution is confused with every individual constitutional law and a distinction is not made between a principle like "the German Reich is a Republic" (Art. 1) and individual provisions like "the civil servant is protected from intrusion into their personal papers" (Art. 129). The essence of a commissarial dictator must thereby be entirely misconstrued.

(c) The constitution safeguards a series of so-called *basic rights*. The individual constitutional law provision of such basic rights' guarantees is distinguishable from the guarantee itself. Wide-ranging intrusions into the guaranteed basic rights are permitted via constitutional and statutory norms. But as soon as the basic right is *abolished*, the constitution itself is violated. In a bourgeois Rechtsstaat, such an elimination of rights may not be undertaken through a constitution-amending statute. On this, cf. below § 14, p. 177.

(d) A *constitutional dispute* in the actual sense does not involve each of the many constitutional law details. Such a dispute concerns only the constitution as fundamental political decision. On this, cf. below § 11, III, p. 112.

(e) The *oath to the constitution* (Art. 176) does not mean an oath regarding every single constitutional norm, nor [28] does it constitute a blanket (immoral) oath referring to the amendment procedure and containing the consent for and submission to everything that comes about by way of Art. 76. One cannot swear an oath to an amendment procedure. The particularity and distinctiveness of the oath is that oath-takers bind themselves *existentially*. The oath to the constitution is such a bond to the form of political existence. This oath is to the constitution in the actual and positive sense. In other words, it signifies an acknowledgement of the fundamental political decisions contained in the Weimar Constitution. This is a recognition that reinforces these decisions and out of which a constitution in the substantive sense is first constituted at all (see the Bonn dissertation of E. Friesenhahn, *Der politische Eid*, Bonner Abhandlungen Heft 1, 1928).

(f) *High treason* is an attack on the constitution, not on the individual constitutional law. See below § 11, IV, p. 119.

(g) Constitutional *law* provisions can continue to be valid as statutory provisions after the setting aside of the constitution, even without the issuance of a special statute (cf. the examples below at § 10 II, 2, p. 94). Self-evidently, the *constitution* that is set aside no longer comes into consideration.

(h) According to Art. 148, 3, p. 2, every school-age child receives a copy of "the Constitution" at the end of their mandatory schooling. Naturally, it does not contain the extensive and difficult collection of constitutional *laws* in the formal sense, which have been issued since 1919 in conformity with the qualified amendment procedure of Art. 76. Not once is a copy of the constitutional laws of 30 August 1924 (*Reichsgesetzesblatt* II, pp. 235–357), issued on the basis of the London Protocols of the 16 August 1924, passed out to schoolchildren. Despite Art. 178, 2, p. 2, it is just as unlikely that a copy of the treaty of the 28 June 1919, signed in Versailles, would be distributed.

III. *The Compromise Character of the Weimar Constitution.*

1. The Weimar Constitution is a constitution because it contains the above (under II 1) enumerated, fundamental political decisions regarding the German people's concrete form of political existence. However, in the details of the constitutional *law* order as well as in special declarations and programs incorporated into the constitution, there are some compromises and ambiguities not containing a decision. [29] Put more accurately, through these compromises and indistinct elements, the coalition parties attempted to evade just such a decision. These decisions, of course, which the political situation immediately calls into question, cannot be avoided in the constitution. For otherwise there is no constitution at all. If a "constitution-making" assembly would attempt to evade a decision here, then the decision falls outside of the assembly, and it is to be settled through either violent or peaceful means. In the latter case, it can be that a simple statute or even a mere precedent occasions the decision. This is because the precedent's consequential effect is only explicable by the fact that one was able to recognize in it the will of the people as the bearer of the constitution-making power.

During the formulation of the constitutional laws of 1875, the French National Assembly attempted to hold open the possibility of a reintroduction of the monarchy. These constitutional laws, therefore, contained no clear decision on the one question to be decided, monarchy or republic? The constitutional laws were a "constitution of anticipated monarchy" (J. Barthélemy). The decision occurred later partly in the statute of 14 August 1884 (on the extension of § 3 Art. VIII of the constitutional law of the 25 February 1875), which provided that the republican state form cannot be an object of a proposed constitutional amendment. But partly, in fact, the decision was already reached through the position of the French people. In 1875, a republican majority had been elected in the assembly. In 1877, through Mac-Mahon's attempt to dissolve the assembly, it was settled that once again a republican majority had been elected. The disapproval of the people regarding the methods of the "attente monarchique" was so strong and clear that this unsuccessful dissolution became a precedent of unheard-of scope. More specifically, the right of the president to dissolve parliament as well as the veto right of the French president have since then become practical nullities. Despite the clear text of the statute, it can no longer be exercised. All the consultants' reports by jurists, which base themselves on this text and make reference to the fact that the right is still formally valid and is not set aside through a statute amending the constitution (cf., for example, the interesting survey in the *Revue des Vivants*, September 1927, p. 259ff), have as yet been able to change nothing in regard to the effect of this precedent from 1877. The remarkable power of such an individual case is the fact that the political decision of the French people for the republic and against the monarchy was made through the aforementioned rejection of Mac-Mahon's "coup d'état," a decision that the National Assembly attempted to evade in the constitutional laws of 1875. However, as soon as this sense of the precedent is clearly recognized and acknowledged, the dissolution authority can receive its actual and accepted meaning and become effective again in a practical sense.

2. The Weimar Constitution is a constitution, not merely a series of constitutional laws. It contains the fundamental political decisions for a constitutional democracy. But in the constitutional declaration as well as in individual directives, especially of the Second Part under the heading "Basic Rights and Duties of [30] Germans," there is a hodgepodge of programs and positive provisions, which provides the foundation for the most diverse political, social, and religious matters and convictions. Bourgeois guarantees of personal freedom and private property, all of an individualistic variety, socialist programmatic principles, and Catholic natural law are frequently jumbled together in an often somewhat confused synthesis. In this regard, one must keep in mind that in general a compromise is hardly possible between the ultimate oppositions of genuine religious convictions, just as little between genuine class oppositions. At the very least, such compromises are quite difficult. When a constitution is at issue, a compromise will only be possible when the will to political unity and state consciousness strongly and decisively outweighs all religious and class-based oppositions, so that these religious and social differences are rendered relative. The fundamental political questions, posed directly in the political situation of 1919 — therefore, the questions: Monarchy or republic? Constitutional monarchy or the dictatorship of councils? — could not and have not been evaded. A compromise would have been impossible, and if it had come about, then, as noted, it would have only resulted in a dubious decision. The character of a written constitution would have been undermined; the decision would have been reached by way of customary law or practice, but especially through precedents like the events in France after 1875.

Apparently, however, the Weimar Constitution does not contain all the fundamental political decisions that had to be faced under the circumstances of the year 1919. The great choice, bourgeois or socialist social order, was seemingly settled only through a compromise. The Second Principal Part of the Weimar Constitution shows "a mixed character" in its provisions on the Basic Rights and Duties of Germans, which is "to a certain degree a middle stage between bourgeois and socialist perspectives" (thus the socialist delegate Katzenstein, *Bericht und Protokolle des Achten Ausschusses der verfassungsgegebenen Deutschen National Versammlung*, Berlin, 1920, p. 186). In reality, however, only a series of social reforms are introduced, presented partly as a program, while distinctive political consequences had not been drawn from the principles of socialism. The fundamental decision was made throughout the Constitution for the bourgeois Rechtsstaat and constitutional democracy. One wanted [31] "to disagree not about principles or about worldviews" and "to find common ground regarding the regulation of individual relations" (Düringer, *Bericht und Protokolle*, p. 186). But in the given circumstance, the principal either-or was unavoidable. The decision must already have been made to go with the existing social *status quo*, in particular the retention of the bourgeois social order, because even the Social Democrats emphatically rejected the other decision, which was a consistently executed socialist revolution in accordance with the Soviet type of constitution ("We Social Democrats reject the excessive sharpness and decisiveness of the Soviet constitution," Katzenstein, *Bericht und Protokolle*, p. 186). Delegate Martin Spahn expressed what must result in this situation. "Determining the relationship of the state to social movements extends beyond the realm of the traditional constitution," he argued. "I intend to continue to adhere to the traditional standpoint and not to place us on the ground of the social movements arising through revolution, since the development is not yet concluded and today we cannot discern, which direction it can still take" (*Bericht und Protokolle*, pp. 185/6). Of course, the "traditional constitutions" were in no way constitutions that did not take account of "the relationship of the state to social movements." They were constitutions of the bourgeois Rechtsstaat, and, as such, they contained the decision for certain principles of bourgeois freedom to be discussed more fully below (§ 12), specifically basic rights and separation of powers. The statement of delegate Martin Spahn, therefore, meant nothing other than that the question, bourgeois Rechtsstaat or proletarian class-based state?, had been decided in favor of the bourgeois Rechtsstaat. A decision was unavoidable and inescapable.

3. In contradistinction to these genuine decisions on questions of principle, also in contrast to genuine compromises on details not involving principles, compromises through which organizational and substantive details found their objective regulation and order, the provisions of the Weimar Constitution still contain a series of compromises that are *not genuine* and are constituted entirely differently. One could term these apparent compromises because they reach no substantive decision through reciprocal compliance. Its essence, rather, is simply the drawing out and postponing of this decision. [32] For the compromise consists in finding a formula that satisfies all contradictory demands and leaves, in an ambiguous turn of phrase, the actual points of controversy undecided. So the constitution contains only an external, semantic jumble of substantively irreconcilable matters. Such apparent compromises are in a certain sense effective compromises, for they would not be possible if there were no consensus between parties.

But the understanding does not affect the issue in question; one only agreed on postponing the decision and to keeping open the most varied possibilities and interpretations. The compromise does not involve the objective resolution of a question in the form of mutual compliance with substantive principles. Instead, the agreement is satisfied with a dilatory formula that takes account of all opposing claims. Examples of these dilatory formal compromises are also found in the Weimar Constitution. That is immediately understandable in view of the composition of the Weimar National Assembly. In his work on the Weimar Constitution, E. Vermeil (Strassburg 1923, especially p. 223) portrayed the contradictions within the National Assembly and the absence there of a "homogeneous and coherent theory." Dilatory compromises were unavoidable given the strong religious and social oppositions inside Germany and during such a critical situation as the summer of 1919, if the process of constitution making were to come to a conclusion at all. Under the presupposition that the essential *political* decisions are reached, no reasonable grounds speak against one postponing the decision of other questions and leaving aside for the time being all religious and social oppositions. Nevertheless, it would be foolish and a sign of a deficient capacity for juristic distinction to confuse the dilatory formal compromise with a genuine substantive compromise and to assume that substantive oppositions of a principled type be handled in the long term with the method of such formal compromises.

The typical examples of dilatory formal compromises are found in the Second Principal Part of the Weimar Constitution, especially in the third and fourth sections, which regulate the relationship between church and state and between the state and schools. Church and state are not separated from one another under the Weimar Constitution. More specifically, the church is not treated as a private society; so religion is not treated as a "private matter." The state is not "secularized." The demands of radical bourgeois liberalism and the program of Social Democracy, which is thoroughly liberal in these [33] so-called cultural-political questions, are not met. Consequently, according to the Weimar Constitution, religion cannot be a private matter because religious societies remain public law organs to the extent they were before (Art. 137). When religion is something purely private, then what should be understood as the "public" character of religious bodies would be inconceivable. The state cannot radically separate itself from an aspect of public life, which is acknowledged as public. The fact that religious instruction is recognized constitutionally as a compulsory subject in schools (Art. 149, sec. 1), along with the recognition of Sunday and holidays (Art. 139), makes a radical separation of church and state impossible. On the other hand, there should be no "state church" (Art. 137, 1), apparently also not in the degree to which the Prussian state previously made the Christian religion the foundation of public life (On Art. 14 of the Prussian Constitution of 1850, see Anschütz, *Die Verfassungsurkunde für den Preussischen Staat*, 1912, p. 260ff.). The question of whether *public* life in Germany should retain a distinctly Christian character is not clearly answered in the negative. That is of great practical importance for the daily state practice and communal administration and for the use of state supervisory concepts such as "public order." Compare the decision of the Prussian High Court for Administration, vol. 43, p. 300, that reads: "According to its historical and constitutional formation in the Prussian state, the Christian religion is a part of the public order and, consequently, is placed under the protection of state authorities." Elsewhere in the Constitution there are the beginnings of an effective separation of church and state. Art. 138, for example, provides for a discontinuance of state services to the religious societies through Land legislation. "State services to religious societies based on statute, contract, or special legal title," it reads, "will be discontinued through Land legislation." "The guiding principles for this transfer of authority are established by the Reich." This apparently corresponds to the demand of Democrats and Independent Socialists for full *financial* separation. But the question is whether this order for a transfer of authority under Art. 138 means simultaneously the *prohibition* of additional state services to the church. One side contends this (Israël, *Reich, Staat, Kirche*, 1926, p. 19), so that it is concluded from the rationale of Art. 138 that valid Reich constitutional law prohibits any future expenditure of state resources for the church. In a "tactically clever manner," the other side was able to ensure that the parties of the right and the Center, both in committee and in the plenum of the National Assembly, side-stepped discussion of these points and thereby prevented incorporation of a prohibition into the text of the constitution (E. R. Huber, *Die Garantie der kirchlichen Vermögensrechte in der Weimarer Verfassung*, 1927, pp. 5/6). That means the question of financial separation would not be decided and should not be decided. As is the case in most such suspensions of decision, the result is the retention of the *status* [34] *quo* ante. Overall, one can say that according to the provisions of the Weimar Constitution, the state is certainly separated and distanced from the church, and thus deprived of its influence. But one cannot say the contrary, that the church has been separated from the state.

The so-called *school compromise* of Art. 146 contains the second example of a dilatory formal compromise. Section 1 establishes the basic principle of the community (integrated) school. In section 2, "however," the "will of the guardians," that is in practical terms the confessional school, is set alongside it as an autonomous principle. In Art.144, the basic principle of the state school is recognized. This principle states that the local communities can participate in the state's supervision of schools, while the religious societies are not named. According to Art. 149, 1, however, religious instruction is a compulsory subject in schools and "to be offered in agreement with the basic principles of the affected religious societies." The perspectives of a strictly implemented *state school,* one determined by the will of the *guardians*, a *confessional* school and a *free* school are validated indiscriminately. When it comes to the practical execution of a school statute on the basis of Art. 146, a collision between these principles is unavoidable. It can be resolved through a simple "yes" or "no" or through substantive compromise and reciprocal concessions. But the fact that *principles* are recognized equally without distinction does not contain a substantive decision, or even a genuine compromise decision. Instead, it only refers to a subsequently concluded compromise, a compromise, in other words, that temporarily postpones the decision.

These two examples of dilatory formal compromises are of great juristic significance, because they show that some constitutional provisions do not contain a decision at all, not even a compromise decision. As noted, it can be politically clever and reasonable to postpone the decision in such a way. Nevertheless, the peculiarity of the dilatory formal compromise must remain evident, because otherwise the juristic interpretation of that type of constitutional provision ends in a hopeless confusion. When the "intention of the statute" should be certain, and when there is actually no intention other than not to have one in this matter for the time being, thereby postponing a decision, then all the semantic artistry, all the poring over of the history of the provision, even all the private statements of the participating delegates, always only lead to the result that one word of the statutory text is played out and emphasized against another, as is one clause against another, all without a persuasive demonstration being possible—that is to say, assuming it proceeds in an intellectually conscientious manner. When the [35] legislator establishes such formulas, that just means the different parties and principles can make reference to the text of the constitution. Herein lies the explanation for the fact that currently (fall 1927) the educational law implementation of the so-called school compromise (Art. 146) presents the picture of an eternal discussion without a chance of conclusion, in which both parties refer to the text of the constitutional law with complete conviction, and in which exceptional jurists like R. Thoma and K. Rothenbücher as well as the Prussian government raise claims of constitutional injury and unconstitutionality in reference to the government's draft law (cf. W. Landé, *Aktenstücke zum Reichsvolksschulgesetz*, Leipzig 1927, pp. 112, 113, 125). The substantive decision is rendered as a political decision through the educational law itself, in other words, when it comes to the execution of the formal compromise, not through juristic interpretation and consultant reports. Where no will or determination is at hand, then even the greatest legal acumen has lost its justification. All "normative" consideration ends in a miserable linguistic manipulation.

If the Weimar Constitution contains nothing besides such dilatory compromises, its value would certainly be illusory, and one must understand that the fundamental decisions are reached *outside* of the constitutionally provided procedures and methods. However, the substance of the Weimar Constitution lies in the fact that it reaches the fundamental political decisions concerning the political form and principles of the bourgeois Rechtsstaat clearly and unambiguously. Without this political decision, its organizational provisions would only be the norms of something that merely functions without substance, and its individual statutory provisions would only mean a tactical victory, which was achieved by some party coalition in a favorable moment in order to protect its partisan special interests against shifting parliamentary majorities.

From a radical socialist perspective, one could consider the German people's decision in the Weimar Constitution not essential and say that the actual question

of the situation of the year 1919 involved the class opposition between the capitalist bourgeoisie and socialist proletariat, and in this question the Weimar Constitution also contains only an unclear, dilatory formal compromise. That is incorrect.
The Weimar Constitution reaches a decision in this regard: the German Reich is
a constitutional democracy. What is designated as a compromise in this socialist
claim is, in fact, not a compromise to a greater extent [36] than is social democracy
and the Second International itself, which is a compromise of liberal, democratic,
and socialist ideas. At the very least, the political choice, republic of councils with
dictatorship of the proletariat *or* liberal Rechtsstaat with democratic state form, is
clearly settled.

§ 4.

Ideal Concept of the Constitution

("Constitution" in an exemplary sense,
thus named because of a certain content)

I. For political reasons, that which is designated as a "true" or "genuine" constitution often only corresponds to a particular ideal of the constitution.

A consequence of the manner of speaking typical of political conflict is that every struggling party recognizes as a true constitution only the constitution corresponding to their political demands. If the principle political and social oppositions are very strong, it follows closely that a party denies the name of constitution in general to any constitution that does not satisfy its demands. In particular, the liberal bourgeoisie established a certain ideal concept of constitution in its struggle against the absolute monarchy and identified it with the concept of constitution in general. One spoke only of "constitution" when the demands of bourgeois freedom were fulfilled and a decisive political influence was secured for the bourgeoisie. An especially differentiated concept arose in this way. More specifically, it is no longer self-evident that every state has a constitution. Yet there are states with and those without a constitution, "constitutional" states and "nonconstitutional" states. One even speaks of a "constitutional state constitution," of a state constitution that corresponds to a constitution more precisely, which would be nonsensical if a particular political program did not lie behind the concept of a constitution.

The so-called positivistic state theory also established an identity between "constitution" and "constitutional state constitution" (G. Jellinek, *Staatslehre*, p. 499). In this regard, the political success of a movement is reflected in the state and constitutional theory of the day. Nineteenth-century public law theorists in general also have a definite ideal of the constitution, a liberal-bourgeois one in particular, which they implicitly subordinate to their juristic deductions, even if they anticipate several theoretical distinctions. Otherwise, in the nineteenth-century concept of a constitution, the ideals of liberal-bourgeois freedom connect themselves to the ideal of democratic self-determination of the people. Cf. the definition of the constitution in Lorenz von Stein above at § 1, p. 6. [37]

Confusion and lack of clarity arise easily through the combination of an ideal concept of constitution with other concepts of the constitution or through the linkage of diverse ideals of the constitution. When parties with contradictory opinions and convictions achieve political influence, they express their political power by giving concrete content to the concepts of state life, such as freedom, justice, public order, and security, all of which are necessarily undefined. It is self-evident that "freedom" in the sense of a bourgeois social order resting on private property means something other than a state dominated by a socialistic proletariat, that the same circumstance which appeared in a monarchy as "endangerment of the public peace, security, and order" would be judged differently in a democratic republic, etc. For the manner of expression characteristic of bourgeois liberalism, there is a constitution only when private property and personal freedom are ensured. Everything else is despotism, dictatorship, tyranny, slavery, or whatever the designations may be, not a "constitution." For a consistently Marxist perspective, on the contrary, a constitution that recognizes the principles of the bourgeois Rechtsstaat, those concerning private property in particular, is either the constitution of an economically and technically backward state or a reactionary sham constitution, a meaningless juristic façade concealing the dictatorship of the capitalists. Take another example. In terms of a logically consistent "secularization," which is a state with a strict separation of church and state, a state that does not maintain this separation is not free. On the contrary, for a certain type of confessional and religious conviction, a state only has a true constitution when it respects the social and economic property position of the church, guarantees the free public activity and self-determination of the church, and protects its institutions as a part of the public order, etc. Only then will the church concede that one can speak of "freedom." For this reason, there are just as many possible concepts of freedom and constitution as there are political principles and convictions.

II. *The Ideal Concept of the Constitution of the Bourgeois Rechtsstaat.* A particular ideal concept established itself so successfully during the historical development of the modern constitution that since the eighteenth century only those constitutions [38] corresponding to the demands of bourgeois freedom and containing certain guarantees of this freedom are designated constitutions.

1. *Constitution = a system of guarantees of bourgeois freedom.* This concept of a constitution rests on the division of free and non-free constitutions, a division that is in itself boundlessly ambiguous but receives its concrete meaning from an expression of Montesquieu. It is traceable to a clause of the "Esprit des lois," bk. XI, chap. 5 and 7, which reads: "A few constitutions have the glory of the state (la gloire de l'état) for their direct object and purpose, others the political freedom of the state citizens." With this, the fundamental distinction of freedom and power, *liberté* und *gloire*, is established. Apparently, Montesquieu himself treats both as still equally valid and equally valuable directives for state life. With the advance of the liberal bourgeoisie, bourgeois freedom became the defining directive, though not

for the political life of the state in general and especially not for its foreign policy, but certainly for the realm of constitutional legislation. The example of the United States of America and of the French revolutionary constitution provided this type its imprint and determined the schema of its type of constitution. Only those constitutions which contain a few guarantees of bourgeois freedom, discussed immediately below, will be viewed as free constitutions deserving the name "constitution."

Esmein only treats "free constitutions" in his comparative constitutional law, for example. For him, those are the constitutions of England, the United States of America, and France, as well as those constitutions they influenced and that correspond to their type. The constitutions of the German constitutional monarchy and the German Reich Constitution of 1871 are not considered, because they are not a free constitution of this type. The Weimar Constitution of 1919, by contrast, is considered in its new editions (since 1921).

The recognition of basic rights, separation of powers, and a minimum degree of the people's participation in the legislative power through a popular assembly are deemed valid as constitutional guarantees of bourgeois freedom. Additional demands supplement these, always according to the political situation. In the nineteenth century, for example, there is the demand for a parliamentary government, which is designated a free government,[1] and which provides the justification for the fact that that the German constitutional monarchy without a parliamentary [39] government is not understood as a free government, while the nonparliamentary government of the United States of America nevertheless counts as one.

2. *Constitution* = the so-called *division* (more accurately, *separation*) of *powers*.[2] The so-called division of powers discussed below (§ 15, p. 182), with its separation of legislative power, administration, and the judiciary, has been valid since the eighteenth century in the special sense of being necessary to a free and genuine constitution. It contains the organizational guarantee against the misuse of state power. The proclamation of basic rights signifies only the establishment of a general principle of individual freedom, though still not its organized execution through a state structure that is defined by the goal of bourgeois freedom. Given this, it is understandable that the "division of powers" becomes the defining characteristic of the constitution. According to this understanding, where it is not instituted or where it is eliminated, then *eo ipso* despotism, absolutism, dictatorship are dominant. All of these designations receive their juristic sense through an opposition and are not simple political expressions. They denote the denial of the organizational principle of the separation of the legislative, executive, and judicial powers.

Thus, the oft-cited Art. 16 of the French Declaration of the Rights of Man of 1789 states (after the model of the North American constitutions, for example, Massachusetts and New Hampshire) that "every social order, in which the guarantee of the basic rights is not secured and the separation of powers is not provided, *does not have a constitution.*" (Toute société dans laquelle la garantie des droits n'est pas assurée, ni la séparation des pouvoirs déterminée, *n'a pas de constitution*) The same is true of German Idealism's understanding of the philosophy of state, especially that of Kant and Hegel (cf. below § 12, p. 127). It is significant for the Weimar Constitution that even Hugo Preuss shared this understanding and adopted this standpoint for his first drafts of the Weimar Constitution, which he retained in principle even during the additional proceedings. His understanding, more specifically, was that the *organization* of the state exercise of power for the guarantee of bourgeois freedom, which was also for him the defining directive, is even more important than the proclamation of basic and liberty rights.

3. *Constitution = written constitution* (constitutional proclamation). The political demand of a written constitution leads to an additional equivalency: constitution = written constitution. As presented above (§ 2, II, p. 13), this equivalency is first a confirmed *contract* (between prince and estates or popular assembly), then a written constitutional *law*. Political circumstances account for this manner of speaking. In medieval times, agreements between the prince and his [40] vassals or estates had been fixed in written form and designated as "Charte," of which the "Magna Charta" of 1215 is the most famous example. These charters were, in fact, reciprocal agreements, so-called Stabilimenta, between both parties, guarantees of the privileges of the vassals or estates and, more specifically, the services they owe in return. They were, as Bernatzik pithily states, a "mutually beneficial relationship." Consequently, there is something here that is essentially different from a modern constitution in the sense of a total political decision. *Cromwell's* "Instrument of Government" from the year 1653 is the first example of a modern written constitution. Cromwell himself expressed the purpose of this instrument. There must be a lasting, inviolable rule against the shifting majority decisions of parliament; in every government must reside something fundamental, something like a great charter, which is constant and unchanging. The ambiguous word "fundamental" receives the sense of something absolutely unbreakable. For example, that a parliament can never declare itself a permanent body constitutes such a fundamental principle. If the legislature, specifically the parliament, could change that, there would no longer be any security, etc. Cromwell's efforts remained unsuccessful. The modern practice of the written constitution first begins with the English colonies in North America. As they separated themselves from England and declared themselves independent states, they formulated their constitutions in written form. A "congress" in 1776 prompted all these states to undertake these actions. Since the French Revolution of 1789 and the first modern written constitutions on the European continent, the 1791 French constitution, constitutions with a typical content occurred regularly during the founding of states and after revolutions, the scheme of which

till now corresponded mostly to the basic schema, discussed below (§ 12, p. 126), of the bourgeois Rechtsstaat with basic rights and separation of powers. The Weimar Constitution also still follows this schema. The Soviet Republic constitution of 11 July 1918 abandoned the schema of the bourgeois Rechtsstaat and established a new type of constitution, the socialistic soviet constitution.

III. The ideal concept of the constitution dominant today still corresponds to the bourgeois Rechtsstaat's ideal of a constitution. When one looks past Bolshevist Russia and fascist Italy, one can say that this ideal concept is still valid in most [41] states of the globe. The peculiarity of its ideal of a constitution is that an organization of the state is undertaken with a perspective that is critically and negatively disposed toward state power—protection of the citizen against the *misuse* of state power. Not so much the state itself as the means and methods of its control are organized. Guarantees against state overreaching are created and obstacles to the exercise of state power are sought. A constitution that contains nothing other than these guarantees of the bourgeois Rechtsstaat would be unthinkable. For the state itself, the political unity, hence that which is to be governed, must be present or simultaneously organized. The aspiration of the bourgeois Rechtsstaat, however, is to repress the political, to limit all expressions of state life through a series of normative frameworks, and to transform all state activity into *competencies,* which are jurisdictions that are precisely defined and, in principle, *limited.* Thus, it is evident that the bourgeois Rechtsstaat component can constitute only a part of the entire state constitution, while another part contains the positive decision over the form of political existence. This means that the constitutions of today's bourgeois states are always composed of two components: On the one hand, the principles of the Rechtsstaat for the protection of bourgeois freedom against the state and, on the other hand, the political component, from which the actual state form (monarchy, aristocracy, or democracy, or a "status mixtus") is derived. In the connection between both these components lies the peculiarity of today's constitutions of the bourgeois Rechtsstaat. This duality determines its total structure, and by way of central concepts, such as the concept of the statute, it leads to corresponding dualisms. The following exposition of the basic scheme of the modern constitution (§ 12, p. 126) and of the relationship of state form and legality (§ 16, p. 200) receives its fundamental outlines and its essential structure through it. [42]

§ 5.

The Meanings of the Term "Basic Law,"
Basic Norm or Lex Fundamentalis

(Summarizing Overview)

I. *Overview.*

1. In a general, not precise sense, all statutes or agreements that appear to be of special political importance to the persons or groups politically influential at the time are called "basic laws."

Thus, the numerous agreements, concessions, privileges of the German estates in regard to the German Kaiser are termed basic laws (leges fundamentales). On this, cf. below p. 48. The idea of political unity differentiates itself. The concept of the basic law also becomes pluralistic and relative.

2. Basic law = an *absolutely unbreakable* norm, which may be neither changed nor violated by conflicting norms.[1]

Cf. the statement of Cromwell above, p. 40.

3. Basic law = every *relatively unbreakable* norm that may be changed or violated by conflicting norms only under qualified prerequisites. See above p. 18.

4. Basic law = the last *unified principle* of political *unity* and of the entire *order.* In this instance, the term is an expression of the absolute concept of the constitution. See above p. 4.

5. Basic law = *every individual principle* of state organization (basic rights, separation of powers, monarchical principle, the so-called representative principle, etc.).

6. Basic law = the last *norm* for a system of normative attributions. The normative character stands out here and, above all, the "law" in basic law is emphasized. See above p. 7.

7. Basic law = every organizational regulation of jurisdiction and procedure for the politically most important state activities. In a federation, this includes even the setting apart of the rights of the federation from those of the members.

8. Basic law = every *limitation* of state power or activity through a normative framework.

9. Basic law = constitution in the positive sense, whereby the so-called basic law does not have a statutory norm, but rather its essential content is the *political decision* (above p. 21). [43]

II. These different meanings are united in a generally diverse form, in which the one or other side, unbreakable character, unity, order of a principled variety, limitation function, etc., are variously emphasized and can be put in the foreground. One may generally say that the concept renders itself relative and pluralistic as soon as the consciousness of political existence undermines itself, while the idea of *unity* stands out when this consciousness becomes vibrant again. Otherwise, the different meanings are often jumbled together with confusing superficiality.

A widely disseminated textbook of the eighteenth century, Vattel, *Droit des gens,* chap. III § 27, thus answers the question, what is a constitution? with the following statements. A constitution is "the fundamental regulation that determines the type and manner in which the public authority should be exercised" (that would be only partly an order function, partly a limitation function). "In it, the form in which the nation as political body acts becomes visible" (the idea of the represented political *unity*); "how and through whom a people should be governed, which are the rights and duties of the governed" (once again, the partly *organizational,* partly *restrictive* meaning of the constitution). "The Constitution is nothing other than the determination of the *order* in which a nation sets for itself the goals and advantages of the political society that are to be achieved together" (*Société Politique*), etc. In the nineteenth century, the definition of the concept of the constitution is made more difficult by the fact that the ideal concept of the bourgeois Rechtsstaat is lumped in with the concept of the constitution (above § 4, p. 37). But the difficulties that stand in the way of a clear distinction are extraordinarily large even independent of this complication. One could bring up, for example, the "definition of the basic laws of the federation," which was proposed as a supplement in regard to Art. 13 of the Federal Act of the German Federation. The editorial commission in its report (Protocol of the 22d Meeting on 16 April 1820) remarked that the concept of a basic law is "one of the simple concepts mentioned above, which scholastic definitions will more likely render obscure than further clarified and strengthened." In 1819, however, a federation commission established to provide an expert, authoritative definition of this concept suggested: "1. *Basic laws* of the German state federation are those contractual provisions which involve the establishment of the federation, the association of its members, the authoritative definition of its purpose as well as of the entirety of the participation of the individual members of the federation in its exercise. The Federation *constitution* is formed through these contractual provisions" (there are, therefore, basic laws—plural!—distinct from *the* constitution). 2. The provisions about *organic* institutions, "organic" "because through them the body of the federation received its tools," so to speak, and "the decisions that for this purpose the federation understood as enduring, general norms can rightly be attributed to the basic laws." 3. The remaining federation laws are only negatively determined: there are *no* basic laws (Klüber, *Öffentliches Recht des Teutschen Bundes,* 3d ed., 1831, p. 60). This definition of the concept also contains several of the different perspectives that are to be distinguished for a clarification of the concepts of basic law and constitution. Otherwise, the ambiguity of the word "basic" in usages like basic norm certainly contributes to the arbitrariness of such expressions. A similar process recurs in regard to the "basic" rights. See below § 14, p. 163.

In the constitutional conflicts of the nineteenth century, the concept of a constitution changes with the political situation and the interests of the conflicting parties. [44] Overall, the constitution and the limitation of the state through the bourgeois Rechtsstaat are rendered equivalent, as it is elaborated above in § 4 and even further in the course of this investigation, in particular in the second section (p. 200ff.).

Rendering the constitution relative by reducing it to individual constitutional law results in the dissolution of the constitution. This understanding of the constitution as individual constitutional law still seems dominant in Germany.

III. In the following discussions, the term constitution is used in the sense of the *positive* constitutional concept developed above. In particular, constitution and constitutional law are always strictly distinguished.

Meanings of the "Basic Law"

§ 6.

Origin of the Constitution

I. *A constitution arises either through one-sided political decision of the subject of the constitution-making power or through reciprocal agreement of several such subjects.*

A constitution in the sense of a status identical to the entire condition of the state arises self-evidently along with the state itself. It is neither issued nor agreed upon, but it is rather the same as the concrete state in its political unity and social order. Constitution in the positive sense means the formation of this political unity by conscious act, through which the unity receives its particular form of existence. There is a constitutional contract or constitutional agreement when several political unities and independent bearers of the constitution-making power together reach such a decision reciprocally defining their political status. (Both expressions "contract" and "agreement" are not distinguished here, although, in fact, the exceptional quality that Binding and Triepel conferred on the concept of agreement [agreement as fusion of different, substantively equal wills] should not be misconstrued.)

II. *Historical overview of the origins of the modern European constitutions.*

1. The political situation of the late medieval period (from the thirteenth until the sixteenth century) is often designated the "state of estates." Political unity as such had become problematical factually and in terms of consciousness. The traditional military constitution based on fealty had dissolved, and vassals became mostly independent. Where estate associations formed (higher aristocracy, gentry, spiritual authorities, the urban bourgeoisie), these were based on contracts validated through oaths by the members. These estates concluded contracts of diverse sorts among themselves and with their own princes, but also with foreign princes. Their contracts with their own princes involved the guarantee of privileges, [45] limitations of princely power, and often even the right of armed resistance. One cannot denote these countless agreements as constitutions of a state, as it is in general mistaken to apply concepts of modern public law to such medieval relationships. The actual object of modern constitutions, the type of existence and form of existence of the political *unity*, was not the object of these agreements. In the "state" of estates, one may speak neither of a monarchical nor of a dualistic or pluralistic state; at most one may speak of a jumble of well-earned rights and privileges. In numerous charters, concessions, letters, etc., a multitude of special interests were "anchored." The collective appears as a process of dissolution of a previously existing political unity. Only to this extent is the political unity still presupposed, as it is that which dissolves itself and at whose cost estate groups and organizations share in the spoils. The agreements, therefore, establish no political unity

and should also not contain the comprehensive decision. However, because they limit and control the exercise of princely power, the constitutional aspirations of the nineteenth century were able to attach themselves to them, and in the constitutional struggles of the nineteenth century it was possible not only for the princely governments to speak of "estate constitutions," but also for the bourgeoisie to often make reference to such estate agreements and see in them the model of a constitution. This was the case above all in the small German states.

The English *Magna Carta* of 15 June 1215 is in particular often deemed the model and precursor of the modern free constitutions. England's public law development certainly took a distinctive course, because the medieval feudal masters and estates (higher aristocracy, knights, and English bourgeoisie) and their representation (the House of Lords and the House of Commons) made the transition into modern state relations through a gradual and imperceptible development. In the struggle against the king, the English Parliament appeared as the bearer of the national, more specifically, of the *political* unity, while in other European lands it was the absolute prince who brought about political unity in the struggle against the medieval estates. In England, medieval ideas and institutions were able to develop into modern state institutions without clearly demarcated changes. Apart from this, however, the Magna Carta of 1215, considered historically, is only one of many examples of medieval [46] agreements between prince and feudal master. It is one "stabilimentum" in a document between King John and his barons. Their legal nature had been understood quite differently. One designated them as a *statute* because they were guaranteed by the king and had the form of a royal grant, or as a public law contract in the form of a royal *award* (Stubbs, *Constitutional History* I, p. 569), or even as a private law *contract* (Boutmy, *Études*, p. 40). According to Anson, it is both a *constitutional law* and a *declaration of rights* as well as a *contract* between prince and the people! However, as William Sharp McKechnie (*Magna Carta*, 2nd ed., Glasgow 1914, p. 104ff.) demonstrated, it is wrong to apply any of these modern public law distinctions to medieval circumstances. The Magna Carta, according to McKechnie, is a stabilimentum, specifically, a settlement or agreement without any precise public law significance. The written form and inclusion of a few expressions of principle, both to the same limited degree, do not at all prove it was a constitution. The name "*Magna* Carta" is not at all explicable historically in reference to the fact that there is a basic law in the sense of a modern constitution. It is explicable instead in reference to the opposition to a "*Parva* Carta" or "Carta foresta" of 1217 concerning a hunting law. The original name is "Carta libertatum" or "Carta Baronum." Only centuries later, in the seventeenth century, through the struggle of the English Parliament against the absolutism of the Stuarts, did the Magna Carta become the precursor of a free constitution and was defined in a modern sense. But it would be a historical error to view the Magna Carta even as something only approaching a modern free or democratic constitution. When in the Magna Carta certain rights for protection against the misuse of royal authority are guaranteed to every "free man" (freeman), that is entirely different than a modern declaration of human and civil rights. The "free man" was at that time only the baron, who alone counted as homo liber or just as homo (McKechnie, p. 115). Historically, therefore, the Magna Carta is only the agreement of the feudal aristocracy with his feudal master, to whom the aristocracy renew their oath of fealty in exchange for guaranteed rights. The political effect of this Magna Carta model rests on the mythical idea that particular parties make of it. In terms of their content, the sixty-three chapters in the Magna Carta involve limitations on the feudal power of the king, limitations of his judicial authority (no free man may be arrested or imprisoned other than through a court of his peers or according to the law of the land), restrictions on the law of rents, and, above all, the initiation of a committee charged with offering resistance in the case of the failure to comply with these provisions (cf. Gneist, *Englische Verfassungsgeschichte*, p. 240; Richard Schmidt, *Allgemeine Staatslehre* II, 1903, p. 490ff.).[47]

In terms of form, the Declaration of Rights of 1688 (Bill of Rights) is a contractual settlement between the Prince of Orange, who had been called to the throne by the English Parliament, and this parliament. In this context, however, parliament appears as the representative of England's political unity. The Bill of Rights contains thirteen clauses against the misuse of royal power (no suspension of the laws through the king; no inheritance of financial payments on the basis of royal prerogative; right of petition for subjects; no standing army without the consent of Parliament; right of Protestant subjects to bear arms; free elections of parliamentary members; freedom of speech and debate in parliament; cf. Gneist, *Englische Verfassungsgeschichte*, p. 614ff). One can already speak here of constitutional law provisions in the modern sense because the idea of political unity is already clear and the agreement between Parliament and king did not at all constitute the unity whereby the Parliament emerges as the representative of the unity. Instead, this agreement presupposed the unity.

2. In most European states, political unity was the work of princely absolutism. In the German Reich, however, medieval conditions were preserved until the end of the Reich in 1806. Moreover, new political unities, states like Prussia, Bavaria, Württemberg, Saxony, formed in the territories of the Reich. As a whole, the Reich in the eighteenth century remained only a heterogeneous composite of still developing political formations and fragments. Hegel best formulated this circumstance in his youthful writing on "The German Constitution" (1802): "The German state structure is nothing other than the sum of the rights that the individual parts took from the whole"; its "constitution" and "justice" consists in the fact that one "carefully guards against any other power remaining for the state" (*Hegels Schriften zur Politik*, Lasson edition, pp. 13/14). The question has been discussed since the seventeenth century whether this peculiar conglomerate is a *mixture* of state forms (specifically, limited monarchy and aristocracy), a "status mixtus," or a *system* of states, that is, a federal formation. Pufendorf provided the only possible intellectually honest answer (in the famous treatise "De Statu Imperii Germanici," published under the name "Severinus de Monzambano," 1667, chap. VI § 9, edition of Fritz Salomon, 1910, p. 126): this formation is an abnormality and is comparable to a "monstrosity." Considered normatively, it was an ideal case of a Rechtsstaat on the "founda-

tion" of the principle "pacta sunt servanda." The "constitution" consists of numerous agreements, contractual privileges [48], concessions, etc., which were protected judicially through nontransparent procedural possibilities. The most prestigious and politically powerful estate of the Reich, the electors, reaffirmed and expanded these rights during every new election of the Kaiser through new electoral capitulations. Since the seventeenth century, these electoral contracts and textually fixed electoral conditions were designated *leges fundamentales*.[1] Even the exercise of high political powers, such as the legal opinions of a prince or other "estates" as prerequisite of an enforcement action, were ultimately bound to a trial procedure and to the consent of the other estates. Not once during the notorious breaches of the peace and open rebellion was the Kaiser permitted to declare an imperial estate in violation without the "conscious support" of the electors. As Pufendorf rightly explains, the monstrosity of this circumstance is that the Kaiser cannot burden the estates with anything against their will, but these estates can certainly obtain every advantage for themselves at the expense of the Reich and can anchor them in "fundamental laws."

The demise of Wallenstein in 1634 eliminated the last possibility of creating out of the German Reich a unity that existed politically on a national level. In 1630, Wallenstein was already the victim of the enmity of the electors and the estates. Motivated by confessional concerns and the cause of legitimacy, the Kaiser himself stood on the side of the estates and, in particular, could not understand the religious tolerance that would have been the prerequisite of Germany's state unification, thus accepting Wallenstein's manner of thinking on the issue. The conclusive victory of the estates' particular interests over the Kaiser is documented in Ferdinand III's electoral concession of December 1636. It states that even in the "most extreme necessity" the Kaiser was not permitted to raise rents without at least asking the electors ahead-of-time; even during the notorious breach of peace a trial was necessary to declare the exclusion and facilitate the enforcement action. Even in the most extreme case of emergency (in extremo necessitatis casu), the Kaiser must consult the electors (cf. Carl Schmitt, *Die Diktatur,* pp. 95/96).

3. On the European continent, in Spain, France, and in the German territorial states, the modern state develops by the prince becoming "absolute." In other words, the modern state develops when the prince sets aside the well-earned feudal and estate rights and ruptures and eliminates the principle of the *legitimacy of the status quo*, on which the feudal condition rested. [49] The political formations originating in this way were absolute monarchies. The "absolute" character lies in the fact that the prince is "legibus solutus." For political reasons, on which he alone decides, the prince has the authority and capacity to disregard the legitimate demands of the estates and the existing privileges and agreements. The word "state" expresses the special character of this modern political formation especially aptly because it connotes the linguistic and intellectual connection with the word "status." For the comprehensive status of political unity renders relative and

Origin of the Constitution

absorbs all other status relationships, in particular those of the estates and the church. The state, or the *political* status, thus becomes the status in an absolute sense. This modern state is sovereign; its state authority is indivisible; its closed quality and its impenetrability (impermeableness) follow from the essence of political unity. In terms of world history, the concept of sovereignty in particular had a grand function: the overcoming of the legitimacy of the (feudal and estate-based) *status quo* at that time.

The first depiction of modern public law, the *Six Books of the State* by Bodin (1577), clearly demonstrated this decisive point. Sovereign is whoever has the highest power, not as civil servant or commissioner, but rather continuously and on their own authority, that is, by virtue of their own existence. He is bound by divine and natural law. However, that is not at issue at all in the question of sovereignty. At issue, rather, is only whether the legitimate *status quo* should be an insurmountable hindrance for his political decisions, whether anyone can compel him to be responsible, and who decides in the case of conflict. When the time, place, and individual circumstances demand it, the sovereign can change and violate statutes. His sovereignty emerges especially clearly in such actions. In his chapter on sovereignty (Ch. 8, Bk. I), Bodin speaks continuously about ideas such as annulling, squashing, rupturing, dispensing, and eliminating existing statutes and rights. Hobbes and Pufendorf present this essential perspective with systematic clarity during the seventeenth century. The question that always arises is *quis iudicabit*. The sovereign decides about that which advances the public good and the common use. In what does the state interest consist when it demands a rupturing or setting-aside of the existing law? All of these are questions that cannot be settled normatively. They receive their tangible content through a concrete decision by the sovereign organ.

4. As a mixture of liberal and democratic elements, the modern constitution arises in the *French Revolution of 1789*. Its intellectual prerequisite is the theory of the constitution-making power. The state theory of the French Revolution thus becomes a primary source, not only for the political dogma of the entire subsequent period (thus Egon Zweig, *Die Lehre vom pouvoir constituant*, S.V.), but rather also for the positive legal, juristic construction of modern constitutional theory. The [50] constitution-making power presupposes the people as a politically existing entity. The word "nation" denotes in a clear sense a people brought to political consciousness and capable of acting. Historically, one can say that on the European continent, these fundamental ideas of political unity and of national determination arose as a result of the political determination of the absolute monarchy, while in England the continuous development from a medieval construct to national unity was made possible because "the insular condition substituted for a constitution." France, by contrast, conformed to the classic model of a modern European state. There the concept of the nation in its public law meaning was first understood theoretically. However, in the French Revolution of 1789, two different processes and thought systems must be distinguished in constitutional theory terms. First, the French people constitute

themselves as the bearer of the constitution-making power. The people become conscious of their capacity to act politically and provide themselves a constitution under the presupposition of the existing political unity and of the capacity to act that is expressly affirmed at the same time. The process was so effective and pronounced because the fundamental political decision rested above all on the French people becoming *conscious* of their character as a subject capable of acting and of determining its political destiny. In a certain sense, the French people constituted themselves. By giving themselves a constitution, the French people already undertake the additional act of reaching a decision regarding a particular type and form of political existence. The people become nation. Put differently, they become conscious of their political unity. But that does not mean that they did not previously exist and that they also constituted their state through the conscious exercise of their constitution-making power. Political being preceded constitution making. What is not present politically also cannot consciously decide. Political existence was presupposed in this fundamental process, in which a people acts consciously in a political manner, and the act through which the people provide themselves a constitution is to be distinguished from the constituting of the state.

The second meaning of the French Revolution is that it led to a bourgeois constitution of the Rechtsstaat variety, to one, more specifically, that controls and limits the exercise of state power, thereby giving the French state a new type of political existence. [51] When the nation as subject of the constitution-making power opposes the absolute prince and sets aside princely absolutism, the nation puts itself in the prince's place just as absolutely. The quality of absoluteness remains in place with power that is unchanged or that is perhaps even heightened, because in the state the people now identify with themselves in political terms. The *political* capacity of this process leads to a heightening of state power, to more intense *unity* and indivisibility, unité and indivisibilité. When, on the contrary, the exercise of state power should be regulated, divided, and limited through liberal constitutional laws, this "*division* of powers" signifies a revocation and elimination of every type of political absolutism, whether this absolutism is exercised by an absolute monarch or by the absolute nation that is brought to political consciousness. The political greatness of the French Revolution lies in the fact that despite all its liberal and Rechtsstaat principles, the thought of the French people's political unity did not cease to be the deciding directive even for a moment. It remains indubitable that all separations, divisions, limitations, and means of controlling state power operate only inside the framework of political unity. With this unity, however, even the relative character of all constitutional laws is still indisputable. The constitution was not a contract between the prince and the people or, indeed, between some estate organizations, but rather a political decision affecting the one and indivisible *nation* determining its own destiny. Every constitution presupposes this unity.

5. During the *monarchical restoration* (1815–1830), there was an attempt to revive anew the medieval ideas of a contract, or "Charte," concluded between the prince and the estates. In some parts of Germany, medieval ideas and circumstances had remained vibrant. Especially in the midsize and small states, a distinction had not yet been drawn between the medieval procedures under feudal and estate-based agreements, on the one hand, and an act of the constitution-making power, on the other. The counter-revolutionary theory and practice also attempted to make use of medieval ideas in order to evade the democratic consequences of national unity.

In Art. XIII, the 1815 Vienna federal act of the German Federation established that in all states of the German Federation "land-based estate constitutions will prevail." The *estate-based* constitution in the medieval sense would be juxtaposed here to the modern idea of the *representation* of the [52] national unity of the state and would be used as a counter-concept against the elected popular assembly, which represents the entire people. The constitutions that correspond to this provision of the federal act designate themselves sometimes as contracts or agreements. Thus, the constitution of Saxony-Weimar-Eisenach (Karl August) of 5 May 1816 is understood as a "contract between prince and subject." According to Art. 123, changes are possible only through mutual contract between the prince and the estates, etc. Additional examples (Württemberg 1819, Saxony 1831) are found below on p. 64, where the significance of these "constitutions" in constitutional theory terms is considered.

The inner contradiction of such attempts at monarchical restoration is, on the one hand, that the princes could not conceive of giving up the state's political unity in favor of interest representation for the estates. They were not permitted to extend a concept such as the "estates" and the state-dissolving construction of a constitutional contract consistently to its logical conclusion. "Estate-based" representation, therefore, was not permitted to have an authorization for political decision making. On the other hand, however, the representatives must be *political representatives* (not advocates of estate interests) if estate-based representation is to mean anything at all for the constitution. Nevertheless, it was not possible for the princes to recognize these estates as representatives, that is, as representation of the *entire*, politically unified people. For otherwise they would have recognized the people as a political unity capable of action and would have given up the monarchical principle, according to which only the prince is the representative of this political unity and thereby unifies the plenitude of state power in his hands. Both concepts, a constitutional contract concluded with the "estates" and the monarchical principle, were entirely irreconcilable. A consequence of the monarchical principle was that the king, by virtue of the plenitude of his state power, *issued* a constitution. In other words, the king as the bearer of the constitution-making power reached the fundamental political decision that constituted the constitution, but he did so without giving up the constitution-making power. The constitution, then, was not a contract. Instead, it was a *statute* issued by the king. All constitutional legislation of this constitution involved powers that are *limited* only in principle. This means they are only competencies, *jurisdictions*, while the "plenitude of the state power," which is inseparable from the political unity and, in principle, unlimited and incapable of being limited, remained in the hands of the king despite the constitution, if the king did not renounce state power in favor of the parliament. In politically strong monarchies, constitutions establishing a constitutional monarchy were issued on the basis of this monarchical principle. These constitutions were not concluded with the popular assembly. They were imposed. But [53] at least in Germany, where the constitution had been "agreed" upon, the monarchical principle was not given up at all because of the participation of the popular assembly in the determination of the text of the constitutional laws, and the democratic principle of the constitution-making power of the people was not recognized at all (cf. below § 7, II, p. 65).

The French Charte of 4 June 1814 is the model of a modern monarchical constitution. It was issued, or more accurately imposed, on the basis of the monarchical principle, that is to say, under the king's constitution-making power. When it assumed the medieval designation "Charte," that is characteristic of the internally contradictory situation of the monarchy then. For estate-based contracts would have thoroughly contradicted France's singular and indivisible political unity. In fact, the "Charte" was based on the constitution-making power of the king, which had been juxtaposed to the constitution-making power of the people.

6. In the 1830 July Revolution, the political decision was reached in France whether the king or the people were the subject of the constitution-making power. The democratic theory of the people's constitution-making power conclusively triumphed. The advocates of the liberal Rechtsstaat sought to evade the alternative, either sovereignty and the king's constitution-making power or sovereignty and the people's constitution-making power, and they spoke of a "sovereignty of the constitution" (cf. above § 1, II, p. 7). Nonetheless, the question was not answered, only sidestepped and veiled behind the somewhat occult-like image of the constitution-making power of the constitution. All subsequent French constitutions and constitutional laws (1848, 1851, 1875) have the people's constitution-making power for a prerequisite.

7. In *Germany*, the revolution of the year 1848 led generally to the so-called constitutional monarchy, more specifically, to a "dualism" (R. Mohl) of the royal government and the popular assembly, by which both mon-

arch and popular assembly emerged as representatives of the political unity. Such a dualism means only that the decision was postponed. Inside every political unity, there can only be one bearer of the constitution-making power. Consequently, there is the alternative of either the prince promulgating a constitution on the basis of the monarchical principle from the plenitude of his state power, or the constitution is based on the act of the people's constitution-making power, which is the democratic [54] principle. Because they are opposed in a fundamental way, both these principles do not permit themselves to be confused with one another. A compromise, through which the decision is set back and postponed, is naturally possible for a time. Both parts, prince and popular assembly, are then agreed that the decision should be suspended. However, such a compromise is never quite a genuine, substantive compromise. It is, instead, only the dilatory formal compromise discussed above (p. 31). In reality, despite all the concealments and evasions, the constitution rested either on the monarchical or the democratic principle, on the constitution-making power of the prince or that of the people. The "dualism" of these constitutions is unsustainable. Every genuine conflict reveals the simple either/or of the mutually exclusive principles of political form.

If the prince issues a constitution unilaterally, if it is "imposed," it undoubtedly rests on the prince's constitution-making power. If the imposed form of constitution is avoided for political reasons and the constitution is concluded between the prince and the popular assembly, there is a dilatory compromise insofar as the prince does not renounce his constitution-making power and thereby recognizes the democratic foundation of his position. More specifically, the prince recognizes the people's constitution-making power. In the German constitutional monarchies, it has naturally never come to such an acknowledgement of the democratic principle. A dualistic intermediary condition thus results. Theoretically, it was concealed by the fact that it corresponded to liberal ideas, falsely portraying a "sovereignty of the constitution" and, in this way, evading the core political question regarding the constitution-making power. In practical terms, that is, in historical and political reality, this condition of a postponed decision was possible so long as the inner and external political situation remained harmonious and calm. In the critical moment, the unresolved conflict and the necessity of a decision manifested itself. It is not inconceivable that in a long, gradual development, one principle drives back the other slowly and without open conflict, as was the case in England. The states of the European continent, however, did not find themselves in the fortunate position of an unassailable island, which was enormously enriched by a great colonial realm. [55]

The constitutional monarchy existed in Germany until November 1918.

The favorable political and economic position made it possible to disregard entirely this decisive alternative as an uninteresting question. What was not in the "constitution" would be left out of consideration as "not juristic." At the same time, the constitution in the above (§ 2, p. 11) outlined manner was rendered formal and placed at the level of mere constitutional *law*. That passed as "positivism," although it actually never extended beyond the stage of the Louis-Philippe period and the liberal doctrinaires associated with it. This time, indeed, was designated the "epoch of *constitutionalism in its purest form*" by so influential an observer as Lorenz von Stein. Even *after* the transformation of 1918, the empty husk of this type of liberalism sought to conserve itself for a time in Kelsen's "normative state theory." Nonetheless, it was no longer the old liberal belief in the "sovereignty of reason." It was, rather, a contradictory position: on the one hand, the sovereign "constitution" and, on the other hand, its dissolution into individual sets of constitutional norms, which are alterable in a particular process, thereby rendering the constitution relative. The constitution of the German constitutional monarchy now certainly contains a Rechtsstaat limitation of the royal power and displays the dualism of two representatives (prince and popular assembly) typical of constitutional monarchy. However, the monarchical principle was not set aside in Germany. The powers the constitution grants the popular assembly are *limited* in principle. The popular assembly receives certain *jurisdictions* in the area of legislation, while the jurisdictional "presupposition" otherwise is in favor of the monarch. Max von Seydel (*Über konstitutionelle und parlamentarische Regierung*, 1887, *Abhandlungen*, p. 140) gave the best formulation of distinctiveness of this German style of constitutional monarchy: "The parliamentary king cannot resort to state power when his parliament fails to function"; on the contrary the constitutional monarch in Germany "made recourse to state power" when it came to a serious conflict, more specifically, one that involved the question of sovereignty and of the constitution-making power. The monarch remained the bearer of the constitution-making power, which is not to be understood constitutionally and which is unlimited in principle. Because the alternative question, whether the prince or the people had this constitution-making power [56], was at least not decided in favor of the people, this power had to for this reason remain with the prince so long as his political power endured. As in other cases of the suspension of decision, the then-existing *status quo* was unchanged. In other words, the monarchical principle remained in place. If then state theory emphasized that even the prince is only an "organ" of the state and that neither the prince nor the people but instead the state as an "organism" is sovereign, this idea corresponded fully to the liberal method that has already been discussed, the collectivist similarities notwithstanding. The liberal method evaded the question regarding the subject of the constitution-making power and the *representatives* of the political unity that are empowered to decide and which for this purpose constituted a sovereign third. This is the case whether or not the "constitution," which established itself and, therefore, seemingly fell from heaven, is alone sovereign or whether the sovereign "organism" is. The theoretical result was the same. In the case of conflict, however, the political and public law *practice* shows directly who was the bearer of state power and the representative of political unity that decides. It was the king.

During the Prussian conflict between king and provincial assembly, 1862 to 1866, the royal government took the stand that the constitution does not provide for the possibility of the provincial assembly's failure to pass a budget. This case is not regulated and, consequently, the royal government could act freely. The constitution was said to have a "gap" here, and the king could claim for himself the presupposition of unlimited jurisdiction. Such "gaps" are always possible, and an essential part of a constitutional conflict is that one can successfully present claims based on unforeseen circumstances. The uselessness of all normative types of discourse on the "sovereignty of the constitution" reveals itself here especially clearly. During the Prussian conflict of 1862, the royal government's claim regarding a constitutional gap was not only politically successful. It also had theoretical success. The consensus view of German public law experts (cf. Meyer-Anschütz, p. 906) rejected the Bismarckian theory. However, they came to the conclusion that the question is not at all a juristic one. "*Public law stops here.*" The norms, whose meaning and value should nevertheless reside precisely in deciding cases of conflict, do not permit one to draw any answer from them! Consequently, the situation did not change. In the critical case, the monarch representing political unity could, first, find a gap in the constitution and could, second, decide the issue of filling this gap. The many public law nuances with which one confused this simple legal situation have lost today every theoretical and practical value. Nonetheless, it is of special interest historically that the public law of the time ceased to apply precisely where the important and meaningful questions of constitutional law began.

8. The Constitution of the North German Federation of 26 July 1867 presupposed this constitutional condition in the allied states (the minor exception of the three Hanseatic states is entirely disregarded) [57], as did the Reich constitution of 16 April 1871. The homogeneity that is part of every genuine alliance rests first on the national compatibility of the German people and then on the comparability of the constitutional circumstances of the alliance's member states. The federal constitution is a constitutional contract of political unities, which unified themselves into this alliance. An agreement on the constitution, moreover, was *concluded* with a popular assembly, the Reichstag, which is constituted from general elections. On its legal construction, cf. below § 7, II, p. 64.

9. With the transformation in Germany during November 1918, the democratic theory of the people's constitution-making power successfully established itself in practical terms. Theoretically, certainly, constitutional

theory until today (1927) still remains entirely mired in prewar ways of thought. Liberal constitutionalism, which had proved itself a method of formalistic evasion when opposed to the king's constitution-making power, was certainly at first only retained out of habit when opposed to constitutional democracy.

(a) In the period of 10 November 1918 until 6 February 1919 (convening of the so-called constitution-making National Assembly), a "council of people's delegates" led a *provisional government,* which included six members, though only five after December 1918, all under the supervision of the workers' and soldiers' councils. The committees formed under the name "workers' and soldiers' councils" were recognized as the holders of political power and held it until an assembly elected by the entire people according to democratic principles convened, in order to pass constitutional laws.

The Reichsgericht's ruling of 8 July 1920 (*RGZ*, v. 100, p. 26) decided that according to the historical course of events from 7 November 1918 until 6 February 1919 it "cannot go unrecognized that already on 10 November 1918 a new Reich government had been established, which had its pinnacle in the local substructure of the workers' and soldiers' councils in the council of people's delegates. The founding proceeded on a violent path, but it encountered no opposition in the preexisting Reich authority. . . . Thus, the new government established itself without any considerable struggle and maintained itself in this position of power unscathed until it voluntarily handed over its powers to the National Assembly." In the judgment of 4 April 1922 (*RGZ*, v. 104, p. 258, in reference to *RGSt*, v. 53, p. 65, v. 54 p. 149 and p. 152), the question "whether Germany formed a 'republic of councils' in the first months after the Revolution" was left undecided.

This intermediary phase of November 1918 until February 1919 may not be looked upon as if a new, special [58] constitution of the German Reich existed for three months and the German Reich, from 9 November 1918 up until 11 August 1919, would have had three or four constitutions: first, the monarchical constitution of the early Reich until 9 November 1918; then, a council constitution; third, the democratic constitution of the Weimar National Assembly of 10 February 1919; and finally the Weimar Constitution of 11 August 1919. More precisely, in the previously noted three months until 6 February 1919, only a provisional government in the sense of democratic constitutional law existed. In every revolution, one such government must form until the new political decision of the bearer of the constitution-making power takes effect. One can designate this intermediary phase only imprecisely as a new constitution, insofar as a new condition, a new "status," emerges through the successful revolution, of course (cf. above § 1, p. 5). The workers' and soldiers' councils of the previously noted three months, however, considered themselves only as a provisional government and voluntarily surrendered their collective power to the National Assembly as soon as it convened.

Origin of the Constitution

The workers' and soldiers' councils were recognized as the "government." Under their supervision, the available state administrative apparatus with its civil servants continued to conduct business. The existing administrative situation, therefore, was not abolished and the old "state machine smashed," as in the year 1793 under the rule of the Jacobins in France or in 1918 under the Bolsheviks in Russia, in order to establish a fully new organization. The "machine" continued to operate with changed direction. The council of people's delegates assumed control. An agreement of 23 November 1918, reached between the executive committee of the workers' and soldiers' council of greater Berlin (the provisional representative of the workers' and soldiers' councils of Germany) and the council of the people's delegates, provided that political power lies in the hands of the workers' and soldiers' councils of the German socialist republic. It also provided that the Berlin executive committee should exercise its functions until a delegate assembly of Germany's councils convenes and that the council of the people's delegates assumes "executive" functions. All this is not a *constitution* or a constitutional pronouncement, as W. Jellinek, *Jahrbuch des öffentlichen Rechts*, IX, 1920, p. 21, termed it. Rather, it is the legal order of the provisional government. The decision of the general congress of the workers' and soldiers' councils of Germany on 16–18 December 1918 made clear that these workers' and soldier councils consider themselves only a provisional government in the sense of democratic constitutional law.

(b) The *National Assembly*, which was elected under democratic principles (right to general, equal, direct elections) and convened on 6 February 1919 in Weimar, exercised the German people's constitution-making power and formulated the constitutional norms that provided content to the people's political decision as well as norms that were necessary for this decision's execution. [59] The National Assembly was not the subject or bearer of the constitution-making power. It was only its delegate. Until the issuance of this constitutional law, it was bound by no legal restrictions other than those resulting from the German people's comprehensive political decision. Moreover, it was the sole constituted power of the political unity of the German people. As long as its task, the setting of the constitutional framework, had not ended, there were no constitutional restrictions on it. What is often called the *provisional* Reich Constitution (the law on the provisional Reich authority of 10 February 1919), issued by the National Assembly shortly after it convened, could have been changed and violated at any time through a simple majority decision of this assembly, as one could with a mere household provision. In the language characteristic of constitutional theory under the bourgeois Rechtsstaat, this circumstance of concentrating all state power resources in a single office is designated "dictatorship." The distinctive position of a "constitution-making" assembly, which convenes after a revolutionary elimination of the preexisting constitutional laws, is best designated a "sovereign dictator." It is only understandable in reference to the fundamental ideas of democratic constitutional law. So long as the new constitutional law formulation has not yet entered into force, the assembly acts as the sole constitutional magistrate of political unity and the only representative of the state. Everything it does is an immediate consequence of a political power granted it directly, not hemming it in by separation of powers or constitutional control. Consequently, it can undertake any measures that appear necessary in the present situation without any limitations other than those it imposes on itself. Such measures are part of the characteristic content of *dictatorship*. It has no jurisdiction, no competence in the actual sense, that is, in the sense of a sphere of office regulated and delimited in advance. The scope of its power resources and its empowerment stands entirely in its own discretion, and this linkage of empowerment and discretion is a defining characteristic of *dictatorship*. However, because there is no framework of constitutional norms, this dictatorship is not commissarial, which means it is not limited through already existing and formulated constitutional laws. It is, rather, sovereign. Yet, on the other hand, it remains dictatorship; it is a *commission*. It is not itself [60] the sovereign, but instead acts always in the name of and under commission from the people, which can at any time decommission its agents through a political act. In § 1 of the law on the provisional Reich authority of 10 February 1919, the German National Assembly assigned itself the task "of deciding on the future Reich constitution as well as on other pressing Reich laws." It is noteworthy in this regard that the National Assembly could conclude not only pressing Reich *statutes*, but could also institute any *measure* necessary under the circumstances. The expression "pressing Reich statutes" already demonstrates that considered in terms of content, even these statutes were in part only conceived as measures. In Germany, nonetheless, the Rechtsstaat distinction between statutes and measures, which was so vital in the French Revolution, is confused because of a "formal concept of statute" and is now entirely forgotten (cf. below & 13, III, p. 146).

(c) The Weimar Constitution of 11 August 1919 entered into force on 14 August 1919. This ended the position of the National Assembly as a "constitution-making" assembly with the power of a sovereign dictatorship. There was now still only a Reichstag grounded on the new constitution with jurisdictional areas that were regulated and limited constitutionally and were set next to one another in the same constitutional position.

The investigative committee of the Reichstag, installed on 20 August 1919, had the task of considering all the evidence for purposes of determining the causes of the outbreak, of the extension, and of the loss of the war as well as the failure to take advantage of opportunities for peace. The committee already stood under constitutional limitations and could operate only in the context of the powers defined in Art. 34. On this committee, see Erich Kaufmann, *Untersuchungsausschuss and Staatsgerichtshof*, Berlin 1920, p. 18ff.

The Weimar Constitution of 11 August 1919 rests on the constitution-making power of the German people. The most important political decision is contained in the Preamble, which reads, "The German people gave itself this Constitution," and in Art. 1, section 2, asserting that "state power derives from the people." These clauses characterize the positive-legal foundation of the Weimar Constitution as concrete political decisions. More specifically, they characterize the constitution-making power of the German people as a nation, as a unity, in other words, that is conscious of its political existence and is capable of acting. [61]

§ 7.

The Constitution as Contract

(The Genuine Constitutional Contract)

I. *Distinction of the so-called state or social contract from the constitutional contract.*

The numerous state-theory constructions, which ground the state on a *contract*, whether merely constituted or historically mediated, and, through it, attempt to explain its origin legally, are distinguishable from the agreements or contracts, through which a *constitution* arises. Both have often been confused, especially in state-theory debates, which underlie the American free constitutions and in the utterances of French state theorists and politicians of the 1789 Revolution. One linked a particular type of constitution with the ideal concept of a constitution (cf. above § 4, p. 38), then equates this constitution with the state itself and, in this way, viewed the issuance of a constitution, specifically, the act of a constitution-making power, as founding, or constituting, the state in general. When a people as a nation first become conscious of their capacity to act, that type of confusion and equation of the state itself with the constitution is certainly understandable. Nevertheless, one must insist that a constitution, which rests on an act of the constitution-making power of the people, must be something essentially different than a social contract, a "Contrat Social." The democratic principle of the people's constitution-making power means the constitution is established through an act of the people capable of acting politically. The people must be present and presupposed as political unity, if it is to be the subject of a constitution-making power. On the contrary, the constructions of a social, societal, or state contract (the distinctions among these "contracts" need not be discussed here) serve first to found the political unity of the people in general. The social contract, consequently, is already presupposed in the theory of the constitution-making power of the people when one considers its construction necessary at all. The social contract is not at all identical to the constitution in a positive sense. In other words, it is not the same as the concrete political decisions that the subject of the constitution-making power reaches regarding the political unity's type and form of existence, [62] much less to the constitutional *law* rules based on the execution of the previously mentioned decisions.

Fleiner, *Schweizerisches Bundesstaatsrecht,* p. 392, is an example of a recent jumble. "The constitution represents the basic law of state life," he argues. "It is the highest norm in the democracy (sic [Schmitt's]), the foundation of the state, of the contrat social in Rousseau's sense."

1. The constitution of the American state of Massachusetts, drafted by John Adams, was to a great extent characteristic of this type of constitution and a model to be emulated (cf. Charles. Borgeaud, *Etablissement et Revision des Constitutions*, Paris 1893, p. 23). It states in the preamble: "When the purpose of government is no longer fulfilled, then the people can change its government. Political unity stems from the voluntary agreement of individuals. It is the result of a social pact through which the *entirety* of the people (!) reaches a contract with each citizen, and every citizen concludes a contract with the entirety of the people, in order to be governed according to certain rules in the general interest. So it is the duty of the people, when it establishes a constitution, to provide for both a just mode of legislation as well as an impartial and reliable exercise and application of the laws." The entire body of citizens is presupposed as the political unity.

Even in Rousseau the "Contrat Social" establishing the state is distinguished from the lois politiques or fondamentales, which regulates the exercise of state power. Cf. *Contrat Social*, bk. II, chap. 12. Similarly, during the deliberations of the French National Assembly in 1789, the separation is originally clear, and the confusion of the contrat social and constitution first came into play later. Cf. E. Zweig, *Die Lehre vom pouvoir constituant*, p. 330; Redslob, *Staatstheorien*, p. 152ff.

In Kant the contract involved in the "establishment of a bourgeois constitution among the citizens (pactum unionis civilis)" is a distinctive type of general pactum sociale (through which a group of persons bind themselves to a society). The constituting of the bourgeois society is simultaneously the "erection of a bourgeois constitution." The constitution is the act through which the unio civilis first actually arises. Constitution, therefore, is taken in an absolute sense, not in the positive sense used here (*On the Relation of Theory and Practice in Public Law*, see the Vorländer edition, p. 86).

A constitutional *contract* or a constitutional agreement does not *establish* the political unity. It presupposes this unity. It is not the "covenant" on which the local community or the commons rests. This constitutional contract or agreement is instead a "governmental contract" in the widest sense of the term, by which under "government" is to be understood not only the executive in contrast to the legislative and the judiciary, but also the totality of organized state action as well. In the language characteristic of natural law state theory, it is not the *pactum unionis*, nor is it a *pactum subiectionis*. In other words, it is not a contract of subordination under an existing political power, which includes the conditions and limitations for the exercise of state power that is presupposed and already present.

2. The genuine constitutional contract is also to be distinguished from several states concluding a contract among themselves, according to which they form a new *unified state*, so that their previous political existence passes into this new state. Even if the constitution of the new unified state is concluded under the auspices of this contract, the continued validity rests not on this contract, but rather on the will of the constitution-making power of the new unified state.

II. A genuine *constitutional contract* presupposes at least *two* parties that already exist and will continue to exist, [63] and each of which contains internally a subject of a constitution-making power. Therefore, it is a political unity. A genuine constitutional contract is normally a *federal* contract.

On the non-genuine constitutional contract *inside* a political unity, see below under 2.

The international law contract (subordination contract handled under IV, 4, p. 73) can be termed a constitutional contract only insofar as it takes the free right to decide over the type and form of its own political existence of one of the contractual parties to the benefit of the other and, along with this, establishes a constitution in the positive sense.

A new constitution originates through the federal contract. All members of the federation receive a new political, comprehensive status, so that the political unity of the federation as such and the political existence of the federal members exist alongside one another. The distinctive difficulties and circumstances of the federal constitution are considered in the final section of this book. Here, the following must be made clear.

1. The *federal contract between several independent political unities* is a genuine *constitutional contract.*

2. The *"constitutional contract" within a political unity.* The idea of such a constitutional contract is explicable only historically from a special circumstance, the "dualism" of the constitutional monarchy. The question regarding the subject of the constitution-making power inside of a political unity is answered, as was shown above (§ 6, p. 53), in terms of constitutional theory according to a simple either/or, people or prince, either the people as unity capable of political action in its conscious *identity* with itself, or the prince as *representative* of the political unity. In the context of one and the same political unity, the constitution can always only be conferred, not agreed on, because a genuine constitutional agreement would presuppose that several political unities are present. From this, it follows that the numerous constitutional agreements that came about during the nineteenth century in Germany did not solve the question about the subject of the constitution-making power. They signified a compromise, which left the case of conflict undecided. When a constitution that was unilaterally imposed by the prince, thus not agreed on, provides that the constitution can be changed "through means of ordinary legislation," that also signifies such a compromise. For "by way of [64] legislation" means nothing other than "participation and consent of the popular assembly." The constitution in fact does not become a statute thereby, no less than it is a contract. Even so, the confusion lay not far off, which led to the relativizing of the constitutional concept that was examined thoroughly above (§ 2, p. 11f.): constitution equals constitution-amending statute. What it came down to was always the same: the definitive participation of the popular assembly. Obvious contradictions were therefore tolerated without hesitation. The constitution was a *contract.* In other words, it should not be imposed, but rather agreed on by prince and the popular assembly; the constitution was a statute, as soon as the participation and consent of the popular assembly to a statute was necessary.

Examples of constitutional "agreements" (which usually did not preclude that the constitution was, nonetheless, designated as "conferred by the prince") are the Württemberg constitution of 25 September 1819, in which "finally, a *complete reciprocal agreement* over the following points thus came about through the most elevated commitment and the lowliest counter-declaration." Also, the Saxon constitution of 4 September 1831, where "hereby is announced that we . . . have established the constitution of our law, with *the advice and consent of the estates,* to the following extent." Often, the constitution is *decreed* by the prince, but amendment and interpretation are tied to the agreement of the estates. See, for example, the preface and Art. 110 of the Grand Duchy of Hesse's constitution of 17 December 1820. An example of a constitution issued unilaterally by the prince with the proviso that the constitution can "be changed by the ordinary means of legislation" is Art. 106 of the Prussian (imposed) constitution of 31 January 1850.

3. A genuine constitutional agreement was reached at the founding of the North German Federation and of the German Reich, more specifically, a federal contract together with a non-genuine, domestic political constitutional agreement, discussed above in section 2. The pronouncement of 26 July 1867 concerning the constitution of the North German Federation (*Bundesgesetzblatt* p. 1; Triepel, *Quellensammlung,* 4th ed., p. 333) states: "After the constitution of the North German Federation had been *agreed upon* by Us (the King of Prussia), his majesty the King of Saxony, his royal highness the Grand Duke of Hesse, etc., convened with the *Reichstag* for this purpose," etc. In this instance, one must distinguish between the *federal contract* concluded between the allied states (Prussia, Saxony, Hesse, etc.) (that is the actual constitutional agreement), on the one hand, and the agreement reached between the federation and the popular assembly (a *non-genuine constitutional contract*). To the extent that so-called contracts existed within the individual member states of the federation, there were also non-genuine constitutional contracts. [65] The manner of expression typical of the year 1867 naturally no longer had, as had been the case for some time, the sense of relying on medieval ideas of estate-based contracts. It meant only that the constitution should not be imposed. That was a concession to modern ideas, whose result was the previously mentioned compromise, which, though not genuine, was very reasonable in peaceful or, indeed, happy times. Under no circumstances should a constitution-making power for the German people be recognized. However, that a compromise was at all possible, even if only unclearly and half way, signifies, for example, a recognition of the constitution-making power of the people, hence of the democratic principle. The weakness of this contradictory lack of clarity then manifested itself theoretically in irresolvable problems, such as that of the relationship of federated (more specifically, genuine contractual) and constitutional *law* elements in the Reich Constitution. In terms of practical politics, this weakness revealed itself in critical situations, such as

in the world war since the summer of 1917, as the Reichstag began to gain influence on the Reich government.

4. For a *federal constitution on a democratic foundation*, that is, with the constitution-making power of the people, a peculiar difficulty results from the fact that the federation presupposes a definite similarity among its members, a substantial homogeneity (below § 30 III). The national similarity of people in the different member states of the federation, when the feeling of national unity is strong enough, easily leads to contradictions with the ideas of the federal constitution in general. For it lies in the logic of the democratic principle that the constitution-making power of the people as a political unity in regard to national similarity and national consciousness of the people breaks through the limitations of the different states within the federation and substitutes an act of the unified people's constitution-making power for the federation-like constitutional agreement (below p. 388).

The constitution of the German Reich of 11 August 1919 rests on one such act of the German people's constitution-making power. It is not a contract and, consequently, also not a federal constitution. On the contrary, the Reich Constitution of 16 April 1871 left the question open, in line with the compromise on which it rested. Obviously, the inevitable consequence did not go unnoticed. [66] Bierling (*Juristische Prinzipienlehre*, II, Freiburg 1898, p. 356 ff.) states especially clearly and openly that in terms of their "legal effectiveness or validity," the founding of the North German Federation and of the German Reich "must be traced back to the direct *recognition of the entire population* constituted into a higher community through the act of founding." He certainly meant this more in a legal philosophy sense than in a public law one. This recognition should have been expressed prior to the elections to the Bundestag, more precisely to the Reichstag. "Certainly," he continues, "the formulation of law itself proceeded in forms that, seen from a particular perspective, appear as *matters of law*, partly from the standpoint of international law, partly from that of the public law of individual states. The content of the legal formulation, however, naturally extends far beyond the established scope of such international law and public law matters of individual states." That really means the constitution-making power of the German people, therefore, democracy. But the agreed-on "allied" element of the German Reich contained the counterweight to this democratic logic. So until the demise of this Reich Constitution in November 1918, new differences of opinion and disputes arose over and over between the Reichstag, on the one hand, and the Bundesrat and Reich Government, on the other. The Reich Government stressed the federal or alliance foundation of the Reich and presented parliamentarianism (dependence of the Reich Government on the confidence of the Reichstag) and federalism as *absolute* opposites and *completely* irreconcilable matters. Nevertheless, the absolute character of these oppositions lay not in the divergence of forms of organization and institutions. Such a divergence is always only relative and makes numerous practical combinations possible. Rather, it resides in the opposition of the monarchical and democratic principle. This opposition involves the constitution-making power, thus the concrete political decisions over the form of existence of political unity in total. In this context, dilatory compromises, more specifically, postponements and suspensions of decision, are certainly possible, but not a substantive compromise, which could also transform the unavoidable either/or into a harmonious as-well-as.

III. *The genuine constitutional contract is always a status contract.* The general constitutional contract presupposes several political unities as contractual parties, which, as such, have a political status. In its [67] content inheres the founding of a new status for all states participating in the agreement.

This contract is a *free* contract, but only insofar as it rests on the will of the subjects concluding the contract. It is not a free contract in the sense of the modern private law concept of a contract and of a liberal bourgeois social order resting on "freedom of contract."

1. Distinguishing the free contract from the status contract is necessary because the word "contract" is ambiguous. When a medieval author grounded state or government on "contract"; a seventeenth-century philosopher like *Hobbes* used the word "contract"; or, finally, a bourgeois relativist in the twentieth century evaded the traditional ideas that the state rests on a contract by defining the modern democratic-parliamentary state as a "compromise"; then these types of diverse ideas are presupposed in the word "contract" such that it is utterly valueless and purposeless to discuss it without more precise distinctions or to proclaim principles such as *pacta sunt servanda.*

There are three elements of a free contract in the sense of the liberal-bourgeois legal and social order. First, the parties of the contract stand opposite one another as *separate* individuals in private law relations. A contract between two individuals and a contract between two political unities is something so essentially different that the same designation "contract" can involve only peripheral and external similarities in both instances. Second, the free contract between individuals establishes *individual* relations with content that is in principle *definable*, limited, and, thus, *cancelable.* Third, the free contract never involves the entirety of a person. It is subject to cancellation with notification and to dissolution; the total involvement of the person as a whole, moreover, appears immoral and contrary to law.

That is expressed in the statutory provisions of bourgeois law about this "freedom," which had already been proclaimed as a fundamental principle in the French Revolution (Art. 18 of the Declaration of the Rights of Man of 1793 and Art. 15 of the Declaration of Year III, 1795). This principle is also recognized in § 624 of the German Civil Code: "If the relations of servitude are entered into for the life of a person or for a time longer than five years, it can be terminated by the contractor after the passage of five years." The same idea became law in Art. 1780 of the [French] Code civil. The connection between "freedom" of the person and the measurability and limitedness of the service also reveals itself in the details. Cf. E. Jacobi, *Grundlehren* [68] *des Arbeitsrechts*, Leipzig 1927, p. 47 (Enhancement of the degree of subordination through indeterminacy of service). For another example of this connection of definability and freedom, see *Die Diktatur*, p. 37n.

The status contract, by contrast, founds an enduring life relationship that takes into account the person in his *existence* and incorporates the person into a total order, which exists not only in definable individual relations and which cannot be set aside through voluntary termination or renunciation. Examples of such a status contract are engagement and marriage, the establishment of civil servant relationships, and, in other legal orders, vassalage contracts and covenants (conjurations), etc. The *oath* is a characteristic sign of the existential engagement with the entire person. As such, it must disappear from a social order based on free contract.

The direction of historical development proceeds according to the famous formula of H. Sumner Maine (*Ancient Law*, p. 170), "from *Status to Contract*." That is essentially the same line that F. Tönnies presented in his great work "Gemeinschaft und Gesellschaft" as the development from *community to society*. To this historical and sociological insight is added only a short remark, through which the high value of the previously mentioned results should not be diminished, but which nevertheless could perhaps contribute to greater clarity. The juxtaposition of status and contract, community and contract, has something misleading about it because community and status relationships are also established through contract. The social order of medieval times rested on countless contracts, such as vassalage contracts, estate contracts, conjurations. In this context, "contract" means *status* contract; the oath enhances both the duration of the contracts as well as the existential bond of the person. The rejection of the vassalage service by Baptists and other sects signifies the actual beginning of the modern era and of the epoch of free contracts. Werner Wittich portrayed that in work on the Baptist Church that is unfortunately as yet unpublished.

There is still not a historical investigation of the development of the contract concept. One speaks of "contract" indiscriminately. In the historical portrayals of the theory of the status contract, a continuous line is drawn from Marsilius of Padua to Rousseau, without any differentiation within the contract concept. Even Gierke's book on this theme, "Althusius" (3rd ed. 1913), suffers from this defect and places a jurist with still entirely medieval contractual ideas like Althusius alongside Hobbes and Rousseau without taking into account the fundamental change, which in the meantime had occurred in the concept.

2. When the constitution comes about through agreement or contract within an existing political unity, such a contract lacks binding force in regard to the subject of the constitution-making power in cases of conflict.

A *majority* of subjects of the constitution-making power would eliminate and destroy the political unity. Where the process of dissolution sets in, such *"state contracts" arise inside the state.* If an estate-based or another organization succeeds in giving contracts internal to the state the character of *constitutional laws* [69], it has attained the highest degree of a state obligation that is still possible without eliminating political unity. However, if the "state contract" has the sense of bringing about not only the qualified amendability of constitutional law, but instead even the limitation and elimination of the constitution-making power, then political unity is destroyed and the state is in a completely abnormal circumstance. All juristic constructions of this condition are useless. That was the position of the German Reich since the sixteenth century (above p. 47). Obviously, such a process of dissolution can begin anew at any time.

3. If a constitution rests on agreement or contract, then the *legal foundation of its validity* is the *political will* of the allied partners and the *existence* of the federation that rests on it. The federation is a *comprehensive status* that encompasses the status of every member state. Beyond the merely contractual, individual obligation, every member state is altered as an entirety (on this, see the expositions on the concept of the federation below at § 29, II 3).

The legal ground of a constitutional contract is not at all the general principle *pacta sunt servanda.* Still less is this principle a constitutional clause or a constitutional law. It is not possible, therefore, to ground a federation or some community on this principle as one could on its "constitution."

A. Verdross attempted to ground the community of international law on the principle "pacta sunt servanda" (*Die Verfassung der Völkerrechtsgemeinschaft,* 1926). In this principle, he sees the "basic norm," which should be the "constitution" of this "community." Apart from the fact that a constitution is a concrete political decision (above p. 23), not a norm; overlooking, moreover, the obscurities in the concept of this "community"; the following is worth mentioning.

(a) The principle "pacta sunt servanda" is not a norm. It is perhaps a *basic principle,* though not in the sense of a legal rule. Cf. H. Heller, *Die Souveränität,* 1927, p. 132, where this distinction of norm and basic principle is treated in an exceptional critique.

(b) The principle "pacta sunt servanda" states that one can obligate oneself legally through contracts. Today, that is something self-evident, and it is neither a norm nor the moral foundation of the validity of norms. It is, moreover, either a fully tautological duplication and hypostatization, or it states that the concrete contract is not valid. What is valid, rather, is only the general "norm" that contracts are valid. If the "norm" that contracts are generally valid is appended to every single valid contract, then that is an empty fiction. For the [70] individual contract is valid and is legally binding by virtue of positive law and not by virtue of the norm "pacta sunt servanda." Such fictional additions and hypostatizations are possible in unlimited numbers. Every norm is valid, because the general norm is valid that there are norms, which should be valid, etc. They are entirely meaningless for the establishment of a concrete, existing political unity.

(c) Considered in terms of legal history, the principle "pacta sunt servanda" had a special meaning so long as it was self-evident that one could obligate oneself through "pacta." The turn of phrase "pacta sunt servanda" may trace its historical origin back to the formula of the Roman Praetor, who could declare that certain contracts are to be treated as valid in the execution of his office: "Ait Praetor: Pacta conventa quae neque dolo malo, neque adversus leges, plebiscita, senatus-consulta, edicta principum, neque quo fraus cui eorum fiat, facta erunt, *servabo*," Dig. 2, 14, 1.7 § 7, or "(D)olo malo ait Praetor pactum *se non servaturum*," eod. § 9. Cf. Lenel, *Edictum Perpetuum,* 3rd ed., 1927, p. 65. In this formulation, the principle has a concrete content. The *Praetor* presents the agreements, for which he secures protection and execution through the official power to decide. On the contrary, the general principle "pacta sunt servanda" says nothing about *which* contracts are valid and binding, therefore, which of them is to be enforced. It always only repeats the same principle that valid contracts must be carried out; in other words, they are valid.

(d) The principle "pacta sunt servanda" does not have a value in terms of legal science, neither theoretically nor practically. That contracts must be upheld under the presupposition that they are valid is self-evident. It is just as self-evident, however, that only valid contracts need be upheld and that first of all a valid contract must be present. The question always concerns either the presence of a contract, more specifically, of an effectively genuine agreement of intention in the concrete case, or grounds for nullification, elimination, disputation, possibilities for withdrawal, inappropriateness or immorality of the contract, impossibility of its fulfillment, unforeseen circumstances, etc. No one would dispute that contracts must be upheld. The conflict involves only doubt and differences of opinion over whether in concreto a contract is present at all, whether this contract is valid, whether special grounds for invalidity or elimination come into consideration, etc.

(e) In fact, the question is *quis iudicabit*? *Who decides* whether there is a valid contract, whether the grounds to dispute it are persuasive, whether a right to withdraw is provided, etc.? If the question is properly posed in such a manner, it is revealed that the principle "pacta sunt servanda" neither states anything substantive for a decision and, consequently, has no normative value at all, nor provides for *who* decides. An answer to the questions that are solely under consideration is not to be derived from this principle. [71]

(f) The value of the principle is thus reduced to the significance of a saying that the traditional notaries public loved to place on the envelopes of their documents or in their offices. The *political* sense of the emphasis of such principles, however, can only be that a supposition tacitly intervenes to the effect that all the currently concluded contracts are also *valid*. The "norm" pacta sunt servanda then is one of the means in the great system of legitimacy of the existing political and economical *status quo*. Above all, it stabilizes the existing tribute obligations and gives them the sanctity of legitimacy and of morality.

IV. 1. *Only a federal constitution can arise through contract or agreement, and only a constitution of those states becoming federation members can do so.* The constitution of an independent state cannot rest on the international law contract of *third* states. Self-determination inheres in political existence. The constitution in the positive sense is an expression of this possibility of choosing, by virtue of its own decision, the type and form of its *own* existence.

When an international law contract regulates the government and administration of a third land, this land becomes the *object* of foreign agreements and compromises. That means a *denial* of political existence. A constitution in the positive sense is impossible.

The Saar area is not a state. The so-called *Saar statute* regulates the "government" of the Saar area until the popular vote about and the conclusive decision on the disposition of the territory by the "League of Nations" occurs (League of Nations *Assembly* or *Council* of the League of Nations?). The League of Nations serves as a "trustee." A "governmental commission" with five members drawn from different nationalities exercises governmental power on the basis of the "Saar Statute" (addition to Art. 49 of the Versailles Treaty). That is still much less the Saar area's "constitution" than the colonial legislation of the mother country is the constitution of the colony. Constitution in the positive sense means essentially definition of its *own* form of existence.

Even the so-called *mandate* areas, which under Art. 22 of the League of Nations Charter are ruled and administered by a mandate state, do not have a constitution in the positive sense. They are either colonies (B and C mandates) or (the so-called A mandate) protectorates (below 4) with the exceptional circumstance that there is an undefined (for the time being still problematical) supervision by the "League of Nations" (League of Nations Council, Mandate Commission). According to Art. 22, the peoples of these areas are *"not yet capable of leading themselves* under the especially difficult conditions of today's world" (se diriger eux-mêmes; to stand by themselves [Schmitt's English rendering]). This also means that they cannot have a constitution in the positive sense.

2. An international law contract as such is never a constitution in the positive sense. It can also not be part of the constitution of an independent state. The federal contract (even in the federation of states) is not a "pure international legal" agreement. On this, cf. below § 30, p. 380. On the constitutional *law* guarantee of international legal obligations, see below 5. [72]

According to Art. 178, 2, the "provisions" of the Treaty of Versailles "should not be affected by the constitution." This clause of the Weimar Constitution does not signify a renunciation of the political existence and right to self-determination of the German people. It states only that the German Reich does not intend to rely on constitutional provisions to evade the binding obligations of this treaty under international law. The political situation of the year 1919 accounts for this express declaration (on this, see the very interesting piece by Wittmayer, pp. 20/21). Apart from this fact, it is a generally recognized principle in terms of international law that a state cannot evade its still valid international legal obligations because of domestic public law obstacles or lack of capacity. "If there is an undisputed principle of international law, it is this one" (Triepel, *Völkerrecht und Landesrecht*, 1899, p. 303). The declaration of Art. 178, 2, of the Weimar Constitution, therefore, does not have an independent, constitutive content. It would be imprecise to say that the provisions of the Versailles Treaty have "precedence" over those of the Weimar Constitution. It would also be simply nonsensical to designate a change in the Versailles Treaty as a change in the Weimar Constitution and, for example, to demand a constitution-amending statute for a return of the Saar area to the German government before the year 1935. A purely international law duty is not part of the constitution in the positive sense. Consequently, an undertaking that is directed at its elimination is never also high treason in the sense of criminal law. One cannot rely on an international legal duty of the state to justify treason toward a land. An international law duty is not affirmed through the civil servant's oath (Art. 176), etc.

When the content of the London Protocols of 16 August 1924 (the so-called Dawes Plan) became part of Germany's state legislation through a series of constitution-amending statutes of 30 August 1924, this action had the juridical consequence that the domestic adjustment to a change of the plan must be by means of a constitution-amending statute (more specifically, brought about through the procedure of Art. 76). In this instance, the "form" of constitutional law is only a technical juridical means. It would also be incorrect at this point to say that the Dawes Plan is a part of the German constitution. It is affirmed through the civil servants' oath (Art. 176), protected through the criminal law provisions against high treason, and, according to Art. 148, 3, it must be handed out to German schoolchildren at their discharge from school, etc.

3. If a constitutional provision stipulates that "the generally recognized rules of international law" should be valid "as binding components" of the state's law (Art. 4), that means that for the content of certain international legal norms the formal *reconfiguration* (transformation) of the state's law occurs generally. When speaking of norms here, one means generally recognized *rules* in particular, above all those of the recognizing state itself, general norms, not specific contracts, in other words. The thorough change or transformation remains the essential process because the legal foundation ("auctoritatis interpositio") for the validity of the state is thereby created. The transformation is generally only ordered, so far as it is a matter of the generally recognized rules of international law. These rules [73] become generally recognized through state statutory law; they do not become constitutional laws or, indeed, a component of the constitution.

Hugo Preuß considered a provision like Art. 4 an "incorporation of the Reich as a democratic Rechtsstaat into the international legal community" (according to a statement reported by A. Verdross, *Die Einheit des rechtlichen Weltbildes*, Tübingen 1923, p. 111). If the article really had this meaning, the German constitution would be the constitution of a member state of the federated "international legal community" and the written law of this federation would be a part of the German constitution. Obviously, Preuß did not intend to present such a fantastic claim, but rather only to stress the loyal action of the German Reich toward international law. The "international legal community" does not at all have the structure that permits such "incorporation," as a state is incorporated into a genuine federation. The international legal community is not a stable organization. It is only the reflection of the coexistence of independent political unities (on this, see the theory of the basic concepts of federation law below at § 29, I, 1). So Preuß's statement proves very little, despite its remarkable wording. One is not permitted to conclude from this that the "general rules of international law" are German constitutional laws, and one cannot yet correctly speak of the components of the German constitution in the positive sense. Verdross (*Verfassung der Völkerrechtsgemeinschaft*, p. 116) speaks of an "anchoring of general international law in the constitution" and claims that because Art. 4 (just as well as Art. 9 of the Austrian federal constitution, which is essentially in agreement) is part of the constitution, it could be set aside again only by means of a constitutional amendment. That is correct insofar as a constitutional law provision can be set aside again only through constitutional law. In this way, however, "general international law," more precisely, the dozen individual, generally recognized rules of international law, did not become constitutional law of the German Reich. J. Schmitt, *Zeitschrift für badische Verwaltung und Verwaltungsrechtspflege*, 1921, p. 201, and G. A. Walz, *Die Abänderung völkerrechtsgemässen Landsrechts* (Völkerrechtsfragen, Heft 21, 1927, p. 150), are both incorrect. They assume that beyond the transformation-effect of Art. 4 there is still an obligation of the German legislator in regard to the transformed content. The principles that are viewed as "generally recognized rules of international law" are valid as "Reich law," nothing more. They are Reich statutes like other valid Reich statutes. Correct in this regard are Anschütz, *Kommentar*, pp. 49–50, and Giese, *Kommentar*, pp. 57–58.

4. It can only be a matter of the forms of subordination and dependence when the comprehensive political status of a state concluding a contract is determined through an international law contract, which is not a federal contract (and, consequently, does not change the status of *every* party concluding the contract in regard to the membership in the federation). The contract then contains an *elimination* of the constitution-making power of the state that became dependent.

Examples of such international law contracts are the *protectorate* contracts of the nineteenth and twentieth centuries. However, even *intervention contracts* with a right to intervene standing in the discretion of the intervening state change the status of a political unity when the intervention signifies a decision over existential political concepts, such as protection of *independence* from foreign influence, public *security*, and *order*, and when on the basis of the right to intervene the decision on these concepts is placed in the hand [74] of the state empowered to intervene. For an example, cf. the agreements between the United States of America and the Republic of *Cuba* of 22 May 1903 (Strupp, *Documents* II, p. 236 f), on the one hand, and between the United States with the Republic of Panama of 18 November 1903 (Strupp, p. 346 f), on the other. See, moreover, the legal and political position of Haiti, Santo Domingo, Nicaragua, and even Egypt (on the basis of the English Declaration of 28 January 1922).

Art. 102ff. of the Versailles Treaty contains another example of the elimination of the autonomous decision affecting these existential concepts. The principal major powers *founded* (constituée) the Free City of Danzig. The Free City constitution was composed by "representatives called to service through the established process," in agreement with a high commissioner of the League of Nations, and it is guaranteed by the League of Nations. That is not a constitution in the positive sense, more specifically, not a free decision on the type and form of its own political existence.

Neither the Treaty of Versailles nor the agreements of the London Protocols of 16 August 1924 are international law contracts of this type. As large and pressing as the burdens of the German Reich are and as immense and destructive as the opportunities for interference by the allied powers, the decision about these existential concepts is not directly transferred to a foreign power. Even the fact that the incorporation of Austria into the German Reich is made contingent on the consent of the

Council of the League of Nations (Art. 80 of the Versailles Treaty) and that Art. 61, 2, thus becomes temporarily meaningless does not eliminate the political existence of the German Reich. It is incorrect, therefore, to deny the German Reich the character of a sovereign state, as is the case without a clear concept of sovereignty in the treatment by H. Gerber, "Die Beschränkung der deutschen Souveränität nach dem Versailler Vertrage" (*Völkerrechtsfragen*, Heft 20), Berlin 1927.

5. If the content of *certain* international legal agreements is taken up into the constitutional laws of a country by virtue of international legal obligations, that still need not entail an abrogation or even only a diminishment of the political independence of the state, which thereby guarantees international legal obligations through the public law form of constitutional laws. It can involve a juridical-technical method of protection against change by way of simple legislation. The difference between a constitution in the positive sense and individual provisions of constitutional law becomes especially clear here. In terms of public law, the content of these international legal agreements is protected through qualified alterability. The form of a constitutional law serves this purpose. Such provisions, however, are not acts of a people's constitution-making power. They do not eliminate the sovereignty of a state and, in the interest of an international legal obligation, only use the relative concept of constitutional law as a formal-technical means, in order to reinforce the internal state validity.

For example, the international law treaties for the protection of national and religious minorities concluded between the allied and associated principal powers, on the one hand, and Poland (28 June 1919), Czechoslovakia (10 September 1919), [75] the Kingdom of Serbo-Croatia (10 September 1919), and middle and east European states, on the other (additional examples in H. Kraus, *Das Recht der Minderheiten*, *Stilkes Rechtsbibliothek*, vol. 57, Berlin 1927). In these so-called minority protection treaties, the following provision of Art. 1 is regularly found: Poland (in regard to Czechoslovakia or the Kingdom of Serbo-Croatia, etc.) obligates itself to recognize the protective provisions as *"basic laws"* (lois fondamentales) that no statute, decree, official action may oppose or contradict. The same goes for Art. 65 and Art. 73 of the German-Polish agreement on Upper Silesia of 15 May 1922, *Reichgesetzesblatt* II, p. 271, 278). In this instance, the word "basic law" has the relative sense of constitutional law.

§ 8.

The Constitution-Making Power

I. *The constitution-making power is the political will, whose power or authority*[1] *is capable of making the concrete, comprehensive decision over the type and form of its own political existence.* The decision, therefore, defines the existence of the political [76] unity in toto. The validity of any additional constitutional rule is derived from the decisions of this will. The decisions as such are qualitatively different from the constitutional norms that are legislated on their basis.

1. A constitution is not based on a norm, whose justness would be the foundation of its validity. It is based on a political decision concerning the type and form of its own being, which stems from its political *being.* In contrast to any dependence on a normative or abstract justice, the word "will" denotes the essentially existential character of this ground of validity.

The constitution-making power is political *will*, more specifically, concrete political being. The general question of legal philosophy, whether, according to its essence, a law is command, therefore will, or whether it is *norm*, in other words, *ratio* and justice, has definitive meaning for the concept of law in the sense of the Rechtsstaat. Cf. below § 13 in this regard. That the *constitution* must be understood as an *act of will* still does not signify a resolution of this general question. No less at issue is the traditional and eternal metaphysical dispute, which repeats itself in the most varied forms in the diverse areas of human thinking, whether something is good and just, because God wills it, or whether God wills it, because it is good and just (on this, see a few examples in Gierke, *Althusius,* p. 14 n.). Independent of the question of whether the law in general is essentially command or *ratio*, one may say that the constitution must be a decision and *every act of the constitution-making power* must necessarily be *command.* It is, as Boutmy (p. 241) puts it, an "acte impératif."

2. In terms of its content, a constitutional *law* is the enabling legislation of the constitution-making will. The comprehensive decision contained in this will thoroughly provides the constitutional law's presupposition and foundation. If additional individual norms are written into the "constitution," that only has a technical juristic meaning of protection against amendment through qualified amendment procedures (cf. above § 2, p. 16).

3. To the same limited degree that an organizational decree exhausts the organization's power, which its supreme command and authority [77] holds, the issuance of a constitution can exhaust, absorb, or consume the constitution-making power. The constitution-making power is not thereby expended and eliminated, because it was exercised once. The political decision, which essentially means the constitution, cannot have a reciprocal effect on its subject and eliminate its political existence. This political will

remains alongside and above the constitution. Every genuine constitutional conflict, which involves the foundations of the comprehensive political decision itself, can, consequently, only be decided through the will of the constitution-making power itself. Also, every gap in the constitution, in contrast to the lack of clarity in terms of constitutional *law* and differences of opinion in detail, is filled only through an act of the constitution-making power. Every unforeseen case, whose decision the foundational political decision effects, is decided by it.

4. The constitution-making power is unified and indivisible. It is not a coordinate, additional authority (legislative, executive, judicial; cf. § 14) alongside other "powers" that are distinguished from one another. It is the comprehensive foundation of all other "powers" and "divisions of powers."

Through the confusion of constitution and constitutional law, another confusion of constitution-making power with a competence for constitutional law revisions has emerged, a confusion that frequently leads to the placement of this jurisdiction alongside other "pouvoirs" as "pouvoir constituant." On this, cf. below § 10 IV, p. 98.

II. *The subject of the constitution-making power.*

1. According to the medieval understanding, only *God* has a potestas constituens, so far as it is spoken of at all. The clause "All power (or compulsion) is from God" (Non est enim potestas nisi a Deo, Rom. 13:1), means God's constituting power. Also, the political literature of the Reformation period above all adhered to the theory of the Calvinist monarchomachs.[2]

Althusius, *Politica*, Ch. XVIII, 93; XIX, 19ff. The *people* in Althusius already have a potestas *constituta*. The secularization of the concept of the constituting power first emerges later. Under no circumstances may one combine the concepts of a devout Calvinist like Althusius and those of a romantic deist like Rousseau, as does Gierke in his famous work on Althusius.

2. During the French Revolution, Sieyès developed the theory of the *people* (more precisely of the *nation*) as the subject of the constitution-making power. In the eighteenth century, the absolutist prince had not yet been designated the subject of the constitution-making [78] power. Yet this was only because the thought of a free, comprehensive decision reached by persons with regard to the type and form of their own political existence was at first only gradually able to take the form of a political deed. In the eighteenth century, the aftereffects of the Christian theological images of God's constituting power, despite all clarification, were still strong and vital. The American Declaration of Independence and the French Revolution of 1789 signify the beginning of a new epoch, which is not defined by the extent to which the originators of these great precedents were conscious of the scope of their action. In the American Declaration of Independence of 1776, the entirely new principle is not yet recognizable with complete clarity, because a new political formation arose and the act of constitution-

making converged with the political founding of a series of new *states*. It was quite different with the French Revolution of 1789. No new political formation, no new state arose there. The French state existed prior to it and continued to exist after it. This case involves people themselves determining the type and form of their own political existence. When the question of the constitution-making power was consciously posed and answered, the fundamental novelty of such a process was much clearer. With complete awareness, a people took its destiny into its hands and reached a free decision on the type and form of its political existence.

That revealed itself immediately as the Estates General, convened by the king on 17 June 1789, constituted itself as the *constitution-making National Assembly*. The estates constituted themselves without being legitimated through a formal commission, as the commissioners of the people exercising its constitution-making power and derived their powers from this constitution-making power. Sieyès formulated the theory of the "pouvoir constituant" of the nation. He rightly designated it an act of the Revolution that the Revolution immediately at its inception established the difference between constitutive and constituted power. Despite the great influence of the American model, the year 1789 first signifies the beginning of the new political principles.

The American constitutions of the eighteenth century lacked a genuine constitutional theory. The most important historical source for the theoretical foundations of this constitution, *The Federalist* [*Papers*], offers insight mostly only into practical organizational questions. The people provides itself a [79] constitution without distinguishing the general "covenant," which the localities and the society founded, from every other act of constituting a new political unity and from the act of the free political decision on the particular form of existence. On this, cf. above § 7 I, p. 61.

According to this new theory, the *nation* is the subject of the constitution-making authority. Nation and people are often treated as equivalent concepts. Nevertheless, the word "nation" is clearer and less prone to misunderstanding. It denotes, specifically, the people as a unity capable of political action, with the consciousness of its political distinctiveness and with the will to political existence, while the people not existing as a nation is somehow only something that belongs together ethnically or culturally, but it is not necessarily a bonding of men existing *politically*. The theory of the people's constitution-making power presupposes the conscious willing of political existence, therefore, a nation. Historically, that was first possible after France had become a state unity through the absolute monarchy, whose existence had always been presupposed as something self-evident despite the frequent adoption of new constitutions and changes in the then existing constitution. In its political existence, the French people first found its form as a nation. The conscious decision for a particular type and form of this existence, the act through which "the people gives itself a constitution," presupposes the state, whose type and form is being determined. However, for the act itself, for the exercise of this will, there can be no procedural provisions. This applies no less to the content of the political decision. "It is sufficient that the nation wills it." This principle of Sieyès portrays the essence of this process with greater clarity. The constitution-making power is not bound by legal forms and procedures; it is "always in the state of nature," when it appears in this capacity, which is inalienable.

All constitutionally constituted powers and competencies are based on the constitution-making power. However, it can never constitute itself in terms of constitutional law. The people, the nation, remains the origin of all political action, the source of all power, which expresses itself in continually new forms, producing from itself these ever renewing forms and organizations. It does so, however, without ever subordinating itself, its political existence, to a conclusive formation.

In some of Sieyès's writings, the "pouvoir constituant" appears in its relationship to every "pouvoirs constitués" as a metaphysical analogy to the "natura naturans" and its relationship to the "natura naturata" of [80] Spinoza's theory. It is an inexhaustible source of all forms without taking a form itself, forever producing new forms out of itself, building all forms, yet doing so without form itself (cf. die Diktatur, p. 142). But it is necessary to distinguish the positive theory of the constitution-making power, which inheres in every constitutional theory, from the aforementioned pantheist metaphysic. They are in no way identical with one another. The metaphysic of the potesta constituens as well as that of the analogy to the natura naturans is part of the theory of political theology.

Even the attempt to establish a definitive representative or interpreter of the people's will in some binding manner contradicts this theory. Considered formally, the French National Assembly of 1789 was not a constitution-making assembly. Convened by the king, it stemmed from elections to an assembly of three estates, nobility, clergy, and the third estate, with particular instructions from the voters. That is not an objection, however, against its democratic right to constitute itself as constitutive assembly. It could appeal to the will of the French nation against the king.

Sieyès bound the antidemocratic theory of the representation of the people's will through the constitution-making National Assembly with the democratic theory of the constitution-making power of the people, which directed itself against the existing absolute monarchy. The constitution was formulated only by the National Assembly (therefore, neither by the people nor by the king). It would have been consistently democratic to let the people itself decide, for the constitution-making will of the people cannot be represented without democracy transforming itself into an aristocracy (cf. below § 15, p. 217). Nonetheless, democracy was not at issue in 1789. It was, rather, a constitution of a liberal, bourgeois Rechtsstaat. The constitution of 1791 was typical of a constitutional monarchy. The "nation" had two representatives, king and legislative body (popular assembly). The issue of who represented the nation by the proclamation of the constitution, the National Assembly or the king, was a clear question of power and already showed the distinctive, characteristic intermediary position of the liberal bourgeoisie. In opposition to the king (therefore the monarchy), there is the appeal to the "will of the nation," while in opposition to the people (therefore, the democracy), there is the appeal to the "representative" institution. Of course, the king could also be representative of the nation, but his representative capacity in regard to the exercise of the constitution-making power of the people was called into question. The attempts to provide the king influence on the formation of the constitution as representative or interpreter of the people's will in the constitution-making assembly were unsuccessful (Redslob, p. 71).

3. During the monarchical restoration, 1815–1830, the king becomes the subject of the constitution-making power. By virtue of the "monarchical principle," the plenitude of state power remains with the king, even if he binds himself to the consultation of the estates in regard to the exercise of certain rights in limited scope. The theory of a constitution-making power of the king had been presented occasionally and without success in the constitution-making National Assembly of 1789 (Redslob, p. 69). During the restoration, [81] however, it became theoretically necessary to oppose a constitution-making power of the king to that of the people, which was established as a clear thesis of the French Revolution.

For evidence, see *Diktatur*, p. 195n., and Perny, *Le pouvoir constituant sous la monarchie de Juillet*, Pariser thesis 1901, p. 13. E. Zweig, *Pouvoir constituant*, p. 3, speaks imprecisely when he states that "political science has delivered no technical expression of such a type (as constitution-making power of the people)" for the "organizational hierarchy of the monarch."

Theoretically, moreover, the position of the monarchy was especially difficult. In specific terms, it is possible to apply the democratic theory of the people's constitution-making power without modification to the monarchy, a hereditary monarchy in particular, only as a defensive move based on a superficial antithesis. For the nation can change its forms and give itself continually new forms of political existence. It has the complete freedom of political self-determination. It can be the "formless formative capacity." The hereditary monarchy, by contrast, is an institution that is bound to a family's hereditary order of succession and is in itself already formed. A dynasty cannot be considered, as can the people or nation, the origin of all political life.

4. Even the organization of a "minority" can be the subject of the constitution-making power. The state then has the form of an *aristocracy* or *oligarchy*. Nevertheless, the expression "minority" is prone to misunderstanding because it derives from the numerical and statistical ideas of today's democratic methods and presupposes a minority like that of a political party. Naturally, an electoral minority cannot be the subject of the constitution-making power, just as little as a party in today's sense of a human association resting on "free competition" could be. Certainly, however, a stable organization as such can reach the fundamental political de-

cisions on the type and form of the political existence. In other words, it can establish a constitution without appealing to the will of the majority of state citizens. As in ancient or medieval aristocracies, that can be a circle of certain *families*, or an *order*, or another group that is formed internally. The nineteenth century does not know such cases of constitution-making power. In the twentieth century, the rule of the "councils" in Russia in its connection with the communist organization, as well the rule of the "*Fascio*" [82] in Italy, contained elements of a new type of aristocratic forms. But the theoretical and practical construction is still not at all clear and does not conclusively renounce appealing to the will of the people, for whose true and unfalsified expression the prerequisites should first be created. Its regime, therefore, is dictatorship also in the sense that it is only a transition, and the conclusive decision over the type and form of the political existence is still to be reached. The only thing conclusively decided is the rejection of the *liberal* method of majority decision in secret and equal individual votes of all separate state citizens as well as of the principles of the *bourgeois Rechtsstaat* (basic rights and separation of powers; on these, cf. § 12, p. 126). Certainly to that extent, there is an act of constitution-making.

III. *Initiation of the constitution-making power.*

1. There cannot be a regulated procedure, through which the activity of the constitution-making power would be bound.

2. The activity of the constitution-making power of the monarch regulates itself simply through the fact that the absolute monarchy is an existing institution. In this instance, there is already a constituted organization. That has an advantage, both practically and theoretically, which consists in the fact that a stable entity is provided, whose expressions of will are clear. The practical and theoretical weakness, however, is perhaps greater still. For the organization and institution of the monarchy rests on the monarchical principle; in other words, it rests on the hereditary succession in a family. Consequently, it is not actually based at all on distinct political concepts, but instead on concepts of family law.

The king initiates his constitution-making authority by issuing a constitution out of the plenitude of his power, imposing it through unilateral action. He can come to an understanding with representatives of the estates or of the people and commit himself to seek their consultation and consent. As elaborated above (§ 6, II, 7, p. 53), that still does not require a renunciation of the constitution-making power, nor does it entail recognition of the people's constitution-making power.

3. The people initiate their constitution-making power through some recognizable expression of their direct comprehensive will, which is targeted at a decision on the type and form of the existence of the political

unity. Special questions and difficulties stem from the distinctiveness of the subject of this constitution-making power. [83]

(a) The people as bearer of the constitution-making power are not a stable, organized organ. The people in this capacity would lose their nature, when they direct themselves to the daily, normal functioning and the regular completion of official business. According to their nature, the people are *not* a magistrate, and even in a democracy they are never the responsible officials. In a democracy, on the other hand, the people must be capable of making political decisions and acting politically. Even if they have a determinative will only in less definitive moments and express themselves recognizably, they are nevertheless capable of and in a position for such willing and are able to say yes or no to the fundamental questions of their political existence. The strength as well as the weakness of the people lies in the fact that they are not an organ that is supplied with defined competencies and that completes official business in a regulated process. As long as a people have the will to political existence, the people are superior to every formation and normative framework. As an entity that is not organized, they also cannot be dissolved. So long as they exist at all and intend to endure, their life force and energy is inexhaustible and always capable of finding new forms of political existence. The weakness is that the people should decide on the basic questions of their political form and their organization without themselves being formed or organized. This means their expressions of will are easily mistaken, misinterpreted, or falsified. It is part of the directness of this people's will that it can be expressed independently of every prescribed procedure and every prescribed process. In the political praxis of most countries, the will of the people is determined in a process of secret individual votes or secret elections (cf. below under 3). But it would be an error, an undemocratic one in particular, to consider these methods of the nineteenth century without further explanation for an absolute and conclusive norm of democracy. The will of the people to provide themselves a constitution can only be made evident through the act itself and not through observation of a normatively regulated process. Self-evidently, it can also not be judged by prior constitutional laws or those that were valid until then.

(b) The natural form of the direct expression of a people's will is the assembled multitude's declaration of their consent or their disapproval, the *acclamation*. In modern, large states, the acclamation, which is a natural and necessary life expression of every people, has [84] changed its external form. In these states, it expresses itself as "public opinion" (below § 18, p. 246). However, the people can always say yes or no, consent or reject, and their yes or no becomes all the more simple and elementary, the more it is a matter of a fundamental decision on their own existence in its entirety. In times of peaceful order, these types of expression are rare and unnecessary. That no special will is perceivably expressed simply signifies the enduring consent to the existing constitution. In critical times, the no that directs itself *against* an existing constitution can be clear and decisive only as a negation, while the positive will is not as secure. Nevertheless, often in this negation, there is a direct, independent affirmation of a form of existence, which is contradictory and evident to others. In November 1918, the German people rejected the preexisting monarchical principle. That self-evidently signifies a republic. However, this means that the additional formative possibilities of this republic, the bourgeois (constitutional) democracy of the liberal Rechtsstaat or socialist council republic, were not yet foreclosed. The no in regard to a republic of the bourgeois Rechtsstaat variety could once again mean something different depending on the circumstances, a return to monarchy, dictatorship, council system, or some other political form. The people's constitution-making will always expresses itself only in a fundamental yes or no and thereby reaches the political decision that constitutes the content of the constitution.

(c) The constitution-making will of the people is an unmediated will. It exists prior to and above every constitutional procedure. No constitutional law, not even a constitution, can confer a constitution-making power and prescribe the form of its initiation. The further execution and formulation of a political decision reached by the people in unmediated form requires some organization, a procedure, for which the practice of modern democracy developed certain practices and customs. These are considered below.

4. In modern democracy, the practice of a democratic national assembly, the so-called constitution-making national assembly, which is elected according to the basic principles of the general and equal right to vote, developed as an accepted "democratic" procedure. Above all, then, it is followed when the constitution has been eliminated [85] and a new one should be established. Nevertheless, the convening of a "constitution-making national assembly" is not at all the only conceivable democratic procedure. In modern democracies, moreover, still other types of the execution and formulation of the constitution-making popular will emerge.

(a) *The national assembly that drafts and passes constitutional legislation* is an assembly elected according to fundamental democratic principles. It is specially commissioned for the formulation and legislating of constitutional provisions, drafts the text of constitutional laws, and passes them. Constitutional norms that come about in this way enter into force via the assembly's majority decisions without a popular vote (referendum) on the accepted draft taking place, consequently without confirmation by the state citizens who are entitled to vote.

See, for example, the Weimar Constitution of 11 August 1919 (Art. 181). "The German people," it reads, "has drafted and passed this constitution through its National Assembly. It enters into force on the day of its promulgation." It would be noteworthy in this regard that the National Assembly only drafted the constitutional formulation and the German people, naturally as the bearer of the constitution-making power, cannot be called upon to undertake a formal act, such as the passage of a statute. This article of the Weimar Constitution, therefore, only means that the constitutional norm should enter into force on the basis of the majority decision of the National Assembly without an additional special act of the German people, who formally give their consent. This consent, moreover, was already expressed in the election to the National Assembly.

Even the 1791 French constitution entered into force through majority decision of the constitution-making National Assembly without a plebiscite having taken place. On the additional peculiarities of the origin of this first modern constitution of Europe, cf. below under e.

(b) The assembly (convention) that *drafts* constitutional norms followed by a popular vote (referendum) or other express confirmation, direct or indirect, of the drafts by the state citizens with the right to vote.

The word convention is the technical expression for an elected body entrusted exclusively with the drafting of constitutional legislation. The expression stems from the English Revolution. The "conventions" of 1660 and 1689 were provisional governments for the production of a proto-constitutional condition (E. Zweig, *Pouvoir constituant*, p. 49). Through the practice of the American states and the famous example of the French National Convention of 1792, the word retained the meaning of an assembly that produces the draft of the constitutional legislation.

By the decree of 21 September 1792, the French National Convention established as a basic principle that any constitutional legislation must be confirmed expressly by the people ("qu'il ne peut y avoir de Constitution que celle qui est acceptée par le peuple"). Consequently, the constitution of the Convention of 24 June 1793 was presented to the people for approval, to the nominating assemblies specifically [86]. It was almost unanimously accepted (Duguit-Monnier p. XXXXI). Despite this, however, it did not enter into force, because the National Convention suspended the proto-constitutional condition and instituted the dictatorship of the Jacobins (le gouvernement révolutionaire), during which government was conducted through *measures*, not by formal legislative acts, etc. The same National Convention later concluded another constitution, that of the Year III of 22 August 1795 (the so-called Directorial Constitution). It was also proposed to the consent of the electors and was accepted with a great majority (Duguit-Monnier, p. LXII).

(c) Special circumstances at the constitutional convention for a federal state constitution. In this instance, the constitution can be submitted to the people of the individual member states for their consent.

The federal constitution of the United States of America of 1787 was drafted by a constitutional *convention*. It was then set before the *Congress* of the assembled states, which, in turn, recommended its acceptance to the people of the individual states. Finally, it was accepted in each of the thirteen states through special ratifying conventions, in other words, assemblies elected exclusively for this purpose. On the great difficulties of this process and the often very slight accidental majorities, cf. the portrayal in James Beck, *Die Verfassung der Vereinigten Staaten*, Ch. XV, German edition by A. Friedmann, 1926, p. 207ff.

The Weimar Constitution was not specially ratified by the enfranchised state citizens of the individual Land governments, also not through the national assemblies of these Land governments. In the debates on the Weimar Constitution, however, the Bavarian delegate v. Preger and the deputy Beyerle considered the ratification of the Reich Constitution through the individual state national assemblies necessary (*Protocol*, pp. 24/26). H.Preuß, who, as Poetzsch, *Kommentar*, p. 11, rightly remarked, had democratic logic on his side, opposed this very decidedly. On this, cf. above § 7, p. 65, below § 30, p. 388.

(d) General popular vote (plebiscite) on a proposal or a new order and regulation, both of indeterminate origins.

The practice of the Napoleonic plebiscites was present in the consular constitution of the Year VIII, 1799 (three consuls, among them Napoleon Bonaparte). The plebiscite was provided for in Art. 95, but before its acceptance the constitution was already considered as valid constitutional law. The practice of plebiscites was also present in the Senatus-Consult of the Year XII (1804), with Napoleon as emperor of the French, and the empire being made hereditary in the Bonaparte family. Similarly during the Hundred Days of 1815, there was a plebiscite on the "Acte Additionel." Note also the plebiscite of 14 December 1851. The President of the Republic, Louis Napoleon, was commissioned with powers of government under a wide-ranging delegation of authority for constitutional legislation. Finally, there is the plebiscite of 21/22 November 1852 on Napoleon III as Emperor of the French.

All these plebiscites resulted in overwhelming majorities voting "yes." The Napoleonic government influenced the election rather strongly and ruthlessly. The governmental electioneering damaged the prestige of the plebiscite and rendered it suspicious to democratic sensibilities. Theoretically, this method corresponds thoroughly to the democratic principle and to the idea of the people's constitution-making power. That during these votes the people responded "yes" to every new order is explicable incidentally not only in reference to electioneering, but also from the fact that the French people at the time had no desire other than for civil peace and order. The majority of state citizens are generally inclined to leave political decisions to others and to respond to questions posed always such that [87] the answer contains a minimum of decision. Consequently, they will readily consent to an accomplished fact. During these Napoleonic plebiscites, "no" would have meant insecurity and disorder, while the "yes" constituted only belated consent to an accomplished fact, therefore, the minimum of its own decision (on this, cf. below the critique of the principle "majority decides," § 21, p. 278).

(e) Exceptions and special cases in this democratic practice.

As noted (p. 78), the 1791 French constitution was concluded by a national assembly, which was not selected according to basic democratic principles of the general right to vote, but rather came about because, among the commissioned representatives of the three estates (nobility, clergy, bourgeoisie), those of the third estate constituted itself as the constitution-making National Assembly on 17 June 1789. In these questions of democratic constitutional theory, it would be an especially misdirected formalism to deny this first national assembly the character of a commissioner of the people's constitution-making power. The will of the French nation was undoubtedly validated. By contrast, the procedure of a special election or vote has only relative significance.

The constitution of *Czecho-Slovakia* of 29 February 1920 was not concluded by

The Constitution-Making Power

a national assembly selected according to the fundamental principles of the general right to vote. It was selected by an assembly that was comprised only of party delegates from the Czech and Slovak parties. Of the 13.6 million inhabitants of this state, almost 5 million, or all non-Slovak inhabitants, in particular the German portions of the people, were not represented. A ratification by popular vote did not take place. (On this "imposed" constitution, see Franz Adler, *Die Grundgedanken der tschechoslowakischen Verfassung, Quellen und Studien,* edited by the Osteuropa-Institut in Breslau, "Recht" Department, new series, vol. III, 1927, pp. 10/11, F. Weyr, *Jahrbuch des öffentlichen Rechts* XI, 1922, p. 352.)

§ 9.

Legitimacy of a Constitution

I. *Types of constitutional legitimacy.* A constitution is legitimate not only as a factual condition. It is also recognized as a just order, when the power and authority of the constitution-making power, on whose decision it rests, is acknowledged. The political decision reached regarding the type and form of state existence, which constitutes the substance of the constitution, is valid because the political unity whose constitution is at issue exists and because the subject of the constitution-making power can determine the type and form of this existence. The decision requires no justification via an ethical or juristic norm. Instead, it makes sense in terms of political existence. A norm would not at all be in a position to justify anything here. The special type of political existence need not and cannot legitimate itself. [88]

Two types of legitimacy, dynastic and democratic, may be distinguished historically. These types of legitimacy, in turn, correspond to both subjects of the constitution-making power, prince and people, which matter historically. Where the idea of *authority* is predominant, the king's constitution-making power will be recognized; where the democratic idea of the *maiestas populi* prevails, the constitution's validity rests on the people's will. So one can speak of constitutional legitimacy only in historical terms and under the perspective that distinguishes among dynastic and democratic legitimacy. In this regard, it is actually a question of a political unity's form of existence.

II. *The legitimacy of a constitution does not mean that a constitution originated according to previously valid constitutional laws.* Such an idea would be thoroughly nonsensical. A constitution does not generally come into being according to rules that stand above it. Moreover, it is inconceivable that a *new* constitution, in other words, a new, fundamental political decision, subordinates itself to an earlier constitution and makes itself dependent on it. Where a new constitution results during the elimination of the earlier constitution, the new constitution is not "illegitimate," because the old one is abolished. Otherwise, indeed, the old, displaced constitution would continue to be valid. The question of the agreement of the new with the old constitution thus has nothing to do with the question of legitimacy. The legitimacy of the Weimar Constitution rests on the German people's constitution-making power. That this constitution came about with the elimination of the earlier constitution of 1871 could at most lead to its being considered illegitimate from the standpoint of dynastic legitimacy, the constitution-making power of the monarch, but no more. Conversely, from the standpoint of democratic legitimacy, every constitution issued by the king on the basis of the monarchical principle, every imposed constitution, is just as illegitimate. However, it is completely impossible to measure a new constitution by whether it came about by way of the preservation of prior constitutional rules and formalities, as would be the case, for example, by posing the question whether the provisions of the Weimar Constitution arose in line with the procedural rules, which the old Reich Constitution contained in Art. 78 on constitutional changes. A new constitution cannot [89] subordinate itself in this way to previous norms that are no longer valid. And it is a meaningless conceptual game, one stemming only from a misunderstood need for "normative order," to even pose the question of whether in the case of an unquestionably valid new constitution the prescriptions for revision of a currently invalid prior constitution were followed.

W. Burckhardt, "Verfassungs- und Gesetzesrecht," *Politisches Jahrbuch der Schweizerischen Eidgenossenschaften*, vol. XXVI, 1910, p. 48, aptly asks, "Can one reasonably measure the legality of a new constitution by reference to the prescriptions of its predecessor? That is the question. If the present constitution is illegal, because its originators did not adhere to provisions of the prior one, then one must provisionally ask, whether the previous constitution itself was legal, etc. And when one ambles back through time and encounters *one* illegal constitution, would all others be illegal simply because it was not possible to establish the constitution with the sanction of the past, even though it derived its justification for existence from the present. What sense or purpose would this entire conclusion on the legality of a constitution have? It would be blowing hot air." When otherwise Burckhardt poses and rejects the general question "Can a constitution prescribe in legally binding manner how it should be changed?" (p. 46), this general rejection rests on the oft-discussed confusion of the constitution in the genuine sense with constitutional laws. How constitutional laws should be changed can be prescribed through constitutional law.

Unfortunately, expressions such as "legitimacy" or "illegitimacy" are nevertheless often used in the sense that one intends to designate a constitution as "legitimate" only when it came about in accord with a previously valid, constitutionally regulated process of constitutional revision.

The Reichsgericht states in its well-known decision, *Zivilsachen*, vol. 100, p. 25, that "the new state authority (of the workers' and soldiers' councils) created by the transformation cannot be denied public law recognition. The illegality of its founding is not an argument against it, because the illegality of the founding is not an essential distinguishing mark of state authority. The state cannot exist without state power. With the elimination of traditional authority, the newly established authority sets itself in its place." These principles demonstrate directly the meaninglessness of the question of whether the Weimar Constitution came about "legally" through the process of Art. 78 of the suspended constitution. They certainly only speak of the "state power," not of the "constitution." However, they are valid in the properly understood concept of the constitution even for the Weimar Constitution. Therefore, they are also rightly carried over to the Weimar Constitution, as is done in Anschütz, *Kommentar*, p. 5, for example. Three things are noteworthy. First, one cannot speak of the legitimacy of a state or of a state authority. A state, or the political unity of the people, exists in the sphere of the political specifically. The state is as little able to advance a justification, such as legality, legitimacy, etc, as the individual living person must or could justify his existence normatively in the sphere of private law (cf. Schmitt, "Der Begriff des Politischen," in *Archiv für Sozialwissenschaften*, vol. 58, 1927, p. 1ff.). Second, the state and state [90] authority are the same. There is no state without state authority and no state authority without the state. The replacement of persons, who exercise state power, and the alteration of the state order do not eliminate the continuity of the political unity. Third, the elimination of the existing constitution and the issuance of a new constitution involve the question of the constitution-making power (cf. on this below at § 10). The legitimacy of a constitution also involves this question of the constitution-making power, but not the question of the agreement with the rules of no longer valid constitutional laws.

The prevalent manner of speaking confuses the constitutionality of a constitution with the permissibility of a constitutional change. *Constitutional constitution*, however, is either something entirely senseless or a thoroughly empty banality. If the constitution itself decides that it is constitutional and is subsequently recognized as constitutional, it cannot thereby acquire a new capacity. Every valid constitution is self-evidently constitutional. A norm cannot legitimate itself. Its validity rests on the existential will of those who issue it. But should "constitutional constitution" only mean constitutional in the sense of constitutional laws that are no longer valid, the contradiction is immediately clear. For laws that are no longer valid cannot confer a valid and legally significant capacity.

III. *Dynastic legitimacy* rests on the authority of the monarch. Since an individual, isolated person seldom attains this level of political significance through his individual existence, the prince's constitution-making power also cannot remain permanently with the individual prince. The prince's constitution-making power leads to dynastic legitimacy, which rests on the historical presence of a *family* connected with the state, on the continuity of the dynasty, and on the *order of succession*.

Democratic legitimacy, by contrast, rests on the idea that the state is the political unity of a *people*. The people are the subject of every definition of the state; the state is the political status of a people. The type and form of state existence is determined according to the principle of democratic legitimacy through the free will of the people.

The people's constitution-making will is bound to no particular process. However, it was demonstrated above that the current practice of democratic constitutions elaborated certain methods, whether it is the election of a constitution-making assembly or it is a popular vote. These methods are frequently bound up with the idea of democratic legitimacy, so that one inserts a certain process into the concept of legitimacy. One only designates as truly democratic such constitutions that have found the consent of a majority of enfranchised state citizens in the secret ballot procedure. The extent to which these methods of secret, individual ballots are openly problematic from the perspective of a genuine democracy [91] was already discussed and will be even more precisely elaborated below. The tacit consent of the people is also always possible and easy to perceive. A conclusive action is discernible in the mere participation in public life a constitution provides, for example, an action through which the people's constitution-making will expresses itself clearly enough. That is valid for the participation in elections, which brings with it a certain political condition.

Bierling, *Juristische Prinzipienlehre*, 1898, II, pp. 363/64, states that every "imposed legal norm can attain a true legal validity first through a subsequent recognition by the legal comrades to the same degree that some revolutionary legal establishment can." It is always "only the general recognition of established norms" that brings about legality. And, on p. 357, he argues that "the institution of elections to this already constituted Reichstag (1867) contains a thoroughly clear, advance recognition of the constitution agreed upon by the Reich government with the Reichstag."

In this way, therefore, the character of democratic legitimacy can be attributed to the most diverse constitutions in that it is based on the people's ever-present, active constitution-making power, even if that power is also only tacit.

§ 10.

Consequences of the Theory of the Constitution-Making Power, of the People's Constitution-Making Power in Particular

I. *Continuous presence (permanence) of the constitution-making power.* The constitution-making power activates itself through the act of the fundamental political decision. Execution and formulation of the decision can be turned over to special commissioners, such as a so-called constitution-making national assembly, for example. Also, a constitutional power for "changes" or "revisions" of constitutional laws can exist on the basis of the constitutional norms that arose in this way. But the constitution-making power itself is distinguishable from this. It cannot be delegated, alienated, absorbed, or consumed. It remains always present depending on the circumstances. It also stands alongside and above every constitution derived from it and any valid constitutional provision of this constitution. [92]

Sieyès emphasized the inalienability of the pouvoir constituant of the people. It is noteworthy that the issue in Sieyès is only the democratic theory of the people's constitution-making power, with which one opposed royal absolutism. The people's authority for constitution-making can be abolished. When its political existence is preserved, another subject of this power, for example, a monarch, emerges as bearer of the constitution–making authority. However, the capacity for constitution-making is not extinguished by an act of initiation. Just as little does it rest on some legal title. When the monarch voluntarily renounces his constitution-making authority and thereby recognizes the people's power in this regard, this capacity of the people does not rest at all on the legal title, which would consist in the king's renunciation. It has its ground of validity exclusively in its political existence.

The French constitution of 24 June 1793 formulates the democratic principle of the constitution-making power of the people in Art. 28: "A people always has the right to revise, to reform, and to change its constitution" (Un peuple a toujours le droit de révoir, de réformer et de changer sa constitution). This is word for word also the draft of the Girondist constitution of 1793, Art. 93. This formulation is especially interesting in that it contains not only the right to constitutional amendment (revisions), but rather also a right to eliminate the constitution.

For reasons of political and juristic convenience, an ever more influential way of thinking proceeds from the assumption that a constitution can only be eliminated if the constitutionally regulated process for changing constitutional laws is observed. In this instance, the argument, "because what should not be, cannot be," leads to consequences that are obviously senseless.

Where the constitution-making power exists, there is also always a constitutional minimum, which need not be impinged on by statutory violations of constitutional laws, revolution, and coup d'états, when only the constitution's foundation, the constitution-making power, remains, whether it is of the king or of the people. The practice of the Napoleonic plebiscite (above § 8, III, 3 d, p. 86) rests on the democratic principle of the people's constitution-making power. Constitutional violations could thus be easily corrected through the consent of the people. Nonetheless, it is already clear that one must distinguish among the statutory violation or elimination of *constitutional laws*, the abolition of the *constitution*, in particular the foundational political decisions that comprise it, and the *constitution-making power* (of the king or of the people). Under some circumstances, the revolutionary elimination of a constitution can even be designated somewhat rightly as mere constitutional change, but naturally only when one presupposes this permanence of the subject of the constitution-making power.

Hence, in the committee debates on the Weimar Constitution, H. Preuß discusses the fact that the Weimar Constitution, which certainly came about by way of the revolutionary elimination of the previous Reich Constitution, signifies a "constitutional change." "We are only undertaking [93] a constitutional change occasioned by special circumstances and unusual events" (*Protocol*, p. 28), he points out. That is a striking statement from the mouth of an outstanding teacher of public law and an extraordinary expert on democratic constitutional law. This statement is explicable in reference to the idea that the previously existing German Reich rested on the will of the German people and, consequently, in fact on its constitution-making power, even if this idea is not clearly formulated. Then, the new constitution would have perpetuated this permanent minimum. Anschütz (*Kommentar*, p. 3) states that "the Revolution has not destroyed the Reich; it only changed its constitution." If it is intended with juristic exactitude, even that claim is only explicable in reference to the permanence of the German people's constitution-making power. It would be certainly more precise to speak here of the elimination of the constitution than of a change of constitution (cf. below § 11, I, p. 99).

II. *Continuity of the state during the elimination and statutory violation of the constitution, to the extent that only the constitution-making power remains unchanged.*

1. A constitution that originated as an act of the constitution-making power is derived from this power and can, therefore, not in itself bear the continuity of the political unity. Constitutional legislation, which rests on the foundation of this constitution and only signifies the execution of the ultimate political decision, is even less capable of establishing such a form of continuity. The political unity as an entirety can continue to exist despite changes in and changes of the constitution. If a constitution is eliminated or a constitutional law is violated by statute, that is always unconstitutional or an unconstitutional law, for a constitutional law cannot violate itself or eliminate itself under its own power. However, the constitution-making power need not be abolished in the process. If it activates itself anew in response to the new condition, the new constitution rests on the same principle as the previous one, which is now eliminated, and it is a product of the same constitution-making power as this earlier constitution. The continuity

lies in the common foundation, and the question of state continuity can be posed neither in terms of international law nor public law.

During the French Revolutions and coup d'états of 1848, 1851, 1852, and 1870, it came down to a change of a constitution by statutory violation or by the elimination of previously existing constitutions. It did so, however, by retaining and recognizing the constitution-making power of the French people. The problem of a discontinuity of the French State was not raised.

2. It is generally recognized that *in terms of international law*, or law in relation to other states, the continuity of the political unity is not eliminated in this instance.

The consequence of this continuity *in terms of public law* is that the previous statutes and decrees, so far as they do not contradict the new regulation [94], are still directly valid without a special act of acceptance (without reception). Even provisions in previous constitutions can remain in force from that point on as simple statutes.

The provision of Art. 75 of the French Constitution of Year VIII (1799) on the consent of the government during judicial prosecution of administrative officials thus remains valid, despite any eliminations of constitutions and statutory violations of constitutions that have occurred in the meantime. On this, see Esmein-Nézard, pp. 580/81. Under the constitutions of the German constitutional monarchy, which resulted from the Revolution of 1848, there was continuity on the basis of the monarchical principle. Even in this instance, the previously existing statutes, cabinet orders, etc., remained valid without special reception.

On the continuity of the German Reich during the transformation of November 1918 and after the Weimar Constitution, cf. below III, 2.

III. *The problem of continuity in the change of the subject of the constitution-making power (constitutional elimination).*

1. A revolution can abolish not only constitutional legislation and the constitution, but also the previous type of constitution-making power, which is the very foundation of the prior constitution. By means of a democratic revolution, for example, the constitution-making power of the monarch can be eliminated, and through a coup d'état or a monarchical revolution, the constitution-making power of the people can be as well. Then, there is an exchange of the constitution-making power and a complete *annihilation of the constitution*.

Some examples are 1789 and 1793 in France (elimination of the king's absolute monarchy); and 1917/18 in Russia (elimination of the czarist monarchy).

During such revolutions, the new government challenges the continuity of the political unity in two important cases.

The Jacobin government of 1793 took the position that a free people need not pay the debts that a "tyrant" (the previous monarchical government) incurred. During the Genoa conference in May 1922, the Russian Soviet government appealed to this precedent to renounce payment of czarist Russia's debts. In the totality of this question of the fulfillment of prior Russian government obligations, the argument of interest here is the one that touches on the claim that there is no continuity during a change of the constitution-making power. Both cases, 1793 and 1917, may be the only examples of rejecting continuity.

However, it corresponds precisely to the logic of a democratic constitution to assume continuity even in such cases. For the logically consistent democratic theory knows no legitimate constitution other than a constitution based on the people's constitution-making power. [95] Therefore, it is possible to attribute the staying power of any constitution to the express or tacit will of the people, whatever type of *government* it is in terms of the form of the exercise of this will. Otherwise, according to this theory, there is no state and no political unity. Instead, there is a senseless power apparatus, a system of despotism and tyranny.

That is Rousseau's theory of the "Contrat social." Indeed, he does not speak of a special and distinctive constituting power of the people. However, he certainly does discuss the lois politiques or lois fondamentales, which regulate the relations of the sovereign (of the people) to the government (bk. II, chap. 12). These statutes are constitutional laws, and, as such, they are relative. In other words, they are derivative and limited in principle. They rest on the sovereign will of the people, and they can establish a monarchical, aristocratic, or democratic form of government. But the people always remain sovereign. Even the most absolute monarchy would be only a governmental form and dependent on the sovereign will of the people.

2. *Continuity of the German Reich 1918/19.* When a state rests on a national foundation, and when the people has a conscious will to political existence on the basis of this national unity, it is always possible to treat this will as the definitive ground of *every* state constitution. A *subsequent* construction of the people's constitution-making power is easy to find here. The German Reich under the 1871 constitution can be considered a state, which rests on the national will of its people. It was not only an alliance of the governing member states, but, as Anschütz (Kommentar p. 2) aptly states, "above all things also the German state as comprehensive state, as national community." The German people also had the will to political unity on a national basis, even if not yet the will to eliminate the monarchical principle and to give itself a constitution exclusively by virtue of its own political decision. That the constitutional condition as it was since 1871 had the consent of the German people cannot be disputed after the acclamation of the war of 1870 and the founding of the Reich of 1871. This constitution was, indeed, (cf. above § 7, p. 64) even agreed upon by a Reichstag elected by the German people. The subsequent construction of a democratic foundation is not a fiction, therefore, although the German people's constitution-making power was by no means recognized in the constitution of 1871, and even though the monarchical principle is actually presupposed in the constitutional monarchies of the individual states. [96] This intention of the German people to achieve political unity on a national basis even remained present after November 1918 and is sufficient to produce, on a democratic

foundation, a continuity between the German Reich under the Weimar Constitution of 1919 with the Reich under the 1871 constitution.

The question is among the most controversial issues of the public law literature to date on the Weimar Constitution, although the practical consequences of the varied responses are not very different. They differ neither in terms of international law, for the transition of the international law obligations of the traditional Reich to the new one is not disputed and declared only as succession, or in terms of public law, for through the transitional statute of 4 March 1919 the domestic legal continuity is expressly decreed. Anschütz, *Kommentar*, pp. 8, 9, and Stier-Somlo, *Grundriß* (1924) I, p. 52ff., assembled the literature on the disputed question.

(a) The previous distinctions among constitution, constitutional law, and constitution-making power account for the fact that the revolutionary abolition of the Reich Constitution of 1871 is by itself still no reason to deny the continuity between the two constitutions. It is also incorrect to say that every "legal," constitutional discontinuity simultaneously contains an elimination of the identity of political unity. The constitutional laws are valid only on the basis and in the context of the constitution in the positive sense. The constitution, in turn, is valid only on the basis of the will of the constitution-making power. There can be a discontinuity within each of these three levels without a state discontinuity resulting. As explained above, if it is impermissible to judge the legitimacy of a new constitution according to the norms of the eliminated constitutional laws, it is just as incorrect to deny the continuity of the German Reich of the Weimar Constitution, therefore, because the constitution did not come about as a "constitution-amending statute" in accordance with Art. 78 of the abolished constitution.

F. Sander, "Das Factum der Revolution und die Kontinuität der Rechtsordnung," *Zeitschrift für öffentliches Recht*, I, 1919, p. 132ff.; Rauschenberger, *Staatsstreich und Revolution*, 1920, p. 13ff.; and Stier-Somlo, *Grundriß*, I, pp. 53/55, are thus all incorrect.

(b) It is more significant when a discontinuity derives from a "conscious break with the past." The merit of this argument is the reference to the change of constitution-making power. The previous constitutional condition rested on the monarchical principle; the new one rests on the German people's authority for constitution making. There is not only an elimination of constitutional laws and a [97] change of the constitution, but there is also then a change of the constitution-making power.

(c) There is an additional element that permits the change of the constitution-making power to appear even more clearly. Not only did a new subject of the constitution-making power emerge, but also an established constitution, instituted through a unilateral act of the entire German people, was set in place of the previous federal constitution, which, as such, rested on an agreement among the allied states.

In the following authors, the different perspectives of b and c are linked, mostly, however, without any special interest in the essence of the constitution-making power and without the necessary distinction between constitution and constitutional law. But the linkage of b and c always results in a discontinuity of the old and new Reich. See Kahl in the committee hearing of 5 March 1919, *Protocol*, p. 23, and in the essay "Die drei Reiche," *Festgabe für O. Liebmann*, 1920, p. 79ff.; Nawiasky, *Bayerische Verfassung*, p. 66; Wittmayer, *Weimarer Verfassung*, p. 4; and Giese, *Kommentar*, p. 16.

This justification would be appropriate, if the question of the constitution-making power in the previous constitutional situation would have been decided unambiguously and if the German Reich of the 1871 constitution had not already have been a form of the national unity of the German people. In this way, however, it becomes possible that the *new*, democratic constitution sees in it the singly determinative perspective and that there is a continuity of the German *people* and its will to political unity on a national basis. Consequently, one must respond affirmatively to the question of continuity. With the Weimar Constitution, the German people do not *intend* to deny its identity with the German people of the 1871 constitution. As it states in the preamble of the Weimar Constitution, the German people intend to renew the Reich of 1871, but not found a new Reich. Precisely because it is a democratic constitution, the new constitution does not found a new German state. It only signifies that a people, which previously believed itself capable of existing politically solely on the basis of the monarchical principle, perpetuated its existence by virtue of its own political decision in the form of a constitution, which it provided itself when the monarchical principle was displaced.

In the drafting history of the Weimar Constitution, this emerges most clearly in the statements of F. Naumann and H. Preuß (*Protocol*, p. 24/25). Preuß even speaks only of mere change of constitution (cf. above § 10, I, p. 92). On this, see further K. Beyerle (*Protocol*, p. 25): "We are perpetuating the old Reich." E. Vermeil, *La Constitution de Weimar*, Straßburg 1923, pp. 66, 273, however, praised Wittmayer for the good democratic attitude he demonstrated through his discontinuity thesis, but he must nevertheless affirm that certainly even the democrats in Weimar wanted continuity. [98]

IV. *The distinction of the constitution-making power of the people from every constituted authority, specifically that based on constitutional law.*

1. Every constitutional rule based on the constitution and that proceeds in the context of constitutional competencies is essentially of a different nature than an act of the constitution-making power. Even the constitutional powers and competencies of the "people," which is to say the state citizens entitled to vote, such as, for example, the election of the President according to Art. 73, the election of the Reichstag according to Art. 20, and the referendum according to Art. 73, are all not powers of the sovereign people, who give themselves a constitution and engage in acts of the constitution-

making power; they are, rather, competencies in the context of the constitution that is already provided.

While the Weimar Constitution is valid, it would be impermissible to sanction any statute in violation of constitutional laws simply because it was passed by a popular initiative. According to Art. 73, the people have only constitutional authority and no powers that are more elevated than those of the Reichstag. The people are also not made superior to this Reichstag. A statute that comes about by way of the popular initiative under Art. 73 can be eliminated through a statute that results from a simple majority decision of the Reichstag (Anschütz, *Kommentar*, p. 224), etc.

2. Above all, it is incorrect to designate the authority, empowered and regulated on the basis of a constitutional law, to change constitutional provisions, to revise them in other words, as the constitution-making power or "pouvoir constituant." Also, like every constitutional authority, the authority to amend or revise constitutional laws (for example, according to Art. 76) is a statutorily regulated competence. This means it is in principle bounded. It cannot transcend the framework of constitutional regulation on which it rests.

On this, cf. below § 11, II, p. 102. Therefore, the attempts to equate the "pouvoir constituant" with this constitutionally regulated authority of revision and to designate that as a "formal concept" of the constitution or of the pouvoir constituant are incorrect. Therein lies the fundamental error of the book by E. Zweig, *Die Lehre vom pouvoir constituant*, 1909. The discussion of W. Hildesheimer, *Über die Revision moderner Staatsverfassungen*, Tübingen 1918, p. 75, rests on the same error.

3. This distinction persists even in states in which a constitutional statute can be concluded by way of the simple legislative process [99], as in England by virtue of the so-called sovereignty of the English Parliament. It would be incorrect to claim that through a "simple majority decision of Parliament," England could be changed into a soviet republic.

§ 11.

Concepts Derived from the Concept of the Constitution

(Constitutional Change, Statutory Violation of the
Constitution, Constitutional Suspension, Constitutional
Dispute, High Treason)

I. *Overview.* The following concepts must be distinguished from one another:

1. *constitutional annihilation*, which is the simultaneous abolition of the existing constitution (not only of one or more constitutional laws) and of the constitution-making power that supports it (cf. above § 10, III);

2. *constitutional elimination*, or the abolition of the existing constitution, retaining, however, the underlying constitution-making power (on the change of the constitution, coup d'état, cf. above § 10, II);

3. *constitutional change* (revision) as a change in the text of previously valid constitutional laws, which also includes the elimination of individual constitutional provisions and the reception of individual new constitutional law directives.

The term constitutional change (constitutional revision) is imprecise because it does not treat changes of the constitution itself. Instead, it only considers changes in constitutional law provisions. Nevertheless, the expression is common today, so it will be retained.

(a) Constitution-disregarding constitutional changes are constitutional changes that take place without fulfillment of the constitutionally prescribed process for such constitutional changes.

(b) Constitution-regarding constitutional changes, defined as constitutional changes occurring through fulfillment of the constitutionally envisioned process for such changes or revisions (constitutional revision in the actual sense).

4. *Statutory constitutional violation* is the infringement of constitutional provisions in one or several particular individual cases, but only as exceptions under the presupposition that the [100] violated provisions continue to be valid. They are otherwise unchanged, therefore, neither permanently abrogated nor set aside (suspended) temporarily.

In a formulation apt for the practice of public law under the Weimar Constitution, E. Jacobi made the expression "statutory violation of the constitution" serviceable in scholarly terms for the first time in his report on the dictatorship of the Reich President under Art. 48 for the *Veröffentlichungen der Vereinigung Deutscher Staatsrechtslehrer*, no. 1, Berlin 1924, p. 109, 118.

(a) Constitution-disregarding violation of the constitution is the exceptional infringement of a constitutional provision without consideration of the procedure for constitutional amendments.

A state president, for example, dissolves a parliament incapable of acting because of its splintered party composition, although the constitutional provisions do not provide for this dissolution, or perhaps even (like Art. 68 of the French constitution of 4 November 1848) expressly prohibit it, as with the coup d'état of the president of the Republic, Louis Napoleon, on 2 December 1851.

An additional example is the extension of the legislative period of a parliament for a single instance through a simple statute, despite constitutional regulation of the duration of the legislative period.

(b) Constitution-regarding violation of the constitution is the exceptional infringement of a constitutional provision for one or several particular individual cases, whereby either a constitutional law permits such an exceptional violation (for example, Art. 48, 2, of the Weimar Constitution) or whereby the procedure prescribed for constitutional amendments is nonetheless observed.

For example, the one-time extension of the legislative period of parliament through the constitutionally regulated process of a constitutional amendment or the one-time extension of the term of the President, as was the case with the statute of 27 October 1922 (*Reichsgesetzesblatt*, p. 801), passed in the form of a constitution-amending statute (according to Art. 76): "The President, elected by the National Assembly, holds his office until 30 June 1925."

5. *Constitutional suspension* as the temporary setting aside of single or multiple constitutional provisions.

(a) Constitution-disregarding constitutional suspension is the setting aside of constitutional provisions without a constitutional regulation providing for this suspension or, for example, with disregard for an available procedure of suspension.

(b) Constitution-regarding constitutional suspension is the provisional setting aside of constitutional provisions with the retention of the constitutional provisions providing for such a suspension, for example, according to Art. 48, 2, p. 2. Setting aside of one, several, or all of the seven basic rights [101] articles enumerated in this clause: 114, 115, 117, 118, 123, 124, 153.

II. *Constitutional changes of the constitution (revision and amendment of the constitution).*

1. Constitutional law can stipulate that different offices have the authority to make a change in constitutional law provisions, and constitutional law can regulate these changes as well.

(a) An assembly convened exclusively for this purpose, which only has the task of concluding such a constitutional amendment.

For example, Art. 8 of the French Constitutional Law of 25 February 1875. Both legislative chambers (Chamber of Deputies and the Senate) unified themselves into one National Assembly, an "assemblée nationale," when a constitutional provision should be revised. Such a constitution-amending national assembly is to be distinguished from a constitution-making national assembly that convenes after a revolution (more specifically, after an annihilation or elimination of a constitution) and is the bearer of a sovereign dictatorship.

Art. V of the American federal constitution of 1787. The Congress (House of Representatives and the Senate) is required to call a *convention* when two-thirds of both houses consider the proposition of a constitutional amendment necessary or when the legislative bodies of two-thirds of the individual states petition it. Constitutional changes are possible if they are ratified by the legislative bodies of three-fourths of the individual states or by the conventions in three-fourths of these states (always after the Congress has suggested the one or the other type of ratification).

(b) Legislative bodies by way of legislation (with or without special hurdles), however with ratification of the enfranchised state citizens by an obligatory popular vote (referendum).

Federal constitution of the Swiss Association of 29 May 1874, Art. 118, provides that the federal constitution can be revised, entirely or in part, at any time. Art. 119 stipulates that complete revision of the federal constitution occurs by way of federal legislation. Regarding the altered portion, according to Art. 123, the revised federal constitution enters into force when it is accepted by the majority of the citizens participating in the vote and by a majority of the cantons (referendum combined with ratification through the cantons).

On the sense of the words "by way of legislation," cf. above § 7, p. 63.

(c) Legislative bodies by way of legislation without the obligatory confirmation through a popular vote, but under qualified conditions (such as qualified majority, repeated concluding draft, etc.).

Art. 76 of the Weimar Constitution: "The Constitution can be changed by way of legislation. However, decisions of the Reichstag regarding amendment of the Constitution only come about when two-thirds of the statutorily mandated quorum are present and at least two-thirds of those present consent." Also in the Reichsrat, a two-thirds majority is required for constitutional changes. As noted, [102] the word "Constitution" in the text of Art. 76 is imprecise, and it would correctly read "constitutional laws."

(d) In a *federal constitution*, the federal legislative procedure for changes in constitutional laws can replace a contractual change of the federal contract itself. Where there is this possibility of a change in the federal constitution, the federation already distances itself from its federated foundation and develops itself into a unitary state. During this transition phase, the federated character can be preserved by the fact that the confirmation of a majority of states, simple or qualified, is needed for the change or that a minority can block the change.

Some examples are Art. V of the American federal constitution of 1777 [*sic*], above under a. Art. 123 of the Swiss federal constitution of 1874, above under b. Art. 78a of the 1871 Reich Constitution, under which "amendments of the constitution are the product of legislation. They count as rejected when they have fourteen votes against them in the Bundesrat." This provision of the Bismarckian constitution first affirmed a so-called "competence for competencies" of the federation.[1] Second, it recognized the Reichstag's right to participate in legislation, in particular even its right of initiative according to Art. 23a. On this, cf. Seydel, *Kommentar*, pp. 412/13.

2. *Boundaries of the authority for constitutional amendments.*

If the procedure for a constitutional amendment is regulated constitutionally, this establishes a jurisdiction (competence) that is not self-evident. The constitutionally regulated jurisdiction of legislative bodies to issue statutes through the constitutionally regulated process, which is the simple legislative competence, does not in the least also establish for the legislative body alone any jurisdiction to change constitutional provisions, more specifically, to change the basis of this competence. The jurisdiction for constitutional amendment is not a normal jurisdiction in the sense of a competence, in other words, of a regulated and bounded set of tasks. For changing constitutional laws is not a normal state function like establishing statutes, conducting trials, undertaking administrative acts, etc. It is an extraordinary authority. As such, however, it is not thoroughly unlimited, for it remains an authority that is constitutionally shared. Like every constitutional authority, it is limited, and, in this sense, it is a genuine competence. In the context of a constitutional regulation, there can be no unlimited authority, and every jurisdiction is bounded. Even a "competence-competence" can be nothing without limits, if the expression is not to become meaningless and the concept of competence is not to dissolve altogether. When understood properly, competence-competence is [103] something other than sovereignty, which had been often confused in the public law literature of the prewar era.

The structural peculiarities of a federation, in which constitutional principles from a federal and unitary state, but also those from monarchical and democratic ones, were linked (cf. below § 30, p. 386), accounts for the controversy over competence-competence of the Reich. On this, see Haenel, *Staatsrecht*, p. 774ff.

The boundaries of the authority for constitutional amendments result from the properly understood concept of constitutional change. The authority to "amend the constitution," granted by constitutional legislation, means that other constitutional provisions can substitute for individual or multiple ones. They may do so, however, only under the presupposition that the identity and continuity of the constitution as an entirety is preserved. This means the authority for constitutional amendment contains only the grant of authority to undertake changes, additions, extensions, deletions, etc., in constitutional provisions that preserve the constitution itself. It is not the authority to establish a new constitution, nor is it the authority to change the particular basis of this jurisdiction for constitutional revisions. For example, it is not permissible to use the qualified majority procedure of Art. 76 to change Art. 76 such that constitutional amendments are undertaken through simple majority decisions of the Reichstag.

(a) *Constitutional amendment, therefore, is not constitutional annihilation* (above I, 1).

The offices with jurisdiction over a decision on a constitution-amending statute do not thereby become the bearer or subject of the constitution-making power. They are also not commissioned with the ongoing exercise of this constitution-making power. They are not, for example, a latent, always present constitution-making national assembly with the powers of sovereign dictatorship. A constitutional amendment that transforms a state resting on the monarchical principle into one ruled by the constitution-making power of the people is not at all constitutional. When one occasionally engages in discussions over what constitutes the "juridical" component of the system, in order to transform the old Reich Constitution by legal means into a modern democracy at the beginning of November 1918, then that is a meaningless game, as elaborated above and as also deduced from the correct concept of constitutional amendment. By legal means, this constitution could not at all be transformed into a democratic one. The voluntary renunciation of the [104] monarchical principle by the monarch would have only signified a renunciation of the conflict and would have facilitated a *peaceful* exchange of the constitution-making power. But the new subject of the constitution-making power would not have become the legal successor of the monarch, because in this sphere there cannot be a legal succession at all. It is exactly the same in the opposite case. A constitution resting on the constitution-making power of the people cannot be transformed into a constitution of the monarchical principle by way of a constitutional "amendment" or "revision." That would not be constitutional change. It would be instead constitutional annihilation.

Democratic principles require a special act of the people's constitution-making power for the monarchy to be reintroduced under the Weimar Constitution. This is the case whether this change results from a decision of a "constitution-making" national assembly or from a special plebiscite, which in the context of the Weimar Constitution would be distinguishable from a referendum according to Art. 73. The new monarchy, however, would then rely on the constitution-making power of the people. It would not be a state form and a restoration of the monarchical principle, but rather only a governmental form. The restoration of the monarchical principle could only be achieved through a constitutional annihilation. In this context, the procedure of Art. 76 does not come into question at all. With the help of Art. 76, the principle of Art. 1, 1, "the German Reich is a republic," can in no way be transformed into the principle "the German Reich is a hereditary monarchy under the hereditary line of succession of the family Hohenzollern." It would be another, psychological question whether perhaps the German people, whose need for the appearance of legality is stronger than its political sense, would sooner accept an elimination of the prior constitution carried out by way of Art. 76 than an attempted constitutional annihilation via a putsch or revolution.

(b) *Constitutional amendment is not an elimination of the constitution* (above I, 2). Even if the constitution-making power is preserved, another political decision may not substitute for fundamental political decisions that constitute the constitution (in contrast to constitutional law rules). The democratic right to vote, for example, could not be replaced by a council system under Art. 76. The federalist elements, which are today still retained in the constitution, could not simply be eliminated according to Art. 76, so that in a single stroke the German Reich would be transformed into a unitary state by a "constitution-amending statute." "By means of Art. 76," it is not only politically, but also constitutionally impossible, simply to eliminate Bavaria or to declare Prussia a land of the Reich against its will. The position of the President, for example, could also not be transformed into that of a monarch through a "revision" of Art. 1, 1, or Art. 41 [105], etc. The fundamental political decisions of the constitution are a matter for the constitution-making power of the German people and are not part of the jurisdiction of the organs authorized to make constitutional changes and revisions. Such amendments bring about a change of constitution, not a constitutional revision.

Even if a complete revision of the constitution is being considered, then the just elaborated distinction must be respected and the resulting limits of the authority of revision are to be fulfilled. Despite the term "total revision," that is recognizable in the wording of the constitutional rule through closer consideration of the constitutional provisions permitting such a total revision. The *French* constitution of 4 November 1848 provided in Art. 111, for example, that the constitution could be changed (modifié), and, indeed, "entirely or partially" (en tout ou en partie). It regulates the procedure for this revision. No interpretation of the letter of the provision could lend the word "en tout" the meaning that by legal means of constitutional revision a monarchical constitution of the Napoleonic style, for example, however new, could have been established. For in its preamble (préambule) the same constitution of 4 November 1848 definitively proclaimed a republic for the state form of France, declared in its Art. 1 that sovereignty resides with the entirety of the French state citizens, that it is inalienable and inexhaustible, and that no individual and no part of the people could claim its exercise, etc. Art. V of the *United States* Constitution provides for amendments. However, it also provides that "no state may be deprived of an equal vote in the Senate without its consent," from which it self-evidently follows that it first of all may not be justly deprived of its independent existence. According to Art. 118 of the *Swiss* federal constitution, a "total revision" is possible at any time. Fleiner, *Schweizerisches Bundesstaatsrecht*, p. 396ff., does not define this concept more precisely and only says that under a partial revision, one understands "the issuance of a new or the abrogation or alteration of an existing individual article of the federal constitution." It is uncertain to what extent the total revision under the Swiss federal constitution can produce a completely new constitution (that is, a change of the political decision over the type and form of state existence), because the Swiss constitution is purely democratic and because even in a "total revision" one cannot seriously be thinking of an elimination of this democratic foundation or of the democratic state.

If a particular constitutional change is prohibited by an explicit constitutional provision, it is only a matter of a confirmation of the distinction of constitutional revision and the elimination of the constitution.

Take, for example, Art. 2 of the French constitutional statute of 14 August 1884: "La forme républicaine du Gouvernement ne peut faire l'objet d'une proposition de revision."

That is even the case when constitutional changes offending the spirit or the principles of the constitution are expressly prohibited.

For example, § 112 of the Norwegian constitution of 17 May 1814 reads: "When experience shows that some part of the present constitution [106] ('constitution' = 'basic lot' in the French collection of Laferrière-Batbie, p. 391, with 'loi fondamentale' rendered as 'constitution' in an official translation made available to me by the esteemed colleague Dr. Wolgast) of the Kingdom of Norway must be modified, then . . . (the procedure follows). *However, such a change* (in the French text 'changement,' in the official translation 'amendment') *may never contradict the principles of the present constitution; it may only modify particular individual dictates without changing the spirit of the present constitution"* (certaines dispositions qui n'en altèrent pas l'esprit). Cf. on this Wolgast, "Die richterliche Prüfungszuständigkeit in Norwegen," *Hirths Annalen* 1922/23, p. 330f. The prevailing view in Norway (Morgenstierne) appears to accept a competence for judicial review even in regard to the statutes coming about via § 112. On the constitutional amendment of 1913 (after which constitutional changes were concluded by parliament, the Storting, without participation of the king), see F. Castberg, "Die verfassungsrechtliche Gesetzgebung in Norwegen in den Jahren 1914–1921," *Jahrbuch des öffentlichen Rechts* XI, 1922, p. 227; also Morgenstierne, *Jahrbuch des öffentlichen Rechts* VIII, 1914, p. 373f., and Erich, "Studien über das Wesen und die Zukunft der monarchischen Staatsform," *Blätter für vergleichende Rechtswissenschaft*, 1918, 184ff. In a provision like this § 112, it is otherwise also clear that the article itself cannot be eliminated by way of the procedure for constitutional revision.

The question of the boundaries of the authority for constitutional amendments or revisions has hardly been handled yet in constitutional theory. A noteworthy exception is the essay by William L. Marbury titled "The limitation upon the amending Power," in *Harvard Law Review* 33, 1919/20, p. 223ff., where it is rightly claimed that the authority to alter and extend the constitution cannot be boundless and has not been conferred, in order to eliminate the constitution itself.

The author of this essay relies on the fact that Art. V of the American federal constitution already contains a boundary for the authority of revision, because according to this article no individual state may be deprived of its equal voting rights in the Senate without its consent. The essay has set for itself the practical goal of initiating the review of the permissibility of the Eighteenth Amendment of 1919 (prohibition of the manufacture, sale, facilitation of the importation and exportation of intoxicating liquors) by the United States Supreme Court. This constitutional change had come about in the process prescribed for a constitutional amendment. To review its validity meant determining the substantive boundaries of the amendment authority. The Supreme Court, however, did not undertake such a review, and the previously mentioned essay did not achieve its practical goal. But one cannot say that the attempt remained unsuccessful and meaningless. On this, cf. the presentation in Eduard Lambert, *Le Gouvernement des juges*, Paris 1921, p. 112ff. The core thought of the essay is also correct and will sooner or later show its practical significance. It demonstrates, more specifically, that the authority for constitutional amendments conferred by the constitution is in principle limited and that the constitution itself as a foundation must remain inviolate. It also shows that it is a misuse of the amendment competence to issue ordinary statutes by way of the amendment procedure and, in this way, to guard against changes.

(c) *Constitutional amendment is not a statutory violation of the constitution* (above I, 4). A statutory violation of the constitution [107] does not alter the constitutional norm. Rather, it constitutes an individual order that deviates from the norm in a single instance while preserving the general validity of the norm in other cases. This does not constitute a change of the constitutional law. It is simply presupposed that the constitutional law in question continues to be valid. Such statutory violations of the constitution are in essence measures, not norms. Hence, they are not laws in the Rechtsstaat sense of the word and, consequently, also not constitutional laws. Their necessity derives from the special condition of the individual case or from an unforeseen abnormal situation. When in the interest of the political existence of the whole such statutory violations and measures are used, the superiority of the existential element over the merely normative one reveals itself. Whoever is authorized to take such actions and is capable of doing so, acts in a sovereign manner. Since the sixteenth century, therefore, the question regarding sovereignty and "absolutism," considered in legal history terms, involved a statutory rupture of the existing legitimate order. The prince was "legibus solutus." In other words, according to prevailing conditions and without being hindered by limitations of valid laws and contracts, he was authorized and in a position to undertake the necessary measures in the interest of political existence. On this point, Gierke (*Althusius*, p. 281) states that "it was naturally agreed that the legislature could change and abrogate as well as establish norms in the same degree. Since the beginning of the sixteenth century, however, a lively controversy arose over whether up until the eventual elimination the legislature is bound or not by its own laws or by those of its predecessor." The *lawmaker* as legislator can only establish statutes, not violate them. The question did not involve lawmaking, but rather sovereignty, or the existential superiority over the norm. Even for the modern Rechtsstaat, these statutory ruptures are the criterion of sovereignty. The difficulty lies in the fact that the bourgeois Rechtsstaat takes its point of departure from the idea of being able to comprehend and to limit the entire exercise of all state power without exception in written laws. In this way, political action of any given subject, whether it is the absolute monarch or the people come to political self-consciousness, even sovereignty itself, is no longer possible. Instead, a diverse range of fictions must be set up, such as that there is no longer any sovereignty at all, or, what is the same thing, that the "constitution," [108] more precisely, constitutional norms, are sovereign, etc. (cf. above § 1, II, p. 8). In reality, however, it is precisely the essential political decisions, which elude normative definition. The fiction of the absolute normative quality then has no consequence other than that such a fundamental question like the one regarding sovereignty is left unclear. For the inevitable sovereign actions, a method for *apocryphal acts of sovereignty* develops.

The organs authorized for a constitutional revision do not become sovereign at all as a result of this jurisdiction. The previous discussion makes that self-evident. They become the subject or bearer of the constitution-making power to the same limited degree. It is also not possible, for example, to designate the "procedure" as such as "sovereign," whereby only an additional fictional personification would be created and nothing explained. On the other hand, it is a small step from the legislature authorized to establish statutes that violate ordinary law to one empowered to make constitutional changes via statute that violate constitutional provisions. If, however, the issue is the political necessity of such ruptures, respect for the constitution expresses itself by how the procedure for constitutional amendment is observed, yet without changing the constitutional text. So long as this method is not misused, one may assume that it does not contradict the spirit of the constitution. It is captured in Carl Bilfinger's apt formulation (*Archiv des öffentlichen Rechts* 11, 1926, p. 174). This method is "overwhelmingly accepted as a procedure, one that, indeed, is not correct but is nevertheless not directly unconstitutional, as would already be the case prior to the transformation. Even under the new constitution, a constant practice of ruptures has developed, which expresses itself conclusively in the promulgation formula of 'constitution-amending' Reich statutes ('after it is determined that the demands of constitution-amending statutes are fulfilled')" (the same can be seen in H. Triepel, *33. Deutscher Juristentag 1924, Verhandlungen*, p. 48). Nonetheless, it would be erroneous to believe that any instance of unconstitutionality could be permitted or made constitutional again through a constitution-amending statute in the German Reich, therefore, according to Art. 76 of the Weimar Constitution, or to believe that something would in fact be achieved by demanding an explicit change of the *text* of the constitutional provision and disregarding "tacit" ruptures (cf. the [109] *Verhandlungen des 33. Deutschen Juristentages 1924*, in particular the contribution of the Count zu Dohna). More precisely, it is necessary to remain conscious of the distinction between constitution-amending statutes and pure acts of sovereignty and not to overlook the fact that the procedure of Art. 76 serves two completely different goals under the current practice of the Weimar Constitution: first, the procedure of the constitutional revision and, second, the facilitation of apocryphal acts of sovereignty.

The prior practice of Art. 76 led to the execution of indiscriminate individual orders that take the form of a constitution-amending statute in accordance with this article and that violate constitutional provisions. The feeling for the political and constitutional scope of this practice does not seem to be very vital among responsible politicians, and it is understandable when excellent teachers of state law, such as Hugo Preuß (*Deutsche Juristen Zeitung*, 1924, Sp. 653) and H. Triepel (*Deutsche Juristen Zeitung*, 1926, Sp. 845), protest against it. Indubitably, it would be an act of sovereignty exceeding the bounds of the typically permissible when an initiative under Art. 73 would be precluded by a constitution-amending statute for a particular matter, as the Reich government attempted to do with the draft of a so-called strangulation statute concerning the revaluation issue (Triepel, *Deutsche Juristen Zeitung*, 1926, Sp. 845; C. Schmitt, *Volksentscheid und Volksbegehren*, 1927, p. 17). On the other hand, for example, a closure statute for pending trials of a particular type, such as the trials regarding the assets of the former ruling families at the Land level, would be permissible. As noted, however, one must not overlook that an apocryphal sovereign action is at issue here.

(d) *Constitutional amendment is not constitutional suspension* (above I, 5). The temporary setting aside of individual or of all constitutional provisions is often imprecisely designated as the putting out of force or suspension of "the constitution." The constitution in the actual sense, the fundamental political decisions over a people's form of existence, obviously cannot be set aside temporarily, but certainly the general constitutional norms established for their execution can be precisely when it is in the interest of the preservation of these political decisions. In particular, legislation for the protection of bourgeois freedom, which is typical of the Rechtsstaat, [110] is subjected to a temporary suspension. More specifically, as will be shown below, they do not transcend the principle of a *political* form of existence in the actual sense. Instead, they only entail the limits of political action. In instances of the endangerment of the *political* form of existence, they must appear as a hindrance to state self-defense. During disturbances of public safety and order, in dangerous times like war and domestic unrest, constitutional limitations such as these are suspended. Both constitutional as well as simple statutory norms for the protection of bourgeois freedom would be violated by statute not only in the individual case. They would also be set aside generally for a certain time, so that the limitation of political action, which constitutes its actual purpose and content, does not apply for this period.

Such cases demonstrate most clearly that structurally the modern constitutional state is composed of two diverse components. There is a series of state power *restrictions* from the bourgeois Rechtsstaat and a system of *political activity*, whether it is monarchical or democratic. The liberal representatives of the bourgeois Rechtsstaat ignored this problem, and, driven by mistrust, they contemptuously rejected the state of exception, state of war, state of siege, etc., when they were unsatisfied with the example of the model land of bourgeois freedom, England, where indeed even the Habeas Corpus Act of 27 May 1679 is suspended during domestic unrest. The American federal constitution of 1787 provides for the possibility of a suspension of the Habeas Corpus Act in Art. I, paragraph IX, 2. The French constitution of the 22 Frimaire VIII (Consular Constitution of 13 December 1799) contains the first example of the suspension of a "constitution." According to Art. 92, the constitution can be suspended for all areas in which armed uprisings threaten the security of the state. That was termed "suspension de l'empire de la constitution." The manner of expression is explicable from the fact that one designated as the constitution only the bourgeois Rechtsstaat component (basic rights and separation of powers) (cf. above § 4, p. 38) and identified it with the constitution in general. It is thus also the case with Art.130 of the 1831 Belgian constitution. The *constitution* can be neither entirely nor in part suspended: La Constitution ne peut être suspendue en tout ni en partie.

In the course of the nineteenth century, the so-called state of siege, war, or exception developed into a legal remedy. Certain constitutional norms are suspended, especially the constitutionally guaranteed access to ordinary courts, personal freedom, freedom of assembly, freedom of the press, etc. The protection from discretionary intrusions of state officials into these spheres of freedom then erodes to an extent specified by statute. The Prussian law on the state of siege of 4 June 1851, which according to Art. 68a of the [1871] Reich Constitution, is valid in wartime for the entire Reich except Bavaria, enumerates in § 5 the following articles that can be rendered invalid for a specified period and in a particular district: 5 (personal freedom), 6 (inviolability of living quarters), 7 (access to ordinary courts), 27, 28 (freedom of opinion, freedom of the press), 29 (freedom of assembly), 30 (freedom of association), 36 (suppression of domestic unrest and execution of the laws by the civil authorities and, at their request, through armed force). [111]

Art. 48, 2, p. 2, provides for the possibility of placing in abeyance seven constitutional articles that guarantee basic rights, either entirely or in part: 114 (personal freedom), 115 (inviolability of living quarters), 117 (privacy of the mail), 118 (freedom of opinion, in particular freedom of the press), 123 (freedom of assembly), 124 (freedom of association), 153 (private property).

The affected constitutional provision is not valid for a specified period. The constitutional restrictions and limits of official activity the provision contains do not apply to any official with proper authorization. Neither these constitutional provisions nor the statutory norms resting on them form a limit on the official's actions. The suspension does not mean a rupture in the individual case, for no valid statutory provision is violated. Put more precisely, its validity is not eliminated. Nor is there a change, for after the termination of the possible suspension, which is always only temporary, the suspended provision again enters into force unchanged.

In Art. 48, 2, 1, the President is empowered to enact *measures* that he deems necessary for the reestablishment of public security and order. This clause contains the rule for a typical dictator, whose nature includes (a) that the dictator is authorized to issue measures that are defined by circumstances and that are neither an act of the legislature or of the judiciary. Nor could this clause provide some conclusively regulated procedure. Also, part of its nature is (b) that the content of the authorization cannot be defined ahead of time in factual terms, but instead is dependent on the discretion of the empowered person. Herein lies no general legislative grant and factually defined delegation. The content of the authorization is only dependent on the fact that those authorized consider something necessary under the circumstances (cf. above § 6, II 9b, p. 59). Art. 48, 2, 2, conferred on the President the additional, entirely differently constituted authority to suspend the seven basic rights articles that are enumerated there, *rendering them invalid* in more specific terms. That the authorization for any *measure* that is necessary under certain circumstances only means the authorization to proceed energetically without regard for statutory limits, *to act*, to initiate legal ruptures, but not to place statutory provisions in abeyance. There is a second grant of authority extending beyond the mere authorization for the President to proceed energetically in the invalidation of statutory provisions, but it is limited to the seven enumerated basic rights articles of clause 2.

The theory of the "inviolability of the constitution" (*Die Diktatur des Reichspräsidenten*, Berlin 1923, *Verhandlungen des Deutschen Juristentages 1925*; also *Gedächtnisschrift für Emil Seckel*, 1927, p. 430f.) presented and defended emphatically and with great insight by Richard Grau, is directed against this interpretation of Art. 48, 2. The theory rests on the thoroughly correct idea that the constitution [112], even in regard to a wide-ranging commissarial dictatorship, must not be infringed on, an idea, however, that no one reasonably disputed. The question is not whether the constitution is exempt from infringement. That is self-evident. The question, rather, is what "constitution" means here. R. Grau's opinion remains mired entirely in the often discussed, uncritically adopted confusion of the *constitution* in the actual sense with every single *constitutional* provision. According to Art. 48, the President's commissarial dictatorship serves the purpose of protecting and defending the *public security and order*, in other words, the existing constitution. Protection of the constitution and protection of every single constitutional provision are no more identical with one another than are the inviolability of the constitution and that of every single constitutional provision. When every single constitutional provision becomes "inviolable," even in regard to the powers of the state of exception, the protection of the constitution in the positive and substantial sense is sacrificed to the protection of the constitutional provision in the formal and relative sense. The purpose of Art. 48, 2, is perverted into its opposite. Specifically, the constitution is not "inviolable"; just the individual constitutional provision is. In other words, the individual constitutional provision is an insurmountable obstacle to an effective defense of the constitution.

III. *Constitutional disputes.* The concept of constitutional dispute must be derived from a properly understood concept of the constitution. A mere violation of a constitutional provision does not make every dispute of an interested party into a constitutional dispute in the actual or, as Haenel (p. 567) puts it, "in the eminent sense" of the word.

1. A constitutional dispute is not a so-called constitutional complaint. More specifically, it is not a general legal instrument of the individual, through which a violation of constitutionally protected rights can be vindicated against an official act.

An example of a constitutional complaint is the Swiss federal constitution of 4 May 1874, Art. 113, 3, according to which the Federal Court rules on "complaints concerning violations of the constitutional rights of citizens." Art. 178, 1, of the Organizational Statute of 22 March 1893, however, stipulates that only a violation of constitutionally protected rights by a *canton* or a *canton-level* (not federal) official can be challenged before the Federal Court. Otherwise, there is hardly a restriction. Every official act, a canton-level statute, a judicial decision, or an administrative act, can be challenged by any inhabitant authorized to act, whether a national or a foreigner, with the justification that there is a violation of the objective right of the federal constitution or of a canton constitution. In regard to the violation of basic rights (especially important individual rights), the individual is also protected when these rights are secured only through simple statute. For the resolution of the complaint, recourse can be made to a simple statute. [113] Hence, the entire state activity at the canton level is supervised by the Federal Court. In particular, the much discussed Art. 4 of the Swiss federal constitution (every Swiss national is equal before the law) facilitates a wide-ranging control, above all not just when the civil remedy for the violation of a subjective right of the complaining party is demanded, but also when, in so-called reflex effect of the objective right, the legal instrument is provided (Fleiner, p. 445/56). This general constitutional complaint is designated "public law recourse." It has the meaning of a legal protection for the individual, and yet it also has a public law sense, specifically public law in a federal state. When Fleiner, p. 443, considers this limitation of the Organizational Statute of 1893 (recourse against acts of the canton, not against federal acts), it is, indeed, noteworthy that the distinctive federal public law rationale of the provision is revealed in this restriction.

2. In the German public law theory, the word "constitutional dispute" receives its peculiar meaning through two elements.

(a) The first element is the structure of a *federal* constitution, whereby it does not matter whether a constitution of a state federation or of a federal-state is under consideration. The federation as such has a political and public law interest in constitutional disputes within a member state, which is different from the interest in constitutional complaints and from the general supervisory interest. In the course of the nineteenth century, this political and public law interest led to special institutions in the historical development of German federal public law. Every federation rests on the principle of the homogeneity of its members. In particular, the constitution of the member states must demonstrate a minimum of homogeneity (cf. below § 29). For this reason, every federation has a certain right to intervention, a right of "intermediation," as it is called in the German Federation, while, by contrast, the member states attempted to avoid such intermediations whenever possible in the interest of their independence. This produces a specially constituted regime for constitutional disputes within member states. Constitutional disputes could be settled through the mediation of the federation, by a panel of judges, by a court, or by way of federal legislation. A genuine constitutional dispute inside a member state must interest the federation, if not directly, then in any case under certain circumstances, and it thereby becomes a federal affair. Hence, it is understandable that the concept of constitutional dispute was introduced into the German public law through a 30 October 1834 decision of the German Federal Assembly.

Through this federal decision (*Protokolle der deutschen Bundesversammlung 1834*, p. 927ff.), the federation members obligate themselves in those cases where errors arise in a member state "between the government and the estates over the interpretation [114] of the constitution or over the boundaries of the participation granted to the estates during the exercise of certain rights of the regent, above all through the rejection of the means necessary for leading a government appropriate for the federal obligations of a Land constitution, and that all constitutional means and those compatible with existing statutes" had been undertaken unsuccessfully to abandon the decision of such disputes through arbitration before the mediation of the federation is petitioned. On this, cf. Zachariae, *Das deutsche Bundesrecht*, II, 1854, § 279, p. 770; also G. v. Struve, *Das öffentliche Recht des deutschen Bundes*, II, 1846, p. 39.

(b) The other element is the structure of the *constitutional monarchy* in Germany, which represents an intermediary position between the monarchic and the democratic principle and makes it possible to treat government and estates, prince and popular assembly, dualistically as two parties that stand opposite one another and whose relations are regulated by the constitution. Hence, the constitution can be treated as a contract (cf. above § 7, II, 2), whose parties are the government and the popular assembly. Constitutional disputes are defined not only by the object of the dispute (the constitution), but also by the parties (government and popular assembly).

The question is not whether the linguistic usage is determined unequivocally by the federation decision of 1834 and whether only a conflict between the government and the popular assembly can be designated a constitutional dispute. Art. 76, 2, of the 1871 Reich Constitution also uses the word in this sense.

Art. 76, 2, stipulates that "in federal states whose constitution does not provide an official to decide such constitutional disputes, the Bundesrat must mediate the dispute amicably on petition of one of the parties, or when that does not occur one must bring the parties to a settlement via federal legislation." The practice of the Bundesrat corresponded to the historically grounded interpretation of the concept of constitutional dispute, as did the prevailing opinion of public law scholars. On this, cf. Laband, *Staatsrecht*, I, p. 261; Seydel, *Kommentar*, p. 407; also Haenel, *Staatsrecht*, I, p. 568 (at least as a rule; only under extraordinary circumstances does it intend to provide the individual state citizen or member of a nonconstituent representative body a right to resolution of constitutional disputes).

In Art. 19, the Weimar Constitution provides that constitutional disputes inside a Land are decided by a Staatsgerichtshof. Meanwhile, this Staatsgerichtshof was established in accord with the Reich statute of 9 July 1921 (*Reichsgesetzesblatt*, p. 905). The Art. 19 provision is rooted entirely in the development of the German federal state. It does not introduce a federal supervisory power of the Swiss constitutional complaint variety, but instead presupposes the German legal concept of the constitutional dispute. [115] In the deliberations on the Weimar Constitution, that is unequivocally emphasized (*Protocol*, p. 411, Privy Counselor Zweigert of the Reich Justice Ministry against the opinion of Kahl, who designates every dispute involving the substance of the constitution a constitutional dispute, even if it does not occur between the government and the popular assembly).

3. The interpretation of the term "constitutional disputes" in Art. 19 has already produced viewpoints in the public law literature that distance themselves greatly from the historical development of the term.

A Kiel dissertation by Dose, *Die Zuständigkeit des Staatsgerichtshofes zur Entscheidung von Verfassungsstreitigkeiten*, 1923, provides the historical interpretation in the narrowest sense. According to an opposing understanding, every individual state citizen can be a party to such a dispute and be actively affirmed in his or her position. See, for example, Poetzsch, *Kommentar*, p. 72 ("it does not matter who appears as a party in this way"); Poetzsch, *Archiv des öffentlichen Rechts*, 42, p. 91ff. (though rather restrained, on the question of basic rights); Anschütz, *Kommentar*, p. 106; Giese, *Kommentar*, p. 101 ("even a state citizen"). According to a third opinion, only the highest state organs or parts of them can lodge a complaint. See W. Jellinek, "Verfassung und Verwaltung," II (*Staatskunde*, 1925, p. 29). The prior practice of the Staatsgerichtshof for the German Reich extends very far in terms of the recognition of standing and active affirmation of one's position. Thus, for example, the factions of Land legislatures are recognized as parties against the state's ministry (decision of the provisional Staatsgerichtshof of 12 July 1921; published in *Archiv des öffentlichen Rechts* 42, p. 79, with very noteworthy remarks by Poetzsch; and the decision of 21 November 1925, *RGZ*, vol. 112, p. 1*),[2] as is the local affiliate Nassau of the former high Reich nobility against the Prussian State Ministry, decision of 10 May 1924 (*RGZ* 111, 1*, p. 5*), where it was decided that "in regard to their property and family relationships, therefore, the petitioners claim to have a right of self-legislation, which rests not merely on a delegation of the state power of the Land.... The dispute over the existence and scope of such a right represents a constitutional dispute in the sense of Art. 19." Localities are also recognized as parties (*Deutsche Juristen Zeitung*, 1922, Sp. 427), etc.

The received historical interpretation, which limits the constitutional dispute to a conflict between the government and the popular assembly, can no longer be held in its traditional simplicity. It was only possible as long as the constitution, with a dualism characteristic of the constitutional monarchy, could be understood as a contract between the prince and the estates, government and popular assembly. In a purely democratic constitution, which the people establish by virtue of their constitution-making power, such contractual relations and, consequently, also such party roles are no longer possible. On the other hand, one must reaffirm that not every conflict of some interested party is considered a constitutional dispute merely because some constitutional provision is involved, and that even here the constitution has to be distinguished from individual constitutional provisions. [116] An unlimited opportunity for popular complaints of any type should not be granted to every state citizen or even to every "world citizen." Art. 19 does not mean that the protection of the constitution in general should be entrusted to the citizens of the state.

There have been constitutions that generally entrust the protection and defense of all constitutional rights to state citizens. Thus, Art. 110 of the French constitution of 14 November 1848 states that "l'assemblée nationale confie le dépôt de la présente Constitution et les droits qu'elle consacre, à la garde et au patriotisme de tous les Français." When state president Louis Napoleon was denounced because in the matter of the Roman Republic he flagrantly violated the constitutional rights of the popular assembly in the interest of the pope, a minority of the leftist parties on 12 June 1849, appealing to Art. 110 of the constitution, attempted to call the population of Paris to arms. The attempt misfired in an especially pitiful manner (on this, see Emil Bourgeois and E. Clermont, *Rome et Napoléon III*, Paris 1907, p. 190/91).

The Weimar Constitution provides the individual state citizen a right to petition (Art. 126), and it provides minorities of state citizens the opportunity to initiate a referendum via a popular initiative (Art. 73, 2) or to introduce a popular legislative procedure (Art. 74, 3). But it recognizes neither a popular complaint nor a right of the individual to armed resistance. From the democratic principle, nothing arises in the way of a general complaint authority or of the active affirmation of individual petitions.

The uncertainty, one can say confusion, in the delimitation of the roles of parties in constitutional disputes rests ultimately on the fact that the Weimar Constitution, like every modern constitution, is a mixture of liberal (Rechtsstaat-based) and democratic (political) components (cf. below § 16). A logically executed, purely individualistic-liberal understanding, disregarding all distinctively political elements of the constitutional structure (whether it is a monarchical, democratic, or federal state), must provide every individual person, not only every state citizen, with a right to petition against the state in every violation of objective law. Thus, a court on the state and against the state would develop out of the Staatsgerichtshof. Indeed, every violation of a statute would at the same time be a violation of the constitution. The limitation on constitutional disputes inside a Land would then be unreasonable, and it must, as W. Jellinek ("Verfassung und Verwaltung," *Staatskunde*, II, 1925, p. 29) says, appear "odd" that a dispute resolution mechanism is not envisioned for constitutional disputes in the Reich. [117]

In contrast to this, one must affirm the viewpoint that "not every conflict over the meaning of a constitutional article is a constitutional dispute; it depends on the subjects contesting the issue" (R. Thoma, *Archiv des öffentlichen Rechts* 43, p. 283). A Staatsgerichtshof for the settlement of constitutional disputes should only decide on disputes involving the *constitution*, not those concerning constitutional details. Therefore, only the *"principal institutions"* of the constitution (as Haenel, p. 92, states) come into consideration as parties of such a dispute. More specifically, this includes only the highest offices, whose direct purpose is the organization and execution of the political decisions providing the constitution its content. As before, this means above all parliament and government. This applies secondarily to the other highest organizations, but always according to the character of the political institution in question. Only these primary organizations can directly violate the constitution, and only between them can there be a genuine constitutional dispute. If the practice of the Staatsgerichtshof up to now has expanded standing to sue, in particular recognizing minorities of Land parliaments as parties, then one can allow this expansion to stand as constitutional custom. On the other hand, the judgment of 10 May 1924 (*RGZ* 111, p. 5*), which treats a local branch of the former high imperial nobility as a party, clearly goes too far.

4. Another question is to what extent is it advisable to resolve *doubts and differences of opinion about the interpretation of constitutional laws* by a judicial procedure. For a resolution of such doubts, in particular the issue whether a statute or a decree is reconcilable with constitutional provisions, a special judicial procedure can be envisioned, in which a court decides. This court is designated a "Staatsgerichtshof" or even a "constitutional court."[3]

A Czechoslovakian statute of 9 March 1921 provides that a *"constitutional court"* decides exclusively about whether a statute or an emergency decree contradicts the constitution. The Austrian federal constitution of 1 October 1920 envisions a *"constitutional court"* in Art. 139 and Art. 140. For the German Reich, cf. the suggestions of Triepel in the *33. Deutschen Juristentag, Verhandlungen*, Berlin 1925, p. 64. See additionally, W. Jellinek, *Veröffentlichung der Vereinigung Deutscher Staatsrechtslehrer*, 1925, no. 2, p. 38ff., and the "Entwurf eines Gesetzes über die Prüfung der Verfassungsmässigkeit von Reichgesetzen und Reichsverordnungen," reprinted in the essay by R. Grau, *Archiv des öffentlichen Rechts*, new series 11, 1926, p. 287ff. According to § 1 of this draft, the Staatsgerichtshof for the German Reich (in the exercise of § 18 Nr. 1 of the statute on the Staatsgerichtshof of 9 July 1921) resolves doubts and differences of opinion over whether [118] a "legal provision of the Reich law is contrary to the Reich Constitution." Reichstag, Reichsrat, or Reich government could request the decision of the Staatsgerichtshof. R. Grau distinguishes between a *genuine Staatsgerichtshof* (which, "with judicial independence, is called upon to decide between political factors . . . in all circumstances") and a *constitutional court*, which "in questions of constitutional law has to decide as a trustee of the constitution in place of other courts."

Of course, by a constitution-amending statute, it could be ordained for the German Reich that some officials, associations, or even individual state citizens have the opportunity to occasion the court decision about whether a statute or a decree infringes on a constitutional provision of the Weimar Constitution, for example. In the many cases of doubt, to which the individual constitutional provisions of the Weimar Constitution give rise, it is not unreasonable to advocate the institution of a constitution-interpreting court of law, as did Count zu Dohna and H. Triepel at the Thirty-third Meeting of German Jurists (1924) and by Anschütz and Mende at the Thirty-sixth Meeting of German Jurists (1926). In response to the ambiguity of the earlier constitutions of the constitutional monarchy, Rudolf Gneist (*Der Rechtsstaat*, 1872) already raised an equivalent demand as a requirement of the Rechtsstaat. But the type of law court that decides all disputes of constitutional interpretation would, in fact, be a high political institution. This is because it also—and above all—would have to decide these doubts and differences of opinion, which result from the peculiarities of the dilatory formal compromises (above § 3, III, p. 31), and it would actually reach the substantive decision that was postponed through the compromise. So the establishment of such a court of law in Germany today would already necessarily require a constitution-amending statute in line with Art. 76.

It is a murky fiction to separate legal questions from political questions and to assume that a public law matter permits itself to be rendered nonpolitical, which, in fact, means to be deprived of the character of a state. Anschütz (*Verhandlungen des Deutschen Juristentages 1926*, Berlin 1927, p. 13) wants to submit all disputes about the interpretation and application of the Reich Constitution to a Reich-level Staatsgerichtshof. However, he deems it "self-evident" that the court of law may decide only legal questions in contrast to political questions. "I do not believe," he says, "that on this issue anything further is to be said." I fear that the question just begins at this point. In place of a court of law with its appearance of judicial formality, a political organ, decides with more integrity, such as a "senate" in the style of the Napoleonic constitutions, which envisioned a so-called Sénat [119] conservateur for the protection of the constitution: for example, Title II of the Constitution of the Year VIII (1799), Art. 15ff.; Title VIII of the Senate Consul of the Year XII (1803), Art. 57ff; Title IV of the constitution of 14 January 1852, Art. 29; Art. 26 of the Senate Consul of 14 March 1867. Otherwise, there is the danger that instead of a juridification of politics, a politicization of the judiciary emerges, which undermines the prestige of the judiciary.

IV. *The constitution as object of attack and protection in cases of high treason.* The criminal law provisions regarding high treason essentially have the protection of the constitution as an object. The criminal law instruments that define high treason speak above all of an attack on "the constitution." At the same time, other objects of attack, such as the person of the prince or the territory of the state, lose general significance. In a state that rests on the foundation of the monarchical principle and in which, therefore, the monarch is the bearer of the constitution-making power, an attack on the person of the monarch is one directly on the constitution itself. The most important case of high treason, however, is the so-called constitutional high treason in the strict sense, whose character is today defined mostly as an undertaking directed "toward violent change of the constitution."

Thus § 81, 2, of the German Reich's Criminal Code of 1871 reads: "Whoever endeavors to violently change the *constitution* of the German Federation or of a federal

The Concept of the Constitution

state." § 86 of the Reichstag's proposed statute of 1917 stipulates "whoever changes the Reich *Constitution* or that of a Land with violence or threat of violence." It is the same with § 85 of the 1926 Reichstag proposal (cf. Leopold Schäfer's synoptical presentation of the German draft criminal statutes, Mannheim 1927, p. 62/3).

The criminal law literature on this defining factual characteristic of the "change of the constitution" shows that not every individual constitutional law is at issue and that the so-called formal concept of the constitution leads to a true absurdity. More precisely, only the "fundamental state institutions" or "the foundations of political life" are designated as the constitution. It is rightly emphasized that "not every attack on the constitutional document, not every violation of a provision of the constitution," represents high treason against the constitution. "High treason against the constitution is older than any constitutional document, and our constitutions contain provisions that differ most in terms of importance" (Binding). Consequently, factual definitions are also found in the older criminal law provisions concerning high treason, which better characterize the process than "change of the constitution," a term prone to misunderstanding. The General Law of Prussia, [120] for example, part II, 27, § 92, the model of the later conceptual definitions, calls high treason an undertaking that "is directed toward a violent transformation of the state constitution." Other criminal law provisions speak of the fact that the constitution should be *suppressed* or that it should be *overturned*, either wholly or in part, or that it should be eliminated in its *principal components*, etc. Even here the necessity of distinguishing the constitution in the positive and substantial sense from individual constitutional dictates is evident throughout.

The criminal law scholarship on this issue is thoroughly of one mind. See, for example, F. van Calker in *Vergleichenden Darstellung des Strafrechts*, special part, 1906, p. 19, v. Liszt, 20th ed., p. 551; and Frank, *Kommentar*, Nr. 2 to § 81/2. Above all, however, see K. Binding, *Lehrbuch des gemeinen deutschen Strafrechts*, special part II, 2, p. 435, and Count zu Dohna, *Deutsche Juristen Zeitung*, 1922, Sp. 81/82 (on the draft of the enabling act), who argues: "Indeed, then, high treason as an internally closed factual definition only permits itself to be distinguished from attacks on state institutions that are not qualified in this way, when one affirms that in the first case the intention must have been directed toward the alteration of the legal structure of the state." Additional literature is found in the Heidelberg dissertation of H. Anschütz, *Der Verfassungsbegriff des Tatbestandes des Verbrechens des Hochverrats*, 1926, p. 28ff. (manuscript). The Reichsgericht (Sächsische Archiv III, p. 366) attempts to provide the proper distinction. "The point of departure," it argues, "is that the statute (the criminal statute), when it speaks of constitution, means the constitutional document. Not all provisions of the constitutional document," it continues, "can be objects of a constitutional violation. Not every attempt to eliminate a constitutional organization represents an attack on the constitution. More specifically, objects of attack are only those components of the constitution that form the *foundations of the state's political life*, and this is certainly without regard for whether or not their regulation occurs directly in the constitutional document."

High treason, therefore, is only an attack on the constitution in the *positive* sense presented here (§ 3, p. 23). A further question is whether there are additional distinctions *within the factual definition of high treason* that are not a result of the necessary one between the annihilation and elimination of constitutions (above p. 99). As the concept is mostly defined today in the theory and practice of criminal law, these essential distinctions become valid only in the context of the *enforcement* of criminal sanctions. In this instance, these distinctions certainly appear very clearly. For in a democratic constitution, it is self-evidently not the same whether an undertaking only serves to set in motion the constitution-making power of the people, making it actually only an appeal to the people, whose constitution-making power can be suffocated by an apparatus of organizations and competences, or whether this constitution-making power itself [121] should be eliminated. It is also not the same whether the goal of the enterprise of high treason is a restoration of the monarchical principle or a dictatorship of the proletariat. Just so, in a monarchy it would be natural to judge differently the issues of whether the democratic principle should replace the monarchical one or whether in the context of the monarchy a coup d'état can possibly serve the monarchical cause.

The core of all such distinctions lies in the fact that a concept like "constitution" cannot be broken down into norms and normative elements. The political unity of a people has its concrete form in the constitution. Infractions like high treason or treason in a Land protect political existence, not the formalities, which are envisioned for changes in the constitution, and not any other values and imperatives. Consequently, in regard to factual definitions like high treason or treason against a Land, the attack on the constitution can also never be justified by the fact that some international law obligation or norm puts the state or the state officials in the wrong. The concrete existence of the politically unified people is prior to every norm. [122]

PART II

THE RECHTSSTAAT COMPONENT OF
THE MODERN CONSTITUTION

§ 12.

The Principles of the Bourgeois Rechtsstaat

I. [125] In this context, what is understood as the modern, bourgeois Rechts-staat is a type of constitution to which the majority of today's constitutions conform. For this reason alone, this type of constitution is called "modern." Therefore, there is no value judgment at all associated with the word, in the sense of progress, timeliness, or the like.

1. The principles of the modern, bourgeois-Rechtsstaat constitution correspond to the constitutional ideal of bourgeois individualism, so much, indeed, that these principles are often equated with the constitution as such and "constitutional state" is given the same meaning as the "bourgeois Rechtsstaat" (above § 4, p. 36f.). In the first place, this constitution contains a decision in the sense of bourgeois freedom: personal freedom, private property, contractual liberty, and freedom of commerce and profession. The state appears as the strictly regulated servant of society. It is subordinated to a closed system of legal norms, or it is simply identified with this system of norms, so that it is nothing but norm or procedure. Despite its legal and norm-bound character, the Rechtsstaat in fact always remains a *state*, so it still contains another distinctly *political* component besides the bourgeois Rechtsstaat one. More on this linkage and mixture will be presented below (§ 16, p. 200). This means there is no constitution that, in its entirety, would be nothing more than a system of legal norms for the protection of the individual against the state. The political element cannot be separated from the state, from the political unity of a people. And to render public law nonpolitical would mean nothing other than to deprive public law of its connection with the state. The Rechtsstaat aspect, more precisely, is only one part of any modern constitution. Thus, what F. J. Stahl said about the Rechtsstaat is still quite apt today. "It does not at all signify the goal and content of the state, [126] but rather only the means and commitment to realize these" (Stahl, *Staats- und Rechtslehre*, II, p. 137). An outstanding representative of the theory of the bourgeois Rechtsstaat, Rudolf Gneist, declares that even every opponent of Stahl's views could "affirm" this principle "verbatim" (Gneist, *Der Rechtsstaat*, 1872, p. 60).

This Rechtsstaat component, however, is so meaningful for and characteristic of the modern constitution and is, moreover, such an internally complete system of principles, that it is necessary and appropriate to portray and treat it separately.

2. According to its historical development and fundamental schema, which is still dominant today, the modern bourgeois Rechtsstaat constitu-

tion is first of all a *free* constitution, particularly in the sense of *bourgeois freedom*. Its sense and goal, its τέλος, is in the first instance not the power and glory of the state, not *gloire* as per Montesquieu's categorization (above § 4, p. 38). It is, rather *liberté*, protection of the citizen against the misuse of state authority, and, as *Kant* says, it is instituted "in the first place according to the principles of the freedom of the members of a society as persons."

See Kant, *Zum ewigen Frieden*, II, 1, "Definitivartikel" and "Vom Verhältnis der Theorie zur Praxis im Staatsrecht," Vorländer edition, *Phil. Bibl.* 47, p. 87. In the latter, Kant writes: "Merely as a legal circumstance, therefore, the bourgeois condition is founded a priori on the following principles: 1. freedom of every part of society as persons; 2. equality of these parts with every other one as subjects; 3. autonomy of each part of a common system as citizens." Kant's formulations are relevant here because they contain the clearest, most conclusive expression of these principal ideas of the bourgeois Enlightenment, which until then had not been replaced by a new, ideal foundation.

3. From the fundamental idea of bourgeois freedom follow two consequences, which constitute both principles of the Rechtsstaat component of every modern constitution. First, there is a *principle of distribution*. The individual's sphere of freedom is presupposed as something prior to the state, in particular the freedom of the individual is *in principle unlimited*, while the authority of the state for intrusions into this sphere is *in principle limited*. Second, there is an *organizational principle*, which facilitates the implementation of this distributional principle. State power that is in principle limited is *distributed* and comprised in a system of defined competencies. The principle of distribution—individual freedom that is in principle unlimited and a grant of power to the state that is in principle limited—[127] finds its expression in a series of so-called basic or liberty rights; the organizational principle is contained in the theory of the so-called separation of powers, more specifically, the separation of different branches of the state exercise of power, whereby the separation of law-making, government (administration), and application of the laws—legislative, executive, judicial—above all comes into consideration. This division and separation serves the interest of the reciprocal regulation and limitation of these "powers." Basic rights and separation of powers denote, therefore, the essential content of the Rechtsstaat component of the modern constitution.

For this reason, Art. 16 of the *Declaration of the Rights of Man and Citizen of 1789*, which was already quoted, rightly states that a state without basic rights and without separation of powers does not have a constitution, in particular, not a constitution in the sense of the bourgeois Rechtsstaat's ideal concept of a constitution. For Kant, every state contains three intrinsic powers, the "generally unified will in the form of a person divided in three parts as legislator, governor, and judge" (*Rechtslehre*, part II, *Das Staatsrecht* § 45, Vorländer, p. 136). Only a state with a division of powers has the "constitution solely conforming to law." It is a "pure republic," because the *rule of law* (in contrast to the rule of men and to arbitrariness) can only be realized through the separation of the legislator from legal application and from the judiciary. Every elimination of this distinction means "despotism" (*Zum ewigen Frieden*, section II, 1., "Definitivartikel," Vorländer, p. 129). Even Hegel retains the distinction, when he also rejects a mechanical and abstract separation (*Rechtsphilosophie* § 269, Lasson, p. 206; additionally pp. 220 and 357). In his early work on the German constitution, 1802 (Lasson, p. 3n.), he terms despotism a state without a constitution, probably under the influence of Art. 16 of the Declaration of the Rights of Man and Citizen of 1789.

The idea had been expressed in the American constitutions before that Declaration of 1789. The Declaration of the Rights of Virginia (1776) states in Art. 5 and in the text of the constitution itself that each of the three powers must form a specially separated distribution; that none may exercise the function of the others; and that no one may clothe a public function in more than a department. This is comparable to other American constitutions, although the federal constitution of 1787, which realized the principle especially consistently, contains no express proclamation. The French constitution of 1791 repeats Art. 16 of the human rights declaration and demands the separation of powers (séparation des pouvoirs). The Jacobin constitution of 1793 does not speak of distribution or separation of powers. Nor does the Girondist constitutional draft (*Condorcet*). In Art. 29 of its rights declaration, it is content to state the necessity of "a limitation of the public function through statute" and of the guarantee of the responsibility of all public officials. By contrast, the constitution of 1795 (Constitution of the Directory of the Year III) once again proclaims expressly (Art. 22 of its Declaration of the Rights of Man and Citizen) that "the social guarantee cannot exist, if the distribution (division) of powers is not introduced, and when their boundaries are not determined and the responsibility of the public officials is not guaranteed." The French constitution of 4 November 1848 declares in Art. 19 that the separation (séparation) of powers is the first condition of a free government. The constitutions of the second Reich (Art. 1 of 14 January 1852 and Art. 1 of 21 May 1870) state that "the Constitution recognizes, reinforces, guarantees the [128] major principles proclaimed in 1789, which are the foundation of the public rights of the French." Not with the same doctrinal principles, but nevertheless as an express determination, the Frankfurt constitution of 28 March 1849 (§181) stipulates that adjudication and administration are separate from and independent of one another. This separation proved acceptable because the aim was just protection against the monarchical government; defense against the legislature was not considered since this question was deemed resolved through the consent of the popular assembly. The basic rights of the Germans were proclaimed at the same time.

4. Even where basic rights and separation of powers are not explicitly expressed or proclaimed in a modern Rechtsstaat constitution, they must be valid as principles of the bourgeois Rechtsstaat, and they must be part of the positive-legal content of every constitution that contains a decision for the bourgeois Rechtsstaat.

On the fact that the basic rights (human and civil rights of 1789) continue to be self-evidently valid for the French public law, with positive-legal significance, although the present constitutional laws of 1875 no longer enumerate them, cf. A. Lebon, *Das Verfassungsrecht der französischen Republik*, 1909, p. 174. The principles of the Declaration of the Rights of Man and of the Citizen of 26 August 1789 are so firmly entrenched in the consciousness of the French that their reaffirmation in the constitution is superfluous. See also Esmein-Nézard, I, p. 561, and Duguit, *Droit Constitutionnel*, 2nd ed., II (1923), p. 159, III, p. 563.

5. In its Second Principal Part, the *Weimar Constitution* enumerates the basic rights and duties of Germans. The bourgeois Rechtsstaat's fundamental principle of distribution is recognized, even if the impact of this recognition is diluted and obscured by the fact that diverse individual provisions, including social reformist programs and other matters that for political reasons were included in the constitutional text, are placed directly and unsystematically next to and between the actual basic rights. The Rechtsstaat-based organizational principle of the separation of the three powers is not expressly declared. However, it lays the foundation for the organizational provisions of the First Principal Part and becomes recognizable even in the headings of the individual sections (Reich legislation, Reich administration, legal adjudication). The federal state organization of the Reich also presupposes the separation of powers, because the distribution of jurisdictions between Reich and the Lands is not thoroughly regulated according to content. It is regulated differently for legislation, administration, and the judiciary. The organization of Reich officials rests on the usual distinction between legislation and government. Then, inside of the government, [129] a distinctive distribution of government powers between President and Reich government is again undertaken. Ultimately, the Reichsrat was not organized as a chamber of states, so that it could receive a share of the administration. As a chamber of states specifically, that is, as a legislative organ, the Reichsrat would have to remain separated from administrative affairs according to the basic principles of a logically consistent distinction between legislation and administration (H. Preuß, *Protocol*, p. 120).

The principle of separation of powers is valid even for other constitutions as a necessary element of the Rechtsstaat. In its character as a Staatsgerichtshof, the Swiss Bundesgericht gave expression to the basic principle that "every citizen can expect the different powers of the state not to overreach their boundaries," regardless, moreover, of whether the basic principle of the separation of powers is declared expressly in the canton constitution or whether it results on its own from the distinction between the legislative, judicial, and administrative power (References in Fleiner, *Schweizerisches Bundesstaatsrecht*, p. 447, nn. 21 and 23).

II. *The concept of the Rechtsstaat.* The current Rechtsstaat concept is defined from the perspective of bourgeois freedom. In this way, the ambiguous term "Rechtsstaat" receives a distinctive sense.

1. According to the general meaning of the word, every state that respects unconditionally valid objective law and existing subjective rights could be designated a Rechtsstaat. That would mean that the *status quo* that is in force would be legitimated and perpetuated and that "well-earned rights," whether of individuals or of some associations and corporations, are considered more important than the political existence and security of

The Bourgeois Rechtsstaat

the state. In this sense, the traditional German Reich, the Roman Empire of the German Nation, was an ideal Rechtsstaat in the period of its dissolution. Its character as a Rechtsstaat was due to nothing other than the expression and means of its political decline. The well-earned rights of some estates or vassals could hinder any political action. With the destruction of the Reich's political existence, even all these well-earned rights themselves were certainly also eliminated.

Thus, Bluntschli (Article "Rechsstaat" in his *Staatslexikon*) can say the fealty state is a Rechtsstaat, or Max Weber (*Wirtschaft und Gesellschaft*, p. 745) can claim that the medieval Rechtsstaat was a Rechtsstaat of subjective rights, "a bundle of well-earned rights," while the modern Rechtsstaat is an objective legal order, more specifically, a system of abstract rules. In his book on the Rechtsstaat, Gneist also speaks of this Rechtsstaat in the German Reich, but only because of its carefully composed jurisdiction, which was defined for the protection of the rights of all against everyone else, [130] especially even for the protection of subjects against orders and decrees of the Land authority that violate rights. However, he does not fail to see that this system leads to the dissolution of the state, because it rests on the intermingling of private and public rights (p. 52).

2. In the sense of the bourgeois Rechtsstaat, the word receives its meaning at first through a series of oppositions. Like some designations of this type, it above all has a polemical sense. The Rechtsstaat signifies opposition to the power state, the oft-discussed opposition of *liberté du citoyen* to the *gloire de l'état*. An additional meaning lies in the contrast to the ordered, welfare, or any other type of state that does not limit itself to only upholding the legal order. Under legal order is understood a bourgeois legal order, which rests on private property and personal freedom and considers the state to be the armed guarantor of this bourgeois order, peace, and security.

3. The concept of the bourgeois Rechtsstaat receives a more precise sense if one is not just content with the general principles of bourgeois freedom and the protection of justice in general but, instead, sets up certain *organizational criteria* and elevates them to being the defining feature of the true Rechtsstaat. Naturally, the general foundation of the organization always remains the principle of the separation of powers. Nevertheless, during the political struggle of the free bourgeoisie, different additional consequences result from the principle, which leads to the fact that individual special demands are stressed and made prominent.

(a) A state only counts as a Rechtsstaat when intrusions into the sphere of individual freedom may be undertaken solely *on the basis of a statute*. It is only a state, therefore, whose administration, according to the expression of O. Mayer, is dominated by the "reservation" and "priority" of the statute. The polemical aspiration of this specialization of the concept is directed against the administration. Put into political terms, it is set against the power instruments of the royal government, military and civil officialdom. A state is a Rechtsstaat only when the entire administrative activity, in particular the police, stands under the reservation and priority of the statute and when intrusions into the individual's sphere of freedom are permitted only on the basis of a statute. The principle of the legality of administration becomes the distinguishing mark. The guarantee of bourgeois freedom lies consequently in the statute. Which guarantees against the misuse of the [131] statute are provided is an additional question, about which, however, the German bourgeoisie had become less conscious in the nineteenth century, because all its theoretical and practical interest was claimed by the struggle against the royal government and the royal administration. On this, cf. below § 13.

(b) A state only counts as a Rechtsstaat when its entire activity is wholly comprised in a sum of precisely defined competencies. The division and separation of powers contains the fundamental principle of this general *calculability of all expressions of state power.* The demand of calculability originates from the bourgeois Rechtsstaat principle of distribution, according to which the freedom of the individual is in principle unlimited. Every state authority, by contrast, is in principle limited and, consequently, calculable. General calculability is the presupposition of general controllability. All state activities, even legislation and government, end in an operation that is ongoing and calculable in terms of a previously defined norm. Everything is caught up in a network of competencies. The most extreme competencies, even a "competence to define competence," are never in principle unlimited, never "the plentitude of state power." It is, rather, always a controlled power, the overstepping of which could set into motion a formal judicial procedure. Legality, controllability, and conformity to jurisdictional boundaries and to judicial forms thus provide the closed system of the bourgeois Rechtsstaat. The constitution appears as the basic law of this system of statutes. One finesses the fact first that the constitution is nothing other than a system of statutory norms, second that this system is closed, and third that it is "sovereign." More specifically, at no point is the system ruptured, nor can it be influenced, either for the purpose or necessity of political existence.

(c) As it is guaranteed in Art. 102, the *independence of judges* is termed an especially important organizational mark of distinctiveness of the bourgeois Rechtsstaat. Nevertheless, it is inadequate to guarantee independence for private legal disputes and for criminal matters. That would be routine and was always the case for the most part in all well-functioning monarchies. The interest of the liberal bourgeoisie struggling for the Rechtsstaat was above all in a judicial supervision of the royal government's actual instrument of power, [132] in particular of the administrative officialdom.

This explains the fact that a broader linguistic usage designates only a state with *judicial supervision of administration* as a Rechtsstaat. For a time, the enthusiastic opposition against the "all-powerful bureaucracy" extended to the demand for making the doctrine of the *civil courts* applicable to the administration. "Justice and statute can only attain true significance and power, where it already finds a court judgment serving its realization." This fundamental principle of Rechtsstaat thinking is found in the famous piece of writing of the Hesse appeals' adviser Bähr (*Der Rechtsstaat*, Cassel 1864). The distinctiveness of his idiosyncratic writing lies in the fact that only the ordinary civil courts are viewed as these judicial bodies and in such a way that the entire state life can be subjected to the control of county and appellate judges. Thus, the Rechtsstaat becomes the so-called *judicial state*.

By contrast, in states with a more significant political life, especially in Prussia, the necessity of a special *administrative law adjudication* was always recognized. Above all, even Rudolf Gneist in his frequently mentioned work on the *Rechtsstaat* (1872) demanded a special administrative jurisdiction, after Lorenz von Stein in his *Verwaltungslehre* (Stuttgart 1865) opposed the aforementioned private law constructions and demonstrated the distinctiveness of administrative power. Organizationally, the administrative law adjudication became a defining feature of the Rechtsstaat. In an idiosyncratic manner, Gneist bound the Rechtsstaat concept together with that of local self-government as a voluntary activity of propertied and educated state citizens. The foundational idea of his understanding is the necessity of integrating society (specifically, the propertied and educated bourgeoisie) into the state, an idea whose systematic presupposition is found in Lorenz von Stein. What Gneist had in mind is best recognized in his claim that "the institutions of administrative jurisdiction in the constitutional state can no longer be constituted exclusively from the professional civil service." "More precisely," he continues, "it needs an organic formation out of the womb of the society (by that is meant the voluntary activity of educated state citizens who are not civil servants). In this new formation lies the *Archimedean point of today's Rechtsstaat*" (pp. 159/160). [133]

The organizational criterion of the bourgeois Rechtsstaat thus becomes ever more differentiated. One can generally say that according to the current interpretation it is sufficient, if, for the area of administrative law in particular, special courts with independent judges are organized as administrative courts that decide cases with procedures taking a judicial form. The regulation established by the Prussian administrative statute of 30 July 1883 would satisfy the minimum for this type of Rechtsstaat, although no possibility of general complaint is provided that is in accord with the form of bourgeois adjudication. Instead, the so-called enumerative principle holds; under it only those affairs expressly permitted by statute can be brought before the administrative courts (often designated as a system of legal actions).

4. The fully realized ideal of the bourgeois Rechtsstaat culminates in the conformity of the entire state life to *general judicial forms.* Under this Rechtsstaat ideal, there must be a procedure for every type of disagreement and dispute, whether it is among the highest state officials, between officials and individuals, or, in a federal state, between the federation and the member states or among member states, without regard for the type of conflict and object of dispute, a process in which decisions are reached according to a procedure in accordance with legal forms. It is certainly often overlooked that the most important presuppositions of this type of procedure are valid, general norms. For the judge is "independent" only so long as there is a valid norm on which he is unconditionally dependent, whereby under "norm" is understood only a general rule determined in advance (below § 13). Such a rule's validity alone provides the judge's decision with its legal force. Where this type of norm is absent, nothing more than a mediating procedure can come into play, and its practical success is dependent on the authority of the mediator. If the significance of the mediator's proposal to intercede is dependent on the *power* of the mediator, then a genuine mediation is no longer present, but rather a more or less accepted *political* decision is. The judge as such can never have power or authority that is independent of the validity of the statute. Even without political power, a mediator or an arbitrator can continue to enjoy a more or less great personal prestige, though only under the double presupposition that, first, [134] certain ideas of appropriateness, dignity, or particular moral premises are common to the disputing parties and that, second, the opposing views have not yet reached the most extreme degree of their intensity. This constitutes the boundary of all judicial forms and of any arbitration effort. The state is not merely a judicial organization. It is also something other than a merely neutral member of a conflict resolution body or an arbitrator. Its essence lies in the fact that it reaches the *political decision.*

5. *The problem of political justice.* In disputes that must be decided by the courts of general jurisdiction—civil, criminal, or administrative courts—according to the factual circumstances or object of dispute; and if a general judicial formality were to be fulfilled; then the political character of the disputed question or the political interest in the object of dispute can emerge so strongly that the political distinctiveness of such cases must be considered even in a bourgeois Rechtsstaat. This constitutes the actual problem of political justice. This question does not at all involve settling conflicts of political interests via a formal judicial procedure without regard to the recognized norms of decision. Therefore, it does not entail artificially

making these oppositions into legal disputes. Quite the contrary, because of its political character a special procedure or order is provided for special types of genuine legal disputes. Naturally, that emerges seldom in the realm of private law adjudication, but it does certainly in criminal matters or in disagreements with an object of dispute that has a public law character. It is always a matter of the distinctive distortion of the judicial forms associated with the Rechtsstaat. The issue, in other words, is the consideration of the political character of legal disputes in reference to organizational or other peculiarities, through which the Rechtsstaat principle of conformity to *general* judicial formality is weakened.

The following are the most important examples.

(a) Exceptional treatment of *political crimes* by criminal courts, in particular high treason and treason against a Land. According to German law (for example, the Law on Court Organization § 134), the Reichsgericht is in the first and final instance competent in cases of high treason, treason against a Land, treason in wartime against the Reich as well as of the crime against the §§ 1, 3 of the Law against the Betrayal of Military Secrets of 3 July 1914. In § 13 of the Law for the Protection of the Republic of 21 July 1922 (*Reichsgesetzesblatt*, I, p. 585), [135] a special *Staatsgerichtshof* was declared to have jurisdiction over a series of political infractions, whose jurisdiction, however, since 1 April 1926 (Law of 31 March 1926, RGBl. I, p. 190), is again returned to the ordinary courts to the extent that the case involves criminal matters.

In other states a *second chamber* has jurisdiction as a Staatsgerichtshof for special political trials, the model being the English upper house (which today, however, has become powerless). Hence, Art. 9 of the French Constitutional Law of 24 February 1875 provides that, through an internal administrative decree of the state president, the *Senate* is established as a court of law (Cour de justice) and recognized as competent in regard to charges that the Chamber of Deputies has raised against the president of the republic or against a minister, additionally in regard to endeavors directed against the security of the state (attentats commis contre la Sûreté de l'Etat). In this capacity, it has considered a few famous cases (*Boulanger, Deroulède*). Other French constitutions provided a special Staatsgerichtshof for such cases, thus, for example, the constitutions of the Year III (1795), of 4 November 1848, and of 14 January 1852.

(b) *Ministerial and presidential indictments* raised by the popular assembly and decided either by a second chamber or by a special Staatsgerichtshof presuppose a *legal* obligation.

See, for example, Art. 59, which stipulates that "the Reichstag is authorized to raise charges against the President, the Chancellor, and Reich ministers before the Staatsgerichtshof for the German Reich, claiming that these officials intentionally violate the Reich Constitution or a Reich statute. The petition for the lodging of the indictment must be signed by at least one hundred members of the Reichstag and requires the consent of the majority prescribed for constitutional amendments."

The details are regulated by the Reich Law on the Staatsgerichtshof of 9 July 1921 (*Reichgesetzesblatt*, I. 905). For an example of the jurisdiction of a *second chamber* as a Staatsgerichtshof in petitions against ministers of the French Senate under the Constitutional Law of 24 February 24 1875, cf. above under a.

The public law significance of the ministerial petition is displaced by the *parliamentary* "responsibility" of ministers. As political responsibility, this parliamentary accountability is often contrasted to "public law" responsibility (ministerial petition before a Staatsgerichtshof). Nevertheless, in this context, the word "responsibility" is imprecise and ambiguous (cf. below § 25, p. 320f), and, above all in "public law terms," it is not in contradiction with "political" responsibility. For nothing that affects the state can be nonpolitical. A procedure, however, against a minister or president, which is introduced through a parliamentary petition and is concluded by the legally valid decision of a Staatsgerichtshof, is either an exceptional *criminal* proceeding or not adjudication at all. The regulation established by the just cited Art. 59 is especially unclear and contradictory. A *culpable* violation of the Constitution or Reich statute is [136] discussed. The Constitution, therefore, is placed together with some "Reich statute" in a misunderstanding of its character. At least for a Reich minister, the consequence is that a confusing assemblage of responsibilities comes into play. Along with accountability under civil law and the general criminal law, which, for example, is grounded in high treason or treason against a Land, a "parliamentary responsibility" according to Art. 54 resides with the Reich ministers. Additionally, then, there is this responsibility regulated in Art. 59. It no longer has a distinctive meaning today. Like some other provisions of the Weimar Constitution, it exists only as a residue of the constitutional circumstances under the constitutional monarchy. In comparison with the criminal law procedure, it could at most serve political passions or express goals, if it were to become practical at all. The case of the presidential petition is something else altogether. This did not become superfluous in the same way through "parliamentary responsibility." However, even it has no independent significance compared to a criminal proceeding because of high treason or treason against a Land. Either it is a genuine case of political justice—then the jurisdiction of other courts must be excluded, and it may not come to a double criminal proceeding under violation of the principle "ne bis in idem."—or it is not adjudication at all, which means one should not choose a formal judicial procedure.

(c) Genuine *constitutional disputes* are always political disputes. On their resolution, see above § 11, III, p. 112.

(d) Resolution of doubts and differences of opinion over the constitutionality of statutes and decrees by a special court (Staatsgerichtshof, constitutional court, constitutional court of law, cf. above § 11, III 4, p. 117) is not a genuine trial outcome. It is, nevertheless, of interest in this connection because it contains a limitation on the general jurisdiction for court review.

It is often termed a Rechtsstaat requirement that the courts review the constitutionality of the statutes they apply. See, therefore, H. Preuß in the constitutional committee of the Weimar National Assembly, *Protocol*, pp. 483/4, where he appealed to Gneist and designated the exclusion of the power of judicial review through Art. 106 of the Prussian constitution of 1850 as the "obvious reactionary victory over the Rechtsstaat of 1848." This stance still presupposes a quite unviable separation of (constitutional) *law* and *politics*. Even the judge is in the "process" of political "integration" (R. Smend), in which the political unity forms, and in particular a decision on "constitutionality" is [137] never a nonpolitical one. As Hofacker puts it, "The question of constitutional review of statutes other than by legislative offices is, in fact, a political question of extraordinary significance, as it affects the rank and the dignity of the legislature. Such political questions cannot be resolved by legal scholarship alone" (Hofacker, *Der Gerichtssaal*, vol. XCIV, 1927, pp. 221/2). Consequently, the statutes that transfer the decision to a special court of law often provide that only certain top officials or political bodies can appeal to this court of law. In the case of Art. 140 of the Austrian federal constitution, for example, only the federal government or the government of a Land can appeal to the "constitutional court of law." According to the Czecho-Slovakian statute of 9 March 1921 discussed above (§ 11, III 4), only the highest court, the Supreme Court, the Supreme Administrative Court, the Electoral Court, the House of Deputies, the Senate, or the Karpatho-Russian Land Parliament can lodge a petition for a decision. Art. 13, 2, provides that in regard to doubts and differences of opinion over whether a Land legal provision is reconcilable with Reich law, the competent *central* authorities of the Reich or of a Land can call for the decision of a high court (according to the law of 8 April 1920, *Reichsgesetzblatt*, p. 410, of the Reichsgericht). According to the 1926 draft of a German Reich statute regarding the review of the constitutionality of Reich statutes and Reich decrees, the Reichstag, the Reichsrat, or the Reich government can call for the decision of the Staatsgerichtshof. The draft, however, excludes contracts with foreign states and the statutes that are contingent on them. This German draft is noteworthy in that it does not exclude the competence of judicial review. On this draft, besides the essay by R. Grau, *Archiv des öffentlichen Rechts*, new series 11, 1926, p. 287ff., see above all F. Morstein Marx, *Variationen über richterliche Zuständigkeit zur Prüfung der Rechtmässigkeit des Gesetzes*, Berlin 1927, p. 129ff., whose discussions are of special interest because of their principled *Rechtsstaat* arguments and (in reference to O. Bähr and R. Gneist) because he derives the "full competence of judicial review" from the *idea of the Rechtsstaat* (p. 150). However, the institution of a special court of law for decisions on the constitutionality of a statute reveals a politically motivated distortion of the Rechtsstaat logic.

(e) Special treatment of *government acts* or specific *political acts* in the area of adjudication. In some countries, in particular France and the United States of America, where review of executive acts by an ordinary court with general jurisdiction or by an administrative court is permitted, the practice led to the exception of government acts or "political acts" from this court supervision, so that these acts escape any ordinary court or administrative court review. The demarcation of the political from other acts is certainly controversial. A definite, automatic distinguishing mark of the "government act" did not previously result in the aforementioned practice.

See Jèze, *Les principes généraux du droit administratif*, I, 3rd ed., 1925, p. 392, who views the distinction only as a matter of the "opportunité politique," and R. Alibert, *Le contrôle juridictionel de l'administration*, Paris 1926, p. 70ff. There is additional literature in R. Smend, "Die politische Gewalt im Verfassungsstaat und das Problem der Staatsform," *Festgabe für Kahl*, Tübingen 1923, p. 5ff. [138]

(f) *Electoral reviews* of the politically most important elections (elections to parliament or for the head of state). The review of elections in itself belongs in the realm of administrative adjudication. Electoral review is organized in a special manner only because of the political significance of the most important elections. For historical reasons, review of parliamentary elections is often turned over to parliament (thus Art. 27, 1a). Often, however, a special electoral review commission is also formed,[1] which is composed in a different way, in order to be fair both to the objectivity of the electoral review and, at the same time, to the special political interest of this process.

See, for example, Art. 31, which stipulates that "in the Reichstag an Electoral Review Commission is formed. It also decides the question of whether a deputy has lost member status.

The Electoral Review Commission is composed of members of the Reichstag, which selects them for the election period, and from members of the Reich administrative court, which the President orders on suggestion of the presidium of this court."

This Electoral Review Commission, formed for the Reichstag, also examines the results in the election of the *President*. See § 7 of the Law on the Election of the President of 6 March 1924 (*Reichgesetzesblatt* I, p. 849).

§ 13.

The Rechtsstaat Concept of Law

I. *Law and statute in the bourgeois Rechtsstaat.*

1. The bourgeois Rechtsstaat is based on the "rule of law." To this extent, it is a *statutory state*. But the statute must retain a connection with the principles of the Rechtsstaat and of bourgeois freedom, if the Rechtsstaat is to remain in place. If everything that some person or an assembly dictates is without distinction law, then every absolute monarchy is also a Rechtsstaat, for in it the "law" rules, specifically the will of the king. The current Soviet Republic and the dictatorship of the proletariat would also be a Rechtsstaat, for there is even a legislature and, consequently, laws. If the "rule of law" should retain its connection with the concept of the Rechtsstaat, it is necessary to incorporate certain *qualities* into the concept of the law, through which it is possible to distinguish a *legal norm* from a *command* based on mere will or a *measure*.

Professors Alexejew (cf. *Jahrbuch des öffentlichen Rechts*, XIV, 1926, p. 326) and Timascheff treat the Soviet Republic as a state in which there is written and [139] settled law that does not, however, have the character of the *statute*. On this, see the especially interesting remark of Mirkine-Guetzevitch, *Revue du droit public*, 42 (1925), p. 126: the norms of a class dictatorship are not laws, because *fact* has priority over *right*; that is not a form of "legality." Obviously, in any case, not every measure of the competent legislature can be "law," if a connection between the concept Rechtsstaat and the rule of law is to exist.

2. Bourgeois freedom and all the individual, organizational marks of the Rechtsstaat developed above (§ 12, II, p. 129) presuppose a certain concept of law. "Rule of law" is an empty manner of speaking if it does not receive its actual sense through a certain opposition. This fundamental idea of the Rechtsstaat contains, historically as well as intellectually, the rejection of the rule of *persons*, whether it is an individual person, an assembly, or body whose *will* takes the place of a general norm that is equal for all and is determined in advance. The rule of law means above all and in the first place that the legislature itself is bound by its law and its authority becomes legislation, not the means of an arbitrary rule. The bond of the legislature to the law, however, is only possible so long as the statute is a norm with certain properties, such as rectitude, reasonableness, justice, etc. All these properties presuppose that the statute is a *general* norm. A legislature, whose individual measures, special directives, dispensations, and legal ruptures are just as valid as its statutes containing general norms, cannot conceivably be bound by its own statutes.

The bourgeoisie struggling for its freedom and its Rechtsstaat adopted a concept of law that rests on an old European tradition and was brought to the modern age from Greek philosophy by medieval scholasticism. Law is not the will of one or of many persons, but rather something *generally reasonable*; not *voluntas*, but rather *ratio*. This is valid without distinction of state form for monarchy, aristocracy, and democracy. Consequently, Aristotle distinguishes a democracy in which the law (νόμος) rules from another type of democracy, in which popular decisions (ψηφίσμτα) and not the laws rule. "In democracies," he argues, "that are bound to the law, no demagogues emerge. Instead, the most capable citizens have the chair. However, where the laws do not have the highest authority, demagogues arise. For there the people become a monarch, specifically a many-headed one" (*Politics*, bk. IV, chap. 4, nr. 4). Even for Thomas of Aquinas, law is a "rationis ordinato" in contrast to the will of the individual that is darkened by passions [140] or of a mass of persons. On the development in the sixteenth and seventeenth centuries, see Gierke, *Althusius*, p. 28off. Suarez traces the bond of the legislature to its own laws back to the fact that they represent this one "regula virtutis" that is derived from the "ius naturale" by reason, which consequently is also valid for the legislature, because it is self-evident that a mere act of will cannot be binding when the legislature enacts something different.

The proponents of state *absolutism* presented the clearest contrast to this Rechtsstaat concept of law. Hobbes coined the classical formula here: auctoritas, non veritas facit legem (*Leviathan*, Ch. 19). The law is will and command, not a wise council. It is valid merely as command, not by virtue of moral and logical qualities. The awareness about the Rechtsstaat concept of law became stronger in the struggle against this absolutist concept of law and the principle of the representatives of absolutism, specifically, that the prince is legibus solutus. The *Monarchomachs* reaffirmed this Rechtsstaat principle (cf. Gierke, *Althusius*, p. 280). And even in England, Rechtsstaat consciousness did not disappear despite the alleged omnipotence of the English Parliament. Locke provides the classic Rechtsstaat formulations and speaks of previously established positive laws (antecedent, standing, positive laws), while all ex post facto laws are contrary to law. What can happen absent a norm (without a *rule*), because it is dependent on circumstances, is not a part of legislation (cf. the evidence in *Diktatur*, pp. 41/2). According to Bolingbroke, the true state is established like the cosmos. Led by an all-wise being and governed by another that is all-powerful, the order of the cosmos rests on the linkage of wisdom and power, which means for him legislative and executive, that is, parliament and monarch. The parliament issues laws, which should be valid without exception. The parliament is the *wisdom* of the state,[1] and it prescribes rules for the *power* of the king. Neither god nor the king can violate a law (*Phil. Works*, V, p. 147). Like Locke, Montesquieu justifies his theory of the separation of powers by stating that if the same body that issues statutes also controls the executive, then it could destroy the state through its volontés générales; and as the executive, moreover, it could annihilate any individual citizen through its volontés particulières (bk. XI, chap. 6 of the "Esprit des lois"); the separation of the legislative and executive branches should stymie this linkage of general norms and discrete individual commands; a government is despotic when it "can issue discrete individual commands without being bound by general, stable, and enduring laws." This idea of the subordination to a general, "inviolable" norm, which is capable of a genuine bond (according to the expression of Otto Mayer), is the cornerstone of all Rechtsstaat thinking. It reveals itself in the legal definition of the Girondists' draft constitution of 1793, Section II, Art. 4: les caractères qui distinguent les lois sont leur *généralité* et [141] *durée indéfinie*, while the decrees are determined by local and particular application and by the necessity of a periodic or occasional renewal. This constitution, moreover, recognizes measures (mesures). In particular, the actions of the state of exception in Art. 7 are designated as such measures.

The German state theory of the eighteenth and nineteenth centuries retained this concept, so long as it was still conscious of the principles of the bourgeois Rechtsstaat. For Kant, a government" that was simultaneously a legislative branch, and a legislature that would at the same time engage in government acts, is "despotic." Kant's thinking is entirely in line with that of the Rechtsstaat with a separation of powers, in which the "law itself is dominant and not a particular person" (*Zum ewigen Frieden*, 2d section, 1., "Definitivartikel," Vorländer ed., p. 199; *Rechtslehre*, part II, *Das öffentliche Recht, Beschluss*, Vorländer, p. 186, etc.). Also for Hegel, the law is the current truth in a general form (*Rechtsphilosophie*, p 210). The legislative power expresses the general, the executive the particular (p. 358). The political avant-garde and the juristic theorists of the Rechtsstaat also presuppose unconditionally the general concept of law. "The law," as R. Mohl puts it, "is an establishment that is essentially meant to last for the long-term. In regard to any of these types of formal law (constitutional statute, simple statute), the *generality* of the command is an essential property. Regulation of a certain legal case through a special statute is not permitted to the extent it involves an accomplished fact. Consequently, the already existing fundamental principles are definitive." Lorenz von Stein states in his *Verwaltungslehre* (1st ed.1865, p. 78) that "according to its higher essence, the statute always stems from the entire consciousness of state life and, therefore, also always intends to achieve its goals." "On the one hand," he continues, "the statute intends to grasp *similarity* in all factual relationships and define the will of the state precisely for this similarity in all its different forms." The statute, consequently, must determine "all its objects similarly and in a unified way." The decree, by contrast, takes its point of departure above all else from the *factual situation*, "specifically, from its distinctiveness and its changing character." Even in Rudolf Gneist, both in his "Rechtsstaat," 1872, as in other writings of this liberal avant-garde fighter for the Rechtsstaat idea, the concept of the statute as a general, stable norm, in contrast to individual orders and statutory violations of the law, is always presupposed, whether or not it may be ordained by the will of an absolutist prince or by the majority decision of a parliament.

3. The Rechtsstaat concept of law, therefore, stands in a certain tradition. One may easily add to the examples just introduced.[2] Because natural law lost its evident quality, the different properties [142] of the statute (justice, reasonableness) under consideration now became problematical. Even the appeal to "good faith and credit" as a general legal principle (thus the announcement of the committee of the judges' association of the Reichsgericht against the power claims of the legislature, *Juristische Wochenschrift* 1924, p. 90) cannot substitute for these natural law convictions in politically and economically difficult times. But a property cannot be renounced without displacing the Rechtsstaat itself, without, in other words, giving up the *general* character of the legal norm. Herein lies the last guarantee of the traditional Rechtsstaat distinction of law and command, of *ratio* and will, and with it the last residue of the bourgeois Rechtsstaat's ideal foundation

generally. When H. Triepel criticizes the misuse of the legislative authority of the Reichstag by stating that "the statute is not sacred, only justice is, for the law is subordinate to justice" (*Festgabe für Kahl*, 1923, p. 93), the consciousness of this long-established Rechtsstaat tradition expresses itself. However, the opposition is not that of law and justice, but rather that of a properly understood concept of law in contrast to a helpless formalism, which designates everything as law that results from the procedure prescribed for legislation. It is thus also factually justified, yet still subject to misunderstanding owing to its manner of expression, when J. Goldschmidt forms the word "nomocracy" for the struggle against the misuse of the legislative power (*Juristische Wochenschrift* 1924, p. 245ff.). That which is directly lacking is the nomos, and the misuse lies in the failure to recognize what remains as a minimum of the traditional rational concept of a genuine statute, in the failure to recognize the general character of the legal norm. Everything that one can say about the rule of law or the rule of the norm, all turns of phrase about the "normative quality," are in themselves contradictory and confused, if this general character is given up and any conceivable individual command, any measure can be valid as a "norm" or a "statute." [143]

II. *The so-called formal concept of law.* The problem of the Rechtsstaat concept of law is made more difficult by the fact that the Rechtsstaat component of a constitution is not itself sufficient and that alongside the Rechtsstaat concept of law stands a *political* one.

Before this duality of the concept of law can be considered, however, the distinctiveness of the so-called formal concept of law must be clarified. For the concept of law and the Rechtsstaat are much obscured, because one transfers the legislative procedure and jurisdiction to state acts other than legislative ones for political reasons and on account of the force of necessity. This produces the concept of "formal law," which then appears as an opposition to "material law."

1. The consequence for the formal concept of law is law becomes that which is issued by the offices authorized for legislation and in the prescribed procedure for legislation. A delegation and expansion of jurisdictions and procedures is in itself nothing unusual, and a formalization of the concept is not itself disadvantageous. For example, it is possible to apply the decision-making procedure for legal disputes to other matters, such as disputed elections or criminal exonerations. Then one can speak of a "legal dispute in the formal sense" and say that election review or criminal exoneration is a legal dispute. More generally, one could designate all official business as "adjudication" that a judge settles under the protection of judicial independence, etc. With that type of formal definition, one comes out

well in individual areas of legal practice. Such definitions have the practical value of a useful technical means of assistance in a very restricted context. For a criminal law judge or a forest official, for example, the question can arise as to which animals are designated as "wild," and it can be practical to answer that those animals are wild which someone with a hunting license, exercising his right to hunt, is entitled to kill outside of the statutory closed season. Or an official of the public grain company could define bread as that which the possessor of a bread card is entitled to obtain on the basis of his bread card, etc. In this way, there arises a series of formal conceptual definitions that have a certain technical-practical meaning, and with them one can work in a specialized practice area up to a certain point. They are, in fact, [144] not conceptual definitions, but rather partly abbreviations, partly fictions, and have the relative and limited value of such abbreviations or fictions. However, it would be absurd to see this as the distinctive juristic method in this and to believe that a serious problem of jurisprudence permits itself to be handled scientifically in such a manner.

2. That is most valid for constitutional provisions. If it is characteristic of the organization of the constitutional monarchy that a statute comes about only in consultation with the popular assembly; and if the popular assembly struggles to extend the scope of its consultative powers and to participate in all possible politically important acts, approval of taxes, proposal of the yearly budget, declaration of the state of siege, declaration of war, appointments, pardons, concessions on important business enterprises, incorporation of an administrative area into another, territorial changes, etc.; then it is a simple sleight-of-hand of linguistic technique and nothing more when it is constitutionally stipulated that such political acts come about "in the form of the statute," or when by way of custom it is established that for such acts the legislative procedure is used. The meaning and significance of the "formal" concept exhausts itself in the fact that the popular assembly (the parliament) nevertheless has the same participatory role in and jurisdiction for such acts as it does in legislative acts, although they are not acts of legislation. Just as one can settle any conceivable issue "according to judicial forms," one can also do so "in the form of a statute." The formal element does not have any significance at all as such. It is to be viewed as "form" not in some special or eminent sense, but rather only as an abbreviating definition for an extraordinary expansion of the jurisdiction of certain offices.

The legislative process, therefore, can be extended to matters other than acts of legislation through express constitutional provision or by the exercise of customary law. The Weimar Constitution contains a series of examples that partly correspond to the typical constitutional regulation of modern states and that are partly new and distinctive.

For examples, see the following provisions. Art. 85 provides that "the budgetary plan is established *by statute* before the beginning of the budgetary year." Art. 87 stipulates: "Funds in the form of credits may be established only in cases of dire need and, as a rule, only for expenditures for recruitment purposes. Such an establishment as well as assumption of a security service by the Reich may only be pursued on the basis [145] of a *Reich statute.*" "The alteration of the territory of Lands and the new formation of Lands within the Reich," according to Art. 18, I, 2, "take place through a *constitution-amending Reich statute.*" Under Art. 45, 3, the "declaration of war and conclusion of peace require *a Reich statute.*" Art. 51, 1, provides that "in case of incapacitation, the Chancellor will initially substitute for the President. If the incapacitation lasts for longer than anticipated, a *Reich statute* regulates the substitution." "The Reich via statute," according to Art. 156, 1, "can execute a transfer of expropriated private economic enterprises into common property without needing to pay compensation for socialization during the application of the valid provisions for expropriation, broadly understood."

However, nothing further results from such extensions and delegations of authority than that, constitutionally or in terms of customary law, offices authorized for legislation complete certain actions through the legislative process. It would be more than unreflective to draw the additional conclusion that the offices with jurisdiction for legislation could thus settle anything conceivable in the form of a statute and do so without restraint. It would be equally thoughtless to conclude that everything these offices touch with the magic wand of the legislative process are now transformed into a statute, so that the "rule of law" means nothing more than the rule of the offices entrusted with legislation. Such a result would be just as illogical as using the formal concept of adjudication to give the judge a boundless grant of authority and to remove him from any control, for example, empowering him to address cases without a genuine legal dispute, the so-called uncontested legal proceedings, all under the cover of judicial independence. It is self-evident that despite this expansion of his jurisdiction, the judge can only handle such matters that, in fact, are either acts of the judiciary or for which its jurisdiction is expressly justified. No one will assume that he may undertake some governmental act merely because it is cast in the form of a trial and can do what he considers necessary simply by relying on his independence. For the formal concept of law, however, this simple factual situation seems hardly to have been noticed. G. Jellinek (*Gesetz und Verordnung*, p. 232) states that "all forms by means of which a person is capable of affecting others are at the disposal of the state." The writings of Laband (*Staatsrecht* II, p. 63) are even more remarkable and characterized by the absence of any Rechtsstaat consciousness. [146] "Through a statute," he argues, "a pending legal dispute can be decided, the validity or invalidity of an act of the government can be expressed, an election can be recognized and nullified, a pardon or amnesty can be issued. In a word, there is not an object of the entire state life, indeed, one can say, not even an idea that cannot be made into the contents of a statute." That is completely wrong-headed. And if it is understood and intended, as unfortunately tends to occur without proper reflection, that legislative officials can empower themselves for anything if it is given the form of a statute, then that is improper and false. Apart from the previously discussed delegations that require a special constitutional title, the legislative process comes into consideration only for statutes understood in the sense of the Rechtsstaat.

III. *The political concept of law.* The possibility of the confusion of this so-called concept of law is explicable above all in reference to the fact that there is a political concept of law, which stands independently alongside the Rechtsstaat concept of law. The expression "political concept of law" is not meant as a contradiction to a juristic concept of law. Juristically, that is, for legal scholarship and in particular for a constitutional theory, both concepts of law are objects of scholarly treatment in the same way. Both concepts of law are part of a modern constitutional theory, because there is not a modern constitution without both of these differentiated components, the Rechtsstaat and the political elements, to which the dualism of both concepts of law correspond. In this context, "political" means a concept of law that, in contrast to the Rechtsstaat, results from the political form of existence of the state and out of the concrete manner of the formation of the organization of rule. For the Rechtsstaat understanding, the law is essentially a norm. It is, specifically, a norm with certain qualities, a legal (an appropriate, reasonable) rule of a *general* character. Law in the sense of the political concept of law is concrete *will* and *command* and an act of sovereignty. Law in a state conforming to the monarchical principle is, consequently, the law of the king. Law in a democracy is the will of the people; lex est quod populus jussit. A logically consistent and complete Rechtsstaat aspires to suppress the political concept of law, in order to set a "sovereignty of the law" in the place of a concrete existing sovereignty. In other words, it aspires, in fact, to not answer the question [147] of sovereignty and to leave open the question of which political will makes the appropriate norm into a positively valid command. As noted (p.108), this must lead to concealments and fictions, with every instance of conflict posing anew the problem of sovereignty. The point of departure in this regard is that alongside the Rechtsstaat concept of law, moreover, together with the juristic-technical aid of the so-called formal concept of law, there is still a political concept of law, which is not capable of eliminating the Rechtsstaat element.

1. When the liberal bourgeoisie intended to achieve its Rechtsstaat ideal in the nineteenth century, it could not be satisfied with setting up legal principles and norms against absolutism. In opposition to the concrete existing state institutions of the monarchical principle, it had to demand just as concrete, differently constituted political institutions. One struggled not only

for the Rechtsstaat *in abstracto*, but above all for the rights of the "popular assembly," in particular, for an expansion and extension of the authorizations and competencies of parliament. Ultimately and politically, that led to democracy. One could see the organizational guarantee of the Rechtsstaat reflected in different institutions. Together, however, they also led to the fact that there was a demand for the popular assembly having the most far-ranging consultation power possible. That corresponded to the natural direction of a political struggle against a strong monarchical government. In such a political position, each of the different demands—Rechtsstaat concept of law and widest possible consent power for the popular assembly—had to bind themselves together. As long as the princely government itself was still so strong that its power constituted a danger for the Rechtsstaat, the diversity of these two demands was hardly recognized and a blending of two diverse concepts of law occurred—the Rechtsstaat concept of law as a *norm* characterized by certain qualities and the democratic concept of law as the *will* of the people—whereby at that time the people were replaced, entirely self-evidently and for the most part tacitly, by the will of the popular assembly, of the parliament. The popular assembly's consent power is of course understood only as a distinguishing characteristic of the concept of law, which was derived from the political-democratic concept of law. [148]

2. A concept of law, which is valid as a "substantive" concept of law, also has a political character, because it is not a "formal" one. According to Anschütz, law is a legal norm, a provision through which the state turns itself toward its subjects, "in order to establish the boundaries of the permissible and the required that exist between *itself and its subjects.* For it is the essence of any law in the substantive sense that it sets limits to personal *freedom* in general, to *property* in particular" (Anschütz, "Gesetz," in Stengel and Fleischmann, *Wörterbuch des Staats- und Verwaltungsrechts*, II, p. 215). Anschütz argues that there was "at the time, 1848, as was the case previously and is today, only a substantive concept of law that . . . intends to define and actually defines the 'freedom and property' formula." Article 62 of the Prussian constitution of 31 January 1850 ("the legislative power is exercised in common by the king and by two chambers") presupposes it. This means that it requires a statute developed in consultation with the popular assembly to make incursions into freedom and property and that a royal decree is not a sufficient basis for such incursions. In order to understand this concept of law (statute = limitations of freedom or property), it is necessary to take account of the political circumstance from which it arose. In the political struggle against a strong royal government, the consultation power of the popular assembly as the law's defining characteristic must be ever more strongly emphasized and, in the end, be deemed definitive. If the popular assembly's consent power is, above all, politically a part of the law,

the politically simple, although logically false reversal, becomes explicable. What comes about with the consent of the popular assembly is a law. The rule of law then means the consent of or ultimately rule by the popular assembly. The bourgeoisie attempted to protect itself against intrusions into personal freedom and private property, and, as something characteristic of the Rechtsstaat, it raised the demand that such intrusions may be undertaken only on the "basis of a statute." A component of the law in this sense is, indeed, the consent power of the popular assembly, in other words, the representation of those affected by the previously mentioned intrusions. A *decree* issued by the king, by contrast, whether or not it otherwise may be just, reasonable, and appropriate and corresponds to all the qualities of a true legal norm, would not be considered law. "Politically," G. Holstein argues, "the liberal movement pursued a double goal. First, it attempted to achieve defining influence on the formation of political will [149] of the state totality, but it also protects the sphere of individual freedom of the citizens, which still remains an object of state action. The liberal movement considered both goals realized when it guaranteed the commensurate influence for the popular assembly on the lawmaking process (Holstein, "Die Theorie der Verordnung im französischen und belgischen Verwaltungs-recht," *Bonner Festgabe für E. Zitelmann*, 1923, p. 362). The primary interest of the public law literature thus revolves around this political distinction between statute and decree. One attempted "to regulate by *statute* all collisions of the state power with persons and property," although R. Gneist (*Rechtsstaat*, p. 159) already correctly recognized that the boundary between statute and decree is to a great extent random. He also recognized that in no state did statute regulate all intrusions into personal freedom and property. The political situation demanded a simple formula in order to demarcate the boundary between statute and decree, in particular, the power of the popular assembly from that of the king. The fundamental, qualitative criterion of the Rechtsstaat concept of law was lost because of this interest in a secondary, though politically useful, criterion of the Rechtsstaat concept of law. The book by G. Jellinek, "Gesetz und Verordnung" (1887), discussed above, is an example of this displacement of theoretic interest.

In the constitutional struggles of the nineteenth century, therefore, it was a matter of establishing that intrusions into freedom and private property may be undertaken "only on the basis of a statute." Also in this regard, the politically simple, but logically false, reversal occurred again. Law is an intrusion into freedom and private property. For example, all of G. Anschütz's discussions of the "substantive" concept of law assumes this perspective. These discussions rest on the correct recognition that every constitutional regulation of legislative authorizations *presupposes* a substantive concept of law. However, they understand this presupposition not in the genuine

Rechtsstaat sense of the concept of the law as a norm with certain qualities, but rather in the sense of the just discussed political concept. Naturally, intruding on freedom and private property cannot be the direct essence of the statute, for all other possible acts, permissible and impermissible, do so as well. The issue concerning this concept of law at the time, 1848, was only to secure constitutionally the popular assembly's consent power in regard to such intrusions and to prevent the princely government from undertaking such intrusions by way [150] of decree without participation by the popular assembly. The actual Rechtsstaat guarantee consists in the fact that such intrusions may be undertaken only on the basis of a statute, whereby the statute corresponds to certain substantive *qualities*. In the context of the political struggle, the differently constituted political-democratic guarantee, which consisted in the popular assembly's consultation power and was directed against princely absolutism, allied itself with this Rechtsstaat guarantee. The Rechtsstaat guarantee directs itself against every absolutism and places substantive limits on *any* political concept of law, be it monarchical or democratic. It does so by assuming that for any legislative intrusion into freedom and property to be considered law, it must contain a norm with certain qualities. In the reality of the political conflict, however, it was always only a struggle against the absolutism present at that time. Consequently, the struggle against the monarchial absolutism existing in 1848 meant a fight for democracy.

3. The ideal of the Rechtsstaat remains in place to thoroughly comprise all possibilities of state action in a system of norms and, through it, bind the state. In practical reality, however, a system of apocryphal acts of sovereignty forms (above § 11, II, p. 108). If this practice is generally recognized today in all manifestations of the bourgeois Rechtsstaat, that lies not in an intentional constitutional regime, but rather in the fact that a political concept of law proves itself stronger in opposition to the Rechtsstaat concept of law. In the sense of democratic constitutional law, for example, it is logically consistent that the popular assembly undertakes such acts of sovereignty, so long as it can identify itself with the people without contradiction. The respect for the Rechtsstaat concept of law seeks to express itself in the fact that the forms of a constitution-amending statute (Art. 76) are respected. In terms of constitutional theory, however, it is necessary to differentiate between them here, and in practical terms the distinction is also meaningful. Above all, it is meaningful because in a democracy that is established in a logically consistent way one must become aware of the actual implications and obviously because the electorate, instead of the parliament, establishes itself as the bearer of the political will. [151]

IV. *The meaning of the general character of the legal norm.*

The organizational achievement of the Rechtsstaat depends on preserving the legal norm's general character. In the central presupposition, not in organizational details, lies what one can designate, using Rudolf *Gneist*'s expression, the "Archimedean point of the Rechtsstaat."

1. The system of the so-called division, or rather the separation of legislation, administration, and adjudication from one another, is only meaningful as long as the law is understood as a general norm. When on the basis of a constitutional rule certain state posts are authorized to issue laws in a special procedure, a concept of law is already self-evidently presupposed. Politically, it would be a misuse of the term *statute*, and, logically, it would be the equivalent of a magic trick, to reverse the relationship between law and general norm by simply designating as law ("law in the formal sense") anything that officially authorized legislative bodies produce via the legislative process. The concept of law in the formal sense, as shown above (II), has a relative and limited legal status. However, it is also impermissible to forget the substantive presuppositions of the distribution of jurisdiction among legislation, administration, and adjudication. When constitutional law makes provision for who should legislate, obviously that does not mean that this legislature should use the procedure for legislation in order to conclude trials or to undertake administrative acts and governmental actions. In a Rechtsstaat, "the law" should rule, and the entire state activity stands under the statutory reservation. The offices authorized for legislating should be directly prevented from establishing, in place of the rule of a norm, their own rule enabling them to no longer distinguish any given individual commands, measures, and orders from "statutes." A merely formal concept of law, such as that law is anything the lawmaking bodies ordain via the legislative process, would transform the rule of law into an absolutism of legislative offices, and any distinction of legislation, administration, and adjudication would be eliminated. If that were valid constitutional law today, the entire Rechtsstaat struggle against the absolutism of the monarch would be ended in the sense that [152] the multiheaded absolutism of the transitory partisan majority would replace monarchical absolutism.

2. The distinctive construction of the Rechtsstaat protection rests on the distinction of the general statutory regulation and the application of these rules by the judge or an administrative official. The intrusion into freedom and property occurs *not by a statute, but rather on the basis of a statute*. In state practice, the guarantee of private property, for example, as one of the foundations of the bourgeois Rechtsstaat, developed into a right to expropriation, whose meaning erodes if the distinction between general statute and specialized statutory application erodes. The regulation of the law of expropriation generally determines under which presuppositions and through which procedure expropriation is permitted. This general norm is applied to the concrete case, and the expropriation is carried out by an act

of administrative officials (distinct from the legislative branch). The statute is the basis for, the general presupposition of, but not the instrument of the expropriation. For this reason, the guarantee of the liberty rights of individuals includes over and over again the turn of phrase that an intrusion into the guaranteed sphere of freedom is permissible only *on the basis of statutes.* Art. 114, for example, provides that "the freedom of the person is inviolable. An infringement on or deprivation of personal freedom by public authority is only permissible on the basis of statutes." Or take Art. 115, which stipulates that "the living quarters of every German is for him a sanctuary and is inviolable. Exceptions are permissible only *on the basis of statutes.*" In the same manner, Art. 153 reads that "the expropriation may occur only *on a statutory basis.*" This provision rules out the possibility that the concrete intrusion, such as the act of expropriation itself, assumes statutory form and, for example, that an expropriation takes place *through* a law in the formal sense. Should such a "statute" be permissible as an exception, the turn of phrase "by statute" is being used appropriately. For example, it is constitutionally mandated in Art. 156 that in the socialization of individual economic enterprises, the Reich can transfer expropriated private economic enterprises into common property *by statute.*

Cf. the examples above II, 2, pp. 144/45. With regard to the law of expropriation, M. Layer, "Principien des Enteignungsrechtes," Leipzig (*Staats- und völkerrechtliche Abhandlungen*, ed. by G. Jellinek and G. Anschütz), 1902, p. 177, remarks:"absolutism has certainly taken it thus far (that in particular the public interest was the legal ground [153] for the expropriation). However, now it is a *statutory norm*, and that is already a great difference." A theoretically and practically interesting instance of this Rechtsstaat distinction between statute and statutory application is found in § 2, 4, of the Prussian mining law of 24 June 1865 and 18 June 18 1907. See Brassert-Gottschalk, *Kommentar zu diesem Berggesetz*, 2d ed., 1913, p. 34, on the deliberations concerning § 2, 4. The house of deputies intended to select this version: "The application takes place by statute." It was altered in the upper house at the suggestion of Dernburg, who suggested that "the application order occurs by statute, because there are practical as well as even constitutional doubts in always regulating application by statute and thereby intruding in the jurisdiction of state executive power." See *Stenographische Berichte* 1907, pp. 294, 341ff. The formulation "on the basis of a statute" (in contrast to "by statute") is simply essential for the Rechtsstaat-type elaboration of the law of expropriation, and the manner of expression of § 164 of the Frankfurt constitution of 28 March 1849 is characteristic of this: "An expropriation can only be undertaken out of regard for the common good, only on the basis of a statute, and in exchange for just compensation." It is symptomatic of the dissolution of the bourgeois-Rechtsstaat consciousness that that type of clear expression was no longer understood and that not one of the commentaries on the Weimar Constitution as yet distinguishes an expropriation on the basis of a statute from an expropriation by statute. Even such an insightful and, moreover, Rechtsstaat-minded jurist as Richard Grau has resisted the attempt to restore the traditional and self-evident distinction (Carl Schmitt, *Unabhängigkeit der Richter, Gewährleistung des Privateigentums, Gleichheit vor dem Gesetz*, Berlin 1926) and to

The Rechtsstaat Concept of Law

contradict the claim that the constitutional regime of the Weimar Constitution was also intended to provide the Reich a *substantive* law of expropriation ("Der Vorrang der Bundeskompetenz," *Festschrift für Heinitz*, 1926, p. 403). For this purpose, he refers to a statement in the *Protocols*, p. 74. The expression of the deputy Delbrück reproduced there states only that it could be necessary in many cases, "for example, if a railroad should go through more states," to regulate the substantive law of expropriation through Reich legislation, whereby "substantive law of expropriation" obviously means something other than the authority to undertake the concrete act of expropriation. Then, Delbrück also continues to speak entirely self-evidently only of "statutory regulation." In this context, Beyerle suggests assigning the law of expropriation to Reich legislation only so far "as there is a need for the issuance of equivalent Reich provisions." He even speaks here only (with the assent of Delbrück) of the Reich as *legislature.* M. Spahn states that "the law of expropriation must be regulated unconditionally in a unified manner, above all in regard to the question of compensation." The misunderstanding of Grau is very characteristic precisely in its confusion of substantive law of expropriation with the concrete act of expropriation.

3. Under the Weimar Constitution, the distinction of law from acts of the administration or of the judiciary receives an even more special meaning, because the Constitution preserves elements of the federal state in the organization of the German Reich. The Weimar Constitution distributes competencies between Reich and individual German Lands such that in its first section it initially designates the objects for which the Reich has jurisdiction in terms of legislation. In regard to administration, by contrast, it adheres to the fundamental principle of Art. 14, under which "Reich laws are executed by the officials of the individual German Lands [154] to the extent that Reich statutes do not provide for something else." In a federal state organization, where the distribution of jurisdictions between the Reich and the individual state is not fully regulated in terms of subject matter, but rather differently according to whether it involves legislation, administration, or adjudication, a complete destruction of the constitutional system would result if the Reich legislature with the jurisdiction over an issue could misuse the form of the statute for any given individual measure, administrative act, decision, etc.

According to Art. 7, 16, for example, the Reich has the legislative jurisdiction for mining. Through this provision, it receives the authority to issue a mining statute. For instance, it can eliminate the Prussian mining statute of 24 June 1865 while it issues a Reich mining statute, but nothing else. It cannot intervene "by law" in the form of a Reich statute in the mining *authority* of the states [Lands] in the individual case and, in an individual state (apart from the explicitly permitted case of Art. 156), for example, order the granting of a mining concession for a particular mine installation. It received no mining *authority* in general. Nonetheless, it acts within its jurisdiction in regard to railroad legislation according to Art.7, 19. The legislative competence for the railroad system does not establish a railroad authority, which, rather, is established in Art. 90. The issuance of a single order in the area of administration does not, consequently, also constitute a "utilization" of the legislative right in the sense of Art. 12, but, depending on the circumstances, it is a violation of Art. 15. Against the misuse of legislation for supervisory purposes, see H. Triepel, *Die Reichsaufsicht*, 1917, p. 129.

4. The bourgeois Rechtsstaat is based on the freedom and the equality of state citizens. That the concept of bourgeois freedom presupposes the concept of law denoted here as pertaining to the Rechtsstaat was discussed above under 2. But also the correctly understood concept of *equality* leads to the same understanding of the statute. Today, almost every constitution states that all state citizens are "equal before the law." The Weimar Constitution has expressed this principle in Art. 109, 1: "All Germans are equal before the law." Equality before the law means not only equal application of a statute that has already been issued, but also protection against statutory violations of the law, dispensations, and the granting of privileges, regardless of their form. From the extensive range of disputed questions to which the principle of the equality before the law led, only one is of interest here. *Equality before the law is immanent to the Rechtsstaat concept of the law.* In other words, law is that which intrinsically contains equality within the limits of the possible, therefore a general norm. There is no equality before the individual command because, in terms of content, it is entirely determined by the individual circumstance of the single case, while the law [155] in the sense of the Rechtsstaat means a normative regulation, which is dominated by the idea of justice, and under which equality means justice. The properly understood concept of equality is bound up with the correctly understood concept of law. Hence where special commands or mere measures are concluded, there is no law and no equality. The order that Mr. X is to be expelled from the Land is not something in reference to which one could reasonably speak of "equality." It involves only an individual, particular person, a single factual situation, and exhausts itself in this command. Faced with the concrete command that Mr. X is to be expelled from the state, it is entirely nonsensical to say that all Germans could be expelled equally as well. Neither Mr. X, whom this command affects, nor some other persons who are not affected by it could be termed "equal" here. Equality is only possible where at least a majority of cases can be involved, in particular where there is a general regulation.

Art. 109, therefore, prohibits exceptional laws in the actual sense, that is to say, statutes directed against a certain person or a majority of particular persons for individual reasons. Even the legislature is bound by this provision. On the controversy, see issue 3 of the *Veröffentlichungen der Vereinigung der deutschen Staatsrechtslehrer*, with the reports by E. Kaufmann and H. Nawiasky, 1927, and H. Triepel, *Goldbilanzenverordnung und Vorzugsaktien*, Berlin 1924, p. 26ff. Cf. Anschütz, *Kommentar*, p. 304; Leibholz, *Die Gleichheit vor dem Gesetz*, Berlin 1925, and *Archiv des öffentlichen Rechts*, new series 12, p. 1ff.; Aldag, *Die Gleichheit vor dem Gesetz in der Reichsverfassung*, 1925; Carl Schmitt, *Unabhängigkeit der Richter*, 1926, and the discussion of the commentary by Anschütz, *Juristische Wochenschrift*, 1926, p. 2271; and E. v. Hippel, *Archiv des öffentlichen Rechts*, new series 11, p. 124ff.

5. Even any further elaboration of the Rechtsstaat and every guarantee that is distinctive of the Rechtsstaat presupposes the general character of the statute. The *independence of judges* from internal administrative commands, for example, has its essential correlate in the *dependence* of judges on the *statute.* Dependence on the statute means something other than dependence on the commands and special instructions of a superior. It even means something quite the opposite. If the legislature may use the form of the statute for individual commands to the judge, the judge is no longer independent, but instead is dependent on the offices authorized for legislation, and if these may use their legislative jurisdiction for special instructions and "imperious orders" to the judge, then through it they are simply the superiors of the judge. Judges are independent only so long as the general character of the statute [156] is retained. Another example is the traditional Rechtsstaat principle *nulla poena sine lege*, which presupposes a general norm and would transform itself into the opposite of Rechtsstaat-like protection, if through a majority decision of the legislative body in the form of a statute, "by law," Mr. X could be condemned to death or thrown into prison. The *factual circumstance* of an action is generally valid today as a prerequisite of a punishment. The concept of the factual character could even be made into the basic concept of a system of criminal law, as occurred in Beling's "Lehre vom Verbrechen" (1906). However, factual circumstance, "typicality," and other ideas above all mean that something is capable of being subsumed under a general norm. The concept of fact in Albert Hensel's system of *tax law* ("Steuerrecht," in the *Enzyklopädie der Rechts- und Staatswissenschaften*, 2nd ed. 1927, pp. 34, 42ff.) found a usage that was typical of the Rechtsstaat in the same way. The concept of factual circumstance is useful for understanding the subordination to authority of those with tax obligations (of the tax debtors, as Hensel says) as a mere consequence of the fact that the state "is entitled, here as in all other areas of legislation, to establish norms, that it, moreover, has to fulfill the purpose of the statute through its own offices under application of its own coercive powers (but only if a concrete claim has arisen through factual realization!)." All these constructions are displaced along with the presupposition of a general norm and show that the subordination of state officials to the statute, every organizational execution of the protection of bourgeois freedom, and every single bourgeois-legal demand rest on this concept of the statute as a general norm. Any other properties of the statute as a substantive-rational, just, and reasonable order have become relative today and rendered problematical. The natural law belief in the law of reason and reason in the law has been displaced to a great extent. What protects the

bourgeois Rechtsstaat against complete dissolution in the absolutism of shifting parliamentary majorities is only the factually still present residue of respect for this general character of the statute. Not as if that were a completely exhaustive definition of law in the material sense. However, it is the general, logical, [157] unavoidable minimum. "The law can be bad, unjust, but this danger is reduced to a minimum because of its general and abstract composition. The protective character of the law, indeed, its *raison d'être* itself, lies in its general character. (Duguit, *Manuel de Droit constitutionnel*, 4th ed. 1923, p. 97; *Traité de Droit constitutionnel*, vol. II, 1923, p. 145f.).

§ 14.

The Basic Rights

I. *Historical overview.*

1. *The American Declarations of Rights.* The Magna Carta of 1215 (above § 6, II 1, p. 45), the Habeas Corpus Act of 1679 (protection against arbitrary arrests and right to judicial hearing), and the Bill of Rights of 1688 (above § 6, II 1, p. 46) are often termed the first declaration of basic rights. They are, in fact, contractual or statutory regulations of the rights of English barons or citizens, which in the course of a gradual development certainly assumed the character of modern principles, but they do not correspond to the original meaning of basic rights. The history of the basic rights, more precisely, first begins with the declarations the American states established in the eighteenth century to justify their independence from England. As Ranke expressed it, this is really the beginning of the democratic, more accurately, of the liberal age and of the modern bourgeois, liberty-based Rechtsstaat, although these American declarations designate themselves still as "Bills of Rights" in connection with the English tradition. The state of Virginia issued the first and, according to G. Jellinek (*Die Erklärung der Menschen- und Bürgerrechte*, p. 18), the model declaration on 12 June 1776, then Pennsylvania (11 November 1776) and others followed. Nevertheless, not all thirteen states of the Union issued such declarations. The federal constitution of 1787 contained no such declaration of basic rights. It first incorporated basic rights in a few supplementary amendments (Amendments 1789–1791). The essential basic rights of these declarations are freedom, private property, security, right to resistance, freedom of conscience, and religious freedom. The securing of these rights constituted the purpose of the state.

According to the prevailing interpretation, which rests on the essay by G. Jellinek, *Die Erklärung der Menschen- und Bürgerrechte*, 4th ed., [158] 1919, the idea of these different basic rights developed out of religious freedom. The controversy over the historical correctness of Jellinek's presentation cannot be entered into here (see a literature comparison by W. Jellinek in the preface of the fourth edition of the just named essay, which he edited; see also Hashagen in the *Zeitschrift für die gesamten Staatswissenschaften* 1924, p. 461; Karl Becker, *Declaration of Independence*, New York 1922; and G. v. Schulze-Gaevernitz, "Die geistesgeschlichtlichen Grundlagen der anglo-amerikanischen Welt-Suprematie," *Archiv für Soziale Wissenschaft* 58 (1927), p. 76 n. 19.

For the systematic treatment of the modern Rechtsstaat, the important thing is that the idea of basic rights contains the fundamental principle of distribution, on which rests the free bourgeois Rechtsstaat that is implemented with logical consistency. That means that the liberty sphere of the individual is *unlimited* in principle, while the powers of the state are *limited* in principle. The state during antiquity knew no liberty rights, because a private sphere with an independent right against the political community appeared inconceivable and the idea of freedom of the individual would be independent of the political freedom of his people and of the state would have been considered absurd, immoral, and unworthy of a free man. Christianity appeared in a world dominated by the Roman Empire, whose political universe included a "cosmos" that was pacified and, consequently, rendered nonpolitical. This characteristic of the political universe ended as the Roman Empire disintegrated with the migration of peoples. But the theory of the entire medieval period retained the idea of the political universal. The pope and the emperor were its bearers. With the sixteenth century, the theory of the political universal, even its fiction, became impossible, because the sovereignty of the numerous states formed then was recognized and the world had obviously now made a transition into the condition of a political universe that was pluralistic. Christianity and the representatives of the Christian church were in an entirely new situation. A new organization of religious life in the form of national churches developed from the state. The theoretical basis of the organization was often very unclear. But, in political practice, it was dominated very clearly by the idea that the definitive grouping of persons is determined by *political* allegiance and religion. Hence, religious life cannot be a private affair. The Baptists and the Puritans first gave a completely new answer. In the logic of their posture toward the state and toward every social bond lay an absolute *privatization* of every religion. However, that did not mean that religion lost its value—quite the opposite. The state and public life generally were rendered relative and devalued. Religion as the highest and the absolute thing becomes the affair of the individual. Everything else, every type of social formation, church as well as state, becomes something relative, and it can derive its value only as a means of assistance to every absolute value, which is alone definitive. That religious freedom represents the first of all basic rights is thus unconditionally correct even without regard to the [159] historical details of the development in a systematic sense. For with it the fundamental principle of distribution is established. The individual as such is the bearer of an absolute value and remains with this value in his private sphere, so his private freedom is something that is in principle unlimited. The state is only a means and, as such, relative, derivative, limited in each of its powers, and controllable by the private sphere.

2. *The French Declaration of the Rights of Man and of the Citizen of 26 August 1789* establishes as the most important basic rights those of freedom, property, security, and the right to resistance, but not freedom of religion or freedom of association. Despite all the historical connections, there is something essentially different here than with the American declarations. The concept of state citizen is presupposed in the French declaration, and an already existing, national state is perpetuated there. Unlike what occurred in the American colonies, a new state system is not established on a new foundation. As stated in the introduction, the French declaration should offer a celebratory reminder to all members of the community of their rights and privileges. By complying with these rights, the state authority should gain greater respect. The new distributive principle of private freedom, therefore, does not appear in its unconditional logic. It does

so, rather, only as a modifying element in the context of an existing political unity.

The later French constitutions (1793, 1795) once again contain declarations of rights in unchanged form. However, the 1795 constitution (the Directory Constitution) contains, according to the heading, not only declarations of rights but also the duties of persons and of citizens. The constitution of 4 November 1848 refers to the principles of 1789. The currently valid constitutional laws of 1875 contain no special declarations. The human and civil rights of 1789 are valid even without special proclamation as the self-evident foundation of the state order (cf. above § 12, I 4, p. 128).

3. In Germany on 27 December 1848 (section VI, §§ 130ff. of the constitution of 28 March 1849), the Frankfurt National Assembly proclaimed, under the heading "The Basic Rights of the German People," the right to accommodation and emigration, equality before the law, freedom of the person, privacy of mail, freedom of opinion, freedom of belief and conscience, freedom of assembly and association, private property, and the right of [160] access to ordinary courts. The Frankfurt Federal Assembly of 1851 declared the constitutional work of the Frankfurt National Assembly null and void. Strongly under the influence of the Belgian constitution of 7 February 1831, the Prussian constitution of 30 January 1850 contains the catalog of rights as it was elaborated in the course of the nineteenth century: equality before the law, personal freedom, inviolability of living quarters, access to ordinary courts, prohibition of exceptional courts, inviolability of private property, freedom of emigration, freedom of religion (nevertheless, the Christian religion provides the basis for institutions connected to the exercise of religion), free expression of opinion, freedom of the press, freedom of assembly, and freedom of association.

Bismarck's Reich Constitution of 16 April 1871 contains no such catalog of "basis rights."

The heading of the Weimar Constitution's Second Principal Part is "Basic Rights and Duties of the Germans." Under this heading, one finds in part the rights that are typically enumerated, such as equality before the law in Art. 109, personal freedom in Art. 111, inviolability of living quarters in Art. 115, privacy of the mail in Art. 117, right of the free expression of opinion in Art. 118, freedom of assembly in Art. 123, freedom of association in Art. 124, and private property in Art. 153. This section also partly contains diverse individual provisions and programmatic principles, etc. The right of access to ordinary courts and the prohibition of exceptional courts stand in the First Principal Part under Art. 105.

4. In January 1918, the All-Russian *Soviet* Congress proclaimed a Declaration of the *Rights of Working and Exploited Peoples*, which became section I in the constitution of the Russian Soviet Republic of 5 July 1918.

According to the Bolshevik reading, the basic rights of a free, bourgeois Rechtsstaat are only the instruments of the capitalist rule of private property. In the proclamation of 1918, the principles of a new state system are supposed to be set up. The private property in land, mineral and water resources, and factories and banks are eliminated, and the struggle against the imperialism of capitalist powers, the brotherhood of all the workers and of the exploited of the world, and the freedom of the exploited people of Asia and the colonies are proclaimed. "In order to ensure a true freedom of conscience to those who work, the church is separated from the [161] state and education from the church; the freedom of religious and antireligious propaganda is legally accorded to all state citizens." Freedom of the press and freedom of association and assembly are valid only for the working class and those involved in agriculture. Added to this is a series of other political provisions. In its first part, the constitution of the Union of Socialist Soviet Republics of 6 June 1923 contains only a "Declaration on the Founding of Socialist Soviet Republics," in which the opposition to world capitalism is proclaimed, but it does not contain the enumeration of the 1918 declaration. Nevertheless, this is repeated in the constitutions of the individual member states, especially in the constitution of the Russian Socialist Soviet Republic of 1925 (cf. Alexejew, "Die Entwicklung des russischen Staates in den Jahren 1923–1925," *Jahrbuch des öffentlichen Rechts* XIV, 1926, pp. 324, 402).

II. *The historical and legal significance of the declaration of basic rights.* The declaration of basic rights means the establishment of principles on which the political unity of the people rests and whose validity is recognized as the most important presupposition of the fact that this unity always produces and forms itself anew. It also means that the integration of the state unity occurs, in the words of Rudolf Smend. If through a great political act a new state system is founded or through a revolution a completely new principle of state integration is established, then a declaration is a natural expression of the intention, in the decisive moment, to give a certain turn to its own political destiny. That holds true for the declarations of the American states of 1776, for the French declaration of 1789, and for the Russian one of 1918. In these instances, the "proclamation of a new state ethos" is involved, the "constitutive total purpose" of the constitutional being of the state is "announced in triumphant form" (Smend, "Bericht," *Archiv des öffentlichen Rechts*, New Series, 1927, p. 105). In Germany, the attempt that the 1848 Revolution made in this direction failed. The Bismarckian constitution of 1871, as Smend aptly stated, received its state ethos from the monarchical states, which formed the federation. These states generally had a catalog of "basic rights" in their constitutions, so that even the practical goal of a new proclamation faded from view. The Weimar Constitution of 1919 was entirely different. In its introductory text, it states that [162] the German people is motivated by the will, through this constitution, to "renew and strengthen its Reich in freedom and justice, to serve internal and external peace, and to promote social progress." In the second main section, alongside the catalog of so-called basic rights as it was formed in the course of the nineteenth century, one still finds additional fundamental declarations. And the question is to what extent is the proclamation of a "new state ethos" present in a manner similar or identical to the other great historical precedents? Friedrich Naumann consciously intended to provide such a proclamation (*Protocol*, p. 176f.). Influenced by the Russian declaration of "rights of the working and exploited peoples," he stated that "the most recent contemporary constitution, the Bolshevik-Russian constitution of 5 July 1918, is, so to speak, the direct rival of the constitution that we are now producing." Consequently, for the new German state, which was meant to be neither a bourgeois-individualist nor a Bolshevik-socialist state, but rather a social one, he wished to affirm its ideal foundations and principles. If that did not come about, it would be a "deficiency in the body of the state that we want to restore." But the Weimar National Assembly did not share the political pathos of this way of thinking. The Constitution's second main section only amounted to a jumbling of diverse principles, an interfactional compromise program that, because of its "mixed character" (*Protocol*, p. 186), cannot be equated with the great precedents. Such proclamations do not "produce" themselves according to just any wishes and ideals, however well intentioned, but rather presuppose that through its declaration a people assumes the risks of a completely new political grouping based on an understanding of friend and enemy, and is resolved to defend the new principles of its state in the struggle even against a powerful external political enemy. The signing of the Versailles Treaty, however, preceded the declarations of the Weimar National Assembly.

The historical-political significance of the "Basic Rights and Duties of the Germans" of 1919, therefore, is different than that of the proclamations of 1789 or 1918. Nevertheless, the principles established in the Second Principal Part of the Weimar Constitution have fundamental significance for the constitutional and public law of the German Reich. They contain a comprehensive political decision of the [163] German people concerning the type of their existence, and they provide the German Reich in its present form the character of a constitutional democracy. In other words, it is a constitutional state resting on democratic principles, yet one that is modified by the principles of the bourgeois Rechtsstaat. Legislation, adjudication, and administration receive their definitive guidelines through it. No German law may be interpreted or applied in contradiction to them, and no German law may nullify a genuine basic right. These fundamental principles can be eliminated neither by simple statute nor by a constitution-amending statute according to Art. 76. Instead, they may be eliminated by a new act of the constitution-making power of the German people.

III. *Substantive distribution of the basic rights.*

1. The basic rights are distinguishable from other constitutionally secured and protected rights. Not every basic right in the Rechtsstaat constitutions is guaranteed by a constitutional rule, and vice versa, nor does every protection against amendment through simple statute by itself signify a basic right. Art. 129, 3, 3, constitutionally guarantees that civil servants have a right to the privacy of personal papers, and Art. 149, 3, guarantees that theological faculties are retained in universities, but these do not constitute basic rights. Rather opaquely, any possible demand and right considered important is designated a basic right and "anchored in the constitution." For a concept that is useful in scholarly terms, one must affirm that the basic rights in the bourgeois Rechtsstaat are only such rights that can be valid as rights *prior to* and *superior to* the state and that the state confers not according to the standard of its laws. Instead, the state recognizes that these rights are given prior to it and protects them on this basis. The state also accepts that it may intrude on these rights only to a degree that is in principle definable and then only through a regulated procedure. According to their inner nature, therefore, these basic rights are not legal entitlements, but rather spheres of *freedom*, from which rights, more precisely, defensive rights, stem. That character of rights is most clearly evident in the liberty rights, which historically signify the beginning of the basic rights. Under this idea, freedom of religion, personal freedom, property, right of free expression of opinion exist *prior to* the state and receive their content not from any statutes or according to the standard of statutes or within the limitations of [164] statutes. On the contrary, they designate the free play of individual freedom, which is, in principle, unregulated. The state *facilitates* their protection and herein generally finds the justification of its existence. The individual's *right to resistance* is the most extreme instrument of protection of these rights. It is not merely an inalienable right, but also one that is not organizable. It is essentially part of the genuine basic rights.

The great historical portrayal of the theory of the right to resistance that K. Wolzendorff provided in his book, *Staatsrecht und Naturrecht*, Breslau 1916, fails to recognize that the individual right to resistance has a suprastate quality that does not lend itself to organization. Wolzendorff especially praised the theories and drafts of Condorcet, through which the right to resistance of the individual is "diverted" into a legal organization. But this organizing and "diverting" only means that the individualistic right to resistance transforms itself into a mere legal instrument and that the human and liberty rights transform themselves into a right to petition for redress, which is granted, regulated, and rationalized by the state. The funda-mental principle of distribution—specifically, human freedom, which is in principle unbounded, and the state, which is in principle bounded—is thereby given up. The individual no longer has basic and liberty rights, but instead has certain procedural opportunities for seeking redress "according to the standard of the law."

2. The basic rights in the actual sense are essentially rights of the free *individual person*. They are rights, in other words, that the individual per-son has against the *state*. What Richard Thoma (*Festgabe für das preußische Oberverwaltungsgericht*, 1925, p. 187) says applies to every genuine right. "Basic right guarantees," he argues, "are pauses in the eternal pendular process of *the man versus the state*" [Schmitt's English in italics]. Part of this concept of rights, however, is the understanding that the individual, by virtue of his own "natural" right, comes into opposition to the state and may not eliminate entirely the idea of individual rights that are prior to and above the state, so long as one can speak at all of basic rights. Rights that are delivered over to the whim of an absolute prince or to a simple or quali-fied parliamentary majority cannot genuinely be designated basic rights. Basic rights in the actual sense are only the liberal human rights of the individual person. The legal meaning of their recognition and "declaration" is that this recognition signifies the acknowledgment of the fundamental distributional principle of the bourgeois Rechtsstaat, which is a sphere of individual freedom that is in principle unlimited and an opportunity for intrusion by the state that is in principle limited, definable, and subject to review. That these genuine basic rights are valid for every person without regard to state membership is a further consequence of human rights exist-ing prior to the state. They are individual rights, or, put differently, rights of the isolated individual person. Basic rights in the [165] actual sense are hence only individualistic liberty rights, not social demands.

Among these rights are freedom of conscience, personal freedom (in particular protection from arbitrary arrest), inviolability of living quarters, privacy of the mail, and private property. In regard to these liberty rights, the single individual is considered isolated. The Weimar Constitution enu-merates them in the first section of the Second Principal Part under the heading "The Individual Person." Under this heading, in fact, rights other than actual basic rights are also enumerated, while the individualistic proto-right, freedom of religion and conscience, is treated in the third section under the heading "Religion and Religious Societies" (Art. 135, 136).

But even the rights of the individual in connection with other individuals must still be considered genuine basic rights as long as the individual does not leave the nonpolitical condition of mere social relations and so long as only the free competition and the free discussion of the individual is recog-nized. Such rights, however, could easily lose their nonpolitical character and thereby cease to be individual liberty rights. They could also no longer correspond to the distributional principle, and then they could even lose the absoluteness of the principle's protection along with their individualistic-human character. The necessity of regulation and legislation then results from the fact that these rights do not remain in the sphere of private relations. Instead, they contain social catalysts, which include the free expression of opinion, freedom of speech and of press, freedom of worship, free assembly, and freedom of association and of collaboration. As soon as the freedom of collaboration leads to coalitions, or associations, that struggle against one another and stand opposed to one another with specific, social instruments of power like strikes or lockouts, the boundary of the political is reached and an individualistic type of basic and liberty right is no longer present. The right to form coalitions, right to strike, right to work stoppage are not liberty rights in the sense of the liberal Rechtsstaat. When a social group gains such opportunities for struggle, whether through express constitutional provisions or through acquiescence in the practice, the basic presupposition of the liberal Rechtsstaat simply no longer applies, and "freedom" still does not mean the individual's opportunity for action, which is in principle unlimited. On the contrary, [166] it means the unhindered exploitation of social power through social organizations.

3. All genuine basic rights are *absolute* rights in that they are not guaranteed "according to statutes." The content of such rights results not from the statute. Instead, the statutory intrusion appears as an exception to them, as the generally regulated exception that is limited and definable in principle. It is part of the bourgeois Rechtsstaat's fundamental distributional principle that the freedom of the individual is presupposed and the state limitation appears as an exception. Also, the Weimar Constitution's manner of expression often (not always) corresponds to this principle, whose significance Kurt Häntzschel (*Zeitschrift für öffentliches Recht*, V, 1926, pp. 18/19) showed at the same time he demonstrated the importance of this distinction between absolute and relative basic rights. Art. 114, for example, states that "the freedom of the person is inviolable. An infringement or deprivation of personal freedom by the public authority is permissible only on the basis of statutes." Or take Art. 115, which provides that "the living quarters of every German is for him a sanctuary and is inviolable. Exceptions are permissible only on the basis of statutes." It is similarly the case with Art. 117, which reads, "the privacy of letters as well as of the mail, telegraphs, and telephone calls is inviolable. Exceptions can be established only by Reich statute." As Häntzschel states, other rights recognized by the Weimar Constitution are "relative from the outset in that they are guaranteed 'within the limits of' or 'according to statute,'" such as the freedom of occupation or of contract in Art. 151, 3, which stipulates that "the freedom of trade and occupation is

ensured according to Reich statutes." See also Art. 152, which provides that "during economic transactions, contractual freedom is valid according to statutes." Even private property is apparently not an absolute right in the formulation of Art. 153. At this point, a contradiction between the first and second clause of the article reveals itself. "Property is guaranteed *by the Constitution!* [Schmitt's italics and exclamation point]. Its content and its limits are derived from statutes" (cf. p. 172).

The language of the constitutional rule is not always clear and unambiguous. That expresses itself very noticeably in the most important social liberty right, in the origin of all other social liberty rights, and in the presupposition of the liberal idea of free discussion, the right of free expression of opinion with its consequences for freedom of speech and the press. Art. 118 states with a turn of phrase that is subject to misunderstanding that "every German has the right, within the limits of general laws, to express freely his opinion through word, writing, imprint, image, or in any other manner." The words "within the limits" appear to designate a limited right from the beginning [167], such that the right of free expression of opinion in the Weimar Constitution would not be treated as an absolute basic right. This result, which, however, is actually improbable, is also not justified by the obviously unclear wording. The history of this clause's origins (cf. *Oberverwaltigungsgericht*, vol. 77, p. 514) offers no special opportunity for enlightenment. One could discern from it that in the formulation "within the limits of the general laws," the word *general* can simply be left out, because it entered the text through an editorial change (likewise Kitzinger, *Reichsgesetz über die Presse*, p. 203). The formulation would then mean that the right of free expression finds its boundaries in statutory provisions for the protection of other legal instruments. However, this is not yet going so far as to say that the idea of the basic rights' distributional principle—that the freedom of the individual is in principle unbounded and the possibility of limitation through the state is in principle bounded—is displaced altogether.

According to Häntzschel ("Reichspressgesetz," *Archiv des öffentlichen Rechts* X, 1927, p. 228) and Rothenbücher ("Deutscher Staatsrechtslehrertag," *Archiv des öffentlichen Rechts* XIII, 1927, p. 101), the word *general* in the formulation "within the limits of general laws" can be left out. It also refers not only to criminal laws (as in Art. 124), so that the protection is more limited under Art. 118. However, all statutes and administrative measures directed against the expression of opinion as *such* should be excluded. "General laws" in the Art. 118 sense would all be statutes that protect a legal entitlement without direct regard to a particular opinion that deserves protection in itself. In this context, Rothenbücher rightly emphasizes that "opinion" signifies a public position of the fundamental type. Even Smend ("Bericht," *Archiv des öffentlichen Rechts*, new series 13, p. 107) distinguishes among protected legal entitlements, and yet he incorporates a balancing of interests into the question, which could easily render relative the absolute value of the entitlement of free expression of opinion. "General laws in the sense of Art. 118," he argues, "are statutes that have precedence over Art. 118, therefore, because the social entitlement protected by them is more important than the freedom of opinion." That no longer corresponds, however, to the idea of the fundamental distributional principle. A liberty right is not a right or entitlement that can enter into a balancing of interests with other entitlements. For the principle of basic rights, there is nothing more important than freedom, and the question is only finding the standard to limit state intrusions, statutes as well as administrative acts, to make them definable and, through this, subject to review.

The prevailing opinion today seems to incline toward recognizing that limitations of the right of free expression of opinion resting on a statutory foundation continues to be valid as before and that under the general laws are understood not only criminal laws but also police authorizations like § 10 II 17 *Allgemeines Landesrecht* [General Law of Prussia] (Anschütz, *Kommentar*, p. 323; R. Thoma, *Festgabe*, 1925, p. 213). For individual provisions, however, (for example § 9 of the Prussian statute of 12 May 1851 or § 5 of the Reich press statute) exceptions are once again made. Art. 118 should eliminate them. The correct interpretation may incline toward recognizing that the words "within the limits of the general laws" mean only the general statutory reservation. Yet there is an adverbial sense to the word *general* that means "as is generally the case with basic rights." It also means that the principle of the general character of the statutes, which is part of a truly general statutory reservation, may be violated and, at the same time, that the court ruling that a statute directed against the right of free expression of opinion as such is impermissible. Herein lies the great meaning of Rothenbücher's thesis.

The formulation of Art. 118, which is acknowledged as unclear and ineffective, eliminates this basic right not as a genuine basic right. In the Weimar Constitution, it should be guaranteed with the usual catalog of basic rights, but with two special limitations. The first is to facilitate a campaign against artistic trash and filth as well as for the protection of youth [168] during public performances and showings (Gesetz zur Bewahrung der Jugend vor Schund- und Schmutzschriften vom 18. Dezember 1926, *Reichgesetzesblatt* I, p. 505). The second is to grant constitutional permission for film censorship (Lichtspielgesetz vom 12. Mai 1920, *Reichgesetzesblatt*, p. 953). This last limitation is of special interest for the development of the liberal basic rights in general, for it shows that with the increasing intensity of the social subordination of the individual and with the changes in communication technology, the traditional liberal principle of distribution is displaced and the idea of the unlimited freedom of the individual becomes a mere fiction. Because a certain technology of communication and of imparting opinion, film technology, is excepted from the means of free expression of opinion, the liberty right of the free expression of opinion is apparently already given up. Nevertheless, it may perhaps be said that film technology does not signify a technology of expression of opinion in the same sense as writing and printing. As Rothenbücher aptly stressed, opinion in particular means public expression of opinion of fundamental importance. Regarding the freedom of expression of opinion, it is, in fact, a matter of the principle of free discussion, which for the liberal idea is the actual means of integration of a social unity. Discussion presupposes, however, first, human thoughts and, second, thoughts expressed through human language. Writing and print (the press) are means of the dissemination of ideas. Film, by contrast, so far as it is not simply posted writing, is only image and mimetic portrayal. It is not language and thinking mediated through the spoken or written human word. It is not a bearer of a genuine discussion. An ideal justification for it may lie in the fact that the entire film technology is exempted from the right of the free expression of opinion. Otherwise, it is precisely this meaning of film that shows how much the demand for liberal discussion has diminished. The political problem of the influencing of the masses through film is so significant that no state can leave this powerful psycho-technical apparatus uncontrolled. The state must remove film from politics, neutralize it. In fact, because the political is unavoidable, the state must place it in the service of the existing order, even if it does not have the courage to use it openly as a means of integrating a social-psychological homogeneity.

4. The essentially *democratic* rights of state citizenship are a thoroughly different type. They can also be designated as basic rights, but in an entirely different sense than the individualistic liberty rights. A dualism of the basic rights corresponds to the dualism of the components of a modern constitution of the Rechtsstaat variety (below § 16, p. 200). The democratic rights of state citizenship presuppose the state citizen, the *citoyen*, living in the state, not individual free persons in the extra-state condition of "freedom." This means these democratic rights have an essentially political character. As political status rights (G. Jellinek) or as rights of peoples (Fleiner, *Bundesstaatsrecht*, p. 288), they are rightly distinguished from the individual basic rights. The most important contrast lies in the fact that they cannot in principle be unlimited, cannot be "liberties," and, as such, they do not correspond to the distributional principle of the genuine basic rights. For they operate *inside* the state and involve only a certain, defined degree of participation in state [169] life. They are dominated by the democratic idea of equality and should be conferred on every state citizen in the same scope. According to their nature, they are not valid for foreigners because otherwise the political community and unity cease to exist and the essential presupposition of the political existence, the possibility of the distinction of friend and enemy, is undermined. Among these democratic rights are equality before the law (Art. 109), the right to petition (Art. 126), which, correctly interpreted, is a right of the state citizen and not a general human right, the equal electoral and voting right of the individual state citizen (Art. 22 and 17, respectively), and equal access to all public offices according to capacity (Art. 128).

5. Constituted differently, on the other hand, the essentially *socialistic* rights of the individual are dependent on the positive services of the state. They cannot be unbounded, for every right to the service of another is limited, as is the case, however, with a right of all to state services. That type of right presupposes a state organization that incorporates the right-holding individual. In this way, this individual's right is already rendered relative. It is *conditioned*, specifically, by a rationalizing organization that includes the individual, directs him to his place, and measures and responds to his claim. When a constitutional law proclaims the "right to work," it does not intend to establish a right that is unbounded in principle. Such a "right to work" can exist only in a system of organizations, reports, medical investigations, labor procurement and directives, and obligations for the provision of directed labor, as organized welfare services or in the form of a labor mediation or unemployment insurance, as under the German law of

16 July 1927 (*Reichgesetzesblatt* I, p. 187). According to its logical and juristic structure, such a right stands in opposition to the genuine basic and liberty rights, and it is consequently misleading to speak indiscriminately of "basic rights." The right to work, the right to social welfare services and support, and the right to noncompensatory training and instruction (Art. V 17 of the Soviet constitution of 1918 and Art. 145 of the Weimar Constitution, which is not as extensive) are all examples of this type of right. Art. 119 of the Weimar Constitution supplies another example when it stipulates that "families with many children have a claim to the protection and the social welfare services of the state." Take also Art. 163, 2. "Every German should be granted the opportunity to earn his living through productive labor. To the extent that an appropriate opportunity for work cannot be found for him," it continues, "his [170] necessary living needs will be provided for. Details are determined through special Reich statutes."

IV. *Institutional guarantees are distinguishable from basic rights.*

1. Constitutional provisions can guarantee particular institutions special protection. The constitutional provision can then have the goal of preventing elimination of these institutions by way of simple legislation. In an imprecise formulation, one often also speaks of basic rights, although the structure of such guarantees is logically and legally entirely different from that of a liberty right. Basic rights are not involved, even when subjective rights of individuals or of corporations are linked with the institutional guarantee, which is not necessarily the case. The institutional guarantee is intrinsically limited. It exists only [171] inside the state and is not based on the idea of a sphere of liberty that is in principle unlimited. Instead, it involves a legally recognized institution, which is always something defined and limited and which completes certain tasks and achieves particular goals. Also, the tasks in detailed form may not be specialized and may permit a certain "universality of effect."

These institutional guarantees include the so-called basic rights of localities, for example § 184 of the 1849 Frankfurt constitution. Every locality has as basic rights under its constitution (a) the election of its leaders and representatives and (b) the independent administration of local affairs including the local police under the supervision of the state, which is mandated by statute. Art. 127 of the Weimar Constitution declares that localities and associations of localities have the right of self-government within the limits of law.[1] This principle contains a constitutional guarantee. Specifically, the legal right of self-government is guaranteed by a Reich constitutional law, so that the institution of communal self-government as such cannot be eliminated, and all statutes that, according to their substantive content, completely destroy communal self-government or deprive it of its essential resources are unconstitutional under the Weimar Constitution. By contrast, this provision does not guarantee a right to existence, for example, for the individual locality or for the individual association of localities. Consequently, annexation of one locality against its will is possible under Land law. Also, for example, the content of the legal norms

Summarizing overview of the 1st, 5th, and 6th individual rights considered here

Liberty rights of the isolated individual	Liberty rights of the individual in connection with other individuals	Rights of the Individual in the state as state citizen	Rights of the individual to services of the state
Freedom of conscience Personal liberty Private property Inviolability of Living quarters (privacy of letters)	Free expression of opinion Freedom of speech Freedom of the press Freedom of worship Freedom of assembly Freedom of association (Freedom of coalition already the transition into the political)	Equality before the law Right of petition Equal right to election and to the vote Equal access to public office	Right to work Right to social welfare and support Right to a guardian, training, and instruction
Liberal, individualistic guarantees of the individual sphere of liberty, of free competition, and of free discussion		Democratic-political rights of the individual state citizen	Socialist (diluted social) rights and claims

for self-government under individual Land law, the status quo on 14 August 1919, is not determined. These norms, moreover, can be changed at any time through simple Land statute. In this regard, Art. 127 of the Weimar Constitution distinguishes itself from Art. 70 of the 1920 Prussian constitution, the status quo of which is, according to current legal circumstances in Prussia, distinctly a matter of self-government, so that limitations are only permissible via a statute amending the Prussian constitution.

Other examples of institutional guarantees are the prohibition of exceptional courts (right of access to the ordinary courts) in Art. 105, marriage as the foundation of family life (Art. 119), and Sunday holidays in Art. 139. The wording of the Weimar Constitution regarding private property is contradictory and unclear. Under Art. 153, property is ensured alongside the concrete right of property as a private law institution, as is the right to inheritance (Art. 154). That the Weimar Constitution guarantees private property as an institution, however, cannot mean that it is no longer treated as a basic right. It can mean, though, that the Constitution intended to make private property relative. In public law terms, it also cannot denote that the guarantee of private property through Art. 153 would have a meaning other than the declaration of the inviolability of personal freedom. Personal freedom, naturally, can never be an institution. On the other hand, private property can, indeed, be considered something prior to the state, a natural right existing before all social order, yet it can also be considered a mere statutory institution. Art. 153's formulation makes it appear doubtful whether a [172] basic right is recognized or only an institutional guarantee is intended. The wording of the second clause in Art. 153, 1, "Its content and limits (specifically of property [Schmitt's parenthetical addition]) are derived from statute," contradicts the basic right of the first clause, for the content of a genuine basic right, that of personal freedom, for example, simply does *not* stem from the statute. It is, rather, given prior to it. So under the Weimar Constitution, it would be impermissible to define the content of private property by statute, such that the "whims of authority" (M. Wolff), which lie in the established concept of property, would be transformed into a sum of enumerated individual rights. In the first clause, the guarantee of property is meant as the recognition of a principle, not as the constitutional guarantee of a title without content, because there cannot be a bourgeois Rechtsstaat without private property, and the Weimar Constitution is intended as a *constitution* of the bourgeois-Rechtsstaat variety.

The provisions of the Weimar Constitution regarding *civil servant rights*, by contrast, contain a genuine example of institutional guarantees. They secure the retention of a professional civil service, which "should be servant of the collective and not of a party" (Art. 130). In other words, civil servants should be protected from the state-dissolving consequences of a parliamentary practice characterized by plundering and rigid allegiances. The guarantee of the well-earned rights of civil servants (Art. 129, 1, 3) certainly benefits individual civil servants. It even establishes a subjective right for civil servants. These subjective rights reach beyond legal claims regarding property and wealth to also include those to title and rank, though they do so with different types of legal protection. They even extend to activity in accord with legal and administrative norms (cf. *RGZ*, vol. 104 p. 58; vol. 107, p. 6). All that, however, does not serve the private interests of the civil servant. Instead, it serves the institution of the professional civil service as such. Consequently, a statute that in principle eliminated the professional civil service would be just as unconstitutional as a statute that eliminated communal self-government, the family, or the right to inheritance. There are, therefore, institutional guarantees with and without subjective rights. Even the legal protection and the possibility of redress of claims are constituted very differently. To the essence of the institutional guarantee, however, belongs neither a subjective right nor maintenance of open access to legal channels. [173]

The constitutional guarantee of the freedom of science and for the teaching of science (Art. 142), the so-called "basic right of the German University" (R. Smend, "Staatsrechtslehrertagung 1927," *Archiv des öffentlichen Rechts* XIII, p. 107), also contains an institutional guarantee. Not a basic right in the genuine sense, this provision intends a constitutional protection against elimination through the legislature, as is characteristic of the institutional guarantee. The same is true for the guarantees of Art. 149 concerning religious instruction as a compulsory course of study in schools and the retention of the theological faculties in the universities.

2. There cannot be basic rights of a natural or organized *community* inside of the state. Among these so-called basic rights, an institutional guarantee is present. The family as such can have no basic right in the genuine sense, no more so than can one of its members. The family can only be protected constitutionally as an institution. The same is true of localities or associations of localities. The character of a legal subject can be conferred on the institution; subjective rights can be constitutionally ensured. And it would have been possible, for example, to confer such subjective rights on the localities and associations of localities, while they retained in Art. 127 (in contrast to § 184 of the Frankfurt constitution of 1849) only an institutional guarantee without subjective rights. But even such subjective rights are only constitutional rights, not genuine basic rights in the sense of the fundamental distributional principle of the bourgeois Rechtsstaat. All these institutions exist *inside* of the state, not before it or above it. The genuine basic right presupposes as given the individual with his or her liberty sphere, which is in principle unbounded. An institution cannot be presupposed as given in such a way. The modern state is a closed political unity, and it is, by its nature, *the* status. In other words, it is a total *status*, which renders relative all other forms of *status* inside of itself. The state cannot recognize a status internal to its own that is inalterably prior to or superior to it, the state, and that, therefore, has a public law character with rights equal to the state. To the same limited degree can intermediary organs extend into the state's sphere, either standing above the state or existing independently alongside it. To every such inalterable status that is independent of it, the state cannot have relationships of a public law variety. It cannot have internal relations, in other words, only international legal ones. [174]

The state can constitutionally guarantee subjective rights of the most diverse type for an already organized community that is independent of it. The state can even confer a right to existence. Even those are not basic rights in the genuine sense. When a church, such as the Roman Catholic Church, claims for itself rights prior to and above the state, that can lead to a *contract* between state and church. Then the contract is an act of international, not of public, law, and the state as a closed unity encounters the church as such. The content of this contract may also be provided with constitutional guarantees. More specifically, it is stabilized as constitutional law during the transformation into domestic law. Hence emerges the distinctive protection of such constitutional guarantees. However, international legal obligations of that kind are not part of the constitution of a state and are in no sense the basic rights of those granted rights under international law.

When a state has obligated itself under international law to treat the members of a minority in a certain way, and this obligation with the character of a constitutional provision is transformed into domestic law, no right of the minority as a collectivity emerges. The usual treaties protecting minorities, which have been concluded in different states of eastern and middle Europe since 1919 (above § 7, IV 5, p. 74), contain guarantees of the freedom and equality of the individual members of a minority and rest on the idea of the general human rights of the individual. To this extent, they are basic rights. When beyond this, minorities are guaranteed an extensive so-called autonomy and the minority as such is organized, that signifies an institutional guarantee with or without subjective rights, but not a genuine basic right.

3. The international-law "basic rights" of the states remain out of consideration here. Inside a federation, every member state has a right to existence, which can also be designated a "basic right." But this designation is meant self-evidently in another sense than as a basic right of the individual in the bourgeois Rechtsstaat (cf. below § 29 on the problem of the federation). The "basic" or "fundamental" rights of the imperial electors or other estates of the old German Reich do not need to be discussed. On this issue, see above § 6, p. 44.

V. In the bourgeois Rechtsstaat, *basic duties* are nothing other than constitutional obligations. When they are limited, they can only be duties in the positive-law sense. Duties that are in principle unbounded would contradict the idea of the bourgeois Rechtsstaat. Hence every duty exists only "according to the law," which defines the presupposition and content of the duty. When the Weimar Constitution speaks of basic duties, [175] it is noteworthy that the logical and legal structure of these basic duties is different from that of the basic rights. As Reichstag deputy Düringer rightly remarked in the deliberations of the constitutional committee of the Weimar National Assembly (*Protocol*, p. 184), according to the original idea there are only basic rights, no basic duties of the individual. Because of the nature of the state, the recognition of basic duties takes on the character of a purely liberal Rechtsstaat, and the declaration of the basic duties in the Weimar Constitution's Second Principal Part should just serve this purpose and should emphasize the social character of the German Reich in opposition to the principles of individual freedom. The basic rights are only duties of the state members or state subjects, in particular those persons who stand in the sphere of state power, not duties of humanity generally.

Take, for example, Art. 132: "According to law, every German has the obligation to undertake voluntary activity," a provision that does not yet by itself establish a concrete duty, but instead refers to the statutory provision that renders this duty concrete. Similarly with Art. 133: "All state citizens are obligated, according to law, to provide personal services for the state and the localities." It is exactly the same with Art. 133, 2, 1, which reads, "Mandatory military service complies with the provisions of the *Reich Defense Law.*" See also Art. 145, 1, p. 1, stipulating that "there is a general obligation to attend school." In toto, these basic duties of the Weimar Constitution do not eliminate the bourgeois Rechtsstaat character of this constitution. Its "mixed character" reveals itself in clauses, such as Art. 163: "Without detriment to his personal freedom, every German has the moral duty to activate his spiritual and bodily forces such that it advances the well-being of the whole society."

VI. *Division of the basic rights in regard to the legal protection against state limitations and intrusions.*

1. On the distinction of absolute and relative basic rights, see above III 3. The genuine basic right of the individual is always absolute and corresponds to the Rechtsstaat principle of distribution, according to which the freedom of the individual is in principle unbounded, while the authority of the state is in principle bounded.

From this absolute and in principle unrestricted quality of individual freedom, it does not follow that intrusions and limitations are completely excluded. But they appear as an exception that is calculable, definable, and controllable according to presupposition and content. Such exceptions may only come about on the basis of statutes, whereby statute is understood in the sense of a general norm under the Rechtsstaat concept of law and does not mean just any single act of the king or of the legislative body [176] that has the form of law. Basic and liberty rights stand under the statutory reservation. The protection accorded these rights resides in the fact that the statute in the Rechtsstaat sense must have certain substantive properties, with which it satisfies the idea of the Rechtsstaat principle of distribution (above § 13).

Limitations on personal freedom, etc., are permissible on the basis of statutes, simple statutes in particular, such as those concerning criminal procedure, for example. It must not be overlooked here that in practical terms a certain degree of intrusion has routinely developed. Even where indeterminate concepts, taken abstractly, appear to provide limitless opportunities for intrusion, a drawing of boundaries occurs in practice. Thus, the administrative court review of the police in particular has also reordered the so-called general jurisdiction of the police in the sense of the Rechts-staat statute and, in this way, produced a bounded quality and rendered it definable in principle. The best-known example of such a "general dele-gation" is the § 10 II 17 of the General Law of Prussia, which serves as the legal foundation for police authority: "The office of the police provides the necessary institutions for the preservation of public peace, security, and order and for the deflection of dangers facing the public or its individual members." In this regard, every individual term has led to a series of legal precedents that makes the police intervention calculable and definable and provides ordinary content to the concepts "maintenance" of "public secu-rity" and "order," etc., thereby facilitating court supervision. This series of precedents has even come up with restrictive rules for the so-called police emergency (for example, a mere duty to tolerate, not an obligation to inter-vene actively). Where the normal presuppositions of this practice are not given and, consequently, more extensive, indefinable intrusions become necessary for the case of the *state of exception*, the possibility of a suspen-sion, or the temporary setting aside of the basic rights, is provided for con-stitutionally, as under Art. 48, 2 (above § 11, II, p. 110).

It is frequently said that the positive legal significance of the basic rights consists in the fact that they establish the principle of the "legality of the administration." Otherwise, one seems to assume that to the extent that ex-press constitutional orders do not forbid it, every intrusion into the sphere of liberty that the basic rights ensure [177] is permissible through statute or special statute. Hence, the statutory reservation is misunderstood because the Rechtsstaat concept of the statute is not correctly recognized. It is just as imprecise and misleading to speak of an "authorization" by statute. In regard to the Rechtsstaat significance of the basic rights, of the Rechtsstaat concept of law, and of the fundamental distributional principle contained in them, this "statutory reservation" and the Rechtsstaat principle of legal intrusions into the sphere of liberty must be defined as limitations on the freedom that the basic rights ensure can only occur *on the basis of a statute*, which is to say a general norm, through an act of *statutory application*.

2. The protection of bourgeois freedom ensured by the recognition of basic rights exhausts itself, however, not in this statutory reservation, but rather extends itself even further. The recognition of basic rights in the sense of the bourgeois Rechtsstaat signifies that the Rechtsstaat principles of a modern, free, bourgeois constitution are recognized as an essential component of the constitution itself. That means that these principles are part of the substance of the constitution and, indeed, may be modified by

constitutional legislation; yet their complete elimination is more than a mere constitutional revision. It would thus be incorrect to claim that any statute that eliminates the bourgeois basic and liberty rights could come about by way of a constitution-amending statute under Art. 76. This error is only possible as long as the fundamental distinction of constitution and constitutional law is overlooked. The purpose of a constitutional revision is changing constitutional laws, not eliminating the constitution. Extensive limitations of liberty rights are possible by way of a constitution-amending statute. To the degree that the practice of apocryphal acts of sovereignty is possible (above § 11, II, p. 108), even statutory violations of the Constitution and one-time measures are permissible. However, a statute produced via the procedure of Art. 76 that eliminates personal freedom or another recognized basic right altogether and that would provide an official discretion for incalculable intrusions would be unconstitutional because it abolishes the basic right.

Duguit's view ("Manuel," p. 486, *Traité de Droit constitutionnel*, 2nd ed., vol. III, pp. 561/2) that the liberty rights of 1789 cannot be eliminated [178] through a constitution-revising statute rightly applies to every constitution of the bourgeois Rechtsstaat variety. Thought out to its logical conclusion, however, this principle must lead to the distinction between constitution and constitutional laws (cf. above § 2, p. 26). The fact that the genuine basic rights as an essential, in particular positive-legal, component of the constitution stand above the constitution's *legal* order also certainly underlies Art. 130 of the 28 March 1849 Frankfurt constitution, which provides that "the following basic rights should be guaranteed to the German people. They should become a norm for the constitutions of the individual German states. *No constitution or legislation* of an individual German state should ever eliminate or restrict them." The superiority of the basic rights even over constitutional laws is certainly obscured by the fact that a *federal* regulation of the relationship between the Reich and individual states is established, while at the same time the relationship of basic rights and constitutional law is apparently not addressed insofar as it is an affair of the Reich. Moreover, an analogous lack of clarity is evident in the basic rights of the federal constitution of the United States of America (Boutmy, *Etudes*, p. 94ff.). But apart from this federal law aspect, the question remains whether basic rights can be eliminated by way of a constitution-amending statute. This question was posed by the 18th Amendment of the constitution of the United States of America (prohibition of alcohol). But it was also handled primarily from the perspective of a federal state (William L. Marbury, *Harvard Law Review* 1919/20, p. 223ff.; above § 11, II, p. 106). Nevertheless, it is also of interest in this connection that the question of principle regarding the boundaries of the authority for constitutional changes has also not yet been decided in American practice.

3. Even though with varying degrees of effectiveness, the guarantee of every genuine basic right directs itself first to the posts with the jurisdiction for constitutional revisions, and, in particular, it does so differently depending on whether these offices emerge as bearers of the constitutionally assigned authority for constitutional revisions or as bearers of the au-

thority for apocryphal acts of sovereignty (p. 108). Such a guarantee next directs itself to the posts with jurisdiction for the issuance of simple statutes and finally to the remaining state officials, especially the so-called executive. The opposition movement *against the executive* became noticed primarily or almost exclusively as a result of the political struggles of the liberal bourgeoisie, which in Europe worked principally against monarchical absolutism. The primary interest of this movement aimed at preventing intrusions and restrictions stemming from royal decrees and at subjecting the administration, in particular the police, to law in the form of statutes, thereby enforcing the principle of the legality of *administration*. Because of this historically declared interest in a definite aspiration for basic rights, their principled meaning often remained unnoticed. Entirely overlooked was the central distinction of the general statute as the *foundation* of the concrete act of legal application. Consequently, the variable content of this guarantee's different goals [179] was also overlooked. And because today the legality of administration, in particular that of the police, has become something self-evident, one can—erroneously—treat these basic rights as "useless."

In regard to their legal status, R. Thoma, *Festgabe*, presented the following distinctions among the "basic rights." Some have *"constitutional force,"* in his terms. More specifically, an exception cannot be made on the basis of a simple statute, but rather only by virtue of a constitutional provision and on the basis of a constitution-amending statute. Hence the right of access to ordinary courts and the prohibition of exceptional courts (Art. 105) both have constitutional force. Other, and indeed most, basic rights only have the *"force of law"*; that is to say, exceptions and limitations can be established by simple statute. In this regard, one must again distinguish between whether the Weimar Constitution requires a Reich statute (the so-called *force of Reich statute*, for instance in Art. 117; exceptions from the privacy of the mail can only be declared permissible by Reich statute; or Art. 112, which stipulates that emigration can only be limited by Reich statute) or whether an individual Land statute also facilitates such limitations and intrusions (the so-called basic rights with the *force of individual Land statutes*). Remarkable in this regard is the fact that the most important and fundamental basic rights, such as personal freedom and the inviolability of living quarters (Art. 114 and 115, respectively), only have the force of individual Land statutes, and because the principle of the legality of administration became something self-evident, they are practically "useless." In contrast to this, one must reaffirm the belief that every genuine basic right has constitutional force and cannot be eliminated by constitution-amending statute. Even independent of the principle of the legality of administration, the scope of limitations established by legislation is measured according to the principles of the Rechtsstaat statute, and every basic right also binds the legislature, the Reich as well as the Land legislature. Therefore, it is in no way "useless" when one ignores the principle of the legality of administration as something self-evident.

That R. Thoma can distinguish "constitutional force," more precisely, the "force of constitutional law," from basic rights with merely the "force of law" is explicable first of all from the fact that the concept of the basic rights was impermissibly extended to the most diverse constitutional guarantees, so that, in particular, institutional guarantees could be intermingled and confused with basic rights. In fact, the institutional guarantee establishes a special protection against simple legislation, and Thoma's expression "force of constitutional law" is most apt here. The clearest example of a right with constitutional force is the right of access to ordinary courts, which is guaranteed in Art. 105, specifically with the wording "Exceptional courts are unacceptable. No one may be removed from the jurisdiction of a judge established by law." It is certainly rightly assumed that these two clauses have the same content in the sense that the second sentence is the more general and the prohibition of exceptional courts is only a further specification of the right of access to ordinary courts (E. Kern, [180] *Der gesetzliche Richter*, 1927, p. 234). Moreover, this provision is an exceptional instance of equality before the law (Art. 109). However, this "right of access to ordinary courts" means, in fact, an institutional guarantee. It shows especially clearly how exceptional guarantees enter into the Constitution on the basis of certain historical and political experiences, in order to give effect to a protection against the misuse of the legislative jurisdiction. Another example of this type of special protection is the prohibition of criminal statutes with retroactive force and ex post facto laws, such as Art. 116, which provides that "an action can only be punished when its punishable character was determined by statute before the action occurred."

Such constitutional guarantees are explicable in concrete historical terms from the concern for specific dangers, which one fears because of certain experiences. They serve only indirectly the basic rights' principle and are not themselves "basic rights." They contain a special protection against the misuse of legislative authority, a special guarantee for the security of the separation of powers and for the preservation of the Rechtsstaat concept of law. They prohibit an act of sovereignty by the legislature, which constitutes a rupture of the valid legal order. For the case of an extraordinary endangerment of state security and order, it is necessary to have a special type of regulation that eliminates any of these constitutional bonds and that has led to the elaboration of legal concepts such as state of war, state of siege, and state of exception. A "statutory reservation," in other words, a provision that is determined in advance, definable, general, and subject to review, is only meaningful in regard to genuine basic rights, but not in regard to such institutional guarantees. "Ordinary court," for example, presupposes a court organization and a jurisdictional order, not an unbounded liberty sphere in which one can intervene on the basis of the statutory reservation. The diversity of the constitutional guarantees reveals itself still more clearly when a positive individual provision is constitutionally guaranteed, such as, for example, religious instruction as a compulsory subject in schools (Art. 149, 1, p. 1) and the right of civil servants to the privacy of personal papers (Art. 129, 3, p. 3), etc. It is self-evident that such "guarantees" have "constitutional force." However, it would certainly misconstrue the positive principle of a [181] modern Rechtsstaat constitution if one intended to give such accidental details of the constitutional order a more secure guarantee than the fundamental principle of the basic rights themselves.

4. Several instances of unclear constitutional provisions in the Second Principal Part of the Weimar Constitution are also ultimately explicable from the great lack of clarity over the diverse nature of constitutional guarantees and from the misuse propagated by the term *basic right*. It must be reaffirmed that in a bourgeois Rechtsstaat only the liberty rights of the individual person are considered basic rights because only they can correspond to the fundamental distributional principle of the bourgeois Rechtsstaat, which is a liberty sphere that is unbounded in principle and state authority for intrusions that is bounded in principle. All other rights, however important they are considered and regardless of the legal force of the guarantees and explicit commitments they receive in the constitutional order, can always only confer rights that are limited in principle. That applies to all institutional guarantees. The recognition of the different rights of civil servants, which the Weimar Constitution established in Art. 129 and Art. 130, shows the difference very clearly. Art. 130, 2, provides that "all civil servants are guaranteed the liberty of their political conscience and the freedom of association." At this point, a general human liberty right is combined in a contradictory manner with an institutional guarantee. The civil servant has as such a special status with all that such a concept entails. This status does not exhaust itself in a series of individual commitments. The civil servant has the duty of fidelity, of professional compliance, of official silence, of a dignified bearing even outside the office. This special status is very different from that of being a general "person." One can say that the concept of the civil servant was always very suspect to the radical representatives of bourgeois liberalism. But, in this regard, the Weimar Constitution definitely intends to continue the great tradition of the German civil servant state despite the altered state form and to preserve for the German people the distinctive strengths and values of this civil service. Hence arose the institutional guarantees of Articles 129 and 130. In a manner characteristic of the mixed character of the Weimar Constitution, two principles [182] are again placed side by side and the possibility of conflict is ignored. If implemented with logical consistency, a freedom in the sense of a general human right, which is unlimited in principle, must eliminate the concept of the civil servant. For it would be inconceivable that in regard to his subjective rights

and entitlements the civil servant may lay claim to the advantages and distinctions of his special status, but in regard to his duties he is permitted to make recourse to the in principle unrestricted individualistic "liberties" of the liberal isolated person, the freedoms, in other words, of the non–civil servant. If the civil service should be retained as an institution, then in cases of conflict the special status of the civil servant should be given priority. The status obligations of civil servants have full priority over the guarantees of the freedom of association and of the freedom of political conscience. The fact that certain preexisting limitations on the freedom of association and on the free expression of opinion are being eliminated restricts the meaning of these constitutional guarantees under Art. 130. Otherwise, it remains a fundamental distinction whether the general human right of the freedom of conscience and of association of the single person is secured or whether, under retention of the institution of the civil service, such "liberties" are guaranteed to the civil servants. In the one case, it is a matter of a genuine basic right, which is presupposed as a liberty sphere that is in principle unlimited. The other case involves constitutionally legislated special provisions in connection with an institutional guarantee.

§ 15.

The Separation (So-Called Division) of Powers

The separation of powers contains the second principle of the Rechtsstaat component of a modern, free, bourgeois constitution.[1] It is the organizational principle, the execution of which should ensure that all grants of state power are definable and subject to review.

I. *The historical origin of the separation of powers theory.*

The experiences that the English people had with the rule of their Parliament during the first English Revolution led to theoretical and practical attempts to distinguish and separate the different [183] areas of the exercise of state power from one another. The most important and fundamental distinction that resulted was between law as an enduring, general norm that is binding for all, even for the legislature itself, a law, consequently, that may not violate the constitution in an individual case, and the other instances of the exercise of state will. Cromwell's "Instrument of government" of 1653 counts as the first example of a practical attempt at this division (above § 4, II, p. 40). In opposition to the Parliament he had dissolved three times, Cromwell generally strove to create a strong government capable of acting. In connection with these experiences arose a theory of the necessity of the separation and of the reciprocal control of the different branches of state activity. Harrington (*Oceana*) attempted to draft a complicated system of reciprocal controls and limitations. Locke (*Treatises on government*) distinguished the legislative authority, which establishes general, a priori, stable rules, from the executing and federative power. This final one is the power for external affairs that cannot be bound to general norms, because it is too dependent on the changing foreign policy situation (*Civil government*, § 147, cf. Schmitt, *Die Diktatur*, p. 42). Also already found in Locke is the oft-repeated justification of the separation of the legislative and executive powers that it is not good when the same persons who make the laws also apply them, because a statute immediately loses its character as law when the legislature can use the form of the statute for any given individual commands and measures. It is noteworthy that this justification applies fully to a system of "irreconcilabilities," of incompatibilities. Connected with the distinction of several "powers" is the further organizational idea of introducing additional divisions inside the state realms of activity already distinguished in this way, in order to achieve a maximum of the means of supervision and restriction (checks and controls). The distinction facilitates not only the separation of powers, because otherwise a disconnected jumble of isolated state activities would arise; rather, it also has the goal of producing a balance, or "equilibrium," among them.

The idea of a counterpoise, of a "balance," of opposing forces has dominated European thinking since the sixteenth century. It expresses itself in the theory of the foreign policy balance (at first, of the five Italian states among themselves, then of the European balance of power). It is also expressed in the [184] balance of imports and exports as the trade balance; in the theory of the balance of egoistic and altruistic impulses in the moral philosophy of Shaftesbury; and in the theory of balance stemming from attraction and repulsion in Newton's theory of gravity, etc. On this, cf. the references in *Diktatur,* p. 103. See additionally Karl Pribram, "Die Idee des Gleichgewichts in der älteren national ökonomischen Theorie," *Zeitschrift für Volkswirtschaft, Sozialpolitik und Verwaltung* XVII, 1908, p. 1ff., which views the theory of the static balance between the collective phenomena of the human economy as something peculiar to all mercantilist theories.

The actual progenitor of the constitutional-theoretical teaching of the balance of powers is Bolingbroke, who propagated the idea of a reciprocal control and balancing, however, only in politically engaged writings and essays, not in a systematic exposition. The expressions that he used for this are reciprocal restrictions, reciprocal control, reciprocal delay and detention, etc. Of special significance for the ideal constructions of the English constitution is an idea of the tripartite balance and of the "equilibrium of powers," out of which the free government results: king, upper house and lower house; between king and Parliament (specifically, upper house and lower house taken together), between legislature and executive, between the prerogatives of the king and the freedom of the people. All these should be "balanced." The most important writing on the topic, *The Idea of a patriot King,* 1738, merits consideration. See additionally, the "Dissertation On parties [sic]," 1733/4. The writings mostly appeared as essays in the weekly publication "The Craftsman," 14 volumes, 1726–1736. On this, see Walter Sichel, *Bolingbroke and his Times,* London 1901, II, p. 250 ff. The definitive terms read: to check, to controul, to counterwork, to arrest, to restrain [English in Schmitt's original]. Other expressions appear in the philosophical and in the assorted works (Edinburgh 1775 and 1779). The "patriotic king," as Bolingbroke conceives him, is the chief executive, who already bears the confidence of the people. This is an idea that, according to Richard Schmidt (*Der Volkswille als realer Faktor des Verfassungslebens und Daniel Defoe, Verhandlungen der Sächsischen Akademie der Wissenschaft,* 1924, Vol. 76, p. 34), is traceable back to Defoe, who saw in the people's public opinion a power that could protect the minister against Parliament. All these ideas are of great significance for the construction of modern democracy. Cf. below in the section on the parliamentary system, § 24, p. 304.

Under the influence of Bolingbroke, Montesquieu drafted an ideal image of the English constitution in the famous chapter 6 of the 11th book of his "Espirit des lois" (1748). The definitive statement runs: "In every state, there are three types of public power, the legislative power, the executive foreign power, and the executive domestic political power. On the basis of the first power, the prince or governing authority issues new laws for a certain time or in perpetuity, and he improves or eliminates the older laws. On the basis of the second power, he declares peace or war, sends and receives emissaries, provides for security, and responds to hostile attack. On the basis of the third power, crimes are punished and civil law disputes are settled. This last one is the judicial power." On this third power, *Montesquieu* makes use of the rather suggestive saying that it is "to a certain [185] degree not present," "en quelque façon nulle."[2] Therefore, only the distinction between the legislative and executive branches remains of genuine interest. This principle already makes clear that the executive is by no means only defined by legal application, but rather by the actual activity of the state. Also, it would be incorrect to assign the current practice of the rapid and voluminous production of laws to Montesquieu's "legislative" branch. The goal of his distribution (division) of the different branches of state activity is one power checking the other. "*Le pouvoir arrête le pouvoir.*" In this way, a counterpoise, a balancing, should be achieved.

In the 1787 federal constitution of the United States of America, the system of separations is consciously applied and enforced. In other words, not only are reciprocal checks and controls enforced, but effective *separations* of power are also instituted to a great extent. The legislative branch (divided again into two chambers, the House of Representatives and the Senate, which together form the Congress, that is to say, the legislative body) is separated from the executive (the president), and, when possible, a direct negotiation between both is avoided. The president (the government or executive), consequently, does not have his own power of initiative. This is even the case when he is presented a draft statute to which he objects. Such objections can only be overturned by a two-thirds majority decision of the house from which the draft originates.[3] The president has no power of dissolution against both houses. He is not dependent on the confidence of this legislative body, etc.

The constitution of the year 1791, the first constitution of the French Revolution, speaks for the first time of a *separation* of powers (séparation des pouvoir[s], instead of division, cf. Duguit, *Manuel*, p. 316ff.). Nevertheless, to the same limited degree as the American federal constitution, an absolute separation, more accurately isolation, cannot be instituted. More precisely, a system of reciprocal checks and connections is produced that corresponds to the idea of a balance. [186]

A great multiplicity of expressions and of perspectives on the general principle of organization of the separation of powers derives from this overview. The most general and comprehensive expression may be the phrase "separation of powers" suggested here. "*Separation*" means a complete isolation, one, however, that serves as a point of departure for the wider organization and then in the extended order again permits some connections. "*Division*" correctly means a distinction *inside* one of the several powers, for example, the division of the legislative power into two houses like a senate and a house of deputies (W. Hasbach, *Die parlamentarische Kabinettsregierung*, 1919, pp. 3/4). In this way, a typical organizational schema arises with three powers, legislative, executive, and adjudicative. This triad is generally established, although theoretically perhaps additional "powers" could be and were in fact construed. As noted, there is no constitution of the bourgeois-Rechtsstaat variety whose organizational structure is not dominated by the principle of the separation of powers.

II. *Separation and balancing of powers.* There are two perspectives regarding the separation of powers. First of all, there is the institution of a *separation* of the highest state officials and their jurisdiction, then the establishment of a connection, the reciprocal influencing and *balancing* of the authorities of these distinguished "powers." A certain separation is necessary, so that a distinction is possible. If it can also be instituted without interruption to the point of a complete isolation, it is first and foremost to be viewed as an independent perspective of this organizational principle itself.

1. The schema of a strictly implemented *separation* must result in the legislative, executive, and judicial branches representing three organizations of state activity that are detached from one another. No officials and no part of a department may simultaneously belong to another department, so that the most strictly defined incompatibility exists, in particular an incompatibility between the position of a deputy of the legislative body and that of a civil servant of the state administration, even that of a minister. No administrative civil servant may serve as judge. No judge may serve as administrative civil servant, nor may an official of one department exercise jurisdiction that, according to its substantive content, belongs in the other one. No official of one department may exercise an official power over an official of another one. It would belong to the logic of this strictly implemented separation that the legislative bodies may exercise no influence on the government. A parliamentary government, one that is dependent on the confidence of the majority of the legislative body, would contradict this [187] strict separation and, for this reason, is avoided in the constitution of the United States of America. From the necessity of the separation, however, one could even draw the conclusion that no judicial control over acts of the legislature may take place, which means that the judicial review of the constitutionality of laws, as the highest court of the United States of America exercises it, runs against the logically instituted schema of a separation of powers. In these examples, it is already evident that in regard to the system of a "separation of powers," it is in no way a matter of a historically concrete organization that would be executed fully in every detail, but rather only of a theoretical schema whose construction clarifies the organizational principle.

In the following, it is appropriate to portray one such theoretical schema. Specifically, L = *legislative*, E = *executive* (specifically, government and administration together or one of both; government can once again signify the head of state, king or state president, or the cabinet), J = *judiciary.*

Theoretical Consequences of a Strict Separation:

1. No Effect of E on L (Government in Opposition to Parliament)

(a) *The government has no authority to convene parliament.*

According to Art. 24, "The Reichstag assembles every year on the first Wednesday of November at the seat of the Reich government. The president of the Reichstag must convene it earlier, if the Reich President or at least a third of the members of the Reichstag demands it. The President has an indirect authority to convene the parliament, but the Reich government does not have one as such. According to the federal constitution of the United States of 1787, the president has the authority to convene Congress only in extraordinary cases. It is exactly the same for the executive according to the French Constitution of the Year III (1795, Constitution of the Directory). According to Art. 1 and 2 of the French Constitutional Law of 16 July 1875, the president of the Republic has the authority to convene the chambers of the legislature.

(b) *The government does not have legislative initiative.*

That is the case with the federal Constitution of the United States, though the statutory draft is presented to the president, who signs it and supplies it with remarks.

It is different with Art. 68, according to which the Reich government suggests and passes draft statutes. Moreover, there is the Reichstag's right of statutory initiative. [188]

(c) *No joint vote on statutes.*

It was different under the German constitutional monarchy. Take, for example, Art. 62 of the Prussian constitution of 30 January 1850, according to which statutes come about through a collaborative decision of the king and of both chambers.

A distinctive feature of the federal Constitution of the United States is that the objections of the president against the draft statute can only be overturned with a two-thirds majority of the house from which the draft statute originated.[4] Cf. note b above.

(d) *No enabling acts and no delegation of the legislative jurisdiction.*

Cf. the Constitution of the Year III (1795 Constitution of the Directory), Title V, 45, according to which the legislative body cannot at all delegate its functions to one or more of its members or anyone else. It is different with German public law practice, which contains numerous enabling acts with often boundless delegations (cf. on this H. Triepel, *Verhandlungen des 32. deutschen Juristentages,* 1921, p. 16, and Poetzsch, ibid., p. 42ff.; H. Triepel, *Goldbilanzen-Verordnung und Vorzugsaktien,* 1924, p. 7ff.).

(e) *No executive veto.*

The Weimar Constitution permits no veto by the President or by the Reich government; by contrast, it offers other opportunities for influence (cf. below f).

The French constitution of 1791 offers an example of a suspensive veto by the king.

(f) *No order of a popular initiative by E opposed to a decision of L.*

For a contrasting instance, see Art. 73, 1, which provides that "(a) statute concluded by the Reichstag is to be subjected to a popular initiative before its promulgation, if the President decides to do so within a month."

(g) *No preparation and promulgation of the statute by E.*

The constitutions of the constitutional monarchy and Art. 7 of the French Constitutional Law of 16 July 16 1875 (the president of the Republic promulgates laws) provide otherwise. Additionally, Art. 70 of the Weimar Constitution stipulates that "the President has to process statutes arising in a constitutional manner and promulgate them in the Reich Legal Gazette within the legally required one-month period."

(h) *No dissolution of the legislative body by E.*

It is different with the constitutions of the constitutional monarchy, Art. 5 of the French Constitutional Law of 25 February 1875 (without practical effect since 1877), and Art. 25 of the Weimar Constitution, which reads: "The President can dissolve the Reichstag, but only once for the same reason." [189]

(i) *No authority for pardons by E.*

On the point that the king's authority for pardons was perceived as a violation of the principle of the division of powers and as an intrusion into the legislative branch, see Redslob, *Staatstheorien,* p. 347.

The constitutions of the constitutional monarchy provide otherwise. See, for example, Art. 3 of the French Constitutional Law of 25 February 1875 and Art. 49 of the Weimar Constitution stipulating that "the President exercises the right of pardon for the Reich."

(k) *Freedom from accountability and immunities of the deputies in regard to courts and other officials.*

This is the case with almost all modern constitutions. Take, for example, Art. 36 of the Weimar Constitution, according to which "no member of the Reichstag or of an individual Land parliament may be prosecuted judicially or internally at any time because of his vote or because of statements made in the exercise of his duty or otherwise be made accountable outside of the assembly." Additionally, see Art. 37 of the Weimar Constitution. "No member of the Reichstag," it provides, "or of an individual Land parliament, without approval of the house to which he belongs, may be investigated or arrested during the session because of an action subject to criminal sanction, whether the member is apprehended in the act or at the latest during the following day. The same approval is necessary for any other limitation of personal freedom that impinges on the exercise of the deputy's duty. Every criminal trial against a member of the Reichstag or of an individual Land parliament and every arrest or other limitation of his personal freedom is abrogated on demand of the house to which he belongs for the duration of the legislative session."

Even more extensive privileges of the members of legislative bodies are justified with arguments from the separation of powers. Hence the exemption of deputies from military service and parliament's authority to recall deputies from the front during wartime. On this issue, cf. the report on Accambray's proposed statute, in the book by Léon Accambray, *Qu'est ce que la République?* Paris 1924, p. 356, with the interesting statement by Josef Barthélemy. If parliamentarians could be mobilized for military service, the parliament may not convene; but if the parliament may convene, the parliamentarians may not be mobilized. Note the reference to the separation of powers already in the Convention of 1793, p. 358. The draft statute on the organization of the nation in times of war of 1927 contains the rule expected in these circumstances. It provides that the members of the government who conduct the war and the members of parliament, which is the expression of national sovereignty in war and peace, remain at their duties during the mobilization; if they wish, however, they can join their unit.

(1) *Strict execution of incompatibilities.*

To derive the entire theory of incompatibility from the separation of powers corresponds especially closely to the French understanding (thus Pierre, [190] *Droit politque, électoral et parlementaire*, I, p. 316). This is already clearly the case with the constitution of year 1791 (Title III, Cap. I, Sect. III, art. 4, 5). Even the wideranging incompatibility between the position of a civil servant and that of a deputy, which today is still valid French law, is mostly justified in this way. Art. 21, 2a, of the Weimar Constitution, corresponding to Art. 7, 3, of the Prussian constitution of 1850, provided that "if a member of the Reichstag assumes a compensated Reich office or in a federal state a compensated state office; or if a Reichstag member enters into an office in the Reich or state service that is connected to a higher rank or with a higher remuneration, the member loses his seat and vote in the Reichstag, and he can only regain his position in it through an election." Otherwise, extensive incompatibilities are foreign to German public law ("excluding civil servants from the popular assembly at least does not correspond to German circumstances," according to G. Waitz, *Grundzüge der Politik*, 1862, p. 65). Civil servants (the Prussian Land councils in the Land parliament!), whose participation one was loath to renounce, sat in parliaments. The principle of the separation of powers was mostly overlooked (cf. the ignorant remark in the essay by W. Clauss, *Der Staatsbeamte als Abgeordneter*, Karlsruhe, Heft IX of the *Freiburger Abhandlungen*, p. 5, which until 1927 was the single monographic treatment in the German public law literature). The single systematic expression in the prior German public law literature is found in E. Kaufmann, *Bismarcks Erbe in der Reichsverfassung*, p. 72. The case of a genuine incompatibility in the Reich Constitution of 1871 resulted from the Reich's federal state structure. According to Art. 9, 2a, "no one" could "simultaneously be member of the Bundesrat and of the Reichstag." It is certainly explicable only as an aftereffect of the long struggle against this Art. 9a. that under the Weimar Constitution there is not one instance of an incompatibility between membership in the Reichstag and that in the Reichsrat, whereas in Prussia there is indeed an incompatibility (Art. 33, 2, of the Constitution of 1920) between the Land parliament and the state council. In Art 44, the Weimar Constitution contains an incompatibility that is very important in terms of principle, one that arose from the principle of the separation of powers: "The President cannot simultaneously be a member of the Reichstag." Other incompatibilities of currently valid public law include § 123 of the Reich Budget Order of 31 December 1922, *Reichgesetzesblatt* II, 1923, p. 17 (incompatibility between membership in the Reichstag and the Budgetary Court) and in § 1, 2, of the Code of the German Reich Rail Company, Addendum to § 1, 2 of the Law on the German Reich Rail Company of 30 August 1924 (*Reichgesetzesblatt* II, p. 281). "The members of the administrative council (of the Reich Rail Company)" it provides, "must be experienced experts in the economic life or in the technical aspects of the railroads. They may not be members of the Reichstag, of a Land parliament, of the Reich government, or of a Land government."

Other incompatibilities resting on organizational and structural differences are foreign to German public law, [191] in particular the irreconcilability of a religious office with that of a parliamentary deputy that follows from the difference between church and state. On this, see the discussions in Tocqueville, *La Démocratie en Amérique*, I, p. 358, who views this incompatibility as a safeguard of democracy in America. On so-called *economic* incompatibilities, see below § 19, II, 2, p. 255. Concerning the important question of the incompatibility of parliamentary deputies and civil servants, a significant change of the sense of this irreconcilability is noteworthy, one that is demonstrated in Werner Weber's distinguished 1928 Bonn dissertation on incompatibility. The earlier goal was protection of the independence of deputies (incompatibility in this regard, therefore, is also treated under the separation of E from L). Today, under the rule of parliamentary majorities, the opposite sense becomes valid with the protection of the moral and substantive integrity of civil servants against partisan influence and allegiance.

2. No Influence of L on E

(Parliament opposed to government and administration)

(a) *General prohibition of the preemption of executive acts by L.*

One such preemption is found in Art. 46 Title V of the Constitution of the Directory of the Year III (1795). Today, such a general prohibition is no longer expressed because of the budget law of parliament and its authority for parliamentary supervision.

(b) *No selection of the chief of state or of the government by L.*

Art. 2 of the French Constitutional Law of 24 February 1875 is quite different in that it provides that the president of the Republic is selected by a "national assembly," which is a legislative body arising in such a way that both chambers (Senate and House of Deputies) convene as one body. Also different is Art. 45 of the Prussian constitution of 1920. There the Land parliament selects the minister president without deliberation, and the minister president appoints the other state ministers (the chief of state, however, appoints the state ministry).

The Weimar Constitution, by contrast, strictly implements the principle of the separation (according to the model of the federal Constitution of the United States). Art. 41, 1, stipulates that "the Reich President is elected by the entire German people," while, according to Art. 53, "the Reich Chancellor is appointed and dismissed at his suggestion; the Reich ministers are appointed and dismissed by the President." In this regard, however, cf. section d. below.

(c) *No complaint authority and no court claims of L against E.*

By contrast, see the system of ministerial and presidential complaint by the Chamber of Deputies, with the power of judgment of the other chamber (upper house) serving as a state high court. Hence Art. 9 of the French Constitutional Law of 24 February 1875, discussed above § 12, 5b, p. 135. [192]

The Weimar Constitution honors the perspective of separation insofar as a special Staatsgerichtshof for the German Reich decides on the complaint raised by the Reichstag, Art. 59. (above p. 135).

(d) *No dependence of the government on the confidence of the parliament (no vote of no confidence).*

Hence, the federal Constitution of the United States of America of 1787, the French constitution of 1791, and the constitutions of the German constitutional monarchy.

Art. 54 of the Weimar Constitution differs: "The Reich Chancellor and the Reich ministers require the confidence of the Reichstag for the execution of their office.

Each of them must resign if the Reichstag withdraws its confidence through explicit decision."

(e) *No petition of L for the removal of the chief of state by popular vote.*

Contrast Art. 43 of the Weimar Constitution. "Before the expiration of the term (the period of office of seven years)," it reads, "the President can be removed by popular vote at the instigation of the Reichstag. The Reichstag vote requires a two-thirds majority. By this decision, the President is prevented from further exercise of the office. The rejection of the removal by the popular vote counts as a new election and results in the dissolution of the Reichstag."

(f) *No consent of L to the criminal prosecution of the chief of state.*

Art. 43, 3, is different. It stipulates that "the President cannot be prosecuted under criminal law without consent of the Reichstag."

(g) The very strong, but indirect effects of L on E, which lie in parliament's *budgetary authority,* are not considered a violation of the principle of the separation of powers, so long as the parliament restricts itself to the mere supervision of the budget law and avoids direct instructions and interventions.

3. No Effect of E on J
(Government and administration vis-à-vis adjudication)

The guarantees of *judicial independence,* especially the irremovable and irreplaceable status of the judicial office, facilitates this separation of E and J. Art. 102 of the Weimar Constitution reads that "judges are independent and subject only to the law," while Art. 104 provides that "judges of ordinary judicial claims are appointed for life. They can be deprived of their office against their will, either permanently or temporarily or be placed in another position or into retirement, only by virtue of judicial decision and only for reasons and under the forms that are set by law. Legislation can establish age limitations at which judges enter retirement." These provisions of the Weimar Constitution are placed entirely in the [193] context of the typical Rechtsstaat guarantee of this separation. The organization of a special *administrative adjudication* is also established with the separation of E and J. Cf. section 4a.

4. No Effect of J on E
(Adjudication in contrast to administration)

(a) *Establishment of special administrative courts.*

The establishment of special administration courts constitutes a rejection of ordinary court review of state administration, hence the rejection of the pure adjudicative state. See above § 12, II, p. 132.

(b) *Institution of special courts for the resolution of jurisdictional conflict.*

§ 17 of the German law of judicial organization provides that Land legislation can transfer to special officials the task of resolving disputes between courts and administrative officials or administrative courts over the accessibility of the legal process.

(c) The raising of a complaint of the so-called *conflict during the criminal prosecution of or civil law challenges to civil servants.*

The conflict induces the administrative official to remove the trial from the ordinary courts and bring about a settlement or at least (for the question of exceeding official authority) a preliminary judgment of an administrative official or of an administrative court. The Prussian statute of 16 November 1920 (*Gesetzessammlung* 1921, p. 65) eliminated this cause of removal.

5. No Effect of L on J

(Parliament in contrast to court doctrine)

(a) *Constitutional guarantee of judicial independence.* (On this, cf. section 3 above.)

(b) *Rechtsstaat concept of law.*

Impermissibility of individual commands and of parliamentary justice (above § 13, p. 155).

(c) *No parliamentary investigative committees with judicial powers.*

Art. 19 of the 1920 Danzig constitution provides that "investigative committees may not intervene in a pending judicial or internal administrative review."

The Weimar Constitution does not contain any of that type of guarantee of the separation of L and J. "The Reichstag," according to Art. 34, "has the right and, on petition of one-fifth of its members, the duty to initiate investigative committees. In public proceedings, these committees raise the evidence that they or the petitioners deem necessary. . . . The courts and administrative officials are obligated [194] to comply with formal requests from these committees for the production of evidence; official documents are to be presented to them on demand. The provisions of the law of criminal procedure finds appropriate application to the investigations of the committees and the officials investigated by them, but the secrecy of letters, packages, telegraph, and telephone is unaffected."

That the same set of facts is simultaneously made the object of investigation by judicial officials and by such a parliamentary investigative committee (alongside an investigative committee of the Reichstag perhaps another such committee of a Land parliament) is *in itself* still not considered a violation of the independence of the judiciary, despite the potential negative consequences for evidentiary materials that this entails. On this, see E. Jacobi, *Verhandlungen des 34. Deutschen Juristentages,* 1926, p. 69ff.

(d) *No judicial powers of a legislative chamber.*

It is different with the constitutional provisions that establish the upper house or the Senate as a Staatsgerichtshof for ministerial complaints or for political crimes (see section 2c above).

Tocqueville, *La Démocratie en Amérique,* bk. I, chap. 7, sees a "confusion of powers" in such a "jugement politique," a confusion, however, that is permissible as long as only public servants, but not every citizen, can be affected by this type of justice.

6. No Effect of J on L

(Judiciary opposed to parliament)

An enforcement of this principle of separation in this case would result in the courts not having any jurisdiction to review statutes. For example, the French constitution of 1791, Tit. III, cap. V, Art. 3, provides that the courts may not interfere in the exercise of the legislative power or suspend the execution of statutes. In this regard, it is precisely like the constitution of 1795. Additionally, the Austrian federal constitution of 1 October 1920, Art. 89, provides that "the review of the validity inhering in promulgated statutes is not granted to the courts." The simple statutes concluded by parliament may not be reviewed for their conformity with constitutional provisions. The statutes concluded via the procedure for constitutional revision may not be reviewed for whether they exceed the boundaries of the amendment authority (above § 11, II, p. 103). This power of judicial review is above all rejected by French jurists on the basis of the principle of the division of powers, with the justification that the exercise of the right signifies an intrusion of J into L. See Esmein-Nézard, I, pp. 563, 589ff.; additionally Redslob, *Staatstheorien*, p. 316ff.; but also, for example, Kahl in the constitutional committee of the Weimar National Assembly, p. 485. In contrast to this, the American practice of the judicial [195] review of laws for their constitutionality is justified by the fact that there is no intrusion in the legislative power, because the judge does not eliminate the law, which he considers unconstitutional, but instead only declines to apply it for the individual trial before him. This justification does not violate the principles of Rechtsstaat organization insofar as there is no intrusion of the judge into the legislative power if he declines to apply a statute properly concluded in formal terms, but rather only exercises a control and "restriction."

Since the famous decision of the Reichsgericht of 4 November 1925 (*RGZ* v. 111, p. 322), German legal practice affirms judicial review after other high courts had already previously assumed their jurisdiction for review (cf. Giese p. 210; additionally, *Reichsversorgungsgericht*, 21 October 1924, vol. IV, p. 168; 30 July 1925, vol. V, p. 95). These decisions find support in the consideration that the judge may not apply a law because it is substantively invalid. A simple statute can set itself above "the constitution." In the decision RGZ vol. 111, p. 322, the Reichsgericht states that the fact that the judge is subordinated to the law "does not preclude the denial of validity to a Reich statute or to one of its individual provisions by a judge insofar as it stands in contradiction to other prescriptions that are prior to it and that must be respected by the judge. That is the case when a law contradicts a legal principle established in the Reich Constitution, and if in the issuance of the law the prescribed requirements for constitutional amendment under Art. 76 have not been met." Following that is the interesting clause: "Since the Reich Constitution itself contains no provision, according to which the decision on the constitutionality of Reich statutes may be withdrawn from the judge and would be transferred to another specific office, the authority and duty of the judge to review the constitutionality of Reich statutes must be recognized." That type of a justification evades the actual difficulty. That the courts have such a review power and decide doubtful cases definitively does not at all follow from the fact that no other office is constitutionally provided for the review of statutes. Also, in this regard is the question: who decides? It is not answered by the justification that the Reichsgericht gave. One can say that every state post itself must undertake this review, and that if a state act that is formally in order occurred inside a department, it is only in exceptional cases that one can assume the nullity of the defective state act. And it is precisely as an exceptional case that such an act can be made valid, regardless of whether it is rendered valid by an official or by an individual. W. Jellinek has rightly pointed to the implications of this problem. It is not enough, therefore, to stress the substantive illegality of an unconstitutional law. In regard to such formally correct statutes, it is nevertheless usually a matter of cases in which the unconstitutionality can be thrown in doubt. [196] A simple Reichstag majority will hardly dare an obvious violation of the clear wording of a constitutional provision. However, when it is a matter of the resolution

1. Example: Schema of a *balancing* of *L* and *E*
Reciprocal influence and effect, weight and counterweight

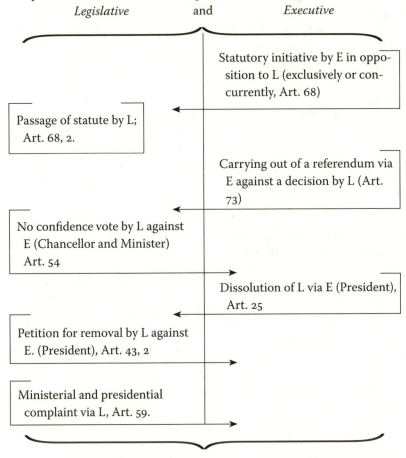

| *Legislative* | and | *Executive* |

Statutory initiative by E in opposition to L (exclusively or con-
currently, Art. 68)

Passage of statute by L;
  Art. 68, 2.

Carrying out of a referendum via
E against a decision by L (Art.
73)

No confidence vote by L against
E (Chancellor and Minister)
Art. 54

Dissolution of L via E (President),
Art. 25

Petition for removal by L against
E. (President), Art. 43, 2

Ministerial and presidential
complaint via L, Art. 59.

The people
hold the balance and are the deciding factor.

of doubtful cases, then the entire problem changes, and it is no longer resolvable by the fact that one renders valid undoubtedly unconstitutional laws. For the question is *not* whether unconstitutional laws are invalid. That is self-evident. The question, rather, is who resolves the doubts about the constitutionality or unconstitutionality of a law. Who, therefore, is competent to make this distinctive decision, and whether the competent officials, in the framework of their jurisdiction, settle any doubts, as does every competent official generally; or whether the courts are competent to resolve such doubts. This question is not settled by the fact that one says the constitution establishes no other office for this purpose and, consequently, the courts are competent to do so.

Nonetheless, I would like to affirm the competence of judicial review in regard to the constitutionality of simple statutes, for with no *influence* of the judiciary on the

2. Example: Schema of a *balancing* (through distribution) inside of *L*

Legislative

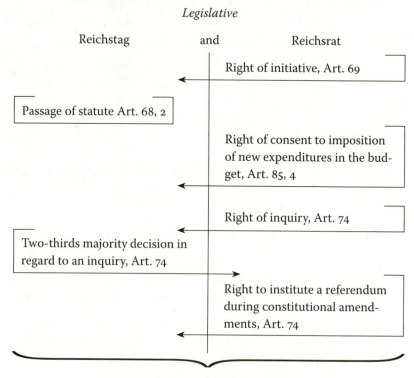

Reichstag   and   Reichsrat

Right of initiative, Art. 69

Passage of statute Art. 68, 2

Right of consent to imposition of new expenditures in the budget, Art. 85, 4

Right of inquiry, Art. 74

Two-thirds majority decision in regard to an inquiry, Art. 74

Right to institute a referendum during constitutional amendments, Art. 74

President and the people
hold the balance and are the deciding factor.

legislative branch the principle of the separation of powers still remains intact. The judiciary is generally not in the position "to intervene and to influence" in the same manner as other state activities. It is bound to the law, and even if it resolves doubts about the validity of a law, it does not abandon the sphere of the purely normative. It restricts, but it does not command. It is not a "power" like the other powers. That is certainly what Montesquieu means when he says that it is "en quelque façon nulle." Consequently, I would see no violation of the Rechtsstaat principle of the separation of powers in the judicial review of the validity of statutes, because there is no "intervention" in the genuine sense (on this question, see above all p. 137 in the previously cited book by F. Morstein Marx, *Variationen über richterliche Zuständigkeit zur Prüfung der Rechtmässigkeit des Gesetzes*, Berlin 1927).

2. The schema of a *balance* of the distinguished or even separated powers leads to opposing effects and influences, in which it is a matter of weighing the mutually held authorities against one another and of bringing them into a balance. Every strengthening on the one side is balanced on the other side, so that no part of the balance receives the surplus. In the current Rechtsstaat, this system is mostly a matter of balancing the excess weight of the legislative bodies, therefore of the parliament. For in consequence of the rule of law, the legislative body itself has a natural

3. Example: Schema of a balancing through distribution inside the executive

Executive (government)

President   and   Government

(Art. 52ff.)

President	Government
1. Art. 41 (politically important competencies of the President, such as international law representation abroad, appointment of civil servants, high command [of the armed forces], measures during a state of exception, and pardons.	
2. Government authorizations in regard to the legislature (dissolution, Art. 25, carrying out of a referendum, Art. 73)	All other governmental authorizations and competencies
3. No dependence on the confidence of the legislature	All other governmental authorizations and competencies
Appointment and dismissal of the Chancellor and ministers; Art. 53	
	General requirement of the countersignature of all the President's official actions by the Chancellor or minister, Art. 50

surplus in the preservation of the Rechtsstaat concept of law. The [197] dependence of the government on the confidence of the parliament and the legal budgetary authority of the parliament work together, so that this surplus can easily become an unrestricted and uncontrolled absolutism. In order to prevent that, one seeks a construction of the "genuine" parliamentarianism to bring the relationship of parliament and government into a counterpoise. Such counterbalanced constructions are of special significance for the Weimar Constitution because its organization of the executive rests on that type of idea. [198]

III. The schema portrayed under II should clarify only an abstract and general outline. Every constitution of a real state must adapt itself to political circumstances, just as the abstract outline of a building must adapt to its foundation and to other natural and substantive facts. The purpose of portraying the ideal schema lies in clarifying in a sketch the organizational principle of the Rechtsstaat component of every constitution that is based on bourgeois liberties. Through a determination both of correspondences with as well as deviations from the schema, the organizational order of a Rechtsstaat constitution becomes more understandable.

It is, therefore, not an objection against such schemata if along with Kant one quotes Swift's witty expression: there are constitutional engineers who balance out the organization of the state as carefully as an architect does a house on which only a sparrow needs to be set in order to disturb the counterbalance and to cause the building to collapse. [199]

The organizational principle of the separation of powers belongs essentially to a Rechtsstaat constitution, and it is right to question whether this principle is given priority even over every constitutional change and revision because of its fundamental significance. From the Rechtsstaat standpoint, the question must be answered affirmatively. Cf. E. Lambert, *Le Gouvernement des juges*, Paris 1921, p. 120ff. But overlooked here is the fact that a constitution of a politically existing people cannot consist only of Rechtsstaat principles. More precisely, these principles only form a moderating component of the constitution, which supplements the political principles (below § 16, p. 200). [200]

§ 16.

Bourgeois Rechtsstaat and Political Form

I. *The constitution of the modern bourgeois Rechtsstaat is always a mixed constitution.*

1. Considered on its own, the Rechtsstaat component with both principles, basic rights (as a distributional principle) and the division of powers (as organizational principle), contains no state form. It is, rather, only a series of limitations and controls on the state, a system of guarantees of bourgeois freedom that makes state power relative. The state itself, which should be controlled, is presupposed in this system. The principles of bourgeois freedom could certainly modify and temper a state. Yet they cannot found a political form on their own. "Freedom constitutes nothing," as Mazzini aptly stated, so in every constitution with the Rechtsstaat component, there is a second part where principles of *political* form are bound up and mixed in with the Rechtsstaat one.

According to a traditional received division, three state forms are distinguished: monarchy, aristocracy, and democracy. This division can be adopted provisionally here. The essential difference among the principles of political form underlying it is considered below (II). The principles of bourgeois freedom, however, change the position and meaning of the elements of political form and make mere *legislative* or *governmental* forms out of *state* forms. The concept of government is once again rendered relative and limited by the priority of the statute and the independence of the judiciary, thereby becoming a system of divisions and controls. With the help of the principles of bourgeois freedom, every state without regard to its state or governmental form can be *limited* in the exercise of state power. An execution of these principles transforms every monarchy into a constitutionally limited, so-called *constitutional* monarchy, in which the constitutional, not monarchical, component is primary. The political principle of democracy is changed in the same way and a *constitutional* democracy emerges out of a pure democratic state. The principles of bourgeois freedom can also bind themselves with any state form to the extent that only the Rechtsstaat [201] limitations are recognized and the state is not "absolute."

All state theorists of bourgeois liberalism stress that every state power must be limited. If they grant validity to a sovereign authority, they attempt to set the concept of a "sovereignty of the constitution" (of the Rechtsstaat principles), which diverts attention from the concept of sovereignty proper, or, more abstractly, the concept of a "sovereignty of justice and reason," in the place of a concrete existing political sovereignty (above § 1, II, p. 7). It is stressed again and again that the sovereignty of the *people* in particular has boundaries and that even in democracy the principles of the basic rights and separation of powers may not be violated. This is the case not only with *Kant* in his state theory speculations. It is above all also the case with the leaders of bourgeois liberalism in its classical period, the nineteenth century. According to Benjamin Constant, "The people do not have the right to strike an innocent party . . . and also cannot delegate this right to anyone. The people do not have the right to violate the free expression of opinion, the freedom of conscience, or the procedure and the protective preliminaries of the judiciary" ("Über die Souveränität des Volkes," *Oeuvres politiques*, 1874 edition, p. 13). Guizot terms the logically implemented democracy chaos and anarchy. In a famous chapter of his book on democracy in America (vol. II, part II, chap. 6), Tocqueville thoroughly considers the dangers of "egalitarian tyranny" under the following heading: "Which type of despotism does the democratic people have to fear." "But I dispute," John Stuart Mill argues, "the right of the people to exercise such coercion (against the freedom of expression of opinion), whether it is by its own (the people's) decision, or whether it is by its government. In this matter, the best government has no more rights than the worst." Mill, *On liberty* (1849), chap. II (on freedom of thought and discussion). The writing of Mill is especially characteristic because, influenced by the events of the year 1848, it shows the opposition of liberal and democratic principles and that the consciousness of this opposition in the meantime has become stronger due to the connection between socialism and democracy. Today, it is possible to recognize the difference between both these principles. On this, see Carl Schmitt, *Die geistesgeschichtliche Lage des heutigen Parlamentarismus*, 1926, p. 21 [*The Crisis of Parliamentary Democracy*, trans. Ellen Kennedy (Cambridge, Mass.: MIT Press, 1985)]. See also F. Tönnies, "Demokratie und Parlamentarismus," in *Schmollers Jahrbuch*, vol. 51 (1927), p. 173f., who elsewhere argues that "private property and division of powers are liberal and not democratic principles." Tönnies, *Deutschen Soziologentag*, 1926, p. 35. Also relevant in this regard is the protest of German law teachers, such as H. Triepel and J. Goldschmidt, against the misuse of the legislative power and the absolutism of majority decisions (above § 13, I 3, p. 142). The distinction is known today even in the United States, whose constitution is indeed consciously built on the opposition between the Rechtsstaat that divides power and democracy, but whose political ideology previously only spoke so unproblematically and optimistically of "democracy" because it did not need to be conscious in a practical sense of the fundamental opposition. Cf. N. Murray Butler (*Der Aufbau des amerikanischen Staates*, German edition, Berlin 1927, p. 253), who argues that "the struggle between freedom and equality has begun. The history of the coming centuries must be written in the terms of this extensive conflict."

This means the modern Rechtsstaat constitution can appear in the form of a monarchy as well as that of a democracy. So long as the liberal principle of bourgeois freedom is genuinely recognized and enforced, only the logically consistent implementation of the Rechtsstaat principle prevents the similarly logically consistent execution of the principle of political form such that there are always only moderated monarchies or democracies. More specifically, [202] there are only those that are limited and altered by the principles of the Rechtsstaat. The constitution of the bourgeois Rechtsstaat variety is first of all a mixed constitution in the sense that the intrinsically independent and complete Rechtsstaat component bonds with *elements* of *political* form.

2. In a wider sense, the modern, bourgeois Rechtsstaat constitution is also a mixed constitution because *inside* the second, political component, diverse principles and elements of political form (democracy, monarchy, and aristocracy) bond with *one another* and are mixed *together.* In this way, this political part of contemporary constitutions corresponds to an ancient tradition, according to which the ideal state order always rests on a connection between and *mixture of different principles of political form.*

The ideal of the mixed constitution derives from Greek state theories and was influenced most strongly by the writings of Aristotle and Polybius. It is noteworthy that the division of state forms into democracy, aristocracy, and monarchy is connected with the distinction of good and bad constitutions because each of the three named state forms can "develop negatively" and just the right mixture of these supplies the best constitution. On this, see Richard Schmidt, *Verfassungsausbau und Weltreichbildung,* Leipzig 1926, p. 23ff. In the "polity," according to Aristotle, ruling and being ruled are linked. That is his actual state ideal, whose concrete execution must always lead to a mixture of political form elements. Polybius sees in the Roman constitution, which is a model for him, the mixture of forms in that the popular assembly (the populus) validates the democratic element, the Senate the aristocratic, and the magistracy the monarchical one. In the political doctrine of the Middle Ages, it is above all Thomas Aquinas, who considers the *status mixtus* the political community's best constitution. See *Summa theologica* I, II; 105, 1 (on this work, see Marcel Demongeot, *La Théorie du Régime mixte chez Saint-Thomas d'Aquin,* Aix thesis 1927).

Since the sixteenth century, the state of the absolute prince suppressed this ideal of a mixed constitution and achieved the ideal of the *pure* constitution, so that, considered historically, the theory of the *pure* (unmixed) constitution appeared as the theory of absolutism. Machiavelli, who otherwise stands entirely in the classical tradition, says, however, that an enduring state system must be either a pure monarchy or a pure republic. He argues that state forms that shift back and forth between both [203] are defective (*Sopra il reformer lo stato di Firenze*). Bodin is also an opponent of the mixed constitution, but Hobbes and Pufendorf after him especially are (de iure naturae et Gentium, VII, 5; § 12, 13, de republica irregulari, § 5 in the *Diss. Academicae* 1675, p. 93 ff.).

In contrast to this absolutist state theory, the theory of the modern Rechtsstaat begins with the mixed state form. The opponents of the absolute prince, the so-called Monarchomachs, advocated it. Many important political theses of the Monarchomachs are traceable to the formulations of Calvin, who declared the aristocracy or a constitution *tempered* by the aristocracy and elements of polity as the best one (vel aristocratium, vel *temperatum* ex ipsa et politia *statum*) in the *Institutio religionis christianae Lib.* IV, c. 20, specifically in an addition to the 1543 edition, § 7 (*Corpus Reformatorum* 29, p. 1105). On Leibniz, cf. Gierke, *Althusius,* p. 179. On the theory of Status mixtus disseminated in the German Reich, see ibid. p. 181ff.

For the further development of the modern Rechtsstaat theory, that which arose in England is by far the most important. Bolingbroke linked the theory of the balancing of powers and of the "equilibrium" (above p. 183) with the theories of the mixed state form (*mixed government*, in contrast to *simple government*), and he saw the ideal connection already realized in the English constitution. The English king represents a monarchical element, the upper house an aristocratic, and the lower house a democratic one. For him, a pure, unmixed form would be arbitrary, "without control," and a monarch governing alone would be despotism, just as democracy governing alone would be anarchy (*Mixed Works*, III, p. 206). The theory of the balance of powers and the theory of the mixed state form pass over into one another here. In his clever way, Montesquieu adopts and modifies these currents of thought in a theory of the decline of the state form. He considers ideal a mixture of aristocracy and monarchy and a well-tempered government (*Esprit des lois*, bks. XI and VIII). Even Burke, who otherwise is an opponent of Bolingbroke, praised the English constitution as *mixed and tempered government*, as a monarchy limited by upper house and lower house (*Works*, V, p. 229). The authors of the *Federalist Papers* (1788), whose arguments are definitive for the federal constitution of the United States, also demand a mixture and tempering that directs itself especially against pure democracy. Finally, the author of most of the draft constitutions of the French Revolution, Sieyès, also had such ideas. In this regard, cf. his formulation from the year 1801 (in E. His, *Geschichte des neueren schweizerischen Staatsrechts*, I, 1920, p. 353, n. 151), where he argues that the foundation of a good constitution must be democratic, the middle part aristocratic, and the capstone monarchical. As an example of the constitutional theory thinking of the German liberals, take H. W. A. v. Gagern, who argues that "it lies in the nature of powers that they be exercised, and in the nature [204] of authority that it attempts to extend itself. Human ingenuity conceived the system of the representative constitution and history elaborated it in order to limit these powers and forms of authority in the state—the monarchical, aristocratic, and the democratic elements—such that they must tolerate one another while existing side by side" (*Über die Verlängerung der Finanzperioden und Gesetzgebungslandtage*, 1827). This statement contains not only the profession of von Gagern's political commitment, but also the political essence of the bourgeois Rechtsstaat in general. Even F. C. Dahlmann states in his *Politics* (§ 99, p. 83, 3rd ed., 1847) that "in order to last, the governmental form of a great state must be built from different components, not those of the same type." He finds in the English constitution such a mixture and division.

3. The bourgeois Rechtsstaat constitution knows actually only *governmental and legislative* forms, whereby "government" as *executive* in the sense of the separation of powers principle is distinguished from the *legislative*. By itself, the Rechtsstaat component means neither a constitution nor an independent state form. Consequently, the Rechtsstaat can comprise political unity neither as such nor as an entirety. The constitution-making power in particular remains always external to this Rechtsstaat component, and the problem of the constitution-making power cannot be resolved either theoretically or practically with the principles and concepts of mere Rechtsstaat legality. As a result, it is mostly either ignored or obscured in a mixture of liberal and democratic ideas and in abstractions, such as "sovereignty of justice" or "sovereignty of the constitution." By contrast, one must be reminded that the question regarding the constitution-making power is

unavoidable and that the response to this question also answers the question about the state form, while the mixture of political forms in the bourgeois Rechtsstaat results from the fact that different "powers" can only be distinguished when they are organized according to different principles of political form. The legislative branch, for example, can be organized democratically, while the executive branch can be set up as a monarchy, etc.

II. *The two principles of political form (identity and representation).*

The difference between the state forms rests on the fact that there are two opposing formative political principles. Every political unity receives its concrete form from the realization of these principles. [205]

1. State is a certain status of a people, specifically, the status of political unity. State form is this unity's particular type of formation. The people are the subject of every conceptual definition of the state. State is a condition, the particular circumstance of a people. But the people can achieve and hold the condition of political unity in two different ways. It can already be factually and directly capable of political action by virtue of a strong and conscious similarity, as a result of firm natural boundaries, or due to some other reason. In this case, a political unity is a genuinely present entity in its unmediated self-*identity*. This principle of the self-identity of the then present people as political unity rests on the fact that there is no state without people and that a people, therefore, must always actually be existing as an entity present at hand. The opposing principle proceeds from the idea that the political unity of the people as such can never be present in actual identity and, consequently, must always be *represented* by men personally. All distinctions of genuine state forms, whichever type they may be, monarchy, aristocracy, and democracy, monarchy and republic, monarchy and democracy, etc., may be traced back to this decisive opposition of *identity* and *representation*. Even the difference, treated above (§ 8, p. 82), between both subjects of the constitution-making power under consideration, people or monarchy, centers around both these opposing principles. Where the people as the subject of the constitution-making power appear, the political form of the state defines itself by the idea of an identity. The nation *is* there. It need not and cannot be represented. This is an idea that gives Rousseau's oft-repeated arguments (*Contrat social*, III, 15) their democratic irrefutability. The absolute monarchy is, in fact, only absolute representation and rests on the idea that the political unity is first produced by representation through performance. The statement "L'Etat c'est moi" means I alone represent the political unity of the nation.

In the reality of political life, a state can no more forgo all structural elements of the principle of identity than one can forgo all structural elements of representation. Even where the attempt is made [206] to realize

unconditionally an absolute identity, elements and methods of representation remain unavoidable, as on the contrary no representation without
images of identity is possible. Both these possibilities, identity and representation, do not exclude one another. They are, rather, only two opposing
orientation points for the concrete formation of the political unity. In every
state, one or the other is stronger, yet both are part of the political existence
of a people.

2. First of all, there is no state without representation. In a fully implemented direct democracy where the "entire people," all active state citizens,
are actually assembled in one place, perhaps the impression arises that the
people act in its unmediated presence and identity as the people and that
one can no longer speak of a representation in regard to the people. "So,
the united people not merely represents the sovereign; it itself *is* this sovereign" (Kant, *Rechtslehre*, II, § 52). In fact, in the extreme case, only all adult
members of the people act and then only in the moment when they are
assembled as the community or as the army. But even all active state citizens, taken as a whole, are not the political unity of the people. They merely
represent the political unity, which transcends an assembly convened at a
particular time and place. The individual state citizen, however, is present
not in his "natural" condition as individual person (precisely what *Rousseau*
always emphasized). He is present as state citizen, as "citoyen." Moreover,
in a modern democracy without a popular assembly that neither is elected
in secret ballots nor that votes in secret, it is immediately evident that the
enfranchised individual ideally votes not for himself as private person, that
the individual electoral precinct represents not a special district inside of
the state, and that in public law terms (in a system of proportional representation with party lists) the individual party list is not there on its own
account, but rather only as the means to bring about a representation of
political unity that is alone essential. Every deputy is considered a "delegate
of the *entire* people," as a representative. That remains an essential element
of today's state, although it long ago became untrue in practical terms. It is
even expressed in Art. 21 of the Weimar Constitution, according to which
"deputies are [207] delegates of the entire people." By the same logic, however, the same must hold for every individual *voter*. Hence, in every detail,
the system of the democratic election rests on the idea of a representation.
If state citizens entitled to vote do not elect a deputy, but the matter itself is
instead decided through a referendum, a so-called genuine plebiscite, and
the question presented is answered "yes" or "no," the principle of identity
is realized to the fullest. But, even then, elements of representation remain
effective because it must also be believed in this regard that the individual
state citizen entitled to vote appears as a "citoyen," not as a private man and

private interest. He must be thought of as "independent," as "not bound to instructions and commissions," and as a "representative of the whole," not of his private interests. At no time or place is there thorough, absolute self-identity of the then present people as political unity. Every attempt to realize a pure or direct democracy must respect this boundary of democratic identity. Otherwise, direct democracy would mean nothing other than the dissolution of the political unity.

There is, therefore, no state without representation because there is no state without state form, and the *presentation* of the political unity is an intrinsic part of the form. In every state, there must be persons who can say, L'Etat c'est nous. Presentation, however, need not be *production* of the political unity. It is possible that the political unity is first brought about through the presentation itself. That is the case in the degree to which the state form approaches absolute representation. But the procedure and method of the production and initiation of the political unity alone are still not a state form. R. Smend (in the essay discussed above, § 1, I, 3, p. 7) suggested distinguishing between "integration" and "representation" as state forms. In parliamentarianism, he sees a "state form in itself," because from the very beginning the state continuously integrates itself through public opinion, elections, parliamentary debates, and votes. But every political unity must somehow be integrated because such unity is not by nature present. Instead, it rests on a human decision. "Integration," therefore, is not a specific principle of form. According to circumstances and the peculiarity of the people, integration may occur just as well through representation as through methods and procedures springing from the idea of identity. Smend juxtaposes integration as "dynamic" to the traditional forms as "static." The fundamental meaning of the concept of integration should not be misconstrued. Integration is not a state form and stands above all not in opposition to representation. One may even say that in its effect genuine representation is an essential factor of the process of integration. Nevertheless, that would be a functional consideration, not a formal one, and it is to be shown below (III) that to represent is not mere functioning. On parliamentarianism as a special system of government (not a state form), see below § 24, p. 305. Parliamentarianism is not *the* form of integration. [208] Considered historically, it is only a certain method of integration, which is rendered concrete in a dual manner. It integrates only the (propertied and educated) liberal bourgeoisie and only in the monarchical state existing in the nineteenth century.

3. In the same way, there is no state without structural elements of the principle of identity. The principle of form of representation can never be instituted purely and absolutely by ignoring the people who are always somehow existing and present. That is impossible because there can be no representation without the public and no public without the people. The concept of representation, however, must be seen in its public law and political peculiarity and be freed from any encumbrance from other concepts such as assignment, interest advocacy, business leadership, commission, trusteeship, etc., because otherwise ideas of a private law and economic-technical variety undermine its distinctiveness. In the nineteenth-century

literature, the lack of clarity is so great that often only with immense effort is it possible to recognize the public law sense of the word representation.

Emil Gerber's dissertation, Bonn, 1925, makes an attempt to clarify these concepts for the period of pre-March liberalism, a period that is especially important and instructive because of the struggle between "representation" and "estate advocacy." Through personal communication, it is known to me that Dr. G. Leibholz plans an extensive exposition of the concept of representation. I do not want to anticipate his work, so I am content to list a few distinctions in the form of theses, which are indispensable for any state and constitutional theory.

III. The components of the *concept of representation*.

1. Representation can occur only in the *public* sphere. There is no representation that occurs in secret and between two people, and no representation that would be a "private matter." In this regard, all concepts and ideas are excluded that are essentially part of the spheres of the private, of private law, and of the merely economic. This includes concepts such as execution, trusteeship, and advocacy of private interests, etc. A parliament has representative character only so long as one believes that its actual activity lies in the public sphere. Secret sessions, secret agreements, and deliberations of some committee may be very meaningful and important, but they never have a representative character. As soon as the conviction establishes itself that what occurs publicly in the context of the parliamentary activity has become only an empty formality and that the true decisions fall outside of this public sphere [209], parliament can perhaps still exercise some useful functions, but it is just not any longer the representative of the political unity of the people.

In F. C. Dahlmann, *Politik*, chap. VI., § 139 (p. 117 of the 3rd ed. of 1847), the concept is still genuine. Set against this alignment (of the estates), the representative constitution takes the rights of the *public* and *collective* as its point of departure. This constitution considers the prince the executive body of a state order, which is undoubtedly superior to him, and it alone is still by far stronger than and towers above the populace and has nothing to do with popular sovereignty. For a populace can certainly have the understanding that government is according to the will of the people without thereby assuming the risk of intending to undertake governing itself. Bluntschli is one of the few nineteenth-century teachers of public law who is still aware of the distinctiveness of the concept of representation as it is expressed in writings on public affairs. In his *Allgemeinen Staatsrecht*, I, p. 488, he elaborates by stating that "representation in public law is entirely different from the equivalent in private law." "Consequently," he continues, "the fundamental principles valid in the latter may not be applied to the former." By contrast, the concept in Robert Mohl already passes over entirely into the private in the bourgeois sense, for example, and is brought under the perspective of business management. "Representation or (!) advocacy," he writes in *Staatsrecht, Völkerrecht, Politik, Monographien*, pp. 8/9, is the institution whereby the subjects, either in their entirety or merely a portion of them, are authorized to influence state business through a small number of persons drawn from the midst of the participants and selected in their name and obligated toward them." In part, the confusion that lies in the intertwining of private law and business ideas explains and excuses itself in reference to the fact that the Anglo-Saxon manner of expression does not care for clear and sharp distinctions. When one considers the extent to which the reference to the English model replaced state theory thinking, one will not expect that the theorists of the nineteenth century themselves distinguish where the English have no interest in the distinction. Moreover, it is still a matter of state theory concepts defining themselves in political struggle only according to some tactically important detail, which is made prominent by the circumstances of the struggle or by an especially pressing political interest. Hence, it came about that ultimately nothing appears to remain for the consciousness of state theory from a concept as comprehensive and systematic as representation other than that the representative is not bound to the instructions and directives of his electors. One has not exerted oneself further to find a systematic explanation of this "independence" and its specific connection with the concept of representation.

From the sociological literature, only one, certainly very important, work is known to me that is meaningful for the concept of representation. That is the essay by Werner Wittich in the commemorative volume for Max Weber, vol. II, p. 278ff., entitled "Der soziale Gehalt von Goethes Roman 'Wilhelm Meisters Lehrjahre.'" The word "representation" does not occur here, but becomes evident from the beginning in the exceedingly apt remarks on "the public sphere," "public person," and "appearance." The crisis of the concept is that the nobility loses its representative position without the bourgeoisie being in the position to create an instance of representation.

2. Representation is not a normative event, a process, and a procedure. It is, rather, something *existential*. To represent means to make an invisible being visible and present through a publicly present one. The dialectic of the concept is that the invisible is presupposed as absent [210] and nevertheless is simultaneously made present. That is not possible with just any type of being. Indeed, it presupposes a special type being. Something dead, something inferior or valueless, something lowly cannot be represented. It lacks the enhanced type of being that is capable of an *existence*, of rising into the public being. Words like size, height, majesty, fame, dignity, and honor seek to express this peculiarity of enhanced being that is capable of representation. What serves only private affairs and only private interests can certainly be advocated. It can find its agents, attorneys, and exponents. However, it is not represented in a specific sense. It is either really present or executed by an instructed delegate, business manager, or deputy. In representation, by contrast, a higher type of being comes into concrete appearance. The idea of representation rests on a people existing as a political unity, as having a type of being that is higher, further enhanced, and more intense in comparison to the natural existence of some human group living together. If the sense for this peculiarity of political existence erodes and people give priority to other types of their existence, the understanding of a concept like representation is also displaced.

That X steps in for the absent Y or for a few thousand such Ys is still not an instance of representation. An especially simple historical example of representation occurs when a king is represented before another king through an ambassador (that is, a personal representative, not through an agent who conducts business for him). In the eighteenth century, one such "representation in the eminent sense" distinguished itself clearly from other processes of interest advocacy.

Vattel's widely distributed, influential textbook of international law states (*Droit des Gens*, 1758 edition, I, p. 42) that "the representative character of the sovereign authority rests on the fact that he represents his nation. The monarch thereby unites in his person the entire majesty, which is due the nation as a united body." "Telle est l'origine du Caractère représentatif que l'on attribue au Souverain. Il représente sa Nation dans toutes les affaires qu'il peut avoir comme Souverain. Ce n'est point avilir la dignité du plus grand Monarque que de lui attribuer ce caractère représentatif; au contraire, rien ne le relève avec plus d'éclat: Par-là le Monarque réunit en sa Personne toute la Majesté qui appartient zu Corps entier de la Nation." Elsewhere (II, p. 304/5), he speaks of the representative character of the envoys, the "Ministres publiques," distinguishes them from the chargés d'affaires, the commission agents, and offers the following definition: "What one calls the representative character par excellence is the ability of the minister to represent his master, so far as it is a matter of his person and his dignity (dignité)." These conceptual definitions underlie the order of ranks of diplomatic agents of 19 March 1815 (*Wiener Kongressakte, Anlage d. Art.* 2). Les ambassadeurs, légats ou nonces ont seuls le *caractère représentatif* (*Strupp*, Documents, I, p. 196). They are of special significance in constitutional theory terms because they express a [211] defining idea of the eighteenth century that passed over directly into the constitutional law of the French Revolution. The principle of the first revolutionary constitution of 1791 is to be understood in this historical context. The French constitution is representative; representatives are the legislative body and the king (Title III, Art. 2, w), while it is said of the "administrateurs" (Tit. III, chap. IV, sect. II art. 2) that they have no "caractère de représentation."

The dispute that surrounded the representative constitution in Germany in the nineteenth century is only understandable in reference to this meaning of representation. The statesmen of the monarchical restoration recognized the political sense of the concept and attempted to substitute estate *interest* advocates for a "representation of the people." In this way, the political value had been taken from the demands of the liberal bourgeoisie. In Art. 13 of the Vienna Federal Act, therefore, the expression "representative constitution" (Constitution représentative) is intentionally replaced by the expression "estate constitution." The weighty controversy over this difference would be inconceivable had it not been a matter of the actual political object of dispute. For if a body that is representative of the entire people stands opposite the king, the monarchical principle is shaken, for this principle rests on the king alone thoroughly representing the political unity of the people. In a transitional and intermediary phase, one can attempt to place *two* representatives of the "nation," the politically unified people, alongside one another, the king and the parliament. That is the idea of the constitutional monarchy; herein resides its "dualism." The French constitution of 1791 rests on this principle and expresses it especially clearly. The constitutions of the constitutional monarchy in Germany avoid those types of precise declarations, but they contain the same dualism. It is the democratic logic of such a state construction that the parliament as the *true* or (as Rotteck, *Vernunftrecht*, II, p. 237 says) "natural" representative of the political unity of the people emerges and forces aside the other representatives. Theoretically and ideally that signifies the actual weaknesses of the constitutional monarchy. Despite all the confusion that reveals itself in the use of the term "representation," the central political meaning of the term always lets itself be recognized.

Representation is part of the political sphere. Hence, it is essentially something existential. One cannot grasp it by subsuming it under general [212] norms. The nineteenth-century monarchy sought to adhere, theoretically and ideally, to the principle of *legitimacy*, thereby retaining an essentially normative foundation while surrendering its representative character. Legitimacy and representation are completely different concepts. Legitimacy alone establishes neither authority nor potestas [power] nor representation. In the period of its most intensive political existence, the monarchy called itself *absolute.* That means *legibus* solutus, or simply the renunciation of legitimacy. The nineteenth century's attempt to restore monarchy on the foundation of legitimacy was only an attempt to stabilize a status quo juristically. Because the political capacity for vibrant forms of representation is lacking, one sought to secure one's position normatively by applying essentially private law concepts (possession, property, family, right to inheritance) to political life. What was still historically vibrant in the monarchy's principle of form did not lie in legitimacy. The example of the politically strongest monarchy, the Prussian kingdom, is clear enough in this regard. A monarchy that is nothing other than "legitimate" is already politically and historically dead.

3. The *political unity as a whole* is represented. There is something in this representation that exceeds every commission and every function. Consequently, not just any "organ" is representative. Only he who *rules* takes part in representation. The government distinguishes itself from administration and business management by presenting and rendering concrete the spiritual principle of political existence. According to Lorenz von Stein (*Verwaltungslehre*, p. 92), the government establishes "the principles." It acts "in the name of the ideas of the state." Through this type of spiritual existence, it distinguishes itself both from an employee on special assignment, on the one hand, as well as from a violent oppressor, on the other. That the government of an established community is something other than the power of a pirate cannot be understood from the perspective of the ideas of justice, social usefulness, and other normative elements, for all these normative concepts can apply even to thieves. The difference lies in the fact that every genuine government *represents* the political unity of a people, not the people in its natural presence.

The struggle for representation is always a struggle for political power. In Germany's constitutional monarchy, the parliament was thus the "people's advocate," but not the representative of the political unity of the people. K. Rieker (*Die recht-*

liche Natur der modernen Volksvertretung, Leipzig 1893, p. 53) defines the people's advocate in the monarchical states of Germany as "a body constituted from the subjects in a special way, which, by virtue of a legal fiction, is the entire people, the totality of the subjects." What is misconstrued here is that the entire people are the political unity. In the monarchy, by contrast, the totality of the subjects are in fact *not* supposed to be the political unity.

4. The representative is *independent,* neither functionary nor agent nor commissioner. With one clause that is in theory generally valid, the French constitution of 1791 contrasts the administration with the representative, stating [213] that "the persons entrusted with the government (administration) of the state have no representative character. They are trustees (agents)" (Title III, chap. IV, sect. 2, art. 2). According to Art. 130, 1, of the Weimar Constitution, the civil servants are "servants of the collective." They are also not representatives.

In the "Contrat social," Rousseau had already distinguished a representative from agents and commissioners, who only deal with a business task (emploi) and are mere civil servants (officers) (bk. I, cap. 1 and 18). The National Assembly of 1789 was still clearly aware of the difference. The difficulty lies only in that one must connect the principle of representation with principles of a constitution that distinguishes among powers. Political unity cannot be divided. Only the nation is always represented. In other words, only the *entire* people are represented. Consequently, the three "powers" do not permit themselves to be represented inside the same political unity. On the other hand, the bearer of a "power," of a "pouvoir," is something different and more significant than a functionary or a civil servant, and one says of him that he *represents the "pouvoir."* It helped that one spoke of a representation anywhere an individual or a constituted body wills something for the body as a whole (so Barnave, *Arch. Parl.* XXIX, p. 331) and stated that the representative has not only a function but also happens to be a "pouvoir." Roederer and Robespierre (pp. 324/5) distinguished the "pouvoirs représentatifs" from the "*pouvoirs commis*"; the "pouvoir représentatif" is "égal au pouvoir du peuple" and independent. K. Loewenstein, *Volk und Parlament nach der Staatstheorie der französischen Nationalversammlung von 1789,* Munich 1922, p. 243, has also noted the opposition of representation and division of powers when he states that "the representative principle is not a concept that is immanent to the division of powers as such." Representation is just a *principle of political form*; the separation of powers, by contrast, is a method of using opposed principles of political form in the interest of the bourgeois Rechtsstaat. The difficulty residing in the connection of representation and division of powers is only resolvable by distinguishing both components of a modern constitution and by separating the principle of the division of powers from the political component of the constitution. The actual principles of form signify as such essential *unity,* which is the opposite of division and distinction. The contradictory connection of both these principles becomes evident (below § 24, p. 303f.) in the attempt to institute a parliamentary government while applying the methods of division and balancing of powers to it. If the representative is handled only as a delegate, who acts as trustee of the interests of voters for practical reasons (because it is impossible that all voters could always and at the same time come together), then representation is no longer present. I would also not (as does J. Barthélemy, *Le rôle du pouvoir exécutif,* 1906, p. 41) speak of half-representation (sémi-représentation). In the interest of scholarly clarity, however, I would prefer to attempt to lend the word a precise meaning again and limit it to the presentation of the political unity as such. A *committee* does not represent. It is, rather, a dependent exponent of a larger complex, which forms the committee for practical-technical reasons. The parliament as representative of the people is not a committee of the people, nor is it one of the electorate.

The word *organ* must be avoided here. It owes its popularity in part to the justified opposition to mechanistic and individualistic-private ideas, in part, however, also to a lack of clarity conveying multiple meanings, a lack of clarity in which difficult distinctions like representation, advocacy, mission, etc., dissolve into a general obscurity. For the critique of the use [214] of this term by G. Jellinek, cf. Carl Schmitt, *Die Diktatur*, p. 141. See additionally, H. Heller, *Die Souveränität*, Berlin 1927, p. 60, Duguit, *L'Etat*, I, p. 8, 238ff., and Barthélemy, *Le rôle du pouvoir exécutif*, p. 25ff. Unfortunately, Gierke's legal-historical investigations are also not always clear insofar as they involve the public law and in particular this concept of representation. In the Althusius's expositions, p. 214ff., the concepts "representation," "vicem gerere," "mandatum," "commissio," "empowerment," "advocacy" are mixed up with one another. That an intermingling also occurs in the historical literature treated there is no reason to extend it. Instead, it makes a disentanglement all the more necessary. The statement of Cusanus, which Gierke, p. 216 n. 15, cites as the first example for the use of the word *representation* (et dum simul conveniunt in unu compendio representativo *totum imperium* collectum est), demonstrates something essential. Specifically, that the representative is not involved in some form of advocacy, but rather in the presentation of a unity of the *whole*. The absolutistic theory is not at all so far removed from the idea of representation as Gierke assumes entirely in the sense of the liberal nineteenth century. Instead, it only reserved for the princes the task of representing political unity. Moreover, this absolutism grasped the idea of representation very clearly and forcefully and thereby first made possible the adaptations of it by the French Revolution and of the nineteenth century (by the monarch to the elected popular assembly).

5. The absolute prince is also the sole representative of the political unity of the people. He alone represents the state. As Hobbes puts it, the state has "its unity in the person of a sovereign"; it is "united in the person of one sovereign." Representation first establishes this unity. Nonetheless, it is always only the unity of a *people* in the political condition that is produced. The personal quality of the state lies in representation, not in the concept of the state.

The value of representation is that its public and personal qualities give political life its character. Notorious matters, such as "secret diplomacy" and "personal rule," have brought this system into disrepute. However, one should at least not overlook one thing: that the secret diplomacy of the holders of public power is a harmless game in comparison to the public diplomacy that secret holders of power carry out through their agents.

6. In summary, it may be said that the state as political unity rests on the connection of two opposing formative principles. The first is the principle of identity (specifically, the self-identity of then existing people as a political unity, if, by virtue of its own political consciousness and national will, it has the capacity to distinguish friend and enemy), and the other is the principle

of representation, through which the government represents the political unity. Implementation of this principle of identity signifies the tendency toward the minimum of government and personal leadership. As this principle is realized to an ever greater degree, the resolution of political affairs occurs ever more "of itself" thanks to a maximum of naturally given or historically achieved homogeneity. That is the ideal condition of a democracy, as *Rousseau* presupposes it in the "Contrat social." One [215] speaks there of direct or pure democracy. What is noteworthy in this expression is the fact that there is actually only direct democracy and the "mediative quality" arises only through the integration of formal elements of representation. Where everything agrees, the decision must result by itself without discussion and without essential oppositions of interests, because everyone wants the same thing. But this condition must be viewed as only an ideal mental construct, not historical and political reality. The danger of a radical implementation of the principle of identity lies in the fact that the essential presupposition, substantial similarity of the people, is misperceived. There is not really the maximum degree of identity. Certainly, however, the minimum degree of government is present. The consequence is that a people regresses from the condition of political existence into one that is sub-political, thereby leading a merely cultural, economic, or vegetative form of existence and serving a foreign, politically active people. By contrast, a maximum degree of representation would mean a maximum amount of government. So long as it is genuinely at hand, it could get by with a minimum of homogeneity of the people and could form a political unity out of national, confessional, or diverse class-based human groups. The danger of this condition is that the subject of the political unity, the people, is ignored and the state, which is never anything other than a people in the condition of political unity, loses its substance. That would then be a state without people, a res populi without a populus.

All divisions of state forms derive from this difference between both principles of form. The traditional division of monarchy, aristocracy, and democracy contains a genuine core and involves something essential because it is traceable to the fact that among these three state forms one of each principle of form is predominant in a different manner. The mere factual number of rulers or governors, however, is not an appropriate principle of division, and it requires no special insight to become critical when it is said that in monarchy one rules, in aristocracy several, in democracy many or all. The division is correct only insofar as the words "to master" or "to govern" contain the element of representation, or the presentation of political unity. In democracy, it is many or all who represent, insofar as every voter, every [216] citizen with the right to vote, as explained above (1.), can be an independent advocate of the whole. Yet in democracy this participation of all state citizens in the state has the sense of producing the self-identity of the then present people as a political unity, not the sense of the act of representing. Correctly understood and ignoring the extremes of the numerical division, Aristotle's state theory retains its classic meaning. The most important thing is that Aristotle in the theory of the "polity" recognized the true state as a linkage of ruling and being ruled, of ἄρχειν and ἄρχεσθαι. The simultaneity of ruling and being ruled, of governing and being governed, signifies a linkage of both principles, representation and identity, without which a state is impossible.

IV. The modern constitution is composed of a *linkage and mixture of bourgeois Rechtsstaat principles and those of political form.* Rechtsstaat principles limit and temper the consequences and effects of political principles in a distinctive way. The states of this modern constitution are constitutionally limited (constitutional) monarchies or constitutionally limited (constitutional) democracies. As will be shown immediately below, however, even elements of aristocratic form are used in the modern "constitution state."

1. One cannot say that the bourgeoisie, as it struggles for its Rechtsstaat in Europe, would always have privileged one of the two principles of political form, identity or representation. The bourgeoisie struggles in the same way against every type of state absolutism, whether it is an absolute democracy or an absolute monarchy. Consequently, it resists extreme identity as well as extreme representation. Its goal was the "parliamentary system" insofar as it aspired toward political institutions of the genuine Rechtsstaat variety, demands that extend beyond that which merely moderate and "temper" the state. This system is the actual political demand of the liberal bourgeoisie. As the subsequent discussion of the different form principles will specify in detail, this system rests on a distinctive linkage, balancing, and relativizing of monarchical, aristocratic, and democratic elements of form and structure. It is significant, nevertheless, both historically and in terms of state theory, that precisely this system assumed the name "representative system" or "representative constitution," [217] so that in almost all European countries during the nineteenth century, the liberal bourgeois Rechtsstaat with a parliamentary government is designated as a state of the "representative system." Kant, who is also already a typical advocate of bourgeois Rechtsstaat thinking in this regard, stated that "every true Republic, however, is and can be nothing other than a *representative* system of the people, one united by all state citizens and established in order to act as trustee for their rights in their name by means of their delegates (deputies)" (*Rechtslehre* § 52, Vorländer edition, p. 170). The question is whether this bourgeois, representative constitution signifies a state form.

These ideas about the parliament or popular assembly still presuppose a genuine representation of the whole, in other words, of the politically united people, or the nation. The parliament is not yet thought of as a committee of interest advocates. This representative character of the popular assembly is adhered to with great determination in opposition to the king, so long as he comes into consideration as the representative of the political unity. In traditional liberal terms, the deputy is a man, distinguished by insight and education, who is concerned only with the political whole as such. Constitutional theory must certainly take account of this ideal type of the deputy, for it confers on the parliament the meaning of a representative elite, of an aristocratic assembly with representative character. And historically it is not only the English Parliament to which Gneist (*Englische Verfassungsgeschichte*, p. 709) and Hasbach (*Die parlamentarische Verfassungsgeschichte*, 1919, p. 261), for example, attributed this representative quality. It is also correct in terms of the idea when parliament is understood as an *aristocratic* or oligarchic assembly. Only in relative terms can it appear as something democratic, in particular through the opposition to the absolute monarchy. With the power of the monarchy and in consequence of rising democratization, this aristocratic and representative character erodes. The deputy became a dependent agent of voters and interest organizations. The idea of representation was displaced by the principle of direct identity, which immediately made the great mass of people appear as something entirely self-evident. But in terms of understanding parliamentarianism and the bourgeois "representative constitution," it is necessary to remind oneself that their fundamental character is aristocratic. [218]

2. I agree with R. Smend's designation of parliamentarianism as a special state form (above p. 207) only insofar as the parliamentary system contains a *distinctive relativity*, *linkage*, and *mixture* of opposing political principles and structural elements that correspond to the special interests of the bourgeois Rechtsstaat. If one applies the distinction of both principles of political form, identity and representation, to the parliamentary system, it becomes evident that a special type of *representation* is present. The rule of parliament is an instance of aristocracy (or, in the degenerate form, oligarchy). Aristocracy is a *mixed* state form in a certain sense. Under the theory of the mixed state form, it is always treated as a form especially worthy of recommendation because it stands in the middle between monarchy and democracy and, consequently, already intrinsically contains a mixture. Even in the previously cited expression of Calvin, for example, aristocracy is preferred to other political formations. The state form of the aristocracy distinguishes itself from democracy in that, in contrast to democracy's unmediated identity, aristocracy rests on a representation. On the other hand, it avoids a representation that is so absolute and thoroughgoing that it signifies representation by an individual person, the monarchy. Even personalism, toward

which a representation strives, is deprived of its innermost logic if a single person no longer represents. So the aristocracy can appear as something moderate and intermediate between two extremes. In this regard, Montesquieu also touched on something essential when he designated moderation (modération) as the "principle of aristocracy." Representation contains the genuine opposition to the democratic principle of identity. The so-called "representative democracy" is the typically mixed and compromise form. It is so, moreover, even down to the last detail of its organizational execution. It is very imprecise to treat the representative democracy as a subcategory of democracy (as does Richard Thoma in the *Erinnerungsgabe für Max Weber*, 1923, II, p. 39ff.). For the representative quality contains the undemocratic element in this "democracy." Insofar as the parliament is a *representation* of political unity, it stands in opposition to democracy. But considered historically, the liberal demand for such a representation in concrete political reality directed itself initially against the [219] absolute monarch, who emerged as sole representative of political unity. A second representative, the parliament, placed itself in opposition to this one. As "representative of the *people*" (although in fact there can only be one representative of the political unity of the people, just as there can only be one representative of the collective), constituted out of elections of the people, this parliament spoke and acted in opposition to the king only in the name of the people. Hence, it represented the political unity not by virtue of its own existence and not in complete independence, even if in regard to the people one reaffirmed that the parliament is an "independent" representative. That was obviously a malleable intermediary position and only a transition. The more the opposing player, the monarchical representation, declined, the more the representation of parliament was also displaced and the representative body transformed itself into a committee of the mass of voters. After the parliament had ceased to represent in opposition to a monarch, it was presented the political task of representing the political unity all the more decisively in opposition to the people, that is, its own voters, and to keep itself independent of the people. Therein lies a great difficulty, for the *election* can, indeed, create a genuine representation and is a method of the aristocratic principle when it has the sense of determining the *best* of the *select few*. If the direction of selection proceeds from below to above, the elected are the *exalted*. On the other hand, the election can also be the mere demand of interest advocates and agents. Then the direction of selection proceeds from above to below, that is, the elected is the dependent and subordinate *employee* of the voters. As soon as standing party organizations as always present, unyielding entities dominate the parliament, the parliament is subordinated to the logic of direct democracy and is no longer representative. Yet as long as the parliament meets the presuppositions of a genuine representation, which was overall still the case in the nineteenth century, one could see in the parliamentary system an exceptional, indeed aristocratic state form. The distinctive political situation of bourgeois liberalism, being wedged between the sovereignty of the princes and of the sovereignty of the people, found its expression in this politically intermediary form.

Even here, there exists the mixture and rendering relative of the principles of form that is characteristic of a constitution of the bourgeois Rechtsstaat type [220]. By no means is a pure aristocracy fully instituted. The aristocratic aspect is only one element of form alongside others. The parliamentary system is not a distinctly political form, but rather a balancing of opposing forms, which uses democratic and monarchical form elements for the purpose of separating powers. For the executive, it uses monarchical forms of organization, such as a *king* or a *state president*, whose authority, moreover, is especially enhanced in the interest of the distinction and balancing of "powers." A head of state, as chief of the executive, is necessarily part of this entire system and is also often constituted exclusively as a *representative* of the people in opposition to the parliament, so that even in republics under the democratic principle, the dualism of constitutional monarchy (king and parliament as both representatives of the nation) appears again. Even the President under the Weimar Constitution should have a "representative" character. He is thus elected by the *entire* German people according to Art. 41. He is also the one who represents the German Reich externally (Art. 45). In several constitutions, the institution of an *upper house* or senate counts as an additional *aristocratic* element, yet one that is independent and supplied with diverse justifications and constructions (below § 23). In typical Rechtsstaat constitutions, such as the Belgian constitution of 1831 (Art. 32), this means that the members of *both* chambers "represent the nation." The *democratic principle* ultimately finds its application above all in the legislature, specifically, in the fact that the people, or the enfranchised state citizens, not only elect officials but also decide substantive questions directly through referendum. Therefore, all elements of form join together, though they are rendered relative and balanced against one another, and this linkage and mixture is the essential thing for the modern bourgeois Rechtsstaat constitution and its parliamentary system.

This means that inside the second part of the modern constitution, inside the elements of political form, a constitutional theory of today's bourgeois Rechtsstaat must first of all elaborate, in sequence and individually, these forms, democracy, monarchy, and aristocracy, in order to see the elements of the mixture of forms and to properly understand its typical linkage, namely the parliamentary system, in its distinctiveness. [221]

PART III

THE POLITICAL COMPONENT OF
THE MODERN CONSTITUTION

§ 17-1.

The Theory of Democracy

Fundamental Concepts

I. [223] *Overview of a few conceptual definitions.*

1. *The relationship between democracy and republic.* Democracy is a state form that corresponds to the principle of identity (in particular, the self-identity of the concretely present people as a political unity). The people are the bearer of the constitution-making power and, as such, grant themselves their constitution. At the same time, the concept of democracy can provide a method for the exercise of certain state activities. It also designates a form of government or legislative form and means that in the system of the separation of powers, one or several of these powers, such as the legislature or the government, are organized according to democratic principles under the widest possible participation of state citizens.

According to the contemporary manner of speaking, a *democracy* as state form is also a *republic.* In terms of the government or legislature, democratic structural elements can combine with the retention of a hereditary monarch. One part of state activity can be organized democratically, another in a monarchic manner. In this case, the state is still mostly designated a monarchy. One can say with J. Bryce that there are "enough republicans who are not democrats, and a few monarchies, such as Great Britain and Norway, that are democracies" (*Moderne Demokratien*, I, German edition, p. 22). Nevertheless, the boundary between the two concepts often becomes fluid even in depictions of democratic public law. Today, "republic" no longer designates the ideal state in the sense of Aristotle and St. Thomas.

Since Machiavelli, moreover, the word "republic" often only negatively involves an opposition to monarchy as state form. In the manner of speaking of bourgeois Rechtsstaat theorists, such as Kant, it means the Rechtsstaat that divides powers. Therefore, it stands in opposition to [224] every "absolutism," whether or not, for example, it may be monarchic or democratic (above p. 200). In this regard, "republic" still retains something of the ideal meaning of the classic tradition.

For the logic of state theory concept formation, it is of particular interest that the form introduced as normal defines the other form *per negationem.* For Machiavelli, for example, all states that are *not monarchies* are republics (Principe, cap. 1). For Richard Thoma, by contrast (*Erinnerungsgabe*, p. 44), all states that are *not democracies* are "privilege states." Kant's logically consistent understanding of the bourgeois Rechtsstaat renders relative all principles of political form by making them into organizational means of the balancing of powers.

2. Most definitions of democracy speak of a "rule of the majority," which refers to the majority of the so-called active citizens, in particular the state citizens with the right to stand for office or to vote. In itself, that need be neither the majority of the state members nor the majority of the inhabitants of the state territory. Recently, however, it has often been said in addition that it is not enough that the majority of the active citizens "rule." More precisely, the claim is that the great mass of the population must still have rights of state citizenship. It is not acceptable for majority rule to obtain inside a minority that has at its disposal a mass of persons who either are without rights or are slaves. Bryce (*Moderne Demokratien*, p. 23) demands that the great mass of the entire population, "for example, at least three-fourths approximately," have rights of state citizenship. R. Thoma (*Erinnerungsgabe*, p. 23) demands that personal freedom must be granted to all those who belong to the people. Therefore, when the "majority" is under consideration, many different types of majority can be meant: specifically (a) the majority of active citizens themselves participating in the vote; (b) the majority of all active citizens, without regard as to whether they participate in the vote or not; (c) the majority of the state members; (d) the majority of the population of an individual Land.

3. As democratic principles, *equality* and *freedom* are often termed compatible with one another, while in fact both these principles are different and often opposed to one another in their presuppositions, content, and effects. In terms of domestic politics, only equality can count properly as a democratic principle. Domestic political freedom is the principle of the bourgeois Rechtsstaat, which acts to modify the principles of political form, whether or not, for example, they are monarchic, aristocratic, or democratic. But, otherwise, neither the concept of equality nor that of freedom may be used without more precise logical and historical distinctions. On the concept of [225] democratic equality, see below II, p. 226. It must be said about the term "freedom" that it is a liberal principle when meant in the sense of an individual freedom accorded to every individual person by nature. It comes into consideration only for the Rechtsstaat component of the modern constitution, but not as a principle of political form. There all are "equally free."

The distinction between freedom and equality, like that between liberalism and democracy, provides the foundation for the book by W. Hasbach, *Die moderne Demokratie*, 2nd ed., 1923. This work considers the problem with very precise evidence and interesting material, but without a systematic state theory approach. It suffers from the polemical, antidemocratic tendencies of the author. R. Thoma (*Erinnerungsgabe*, p. 39) characterized equality and freedom as democratic principles and treated the representative democracy of liberalism as a subtype of democracy in general. Therefore, he did not distinguish between democracy and bourgeois Rechtsstaat or between the principles of political form of democracy (identity) and representation. On the concept of "representative democracy," see above p. 218.

Additional definitions of democracy are "government of the people by the people," "rule of public opinion" (government by public opinion [Schmitt's English]), or a state form where "the general right to vote is the foundation of the whole" (thus R. Thoma). All these definitions or characterizations emphasize only individual elements or effects of the democratic principle of equality, while the actual meaning of these individual elements is to be derived first out of a systematic elaboration of the fundamental concepts of democracy, equality in particular.

4. The greatest lack of clarity arises from the fact that the concept of democracy, like many other political concepts, became an entirely general *ideal concept*, the ambiguity of which, moreover, preserved a place for more diverse ideals and, finally, for everything that is ideal, beautiful, and appealing. Democracy is bound to and identified with liberalism, socialism, justice, humanity, peace, and international understanding. "The way is clear for any statutory, peaceful development," Dr. David, the Social Democratic Reich minister, argued in the Weimar National Assembly. "Herein lies the most genuine democracy." This is a remark that is affirmatively quoted by Konrad Beyerle (*Die Verfassung des Deutschen Reiches*, Munich 1919, p. 7).

This boundless extension of the concept of democracy into a general ideal concept is found among bourgeois liberals as well as the Social Democrats. Liberals like L. T. Hobhouse (*Democracy and Reaction*, 2nd ed., London 1909, p. 140) designate democracy as "the application of ethical [226] principles to politics." In fact, that is simply liberal. Jaurès defines democracy as justice, humanity, a federation of peoples, and peace, which is an interpretation characteristic of the social-liberalism of the Second International and its distinctive connection with the Geneva League of Nations (Kautsky, Bernstein, McDonald, Herriot, Paul Boncour, Thomas, Branting, Vandervelde). Thus, there arise distinctive complexes of ideas in which concepts can no longer be distinguished from another. Notable for this type of consideration is the book by Thomas G. Masaryk, *Les problèmes de la Démocratie*, Paris 1924, with a preface by Albert Thomas.

II. *The concept of equality.* Some general and meaningless equality, which by itself is present without regard for substance or value, does not suffice for the democratic concept of equality. Democracy's precise state form can be grounded only on a precise and substantial concept of equality.

1. *General human equality.* The equality of everything "that bears a human face" is incapable of providing a foundation for a state, a state form, or a form of government. No distinctive differentiations and delimitations may be derived from it; only the elimination of distinctions and boundaries may be. No specially formed institutions can be constituted on its basis, and it can only contribute to the dissolution and elimination of distinctions and institutions that no longer have any validity in themselves. Like every area of human life and thought, religion, morality, law, and economy, poli-

tics also has its particular distinctions. Nothing distinctive, either in religious or moral terms or in political or economic ones, may be derived from the fact that all persons are human. Naturally, the economic distinction of producer and consumer, for example, or the juristic distinction of creditor and debtor, cannot be explained from the fact that they are all persons. Referring to this general humanity can soften certain injustices. It can also moderate them and render them relative. However, such a reference does not constitute a concept. On the contrary, when the human equality common to all should be the sole definitive and decisive consideration, it is no longer possible to implement some distinctive differentiation. The idea of human equality does not contain a juristic, a political, or an economic criterion. Its significance for constitutional theory lies in the fact that it is part of liberal individualism and serves the principle of *basic rights.* [227]

An equality with no other content than the equality that is alone common to all humans would be a nonpolitical form of equality because it lacks the corresponding possibility of inequality. Any form of equality receives its significance and sense from the corresponding possibility of inequality. This equality becomes more intense as the inequality opposing it grows. A form of equality without the possibility of an inequality, an equality that one has exclusively and that cannot be at all lost, is without value and significance.

2. The democratic concept of equality is a *political* concept and, like every genuine political concept, includes the possibility of a *distinction.* Political democracy, therefore, cannot rest on the inability to distinguish among persons, but rather only on the quality of belonging to a *particular people.* This quality of belonging to a people can be defined by very different elements (ideas of common race, belief, common destiny, and tradition). The *equality* that is part of the essence of democracy thus orients itself *internally* and not externally: *within* a democratic state system, all members of the state are equal. The consequence for the political and public law perspective is whoever is not a member of the state is not taken into account under this democratic equality. In this instance, equality does not at all mean that the democratic Athenians do not distinguish themselves from the barbarians or that the democratic people of the United States accept every foreigner as state citizen. The degree to which the foreigner is treated equally does not involve political affairs. It is, rather, a matter of the logic of general liberal liberty rights applied in the nonpolitical sphere (private property, legal protection, etc.).

Consequently, according to the Weimar Constitution, "all *Germans,*" not all persons, "are equal before the law" (Art. 109 RV). According to Art. 4 of the Swiss federal constitution of 29 May 1874, "all *Swiss*" are "equal before the law." Under Art. 19 of the Japanese constitution of 1889, it is "all *Japanese,*" etc. Even the French Declaration of the Rights of Man and of the Citizen of 26 August 1789 at the beginning states that all *persons* are by nature free and equal. As soon as it involves political rights and those of the state, however, it no longer speaks of persons (homme), but instead of *state citizens* (citoyen). See Art. 6 and 13.

3. This democratic equality is the *prerequisite* for all other additional equalities, such as equality of the law, equal right to elected office, equal right to vote, general duty of military service, and equal access to all employment. Hence, the general right to elected office is not the content of democratic equality, but rather the consequence of a presupposed equality. Because all members of the state are presupposed as equal, they must have an equal right to elected office or an equal [228] right to vote, etc. These forms of equality are instances of applied equality, not the essence of democratic equality. Otherwise, political democracy would be a mere fiction and would be based on the fact that state citizens are treated *as if* they were equal. Perhaps today, however, some democratic institutions have only an educational goal and initially treat state citizens equally merely in order to nurture them toward a genuine form of equality. The essence of democracy cannot be derived from this.

If this pedagogic perspective is emphasized in numerous writings on democracy, it is a sign of the fact that the political form of democracy has become no longer clearly understood or else has become problematic. Even in the clever and time-tested writing by A. T. Hadley, *Probleme der Demokratie*, German edition, Stuttgart 1926, the final word and the last resort is "education."

4. This means democratic equality is a *substantial* equality. Because all state citizens participate in this substantive component, they can be treated as equals, having an equal right to election and to vote, etc.

The substance of equality can vary among different democracies and historical periods.

(a) In Greek state theory, awareness of the necessity of *physical* and *moral* similarity was especially strong. As an opponent of democracy, Plato sees democracy's actual mistake in not stipulating strictly enough that the virtue of state citizenship, ἀρετή, is the relevant mark of distinction and in rendering citizens equivalent without distinction, so that "men of the most diverse type find themselves together under one such constitution" (*Politeia* VIII, 11, 557c, p. 331 of the translation by Apelt). It is self-evident, however, that even despite this diversity only free Hellenes, not barbarians and slaves, are part of Greek democracy. Aristotle does not place himself in such an opposition to democracy. According to him, the best state, the "polity," indeed comes very close to that which one today mostly designates as democracy, which is a state where all participate in ruling and being ruled (πάντας ὁμοίως κοινωνεῖν τοῦ κατὰ μέρος ἄρχειν καὶ ἄρχεσθαι). At least in book 7 of the *Politics*, this polity appears as the best state form, in which explicitly the great similarity of the persons living in the state is also presupposed. For it is self-evident that such a state, in which all rule as well as are ruled by others, is not a "polity" for humanity. The barbarians are slaves by nature (φύσει) (*Politics*, I, 1, 5). The slave naturally has no ἀρετή, no feeling of freedom and no sense for the elevated type of existence that man finds in the political condition, specifically, the beautiful and noble life, the εὖ ζῆν. The goal and purpose [229] of the slave is by nature "to belong to another" (ἄλλου εἶναι). The barbarian states are only states in name, for in them slaves are ruled by slaves. Only the free Hellenes by nature have the physical and psychological properties that are part of political existence. Even in democracy, it is always presupposed that political existence consists only of free Hellenes. Aristotle, moreover, expressly states that the equality of the law can be valid only under the equality of birth and power. The equality before the law, then, is only just when those who are subject to the law are equal. "Equality," he argues, "counts as just. However, it is also not equality for everyone, but for those who are equal. Even inequality counts as just, and it is naturally so not for all, but only for those who are unequal" (*Politics*, III, 5, 8).

This discriminating concept of equality differentiates itself for the first time in the philosophy of the Stoa. The difference of peoples and clans, of the Hellenes and the barbarians, dissipates in the face of reason, which is common to all, governs the entire world, and makes all wise men into world citizens of a global state. It is noteworthy that this theory of the world citizen demonstrated a special preference for *monarchy* and gave up the democratic ideal. See J. Kaerst, "Studien zur Entwicklung und theoretischen Begründung der Monarchie im Altertum," *Hist. Bibl.*, vol. 6, 1898, p. 65.

(b) In the medieval theory, the ἀρετή or *virtus* is declared the principle of the aristocracy by Thomas Aquinas. In the "Discorsi," by contrast, Machiavelli presupposes this quality among the citizens of the democracy because democracy would not be possible otherwise. According to Montesquieu, the *vertu* is the principle of the *republic*. He defines this vertu conceptually as "a very simple matter, the love of the republic" (*Esprit des lois*, V, 2). It has nothing to do with education and knowledge. In a democratic republic, it is love of equality, above all sobriety and modesty in terms of demands, frugality (V, 3). It is thoroughly part of the classical tradition to assume that empire destroys democracy because it destroys "virtue" (in contrast to this, cf. today F. Tönnies, who, relying on Goldscheid, states that the democratic state must be rich or become rich; *Verhandlungen des 5. Deutschen Soziologentages*, 1926, p. 35). In Rousseau's theory of the "Contrat social," full comparability is the actual foundation of the state. What the people want is simply good, because they will it. Hence, all want the same thing. In reality no one is outvoted. And when he is outvoted, he has simply deceived himself about his true and better intention. This common will is not at all inclined toward subjecting itself to the transitory majority, for the will of the majority, even the will of all, can also be corrupt and no longer leads to a general will. One does not want to subject oneself to the majority, because it is the majority, but rather because the substantial similarity of the people is so considerable that all intend the same thing based on the common substance. Consequently, the state rests on the homogeneity and self-identify of the people, not on contract. [230] That is the strongest and most logically consistent expression of democratic thinking. The significance of this presupposition of democratic equality demonstrated itself in the practice of the Jacobin dictatorship. The political opponent had no "virtue," that is, not the proper political attitude, no "civisme." He was not a patriot and, thus, *hors de loi*. The degree to which an instance of inequality corresponds to political equality as a necessary correlate becomes manifest especially clearly here.

(c) The substance of democratic equality can be found in commonly held *religious* convictions. Inside religious communities, an equality of all members arises to the extent that all sincerely agree on essentials. In smaller associations, whose members consider themselves the chosen, saintly, or saved, the fact of being chosen, consequently, the inequality of those outside the association, is an especially firm foundation for equality *inside* the community.

For the emergence of modern democracy, the example of the English sectarians under Cromwell is significant. According to a widely held view, the ideas of modern direct democracy appeared for the first time in the Levelers' movement (G. P. Gooch, *The history of English Democratical Ideas in the 16th Century*, Cambridge 1894). On 28 October 1647, these radical sectarians proposed an agreement that was passed on to the Parliament, but it had no further practical significance because Cromwell suppressed the entire movement. This agreement stipulated the dependence of Parliament on the people, and the proportional distribution of electoral seats. As rights from birth (native rights), it stipulated freedom of conscience, freedom from compulsory military service, the elimination of exceptional courts, equality before the law, and security and welfare of the people as the foundation of legislation. Such basic tenets should be established as "fundamental principles" and be submitted to the people for acceptance. The leader of the Levelers, Lilburne, states in the *Legal fundamental Liberties of the people of England* (1649) that this "foundation" of a just government must be submitted to the people for their consent in every county. But such demands of equality, religious freedom, consent of the people naturally are valid fundamentally only for one's fellow believers. Not one of these sectarians also thought of granting these rights to papists or atheists. Incidentally, Lilburne expressly states in the work just mentioned that only those with the proper outlook, the well-affected people [English in Schmitt's original], are entitled to election and "can give their consent to the foundations" (*The Clarke Papers*, edition of C. H. Firth, vol. II, Camden Society, 1894, pp. 257/8). Even here it is not a matter of a general human equality, but only of the equality of the holders of certain religious convictions, who struggle against common opponents, papists, Anglicanism, and a state church. Even in the American colonies, where the emigrant sectarians or Puritans founded new communities, the freedom of conscience was valid only for the like-minded. In Puritan Massachusetts, statutes provided that each person be [231] obligated to participate in the public religious service. Whoever was not a member of the religious community was not treated as a freeman. If someone was excluded thoroughly by the community for three months because of transgressions, he was punished with imprisonment and exiled (Rothenbücher, *Trennung von Kirche und Staat*, 1910, p. 119). To the extent that one is speaking here of democracy, the issue is the fact that a new religious feeling becomes the foundation of a new community, inside of which the community members consider themselves as equal to one another. Even here one cannot speak of a form of human equality without substance. More precisely, the substance of this democratic equality lay in the community of genuine religious belief.

(d) *The national democracy.* The French Revolution of 1789, despite its ideas of humanity and general brotherhood of all peoples, presupposes the French *nation* as a historically given entity. Its constitutions are linkages of the principles of the bourgeois Rechtsstaat with the democratic principles of the constitution-making power of the people (see above § 6, p. 50). In the nineteenth century, the national idea led to new political formations and to the democratization of the states through general compulsory military service and the general right to election. The substance of equality, which is part of all these institutions, resides in the national component. The presupposition of this type of democracy is national homogeneity.

In contrast to the general concept of the people, the nation concept means a people individualized through a politically distinctive consciousness. Different elements can contribute to the unity of the nation and to the consciousness of this unity, such as common language, common historical destiny, traditions and remembrances, and common political goals and hopes. The language is a very important factor in this, yet it is not by itself determinative. What is definitive is the commonality of historical life, conscious willing of this commonality, great events and goals. Genuine revolutions and victorious wars can overcome the linguistic differences and justify the feeling of national belonging, even if the same language is not spoken.

If the nation is understood as the essential substantive element of democratic equality, practical consequences of a special type result. A democratic state that finds the underlying conditions of its democracy in the national similarity of its citizens corresponds to the so-called nationality principle, according to which a nation forms a state, and a state incorporates a nation. A nationally homogeneous state appears then as something normal. A state lacking this homogeneity has an abnormal quality that is a threat to peace. The national principle thus becomes the prerequisite of peace and the "foundation of international law."

The resulting possible solutions vary, if there is not national homogeneity in real political terms, because a state consists of diverse nations or contains national minorities. [232] Initially, there is the attempt at a peaceful reconciliation of differences. In fact, however, that means either peaceful engagement and separation or gradual, peaceful *assimilation* to the ruling nation. The currently existing minority protection under international law (above p. 74) attempts to guarantee a peaceful course of action. Hence, the national minority is protected not as a nation. As a nation, it should not have political rights against the ruling nation, because otherwise with the nationality principle even the principle of the democratic state itself would be eliminated. More precisely, the current international law regime protecting national minorities operates from the perspective of the protection of the single person's individual rights, for whom equality, freedom, property, and the use of his native language is guaranteed as an individual. Here, the openly professed idea of national homogeneity and the prerequisite of democracy are peacefully realized. The other method is quicker and more violent. It is the elimination of the alien component through suppression or *exile* of the heterogeneous population and other radical means. The most important example of this method is the Greek-Turkish Treaty of Lausanne of 30 January 1923, which in accordance with Art. 542 of the Treaty of Lausanne entered into force on 26 August 1923 after its ratification on 24 July 1923. According to the treaty, the Greek population living in the Turkish area is transferred to Greece, and the Turkish population living in the Greek area is transferred to Turkey, without regard for the will of the persons affected by this exchange.

Additional consequences are attributed to such methods of ensuring or realizing the national homogeneity. The first consequence is *control of foreign entry* and expulsion of unwanted foreign elements through *immigration legislation*, as it is implemented in the United States of America and in the English dominions, especially in Australia and the South African Union. The second consequence is development of special forms and *methods of rule for countries with a heterogeneous population*, by which it is a matter of, on the one hand, avoiding open annexation and, on the other hand, of retaining a hold on the most important political decisions, such as those involving colonies, protectorates, mandates, and intervention treaties like those the United States of America concluded with Latin American states (above p. 73). An essential aspect of this method is the fact that the dominated country remains foreign territory in public law terms and that its population does not obtain membership in the state of the ruling country.[1] Laws against foreign domination are the third consequence. Such laws are for the protection of national industry and for the protection against the economic and social power of foreign capital, and they result after war in numerous states. Especially famous cases are the Turkish laws that implement a [233] Turkish domination of the country, and Art. 27 of the 1917 Mexican constitution, which allows ground and mineral resources to be nationalized.[2] Fourth, there is also the more recent practice of the law of state membership, the possibility of expatriation, denaturalization, etc. Fifth, a noteworthy individual consequence is that the constitution of the Czecho-Slovakian state of 29 February 1920 was only established by party delegates of the Czech and Slovak parties and under exclusion of the non-Slavic population (above § 8, p. 87). On this, see the instructive apology by F. Weyr, *Zeitschrift für öffentliches Recht*, I, p. 3, and *Jahrbuch des öffentlichen Rechts*, XI (1922), p. 352ff.

Such effects of democratic homogeneity demonstrate the opposition of democracy as a principle of political form to the liberal ideas of freedom and equality of the individual person with every other person. A democratic state would deprive itself of its substance through a logically consistent recognition of general human equality in the area of public life and of public law.

(e) The Bolshevik policy of the Soviet Republic made an attempt to substitute national homogeneity with the homogeneity of a *class*, of the proletariat. [234]

Art. 20 of the Declaration of the Rights of Working and Exploited People in Section I of the constitution of 10 July 1918 reads: "Proceeding from the solidarity of the working people of all nations, the Russian socialist, federalist, soviet republic guarantees to foreigners, who for work purposes are residing temporarily in the territory of the Russian Republic, and to the working class or the peasantry that are not exploiting foreign work forces all the political rights of the Russian state citizen and concedes to the local Soviet the right to accord such foreigners the protection of the civil law of the Russian state without qualified formalities." Cf. Bogolepow, *Die Rechtsstellung der Ausländer in Sowjet-Rußland, Quellen und Studien des Osteuropa-Instituts in Breslau*, Law Department, new series 4, Berlin 1927, pp. 29, 170ff., who argues that "the solidarity of the working people of all nations is the condition of their equal position in regard to political rights."

Even if this attempt succeeds and the concept of the proletariat is capable of replacing the substance of national homogeneity with a class-based homogeneity, here again a new distinction, proletarian against bourgeois, would also arise and the structure of the political concept of democracy would be unchanged. In place of national differences, that of proletarian and capitalist states would come into play, and through it the grouping of friend and of enemy would receive a new intensity.

5. Democratic equality is essentially *similarity*, in particular similarity among the people. The central concept of democracy is *people* and *not humanity*. If democracy is to be a political form at all, there is only a people's democracy and not that of humanity. Even the concept of *class* cannot replace the concept of the people for democracy. So long as class is a purely economic concept on a thoroughly economic foundation, it does not ground a substantial homogeneity. If class becomes the foundation of

a militant organization and supplies the justification for a genuine friend and enemy grouping, class is no longer a purely economic concept, because a genuinely militant class is no longer an essentially economic entity. It is, rather, a political one. If it succeeds in dominating the state, the class in question becomes the people of this state. The democratic concept of the people always remains in place and contains an opposition both to the concept of humanity as well as to the concept of class.

III. *Definition of democracy.* As a state form as well as a governmental or legislative form, democracy is the identity of ruler and ruled, governing and governed, commander and follower. [235]

1. This definition results from the substantial equality that is the essential presupposition of democracy. It precludes the possibility that inside the democratic state the distinction of ruler and being ruled, governor and governed expresses or produces a *qualitative* difference. In democracy, dominance or government may not rest on inequality, therefore, not on the superiority of those ruling or governing, nor on the fact that those governing are qualitatively better than the governed. They must agree substantively in terms of democratic equality and homogeneity. Hence, when one rules or governs, he may not deviate from the general identity and homogeneity of the people. Consequently, the power or authority of those who rule or govern may not be based on some higher qualities that are not easily obtained by the people, but rather only on the will, on the commission from and confidence of those who are being ruled or governed and thereby actually rule *themselves.* Thus the turn of phrase that democracy is the rule of the people over itself receives its sense as an idea. All democratic tendencies and institutions like equality and equal rights in the most diverse areas (the general right to election and to vote and the ever broader extension of the general right to election and to vote to men and women, reduction of the age of election, shortening of the electoral period, dissolution of parliament) arise from this striving to realize the identity of governing and governed.

The word "identity" is useful for the definition of democracy, because it denotes the comprehensive identity of the homogeneous people. More specifically, it denotes the identity of the homogenous people that includes both those governing and governed. And it denies the difference present in other state forms between the governing and governed. In this regard, it is noteworthy that the difference between representing and being represented does not come into consideration, for that which is being represented is not those governing, but instead the political unity of the whole. In pure democracy, there is only the self-identity of the genuinely present people, which is not a type of representation. What is meant by the word "identity" is the existential quality of the political unity of the people in contrast to any normative, schematic, or fictional types of equality. On the whole and in every detail of its political existence, democracy presupposes a people whose members are similar to one another and who have the will to political existence. Under this presupposition, it is thoroughly correct when *Rousseau* states that what the people will is always good. Such a principle is correct not on the basis of a norm. It is correct because a people's existence is based on its homogeneity.

For the further justification of the word "identity" in this connection, I gladly refer to E. Husserl, *Logische Untersuchungen*, II 2, p. 112, who argues that "every instance of equality refers to a species to which all of them [236] belong. And both aspects of this species are not initially something merely equal and cannot be, since otherwise the most perverse regressus in infinitum would be unavoidable . . . Equality is the relationship of objects that provides the foundation for one and the same species. If it is no longer permissible to speak of the identity of the species, of the respect in which the equality takes place, the talk of equality also loses its foundation. (Cf. on this point the thorough treatment of H. Lipps, *Untersuchungen zur Phänomenologie der Erkenntnis*, part I, Bonn 1927, p. 10ff.) Governing and governed remain in the identity of homogenous substance that constitutes the essence of the democratic state. Democratic equality is never something mathematical, numerical, or statistical. The equality of mathematical quantities is, as H. Lipps, *Untersuchungen*, p. 12, aptly states, "not an equality of things and does not denote an identity. It is, rather, the starting point of an axiom as the irreducible root of certain mathematical theorems."

2. In democracy, state power and government derive from the people. The problem of government internal to democracy lies in the fact that those governing and those governed may differentiate themselves only inside the comparability of the people, which remain equal with one another. For the difference between those governing and those governed, between those who command and those who obey, remains in place so long as there are government and commands generally, that is to say, as long as the democratic state as state exists. Thus, a differentiation of those governed and those governing cannot be displaced. As a genuine political concept, democracy is also far from the dissolution of such distinctions into normative elements of an ethical type or into mere economic functioning. Compared to other state forms, the difference between those governing and those governed can even be enhanced and increased extraordinarily in *material* terms to the extent that only the *persons* who govern and command are still rooted in the substantive similarity of the people. If they receive the consent of and have the confidence of the people, to which they belong, their rule can be stricter and more intense, their government more decisive than that of some patriarchal monarch or a cautious oligarchy. Gambetta considered democracy simply the foundation of an especially strong government. This idea is prominent even among the democratic politicians of the Weimar Coalition. In the debates over Art. 48 during the Reichstag session of 3 March 1920, Deputy Petersen stated that "there is no state form as unobjectionable in terms of securing the means of power as democracy, because it rests on the equal rights of all state citizens." One cannot generally define a political form according to properties like mildness and hardness, ruthlessness or humanity. It is the distinctly liberal, Rechtsstaat component, which linked

itself with the democratic [237] element of a constitution, that leads to the weakening and softening of the power of the state by a system of controls and restrictions. This tendency is not essential to democracy as a political form; it is perhaps even foreign to it. A dictatorship in particular is possible only on a democratic foundation, while for this reason it already contradicts the principles of liberal legality, because it is part of dictatorship that no factually defined, generally legislated competence is provided to the dictator. Instead, the scope and content of his *empowerment* are dependent on his *discretion*, so that there is not a jurisdiction in the Rechtsstaat sense at all.

A democracy must not permit the inevitable *factual* difference between governing and being governed to become a qualitative distinction and to distance governing persons from those governed. In a democracy, whoever governs does so not because he possesses the properties of a qualitatively better upper class opposed to an inferior lower class. That would naturally eliminate the democratic homogeneity and identity. Greater efficiency and specialized knowledge could reasonably prompt the people to entrust comrades who are efficient with the administration and leadership duties. Then, however, someone governs only because he has the confidence of the people. He has no authority that stems from special being. It is all the better when only the best and most efficient of the people are entrusted with governing. But this type of selection and preference for the most capable persons in democracy never allows it to lead to the formation of a special class endangering the qualitative and substantive equality of all, which is the supreme prerequisite of every democracy. Those who govern are rendered distinct *by* the people, not *from* the people, and the denunciation of the nobility by *Sieyès* in 1789 involved the nobility not wanting to be distinguished *by* their fellow citizens, but rather *from* their fellow citizens.

3. Democratic identity rests on the idea that everything inside the state involving activation of state power and government only occurs *within* the confines of the people's substantial similarity to one another. It is clear that all democratic thinking centers on ideas of *immanence*. Every departure from immanence would deny this identity. Every type of transcendence that is introduced into a people's political life leads to qualitative distinctions of high and low, [238] above and below, chosen, etc., while in a democracy state power must derive from the people and may not be set in motion by a person or from a position that is outside of the people and standing above it. State power does not even derive from God. At least so long as the possibility exists that another besides the people itself decides definitively what in concreto God's will is, the appeal to the will of God contains a moment of undemocratic transcendence. The principle "all power derives from God" can possibly mean that a state power is exercised even against the will of

The Theory of Democracy

the people; in this meaning, it contradicts democracy. It does so as well if it means that with the appeal to the will of God, the definitiveness and validity of the people's will is denied. If God, in whose name one governs, is simply not this people's god, the appeal to God's will can lead to the fact that the will of the people and the will of God are different and collide with one another. Then, under democratic logic, only the will of the people must come into consideration, because God cannot appear in the political realm other than as the god of a particular people. That is the meaning of the principle "the people's voice is the voice of God." This saying, which was canonized in the American democracy by Jefferson, in Europe by Mazzini, is more than a manner of speech. With its direct appeal to God as well as to the kingdom of God's grace, it has a polemical sense of rejecting every other governing authority, foreign and domestic, that in the name of God intends to impose its will on the people. The clear implication is the rejection of all political influences and effects not originating from the substantial homogeneity of the people themselves.

The People and the Democratic Constitution

I. The people *anterior to* and *above* the constitution.

Under democracy, the people are the subject of the constitution-making power. The democratic understanding sees every constitution, even its Rechtsstaat component, as resting on the concrete political decision of the people capable of political action. Every democratic constitution presupposes such a people capable of action (above § 10, p. 91). [239]

II. The people *within* the constitution exercising constitutionally regulated powers. In the context of and on the foundation of a constitution, the people as the electorate or state citizenry entitled to vote can exercise certain constitutionally regulated competencies.

1. *Elections.* The voter determines the person who should carry out a state activity. The election can have a double sense of the determination of a representative or selection of a dependent agent.

(a) Election of a representative of the entire, politically united people. Art. 41 of the Weimar Constitution, for example, provides for the election of the President by the entire people. The majority of the state citizens participating in the election with the right to vote determine the election result.

The nonvoting registered voters influence the electoral result through the fact that by their absence they reduce the number of the required votes. The greater the number of nonvoting registered voters, the smaller the number of votes cast, and, concomitantly, the percentage of the total electorate that determines the electoral result decreases. The majority of votes cast counts then as the will of the *entire* people. This will is valid, first, as the will of even the electoral participants who voted for the losing side, and yet also as the will of the nonvoting registered voters, and finally as the will of all state citizens not registered to vote. In a democracy, it is self-evident that the state citizen who is outvoted or the nonvoting state citizen cannot claim that he did not vote for the winning candidate.

(b) Election of a member of a legislative body (popular assembly, parliament, Reichstag, provincial legislature) of the entire state. Even the election under current constitutional law should provide the foundation for a form of representation, although actually this idea is becoming no longer clearly understood and the election, in particular through the methods of the system of proportional representation with party lists, is lent the character of selecting party and interest functionaries.

During an *individual election* in an electoral district, the majority of the registered voters of this electoral district participating in the election select a deputy. The deputy elected, however, serves as deputy of the entire people (Art. 21 of the Weimar Constitution). The majority will of the election participants in an electoral district is valid not only as the will of the defeated voters and those not casting ballots or state members of this district, but rather also as the will of all other enfranchised voters as well as of the state citizens of the *entire state* who are not entitled to vote. Any other construction is not possible because it would make the circle of voters an independent entity and would destroy the political unity.

Apparently, this risk declines with the different methods of the *system of proportional representation*. This system's most important justification is that one designates it as a system in which votes are cast not according to personal and local perspectives, but rather according to *ideas* (J. Jaurès), which is an optimistic understanding in view of the reality of current party life. Yet in this system, the electoral district permits its transformation into a mere technical means of voting; [240] the special meaning of local and territorial electoral districts diminishes along with it. It is also possible to unify and validate votes throughout the entire state that are in the minority in certain districts. In this way, moreover, the necessity of a *runoff election* and, in the current system of lists, also the necessity, even the possibility, of a mid-term or special election diminishes. In this system, the idea of the political unity of the entire people undoubtedly emerges stronger in a territorial sense. Nevertheless, it would be incorrect to consider the system of proportional representation more democratic than other systems. The divisions that occur in this system are indeed not territorial, but extend more profoundly through the entire state. Still, as in other systems, the will of the voters for a list must count as the will of *all other voters.* The deputies of every individual list, that is, of every party, must serve as deputies of the entire people. It must be perceived as true, therefore, that every German national voter also elected the communist deputies receiving mandates to the same extent that the German national deputies represent the communist voters. If the division into electoral districts with individual elections signals an endangerment of territorial cohesion, this system signifies a threat to homogeneity. The different voter groups are no longer aware, and they are incapable of being aware, that they are not selecting their own deputies, but instead only deputies of the entire people.

(c) Local elections do not come into consideration in this context, because they do not involve the political unity as a whole. So from the standpoint of state theory, they must be considered a qualitatively different type of election.

2. Ballot questions. By voting, a state citizen takes a position on a substantive question and provides a substantive answer in some form.

(a) The different methods of referendum, of the plebiscite, and of the popular vote, which are included (on this below § 20, p. 259) under the collective designation "popular vote," belong in this category.

The majority of the votes cast usually decides the issue. In other words, the content of the response counts as an answer to the question posed, which is the answer most voting state citizens gave. At this point, it is already clear that logically, psychologically, and in terms of voting technology, the value of the answer depends entirely on the posing of the question. Specifically, only such answers may be tallied that give a clear and simple substantive answer to a question that is just as clear and simple as well as substantive. In general, the question must be so posed that it can be answered with a simple "yes" or "no." The yes or no of the simple majority of the votes cast then counts as a decision of the entire people. It counts even as the will of those who are outvoted and, moreover, as the will of those who did not participate in the vote as well as those who do not have a right to vote. [241]

If a certain type of electoral participation is required, then enfranchised voters who abstain are the deciding factor even more than in other votes or in elections simply by distancing themselves from the election. Art. 75 provides, for example, that "a decision of the Reichstag can only be suspended by referendum when the majority of enfranchised voters participate in the vote." The petition counts as rejected. Put differently, the question presented counts as denied when the majority of enfranchised voters did not participate in the vote. In this way, the decision is made by those who do *not* vote, thereby making clear that they do not intend to decide. Remarkably, the will of those who express a will is not definitive in this instance. Instead, the will of those who express no will and possibly also have no will is decisive. Their "will" or better "non-will" counts also as the will of those who expressed one (on this issue, particularly in reference to the referendum of 20 June 1926, see R. Liepmann, *Zeitschrift für öffentliches Recht*, vol. VI, 1927, p. 609f.).

(b) Popular initiative (popular legislative petition). A minority is sufficient to register a petition (according to Art. 73, 2, one-twentieth of those entitled to vote, and according to Art. 73, 3, a tenth of those entitled to vote). The petition of the minority is designated as a *popular* legislative proposal, although, in contrast to the aforementioned cases, one cannot say that the will of the enfranchised voters taking part in the placing of the petition counts otherwise as the will of all. The fiction is superfluous and misleading in this context because it would only mean that everything that proceeds lawfully in the context of a democratic state, even every single judicial decision and any individual administrative act, counts as the will of the entire people and of all individual state citizens. More precisely, the decisive thing in such a minority petition is that it can even be registered *against* the will of the majority. The word "people" in this instance has an essentially different sense than in combinations such as "popular initiative" or "popular election." The expression is explicable, rather, in reference to the fact that in a democracy an initiative is normally also part of the realm of activity of the state officials, or of the *magistracy*. One may say with Lorenz von Stein (*Verwaltungslehre*, p. 92) that there can be no government without initiative, even if it shares this with the legislative body. In addition to other meanings, the word "people" has the special sense that it includes a contrast to every state official and magistrate. People are those who do *not* govern, do *not* represent, do *not* exercise organized functions with an official character. If an authority is nevertheless now given to a non-organized part of the state citizens entitled to vote, an authority that, according to its nature, would be a concern of state [242] officials, then the peculiarity of the word "people" lies in the fact that it is precisely *not officials* who are active here. It is always presupposed that an unorganized mass places the petition. If a party with a sufficiently large member count would organize an office, in order to constantly register popular initiatives, the sense of this constitutional rule would be presented falsely, and a "popular" petition would no longer be at issue. A "party" petition would be instead. The distinctive quality of the concept "people" resides in the fact that the people is an entity that is not formed and is never capable of being fully formed.

III. 1. The people *compared with* the constitutional regime (public opinion). Under the democratic theory of the people's constitution-making power, the people stands as the bearer of the constitution-making power outside of and above any constitutional norm. If certain competencies (elections and instances of voting) are assigned to the people by the constitution, their potential for political action and significance in a democracy is in no way exhausted or settled. Compared to all such normative frameworks, the people continue to exist as an entity that is directly and genuinely *present*, not mediated by previously defined normative systems, validations, and fictions. Even if one incorporated constitutional institutions of a so-called direct democracy into the state organization, the people are not excluded from all other relationships. And the fact that individual constitutional powers are assigned to the voters and state citizens entitled to vote still does not transform the people into an administrative organ. It is precisely in a democracy that the people cannot become the administrative apparatus and a mere state "organ." The people is always more than a functioning bureau with the competence for settling official business, and, together with instances of a constitutionally organized activity (popular election and direct popular vote on specific issues), the people in its essence persists as an entity that is unorganized and unformed.

In this context, the concept of the people is defined in negative terms, in particular by the contrast with the system of administrators and magistrates organized by position. Beyond this negation of the official realm, in other areas it is also characteristic of the concept of the people that it can be defined negatively. It would not only generally involve something sociologically essential, if one defined the people negatively in such a manner (for example, the audience in a theater as the part of those present who do *not* perform), but this distinctive negativity also does not permit itself to be mistaken for the scholarly treatment of political theories. In a special meaning of the word, the people are [243] everyone who is *not* honored and distinguished, everyone *not* privileged, everyone prominent *not* because of property, social position, or education. Thus states Schopenhauer: "Whoever does not understand Latin is part of the people." In the French Revolution of the year 1789, the bourgeoisie as Third Estate could identify itself with the nation and the *bourgeoisie* was the people, because the bourgeoisie was the opposition to the aristocracy and to the privileged. Sieyès posed the famous question: what is the Third Estate? He answered that it is the nation. The Third Estate is nothing and should become everything. But as soon as the bourgeoisie itself appeared as a class that is marked by property and that dominates the state, the negation was extended. Now the *proletariat* became the people, because it becomes the bearer of this negativity. It is the part of the population that does *not* have property, does not participate in the productive majority, and finds no place in the existing order. In contrast to the propertied classes, consequently, it appears as the people in an especially intense sense, and an assembly of proletarians is today more a popular assembly than an assembly of industrialists or intellectuals can be. Democracy becomes a proletarian democracy and eliminates the liberalism of the propertied and educated bourgeoisie.

2. This negatively defined entity, the people, is not less significant for public life because of the negativity of its definition. "People" is a concept that becomes present only in the *public* sphere. The people appear only in the public, and they first produce the public generally. People and public exist together: no people without public and no public without the people. By its *presence*, specifically, the people initiate the public. Only the present, truly assembled people are the people and produce the public. The correct idea that supports *Rousseau's* famous thesis that the people cannot be represented rests on this truth. They cannot be represented, because they must be *present*, and only something absent, not something present, may be represented. As a present, genuinely assembled people, they exist in the pure democracy with the greatest possible degree of identity: as ἐκκλησία in the market of Greek democracy; in the Roman Forum; as assembled team or army; as a local government of a Swiss Land. But also where they assemble themselves not through an ordered procedure in a certain place, the distinctive meaning of the people nevertheless reveals itself in the genuine presence of a publicly assembled people. The genuinely assembled people are first a people, and only the genuinely assembled people can do that which pertains distinctly to the activity of this people. They can *acclaim* in that they express their consent or disapproval by a simple calling out, calling higher or lower, celebrating a leader or a suggestion, honoring the king or some other person, or denying the acclamation by silence or [244] complaining. Even in a monarchy, the people inevitably appear in this activity, so long as the monarchy is a vibrant state system generally. When indeed only the people are actually assembled for whatever purpose, to the extent that it does not only appear as an organized interest group, for example, during street demonstrations and public festivals, in theaters, on the running track, or in the stadium, this people engaged in acclamation is present, and it is, at least potentially, a political entity. Often enough, experience has confirmed that every popular assembly, even one that initially appears nonpolitical, intrinsically contains unexpected political possibilities.

Only through such simple and elementary appearances may the essential concept of the public, which, though rather obscure, is essential for all political life, especially for modern democracy, again secure for itself its authority and recognize the actual problem of modern democracy. For genuine popular assemblies and acclamations are entirely unknown to the constitutional regime of contemporary bourgeois democracy. The right of assembly still appears as a bourgeois liberty right that is guaranteed (Art. 124) and as an object of regulation under the law of association and assembly. Whoever confuses the constitution of a democracy with such sets of norms can easily dispute that there is a problem at all. For the organization of democracy, as it occurs today in states with a bourgeois Rechtsstaat constitution, extends beyond directly ignoring the assembled people as such, because, as already often discussed, a distinctive feature of the bourgeois Rechtsstaat constitution is to ignore the sovereign, whether this sovereign is the monarch or the people. Freedom of assembly certainly exists and "popular assemblies" take place during elections and votes. Considered in constitutional terms, the assembled are not the people and do not engage in a public function. Where the people engage in constitutionally sanctioned functions, such as elections and votes, the assembly is *not* directly part of the legally established process. The election or vote, more precisely, is a *secret individual vote.* The method of the secret individual vote, however, is not democratic. It is, rather, an expression of liberal individualism, much in the way that its early advocate in the nineteenth century, Jeremy Bentham, [245] was a typical liberal. In the struggle against impermissible electoral influencing by the government and against other misuses, the demand for secret individual ballots makes sense and is relatively justified. Nevertheless, it is necessary to understand its nature correctly and to be clear that in principle it is part of the circle of ideas associated with liberal individualism and contradicts the political principle of democracy. For the logically consistent execution of the secret individual election and the individual vote transforms the distinctly democratic, or *political,* figure, the state citizen or *citoyen,* into a private man who, from the sphere of the *private,* whether or not this private sphere may be his religion or his economic interest or both together, expresses a private opinion and casts his vote. Secret individual ballot means that the voting state citizen is isolated in the decisive moment. In this way, the gathering of those present and any acclamation has become impossible. The connection among the assembled people and vote is completely broken up. The people elect and vote no longer as the people. In modern democracy, the methods of the popular election and referendum today in no way contain the procedure of a genuinely popular election and of a referendum. Rather, they organize a procedure for an individual vote with the addition of individual votes. This procedure is typical in most democracies today. Alongside the freedom of election, consequently, the Weimar Constitution also guaranteed the *secret ballot* (Art. 125, 22, and 17). According to electoral laws and voting orders, one seeks to provide through a set of safety measures (ballot boxes, envelopes, voting booths, etc.) that the secret is secure and the individual remains "unobserved." In the United States of America and in other Anglo-Saxon countries, complicated machines with registers and buttons were invented in order not only to ensure electoral and voting secrecy institutionally, but also to provide it additional mechanical guarantees. It is fully conceivable that one day through ingenious discoveries, every single person, without leaving his apartment, could continuously express his opinions on political questions through an apparatus and that all these opinions would automatically be registered by a central office, where one would only need to read them off. That would not be an [246] especially intensive democracy, but it would provide a proof of the fact that the state and the public were fully privatized. It would not be public opinion, for even the shared opinion of millions of private people produces no public opinion. The result is only a sum of private opinions. In this way, no common will arises, no volonté générale; only the sum of all individual wills, a volonté de tous, does.

On American methods of secret registration by machines, see Esmein-Nézard, *Droit constitutionnel*, II, p. 323f. On the "safety measures" intended to ensure an "unobserved individual vote" under valid German law, see § 41, 42, 43 of the German Decree on Reich Elections and Votes of 14 March 1924 (*Reichsgesetzesblatt* I, p. 173, with the changes of 3 November 1924, *Reichsgesetzesblatt* I, p. 726 and the report of 6 April 1924, *Reichsgesetzesblatt* I, p. 646), especially § 43 (voting precautions), which provides that "in every voting room, the local official sets up one or several tables with certain precautions, so that every person entitled to vote can handle his ballot unobserved and lay it in the envelope."

That the logically consistent execution of the secret election is not democratic, because it removes the individual state citizen from the public sphere and transforms him into a private man, also stems from the public law quality of this "secret." Considered in public law terms, the current electoral and voting secrecy is *not a genuine secret* at all. According to their discretion, the voters can decide whether to disclose and make this secret public; its preservation is only a right, not a duty of the state citizen. The individual can, indeed, forgo the administrative-technical apparatus, which protects electoral secrecy (on this, see Martin Drath, *Das Wahlprüfungsrecht bei der Reichstagwahl*, Berlin 1927, pp. 69ff.), but only because the execution of the statutory provisions on electoral secrecy is an official matter and not an individual one. Moreover, no one prevents him from communicating how he selected and voted, and it is entirely his private business what meaning he attaches to this secret act. A comparison with a civil servant's official secrecy shows the great public law difference between both these types of secrecy. That is all the more noticeable when according to the democratic understanding the electing or voting state citizen engages in a public function and is not a private person. Under the current regulation of the methods for secret individual votes, however, he transforms himself precisely at the decisive moment into a private man. The electoral secret is the point at which this transformation occurs and the reshaping of democracy into the liberal protection of the private takes place. Herein lies perhaps one of the *arcana* of the modern bourgeois democracy.

The People and the Constitution

3. According to these discussions of the connection between the people and the public, it appears justified that democracy is designated as the rule of public opinion, "government by public opinion." No public opinion can arise by way of secret individual ballot and through the adding up of the opinions of isolated private people. All these registration methods are only means of assistance, and as such they are useful and valuable. But in no way do they fully encompass public opinion. *Public opinion is the modern type of acclamation.* It is perhaps a diffuse type, and its problem is resolved neither sociologically nor [247] in terms of public law. However, its essence and political significance lie in the fact that it can be understood as acclamation. There is no democracy and no state without public opinion, as there is no state without acclamation. Public opinion arises and exists in an "unorganized" form. Precisely like acclamation, it would be deprived of its nature if it became a type of official function. This is not to say that it arises in a secret manner out of nothing. It is influenced and even made by parties or groups. Nevertheless, that can never be recognized legally and made official, and, in some sense, it remains uncontrolled. In every democracy, there are parties, speakers, and demagogues, from the προτάται of the Athenians up to the *bosses* in American democracy. Moreover, there are the press, film, and other methods of psycho-technical handling of great masses of people. All that escapes a comprehensive set of norms. The danger always exists that invisible and irresponsible social powers direct public opinion and the will of the people. But the answer to the problem also lies in the essential presupposition of every democracy. The danger is not great as long as there is a substantive democratic similarity among the people, and as long as the people have political consciousness that can distinguish between friend and enemy. If the substantive prerequisites of democracy are displaced, no organization or statutory norm serves as a remedy. Nothing would be achieved, if one wanted to eliminate the difficulties and dysfunctions of current party life, by recognizing, beyond the technical functions of election and voting, the parties as legal organizations and turning them into authorities. Then other parties would simply have to form, for the essence of the party remains outside of every magistracy organization. There is no democracy without parties, but only because there is no democracy without public opinion and without the people that are always present as the people. Just as a party cannot transform itself into an official organ without losing its party character, so public opinion cannot permit its transformation into an official jurisdiction, in particular because even the people cannot allow itself to be transformed into an official body without ceasing to be the people. The current superiority of the party organizations in contrast to parliament rests on the fact that these party organizations correspond

to the democratic principle of identity insofar as they, like the people, are always present and at hand [248] without representing, while the parliament is meaningful only in the act of representation. Parliament, however, has actually lost its representative character (below p. 319). A genuine identity (itself a mere *part* of the people) is naturally superior to representation that is not genuine.

The Weimar Constitution recognizes no parties. It mentions the word only once in a disapproving sense in Art. 130, which reads: "Public officials are servants of the collective, not of a party." And through the civil service a distinctive element of the civil servant state is built into the Constitution and is secured by an institutional guarantee. Parties (factions) are not recognized in the Constitution. Instead, they are recognized in the house rules of parliamentary democracies like the by-laws for the German Reichstag of 12 December 1922 (*Reichgesetzesblatt* 1923, II, p. 101): the Reichstag president, among others, is informed of the formation of the faction. Fifteen is the number stipulated for the formation of the faction. The legislative initiative is conceived as that of a faction "from the membership of the Reichstag" (Art. 68), because fifteen signatures is part of this initiative (§ 49 of the by-laws of 1922). The legislative initiative of the Reichstag transforms itself in this way into the legislative initiative of a faction. Nevertheless, this is not to say that beyond the realm of the by-laws, the factions or parties would have become an essential constitutional component of the Reichstag and, consequently, the party or faction activity of the individual deputy must be counted as part of the "exercise of his profession" as deputy. That would be an interpretation that makes the deputy into a party or faction bureaucrat and the party or faction into an officially recognized formation, an organization of officials, though it is not one in essence. Consequently, the immunity (freedom from responsibility) of Art. 36 cannot be extended to this party and faction activity or to the statements in faction meetings. More accurately, the boundaries of the previously mentioned freedom from responsibility lie precisely where the President's executive authority finds its boundary (for a differing view, see Anschütz, *Kommentar*, p. 145; a correct understanding is in W. Troitzsch, *Rechtspflege und Immunität der Abgeordneten*, Rostock 1927, p. 84). On the electoral law recognition of the parties, see H. Triepel, *Die Staatsverfassung und die politischen Parteien* (Berliner Universitätsrede, 1927), p. 20, who argues that "electoral laws still sometimes shamelessly mischaracterize parties as 'electoral associations' or 'voters' groups.' Mostly, however, parties appear on the scene already plainly identified, occasionally even in the constitution, as in Thüringen. The disguise has indeed become thoroughly senseless. For the entire system bases itself on the fact that organized parties struggle mightily for electoral victories." On the recognition of party groups in France, see Barthélemy-Duez, *Droit constitutionnel*, 1926, p. 444; consult O. Koellreutter, *Die politischen Parteien im modernen Staat*, especially p. 62ff., on the problem generally.

Despite its incomprehensibility and resistance to organization, public opinion since the eighteenth century is known and treated in the political and state theory literature as a special factor in state life. The philosophers of the eighteenth-century Enlightenment were supporters of an enlightened despotism, but in an enlightened public opinion they discerned the control of all state activity and a secure guarantee against any misuse of state power. Freedom of expression of opinion [249] and freedom of the press became political institutions. As such, they retain the character of *political* rights, and they are no longer the result of the individualistic freedom of conscience and religion, as they are in the American context. The use of press freedom and freedom of expression of political opinion is not only engagement inside the private sphere of freedom. It is also public activity, the exercise of a certain public function that constitutes public control.

In his book on the English constitution (1771), De Lolme speaks of the fact that the people exercise their special authority through public opinion, the "power of censure" (II, chap. 12). In the liberal demands of the nineteenth century, the idea of a liberal freedom combines with this democratic idea, above all in the epoch of liberalism when the idea's actual public law constructions arose, in particular between 1815 and 1848. Benjamin Constant understands parliament (the popular assembly) as "representation of public opinion." Chateaubriand writes in his famous expositions on the freedom of the press (*Mélanges* pp. 238, 247) that even the ministry must derive its authority from public opinion. This is the principle and source—principium et fons—of the ministry in a constitutional monarchy. This understanding of public opinion is not as prominent in Germany. Nevertheless, the pithy, though "double-edged," expression of Hegel deserves mention, according to which everything is simultaneously true and false in public opinion. Critique generally predominates in nineteenth-century Germany. Characteristic of this tendency is the essay by Lothar Bucher of the year 1854, "Der Parlamentarismus, wie er ist," 2nd ed., 1881, which is celebrated by Hasbach precisely because of its arguments on the value of public opinion. In the twentieth century, works that thoroughly treat public opinion as a sociological and political theme, the property of the concept of the *public* and its connection with the present, genuinely assembled people, precisely, therefore, the political, do not clearly legitimate it. That is so even for the work of F. Tönnies, *Kritik der öffentlichen Meinung*, Berlin 1922, which otherwise is the most important sociological investigation on this theme.

James Bryce thoroughly treated the special connection of democracy and public opinion in chapters 76–86, vol. III, of his *American Commonwealth*. The reign of public opinion is true democracy for him. The methods of its determination are still uncertain, and it is often something secret and available only in politically engaged and homogenous peoples. It is often said that in the Anglo-Saxon peoples, in contrast to many other democracies, a true public opinion exists. Dicey, *Law and public opinion in England* (1905), celebrated England precisely for the indirect and firm connection of legislation and public opinion, which finds a parallel nowhere else. Nevertheless, a lively critique began a few years ago even in the writings of Anglo-Saxon authors, for example, the interesting book by Lawrence Lowell, *Public opinion and popular government*, 1st ed., 1913, 4th ed., 1921. The question is whether public opinion can continue to exist as a unified force when a concept like "class" seriously competes with the concept of people and endangers homogeneity. For the bearer of public opinion, which always remains something mystical, though not, for this reason, less important, loses its essence and becomes problematic. Previously, one could speak of the "common man" (the man on the street [Schmitt's English]). As soon as this man becomes a class-conscious proletarian, he changes his nature. The same is true of the other types of this idea world, the "simple [250] worker," "Jacques

Bonhomme," etc. Incidentally, such figures are easily lent a romanticized bucolic quality. They are thus rendered nonpolitical and, consequently, are deprived of their democratic character. So it is in the essay by Arthur Feiler, *Frankfurter Zeitung* of 23 June 1927 ("Die Völker und die Staatsmänner"), which states that "peoples everywhere want nothing else from life than simply this, a little sun, a little nature," etc. Such a bearer of public opinion is, of course, essentially a private man and, in regard to political questions, only wishes to have nothing to do with politics. This is certainly an upstanding and appealing wish, one, however, whose fulfillment unfortunately does not remove politics from the world and does not answer any political question.

The incomprehensibility and resistance to organization of such democratic ideas about public opinion reveals itself in the fact that constitutional regulation uses concepts through whose nonjuridical indeterminacy one intends to intentionally avoid a precise, normative determination. Thus Art. 54 states that "the Reich Chancellor and the Reich minister require the confidence of the Reichstag for the conduct of their office." Art. 57 of the Prussian constitution of 1920 says, moreover, that the government must have the *confidence* of the *people*. Indeed, otherwise legal institutions and procedures cannot constantly organize and comprehend public opinion. However, they can certainly serve to bring it to expression, to validate it, and, beyond its official content, to create an indicator of public opinion. The result of an election or popular vote, together with its indirect substantive meaning—selection of a deputy or answer to a proposed question—still only has this additional meaning, which is certainly strongly diminished through the method of secret ballots, of the dependence on the proposed candidate lists, and on the manner of posing questions. The situation can develop such that public opinion can finally still only express itself through abstention from an election or vote. Legal methods can always only single out a particular factor. It is, in any case, part of the essence of a genuine democracy that the results of elections and popular votes are faithfully regarded as indicators of public opinion. Only occasionally, and especially against obvious injustice and under the impression of political corruption, does it come down to unanimous expressions of the people's will, which, as such, are unmistakable and have the character of a genuine acclamation. An example in this regard was the protest of the German people against the surrendering of the so-called war criminals in the year 1920. In some cases, constitutional methods prevent acclamation. Thus, in the vote of the German people on the expropriation of the property [251] of the former ruling royal families in June 1926, it is easily understandable that an acclamation did not occur, because the provision of Art. 75 made it possible and even advisable for the opponents of expropriation to stay at home (above p. 241). In the English practice, there are indicators of public opinion that are both acknowledged and loyally followed, such as the results of *special elections, new elections,* and large *local elections.* As a result of the list system of proportional representation, special elections and new elections do not take place in the German Reich, so that this important potential means of regulation does not apply. Land parliamentary elections in smaller Lands and local elections can offer no substitute for this regulatory possibility. The most important public law consequence of the review of public opinion in question involves the legal mechanism for parliamentary dissolution, through which this institution receives the character of a *normal* institution. It loses the extraordinary quality, the connection with ideas of conflict or, indeed, coup d'état, as it is still recalled from the undemocratic times of the constitutional monarchy. Whether the dissolution is viewed as something abnormal or not is a determinative factor in the positive-law interpretation of a constitutional provision like Art. 25 (Reichstag dissolution by the President).

IV. *Overview of the meanings of the word "people" for a modern constitutional theory.*

1. People as *unformed,* nonconstitutional entity.

(a) People as subject of the constitution-making power (pp. 77, 238);

(b) People as bearer of public opinion and subject of acclamations (p. 242);

(c) People as those who do not rule or are not officials (in the combination "popular demand," p. 241).

2. People as *constitutionally formed* and organized entity, in which it is noteworthy that the people are actually not formed and organized, but rather there is only a procedure of election or voting and the will of the people comes into being only as result of a system of validations or, indeed, fictions (p. 239). Then people = simple or qualified majority of the voters casting ballots or those entitled to vote.

The other meanings of the word "people" (people = population, people = all state members, people = nation = state) need not be discussed. [252] Joseph Held enumerates nine meanings of the term in *System des Verfassungsrechts*, Würzburg 1856, I, p. 109ff. The interesting thing about his enumeration (in contrast to other attempts, for example, Hans Liermann, *Das deutsche Volk als Rechtsbegriff im Reichsstaatsrecht der Gegenwart* (Berlin and Bonn 1927) is that Held recognizes the distinctive sense of the word, which lies in the negative: among the people belong those who are not ruling and are not officials or magistrates, etc. (above p. 241).

§ 19.

Consequences of the Political Principle of Democracy

I. General tendencies explained by the aspiration for democratic *identity*.

1. Greatest possible number of those entitled to vote and to stand for election, reduction of the voting age, women's right to vote and stand for election.

2. Definitiveness attained when those voting constitute the largest possible majority, in other words, when those voting approach the ideal of unanimity. This idea about the normative character of majorities, however, contains a misunderstanding, and it is possible principally because the methods of liberal individualism, in particular of the secret individual ballot and (since Condorcet) the mathematical orientation toward the mere tabulation of voting results, which is a purely quantitative, arithmetic idea, has obscured the distinctly political concept of democracy.

This certainly also accounts for Kelsen's view (*Wesen und Wert der Demokratie*, 1920), for whom the justice of democracy rests on the fact that it is more just when out of one hundred persons ninety rule over ten than if ten rule over ninety. The political sense of democracy is displaced entirely here. The question of the substance of democratic equality is no longer posed. In Rousseau, by contrast, the consciousness of this difference is still very strong. He still knows that it is in no way democratic, if ninety corrupt persons rule over ten honorable persons and that even the unanimity of all decisions is useless if the substance of democracy, which is vertu for Rousseau, is displaced. Even in unanimity, the will of one hundred slavish persons does not produce a free will, while a nonpolitical will of one thousand politically indifferent persons in combination produces no political will in terms of justice.

3. The greatest possible extension of the methods of *direct election* to the selection of magistrates and officials and the greatest possible *frequency of repeated elections*, quicker electoral turnover, short electoral periods, the *possibility of recall* of elected magistrates, easy *dissolution* of the elected bodies. On the double meaning of elections, see below p. 257.

4. The greatest possible extension of direct *substantive* decision by the state citizens entitled to vote (popular vote). [253]

II. *The state citizen in democracy*.

1. The concept of state citizen is part of the political sphere. The state citizen in democracy is *citoyen*, not private man or bourgeois.

The German word "citizen" comprises both meanings, citoyen and bourgeois. But the opposition of both meanings is as great as the difference between a nonpolitical, ethical-economic liberalism and democracy that is a pure political concept. Hegel's early writing on the scholarly approaches to natural law (Lasson edition, 1802, p. 383) is the first and most important expression of the *bourgeois* as a concept contrary to the state citizen existing in the political sphere. "The potency of this estate (of the bourgeois)," he writes, "establishes itself such that the estate maintains itself generally in property holdings and in the justice that is possible regarding property, and such that . . . any individual, since he himself is capable of holding property, comports himself in the bourgeois manner, generally or as citizen. Peace and the ability to make acquisitions, along with the complete security of their enjoyment, compensate for the political insignificance stemming from estate members being private persons, insofar as those rewards are accorded to the individual as well as to the entirety. However, that the danger for the individual is the absolute uncertainty of all enjoyment, property, and right is deduced from the fact that the security of each individual has tended to benefit the collective insofar as the individual is proud of the bravery and of the necessity that is part of belonging to the first estate (the free and noble, whose occupation is the πολιτεύειν, in particular, that of exposing themselves to the risk of a violent death." Another quotation of Fichte deserves mention in order to show the deep connection of these principles with the German philosophy of the post-Kantian generation. "Humanity divides itself into two basic clans," according to Fichte, "the propertied and the nonpropertied." The first *are* not the state, yet they *preserve* the state, "and the latter is in fact its servant. The propertied are thoroughly indifferent as to who protects them, if they are only being protected; the only goal is to receive protection as cheaply as possible. To those with property, the state is a necessary evil, and one must make every evil as limited as possible" (*Staatslehre*, 1813, *Werke* IV, p. 404). The judgment *Lorenz von Stein* rendered on the bourgeoisie (below p. 309) is also rooted in such ideas. If in his valuable book on Hegel's idea of the state (*Philosophische Forschungen*, ed. K. Jaspers, vol. 4, Berlin 1927, p. 127) J. Loewenstein finds the root of the socialist movement in Germany in the critique of the culture and time period (not in the social misery of the masses, and still less in the economic problem of goods production or distribution), then I agree with him, though with this qualification from the side of *political* consciousness, which recognizes its enemy in the bourgeois.

2. General *equality before the law*, in other words, the elimination and prohibition of all privileges in favor of or to the disadvantage of individual state citizens or certain classes and estates. Such privileges may also not be introduced by statute; not even a "constitution-amending" one could justify them. Herein lies the fundamental meaning of the principle that all state citizens are equal before the law (Art. 109). In particular, that means the following.

(a) Equality of political status. Equal participation of all state citizens in elections and votes, so far as they affect the [254] entire state, is an equal electoral and voting right. The additional subtypes and methods of this electoral right, direct right to election, system of proportional elections, and electoral secrecy, are not the result of democratic principles; other considerations account for them. Among these criteria are partly justice generally and partly justice in the sense of liberal individualism.

(b) The voting and electoral right is not a right in the sense that it would stand at the free disposal of the individual (as does electoral secrecy, whose heterogeneity reveals itself especially in this opposition). However, it is also not a mere "reflex" of constitutional law. It is, rather, a public function, and, in terms of logical consistency, it is equally an electoral and voting duty because it is exercised not by the individual as private man but as state citizen, thus by virtue of a public law status. Nevertheless, most democratic states do not give effect to the logic of obligatory electoral participation and voting in their electoral laws.

Example of the electoral duty is the Belgian constitution, Art. 48, 2 (according to the constitutional revision of 1893), which stipulates that "le vote est obligatoire." The fulfillment of this duty is not ensured by criminal sanctions. On this, cf. Errera, *Das Staatsrecht des Königreichs Belgien*, p. 99. Additional examples are Esmein-Nézard, I, p. 367 and W. Hasbach, *Die moderne Demokratie*, p. 329. For literature on the subject, see Stier-Somlo, *Grundriss*, I, p. 546.

(c) Equal, universal, *compulsory military service*, more precisely, the right and the duty of every state citizen, in accordance with the degree of his ability to defend militarily the state and its order internally and externally. There is a genuine democracy without a general right to election to the same limited degree that there is a genuine democracy without general compulsory military service. Hence Art. 133 ("The compulsory military service is guided by the provisions of the Reich Defense Law") guarantees an essential principle, for it preserves the possibility that every German is obligated to serve according to the standards of the law. According to Art. 178, 2, however, the provisions of the Versailles Treaty have precedence (in whose provisions Art. 173's universal, compulsory military service in Germany is eliminated). The implementation of this democratic institution is prevented. Nonetheless, this international law treaty provision, as presented above (p. 72), does not change the German constitution.

(d) Equal duty to voluntary activity and to personal services (Art. 132, 133).

(e) Equal tax and expenditure obligation. "All state citizens *without distinction* contribute to all public burdens in proportion to their means in accordance with statutes," according to Art. 134. [255]

(f) *No limitations on eligibility for office and no incompatibilities.* Because of the equality of all state citizens before the law in a democracy, individual groups of state citizens cannot logically be excluded from access to certain offices, functions, and especially not from eligibility for election. Also, a parliamentary incompatibility in the genuine sense (to distinguish it from ineligibility) is not permissible, for it means that certain state citizens are, indeed, eligible for election, but if they are elected, they must give up their previous post, activity, or mandate. Yet to the extent that a special status is recognized inside of the general status of state citizen, as among the members of the soldiers' estate, limitations on the eligibility for election and incompatibilities are possible. The same must also be valid for civil servants, because even they have a special status, although, as shown above on p. 181, the sense for this logical consequence appears to be absent in Germany. In a democracy, on the contrary, it may hardly be possible to establish so-called *economic* incompatibilities legally and to provide for members of certain economic professions, bankers, syndicates, etc. that they cannot simultaneously be deputies, as that is attempted today in several states, in order to implement a social and economic independence for the deputy and to render significant again the constitutional "independence" of the deputies (Art. 21). Apart from the practical difficulties of such an experiment and of the many possibilities for an evasion, the theoretical difficulty lies above all in the fact that a statute that mandates such economic incompatibilities would infringe on democratic equality.

On the great doubts that the establishment of economic incompatibilities faces in a democracy, see J. Barthélemy, *Revue du droit public*, vol. 1922, p. 125ff. Until now, the only scholarly treatment of this important question in the German literature is found in the aforementioned Bonn dissertation of Werner Weber, 1928.

3. According to democratic principles, equality in private law is dominant only in the sense that the same private law statutes are valid for everyone, not, on the contrary, in the sense of *economic* equality of private wealth, property, or income. In its consequences and applications, democracy as an essentially political concept involves, to begin with, only the public law. However, [256] the superiority of the public over the private results unconditionally from democracy's essentially political character. As soon as political equality is destroyed or endangered by economic inequalities or by the social power of private property, it can became politically necessary to eliminate, by statute or measure, that type of disturbance or threat. In regard to this necessity, appealing to the sanctity of private property would be undemocratic. Still, such an appeal would be in accord with the principles of the bourgeois Rechtsstaat, whose sense lies precisely in hindering the logical consequences of a political principle, as with democracy, and to transform democracy into a constitutional democracy, which is limited by constitutional law.

III. *Officials* (democratic methods for the selection of officials and civil servants).

1. Equality of all state citizens in terms of equal access to all offices. To the extent that there is the necessity of a substantive qualification and that a certain professional training or technical education is unavoidable, equality is present only under the presupposition of equal capability (Art. 128). For the required examinations that determine the professional training and technical education, no class or status-based privileges may exist, nor may inequalities be introduced even through a numerus clausus provision or concealed in some other way. Equal access to offices also takes from the professional civil service the character of an undemocratic institution. Nevertheless, the elaboration of a civil servant hierarchy could lead

to a contradiction with the democratic equality of state citizens and to an impermissible estate formation, if the highest offices in this civil servant hierarchy are exclusively a product of the professional civil service itself. On the contrary, there is no contradiction if commissioners, who are recallable and do not have civil service status, assume the highest offices. This applies whether or not they are only expert ministers. The essential thing for a democracy is that the leading activity of the government remains dependent on the will and trust of the people. The institutional guarantees of the Weimar Constitution (Art. 129, 130), which constitutionally protect the professional civil service (above p. 181), are thus thoroughly reconcilable with democratic principles. [257]

2. Selection of individual leaders, civil servants, or functionaries.

(a) By *lot.*

Equality is best guaranteed during selection by lot, and certainly the possibility of a distinction according to substantive capacity is also excluded. This method has become impractical today. It came into use in especially broad scope in the Athenian democracy. Plato (*Politeia*, Apelt edition, p. 313), indeed, sees here a definition of democracy: "Democracy arises when the poor achieve victory, execute a part of the opponents of democracy, ban another part, share with the remainder, however, the administration of the state and of the individual lands in complete equality, and permit the predominant part of the ruling authority to be selected by lot." Fustel de Coulanges, *La cité antique*, is of the opinion that the selection of civil servants by lot is not based on the idea of democratic equality. Instead, a religious motive underlies it. But even Aristotle, *The Constitution of Athens*, 22, 5, considers the selection by lot to be the democratic method in contrast to the selection by election, which he views as an aristocratic one.

(b) By *election.* In comparison to the selection by lot, that by election, as Plato and Aristotle correctly say, is an aristocratic method. But it can appear as something democratic in comparison with the appointment by a higher organ or, indeed, to a selection by way of hereditary succession. In the election, both possibilities are present. The election can have the aristocratic sense of a separating out of the better and of the leaders or the democratic sense of a procurement of an agent, commissioner, or servant. In contrast to the elected, the electors can appear as the subordinated or as the superior party. The election can serve as a means of the principle of representation as well as of identity (above p. 219). In the nineteenth century, because of the opposition to the hereditary succession of the monarchy or to the membership in an upper house or house of lords, the election is seen as *the* democratic method. This also accounts for the fact that even today democracy is still defined as a state formation that rests on the general *electoral* right (thus R. Thoma's definition, above 218). However, one must distinguish what sense the election in reality has. If it should justify a genuine representation, it serves as the means of an aristocratic principle; if it signifies only the designation of an instructed delegate, one can view it as a distinctly democratic method. On the so-called representative democracy resting on the election, see above p. 218. The democratic logic leads to the elimination of the election and to the specialized vote by the people in its momentarily present identity.

(c) *Appointment* of the civil servant or functionary by a higher authority counts mostly as an undemocratic method. If it is unavoidable because of the requirements of an expertly led and technically [258] ordered operation and because of the principles of the professional civil service, there emerge different additional methods that should modify and correct these authoritarian methods in a democratic sense, for example, dependence of the highest offices of every department, in particular, the minister, on the confidence of the people or the popular assembly. There is, moreover, the improvement of the appointment system through the recruitment of laypersons serving in honorary, official capacities, such as lay judges and juries and laypersons in administrative committees and administrative courts. The participation of laypersons signifies a participation of the people, where people has the negative sense developed above, that to the people belong above all those who are not professional civil servants.

When Rudolf Gneist, in his famous interpretation of self-government (*Self-government, Kommunalverfassung und Verwaltungsgericht in England*, 3rd ed., 1871), set self-government as honorary official service in opposition to that by professional civil servants, he meant it in a liberal, not democratic, sense. The propertied and educated classes should be installed in the honorary offices so that an integration of the society into the state can be effected. However, it is actually not the people as such that should be participating in the administration of the state through this recruitment to honorary offices. Instead, the bourgeois Rechtsstaat should be secured. For Gneist, the honorary office is the "Archimedean point of the Rechtsstaat."

§ 20.

Application of the Political Principle of Democracy to Individual Areas of State Life

I. *Democracy and legislation.*

1. *The democratic concept of law* is a political, not a Rechtsstaat-based, concept of law. It stems from the potestas of the people and means that law is everything that the people intends: lex est quod populus jussit. On this, cf. above § 13, p. 146. There are no limitations on this *will* stemming from democratic principles. Injustices and even inequalities are possible. One could deny inequality only insofar as one understands equality in an absolute sense that all are subordinated to this will in the same way, which is something that is also the case in the absolute monarchy. Initially, the Rechtsstaat-based concept of law, which transforms democracy into a constitutional democracy, makes possible guarantees against injustices and inequalities. It also facilitates the distinction between statutes [259] and other state acts. For in the absolute democracy the will of the people is sovereign and not only highest law; it is also the highest judicial decision or act of the highest administrative officials etc.

2. Legislative process of the direct democracy. The statutory decision is made by the participation of all state citizens entitled to vote. There are different degrees and scope of participatory immediacy, so one can distinguish among different types of the legislative process of direct democracy.

(a) *Popular legislative process* in the actual sense. In other words, the legislative process is set in motion by a popular *initiative*, and the statutory decision comes about through a popular *vote*. This popular legislative process is distinguished by the fact that state *officials* and the popular *assembly* do not participate in it or participate only as a supplementary organ.

Art. 73, 3, establishes a genuine popular legislative procedure. It is, in other words, a referendum brought about by a popular initiative. Nevertheless, the Weimar Constitution provides for a *deviation* from the established legislative process for this popular legislative procedure. Specifically, the draft statute, proposed by way of popular initiative, is initially presented by the Reich government to the Reichstag for final passage, and the referendum by way of popular initiative does not take place if the Reichstag accepts the desired law unchanged. The other possibilities for a referendum that are provided constitutionally, but are not part of the popular legislative procedure, are unaltered in regard to this statutory decision of the Reichstag. Even in this case, the President can order a referendum under Art. 73, 1. A popular decision in the form of a referendum following a minority veto of the Reichstag is possible under Art. 73, 2, etc. If, however, the Reichstag does *not* accept the draft statute proposed via a popular initiative, a referendum must be held, and this referendum now is a *popular decision in response to an initiative*. Despite the aforementioned diversion into the established legislative process by Reichstag decision (Art. 68), there is a genuine popular legislative procedure, even if it is limited and derivative.

As a routine legislative procedure, this popular legislative process is practically impossible in a modern state. In the contemporary Rechtsstaat under the democratic constitution, hence under constitutional democracy, the popular legislative process is also theoretically possible as an extraordinary procedure, because constitutional democracy rests on the fact that the consequences of pure democracy are modified and legislated jurisdictions take the place of the direct and absolute people's will. The people, however, can exercise no established jurisdictions without ceasing to be the people. So even the statute that comes about via a popular legislative procedure is law in the constitutional rule sense. That is to say, it is the exercise of a legislative jurisdiction, and not, for example, an act of the constitution-making power of the people. This means the bourgeois Rechtsstaat concept of law is presupposed in the constitutional provisions on popular initiatives and referendums (§, p. 138), and an initiative is permissible only for a law in this sense, not for [260] any given acts of sovereignty. Nevertheless, precisely in this respect the characteristic value (above § 18, p. 250) of such procedures validates itself especially strongly. A statute that comes about via the popular legislative process with a large or overwhelming majority has found the acclamation of the people. As such, it can represent a genuine act of sovereignty, and, drawing on the strength of the political, it ruptures the norm of Rechtsstaat legality.

(b) Statutory *decision* by *popular vote on the initiative of the government.*

In modern democracy, it is a rare procedure where the government dependent on the confidence of the people proposes that a statute go directly to a popular vote without involvement of a popular assembly as legislative body. The Weimar Constitution does not recognize this procedure at all. In pure democracy, in which magistrate and actually assembled people stand opposite one another, it is the routine legislative process. According to Roman public law, for example, the magistrate poses the question in the popular assembly (vos rogo, quirites), to which yes (uti rogas) or no is answered. On this, see Mommsen, *Römisches Staatsrecht*, III, 1, 1887, p. 304, who argues that "the citizenry as well as the individual citizen, therefore, completely lack the initiative; they can only answer, not themselves propose the question to the magistrate of whether he is in agreement with this or that. Also, with this procedure, there is practically no getting beyond the simple yes or no or the appointment of certain persons; to ask the citizen, not whether he does or does not intend this, but rather what he intends is certainly legally permitted, yet only executable in exceptional cases" (cf. below p. 277).

(c) *Referendum* in the actual sense is a popular vote on the confirmation or nonconfirmation of a decision of the legislative body. The expression "referendum" is reserved to this case in a purposeful way, in which a decision of the popular assembly is presented to the state citizens entitled to vote for a conclusive decision. It is not advisable to designate indiscriminately all cases of the popular vote (initiatives, plebiscites, etc.) as a referendum without distinction. It is more accurate to say that the concept of referendum includes the decision on the *confirmation* of an action.

Cases of referendum:

(aa) *General obligatory* referendum.

In this procedure, a statute comes about through final passage of an advisory body that prepares the draft and through confirmation of this decision by those entitled to vote.

For practical reasons, this procedure is rare. Even where it is recognized as the democratic method, which is in principle an important and logically consistent one, as it is in the Jacobin constitution of 1793, for practical reasons it must be made dependent on some initiative. For otherwise affirmation is *falsely attributed* to the citizens entitled to vote, if this initiative does not occur. Thus, Art. 59 of the constitution of 1793 provides that if forty days after the distribution of the draft statute to all localities a tenth of the primary voter assemblies in no more than half of the departments have raised no objection (réclamation), the draft is deemed accepted and becomes law. [261]

(bb) *Obligatory* referendum for *special types* of law, in particular for constitutional revisions; moreover, facultative referendum.

See, for example, the Swiss federal constitution of 29 May 1874, obligatory referendum for constitutional laws, Art. 123, according to which "the revised federal constitution, in relation to the revised part of the same, enters into force when it is accepted by a majority of the cantons." By contrast, for simple statutes, there is only a facultative referendum, such as Art. 89, 2, providing that "federal laws as well as generally binding federal decisions that are not of a pressing nature should additionally (specifically beyond the required consent of both councils, National Council and Estate Council) be presented to the people for acceptance or rejection, if it is demanded by 30,000 Swiss citizens entitled to vote or by eight cantons." The exact stipulation applies to state treaties concluded with foreign countries according to section 3, whether they are unlimited in duration or for a duration of more than fifteen years (section 3 accepted on the basis of an initiative in the popular vote of 30 January 1921).

(cc) *Facultative* referendum.

In this regard, the question is raised as to on whom is conferred the referendum *initiative*. Under consideration here is the *legislative body* itself, which has an interest in submitting its decision to the consent of the enfranchised voters, the government, the state president, a *minority* of the legislative *body*, and a *part* of the *state citizens* entitled to vote (this last case contains an *initiative calling for a referendum* in contrast to that discussed under (a), an initiative introducing a popular legislative procedure). In federal states even the individual *Lands* or *cantons* (cf. the example of the Swiss federal constitution under [bb]) are a possibility.

The *Weimar Constitution* recognizes the following possibilities of a referendum initiative: referendum on the order of the President (Art. 73, 1 and 3); referendum at the request of a twentieth of those entitled to vote in regard to a statute, the promulgation of which is interrupted on petition of at least a third of the Reichstag; Art. 73, 2; referendum on demand of the Reichsrat, if the Reichstag concluded a constitution-amending statute against the objection of the Reichsrat (Art. 76, 2). The President's authority to order a referendum includes both the general authority to order one against any statute concluded by the Reichstag according to Art. 73, 1, as well as the special authority to order one resolving differences of opinion between the Reichstag and Reichsrat. Thus, the statute on the referendum of 27 June

1921 (*Reichgesetzesblatt*, p. 790) enumerates five cases of referendum, among which is a referendum in response to an initiative. To this, however, is added a sixth case through § 3 of this (constitution-amending) statute, which provides that if a referendum in response to an initiative takes place, it is not only the desired statute, but also one concluded by the Reichstag that diverges from the popular will, that is the object of the initiative.

(d) Limitations and exceptions. In some democratic constitutions, certain matters are excluded from consideration in referendums, or the ordering of a referendum is restricted in some way.

According to Art. 73, 4, only the President can call for a referendum on the budgetary plan, on spending laws, and on compensation orders. This limitation must be valid for all *monetary statutes*. On this, [262] see Carl Schmitt, *Volksentscheid und Volksbegehren*, 1927, p. 14ff.; on the constitutional limitations of the individual Lands, see esp. p. 15. On the question of the limitations of the popular initiative, see below 4c, p. 264. Limitation through *declaration of pressing need*, Art. 72, 73, cf. p. 278.

3. Establishment of the law through *decision* of a *popular assembly* elected by the state citizens, whose will is valid as that of the entire people (Art. 21, 68, 2). In this instance, the principle of representation takes the place of the principle of identity. The consultation and participation of those entitled to vote can occur only *indirectly*.

(a) The so-called imperative mandate, specifically, the deputy's dependence on the instructions and directions of the voters, would, indeed, eliminate the representative character of the popular assembly, and yet it would not be an appropriate means for the execution of the democratic principle. For it would also contradict the political idea of democracy itself. Because of this dependence on the transitory will of *his* voters, and not on the will of the entire people, the deputy would be dependent on a *part* of those entitled to vote. The additional necessary consequence of this imperative mandate would be the introduction of a special procedure of continuous voting in every electoral district or, under the proportional system of representation with party lists, throughout the entire Land. Then, indeed, voting would be continuous, but not by the people as a unity. It is also revealed here that the people cannot be represented, as *Rousseau* rightly emphasized. The people are either entirely present and engaged or generally not involved, and in this case the people are not represented. Instead, the political unity as a whole is. The idea of representation contradicts the democratic principle of self-identity of the people present as a political unity. An imperative mandate of the medieval style, however, which involves dependence of a deputy on instructions and directions by an estate, other types of organization, or by parties, contradicts the idea of political unity as well as the fundamental presupposition of democracy, in particular of the substantive homogeneity of a people, whose natural and political unity is considered identical.

(b) It is possible to influence and consider the direct will of those entitled to vote in such a way that the *dissolution* of this legislative body is made a normal component of the state organization, [263] if an established legislative organ is a representative body and is thus independent of directions.

The dissolution can be brought about by the following:

(aa) through an order of the head of state, the chief executive in the Rechtsstaat that distinguishes among powers. Hence Art. 25 provides that "the President can dissolve the Reichstag." The monarchical right of dissolution is formed differently and does not come into consideration here (below p. 353).

(bb) through a decision of the ministry (otherwise dependent on the confidence of the body to be dissolved). Thus the English practice formally takes the form of a dissolution order of the head of state, in this case by royal decree. The Oldenburg Constitution of 17 June 1919, § 55 (dissolution of the individual Land parliament), recognizes a formal right of dissolution of the government.

(cc) by referendum on demand of a part of state citizens entitled to vote, therefore, an *initiative for dissolution of the popular assembly* by referendum. Thus numerous German Land constitutions, for example, the Prussian constitution of 30 November 1920, Art. 6 and 14. Additional examples in O. Koellreutter, *Das parlamentarische System in den deutschen Landesverfassungen*, Tübingen 1921, p. 7, n. 2.

(dd) self-dissolution by the popular assembly's own decision. Note several German Land constitutions, such as Prussian constitution Art. 14, for example. Additional examples are in Koellreutter, *Das parlamentarische System*, p. 9.

4. Democratic *legislative initiative.* Even in a democracy, the legislative initiative is by nature an affair of the government (above p. 241). Indeed, the government can share the right of legislative initiative, especially the popular initiative, with other offices, and the legislative body can have a right of initiative (Art. 68, for example). But there can be *no government without the power of initiative.*

(a) The struggle of the popular assembly against the monarchical government led to introducing a legislative initiative by the *popular assembly*, that is, by the legislative body itself. Art 68 corresponds to that understanding, according to which proposed statutes are introduced by the Reich government *or from the floor of the Reichstag*. In the degree to which the perspective of the [264] struggle against the kingly government is displaced, this legislative initiative of the popular assembly can be limited again. Earlier, the individual initiative of every single deputy was restricted by the order of business or statutorily. Thus, according to Art. 68 in combination with § 49 of the order of business of the Reichstag from 12 December 1922, the right of initiative is exercised "from the floor of the Reichstag" by only fifteen deputies (the number of a "faction"). Additionally, however, restrictions resulted for monetary statutes. Here one can recognize a line of restriction that leads to at least the limitation of the popular assembly's expenditure initiative for monetary statutes.

"In the draft budgetary plan," according to Art. 85, 2, "the Reichstag cannot raise or reset expenditures without approval of the Reichsrat." This limitation is valid not only for the one-time budgetary plan law, but for all monetary laws as well (cf. above 2d, p. 261). Additional examples are found in Carl Schmitt, *Volksentscheid und Volksbegehren*, 1927, pp. 27–29.

(b) The striving for direct participation of enfranchised voters has led to a so-called *popular initiative*, which is a legislative initiative from a part of the state citizens entitled to vote.

This legislative initiative of the people is either

(aa) the initiation of a popular legislative process (above p. 259), per Art. 73, 3; or

(bb) the setting in motion of an ordinary legislative process that then is directed toward the legislative body. The Art. 73, 3, rule only seemingly includes this instance of legislative initiative. In fact, there is a *deviation*, introduced for practical reasons, in the ordinary legislative process.

(cc) Referendum initiative (only imprecisely termed "legislative initiative," cf. above 2c, p. 260).

(c) Limitations and exceptions. Under democratic constitutions, certain matters, in particular monetary statutes, are exempted from the popular initiative. The exception contained in Art. 73, 4 (only the President can order a popular initiative on the budgetary plan, expenditure laws, and compensation orders) is also valid for an initiative calling for a referendum.

A few individual German Land constitutions exempt certain subjects (especially financial questions) from the "popular vote," therefore from the referendum *and* from the initiative. Other subjects are exempted only from the initiative. Cf. the examples in Carl Schmitt, *Volksentscheid und Volksbegehren*, p. 15. In any case, the *initiative* of the people is so different from the referendum that the exceptions of the one or the other are not directly the same, and, in a democratic state, they do not speak for the widest possible extension of the popular initiative. [265]

II. *Democracy and government.*

1. The relationship of an *elected* representative assembly (parliament) to the government.

The logic of the democratic principle intends a minimum of representation. The result is that both the parliament (specifically, the elected representative assembly) and the government can be affected, so that first the former, then the latter appears subordinated.

(a) The first possibility is *subordination* of the government to the parliament.

So long as a parliament is elected by the state citizens and representative "of the people"—in other words, as long as it is truly representative of the political unity—it stands opposite the king as a second representative. Demanding the subordination of this royal government to the parliament appears as a requirement and a logical consequence of democracy. Overall, that was the situation in Germany during the nineteenth century under the constitutional monarchy. The requirement of a parliamentary government thus becomes a democratic demand. As a result of such a political situation, democracy and parliamentary government are rendered equivalent and confused with one another. Compared to the representation of the political unity through an hereditary monarchy, the representation of the politically united people through an elected body is by outward appearance something democratic, and the actual, principled opposition—representation and identity—does not become evident.

In this situation, a series of equivalencies arises. First, the government should be dependent on the confidence of the parliament, which is to say the popular assembly and, in particular, the people. Then, dependence on the confidence of parliament and dependence on the confidence of the people are not distinguishable from one another. As the demand for the establishment of parliamentary government becomes stronger and more intense, so also does the conflation of parliamentary government and democracy. In Germany, this connection revealed itself finally during the world war, especially since 1916 and 1917, through the parties that demanded the institution of parliamentary government at the Reich level. Cf. Hasbach, *Die parlamentarische Kabinettsregierung*, 1919, p. 265, with the many exclamation points of outrage in quotations from newspaper commentary. In the aforementioned Art. 57 of the 1920 Prussian constitution it says that "the State Ministry as such and every single state minister needs the confidence of the people for the execution of their duties, which is expressed by the Land parliament." The entire manner of thinking, in fact, presupposes that the government has no direct relation to the citizens entitled to vote and that this relationship is mediated exclusively by parliament. This outlook necessarily does not apply when the government is no longer a royal one in an antidemocratic sense, and when it, independent of the parliament, has or can produce a direct connection with the people by appealing *directly* to the confidence of the state citizens entitled to vote (cf. below under 2). [266]

While all public law and political ideas are dominated by the struggle against a nondemocratic government, it is naturally the case that for democratic ideas the government is understood as something subordinate to the popular assembly. A dualistic relationship of superiority and subordination is almost always constituted, with the people (the enfranchised voters) superior to the popular assembly (the parliament) and the popular assembly superior to the government. Under a widely held idea, this construct is considered a system of *committees.* The popular assembly (the parliament) is a committee of the people (enfranchised voter), while the parliamentary government is a committee of the popular assembly (of the parliament). State organization appears as a committee system with three levels: people, popular assembly, and government.

Application of the Political Principle

Thus Bluntschli, *Allgemeines Staatsrecht*, I, 1868, p. 490, terms the "legislative body" a *"proportional extract,"* although otherwise he is still sympathetic to the distinctive feature of the concept of representation. Nevertheless, it is noteworthy that Bluntschli does not speak of an extract or committee of the enfranchised voters, but rather "of the entire people's organism," so that the concept of representation still does not apply. In this context, he cites the famous expression of Mirabeau of 31 January 1789, according to which the estates are for the nation what a geographic map is for the appearance of the country: a picture showing these relationships like the original. Even this picture involves not only the mere committee and exponents, but also still contains something of the idea of a genuine representation.

In the more recent literature, by contrast, the sympathy gradually disappears entirely. Here are some examples involving the Weimar Constitution. Giese, *Kommentar zur Reichsverfassung*, 2nd ed., pp. 161, 191, argues that "the parliamentary principle considers the ministry an executive *committee* of the popular assembly, even if it does not necessarily derive from its womb." In the subsequent editions, the word "committee" recurs. Cf. the collection in H. Herrfahrdt, *Die Kabinettsbildung nach der Weimarer Verfassung*, Berlin 1927, pp. 10/11. The term committee is entirely absent from discussion in the 7th edition (1927) of Art. 54 as well as Art. 53. In the deliberations of the Weimar National Assembly, the idea of the committee is expressly rejected. Koch (*Protocol*, p. 302) declared rightly that the Reich government cannot be a committee of the Reichstag majority. On the contrary, as a characteristic example of the typical failure to recognize a problem, take H. Nawiasky, *Die Stellung der Regierung im modernen Staat*, Tübingen 1925, p. 7, who proposes a three-level pyramid with the people forming the base. Above this level rests "an advocacy organ," "which to a limited degree represents the will of the people and, consequently, renders it capable of action" (p. 7). "That is the popular assembly, the intermediate level of our pyramid," he argues, and over this, again, a smaller collegium, a "committee with its confidence." "That is the government; it stands at the peak of the pyramid," according to *Nawiasky*. Also corresponding to the idea of the committee is that of a "proportional government," by which the members of the cabinet are determined according to the basic principles of the proportional election of the parliament (thus the understanding of H. Triepel, *Staatsverfassung und politische Parteien*, 1927, p. 22, which cited the Austrian statute of 1920 as an example). The constitutional provision, contained in some Land constitutions (Saxony, Württemberg, Baden among others), that after every new election a reconstitution of the ministry must follow, rests on similar ways of thinking. [267]

The idea of a committee is certainly logically consistent under the perspective of the democratic principle of identity. However, it nullifies the idea of a representation and, indirectly, of the political unity in general.

(b) The second possibility is the government's *superior position* in regard to the parliament. The prior practice of English cabinet government shows the opposite image. The leader of the majority party forms the cabinet, or government, as prime minister, and this government leads the parliament. The idea of a committee recurs here behind that of *leadership* and *administration*, so that in the public law literature the English prime minister is occasionally even designated as the "first among equals," whom the parliamentary majority has to obey. The superior position is explicable from the fact that the government supports itself directly on "public opinion," for which even the parliament is only an expression.

(c) The third possibility is a *counterpoise*, in which neither the parliament nor the government is superior or subordinate. That is possible when the government can produce a direct connection with the enfranchised state citizens at any time. The bearer of the balance is the people. The people *maintain* the balance and are the higher third vis-à-vis factors of equal rank, parliament and government. The progenitors of the Weimar Constitution understood this idea as "genuine parliamentarianism" (below § 24). Even here the organizational problem arises of producing the direct connection (one not mediated by the popular assembly) between the government and the state citizens entitled to stand for election or to vote.

2. *Direct relationship of people and government* can be produced by the following means:

(a) *Direct election* of the government by the state citizens with electoral rights. It is established in the Weimar Constitution for an essential governmental organ that the President is elected by the entire people according to Art. 41. At the same time, however, there is a Reich government dependent on the confidence of the parliament, whose constitutional theoretic design consequently causes special difficulties (below § 27, p. 340f.). The connection between the President elected by the people and the parliamentary government is, on the one hand, produced by the President's *right to name* and to *dismiss* the Chancellor and ministers [268] under Art. 53, and, on the other hand, by the provision of Art. 50, according to which all the President's official actions require the *countersignature* of the Chancellor or of the competent Reich minister. According to this idea, the fact that the entire people select the President in direct election should create an instance of *representation*, even if it is diminished by the possibility of recalling the President under Art. 43, 2 (by popular vote called by a petition of a two-thirds majority of the Reichstag). Under this idea, the German Reichstag is also a representative (Art. 21). As under the constitutional monarchy, two representatives once again stand opposite one another and, moreover, the principle of representation is bound up with the democratic principle of identity.

An outstanding sociologist and state theorist, F. Tönnies, made the suggestion that even the Reich government (Chancellor and the Reich ministers) be elected directly by the people, in *Schmollers Jahrbuch*, vol. 51 (1927). The question is whether this direct election supports the idea of democratic identity or the idea of a representation. If I understand Tönnies correctly, he is seeking here to strengthen the democratic principle.

(b) *Dissolution of the parliament* by order of the government.

The dissolution must, as already discussed (p. 263), be viewed as an appropriate institution of this system. If it is to have a constitutional sense,

Application of the Political Principle

it must be valid for the case of the governmental majority of parliament issuing a vote of no confidence. The direct connection with the people can be produced against the no confidence vote of the parliamentary majority, and, as higher third, the people decides the conflict arising between the government and the popular assembly. Cf. below § 29, p. 358.

(c) An *order of a referendum* on behalf of a governmental organ against the decisions of the parliament. "A statute concluded by the Reichstag is made the subject of a referendum prior to its promulgation if the President provides for it within a month after passage," according to Art. 73.

In the cases (b) and (c), there is an "appeal to the people." Because the parliament can also appeal to the people on its own account against the governmental body (in Germany, against the President via a dismissal petition under Art. 43, 2), the reciprocal opportunities balance one another out (cf. the [269] scheme above p. 197). The people hold the balance. The new elections or popular vote occurring in such cases has the special function of deciding a political conflict among the highest state officials. In this instance, the people act as sovereign above and beyond the statutorily mandated constitutional jurisdiction.

III. *Democracy and relations among states under international law.*

The application of the democratic principle of identity to relations with other states results in the return of the principle of representation and limitation of its application. At this point, moreover, it is most evident that no political unity can exist without representation and that even a pure democratic state must be represented in regard to other thoroughly democratic ones. Despite the great political and social changes among states, the generally recognized rules of international law on diplomatic traffic have hardly changed in the last century. Even today, agreements and customs stemming from a pure monarchical time are valid in the same way despite the development of democracy (cf. above p. 210).

The application of the democratic principle is evident in the fact that for the conclusion of treaties or for declarations under international law, the will of the representative is no longer alone decisive and the concept of ratification itself is brought into disarray, because the concept of representation is not properly recognized. The consent of the popular assembly (of the parliament) or even a popular vote is constitutionally required for agreements under international law to be valid in two senses. First, this consent supplements the ratification by the head of state (the representative) as the special requirement for validity under international law in such a way that it does not force the representative aside. Second, an act of the popular assembly or a popular vote directly constitutes an action under international law, so that the representation by the head of state loses any independent significance and still only affects the formality of the exchange of the ratification documents, while, on the other hand, it remains unclear to what extent the popular assembly or, indeed, even the voting populace represents the political unity in regard to the foreign state.

Art. 45 contains three different possibilities: complete representation, limited representation, and elimination of representation by the head of state. According to section 1, the President represents the Reich in terms of international [270] law; in the name of the Reich, he concludes alliances and other treaties with foreign powers; and he confirms and receives emissaries (full representation). Under section 2, the declaration of war and conclusion of peace by statute (the "ratification" by the head of state is only a formality of international legal conveyance, even if it remains meaningful in international law terms due to the need for confirmation under international law). Section 3 stipulates that alliances and treaties with foreign states that have a connection with Reich legislation require the consent of the Reichstag (here the ratification is a substantively meaningful action of the representative, which the consultation of the popular assembly supplements).

The Reich Constitution of 1871 made the Kaiser the representative of the German Reich under international law. According to Art. 11, 3, insofar as treaties with foreign states involved matters that under Art. 4 belong in the realm of Reich legislation, conclusion of such treaties required the consent of the Bundesrat, and the approval of the Reichstag was necessary for them to be valid law. Under the prevailing understanding, this limitation had only public law significance. As such, it did not involve the full representation of the emperor in regard to other states (Laband I, p. 230, II, p. 137ff.; Meyer-Anschütz, p. 818). In another understanding, the constitution limited the scope of representation (Seydel, *Kommentar*, p. 163), while, according to G. Jellinek, *Gesetz und Verordnung*, pp. 349, 354, the requirement of the popular assembly's consent added a (conclusive) condition to the international law treaty, for "in terms of legal validity the representative can only promise that which it can fulfill itself."

Historically, the limitation of the representation by the head of state stems from the French constitution of 1791, Title III, chap. II, art. 3, section 1. "The legislative body," it reads, "is competent to ratify peace, alliance, and trade treaties; a treaty becomes effective only through this ratification." Additionally, the 1793 and 1795 constitutions (Art. 55 and 333, respectively) stipulate this for all treaties, while the constitution of 1848 (Art. 53) requires the consent of the National Assembly to all treaties. According to Art. 8 of the constitutional law of 16 July 1875, the president of the republic ratifies treaties. However, peace treaties, trade treaties, treaties through which financial obligations of the state are established, and such treaties that affect the personal status and the private property of the French abroad are first "conclusive" when they are passed by both chambers. Withdrawal, exchange, and acquisition of territories all occur via statute.

The Belgian constitution of 1831 makes the king the representative of the state in regard to other states. However, for trade treaties and for treaties burdening the state or obligating individual Belgians, it requires the consent (assentiment) of both chambers, and for territorial changes it demands a statute (Art. 68). This provision is modeled after Art. 48 of the 1850 Prussian constitution. "The king has the right to declare war and to conclude peace," it reads, "even to establish other treaties with foreign governments. If they are trade treaties, or if through them burdens are placed on the state or on individual state citizens, then they require the consent of the chambers in order to be valid." Art. 48 of the Prussian constitution had not been considered a limitation on representation by the most widely held theory (even by Gneist). It is instead viewed as an internal public law requirement, while under Belgian constitutional law there is the requirement of an "obligatory ratification of the chambers" (Errera, p. 49).

The partial revision of the Swiss federal constitution of the year 1921 (Art. 89, 3, of the federal constitution) is of particular interest as an example of the penetration of direct democracy. State treaties with foreigners that are concluded for an unlimited duration or for more than fifteen years [271] must be presented to the enfranchised state citizens (to the people) for acceptance or rejection (beyond the "approval" by the Federal Assembly), if it is demanded by 30,000 enfranchised citizens or by eight cantons. Indeed, *three* types of "ratification" appear: the ratification by the international law representative, the approval also designated as ratification, and the ratification (or rejection of the ratification) by the people (cf. Fleiner, *Schweizerisches Bundesstaatsrecht*, p. 756).

An important consequence in practical terms of this democratic elimination of representation is that the *denial of ratification* counted earlier as something *abnormal*, almost as an insult for the foreign state. Cf. the case of the French-English treaty of 1841 on the suppression of the slave trade, the ratification of which France denied despite signing the treaty and the speech by Guizot in the Chamber of Deputies on 1 February 1843. Now, on the contrary, the reservation of approval by the bearer of state legislative authority becomes self-evident, and the denial of ratification is no longer something abnormal. Cf. the case of the free zones in Savoy, in which the French-Swiss Treaty of 7 August 1921 had been denounced by the popular vote of 18 February 1923 and not ratified by Switzerland. M. Fleischmann, *Deutsche Juristen-Zeitung*, pp. 643ff.). On the general problem of "democracy and foreign policy," there is up to now only one comprehensive monograph, J. Barthélemy, *Démocratie et Politique étrangère*, Paris 1917.

IV. *Democracy and administration.*

1. An administration carried out in accordance with the principle of democratic identity is practically impossible and, according to democratic principles, not even a theoretical problem, because in administration (in contrast to the government) there is no representation. The handling of all public affairs by the enfranchised state citizens would be at most possible only in the framework of a modest local self-government and then only as local (cantonal or provincial) self-government and not as state administration. Democracy, however, is a *political* concept, so its principles affect the determination of political unity as an entirety in terms of legislation and government.

A "democratization" of the administration only involves execution of individual tendencies and reforms corresponding to the fundamental democratic idea or to the program of democratic parties, such as, for example, *election* of civil servants rather than their appointment by a higher official or the selection of functionaries through the electorate of the official district, etc. In a state governed by parliament, the demand of a democratization of the administration easily comes to mean that parties holding only a transitory majority select administrative functionaries. The state and communal civil service thus transforms itself into a party following, whereby the leading civil servants [272] become party functionaries and electoral agents. The Weimar Constitution via Art. 130 seeks to escape these consequences by freeing the civil service from this practice of obedience and corruption. It thereby seeks a "depoliticalized" condition, as one often says, whereby the word "politics" is understood in the inferior sense of "party politics." With the help of an institutional guarantee with constitutional law status under Art. 130, the idea of the political unity of the state is meant to be protected against a partisan political dissolution. Nevertheless, German public law does not go so far as to separate the position of the civil servant from that of the deputy and to create an *incompatibility*, to declare, in other words, the position of a deputy (a party politician) irreconcilable with the position of a public official. The Weimar Constitution did not adopt this logic of the idea of the civil servant state.

2. Even the *recruitment of lay persons* for state administration also often counts as a sign of democratic administration. The voluntary activity of such laypersons is then understood as democratic administration. In this context, the concept of the people in its negative meaning may have determined the linguistic usage. The layperson belongs to the people because he is not a civil servant, so the recruitment of laypersons can count as something democratic (on this negativity of the word "people," see above p. 241).

3. *Self-government* in the sense of local, cantonal, or provincial self-government is often equated with democratic administration. According to *Hugo Preuß's* construction, state activity in a state governed by parliament is only "national" self-government. State and locality are equivalent, and the connection to the state is not essentially different from that to the locality and other associative collective persons (*Gemeinde, Staat, Reich als Gebietskörperschaften*, 1889, p. 189; *Handbuch der Politik*, I, p. 198ff.). In this way, the public law has thus became social welfare law, and from a particular *political* unity the state has become a *social* connection and is rendered nonpolitical. Such a way of thinking is, in fact, liberal and not democratic. Democracy is a *political* concept and, as such, leads to a decisive political *unity* and *sovereignty*. The administrative result can be the most energetic centralization just as well as it can be self-government. The centralized administration of the French state, for example, corresponds to a thoroughly democratic [273] realization of the idea of unconditional national unity. The countermovement against this form of centralism, federalism, regionalism, estate organizations, is for the most part monarchical and antidemocratic. There is naturally also a democratic federalism. But it is incorrect to consider the democratic principle of identity as equivalent to the ideal of the

most extensive communal self-government (in contrast to state administration). The people in a democracy are always the entire people of the *political* unity, not the electorate of a locality or of a county. That the political unity as a homogenous and closed entirety is distinguished in a particular way from all other domestic political groupings and organizations is the essential presupposition of political democracy.

Adolf Merkl, *Demokratie und Verwaltung*, 1923, p. 16, speaks of democratic administration (as opposed to "autocratic" administration) "in the sense of coming into wide acceptance and into power, according to which the staffing of the organization through *election* and *appointment* is determinative for democratic administration and autocratic administrations, respectively. This nomenclature finds application here, however—what cannot be emphasized decidedly enough—only in the interest of an easier understanding and in the full consciousness that in the designated properties the democratic or autocratic character of an institution does not come close to being fulfilled and exhausted. A definition is nonetheless found on pp. 44/5. "But otherwise," it reads, "(in particular apart from the fact that the 'bureaucrats' are not less a part of the 'people' than are party politicians), the fiction of an administration by the people is hardly sustainable. Democratic administration means administration by representatives of a certain political party." And he continues on p. 45 that "in reality, self-government, in all its genuine historical manifestations, is *neither* an *administration* by the *people*, as the *idealizing political legends* put it, nor, however, even an *autocratic administration*, as the *withering political critique* maintains. On the contrary, as it is plainly grounded in the essence of territorial self-government, it is the administration by elected representatives of every majority party that makes itself more or less noticeably unpleasant to the minority parties excluded from the administration as politically 'foreign administration.' With the ideology of self-government under such circumstances, one who does not allow himself to be fooled by political phrases or fictions will not be easily persuaded to support the progressive democratization of the administration."

V. *Democracy and the judiciary.*

1. The judge is bound to the *statute*. His activity is essentially normatively determined. He is not an independent representative of the political unity as such. Considered politically, this adjudication, which is entirely dependent on statute, is "en quelque façon nulle." Even in the bourgeois Rechtsstaat, the problem of political justice is emphasized [274] in the general judicial framework by the presence of special jurisdictions and organizations (above § 12, p. 134). If democracy is basically political form, the judiciary, by contrast, is fundamentally nonpolitical, because it is dependent on the general statute. It follows that in regard to the judiciary unambiguous and compelling consequences cannot be drawn from the democratic principle. One can control adjudication by way of the political concept of law. One can demand further that justice should be "in accord with the people" and that this aspiration affect certain institutions to be discussed immediately below. But the achievement of this aspiration depends to a great extent on the political situation and mood as well as on the political values of

judges at the time. It does not rest on systematic connections of a constitutional type.

Even in a democratic state, the judge must be independent if he is to be a judge and not a political instrument. The *independence* of the judge, however, can never be anything other than the reverse side of his *dependence* on statutory law. Herein lies the great difference of this type of independence from the independence of the deputy of a legislative body, such as the independence of the Reichstag deputy under Art. 21. Independence under Art. 21 should establish a *representation* and thus has a distinctive political sense. The independence of the judge should protect him from all official commands and directives, above all those of the government, or political officials, so it has the opposite purpose, which is the *rejection* of the political. Everything that the judge as judge does is *normatively* determined and distinguishes itself from the existential character of the political, even if it must produce an "integrative" effect, as must all state activity.

In Rousseau's ideal democracy, the identity and homogeneity of the people is so great that even judges and parties want the same thing. See the *Contrat social*, bk. II, chap. 4, sec. 7, where he argues that the volonté générale is the common interest, and, from it, arises a "wonderful agreement" of interest and justice, an agreement that cannot emerge from the discussion of private and particular interests. In his words, the common interest and the common use make, on the contrary, "the norm of the judge identical to that of the party." This situation is a beautiful example in democracy of the elimination of all distinctions and complications by general identity and homogeneity. At the same time, however, it also becomes clear that an absolute identity and homogeneity is impossible, and Rousseau's construction runs in a tautological circle. For with an absolute identity of all with all, no one needs to pursue further legal proceedings for the securing of justice. When everyone wants the same thing, not only does the distinction between judge and party (of which Rousseau speaks) disappear, but the [275] distinction between accuser and accused does as well. Even this difference becomes "identical," and the problem of justice is resolved because there are no longer any legal trials.

2. If a democratic state requires that justice be *"people's justice,"* the will of the people is made the defining perspective for settling litigation. That is a simple matter when the will of the people is only expressed in the general norms of Rechtsstaat statutes. In a democracy, however, the people are sovereign. They can violate the entire system of constitutional norms and settle litigation like the prince in an absolute monarchy, who could resolve legal disputes before courts. The people are the highest judge, just as they are the highest legislator. If under people's justice is understood a practice of democratic power claims, the word designates only the democratized and multiheaded type of cabinet justice. It is not generally meant in this way. One is mostly content to demand that only the judge that bears the confidence of the people can adjudicate legal claims. Under the people, however, is not understood the entire nation, as if it were democratic. Often

Application of the Political Principle

understood rather is only the inhabitants of individual official districts. The confidence could be expressed in such a way that the judges are selected for a specified time or until the inhabitants of the district express a lack of confidence in them. It is also possible for the populace to demand the decommissioning of a judge who has fallen from favor through so-called "recall." The consequence would be that adjudication is dependent on the mood of a district's populace. That is not a democratic requirement from the standpoint of a national democracy.

People's justice, however, could also mean that men or women "from the people" should participate in the resolution of judicial business, especially in adjudication. Here again, the word people has its negative sense (above p. 241) and means only that persons who are *not* professional civil servants, trained jurists, or law teachers participate in adjudication, hence in lay justice, in contrast to adjudication by civil servants and by legal academics (jurists). To this demand corresponds the institution of lay judges or jury courts for the criminal trial. This ideal may hardly be practical in the same degree for the resolution of bourgeois legal disputes and may only mean that *expert laypersons* (a concept that is not [276] entirely without contradiction) are recruited for judicial activity as trade judges.

In conclusion, taken most generally, people's justice can signify a popular justice in the sense of an agreement of court judgments with the legal sensibility of the people. So long as judges are dependent on statutory law, it is first of all a matter for the legislature to make popular laws and, in this way, to create the foundation for a popular justice. During the interpretation of statutes, in particular the application of indeterminate statutory concepts, the judge should conform to the fundamental legal views of his time and people. In normal times and with a people that is homogeneous culturally, socially, and in terms of religious doctrine, that is not a difficult task. If this homogeneity diminishes, then reliance on the fundamental legal views of the people is not a solution to the difficulty. In any case, it would be an error in such a situation to refer the highly political task to the judiciary. Political decision is a matter for the legislature and for the political leadership. The Free Law Movement of the last decades demanded a popular justice, but for the most part it did not take into account the implications in constitutional theory terms, because it did not recognize clearly enough the extent to which the independence of judges and the strictest bond to the statute condition one another and that the law must be a statute. This produces a true bond and is not merely a blanket reference to indeterminate norms and to judicial discretion that politicizes the judiciary.

§ 21.

Boundaries of Democracy

I. Because the one-sided and exclusive execution of one of the two principles of state form, identity and representation, is not at all possible, and because no state system can be fully formed according to the principle of identity without any representation (§ 16, II, p. 204), there is a limit to the absolute implementation of the democratic principle of identity. The theoretic consequence of the principle of identity will, indeed, validate itself again and again in a democracy and appear as something illuminating and self-evident. Nevertheless, a democratic state cannot [277] fully renounce all representation. Democracy finds its first natural boundary.

II. An additional boundary of democracy results from the nature of the *people* in the different meanings of this word.

1. The people as an entity that is not officially organized (above p. 242) become valid in individual moments and only by way of acclamation, hence today as "public opinion."

2. The people as state citizens who elect or vote in a regulated procedure (above p. 239) can (a) *elect* persons dependent on their confidence. In this regard, they are to a great extent dependent on suggestions. The people must transfer to the elected persons the decision of substantive questions according to the scope of their jurisdiction. Or (b) they can reach a *substantive decision* by way of the vote on a question (so-called substantive plebiscite). Such a vote is fully conditioned by the posing of the question resulting from the secret individual ballot. The people can only say yes or no.

That is also the case with the popular initiative. Considered more closely, the procedure in such an initiative is one in which private initiators present a draft law that poses the question of whether this demand should be considered. The portion of the enfranchised state citizens desiring the initiative answer "yes" to the question posed. Art. 73, 3, stipulates that a complete statutory draft is an integral part of an initiative through which a popular legislative procedure should be introduced. Naturally, the vote cannot complete a statutory draft. In regard to the determining whether a tenth (Art. 73, 3) or a twentieth (Art. 72, 73, 2) of those with the right to vote intend the initiative to pass (in the procedure for introduction under § 31 of the law on the referendum of 27 June 1921), "yes" is answered only to the statutory draft presented and to the question of whether this draft law should provide the basis for the initiative. By way of secret individual ballot, more precisely, the people can never pose a question. It can only answer a question posed. Theodor Mommsen's observation about the dependence of the assembled people on the magistrates' posing of the question applies ever more aptly to the procedure of secret individual vote in today's mass democracy.

Summarized in a short thesis, one can say that the people can *acclaim*; in a secret individual vote, they can only *elect* the candidates presented to them and *answer yes or no to a precisely formulated question posed to them.*

III. With the help of the principle of separation of powers, the *practice* of modern democracy has rendered the democratic principle relative to an organizational means of legislation (above p. 260). Moreover, certain *affairs* and *materials*, in particular *financial questions*, [278] and the methods of the so-called direct democracy are often excluded from the process or this procedure is limited to such materials. Finally, the process of direct democracy can frequently be forced aside by *emergency decisions.*

Art. 73, 4, contains an example of such limitations by providing that "only the President can occasion a referendum on the budgetary plan, on expenditure laws, and commission orders." Cf. above § 20, I 2c (p. 262) and I 4c (p. 264).

According to Art. 73, 2, a statute, whose promulgation is interrupted by at least a third of the Reichstag, must be submitted to a referendum when one-twentieth of the enfranchised voters request it. Under Art. 72, however, the Reichstag and Reichsrat can declare a statute *urgently needed* when a third of the Reichstag demands a postponement, and the President can promulgate the statute regardless of this demand, thereby vacating the referendum stipulated by Art. 73, 2. According to Art. 89, 2, of the Swiss federal constitution, a referendum can be requested on a generally binding federal executive decision that is not of a *pressing nature.* The federal statute concerning a popular vote on federal statutes and executive decisions ("referendum statute") of 17 June 1874 provides in Art. 2 that "the decision that a federal executive action is to be treated as pressing is reserved to the federal assembly." Thus, in Switzerland, important affairs like the creation of the associational Office of Land Law (1911) and of the Federal Office for Social Insurance (1912), both of which were added by way of the emergency need clause, could be removed from consideration in the referendum (Fleiner, *Schweizerisches Bundesstaatsrecht*, pp. 403/4).

IV. *Critique of the principle "the majority decides."*

Friedrich Naumann wanted to include this principle in the Constitution, which he thought of as a people's catechism, especially as an expression of democratic principle and democratic outlook. The text of the Weimar Constitution does not contain it. Nevertheless, it is perhaps appropriate to remember that it is ambiguous and unclear.

1. In regard to a ballot question, the word "decides" in the principle "majority decides" only signifies the formal resolution of a substantive alternative, while in an election it signifies the selection of the elected person. On a ballot question, the majority decides in the manner that it answers yes or no to a proffered, formulated question. The principle "majority decides" states that there is agreement on the fact that the question is answered as conclusively as accords with the size of the majority of ballots cast. Whether a decision is in fact reached depends on the correctness of and opportunity for posing an alternative in the form of a simple question.

2. Dependence on the posing of the question means that the numerical majority of the ballots cast only decides *the substantive issue* on an exceptional basis. The substantive decision is often already rendered by the manner of posing the question. But if the will [279] of the people expresses itself occasionally in undeniable acclamation and in a decisive, noncontradictory public opinion, that has nothing to do with the procedure of a secret individual ballot and the statistical determination of the majority. In such cases, it is never certain whether a subsequently held secret individual vote would provide the same result as the aforementioned direct emergence and expression of the people's will. For public opinion is generally only borne by an active and politically interested minority of the people, while the great majority of the enfranchised state citizens are not necessarily politically interested. It is now in no way democratic and would, moreover, be a remarkable political principle that those without a political will should decide in contrast to those with such a will.

3. When it is said that those who pose the question are in a position to decide the substantive outcome through the manner of posing the question, this is meant not only psychologically. The influence of the posing of the question results not only from the selection of the time of the vote or from the possibility of finding suggestive formulations, in which the answer can already be contained and made redundant. These are technical questions of mass psychology, which should remain unexamined here. It also need not be discussed that the mass of the enfranchised voters can often not be adequately instructed and that they lack the necessary expertise and powers of judgment, etc. In a democracy, it is precisely this perspective that may never be brought forward as something definitive, because under the presuppositions of a democratic state system the people are capable of every political decision. For the distinctly political questions directed to the people as a whole, especially in regard to the existential distinction of friend and enemy, technical, specialized information and details of technical expertise must be settled by the competent and responsible technical experts. These matters cannot be handled by the mass of the enfranchised voters. However, they are also not the actual political issue in question. The actual ground of this dependence on the posing of the question lies precisely in the fact that the greatest part of the enfranchised voters generally has the aspiration to behave passively in regard to the decision and to evade the decision. [280] This desire not only explains the high number of abstentions, which is often criticized. Above all, it also accounts for the demonstrable tendency regarding the majority of ballots cast of providing an answer that contains *a minimum of substantive decision*.

That is in accord with all previous historical and political experience. A few apparent contradictions, which one can ascertain in the results of popular votes, re-

	Yes	No
Jacobin Constitution	1,801,918	11,610
(did not enter into force)	(only one out of 44, 000 communities voted against the Republic	
Constitution of the Directory, 1795	916,334	41,892
Consulate Constitution, 1799	3,009,445	1,562
Napoleon as consul for life, 1802	3,568,885	8,365
Napoleon as emperor of the French, 1804	3,574,898	2,569
Supplementary acts (during the One Hundred Days), 1815	1,532,327	4,802
Louis Napoleon's coup d'état approved, 1851	7,439,216	640,757
Louis Napoleon as emperor of the French, 1852	7,824,189	153,145

solve themselves in a simple manner if one takes into account which result actually contains the minimum of decision. It has been noticed that the plebiscites of the revolutionary and Napoleonic governments in France always resulted in a "yes." Cf. above p. 86; also the number of voting results in France (according to Duguit-Monnier) below.

In the referenda in Switzerland, by contrast, the inclination appears to be to say "no," at least in regard to progressive laws, such as the introduction of health and accident insurance, which was concluded by the federal legislative organ in 1890, rejected by referendum in 1900, and first accepted in 1912 by referendum. On this tendency, cf. Curti, *Die Resultate des Schweizerischen Referendums*, 2nd ed. 1911; also Hasbach, *Die moderne Demokratie*, p. 154. One concluded from this tendency that the methods of direct democracy are conservative or, indeed, "reactionary." In fact, the majority of the state citizens answering in secret individual votes are neither reactionary nor progressive, but rather simply nonpolitical, and, as such, these citizens seek to evade the substantive decision, while it is forced to give an answer that constitutes the minimum of decision. The "yes" the French citizens gave in the Napoleonic plebiscites is explained entirely independently of the government's electioneering by the fact that there was in reality an accomplished fact and that the decision was already reached. A "no" here would have contained a new political decision of unpredictable consequences. It was easier to say "yes," and so the majority said "yes." The opposite is the case in the Swiss referenda. If in regard to the proposal of a legislative change the majority answers "no," then it is the "no" that signifies the minimum of substantive decision. For also with the "no" the directly present, given circumstance persists. In other words, the matter remains essentially unchanged, which is a resolution whose "decisional" content is obviously less than the decision for a change.

4. The method of individual secret ballot transforms the enfranchised citizen into an isolated private man and makes it possible for him to express his opinion without abandoning the private sphere [281]. A tabulation of

what private people think privately produces neither a genuine public opinion nor a genuine political decision. It can even be inappropriate to expect such decisions from private people.

At least the majority of professionally engaged citizens would prefer, to the extent that it is not a matter of their direct economic interests, not to be unnecessarily burdened with political decisions. A clear, public example of this aversion to a decision presents itself currently (1927) every time the inhabitants of the German Reich raise the flag. "The Reich colors are black-red-gold," according to Art. 3. "The commercial flag is black-white-red with the Reich colors in the upper inside corner." This provision contains a compromise and not a domestic political decision between the colors black-red-gold and black-white-red. An overwhelming and decisive acclamation of the German people has still not resulted. The result of a secret individual vote would probably be dictated by party discipline and would not provide a majority that seems overpowering to the part of the electorate that was outvoted. Currently, this type of resolution may still not be the most appropriate means of such a decision. Meanwhile, a large part of the population, above all business people, has let it be known publicly that they themselves also do not want to decide in that they either do not fly the flag at all or display a "neutral" one like the provincial flag, the local city flag, the papal flag, or a flag of one's own that is specially prepared for a purpose—as living illustration of the principle the "majority decides."

5. Even in terms of numbers, one cannot simply say that the "majority decides" when the majority of the ballots cast should be the deciding factor. More accurately, it is frequently the case that in reality a small part gives the edge. If on the occasion of a vote of one hundred in all, one part comprises forty-eight yes votes and another part forty-eight no votes, arithmetically both these parts cancel themselves out and the remaining portion of only four out of the hundred decides. That is of great substantive significance in a population splintered into many parties, because not all parties have the same interest in the question posed. The issue of religious schools, for example, can be decided by a small party devoted to protecting tenants, the adherents of which vote for tactical reasons for the one or the other of the parties interested in religious schools, or a question of foreign or economic policy can be decided by a party that is interested, above all, in religious schools, etc. So in fact the "majority decides" only really holds when there is the complete similarity of motivation of all those voting.

6. When the majority is nothing other than the result of a tabulation of ballots cast in a secret individual vote, one can just as well say that "the majority does *not* decide." [282] Such a method of statistical majority determination actually only has the sense of a restricted authorization and limited effective political means for all state citizens to participate in state life. Nevertheless, one may not overlook that there is a type of democracy, and above all parliamentary democracy, that has an interest precisely in having certain conflicts remain latent and left undecided. The procedure for majority determination can become an appropriate and desirable means of

avoiding or suspending political decisions. Politically, it can be simply wiser not to decide and to use the alleged majority decision in this way. Then, the principle the "majority decides" would already belong to the *arcana* of certain political systems, the handling of which extends beyond the framework of a "constitutional theory."

The Theory of Monarchy

I. *The opposition of monarchy and democracy rests on the opposition be-tween both principles of political form, representation and identity.*

The *political principle* of monarchy entails the representation of politi-cal unity. Moreover, there are numerous foundations and justifications of monarchy. But if one ignores the experiential reasons of practical and ratio-nal purposefulness, they may be traced back to a few simple types.

1. The monarchy is *religiously* grounded. In a distinctive sense, the mon-arch is "*of God*," an "image of God," and of godly essence.

The monarchical formulation "from the grace of God," considered from the per-spective of modern ideas, has only a polemical and negative sense and means noth-ing more than that the monarch does not owe his power and authority to another (other than God), not to the church or to the pope, or even to the will and consent of the people. However, the connection of monarchy and religious ideas in no way exhausts itself in this meaning. In terms of intellectual history, a monarch who gov-erns the state appeared always as an analogy to God who governs the world. During medieval times and up into the modern period, the king had a supernatural char-acter for the great mass of the people even in physical terms. As Marc Bloch has shown in numerous examples in his work "Les rois thaumaturges" (*Etudes sur le caractère surnaturel attribué à la puissance royale, particulièrement en France et en Angleterre*, Strassburg 1924), the fact that the king performed miracles and, in particular, healed the sick through laying on of hands was completely of a piece with the vital power of the monarchy. [283] The last attempt to work seriously in practical terms with these religious images of monarchy falls in the year 1825, when Karl X of France still wanted to heal the sick through the laying on of hands, an attempt, however, that only produced a somewhat embarrassing romantic imitation (Bloch, *Etudes*, p. 404). By contrast, during a time in which the king performs miracles, with his entire person he can be considered holy and inviolable, priest and the anointed of the ruling lord. The king's law is godly, that is, of religious origin; the king himself is a governor of God (cf. Gierke, *Althusius*, p. 177; Funck-Brentano, *Le roi*, Paris 1912, p. 166ff.).

This religious grounding of the monarchy passes over into a less precise, his-torical or general irrationalism. The last openly theological argumentation may be contained in the state theory of Bonald, who incorporated the monarch into a series of "unities": a god, a king, a father; monotheism, monarchy, and monogamy. In F. J. Stahl, this theological construction is bound up with other, antirationalist, tradi-tionalist, and legitimist arguments.

2. Even if it easily becomes the religious image of God the father, the monarch as *father* is another justification. The authority and power of the father in the family, the patria potestas, is applied to the state, which is understood as an enlarged family.

Numerous examples and details in Funck-Brentano, *Le roi*, p. 52ff. Especially in his *Politique tirée de l'Ecriture* (1709), Bossuet above all advocates this patriarchal form of argumentation together with the religious one. "L'autorité royale est paternelle," he argues. "La Monarchie a son fondement et son modèle dans l'empire paternal." The patriarchal theory of the monarchy that Filmer, *Patriarcha* (1680), presented is still known today through a few jokes by Rousseau (*Contrat social*, I 2). In fact, this theory involves an adaptation that is to be taken seriously at least in social-psychology terms.

3. Other types of monarchical ideas are not distinctive in the same degree as this religious or patriarchal justification. There is a *patrimonial* monarchy, in which the monarch appears as the bearer of superior and lasting empire and of economic power, above all as the great landholder of the country, dominus, or property owner. In real political terms, that can be a very firm basis for the monarchical position, but it is not a type of argumentation that is characteristic of and peculiar to the monarchical theory, because the social prestige of every great empire can lead to a patrimonial posture. It is just like the feudal monarchy, in which the king is the *leader* of a *following* that is devoted to him personally and serves him for life and death, and to which he guarantees in exchange protection and maintenance in different forms (reception in his home, an allowance, and other types of care). These types of allegiance form themselves in the most diverse ways, without one being able to speak of the monarchy in the sense of a principle of political form, [284] so long as the lord does not receive a divine blessing or patriarchal office. The other historical types of monarchy come just as little into consideration for the ideal justification of monarchy. In the *civil servant monarchy*, as it took shape in European states from the sixteenth to the nineteenth century, the monarch is the pinnacle of a civil service organization, *premier magistrat.* The distinctive monarchical element rests on historically received, non–civil servant state ideas. In the *Caesarist* monarchy, as it was realized in the Bonapartes' empire, the monarch is only a dictator on a democratic foundation. In the course of development, this type of monarchy can become a genuine monarchy. Ultimately, however, the democratic principle supports it, and it turns the monarch into a representative of the political unity borne by the will of the people, who, as such, is constituted by an act of the constitution-making power of the people.

The six types of monarchy enumerated here—theocratic, patriarchal, patrimonial, feudal, bureaucratic, and Caesarist—bind themselves in historically genuine cases of monarchy in different ways, so that every concrete case of monarchy contains in itself several of these elements combined with one another and alongside one another. The monarchy of the German territorial princes of the eighteenth century, such as the Prussian monarchy under Friedrich William I, contained patrimonial elements because of the king's great domain possessions, feudal ones in its relationship with the nobility, civil servant elements because a bureaucratic administrative apparatus, formed according to certain principles, had already arisen from the commissioners of the seventeenth century, and also lay religious elements in the connection with the country's church government. It only lacked any Caesarist elements, which first became possible with general, compulsory military service and general right to vote in the nineteenth century. In his treatise "Democracy and Empire" (1900), Friedrich Naumann sought to transform the German monarchy in the twentieth century into a Caesarist one, an attempt not only without practical results, but also one that was falsely justified in theoretic terms. For a legitimate monarchy cannot falsely attribute to itself another ideal basis. The principle of dynastic legitimacy contradicts the democratic principle of legitimacy. In this instance, there is an unavoidable either/or choice (above p. 54, 88). As soon as legitimacy has become an ideal basis of an institution, the legitimate power can no longer emerge as the bearer of a new political idea. Shortly before the Revolution of 1789 in France, there were attempts at similar constructions of a connection between the existing monarchy and Caesarism and the suggestion was made that the king exercise a dictatorship borne by the confidence of the people (cf. *Die Diktatur*, p. 112). But even if Louis XVI had united in himself all the qualities of a Caesar or Napoleon, the mere fact that he was the legitimate prince would have sufficed to make the fulfillment of such a role impossible for him. A new political principle always appears historically with the new men who bear it.

The genuine idea of monarchy returns in the nineteenth century. The still existing monarchy is justified with either historical-traditional or with sentimental arguments. [285] Different perspectives are combined in the legal and state philosophy of Friedrich J. Stahl. Yet even here the distinctively monarchical aspect of the current of thought is absent, and the argumentation has the effect of a clever plea. One refers to that which developed historically, makes analogies to the personal god, emphatically advances the demand that one should have piety. In reality, however, it is only a matter of *legitimacy.* One can justify the most diverse institutions with historical arguments. But when only the legitimate domestic political *status quo* is actually defended, that is something other than the principle of political form of monarchy. Much less still is the poetic portrayal of kings by Romantics, such as in Novalis and Adam Müller, a monarchical state theory. They make out of the monarch a springboard for moods and feelings. The monarchy hence loses its political, institutional, and even legitimate sense, because not only the king or queen, but rather all possible persons or things, the people as well as the monarch, the revolutionary as well as the loyal servant of his master, on occasion all prompt a sentimental attachment and could become the theme of a poetic beautification. The idea of the *representation* of the state, the monarchy's principle of political form, disappears into the idea that the king is a symbol or type of *ideal.* These concepts no longer had their old power and became a mere occasion for romantic feelings and moods, while the popular assembly emerged as the true representative "of the people," which means in particular of the political unity of the people.

5. The *legitimate* monarchy is not a type of monarchy; it is, rather, an instance of legitimacy.

II. *The significance in constitutional theory terms of the different justifications of monarchy.*

1. All principled justifications of monarchy contain at the core only two ideas, which lead in a distinctive sense directly to monarchy: the idea of a personal *god* and the image of the *father.* None of these ideas belong essentially to the political sphere. Where the monarchy is religiously justified and the monarch becomes a divine creation or one standing in a special connection with God, the idea moves in the theological realm or on the terrain of worldviews, not in the political sphere. [286] If the world is governed as a unity by a single god, and the unity of the state is understood under a monarch as something equivalent or analogous, the primary concept is obviously God and world and not monarchy and state. If the monarch is understood as the father of the state family and the dynastic concept of a hereditary monarchy is derived from it, the idea of first importance is family and not state. Always, therefore, it is nonpolitical ideas and images that constitute the core of the argumentation. The theological or cosmological idea must lead to a world monarchy and eliminate the distinctive connection of the monarch with a certain state and a particular people, which is precisely the political element. For in regard to the idea of the absolute unity of the world, a multitude of states and peoples is incomprehensible. The family is a unity justified by physical lineage and household community, which lacks the character of the *public.* It is not a political entity like the people. Such grounds for monarchy are justifications of mastery and authority in general, but not of a principle of political form in its idiosyncratic peculiarity.

2. The rationalist justifications of monarchy, which emerge since the eighteenth century, are of an entirely different type. The king is nothing other than *premier magistrat* for the philosophy of the Enlightenment, the first and, if it is justified in terms of reason, the most enlightened civil servant, who can best care for the well-being of his less enlightened subjects. But neither the inheritability nor the legitimacy of the monarchy results in this way, and if a prince lacks the aforementioned quality of the enlightened person, the justification does not apply.

In the nineteenth century, the rationalistic and empirical justifications of monarchy are distinguished by the fact that they incorporate the monarch into the Rechtsstaat system of separation of powers. These justifications make a mere governmental form out of the monarchy and render it into the more or less influential *chief executive.* The justifications are different here, but they always take proving the *usefulness* and *appropriateness* of the monarchy as their point of departure. The typical example is the following consideration, which is already found in Mably and de Lolme, but which is also still expressed in Max Weber with great certainty ("Grundriss der Sozialökonomik," *Wirtschaft und Gesellschaft*, III, p. 649). Through the hereditary monarchy, he claims, the highest place in the state avoids [287] political competition. Its worst extreme is thus removed from domestic political struggle. Consequently, conflict becomes more mild and rational, for the politician's striving for power is limited because the highest office in the state is possessed once and for all. "This latter, essentially negative function, which attaches to the mere existence of a king as such, who is chosen according to firm rules, is perhaps, considered purely politically, the practically most important thing" (Max Weber).

The position of the monarch rests above all on the fact that he stands *above the parties*. If the state is transformed into a party state through parliamentarization and democratization, that becomes an especially meaningful position. The king receives a distinctive place in the organization of the different "powers" compared to the legislative and executive. He becomes a neutral authority, a *pouvoir neutre*, an invisible, tempering, and moderating element that balances out all oppositions and frictions between the different state activities and functions, an *invisible modérateur*. This construction is typical of the Rechtsstaat liberalism of the parliamentary monarchy. It stems from Benjamin Constant. Historically, the bourgeois kingship of Louis-Philippe may best correspond to its ideal. Nevertheless, the entire current of thought of a neutral authority is also of direct interest for the establishment of the position of a republican state president.

The role of the *pouvoir* neutre or *modérateur* naturally eludes a formal, constitutional definition. Cf. the discussions of this role of the German president, below § 27, III, p. 351. From time to time, certainly, express constitutional provisions also occur. Thus, the (imperial) constitution of Brazil of 25 March 1824, which in Title V (Art. 98ff.) speaks of the legislative power (pouvoir législative) and then of the emperor in Title V (Art. 98ff.) under the chapter heading "Du pouvoir modérateur," reads "Le pouvoir modérateur est la clef de toute l'organisation politique, il est délégué exclusivement à l'empereur comme chef suprême de la nation et son premier représentant," etc.

3. Every consideration of appropriateness and usefulness, just like all arguments deduced from historical experience, whether they are presented by liberal theorists like Benjamin Constant and Guizot or by antiliberal monarchists like Charles Maurras, are necessarily relative. Viewed from the perspective of historical experience, they are dependent on an important presupposition in that they are valid only for a dynasty that has existed and remained on the throne uninterrupted for generations. [288] With his political influence, the monarch can retire completely and transfer political leadership and all potestas to parliament or to a powerful party leader. Over a long period of time, he can disappear as a factor of political power, but he must retain continuity in regard to the occupation of the throne, if he is to fulfill the functions that justify his position (the neutral authority existing above party, representation of the continuity of the state during crises). If

this continuity is interrupted, any claims on behalf of the monarch fail to persuade, because the monarch is drawn into party conflict and even his role in the system becomes a party matter.

Rationalist arguments from appropriateness are only effective under a monarchy whose political security remains unshaken. It is valid only for a "traditional" monarchy, not for the "new prince," the "principe nuovo," for whom Machiavelli wrote his book about the prince. Machiavelli emphatically states in this famous treatise that it is easy to keep oneself on the throne if, in peaceful times, one rules as a generally honored and respected prince. By contrast, to justify and defend a new monarchical regime is an entirely different political situation. If through the toppling of a dynasty the line of succession is ripped apart, all these justifications and arguments fail. It never applies to a monarchical restoration, because until now each of these has failed: 1660–1688, the Stuarts in England; 1815–1830, the Bourbons in France; in a certain sense even 1852–1870, the restoration of the Bonaparte family under Napoleon III. Charles Maurras says that domestic political party conflicts under democratic politics would lead to appeals for help by foreign governments and the latter's interference in the politics of these democratic states. He names as a classic example the typical tendency in Greek democracies, in which the aristocratic party would appeal to the Lacedaemonians for help and the democratic party would appeal to the Athenians. The same process repeated itself in the Italian states of the sixteenth century, when in Florence one party made the French allies, the other the Spanish or the Germans. This historical experience is without doubt very interesting. Set against it, however, is the other experience that restored monarchies also do not last without external political support, which means allies abroad. One must, indeed, designate the connection of the Stuarts with the king of France, for example, simply as treason from the national English standpoint, and the monarchical policy of the Holy Alliance of 1815–1830 also led to constant interventions. From historical experience alone no noncontradictory political system is possible, and if the monarchy is still only historically justified, then any clear proof and every principle is generally lacking. One can only say that the monarchy arises and passes away like everything in history.

III. *The position of the monarch in the modern constitution.*

The constitutional monarchy rests on the fact that the monarchical principle is restricted by the separation of powers, and the monarch, as an autonomous and independent chief of the executive branch, represents the political unity, while a popular assembly (the parliament) stands opposite him as a second representative. [289] In this way, there develops a separation and balancing that corresponds to the organizational principle of the bourgeois Rechtsstaat. The question of sovereignty, however, is certainly not decided here and remains open. In Germany's constitutional monarchy, the monarchical principle retained its validity during the nineteenth century behind the constitutionally legislated norm; the monarchy was genuine state form, not only governmental form and organizational element of the executive.

For the German constitutions, Friedrich J. Stahl, the theorist of the Prussian constitutional monarchy, successfully elaborated the distinctiveness of the constitutional monarchy in contrast to the parliamentary one. Under this understanding, the essence of the constitutional monarchy lies in the fact that the constitutional monarch still has genuine power, and that his personal will is still somewhat valid and not subsumed in the parliament. He remains "through the firm security of his authorizations a distinct, autonomous factor of state authority" (*Die Revolution und die konstitutionelle Monarchie*, 2nd ed., 1849, pp. 33, 76ff., 93ff.). That was a distinction that was very meaningful in practical terms, but in principle it was only the recognition of a form of legality under a bourgeois Rechtsstaat and of a form of liberalism that moderated the exercise of the monarchical authority. One can term that "constitutional monarchy" and even bring it into opposition to "parliamentary monarchy," although this parliamentary monarchy is also constitutional. Only one must not fail to recognize that the *political* conflict was in principle between monarchy and democracy. The constitutional monarchy is not a special state form. It is, rather, a connection between the principles of the bourgeois Rechtsstaat and the political principle of the monarchy under the protection of the sovereignty of the monarch, which immediately reveals itself during every conflict and in every crisis (above pp. 55, 88). The turn of phrase "constitutional monarchy" leaves open the decisive question as to whether the monarchy ceases to be state form and becomes mere governmental form or whether the monarchical principle remains intact.

In the parliamentary monarchy of the European continent, France under the bourgeois kingdom of *Louis-Philippe* 1830–1848 and Belgium on the basis of the constitution of 1831, the monarch remains the chief of the executive branch. Political leadership, however, is dependent on the agreement with the parliamentary majority. The state form was no longer monarchical. More accurately, the monarchy had become an organizational element in the balancing of powers of the liberal Rechtsstaat. F. J. Stahl terms that "liberal constitutionalism." It distinguishes itself from the German constitutional monarchy (in Stahl's manner of expression) by the fact that the monarchical principle is given up. Consequently, the democratic principle must necessarily become the foundation of the political unity if this should continue to exist. The "constitutional" element pertaining to the bourgeois Rechtsstaat is added to both principles of political form as an autonomous component. The intent behind the constitutional element is to devalue and balance them and bind them altogether. [290]

"Tous les pouvoirs émanent de la Nation" [All powers emanate from the nation], according to Art. 25 of the Belgian constitution. "Ils sont exercés de la manière, établie par la Constitution." [They are exercised in the manner established by the Constitution.] Friedrich J. Stahl distinguishes among the following: 1. radical constitutionalism, for example, the French constitution of 1791, which, therefore, seemed radical to him, because the king only has a suspensive veto in regard to legislation and, consequently, is not a legislative organ, but rather is limited strictly to the executive function; 2. liberal constitutionalism, that is, legislation with a two-chamber system, royal veto, and ministers dependent on the confidence of parliament; 3. genuine constitutional monarchy, such as, for example, under the Prussian constitution of 31 January 1850, in which the government remains in the hands of the king, whose consent is required for a statute, and in which the king convenes, adjourns, postpones, and dissolves the parliament. Like the entire construction of Friedrich J. Stahl, this one is determined completely by the special political circumstance of the German monarchy. Its cardinal point lies in the fact that constitutionalism, in particular, a liberal principle, is correctly recognized as a principle *added* to the political principle of monarchy or democracy, while, as shown above, the core political question, monarchy or democracy, remains open and is not decided through the recognition of a "constitution."

2. The parliamentary monarchy Belgian style is also a constitutional monarchy, but only after the renunciation of the monarchical principle, which entails the transformation of the monarchy as a state form into an organizational form of the executive (government). The term "monarchy" is retained for historical reasons. This retention is, indeed, proper insofar as the monarch can lose all power (potestas), while he continues to exist as authority and, therefore, also to exercise the distinctive functions of a "neutral power" especially well. Political leadership and administration is in the hand of his ministers, who are responsible to the popular assembly and dependent on its trust. The famous formula for this reads: "Le roi règne mais il ne gouverne pas." [The king rules, but he does not govern.] The question posed by a great teacher of German public law, Max von Seydel, what then remains of "régner" if one removes "gouverner?," is answerable in reference to the fact that one distinguishes between potestas and auctoritas (above p. 75) and that the distinctive meaning of authority is made evident in regard to political power.

IV. *The state president in a republican constitution.*

1. In the nineteenth-century development of the Rechtsstaat, the historically received institution of the monarchy had been used and valued in a distinctive manner. As "chief of the executive branch," the king was drawn into the system of the separation of powers with differentiated grants of authority, though always as the pinnacle of a special authority. Hence, from a state form, the monarchy became a mere form of government, though it retained [291] its representative character. For it corresponded to the Rechtsstaat idea of balancing to place another representation in opposition to that by an assembly (the legislative body), so that the sovereign, which, according to democratic principles, is the people, remained in the background and did not emerge initially. The democratic principle (of the self-identity of the people present at the time) was balanced with the principle of representation, and yet the danger that the principle of representation would establish itself *absolutely* eliminated the possibility that two representatives, monarch and popular assembly, would stand opposite one another and be reconciled to one another.

This construction connects in ideal manner the bourgeois Rechtsstaat with a mixture of both principles of political form (monarchy and democracy). So it is typical of the bourgeois-Rechtsstaat constitution and was retained where the monarchy as a form of government had also become impossible and the republic established itself. The nineteenth-century French constitutional development is especially pronounced in this regard. As a result of the repeated breaks in continuity, and in view of the numerous changes in the possessors of the throne that the French people had experienced in the nineteenth century, a monarchical authority was hardly still conceivable. But this Rechtsstaat balancing construct remained intact, as did the design for an autonomous chief of the executive branch, which should have representative character. This state president is the republican version of the monarch of the parliamentary monarchy. He must be retained for reasons of the separation of powers and must be provided with particular grants of authority (for example, dissolution of parliament), so that the government in regard to parliament is balanced out to an indeterminate degree of independence.

Prévost-Paradol developed the state theory construct of this system in several essays and above all in his book "La France nouvelle," 1869. His ideas were of great influence on the French constitutional laws of 1875. In France then, one did not want to permit the election of the president directly by the people, because one still stood under the impression of a dangerous precedent, specifically the coup d'état of 1851 that President Louis Napoleon, who was elected directly by the people, had instituted with great success. Moreover, the political goal of the originators of these constitutional laws of 1875 was certainly directed to the reestablishment of the monarchy. There was an attempt to set up the framework of constitutional norms such that a reinstitution of the monarch be made as easy as possible. The design for the balancing of powers is nevertheless the same. [292]

2. The *Weimar Constitution* adopted this system, and it introduced into the constitution elements of a presidential system alongside such a pure parliamentary one. The President is elected by the entire German people. He has a series of important political jurisdictions, such as the representation of the Reich under international law (Art. 45), appointment and removal of Reich civil servants and officers (Art. 46), high command over the entire Reich defensive force (Art. 47), authority to compel Land execution of Reich laws (Art. 48, 1), authority to issue measures under the state of exception (Art. 48, 2), and right of pardon for the Reich (Art. 50). His grants of authority in regard to parliament, which should provide his position the capacity to act as a counterpoise to the Reichstag, are his authority to dissolve parliament (Art. 25) and to order a referendum against a statute concluded by the Reichstag (Art. 73). Cf. in this regard the overview in the balancing schema, above p. 197.

According to Art. 179, 1, the President fully assumes the authority of the Kaiser by virtue of the statute of 10 February 1919 on the provisional Reich authority and on the basis of the transitional statute of 4 March 1919 (so far as nothing else is provided by law). In particular, he receives organizational authority, which is the power to regulate the establishment, jurisdiction, and activities of Reich officials to the extent that this authority was accorded to the Kaiser. One cannot term that a legal succession, not even an indirect legal inheritance, as does Anschütz (*Kommentar*, p. 435), for the legal foundation is not the same. How much the office of the President is analogous to that of a monarchical chief of the executive is revealed in the institution of equivalent authorities and in the assumption of a comprehensive position. As in other cases, there are elements of a principle of political form that are rendered relative by reducing them into means of organization. These elements of political form are bound up with the principle of the bourgeois Rechtsstaat and opposing elements of political form and are applied to a mixture typical of the bourgeois Rechtsstaat constitution.

§ 23-3.

Aristocratic Elements in Modern
Bourgeois-Rechtsstaat Constitutions

I. The political form of aristocracy rests on the idea of representation. Nevertheless, the logic of this form principle [293] is weakened and moderated by the fact that not a single person, but rather a majority of persons, represents the political entity. Thus, there is in aristocracy itself a certain "modération" (above § 16, IV, p. 218).

The modern bourgeois-Rechtsstaat constitution applies the aristocratic principle's elements of form in a twofold sense. If a parliamentary regime is not initially an aristocratic system, it is nevertheless an oligarchic one (on this below § 24). Moreover, elements of aristocratic form and structure could be used as organizational means for the balancing of powers, so that the democratic and monarchical elements render themselves equivalent. While the monarchical element adapts itself especially well for the design of the executive branch and is even used for this purpose (§ 22, IV, p. 288), the aristocratic element was incorporated into an organization of the *legislature* that *divides* powers, and inside the legislative branch a more or less aristocratic *upper house* stood opposite a democratically conceived lower house. So arises the two-chamber system of the modern Rechtsstaat constitution.

II. *Idea of and justification for the two-chamber system.*

1. The English model was definitive for the introduction of the dual chamber system in most countries of the European continent. This system contained something especially illuminating for the liberal ideas of the nineteenth century. For it allowed itself to be properly brought into harmony with the principle of the separation of powers and, moreover, provided the opportunity to protect the social power of certain estates and classes against a radical democracy. Consequently, it met liberal as well as conservative demands in the same manner. This fact also accounts for the wide distribution of this system. In Germany as in France, most liberals considered the dual-chamber system a reasonable, enlightened institution and construed it differently.

2. The justification for and formulation of the two-chamber system, which became classic for the bourgeois liberalism of the nineteenth century, is found in Benjamin Constant. He understands the upper house as a special representation and attempts to divide this *representation* by devising various matters of concern for it. The elected house of deputies is a "representative" of changing public opinion; the hereditary-based upper

house is "representative of permanence and [294] continuity" ("durée" in contrast to "opinion"). He no longer terms the "royal power" as "neutral" (above p. 287), the executive as enforcement, and the judicial authority as "representative." The idea that a special advocate of stability and quality must be placed alongside a lower house, which is dominated by shifting opinions and majorities and is based on number and quantity, recurs in different forms. Even German liberals have expressly recognized such designs of an upper house.

Bluntschli, *Allgemeines Staatsrecht*, I, p. 512; Gneist, *Englische Verfassungsgeschichte*, p. 675ff.; the formulations of Benjamin Constant in his *Oeuvres politiques*, p. 18.

3. The dual-chamber system must contradict a democracy's political logic, for democracy rests on the presupposition of the unified people's similarity and identity. An autonomous second chamber of acknowledged political significance would endanger the unified character of the entire people and would lead the legislative branch, which counts in a special sense as an expression of the common will, of the volonté générale, directly into a dualism. Where a constitution intends to emphasize the sovereignty of the one and undivided nation and perhaps additionally master political fears of the social power of an aristocracy, the one-chamber system will be fully implemented.

Hence the French constitutions of 1791 and of 1848. For the latter, Tocqueville had advocated the one-chamber system, because under it the president of the French Republic was elected by the entire French people, and only a legislative body that is united and elected by the entire people should stand opposite a president elected by the entire people. On the Swiss aversion to the two-chamber system, see Esmein-Nézard, I, p. 126.

The fact that democracy rests on the presupposition of complete homogeneity and unity accounts for this democratic aversion. For a democratic constitution, the question of the dual-chamber system reduces itself to a clear alternative. *Either* the second chamber expresses substantive peculiarities among the people that are worthy of respect, such as exceptional education, distinctive experience, age, riches, land holdings; then this system signifies a violation of democratic equality and comparability of all state citizens; *or* if it is not a matter of essential differences and peculiarities, it is incomprehensible why these differences and peculiarities should lead to the formation [295] of a special chamber. The Rechtsstaat interest in internal balance and the liberal interest in the protection of valued minorities could easily contradict the logic of the democratic principle. That applies also to the modern attempts to balance other social differences, in particular the opposition of capital and labor, in a second chamber. This opposition is so strong that its organization into two bodies allows the social oppositions to emerge even more noticeably and would further endanger political unity.

III. *The historical types of the two-chamber system.*

1. *The English upper house.*

The assembly of lords, or the upper nobility, such as dukes, counts, and high barons, has convened since the fourteenth century (1332). The members of this assembly were among the vassals of the king and formed the Magnum Concilium, a feudal assembly of vassals that as an *upper house* was separated from the lower nobility, from the knights in particular, who assembled with the deputies of the cities and communities as a house of communes, a *house of commons.* Together with the king, both houses formed the parliament. Each house followed a particular historical development. Till this day, the House of Lords is a chamber of peers, in other words, an upper chamber consisting primarily of hereditary members, who are appointed by the king. Until 1832, actually, homogeneity existed between the two houses, because the majority of the one house corresponded to that of the other, so long as the lower house was not yet selected according to the basic principles of modern democracy, but rather on the basis of a medieval election law of localities that stemmed from many historical accidents, a law by which the lords of the upper house thoroughly dominated the elections to the lower house. In the new development beginning in 1832, the lower house became a house of deputies in the modern democratic sense. The upper house, by contrast, preserved its aristocratic character. Through the Parliament Act of 1911, however, it lost the complete equivalence with the lower house as a defining element in legislation. The king can now promulgate a statute without the consent of the upper house if it is approved unchanged by the lower house inside of a certain period of time in three successive legislative sessions. The upper house now has only a "suspensive veto." This Parliament Act of 1911, moreover, concludes an additional development that had produced finance law. The lower house alone decides so-called monetary statutes, even if the upper house considers them. In cases of disagreement, the Speaker of the lower house decides the question of what constitutes a monetary statute without the consent of the upper house.

At present (summer 1927), there are reform plans to give the upper house part of its former power back. The political meaning of these aspirations is that a conservative upper house should oppose a lower house as an effective counterpoise, a lower house in which, because of the democratic election law, the Labour Party is a lasting determinant of power. The balancing should facilitate the protection of the existing bourgeois order.

2. In most countries of the European Continent, the dual-chamber system was introduced in imitation of the English model. The idealization of English constitutional [296] conditions, which had an important impact on these developments, began with Montesquieu, continued through the entire nineteenth century, and still remained influential among some authors even into the twentieth century.

See Montesquieu, *Esprit des lois*, XI, 6, where he argues that "there are always people in the state who distinguish themselves through birth, wealth, and prestige (honor). If they were to be subsumed in the people, however, the common freedom would be their undoing, and they would have no interest in defending freedom, because most decisions would be directed against them. Their share in legislation, therefore, must take account of their special interest." The rationale for this type of special chamber is that a minority that is valuable to the state should not be outvoted according to fundamental democratic principles.

Resulting from these currents of thought is an *aristocratic chamber of peers*, a "corps de nobles" or house of rulers that stands alongside a genuine popular assembly.

Hence the "chambre des pairs" under Art. 27 of the French Charte of 1814 and Art. 23 of the constitution of the bourgeois kingdom of 1830. The Prussian constitution of 1850, Art. 62, provides that "the legislative power is exercised in common by the king and by two chambers; it is necessary that the the king and both chambers approve every statute." And Art. 65 reads that "the first chamber is composed of members whom the king installs with hereditary rights or for life."

3. Dual-chamber system on the basis of the distinctiveness of a *federal state* organization. A special chamber of member states as an assembly of states is formed alongside the house of deputies that derives from the general elections of the entire people. Thus an "assembly of allied state individualities" (Bluntschli) appears alongside the house of deputies formed on a unitary, democratic basis.

The Senate in the United States of America, alongside the House of Representatives, together form the "Congress"; both the Estate Council of the Swiss Confederations as a delegation of the cantons and the National Council together form (as "two departments") the Federal Assembly. Under § 85 of the Frankfurt constitution of 1849, the Reichstag consists of two houses, the house of states and the house of the people.

In regard to grants of authority and activity, the Reichsrat of the Weimar Constitution (Art. 60–67) in reality approximates a second chamber, though it is not constituted as special representation. It is conceived, rather, only as a delegation of the individual German Lands involved in the legislation and administration of the Reich. In other words, it is seen as an assembly of instructed delegates of the individual Land governments. Through its right of legislative consent (legislative initiative under Art. 69 and right of parliamentary inquiry under Art. 74), the Reichsrat can exercise functions of a second chamber in the system designed to divide powers. By no means, however, does it form a parliament together with the Reichstag. [297]

4. There are consequences for a dual-chamber system in a unitary democratic state stemming merely from the division of powers. A second chamber in the form of a senate is placed opposite the house of deputies in order to implement a division inside of the legislature and through this to create controls and limitations. Such a division is also meant to bring about a more thoroughgoing deliberation and discussion of statutes. Along with this comes the idea already expressed by Bolingbroke (above p. 203) that the upper house must assume a referee function between king and lower house, that is, between the chief of the executive branch and the popular assembly, and it must play a mediating role between them as well.

Where for these reasons the institution of a second chamber in a republic based on the democratic principle results, the question is by which features of its composition does that type of second chamber distinguish itself from the other chamber. It would be undemocratic to create an institution resting on *inheritance* or even only *election for life* in place of the methods of *periodic election*. According to the constitutional law of 1875, the French Senate should receive seventy-five senators from the then existing National Assembly, senators who are later installed for life through cooptation. Nevertheless, that was eliminated again (by statute of 9 December 1884) after a few years. Through selection by inheritance and even by election for life, independence and representation could become so strong that the democratic principle of identity is violated. Consequently, one must be satisfied with less significant differentiations and nuances, such as variations in electoral age, the voters, or the number of deputies, indirect instead of direct election, periodic extensions, by which only a minority is removed from office and newly elected, in order to preserve the continuity of the chambers and variation of the electoral district or of the electoral systems. However, these differentiations are obviously insufficient to form the ideal foundation for an autonomous, politically significant institution.

5. More recently, there has been an attempt to configure the dual-chamber system as a connection between an economic and a political chamber or between an economic parliament and a purely political one, so that ultimately *two parliaments* (not only two chambers) would arise.

When the opposition between upper house and lower house means one between capital and labor, the dual-chamber system is only the full elaboration of a class conflict. However, if one attempts [298] to separate politics and economics and to build the dual-chamber system on this separation, in order to evade this conflict, the effort will not have a chance of success because the decision always lies in the political sphere. That is also true with regard to the construction of two parliaments. When the economic parliament successfully asserts its position alongside the political parliament, in the critical case a conflict must arise if both parliaments are not absolutely homogeneous and, consequently, their duality is absolutely superfluous. If, however, a conflict arises, the parliament that proves itself the decisive part will necessarily become the *political* parliament, because it assumes leadership and, with this, responsibility, regardless of whether it was previously organized as a political or an economic parliament. This objection has implications for the proposals made by Mr. and Mrs. Webb to set two parliaments (a political and a social one) with equal rights alongside one another, as well as for the German proposals that demand an economic parliament in the interest of a liberation of the economy from "politics" (referring to today's type of party politics). On this issue, cf. Tatarin-Tarnheyden, *Die Berufsstände*, Berlin 1922, p. 238; *Schmollers Jahrbuch*, 49 (1925), p. 185; and *Zeitschrift für Politik*, XV, p. 120. See also H. Brauweiler, *Berufsstände und Staat*, Berlin 1925, and *Preussische Jahrbücher*, October 1925, p. 64. Brauweiler is an opponent of the dual-chamber system.

Art. 165 of the Weimar Constitution introduced a *Reich Economic Council* that is conceived of as the organization bringing together a system of worker and employee delegations. These special delegations are linked with district economic councils, which, in turn, are composed such that there is parity between them (employer and employee delegations). Up to now (fall 1927), however, the Council has existed only on the basis of a decree of 4 May 1920 (*Reichgesetzesblatt*, p. 858) establishing the provisional Reich Economic Council manned by delegates from the different economic professions and parts of the economic life. According to Art. 165, 4, the Reich government must present social-political and economic-political draft statutes of fundamental importance to the Reich Economic Council for its consideration. The permanent Reich Economic Council also has a right of initiative to suggest draft statutes, and it can authorize one of its members to advocate the proposal before the Reichstag. Otherwise, it has no right of consultation in the Reich legislative process; it is essentially limited to an *advisory* capacity. One can hardly include this institution of Art. 165 under the scheme of the division of powers, for the Reich Economic Council is not a special chamber, even if its members (as under Art. 5 of the decree of 4 May 1920) count as advocates of the economic interests of the entire people and are not bound to instructions. It is to be regarded just as little as an autonomous economic parliament because an autonomous right of decision must be conceded to a parliament for economic statutes and other affairs. That it is essentially limited to advisory activity also [299] has contributed to the fact that it still only conducts its business in *committees* and that not even the formalities of a public discussion, which are part and parcel of parliament, are observed. Individual grants of authority under administrative law, such as the issuing of permission for the production of kindling (Reich Statute of 18 May 1927, *Reichgesetzesblatt* I, p. 123), change nothing with regard to this conclusion. It could be that here approaches to a distinctive reformation of parliament lie at hand, ones that cannot be understood using traditional ideas of state organization. Nevertheless, it must be said that up till now this Reich Economic Council of the Weimar Constitution is neither a second chamber nor an economic parliament.

IV. *The jurisdiction of and grants of authority to the upper house.* The actual jurisdiction lies in the area of legislation. Nevertheless, the English model can contribute to the transfer of even other jurisdictions, in particular adjudication, and above all political adjudication, to this chamber.

1. *Legislation.*

(a) Positive consent under equal rights to the production of statutory decisions.

The original sense of the dual-chamber system is that formal agreement of both chambers establishes a statute. In the constitutional monarchy, the approval of the king is added to that of the two chambers. According to this understanding, a mere veto or right of parliamentary inquiry would not be sufficient to confer on a body the character of a legislative body. Even an absolute veto is not a right of consent in the legislative process. It is, rather, a distinctive grant of authority that intervenes *from the outside* as a *limitation* on the legal authority of lawmaking. This absolute veto is not conceived of as a form of consent. It is understood as an obstacle to and protection against misuse. Still less can the grant of authority for a suspensive veto that may only postpone legislative decisions count as a right of consent and confer on an organization the character of a second legislative body. In practical terms, however, such a right of parliamentary inquiry is frequently not distinguishable from a right of consent, above all when the holder of this right of parliamentary inquiry simultaneously has an authority of legislative initiative. That such a right of initiative alone cannot confer on an organization the character of a legislative body is self-evident. Other possible limitations, such as the [300] authority of the one chamber to initiate a referendum against the statutory decision of the other chamber or a parliamentary dissolution, hence the opportunity to appeal to the people, likewise do not substantiate a positive consultative authority in the making of legislation.

It was already discussed that the consent of the English upper house is limited through the Parliament Acts of 1911, so that one often speaks of a mere right of suspensive veto (for example, Esmein-Nézard, I, p. 209). Nevertheless, apart from monetary statutes, the upper house remains competent for the deliberation of statutory decisions. The expression "mere veto right" is practically and theoretically imprecise.

The French *Senate* is in regard to legislative initiative a second chamber that is thoroughly coordinate to the Chamber of Deputies. According to the constitutional law of 25 February 1875 (Art. 5), it participates in the dissolution of the parliament. The president of the Republic can dissolve the Chamber of Deputies only with the consent of the Senate. The Senate's right of consultation produces a balance and establishes a type of referee position between the house of deputies and the state president.

According to Art. 74, the Reichsrat of the German Reich has the authority to raise an *objection*. The statute then returns to the Reichstag for an additional reading. So the Reichsrat only reaches a decision on the objection against the vote on the statute. Its decision on the objection is not a vote on the statute. Through repeat consideration by the Reichstag (for which, according to the correct understanding, a single reading suffices), the Reichstag takes a position on the objection, without, however, deciding on it conclusively. The decision, more accurately, is dependent on whether the President orders a referendum or not. If during a repeat reading of proposed legislation only a simple majority of the Reichstag is present, the final parliamentary vote is not law. When the President does not order a referendum, the Reichsrat objection succeeds, and the establishment of the statute is prevented. If during a repeat vote the Reichstag reaches its decision with a two-thirds vote of the members present, the Reichsrat objection is vacated when the President does not order a referendum.

Under Art. 76, the Reichsrat can demand a referendum on a Reichstag statutory decision amending the constitution. The constitutional treatment of its right of objection accounts for this Reichsrat authority. For constitution-amending statutes, Art. 76 prescribes that the passage of such a law requires a qualified two-thirds majority (two-thirds of the legally set member count for the house quorum, two-thirds majority decision of those present). Compared to the first reading of the bill, the two-thirds majority during the additional reading would signify a repetition, not a special qualification, and, in this especially important case, it would vacate the Reichsrat objection if the President [301] does not decide to order a referendum. This result is again corrected through the legal authority of the Reichsrat to demand a referendum in such cases.

(b) Both chambers usually also have the same rights in regard to *legislative initiative*. Nevertheless, almost everywhere there are exceptions to the right of initiative in finance statutes. In this regard, the upper house (house of lords or senate) recedes behind the lower house as the actual "people's" delegation, because the lower house is considered the advocate of those who provide revenues or taxes and, consequently, must also approve finance bills.

The special position of the lower house in monetary bills is traceable to developments in England, where the lower house approves subsidies to the Crown. According to the federal constitution of the United States of America, draft statutes involving the raising of revenue must originate in the House of Representatives, although, as with every other legislative bill, the Senate can approve changes. Under Art. 27 of the Belgian constitution of 1831, the House of Deputies must vote on any statute involving income or expenditures. Art. 62 of the Prussian constitution of 31 January 1850 provides that draft financial statutes and state budgets are first presented to the second chamber, whereas for other statutes the government had the choice of the chamber to which it wanted to present the statute initially. Art. 8, § 2, of the French Constitutional Law of 24 February 1875 provides that financial statutes (lois de finances) are first presented to and voted on by the Chamber of Deputies. Controversy exists over whether the Senate does not have a right of amendment at all for such financial statutes. The question is whether the Senate must either accept or reject statutes in the form passed by the Chamber of Deputies; whether it may incorporate reductions or increases in the individual budget figures, as does the Senate of the United States of America; or whether for these changes it unconditionally needs the government to make use of its right of initiative, so that the Senate can undertake any changes in regard to the chamber decision, however only at the suggestion of the government. An autonomous right of amendment of the Senate corresponds the most to the intention of the originator of the constitutional law of 1875, who had the model of the United States Senate in mind.

According to Art. 69, the Reichsrat has its own legal authority to decide on *statutory proposals*. Additionally, it has the *right of consent* to proposed statutes of the Reich government. For the statutory proposals that arose from the floor of the Reichstag, the Reichsrat does not have this right of consent, making it easy to evade the requirement of Reichsrat consent when a Reichstag fraction introduces the draft statutes. Where no agreement on a government proposal comes about between the Reichsrat and the Reich government, the Reichsrat has an autonomous power of suggestion, which obligates the government to introduce the Reichsrat proposal in the Reichstag.

For *monetary statutes*, according to Art. 85, 2, a coordinate right of participation exists for the Reichsrat insofar as the Reichstag, in the budgetary plan proposed by the government, [302] can pass increases in expenditures and reductions in revenue. Correctly understood, this right of consent (in contrast to a mere right of objection) is valid for all monetary statutes and apparently makes the Reichsrat into a second chamber for this important area. Nevertheless, it must not be overlooked that the Reichsrat has a right of consultation only with the government, not against it; moreover, that this right of consultation can be vacated by a two-thirds majority decision of the Reichstag (Art. 85, 5; on the practice of Art. 85, see Poetzsch, *Jahrbuch des öffentlichen Rechts* XIII, 1925, p. 221; Johannes Heckel, *Archiv des öffentlichen Rechts*, new series 12 (1927), pp. 467/68).

2. The *upper house* (house of lords, senate, etc.) as *Staatsgerichtshof.* In some constitutional provisions, a distinctive jurisdiction of the upper house or the senate for political trials is established in line with the English model, which has become irrelevant in the interim. The Weimar Constitution does not recognize this type of political justice by a legislative body. On this, cf. above § 12, p. 135.

3. Upper house or senate as *"guardian of the constitution,"* in other words, as court of law for constitutional disputes; also as an organ for decisions on the constitutionality of statutes and decrees and for the so-called constitutional complaints (cf. above § 11, III, p. 112).

Based on this is the institution of a "Sénat Conservateur," which can declare statutes and decrees unconstitutional, something that is characteristic of the constitutions of the French empire. Hence the constitutional laws of the Year VIII (1799), XII (1802), of 14 January 1852, Art. 26ff. In these latter provisions, the Senate is explicitly designated the "guardian of the fundamental compact and of public freedoms" ("gardien du pacte fondamental et des libertés publiques").

4. *Upper house* (house of lords, senate) and *parliamentary government.* Both chambers of the dual-chamber system together form the parliament. Consequently, for political responsibility of the government to parliament, the government must be dependent on both chambers, whether each individual chamber enforces this responsibility for itself separately, or whether a consensual decision of both chambers is required. In reality, the democratic development leads to the fact that the upper house or the chamber

corresponding to it loses its influence and transforms the dependence on the parliament into a dependence on the lower house (house of deputies). [303]

That was first decided in England during the nineteenth century (below p. 321). In France, according to Art. 6 of the Constitutional Law of 25 February 1876, the ministers are collectively responsible to *both chambers* (solidairement responsables devant *les chambres*). The responsibility of the government in regard to the parliament is, in practice, primarily a responsibility to the Chamber of Deputies, although theoretically the equal rights of both chambers are retained (Esmein-Nézard, I, p. 234ff.) and, even in practice, confidence and no-confidence votes of the Senate occur (E. v. Hippel, *Jahrbuch des öffentlichen Rechts* XV, 1927, p. 180). On the Senate and parliamentary *dissolution*, see p. 300.

In the German Reich, the demand for a parliamentary government only had the sense of a dependence of the government on the confidence of the Reichstag. The constitution-amending statute of 28 October 1918 thus provided that "the Chancellor requires the confidence of the *Reichstag* for the conduct of his office." By contrast, the same statute states additionally that "for their conduct of office, the Chancellor and his deputies are responsible to both the Bundesrat and the Reichstag." Art. 54 mentions the confidence of the Reichstag; the Reichsrat does not come into consideration. The elements of a second chamber, which are found in the organization of the German Bundesrat or of the Reichsrat, are justified only in the federal state structure of the Reich and do not signify a genuine dual-chamber system (above p. 296).

V. *The division of legislative authority* that exists in the dual-chamber system must lead to the position of a member of the one chamber being incompatible with that of a member from the other chamber. In this context, there must be unconditional *incompatibility* (above p. 190).

The Parliamentary System

I. *Ambiguity of the term "parliamentarianism."*

The different designations often used without specificity and discrimination, such as parliamentarianism, parliamentary government, responsible government, party government, majority government, etc., involve different types of relationships between parliament, that is, the lawmaking body, and the government. However, they also concern very different types of political administration and leadership, of the "ruling power." The use of the word "parliament" is explained by English constitutional conditions with the English Parliament being made the center of an ideal scheme and becoming the model for other systems. But everywhere the greatest differences manifest themselves despite the common model. Thus, different features emerge as definitive characteristics of "parliamentarianism," and if a constitutional regime speaks of the dependence of the government on parliament, of "responsibility," or [304] of "confidence," these words have an entirely different sense in various countries and eras.

1. What mattered in European continental states during the nineteenth century is the fact that the elected popular assembly extended its political influence in regard to the monarchical government. The parliament as lawmaking body sought to extend its power beyond the realm of legislation to that of the government, whether by the extension of a "formal concept of law" (above p. 143) or through supervision of governmental activity, above all, however, by determinative influence on the selection of the leading political figures. From this emerged the idea that parliamentarianism signifies *rule by parliament*, or popular assembly, *over the government*. The principle of the separation of powers would then be eliminated to the benefit of a parliamentary absolutism and the demand of a parliamentary government would become a *purely democratic* demand: dependence of the government on the will of the popular assembly; the government as merely a committee of the popular assembly, therefore, of the parliament; the parliament as merely a committee of the people (above, p. 266).

2. In regard to the democratization of the concept, the separation of powers idea again leads to the parliamentarization of the bourgeois Rechtsstaat. Thanks to R. Redslob, *Die parlamentarische Regierung in ihrer wahren und in ihrer unechten Form*, 1918, this idea gained prominence and influenced the founders of the Weimar Constitution. According to Redslob, the essence of "genuine" parliamentarianism is that the executive is not the subordinated instrument of the parliamentary will such that a *counterpoise*

exists between both powers. How the counterpoise is produced varies because of the government's authority to dissolve parliament and the possibility of the bringing about a referendum (cf. the schema above on p. 197). Be that as it may, this interpretation involves something essential. For the parliamentary system is not a result, nor is it an application, of the democratic principle of identity. Instead, by forming its actual system of government, the parliamentary system is part of a modern bourgeois Rechtsstaat constitution. It rests on an application and mixture of different and even opposing political elements. The parliamentary system uses *monarchical* constructions in order to strengthen the *executive*, in particular the government, and to balance it out against the parliament. It applies the *aristocratic* [305] ideas of a representative body, in some countries even of the dual-chamber system. And above all it uses *democratic* ideas about the power of the people voting directly, rather than the decision of those not represented, to transfer the resolution of the conflict between parliament and government to the people voting in an unmediated manner. In this way, the people emerge as the higher party and as the bearer of the balance in regard to parliament and government. This system first brings to completion the typical and distinctive mixture, which, as shown above (p. 216), is part of the essence of the bourgeois Rechtsstaat. It is not an autonomous political form, neither a special state form nor a special governmental form. But it is a *system* that applies and mixes different governmental and legislative forms in the service of a pliable counterpoise.

I can accept the opinion of R. Smend, according to which parliamentarianism is a special state form only insofar as the parliamentary system signifies a balancing and relativizing of state form elements that is characteristic of the bourgeois Rechtsstaat. The parliamentary system can appear as something dynamic and can be placed in opposition to that which is static because it attempts to produce this balance of political elements. However, it is not something dynamic in the sense that as the "integration" of political unity it came to embody a special principle of form in opposition to other principles of state form. The distinctive quality lies in the connection between and balancing of different elements of form in the service of bourgeois Rechtsstaat principles and of the integration of the bourgeoisie into the monarchical state (above pp. 207/8).

This system of an unstable counterpoise of political forms corresponds in a special way to the political tendencies of the liberal bourgeoisie and of the bourgeois Rechtsstaat. This is because various perspectives on identity and representation, along with monarchical, aristocratic, and democratic structural elements, are all applied indiscriminately. Through mixture and balancing it prevents any absolutism, whether it is of the monarchy, democracy, or parliament itself. In other words, it even prevents the absolutism of an aristocracy or an oligarchy. This balance justifies its distinctive connection with the bourgeois Rechtsstaat, and in this regard it also corresponds to the political situation of the bearer of this idea of Rechtsstaat, that of the liberal bourgeoisie. It is thus *the* political system of the bourgeois Rechtsstaat and suffers only from the deficiency that is unique to this Rechtsstaat idea generally, for it intends to evade the ultimate political decision and logical consequence of the principles of political form. It is even thoroughly consistent logically when this system is simply understood as [306] a further requirement of a "free" state added to the other characteristics of a Rechtsstaat, and a great constitutional theory expert like Esmein (I, p. 243) states that "the parliamentary government in Europe is practically the sole form of complete political freedom and an awe-inspiring system." From the standpoint of the bourgeois Rechtsstaat, it does in fact inspire awe. For indeed the reciprocal balancing of all elements of political form completes the Rechtsstaat component of the modern constitution and protects it, so far as it is possible, from the consequences and possible applications growing out of the political component that constantly threaten it. The unified character of this political component is dissolved, and the potential for political absolutism is taken from the individual, balanced, and mixed elements of form.

3. Corresponding to the use of diverse elements of political form, different types of political administration and leadership (of the "ruling power," the determination of the "politique générale," or of the "guiding principles of politics") are realized. If the monarchical element and the idea of representation of the political unity by a single person predominates over other elements, the parliamentary system can leave open the possibility of the *presidential system*, by which the head of state, the chief of the executive branch, participates autonomously in political administration. If the aristocratic or oligarchic idea of a parliamentary rule is predominant in the system, it reveals itself as a *parliamentary system in the stricter sense*, by which the majority of the legislative body has the political reins, while it determines the guiding principles of politics. But it can also be that the leader of this parliamentary majority has the political leadership and administration, and then there is a *premier system*, in which once again there is a strong element of representation. Finally, it is conceivable that it is not the individual party leader and minister president who handles political administration and provides leadership, but rather a council of ministers, which in such a case is usually a coalition ministry composed of different parties. That is to be designated here a *cabinet system*. These four different parliamentary subsystems will become prominent in the following historical depiction. They are not mutually exclusive. Instead, they form an [307] elastic, comprehensive system. It is necessary to distinguish among these subsystems in order to understand parliamentary government in general, but above all to

understand the exceptionally difficult and rather opaque system established by the Weimar Constitution.

II. *The ideal foundations of the parliamentary system.*

Both the peculiarities of the constitutional regime in detail as well as the distinctive historical and systematic connection of the bourgeois Rechtsstaat with the parliamentary system are only understandable in reference to the ideal foundation and justification of this system.

1. *The historical situation.* In the states of the European continent, especially in France and Germany, liberal and democratic parties, in the struggle against a monarchical government, supported and achieved the "parliamentarization of the government" as a *program.* In England, the parliamentary cabinet government developed in gradual transitions on the basis of diverse precedents without deliberate intent through the relationship of parliament to a dynasty called to the throne by parliament. In France and Germany, it was not possible to forgo a conscious goal. In the nineteenth century, the monarchical government still had an autonomous power that was based on the army and the civil service, and it had to be forced to limit and finally give up its rule by a bourgeois revolution. Consequently, in this context, a principled program and a political theory of the parliamentary system also had to result. In this regard, the so-called "parliamentarianism" was not mere practice and custom, but rather a theory and an idea. But in the same way that English parliamentarianism could be the practical model because of the distinctiveness of the English national character as well as of its political situation, the ideal justification is to be found among the representatives of the French and German liberal bourgeoisie. Much later, in the twentieth century when the actual struggle had been forgotten, one could say of parliamentarianism in Germany that it involves a practical "rule of the game" (Max Weber). To the French or German bourgeoisie of the period 1815 to 1870, it involved something other than the rules of the game and comparable methods that are consciously relativistic. This bourgeoisie [308] took parliamentarianism as a political system seriously and gave it an ideal justification, without which the system is conceivable neither as a whole nor in its individual institutions and norms.

Because of its simplicity, however, the reference to the English model remained a widespread and popular means of proof, and, then as now, it substituted for reflection and political theory among many politicians and theorists. Despite the English model, parliamentarianism developed into a conscious system, simply because the political situation on the European continent, as was the case with continental intellectual history, was entirely different than on the English island. The independent, systematic justification for parliamentary government evolved, both in Germany and in France, particularly in the period of 1815 to 1848. This period of time must be viewed as the classic stage of the parliamentary idea. Among the representatives of the French bourgeoisie, the idea emerges in a stronger and more principled form than in Germany, a fact immediately explained by the differing domestic political situations in both countries. In France from 1815 to 1848, the propertied and educated liberal bourgeoisie, after the experience of the revolutionary and Napoleonic period, was forced into a struggle against the monarchical principle and against the restoration of traditional ideas and institutions. This bourgeoisie had to become conscious of its political position. During the period 1830 to 1848, a political system developed in France in the bourgeois kingdom of Louis-Philippe and in Belgium through the constitution of 1831, a political system held by many, among them an expert teacher like Lorenz von Stein, to be the true ideal type of the bourgeois state. In this system, the ideal of political moderation and of a *juste-milieu* reflected the distinctive intermediary stage of the liberal bourgeoisie between the superseded monarchy and the rising radical democracy that was already partly proletarian. Even these liberals, who had other constitutional ideals than the French bourgeois kingdom or the Belgian constitution of 1831, always took as their point of departure the idea that only *moderate* political parties come into consideration as bearers of a genuine parliamentarianism. In Rudolf Gneist's doctrine of local self-government and the Rechtsstaat, for example, the value of local self-government is precisely that it produces such moderation (*Englische Verfassungsgeschichte*, p. 672). [309]

The frequently discussed opposition of liberalism and democracy manifests itself here in its decisive significance as the opposition of bourgeois Rechtsstaat principles and the consequences of a principle of political configuration. The liberal bourgeoisie stood between the absolute monarchy and the ascendant proletarian democracy. Whether one considers it from an objective standpoint of a scholarly critic or as a politician who deems it conservative or socialist-radical, all observers of bourgeois liberalism have noticed this intermediary position and made it the foundation of their designs. The critical year 1848 revealed the situation very clearly. In regard to the political claims of a strong monarchy, the bourgeoisie vindicated the rights of parliament, those of the *popular* assembly in particular. It vindicated democratic demands, therefore. In regard to a proletarian democracy, it sought protection in a strong monarchical government, in order to save bourgeois freedom and private property. In regard to monarchy and aristocracy, it appealed to the principles of freedom and equality, and, in opposition to a petty bourgeois or proletarian mass democracy, it appealed to the sanctity of private property and to a concept of law rooted in the Rechtsstaat.

In the appendix to "Socialismus und Communismus des heutigen Frankreichs," Leipzig and Vienna 1848, p. 36, Lorenz von Stein points out that the bourgeoisie gradually becomes agitated about the principle of revolution. "However," he argues, "one does not deceive oneself on this point. This agitation is thoroughly negative. It intends nothing definite, not a kingdom, not a dictatorship, not a bourgeois regime; it merely does not want uncertainty of conditions. For the bourgeoisie, the kingdom is the seed of a new revolution; it does not intend it. Dictatorship is anti-freedom; it does not want it. The bourgeois regime is either powerless or it is aristocracy; it does not want it." In a series of essays on the class struggles in France from 1848 to 1850 (in the *Neue Rheinische Zeitung*) and in the essay on the Eighteenth Brumaire of Louis Bonaparte (1852), Karl Marx portrayed the domestic political and social conditions of France and mocked the bourgeois parties, which from the "sole possible form of their united power, from the most violent and complete form of their class rule, the constitutional republic, fled back to the subordinated, incomplete, weaker form of the monarchy." Friedrich J. Stahl considers the Liberal Party in his *Vorlesungen über die Parteien in Kirche und Staat* ([lectures] held between 1850–1857, published in 1863). "However," he argues, "if it comes down to positively carrying out the ideas of popular sovereignty, installing the entire people in power on equal terms, not to subject one class to the authority of another even within the people, it [the party] abandons these ideas; it installs in power only the middle class, the wealthy, educated, that is, just itself. Precisely in the same way, the Liberal Party claims the idea of equality against the nobility, against all estates as such, because, according to the basis of the revolution, it cannot provide an organic formation. Still, should equality be positively instituted, should the class of those without property receive the same rights as the middle class, it forfeits these ideas and makes legal distinctions in favor of the [310] wealthy. The liberal party wants a census for representation and security deposits for the press, allows only the fashionable into the salon, does not guarantee to the poor the honor and polite treatment it does to the rich. It is this *partial execution of the principles of the Revolution* that characterizes the Liberals' party position." The general systematic summary of the position of the liberal bourgeoisie is found in Stein's presentation on the restoration and the July Revolution (*Der Begriff der Gesellschaft*, Gottfried Salomon edition, vol. I, p. 498). Stein attempts to explain the contradictions of this system in reference to the general oppositional tendencies of all living things and, nevertheless, ultimately considers harmony possible. His image demonstrates the contradictions and attempts at balancing so clearly that it must be quoted extensively here:

> By recognizing in particular the personal state authority (of a king [Schmitt's addition]), the constitutional principle of the bourgeois state attributes to this state authority the essence of the personal, the independent will and act. On the other hand, by making the king into the mere possessor of the power to be exercised and every act dependent on the consent of his ministry, it again *deprives* him of precisely this independent personal element. By demanding that the king, or the autonomous state authority in any other form, who stands over the parties of the society, should guide their struggles and hinder their excesses, it places the king *above* the popular assembly in the same way as the community element, which is independent of the concept of the popular assembly according to its higher mission. By contrast, providing statutorily that the king should only execute the will of the majority, it makes him the tool of those elements of society that can achieve this majority. Establishing the

kingdom as the absolute inviolable element and as the source of all state authorities, it takes from the popular assembly the right, which it nevertheless gives to the kingdom, to punish the misuse of power, because its inviolability makes the violation of the right into the non-violation of the right. Because the king swears allegiance to the constitution and acknowledges it as a right of the people, the alternate inviolability of the constitution counters the inviolability of the crown. Nevertheless, this right is such that one who violates it should not be pursued as though the violation were an injury of a right. Consequently, in order not to state an absolute contradiction, the cornerstone of the limited constitution is, in fact, an idea that is absolutely irreconcilable internally. No human insight is sharp enough to resolve this opposition conceptually and to draw a juristic boundary that no longer contains a contradiction between left and right.

2. The intermediary position of the liberal bourgeoisie rests on two different presuppositions, on *education* and *property*. Both together facilitate and support the parliamentary system. If historically they no longer occur together and diverge from one another, the deft construction of a pliable counterweight and the mixture of political forms is displaced. Considered in terms of constitutional theory, each of the two attributes leads to different consequences. Both attributes become valid under the bourgeois Rechtsstaat constitution.

(a) *Learning* is a personal quality. As such, it is capable of being used in the system of *representation*. According to its leading idea, the nineteenth-century bourgeois parliament is an assembly of learned persons representing learning and reason, [311] in particular, the learning and reason of the entire *nation*. Even the concept of the nation is a concept of learning. Only a learned people in the sense of qualities like human will and human self-consciousness is a nation. However, a fully unlearned and, consequently, an unhistorical people, is not one. The parliament is a *general national representation*, a precise term that the Freiherr vom Stein had clearly intended in his farewell statement of 24 February 1809. Until into the second half of the nineteenth century, the advocates of the bourgeois Rechtsstaat and the rights of parliament were still thoroughly clear about the meaning of this attribute. "The most important requirement for all representatives," according to Bluntschli, "is the formation of the spirit. For only the learned man is capable of distinguishing carefully between his personal interests and the interests of the whole and to subordinate the former."

Thus Bluntschli, *Das Volk und der Souverän*, 1831, p. 62. Additionally, see *Allgemeines Staatsrecht*, I, p. 432, on the rule of the "educated middle classes." See Hegel in the treatise on the Württemberg provincial estates, *Abhandlungen zur Politik und Rechtsphilosophie*, Lasson edition, p. 219, where he argues that "the first and foremost of the people are not incorporated into the representatives of the people. Instead, it should be the wisest who are taken, because the former (the people) do not know, but they (the representatives) should know what their [the people's] true and actual will is, specifically, what is good for them." On Gneist, cf. the quote below

p. 313. "The electoral census," G. Waitz states, "can be a means of recognizing the extreme position as a condition for independence and learning. However, it must always apply to the middle class, not to the rich alone." *Grundzüge der Politik*, 1862, p. 64. According to Guizot, who sees in the bourgeois "classes moyennes" the true bearer of political life, the parliament brings together in one place and, therefore, for the public, the particles of reason scattered among the people. The entire political pathos of Guizot, this typical advocate of a bourgeois liberalism, lies in the belief in the parliament as a representation of reason. Also his "Histoire des origines du gouvernement représentatif en Europe," 1851, rests on it. Renan in *L'Avenir de la Science* is also very decisive on this point. "The opinion of the majority," he argues, "does not have a right to force itself, when this majority does not represent reason and the enlightened opinion. The single sovereign of divine right is reason." The belief in rational justice and the normative element (p. 201) entails in particular the belief in learning.

(b) *Property* is not a quality that can be represented. On the contrary, the interests of the property owners are advocated. The right of electoral census ensures that this interest advocacy genuinely comes about. Through it, however, the parliament receives, alongside the quality of a national representation, the character of an interest committee. In this attribute, it is self-evidently not independent, but rather bound to the will of the interests it advocates. The parliament as bearer of the right to tax and set the budget acts as an interest advocate, not only as national [312] representation. The propertied bourgeoisie appeals to the justice of the principle that those who pay taxes must also approve them and supervise their use. As long as the fundamental bourgeois views of private and individual property dominated, a right of electoral census must result, a right where the upward extent of the census can be different in detail, and yet it can still appear as something just and self-evident that only those who pay the taxes and rent may be represented in parliament. Conversely, those not represented in the parliament also need not furnish taxes and rent. The principle to which the English colonies in America appealed in their eighteenth-century Declaration of Independence and that even a liberal like Burke viewed as an axiom reads: "No taxation without advocacy" (whereby in the indiscriminate Anglo-Saxon manner of expression advocacy is designated as representation, as "no taxation without representation"). For if a body no longer represents, but rather only advocates interests, the nonadvocated interests must assert themselves in some way, legal or not. They must either be taken up or suppressed. Consequently, the logic of the democratic principle became irresistible, and, in the course of the nineteenth century, an extension of the general right to vote and the elimination of the right to electoral census, at least for the lower house, was implemented. The parliament now ceased to be representative of a certain type of learning. It became partly an interest advocacy organization, partly a means of expression of public opinion, and it ended in a functional dependence on its electors. It became what one said of the English parliament of the last century: a mere registration machine between electorate and cabinet government.

(c) To the extent that the bourgeoisie still led the political struggle only under the perspective of its economic interest and to the degree that the belief in a representative character disappeared, it was also able to content itself with establishing the required political influence with the help of its economic power and to otherwise make peace with the most diverse governments, such as Bonapartism, a German-style constitutional monarchy, and a democratic republic. The decisive consideration for the bourgeoisie was that private property was not threatened and the influence of the economic interests in the composition of the popular assembly was not endangered. This tendency accounts [313] for the noteworthy occurrence that since 1848 a systematic ideal justification of the parliamentary system has actually no longer been expressed and that today it appears as something outmoded and Biedermeierish; Richard Thoma even says "moldy." After 1848, the form of argument in France becomes in part rigidly conventional, in part skeptically resigned. In Germany, the thought of significant liberal theorists inclines toward parliamentarianism incorporating society into the state (according to Gneist, however, only on the basis of a proper local self-government, *Englische Verfassungsgeschichte*, p. 673) and produces the "thorough resolution of social oppositions in a consciousness of the whole." That is already an expression of the idea that prompted R. Smend to treat parliamentarianism in the special sense as a state form of integration (above p. 305). Nevertheless, Gneist still always speaks of the learned and propertied classes when he demands an incorporation of "society" (for example, *Der Rechtsstaat*, p. 153), and for the voluntary activity that, according to him, is the foundation and presupposition of this incorporation, only bourgeois learning and bourgeois property can be considered. If the parliament really achieves integration of the political unity of the entire people in a distinctive sense, it does that under the presupposition and on the foundation of these bourgeois concepts of property and learning. It is very questionable whether the same system of integration can come into consideration at all for a state with masses of industrial workers.

R. von Mohl in particular has expressed the other, more political argument presented on behalf of parliamentarianism in Germany after 1848. It takes its point of departure from the *dualism* that exists in the constitutional monarchy of Germany between popular assembly and the government, which is impossible in the long term and must be settled once and for all because it constantly leads to conflicts. Indeed, the dualism could also be eliminated to the benefit of the rule by the monarchical government, but, according to Mohl, that would only be possible by way of "corruption." The only other possibility that remains for him is a parliamentary government

("Das Repräsentativsystem, seine Mängel und the Heilmittel, politische Briefe geschrieben 1850," in *Monographien zum Staatsrecht, Völkerrecht und Politik*, Tübingen 1860, p. 34ff., in particular p. 395). The point of departure of this way of thinking [314] is thoroughly correct. The dualism led to conflicts, and these had to be resolved. However, the resolution occurred differently and was not as simple and theoretical as Mohl had thought. Bismarck's overwhelming success decided the question *against* the parliamentary government and in favor of the monarchy. It propped up the German style of constitutional monarchy another half century. Consequently, there is no longer a strong parliamentary ideology in Germany after 1866. In the struggle against parliament, the royal government produced national unity. The idea that the parliament is the national representation to a higher degree than the king could not win out in opposition to this political achievement. The liberal and democratic parties still always demanded a parliamentary government, but their demand lacked the force that a cohesive and committed system of thought expresses. Among the more recent German liberals, who were also indiscriminately designated as democrats, Friedrich Naumann, Max Weber, and Hugo Preuß, the idea that a new social class, the workers, must be incorporated into the state is in part decisive. The distinctively liberal bourgeois integration method, the parliament, is applied to a new class, while there is a failure to recognize the ideal structure of parliament, which is essentially defined by such characteristics as learning and property holdings. Yet on the other hand, operative among these democrats is the political recognition that new forms of national representation must be created, an idea that was perceived as the problem of "leadership selection." Reference was mostly made to the English model, and the demand for a parliamentary government was justified with the argument that according to the experience in England the parliament formed a political elite. The distinctively liberal and bourgeois Rechtsstaat idea is thus given up, and in its place a connection between democracy and social reform enters. The defining quality of the parliamentary system is no longer explicable in this way. For the parliament increasingly ceases to be representative of the political unity. It becomes an exponent of the interests and moods of the masses of voters, and the idea of a selection of the political leadership does not justify a parliament of a few hundred party functionaries. It gives rise instead to a search for a political leadership [315] and administration that is directly borne by the confidence of the masses. If it is possible to find such a form of leadership, a new, powerful representation is created. But that is a type of representation that is *in opposition to* parliament, whose traditional claim to being a form of representation would be eliminated.

3. According to its underlying idea, the parliament of the bourgeois Rechtsstaat is the place in which a *public* discussion of political opinions

takes place. Majority and minority, government party and opposition, seek the correct conclusion through a thorough consideration of argument and counterargument. So long as the parliament represents national learning and reason and unites in itself the entire intelligence of the people, a genuine collective will of the people as a "volonté générale" can form. The people itself cannot discuss. According to Montesquieu, that is the great disadvantage of democracy. It can only acclaim, vote, and say yes or no to a question presented to it. Even the executive should not discuss. It should act, execute statutes, or carry out measures that are necessary because of current conditions. It cannot establish a reasonable, general norm, dominated by the idea of justice, not a statute in the Rechtsstaat sense. In the middle between the people, specifically, the methods of a direct democracy, and the government, in particular, a state authority supported by the military and civil service, the superiority of the bourgeois parliament rests on the fact that it is the site of a reasoned discussion. Monarchical absolutism is mere power and command, arbitrariness and despotism. Direct democracy is the rule of a mass driven by passions and interests. It is, as the liberal Burke states and the liberal Bluntschli with hearty approval quotes (*Allgemeines Staatsrecht*, I, p. 315), "the most shameless thing in the world." Parliament stands between and above both direct democracy and the monarchy as the true mean, which in public discussion finds the reasoned truth and the just norm. The discussion is the humane, peace-loving, progressive means, the opposite of every type of dictatorship and authority. That by way of a rational discussion all conceivable oppositions and conflicts can be settled peaceably and justly, that one can speak about everything and allow oneself to speak with those like oneself is the world-view-like foundation of this liberal parliamentarianism. [316]

Consequently, parliamentarianism is often rightly designated "government by discussion." Cf. in this regard, Carl Schmitt, *Geistesgeschichtliche Lage des Parlamentarismus* [*Crisis of Parliamentary Democracy*, trans. Ellen Kennedy (Cambridge, Mass.: MIT Press, 1985)], pp. 43, 57, 61, 62 [original edition]. See additionally Karl Marx, *Der 18. Brumaire des Louis Bonaparte*. "The parliamentary regime," Marx argues, "lives by discussion. How should it prohibit discussion? Every interest, every social institution is transformed into general ideas, considered as ideas." On the difference between genuine, rational, learned discussion and the social negotiation and interest advocacy, cf. Schmitt, *Crisis*, p. 9 [original edition].

III. *Practical consequences of the fundamental idea of the parliamentary system.*

1. The parliament *represents* the entire nation as such and, in this capacity, issues statutes by way of public discussion and public votes. In other words, it produces reasonable, just, general norms, which provide for and regulate the entire state life.

(a) The *public quality of the negotiations* is the core of the entire system.

It is guaranteed through constitutional provisions. "The Reichstag deliberates publicly," according to Art. 29, for example. Because they are public, all deliberations are printed and published. This is also the case with Art. 30, according to which "accurate reports on deliberations in public sessions remain free of any accountability."

(b) *The protection of deputies against criminal prosecution and against limitations of personal freedom* (Art. 37) is a right of the parliament as a whole, not of the individual deputies. Even this privilege is only an individual consequence of the representative character of parliament. The historical occasions of this special position (arbitrary arrests of deputies by the monarch) are by themselves alone no longer a sufficient explanation for that type of astonishing privilege.

(c) The *committees* of parliament only prepare materials that clearly concern technical details. Beyond this, they are not at all significant and contradict the essence of the parliament as an assembly that decides on the basis of public discussion.

Among the differences between the medieval estate principle and the modern representative principle, Bluntschli, *Allgemeines Staatsrecht*, I, p. 488, enumerates in particular the standing committees formed by the estates. "As a rule," he points out, "the modern state only knows the assembly of the representative body itself; only a full public assembly can represent the people."

(d) Transferring the parliament's legislative authority to parliamentary committees or to the government, *delegation* and [317] *empowerment* for the issuance of statutes, is *impermissible* and unthinkable under a proper understanding of the meaning of public discussion.

In his enumeration of the differences between the estate principle and the modern representative one that was just mentioned, Bluntschli, *Allgemeines Staatsrecht*, p. 485, argues that personal substitution is possible in the type of representation by estates, while a substitution in the *chamber*, by contrast, is only possible insofar as it is ordained "by the whole" representative body. The individual deputy cannot allow himself to be represented. The chamber as a whole cannot delegate its powers, first because it is representative and not functionary, and because, as the arena of public discussion and not a mere trading or business management office, it enacts measures. For an execution of *measures*, facilitating organizations would be self-evidently necessary and permissible. But the opposition of statute in the Rechtsstaat sense and measure also demonstrates its fundamental significance in this context.

2. The *individual deputy* also has representative character.

(a) He is independent of his electors and not bound to orders and instructions (Art. 21).

(b) He has complete freedom from responsibility for all statements made in the exercise of his profession (Art. 36).

He has this freedom from responsibility not as a tribune of the people, who receives immunity for political reasons. Also at work here, more precisely, is the idea of the deputy as a person, who is independent and learned, not self-interested. This deputy is someone who stands above the oppositions of interests and who, in order to be able to discuss freely, requires this immunity and earns it. *The guarantee of his freedom of speech presupposes that he genuinely speaks freely*, that is, on the basis of his own position, independent of commands and instructions and any influences that endanger his freedom. An instructed delegate or a compensated lobbyist does not deserve such freedom of speech. For his protection, it is enough that the general criminal law review of the perception of legitimate interests (§ 193 *Strafgesetzbuch*) also apply to him.

(c) The deputy is *not* able to allow himself to be *represented* in the exercise of his mandate, while with a lobbyist one cannot understand why he may not be recalled and replaced at any time by his client or why he may not be served by any particular assistant and subordinate lobbyist.

(d) A person whose entire livelihood is dependent on or part of a certain organization may not become a deputy. In addition to the division of powers or federal state organization noted above on p. 190, therein lies a reason for certain *incompatibilities* found in the public law of many states, particularly an incompatibility between *civil servants* and *ministers*. A further reason for such incompatibilities is the fact that the parliament should be the bearer of all political life. This means the deputy [318] is essentially a politician, while the civil servant should be neutral in partisan terms. The Weimar Constitution expressly recognizes that in Art. 130, but, at the same time, in Art. 39 (vacation for deputies who are civil servants) it favors the deputies who are civil servants.

(e) The deputy may accept a payment for the exercise of his mandate neither from his voters nor from the state. Hence, he must exercise his office on a voluntary basis and only receive compensation for his expenses. This demand corresponds to the ideal that bourgeois liberalism made both of the deputy as well as of voluntary official service.

In his overview of the differences between the estate and representative principle, discussed above, Bluntschli enumerates the following: estate deputies were accountable to their clients, and they were also compensated by them with room and board; the modern deputy is only accountable to the state and receives the necessary room and board out of the state treasury. Art. 32a provides that "the members of the Reichstag may receive no pay or compensation as such." According to the dominant interpretation in theory and practice (Mohl, Laband, Zorn, since the 2nd ed. of his commentary also M. Seydel), the prohibition referred to pay and compensation out of public as well as private means. The Reich statute of 21 May 1906, § 1 (*Reichsgesetzesblatt*, p. 467), changed this provision by stipulating that "Reichstag members may draw no pay as such. They receive compensation according to the dictates of statute." Parliamentary deputies received free railroad travel since 1873 (during the deliberation on the government's emergency supplementary request for compensation of the private railroads, the statute of 18 February 1874, *Reichgesesetzesblatt*, p. 15, Deputy Sonnemann declared the parliamentary grant unconstitutional!). Art. 40 of the Weimar Constitution provides that "Reichstag members receive the right to free passage on all German railroads as well as compensation for expenses according to the dictates of a Reich statute." Compensation (indemnité) of deputies out of the state treasury had already been introduced (Art. 68 of the Constitution of the Year III, 1795) in France during the great Revolution. From 1817 to 1848 (in the classic period of constitutionalism), by contrast, it counted as unconstitutional that the deputy received compensation for his activity. Since 1875, deputies as well as senators have received a fixed yearly sum as compensation. Until 1911, English members of Parliament received no room and board. The English courts even treated the pay of Labor Party representatives from the unions as impermissible. Only since 1911, deputies drew a fixed sum (400 pounds yearly) from the state treasury. Because members of Parliament grant themselves fixed income by way of statute, their independence in regard to clients can be secured. If, at the same time, the dependence on interest organizations in practical reality nevertheless persists, the deputy thus remains a commissioned lobbyist, and even if the delegates of economic interest associations, syndicates, and secretaries appear in Parliament, the resulting situation is that the state exclusively pays the interested parties for the validation of their economic interests and, moreover, bestows on their attorneys and agents the privilege of free passage on all railroads.

3. Decline of the ideal presuppositions of parliamentarianism in contemporary democracy. [319]

(a) *Discussion erodes.* Parliament in most states (the French Chamber of Deputies may make a noteworthy exception, in some cases) today is no longer the site of reciprocal rational persuasion, where the possibility exists that a part of the deputies convinces the other deputies through arguments and the decision is the result of the public, plenary assembly session. More precisely, stable party organizations form a permanently present form of advocacy by certain fragments of the voting masses. The individual deputy's standpoint is determined by the party; factional discipline inheres in the practice of contemporary parliamentarianism; and individual outsiders are insignificant. The factions oppose one another with a precisely calculated strength in terms of the number of mandates. A public parliamentary discussion is no longer capable of changing their interests or class-based commitments. The discussions in the committees of parliament or outside of parliament in so-called multiparty sessions are not discussion. They are instead business calculations and negotiations. In this instance, the oral exposition of positions serves the goal of a reciprocal calculation of the power and interest groupings. The privilege of freedom of speech hence loses its presuppositions.

(b) *The public sphere erodes.* The public, plenary assembly is no longer the place where decisions are made on the basis of public discussion. The parliament becomes a type of official who decides in secret deliberation and announces the decision's outcome in a public session in the form of votes. Speeches of the different parties precede the vote, following a practice stemming from other times. The specialized committees in which the decision is actually made are not always committees of the parliament itself, but rather meetings of party leaders, confidential, multiparty discussions with the clients of the parties, the interest associations, etc.

(c) *The representative character of parliament and of the deputy erodes.* Consequently, parliament is no longer the place where the political decision occurs. The essential decisions are reached outside of parliament. The parliament thus functions as a bureau for a technical reconfiguration in the state apparatus of officials. [320]

§ 25.

Historical Overview of the Development
of the Parliamentary System

I. *Most important dates of the historical development in England (government by parties, responsible government, alternative government, cabinet government).*

1. From the king's court, the Curia Regis, the *Grand Council* (Great Council [Schmitt's English]), developed since the thirteenth century through the addition of deputies of the county districts and cities. The Grand Council divided itself into an upper house (House of Lords) and a lower house (House of Commons), which is a house of communities (of the enfranchised counties, electoral villages, etc.). See above p. 295. It was significant for the development of the lower house that the lower nobility, in particular the knighthood in contrast to the high nobility, met together with the delegates of the bourgeoisie.

On the other hand, inside the grand council, a *more select council* of the king's confidants, known as the state council, is formed. Inside the grand state council again, the *most select circle* of these confidants, the secret state council or cabinet (Privy Council [Schmitt's English]) forms. The designations are not always in harmony, even less is the public law meaning formally established. When the English kingdom edged toward absolutism (sixteenth century) and in the time of the *Stuarts*, the cabinet was very similar to the council of an absolute king. The king appealed to the members of this cabinet according to his discretion. A dependence of the king on both houses of parliament did not exist and was not demanded.

The development of genuine parliamentary cabinet government first begins as soon as the basic principle of a political agreement between cabinet and parliament is accepted and the judicial methods of political responsibility (ministerial challenge through the lower house, prosecution by the upper house as state high court, so-called impeachment [Schmitt's English]) recedes. The basic principle that cabinet and parliament must agree initially develops unplanned and without principled intention with the ascension to the throne by the King of *Orange*. Often, therefore, the year 1689 is designated as the beginning of the development of parliamentarianism, because the new King *William III* naturally took into his cabinet members of the party that had called him to the throne. In partisan terms, the cabinet was in complete harmony with the parliamentary majority for the first time in 1695. For these reasons, Hasbach, *Die parlamentarische Kabinettsregierung*, 1919, p. 45, designates this year 1695 as the "birth of the first cabinet." In the years 1700 and 1701, the other party, the Tories, comes again into power in the parliament and the king takes members of this party into his cabinet. Insofar as for the first time the dependence of the cabinet on the party then dominant in parliament; and to the extent that a type of exchange of government and opposition party, or "alternative government" [Schmitt's English], is recognizable; this year may be designated as the beginning of parliamentary government. Nevertheless, the king retained the authority to freely appoint and dismiss members of the cabinet. He participates in all sessions of the cabinet, chairs the sessions, and determines the guiding principles of policy. That changes beginning in 1715 because George I no longer participated in the cabinet sessions, allegedly because he did not understand English, but in truth probably (cf. Michael, *Zeitschrift für Politik* 1913, vol. 6, p. 577f.) because his interest in the political affairs of England was not great and he understood himself entirely as a German elector. His actual influence appeared to him not significant enough to take part in the sessions. David Hume writes in his political essays [321]that appeared in 1742 that the consent of the king is "little more than a matter of form." The government, however, remains a royal government. Legally, the king (up until the current day) retains all the government's grants of authority and is only compelled to exercise them through his ministers. Anson formulates it thusly: earlier, the king governed through his ministers; now, the ministers govern through the king.

During the entire eighteenth century, the cabinet's dependence on parliament did not stand absolutely firm at all. Walpole still opposed the requirement of resignation in 1741. A change of the entire cabinet, based in solidarity, first occurs in 1782. Pitt explicitly formulated the genuine premier system for the first time in 1803. According to this system, the head (leader [Schmitt's English]) of the then current majority party, as minister president, forms the cabinet out of party followers. During the entire eighteenth century, it is also an open question as to which part of parliament, upper house or lower house, definitively forms the cabinet. During the nineteenth century, there is the first instance of any cabinet receiving from the majority of the lower house a mark of disfavor, a vote of no confidence, or a disapproval, either resigning or being compelled to attempt to create a new majority through dissolution of the lower house and the calling of new elections. Even the practice of dissolution of parliament and of new elections was initially defined in the nineteenth century, and after 1867 the perspective first emerged that a government that intends to carry out decisive innovations must allow the voters' consent to be given through a new election.

In the culmination of this historical development Parliament has become a mere expression of public opinion, which makes it dependent on this public opinion. In regard to Parliament, the cabinet can produce a direct connection with public opinion, and, in particular, it can dissolve Parliament through royal decree and bring about a decision of the enfranchised voters. According to Anson, the authority to topple the cabinet passed from the king to the lower house and then from the lower house to the people, that is, the voters.

2. For the political and public law evaluation of this development, it is noteworthy that the lower house, which, in this regard, is the definitive part of the Parliament, was in different centuries, from 1700 until the current day specifically, an assembly that was constituted entirely differently in political and social terms.

Until the electoral reform of 1832, even the lower house was composed of the parties of the dominant class, the Tories and the Whigs, and was an overwhelmingly aristocratic assembly of the Medieval system, a "House of Commons" [Schmitt's English]. Counties, villages, corporations, large, enfranchised villages had the right to select a member, an electoral right that was often determined according to bizarre historical accidents. The electoral reform of 1832 eliminated the electoral right of most small communities, in which the nobility or the Crown had simply determined their candidates, and granted a right of electoral participation to bourgeois property holders [322], landowners, homeowners, those engaged in commerce. The number of those entitled to vote rose from approximately a half million to a million. Alongside the still more numerous nobles, now even attorneys determined the type of deputy. Nevertheless, even now the lower house was still not a popular assembly in the modern democratic sense. The casting of ballots remained public, but the deputy was still a person commanding respect and mostly independent from his voters. However, soon a harbinger of a new parliamentary practice became evident: that a parliament was compelled to resign by the voters. From the 1850s onward, the dependence on public opinion counted as a basic principle. Through the electoral reform of 1867 (Disraeli), the urban lower classes also received the franchise (the number of those enfranchised rose to 2½ million). In 1884, agricultural workers were enfranchised (now approximately 5 million with a right to vote). According to both statutes, those adult men who pay a certain rent (in the normal case 10 pounds sterling) for their living quarters were granted the right to vote. A modern division of electoral districts came about for the first time in 1885. And beginning in the war through the statute of 6 February 1918, the franchise became general and democratic in the sense that all men twenty-one years of age or over and, moreover, independent women from thirty years of age have the right to vote without regard to landed property or living quarters.

Consequently, the "parties" of parliament do not signify the same thing in different periods. Until the year 1832, there were essentially two parties within the dominant upper class, which were divided among themselves by political and other differences of opinion, such as those regarding landed property or capital property, but not by deep-seated social ones. The distinction between Tories and Whigs generalizes itself into that between conservatives and liberals, which initially does not signify genuine class opposition. Instead, this distinction is rendered relative by the independent, enclosed unity of the nation that encompasses both parties, and, as such, it presents only differences of opinion, not a friend/enemy grouping. A deeper opposition and a genuine heterogeneity first arose when an Irish national party formed and became obstructionist. Nevertheless, this party was not strong enough to transcend the two-party system of conservatives and liberals and to emerge as an equally significant third party. Moreover, this party is again excluded with the formation of an [323] Irish Free State (Treaty of 6 December 1921). A third party in the full sense first appears after 1900 with the Independent Workers' Party (Independent Labour

Party [Schmitt's English]). Hence, a new social element, potentially even a genuine class opposition, emerged. Moreover, the simple two-party system, with its alternative exchange of majority (government) and opposition party, was disrupted. The elections of December 1923 (customs union election) led to a three-party system, Conservative, Liberal, and Labour Party, and to the formation of a Labour government (Macdonald). The elections of 29 October 1924 temporarily eliminated this circumstance. The Conservative Party received an absolute majority in the lower house, so the new government was again in line with the traditions of the two-party system. Nevertheless, one must not fail to see that this electoral result of 1924 is attributable to an electoral system that facilitated a great disparity between mandate numbers and vote count. In the electorate itself, the three-party system was not at all disrupted.[1]

3. A stable concept of parliamentary government cannot be derived from this English development. There is a series of precedents that are interpreted differently according to political circumstances, and about which one can only say that on the whole during the nineteenth century a sovereign Parliament is, indeed, deemed definitive. But the responsibility for providing political direction lay with the cabinet, and the political decision resided with the voters. In the different stages of this development, [324] various designs, schematizations, idealizations, and interpretations of English parliamentarianism arose from English as well as from other authors and served the liberal bourgeoisie of the European continent in the struggle against princely absolutism. In the eighteenth century, Montesquieu, who, incidentally, was fully conscious of the historical and political imprecision involved, construed from the English constitutional circumstances the ideal of the constitution that distinguishes among powers (*Esprit des lois*, XI, 6). In reality, there was a close connection between government and parliament, which is the opposite of a "division." Elsewhere than in the famous chapter 6 of the eleventh book (book XIX, 27), Montesquieu already names two essential elements of this system, the two-party system and the obligation of the monarch to take his ministers from the dominant party. In this context, incidentally, the construction of the two-party system also contains a significant simplification, because more often there were several parties, transitional groupings, and coalitions. In the nineteenth century, one often understood the parliamentary government in outline form as a subordination of the government under the parliament, whereas under the English system the prime minister leads the parliamentary majority and the Parliament can be dissolved when it fails to maintain its following. Since 1867, it is no longer the Parliament but rather the electorate that definitively serves as the bearer of public opinion. The cabinet (the more selective council of min-

isters inside the ever larger ministry) directs policy and exercises the right of legislative initiative. Finally, the Parliament is still only the point of connection between the electorate and the government. It does not exert political leadership, nor does it render a political decision in the case of conflict.

4. Regarding the idealization and simplification of English parliamentarianism and the attempts to imitate it on the European continent, eminent academics and writers stress the *presuppositions* of this English system.

See, for example, Friedrich J. Stahl, *Parteienlehre*, p. 144ff; Lothar Bucher, *Der Parlamentarismus*, 2nd ed., p. 144; J. Barthélemy, *L'introduction du régime parlementaire en France*, Paris 1904, p. 146ff; Schmoller, *Schmollers Jahrbuch* 1917, vol. 41, p. 1123ff.; and Erich Kaufmann in his essay "Die Regierungsbildung im Reich und in Preussen," *Die Westmark* 1921, p. 208ff.

The effect of such undoubtedly correct findings is generally slight because the English Parliament in the nineteenth century [325] became a mythical image for a great part of the liberal bourgeoisie, for whom the important thing was not historical correctness and accuracy. Nevertheless, a few of the most important ideal presuppositions of English parliamentarianism are briefly mentioned here.

(a) *A two-party system* is the first of these presuppositions. The leader of the majority party forms the cabinet. If he loses the majority, the leader of the other party, the opposition party, forms the cabinet. This simple exchange of majority and minority, government and opposition, ceases when a strong third party appears and coalitions are necessary to form a majority. A widely held view in England is that a coalition government is something abnormal and the coalition government of the year 1915 as well as the subsequent governments have been justified only by the special conditions of the war and the postwar period. The surprising victory of the Conservatives in October 1924 is often attributed to the wish of the English people to return to the old two-party system with simple parliamentary majorities.

(b) From the two-party system results an additional presupposition: *homogeneity of the transitory majority and of the cabinet.*

(c) *The parties are leadership parties* in the grip of prestigious politicians, *leaders* whom they follow and who are in the position to determine the guiding principles of politics under their own responsibility and to form a homogenous ministry from the party faithful. This accounts for the solidarity of the entire cabinet, which means all ministers resign when the prime minister steps down. As soon as a bureaucratized party apparatus enters in place of the political leader, with all its employees, secretaries, invisible contributors, etc., the minister is more or less dependent like every party member. He is the exponent of an organization, not a leader, and, as such, also not in the position to assume political responsibility.

(d) *Elections are single-member district elections.* Each electoral district elects a candidate with a relative majority and without a runoff. This means a noticeable disparity can result between vote count and mandate figures, as during the election of October 1924. The single-member district election makes possible a personal relationship between the electorate [326] and a recognized leader. Even if the election orients itself around substantive questions, such as protective tariffs or free trade, there is always a genuine personal relationship to a leader, who is being acclaimed through the election. The system of proportional representation, by contrast, eliminates the personal relationship. The power of the party organizations becomes stronger, and the parties compose the candidate list, on which are only a few names known to the voter, who casts a ballot for a party and a list or, according to the optimistic interpretation (above p. 239), for an idea. Minorities and splinter parties are taken into account to a great extent. Despite this noticeable disparity between voter count and mandate figures, English electoral law remains committed to the basic principle of the single-member district election. Under this electoral system, it is even possible to monitor the shifts of public opinion through repeat elections, while under the system of proportional representation with candidate lists repeat elections do not occur. Lost with these repeat elections is an important distinguishing characteristic for the determination of public opinion.

(e) The parties are parties in the genuine sense of the word, that is, in terms of a design centered on free competition, not stable organizations of masses that are bound to interests or indeed composed along class lines. The opposition of parties may be in no sense absolute and never rupture the framework of national and social unity. A discussion between parties is only possible so long as common premises are at hand. Even reasonable compromises and a loyal exchange of both parties could then only be established if these parties do not intend to abolish or disqualify one another, but instead conduct themselves according to the rules of fair play. However, as soon as absolute oppositions emerge and confessional, class, or national differences become definitive for the party will, this presupposition no longer applies. The great success of the Conservatives during the elections of October 1924 is certainly explained mostly by the need to express clearly the fundamental presupposition of English parliamentarianism in contrast to a socialist class concept. This need, more specifically, is for political unity on a national foundation.

II. *The course of development in France and Belgium.* The most important difference concerning developments in France and Belgium vis-à-vis those in England lies in the fact that certain formulas are applied to the parliamentary system and constitutionally set in place. Nevertheless, [327] this constitutional solidification cannot entirely comprise political life. In the states of the European continent, consequently, a public law practice and custom has developed alongside the written legal text, which generally first gives to the written formulas their content and shows that despite the constitutional norm new and divergent formations of this system constantly emerge.

1. The constitutions of the French Revolution still do not include parliamentary government. The constitution of the year 1789 rests on the basic principle of the separation of powers, and thus places itself in conscious opposition to a parliamentary government. The Constitution of the Year III (Constitution of the Directorate of 1795) is exactly the same. The Constitution of the Year VIII (1799), indeed, requires a countersignature for governmental acts by a minister and provides that no incompatibility exists between the position of the minister and that of the deputy, so that a closer connection between government and parliament is possible. Nevertheless, these possibilities and approaches of a parliamentary constitution did not unfold in the absolutism of the Napoleonic regime.

2. With the end of the Napoleonic rule in 1815, by contrast, a program of parliamentarianism, constituted according to English models, was immediately established, and its literary heralds were Chateaubriand and Benjamin Constant. The *Charte* of 1814 speaks of a ministerial responsibility in terms of high treason and bribery. Therefore, it only establishes responsibility that accords with judicial forms. But the quality of judicial forms is irreconcilable with the essence of direct political influence. In 1816, Chateaubriand developed the principles of parliamentarianism as unified ministry (système homogène) with collective responsibility in regard to the majority of the Chamber of Deputies, because this "is the most important organ of public opinion." The ministry must address the chamber, answer to it, and resign if it does not find a majority. The practice of Louis XVIII took the chamber majority into account. His successor, Charles X, was overthrown by the July Revolution of 1830.

The constitution of 1830 did not contain a new express provision on the dependence of the government on parliament. Instead, it only repeated the *Charte* of 1814. Nevertheless, the basic principle of a constant regard for the transitory parliamentary majority evolved, and the government of Louis-Philippe counted as an example of a parliamentary monarchy. That could not prevent violent differences of opinion on the king's powers to arise. According to Guizot, it was enough for parliamentarianism that the ministers were responsible and that otherwise there remained an opportunity for the king to carry out his political understanding, while in 1829 Thiers had already announced the formula, which he repeated in a famous 1846 chamber debate, that "le roi règne et ne gouverne pas." The king, more specifically, must abstain from exerting any substantive influence on policy. [328] The controversy, which is also of interest for the current parliamentary conditions in Germany, and which shows the ambiguity of the turns of phrase involving "responsibility," was not carried to a conclusion, but was instead settled by the collapse of the bourgeois monarchy in the Revolution of 1848.

3. The Belgian constitution of 1831 also counts as a constitution of a parliamentary monarchy, although in regard to the constitutional text it is little different from a constitutional monarchy of the German variety. "The distinction rests not on statutory language; it lies, rather, in the application of the constitution to the national public life. It is a rule of a customary character and lives in the spirit of

the constitution. The letter of the law says nothing about it" (Errera, *Das Staats-recht des Königreichs Belgien*, 1909, p. 58). According to the constitutional rule (Art. 63, 64), the ministers are responsible, and they assume responsibility through their countersignature of the king's documents. That sufficed as the legal foundation for a parliamentary government. However, "responsibility" means a form of political dependence in contrast to that validated in a formal judicial procedure (petition of the Chamber of Deputies before the Court of Appeals according to Art. 90), a type of political responsibility whose presuppositions and effect were not more closely regulated. But from this political responsibility one discerned the necessity of an agreement between cabinet and chamber majority and the duty of the king to form a new ministry "after a vote of no confidence in a rather significant question" as well as after a change of opinion made evident by an electoral collapse. Essentially, everything is customary practice.

4. The French constitution of 1848 created the office of a state president, who should be independent in regard to parliament. The constitution demanded the countersignature of the ministers for the official activity of the president, but at the same time it declared the state president "responsible." From this direct responsibility of the president one could conclude that the president has independent political powers, because his responsibility would only receive content through the independent grants of authority. This lack of clarity, which is very characteristic of the parliamentary system, led to passionate discussions over how far the direction of policy was granted to the president and what his "responsibility" actually meant. The National Assembly claimed to dominate the "political system" and alleged that this dominance was part of the essence of a parliamentary government. When the legislative assembly expressed disfavor to the ministers, the state president dismissed the ministry. In doing so, however, he emphasized that he was independent in his political decisions because he was responsible. This interesting controversy was not brought to a conclusion; it was effectively settled by the coup d'état. Louis Napoleon dissolved the National Assembly on 2 December 1851, although the dissolution was constitutionally prohibited. According to the new constitution of 14 January 1852 [329], which was sanctioned by a popular vote, Napoleon III was the director of French politics, first as president, then as emperor. The constitution of 1852 was expressly antiparliamentary. The ministers were responsible only to the head of state, and there was no ministerial solidarity as a whole. Nevertheless, concessions to the parliament were gradually granted. Initially, parliamentary "addresses" were permitted in response to the emperor's annual speech from the throne. The Senatus-Consult of 8 September 1869 states that "the ministers are dependent only on the emperor. They are responsible. They can only be forced out by the Senate in an impeachment proceeding." The lack of clarity of these principles is obvious. Shortly before the outbreak of the war of 1870, the full responsibility of the ministry was recognized in the constitution of 21 May 1870 (Art. 19). That counted as the introduction of a parliamentary government, although at the same time the emperor's independent responsibility was again emphasized. The emperor is "responsible to the French people" (Art. 13). The controversy also did not come to a conclusion. After the military defeat, the empire was eliminated on 4 September 1870.

5. The French National Assembly that convened in 1871 installed Thiers as "Chef du pouvoir exécutif." He was, in fact, a minister president responsible to parliament, who appeared before parliament, and yet who on 13 March 1873 introduced

a statute substituting ministerial responsibility for direct presidential responsibility. This principle entered into the constitutional laws of 1875. These laws provided a state president as president of the republic and allowed him to be elected by the National Assembly, but still bound him to the countersignature of the ministers. The parliamentary government is recognized in the constitutional law of 25 February 1875, Art. 6, with the words: "Les ministres sont solidairement responsables devant les Chambres de la politique générale du Gouvernement et individuellement de leurs actes personnels" [Ministers are collectively responsible to the Chambers for general policy and individually for their personal actions]. The president is only responsible in the case of high treason. He appoints and dismisses ministers, has the right to send emissaries to parliament, and can compel a second reading of a statute. Art. 5 of the Constitutional Law of 25 February 1875 grants him the legal authority to dissolve the Chamber of Deputies with the consent of the Senate. But these powers of the state president lost their political significance and did not lead to the fact that the president can exert a substantive influence on the "politique générale." Most of the four French state presidents who resigned before the expiration of their terms of office, Mac-Mahon 1879, Grévy 1887, Casimir Périer 1895, and Millerand 1924, resigned partly because the lack of political influence of their position seemed unbearable to them.

Not only the state president, but also even the ministry itself, was limited vis-à-vis the Chamber of Deputies in terms of the independence of political leadership. In France, there is undoubtedly a strong tendency to practice parliamentary government such that the chamber majority dictates to the ministers every important position, [330] whereby more often political decisions came about in a committee of the parliament, which then, in fact, was a ministry. The constitutional norm is not exactly an unalterable blueprint. Parliamentary government can mean both political rule of the parliament as well as the direction of politics by a minister president. The policy of Minister President Poincaré suffered a defeat in the elections of 11 May 1924. The electorate declared itself against Poincaré and for the radical socialists. Nevertheless, without another election, Poincaré could form a new cabinet on 23 July 1926, which, indeed, included a few radicals, though it still stood under his political leadership. By not shying away from posing the cabinet question very often, he could carry out his will in opposition to a chamber that was indecisive and splintered into many parties. Even for the parliamentary government in France, therefore, neither the written constitutional text nor the clear content of a firmly established practice is sufficient to give an unequivocal sense to the concept "parliamentary government." One cannot tell whether the state president, minister president, or the chamber majority determines the guiding principles of policy from the fact that a constitutional regime intends to introduce a "parliamentary government."

III. *The course of development in Germany.*

1. The German constitutions of 1815 to 1848 correspond to the monarchical principle as the Vienna Federation Acts of 1815 and the Vienna Concluding Acts of 1820 presented it (above p. 211). The "estates" had a right of consultation in legislation, even the authority to approve taxes. There was no responsibility or, indeed, dependence of the princely government in regard to these estates. The ministers were servants of the prince and nothing else. The 1848 Revolution made the issue in most German states either a consti-

tutional stipulation of constitutional monarchy (as in Prussia) or, insofar as "constitutions" already existed, extensions or changes establishing a ministerial responsibility. Despite this success, the revolutionary movement of the year 1848 did not lead to a parliamentary government. The king of the German-style constitutional monarchy retained political leadership and direction and could also not be forced out of this position by the powers of parliament (consultation in legislation and budgetary rights). If the parliament fails, the king can "withdraw into his state authority" (Max von Seydel). Friedrich J. Stahl established the distinction between constitutional and parliamentary [331] monarchy (above p. 289). The liberal opponents of this system designated it "sham constitutionalism." Nevertheless, in the German state literature of the nineteenth century, only Robert von Mohl seeks to justify a parliamentary government (above p. 313).

In Bavaria, of course, the estate constitution of 1818 did not recognize ministerial responsibility before the estates at all. A statute of 4 June 1848 expanded this constitution, introducing this responsibility and providing for the countersignature of ministers for acts of the king. "A state minister or his deputy," it reads, "who violates state statutes through his actions or failure to act is *responsible* to the estates of the Reich." But the ministers nevertheless remain the servants of the king and dependent on his confidence. The newly introduced responsibility refers only to *illegalities*, not to political leadership as such. This responsibility is regulated such that the chambers can impeach a minister who is accountable for violation of state statutes before a state high court (on this, see Seydel, *Bayerisches Staatsrecht*, 2nd ed., I., 1896, p. 517ff.). A Bavarian statute of 30 March 1850 regulates the procedure of this state high court. Saxony (§ 141ff. of the constitution and statute of 3 February 1831) and Württemberg (chapter 10) definitively set this judicially formal responsibility only for constitutional violations. Baden did so (statute of 20 February 1868) for intentional or grossly negligent violations of the constitution, for violations of rights recognized as equivalent to constitutional laws, or for serious endangerment of the security and welfare of the state. This last fact already passes over into the political. Yet the procedure remains formally judicial and thus loses its political force.

In Prussia, Art. 44 of the constitution of 31 January 1850 provided that "in order to be valid, all governmental acts of the king require countersignature of a minister, who thus assumes *responsibility*." That is designated as political responsibility in contrast to responsibility under criminal law. It does not constitute dependence on the parliament, however. The minister remains the servant of the king (Art. 45). Each of the two chambers (House of Lords and House of Deputies) can demand the presence of the ministers (Art. 60). One of the two chambers can decide to impeach ministers "because of the crime of constitutional violation, of corruption, or of treason" before the monarchy's highest court of law. But the "instances of responsibility," the procedure and the criminal sanction, should first be regulated in a special statute (Art. 61, 2). Because this statute was not established, the chambers were not able to exercise their impeachment authority and responsibility became practically meaningless (on this, see Bismarck in the House of Deputies, *Stenographischer Bericht* II, p. 952; additionally, the supreme report of 26 May 1863, ibid., p. 1322). [332] Responsibility in formal judicial terms was never instituted. It still came down to the fact that the entire realm of the king's military command authority was granted an exception from the requirement of ministerial countersignature. The political influence of the parliament on the government could only validate itself by way of a rejection of the budget and of credits. Even this attempt misfired during the Prussian conflict between the House of Deputies and the government from 1862 to 1866. The House of Deputies refused to consent to the budget, but the government continued to conduct business without a budget and, indeed, declared governing without a budget not a normal circumstance, but also not unconstitutional, because there was simply a "gap in the constitution." This "theory of gaps," presented above all even by Bismarck in the deliberations of the provincial legislature, became accepted constitutional law after Bismarck's victory in Prussia and in the Reich. On this, compare Anschütz in Meyer-Anschütz, p. 906: "Only one thing is certain, the constitution does not intend, cannot intend, that the life of the state stands still during the imminent situation without a budget." If, however, no agreement on the budget comes about between the highest state organs, he continues, "there is not so much a gap in the statute law (that is, in the text of the constitution) as, more accurately, a gap in the law that no conceptual operations of legal scholarship can fill." *"Public law stops at this point,"* Anschütz concludes, "so the question of how to proceed in the absence of a budgetary statute is not a legal question." In fact, it involves a question of sovereignty. Anschütz's response avoided answering the question.

2. For the German Reich under Bismarck's constitution of 16 April 1871, Art. 17, 2, provides that "the orders and instruments of the Kaiser are issued in the name of the Reich and their validity requires the countersignature of the Chancellor, who thus assumes *responsibility.*" The Chancellor, as individual Reich minister, was the sole bearer of this responsibility. Of course, the "responsibility" in itself does not establish a parliamentary government. The Reichstag's authority to refer petitions to the Bundesrat or to the Chancellor (Art. 23a) offers an opportunity for an elaboration of "accountability" to the same limited degree as the right of parliamentary inquiry and the right to direct addresses to the king. These authorizations could have become effective means of political influence through practice and custom and were designated "pseudo rights" by the quasi-official public law theory and mockingly placed on a level with the right to "give a cheer to the Kaiser" (Laband, I, p. 309). Even the emerging confidence or lack of confidence pronouncements of the Reichstag (since 1908) [333] did not count as "public law functions." The question of the Chancellor's responsibility in regard to the Reichstag was confused, moreover, by the fact that the extremely complicated system of the division of jurisdiction between Reich and individual states was partly corrected, and yet still made more complicated, by a practice of personal unions of important Reich posts (Chancellor and State Secretary) with those of the Prussian ministries and Bundesrat delegates. In the federal budget law, only the Bundesrat, and not the Chancellor, engages the Reichstag (E. Kaufmann, *Bismarcks Erbe in der Reichsverfassung,* 1917, p. 63).

The Reich Constitution of 1871 never contained provisions on the formal judicial responsibility of the minister, as they are otherwise found in the constitutions of the constitutional monarchy. A petition by Bennigsen to accept the amendment that "the responsibility and the procedure to validate it are regulated by a special statute" was rejected in the Reichstag when it was deliberating on the constitution (*Stenographischer Bericht*, p. 342). Bismarck saw the significance of Art. 17 and the "responsibility" it establishes. The Chancellor, who originally was thought of as the "undersecretary for German affairs in the Prussia Foreign Ministry," now was "promoted" to the position of a "leading Reich minister." Max von Seydel designated this responsibility of the Chancellor as an "empty formula" in the first edition of his commentary on the Reich Constitution, but corrected this characterization in the second edition (1897, p. 178), because Art. 17 involves less the relationship of the Chancellor to the parliament than to the Kaiser. In regard to the Kaiser, it secures for the Chancellor a ministerial autonomy.

If the liberal and democratic parties of the German Reichstag sought to achieve influence over the policy of the Reich government, an extraordinary argument could be made against the most modest efforts at a "parliamentarization of the Reich government," an argument that did not come into question in the individual German states: the irreconcilability of a parliamentary government with the federal structure of the German Reich. The "irreconcilability of parliamentarianism and federalism" is often put forth as a generally valid principle. That the United States of America also does not recognize a parliamentary government seems to confirm the irreconcilability (E. Kaufmann, *Bismarcks Erbe*, pp. 69/70). [334] Whether an absolute incompatibility exists genuinely now between parliamentarianism and federalism need not be decided here. In fact, the logic of the democratic principle of identity, not parliamentarianism, eliminates the state independence of the member states (see p. 390 below). At least for the German Reich under Bismarck's constitution, the irreconcilability counted as official doctrine. A Prussian declaration in the Bundesrat of 5 April 1884 and a message of the German Kaiser to the Reichstag on 30 November 1885 (*Hirths Annalen des Deutschen Reiches*, 1886, p. 350) referred to the fact that a government controlled by the elected parliament is ill suited for the direction of a great people and is dangerous for a Bundesrat resting on contract in particular. Through a parliamentarization of the Reich government, the Reichstag elected by the entire German people would have obtained definitive influence on the political leadership and the federal authority would no longer have been a power wielded by the allied princely governments. Here one perceived the risk of the German Reich disintegrating. Even under the perspective of the monarchical homogeneity of the federation, a parliamentary Reich government appeared suspect. The discussions and struggles around the Prussian right to vote are from both sides also struggles for the substance of homogeneity, without which no alliance, whether it is a federal state or a federation of states, is possible.

3. During the World War, the German Reichstag's influence on the political leadership increased as the military and foreign political situation worsened. It became evident that the dualism of the constitutional monarchy certainly could function in peaceful and settled times. Such periods also encouraged the view that the decisive question could be permanently suspended, and yet any critical situation revealed the untenability of this opinion. The occasional advances of the Reichstag (in 1908, the so-called crisis of the "personal regime" of Wilhelm II, in 1913 the Zabern case) toward greater authority, were, indeed, unsuccessful, but they are significant as a symptom because they let it be recognized that the natural tendency toward parliamentary government was ever present and only deferred as long as the aftereffect of Bismarck's extraordinary achievement lasted. By contrast, the opposition against this tendency relaxed to the same degree that the government [335] was unsuccessful in foreign policy terms and was finally defeated. One can certainly not compare the German, in particular the Prussian monarchy, with the monarchy of Napoleon III. Nevertheless, an immanent logic of constitutionalism emerges, which is the same in both cases. An expansion of parliamentary power is the domestic political consequence of any military or foreign policy disappointment for a government independent of parliament.

Only in the year 1917 did a theoretically interesting discussion about parliamentarianism occur in Germany, one that had a prospect of practical success (cf. the literature in Anschütz, Meyer-Anschütz, p. 1027). In a few now-famous essays in the *Frankfurter Zeitung* (May/June 1917), Max Weber made a series of suggestions. These included the elimination of Art. 9a of Bismarck's Reich Constitution (the article that established incompatibility between the position of a Reichstag deputy and a delegate in the Bundesrat, so that a Reichstag deputy could not be Prussian minister president, a delegate in the Bundesrat, and Chancellor without renouncing his mandate) and the elaboration of the Reichstag's right of inquiry and the formation of a crown council, to which parliamentarians should belong, in order to personally advise the Kaiser. Max Weber at that time did not demand a parliamentary government in the sense of a government dependent then on the confidence of parliament, still less the elimination of the monarchy. These essays (which in 1918 were brought together in the volume "Parliament and Government in the Reordered Germany") had great influence on the originators of the Weimar Constitution and are a noteworthy source for the evaluation of this constitution in state theory terms. What Max Weber demanded was political leadership according to the model of the statesman party leader in England. Because of the peculiar character of German parties and the splintering of the party system, this party leader ideal necessarily becomes problematical. The continuing theoretical discussion did not misconstrue the difficulty at all. A treatise by R. Piloty on "The Parliamentary System" (1917) declared it a basic ideal of this system that "only party guidance at the rudder could then be permitted." "If one admits all parties and, moreover, all opposing positions on equal terms, then one simply rejects this system," he concludes. But even Piloty's interpretation of the parliamentary system inclines toward granting government authority to the leaders of powerful parties, [336] in order to make their party into the government's program and, by this action, to test themselves together with their program in the leadership of the affairs of the state.

On 19 July 1917, the Reichstag's claim to political supervision of the Reich government was thrust to the fore in the so-called "Peace Resolution." The majority (Center, Progressive Party, Social Democracy, and the left wing of the National Liberals) formulated that famous resolution. "The Reichstag," they declared, "strives for a peace of understanding among and lasting reconciliation between peoples. Coercive territorial acquisitions and political, economic, and financial assaults are irreconcilable with such a peace." Also, there was a demand for the introduction of general suffrage in Prussia, a demand showing how little constitutional limitations and considerations mean here, for in the federal state structure of the Reich such an interference of the Reichstag in Prussian affairs was certainly hardly permissible. The Chancellor Bethmann-Hollweg was dismissed on 14 July 1917. The Kaiser appointed his successor, Michaelis, without letting the Reichstag be heard beforehand or taking its sentiment. But in August 1917 the new Chancellor formed a committee composed of seven leading Reichstag deputies and seven delegates selected from the plenum of the Bundesrat, initially only in order to debate the German answer to the papal peace note. Several already saw in this an acceptance of Max Weber's suggestion that a crown council should be formed. Nevertheless, the growing influence of the Reichstag only involved the civil government, while the authority for command and leadership of the army, what mattered during such a war, naturally remained in the hands of the Kaiser. The subsequent Chancellor, Count Hertling, already had been appointed in agreement with the parliamentary parties and came to an understanding about his government program with the ruling party coalition before entry into office. The Kaiser named his successor, Prince Max von Baden, the last Chancellor of Imperial Germany, not entirely according to the customs or rules of a parliamentary monarchy. "I wish that the German people would collaborate more actively than before on the determination of the destiny of the fatherland," reads the Kaiser's proclamation on the dismissal of Count Hertling from 30 September 1918. "Consequently, it is my will that men who are borne by the confidence of the [337] people participate in broad scope in the rights and duties of the government." Then followed a request to Count Hertling to make suggestions to his successors. Prince Max von Baden remarks on this procedure in his "Remembrances and Documents" (Stuttgart 1927, p. 328, 329). The correct procedure is that an invitation must be issued to the parliament to deliberate on the convening of the new government, before their leader is installed. "In all democratically governed lands of the West," he writes, "the prime minister has a free hand in the selection of his colleagues. Through this initiation of the revolution from above, the idea of the leader was given up." On 3 October 1918, Prince Max von Baden was named Chancellor, and, on 5 October, he appeared before the Reichstag, communicated the guiding principles of his government's policy, and posed the question of confidence.

The constitutional changes that expressly introduced parliamentary government in its complete form into the Reich occurred during the last hour of 28 October 1918 (*Reichsgesetzesblatt*, pp. 1273/74): "For the conduct of his office, the Chancellor needs the *confidence* of the Reichstag." At the same time, the Reichstag's jurisdiction was expanded to include consultation in the declaration of war and the conclusion of peace and the requirement of the ministerial countersignature even in the appointment, promotion, and transfer of the highest officers of the provincial army, as well as the officers of the fleet. In a message, the Kaiser declared himself expressly in agreement and said that "after the completion of the war" the German people would have "a right to claim that no right be withheld that would guarantee them a free and happy future." The Bundesrat and a single Chancellor system are retained in these statutes, but the incompatibility between the Bundesrat and Reichstag (Art. 9a) is eliminated.

These constitutional laws came about without opposition that is worth mentioning. They could no more delay the transformation and save the Reich than the establishment of parliamentary government on 21 May 1870 (above p. 329) could have prevented the fall of the Napoleonic Empire. Nevertheless, the phrasing of these statutes is also significant for the Weimar Constitution. For the expression "the Chancellor requires the confidence of the Reichstag for the conduct of his office" is incorporated into Art. 54. While the political and constitutional developments in France and Belgium built the parliamentary system on a "*responsibility*" [338] of the government, the *dependence on the confidence* of the Reichstag became the formula for the parliamentary system in Germany.

After a half century, therefore, all the demands of the German liberal bourgeoisie of 1848 and from the period of the conflict of 1862 to 1866 came to fruition. The great success of Bismarck's policy had held them up for two generations. Now, their demands were realized, but meanwhile the political and social situation was fully changed and their fulfillment acquired a different sense than it would have had fifty years before. The opposing player, a strong monarchy, had fallen, and the success that the German bourgeoisie had achieved with the introduction of parliamentary government in Germany was in a certain sense enjoyed posthumously.

§ 26.

Overview of the Possibilities for the
Formation of the Parliamentary System

I. *The decisive consideration is the agreement between parliament and government.* This involves the elimination of the "dualism" that Robert Mohl had discussed (above p. 313). The agreement can mean something different in concrete reality. It can be a "firm connection," as Hugo Preuß said in the debates on the Weimar Constitution (*Protocol,* p. 300), or only a general harmony of the political tendency in its entirety. Moreover, it can be produced by an express *subordination* of the government to the parliament or of the parliament to the government. All these different, indeed contradictory, political possibilities are designated by the name "parliamentary system."

II. *Means of producing the agreement.* In this regard, the following comes into consideration:

1. Right of the parliament to *address* the government; right of *parliamentary inquiry*; right to demand *the presence of ministers*; right to demand *explanations* of ministers

In general, is not sufficient to produce "parliamentary" government. [339]

2. Indirect opportunities for influence through use of other constitutional authorities, such as (a) the refusal to consent to government's statutory proposal, (b) budget law opportunities, especially the denial of constitutionally necessary consent to the annual budget and denial of the credits demanded by the government, or (c) the right to form investigative committees

Was also not sufficient in Germany to produce parliamentary government.

3. Constitutional determination of the responsibility before the parliament of ministers who countersign acts of the government	Sufficient in France, Belgium, and Italy to produce parliamentary government, but not under the German constitutional monarchy.
4. Constitutional determination of the dependence on the *confidence* of the parliament	The specifications of German parliamentary government: statute of 10/28/1918; Draft I of the Weimar Constitution of 1/3/1919 (§ 65, Triepel, *Quellensammlung*, p. 9); Draft II of 1/20/1919 (§ 70, Triepel, p. 16); Draft III of 2/17/1919 (Art. 75, Triepel, p. 25); Art. 54, Art. 17.

III. *"Instances" of parliamentary responsibility.* Even if responsibility or dependence on the confidence of parliament is established constitutionally, the factual circumstances attached to this responsibility or dependence, especially the duty to resign, may vary greatly. The formal parliamentary decision by which the lack of confidence in the government is expressed always stands between these factual circumstances. That should be designated as the "fall of the cabinet." The word "fall" should be used (even if it is not entirely exact), as in "outbreak of war"[1] or "collapse of the alliance" (casus belli oder casus foederis), to emphasize the political circumstance that results in a particular political outcome.

In such "cases," the following comes into consideration (from the strongest and most explicit case to the weakest indicator):

1. direct removal by parliamentary decision; [340]

2. express request to resign;

3. explicit withholding of a confidence declaration, if this is constitutionally prescribed;

4. express assignment of blame (vote of censure [Schmitt's English]) or general disapproval (in contrast to assignment of blame or disapproval of individual actions);

5. explicit vote of no confidence to which the constitutional duty to resign is bound (Art. 54);

6. explicit vote of no confidence without a constitutional foundation (French or Belgian practice);

7. rejection of a confidence declaration that is demanded by the government;

8. denial of a confidence declaration that is moved by a party;

9. explicit disapproval of a single action or abstention from action by the government;

10. rejection of an approval motion in regard to a single action or abstention from action;

11. denial of a government draft law (presupposes, as in England, that the government exclusively exercises the initiative; otherwise Art. 68);

12. rejection of any government motion;

13. other votes of the parliament that may end in lack of confidence or disapproval, such as the initiation of an investigative committee, demand for the presentation of documents, challenging "the integrity or legality of governmental actions" (cf. *Regierungsvorlage Entwurf I to Art. 34*);

14. *without* special *vote* of the parliament,

(a) new elections (cf. above p. 266)

(b) dissolution of the party coalition hitherto supporting the government (up to now that has been most frequently the case in the contemporary German practice of the parliamentary system).

Moreover, every affair of the cabinet can be made into "a question of the cabinet," and, in this way, the parliament can be compelled to take a position. Vis-à-vis a parliament whose position is not unanimous and cohesive, there is in this situation perhaps a weapon of the government, so that the means of dependence transforms itself into an instrument of independence (cf. above the example of the government of Poincaré, p. 330).

27

The Parliamentary System of the Weimar Constitution

I. In the deliberations of the Weimar National Assembly, a more exact specification of the parliamentary system was intentionally avoided. One wanted, on the one hand, a "firm connection" [341] between parliament and government; on the other hand, states H. Preuß (*Protocol*, p. 300), the relationship should be "elastic." Nevertheless, the aftereffect of the decades-long struggle against the government manifested itself at the outset. Obviously, many understood parliamentary government as the government of a *committee* of the parliamentary majority standing under the political leadership of parliament itself. At the same time, however, Max Weber's views, the sole powerful idea system left for parliamentarianism, were still very influential. They rested on the ideal of democratic *leadership selection*. Following Weber, Art. 56 declares acceptance for the *prime minister system*. "The Chancellor," it reads, "determines the guiding principles of policy." The Chancellor was thought of as a political leader, and yet there was no intention of retaining the one-chancellor system of the Bismarckian constitution, which relied too much on the circumstances of the previous Reich and on the personality of Bismarck and which was hardly still feasible in practical terms. One formed instead a Reich government as a *collegium* under the superior position and chairmanship of the Chancellor such that collegiality is not eliminated. On the other hand, however, the Reich government should be formed such that the collegium itself should not have the privileged position and political leadership (the "determination of the guiding principles of policy"). The collegiality should be a "political collegiality" (see statements of Preuß, Zöpel, and Koch, *Protocol*, p. 301), not a civil servant–type collegium, to the same limited degree that the priority position of the Chancellor means that he would be a superior in a bureaucratic sense. The Chancellor should, indeed, determine the guiding principles of policy and provide the "overall direction," but not intervene himself in the administration. The deputy Koch compared that significantly with the position of a mayor who does not interfere in the details of the business of the magistrate. Moreover, the *presidential* system was also adopted, creating a counterweight to the power of the parliament in the form of the President. In this way, the government is divided between the President and Reich government in the narrower sense (cf. the scheme above on p. 198). With the incorporation of the presidential system, all four subsystems of the parliamentary system in the Weimar Constitution under consideration are potentially recognized. The reciprocal relationship of the

II. Overview

1. Parliamentary system	2. Prime minister (Chancellor) system	3. Cabinet system	4. Presidential system
Definitive political leadership by the majority of parliament can result from:	*Art. 56* The Chancellor determines the main lines of policy.	Can result from:	Political leadership of the President, possible on the basis of:
Art. 54 Dependence on the confidence of the Reichstag.	*Art. 53* The authority to propose legislation by ministers.	*Art. 53* Appointment of the Chancellor and ministers by the President) in conjunction with:	*Art. 41* Election by the entire people.
Art. 50 (with 54) General requirement of countersignature, by contrast, hardly from:	*Art. 55* Chancellor is chair of the government; connected with the position of chair is *Art. 58, 2*, decisive vote in collective sessions.	*Art. 54* Dependence on the confidence of the Reichstag as a practical consequence of coalition governments.	*Art. 25* Dissolution of the Reichstag.
Art. 59 Ministerial and presidential complaint, responsibility according to judicial form.	*Not determined* is that the Chancellor, along with the Minister of Finance, according to the Budget Order of December 1922, can *prevent* the initiation of expenditures or of an official notification in the draft budget even against the majority of the other ministers.	*Art. 57* Collegial decision making, especially during the drafting of legislation.	*Art. 73* Initiation of a referendum, in conjunction with
		Art. 58 The government reaches its decisions by majority vote. The chair decides when there are equal votes.	*Art. 53* Right of appointment and dismissal of the Chancellor and ministers, the latter by the suggestion of the Chancellor.

different possibilities is the actual problem of parliamentary government in the German Reich under the Weimar Constitution. [342]

III. [343] *The practice of the parliamentary systems of the Weimar Constitution.*

1. *The confidence of the Reichstag.* Art. 54, the constitutional foundation of the parliamentary system under the Weimar Constitution, contains *two clauses.* "The Chancellor and the Reich ministers," the first reads, "require the confidence of the Reichstag for the conduct of their office. Each of them must resign if the Reichstag withdraws its confidence through an express vote." Both principles could lead to different practical results, depending on whether the first or the second clause is emphasized.

(a) The "confidence of the Reichstag," of which *the first clause speaks,* is apparently the confidence of the *Reichstag majority.* Certainly, a minority government then would obviously be impermissible. Nevertheless, the party configurations of the current German Reichstag has led to the outcome that the second clause of Art. 54, in contrast to the first, was definitive, although originally it was only conceived of as a logical consequence and specification of the first clause. The "confidence of the Reichstag" was supposed to mean the confidence of the government party, which had the majority in the Reichstag. But there is not such a majority party in the German Reichstag. Even the coalitions are not firm. They group themselves instead in terms of foreign, domestic, cultural, and social policy under entirely different perspectives.

Under this partisan composition of the parliament, the practice of the parliamentary system must base itself on the second clause of Art. 54, according to which a duty to resign only then first obtains if there is an express, so-called "positive" parliamentary vote of no confidence. Occasionally, the government permits the petition expressing the Reichstag's *confidence* in the government to be placed by a government party (Stresemann government in November 1923, Luther government in January 1926). Votes of no confidence have even been issued at the inception of the government with the formula "The Reichstag approves the declaration of the government and expresses confidence in it" (cf. Poetzsch, *Jahrbuch des öffentlichen Rechts* XIII, 1925, pp. 168/69). The constant exercise of such positive confidence votes would have had to eliminate the current practice of minority and coalition governments. By contrast, so long as no positive confidence votes are demanded and the approval of individual declarations or actions (limited declaration of approval) suffices, a minority [344] government is possible and a coalition cabinet can even assume control of the government when there is uncertainty about the coalition. A government can form itself and retain itself in office, which does not have the confidence of the Reichstag (of the Reichstag majority specifically). The Luther government on

28 January 1926 received only 160 votes for the confidence petition, while 150 voted against the petition. So the confidence petition failed explicitly and the remainder abstained. In any case, confidence in the government was not expressed. It would also be conceivable that a pure civil servant ministry would be established under the tacit, even if always rescindable, *tolerance* of the Reichstag majority without receiving a confidence and a no-confidence vote. In this regard, the practice of the German Reichstag has created the concept of *approval*, in which neither a confidence declaration nor a no-confidence declaration is included. The first clause of Art. 54 ("The Chancellor and the Reich ministers require the Reichstag's confidence for the conduct of their office"), therefore, no longer has the meaning that seems to correspond to its literal sense.

(b) But even the meaning of the *second* clause has changed. The use of coalition governments does not produce express votes of no confidence. The government resigns when the party coalition on which it rests comes apart. Cabinet crises, as Poetzsch (*Jahrbuch des öffentlichen Rechts* XIII, 1925, p. 165) aptly remarks, are, in fact, coalition crises. More specifically, they are crises of the party block that replaces the party capable of governing. The extent to which the definitive political decisions fall outside of the public sphere of parliament reveals itself most noticeably in this practice. The original opinion, from which the creators of the Weimar Constitution took their point of departure, was not validated. Art. 54 has acquired an entirely different sense. The first clause, according to which the government requires the confidence of the Reichstag, is not definitive in practical terms. Definitive in this sense, rather, is the second clause, according to which the government resigns after it receives an express vote of no confidence. This second clause, however, is effective only if it is not applied, in particular when it does not *come* to an explicit vote of no confidence.

A further change of the original idea must be noted when the Reichstag majority concludes an explicit vote of no confidence. [345] Such a Reichstag majority expressing its *lack of confidence* is heterogeneous under the Reichstag's current configuration, and it is different for foreign, domestic, cultural, and social policy questions. Consequently, the majority is ultimately always accidental. Certainly, even the coalition majority, which supports the *government*, is not united and is dependent precisely on whether a foreign, domestic, cultural, or social policy goal stands in the foreground. But at least it is a positive majority that is ready for common action, while the majority expressing no confidence in it rests on a mere agreement in the *negative*. It is widely recognized that this latter form of agreement is in most cases useless logically, juristically, and politically, and yet it is a form of agreement containing definitive public law significance. For the first clause of Art. 54, the confidence of the Reichstag is clearly *not* that of the Reichstag majority, and then what still remains of the confidence of the Reichstag? The consequence for the second clause of Art. 54 is that the *vote of no confidence* is always the lack of confidence of the *majority*, because a formal vote is a majority one that is prescribed without regard to how this majority is composed. So the question arises as to whether the composition of this majority and its reason for the expression of no confidence is absolute, and, in any case, it does not matter if the adding together of the denials of confidence merely produces a numerical majority. The motives of the various parties that vote for or against a decision will always be different. Hence, one must fear entering into a practically impossible detailing of reasons, if at some point one generally begins to note the varied grounds for action of the different parties. Indeed, when the motives contradict themselves so openly, and, for example, German nationals and communists vote for a no-confidence petition, the diversity of reasons obviously excludes the necessary and reasonable correlate of a no-confidence decision, in particular the potential for the formation of a new government that will have the necessary confidence. Then the no-confidence decision is an act of pure obstruction. In this instance, there cannot be a duty to resign, in any case not if, at the same time, the dissolution of the Reichstag is ordered.

2. *"The Chancellor determines the guiding principles of policy"* (Attempted establishment of a prime minister, or chancellor, system. Art. 56). [346]

The first question arising in this context is: for whom does the Chancellor determine the guiding principles of policy? Is the determination valid only in the context of Art. 56, specifically only in relation to the cabinet, so that it only says that the Chancellor determines the guiding principles of policy *in regard to the other Reich ministers*; or is it valid generally, which makes it applicable to every other possible form of political leadership and administration that comes into consideration, such as the *Reichstag* and the *President*? According to its original meaning, the provision is valid generally and is the expression of the aspiration to make the Chancellor a political leader responsible to parliament. The Reichstag can topple him through a no-confidence vote and, in this way, block his policy, but not lead and administer policy itself. Also in regard to the President, the Chancellor appears as the leader, because he is responsible to parliament, while the responsibility of the President can only be made valid indirectly, in a judicially formal procedure (Art. 59), or through a petition for removal via an initiative (Art. 43, 2). Leadership and parliamentary responsibility stand in the closest connection. The relationship to the President is certainly not implemented with logical consistency owing to the admixture of elements of the presidential system, as will be shown below. In constitutional terms, the clause "the Chancellor determines the guiding principles of policy" also has the sense of introducing a prime minister system. It should not merely provide an internal, procedural rule for settling business within the cabinet.

The political leadership of the Chancellor, as it is conceived in Art. 56, must not be understood in a servile way as a type of command authority. Determination of the guiding principles of policy means to lead, not command. A superior or subordinate relationship in the sense of civil service law or the normative character of a trial procedure must not be assumed here. It can be that the leader fails, and then a parliamentary majority, the entire cabinet or even the President, actually assumes political leadership. A constitutional regulation can do no more than define formally a few points of a wide area, which then must be considered in formal terms. Between these points [347] there are multiple possibilities and a wide area of discretion, while their connection never produces a closed form. It would be methodologically false to pose questions in this context regarding unconstitutionality, constitutional change, etc. The political development played out differently than the fathers of the Weimar Constitution intended. However, if one determines that today the Chancellor does not lead politically, because another factor is determinative instead, that is not a declaration of unconstitutionality or of a constitutional change. To the same limited degree that a monarchy ceases to be a monarchy because an energetic minister president like Bismarck under Wilhelm I guides the monarch, so a constitutional change cannot be said to occur if, because of substantive or personal reasons, the Chancellor does not realize the political leadership intended for him. The Weimar Constitution, moreover, never systematically implemented the prime minister system, but instead connected it to and mixed it with other systems. All four systems remain open for political practice; none of them is unconstitutional generally. One can take as one's point of departure the political leadership presupposed in Art. 56 and then show how much the current position of the Chancellor deviates from the ideal of a political leader that Max Weber had in mind. But one must not fail to recognize that the legal regime of the Weimar Constitution knows two such leaders, the Chancellor and the President, with the latter borne by the confidence of the entire people. The present regulation is the result of a compromise of all four subsystems of the parliamentary system. It is, moreover, a compromise of still other contradictory aspirations, such as the democratic ideal of a political leader as Max Weber conceived of it, the mistrust that parliamentarians and firmly organized parties, especially the Social Democrats, feel toward the institutions of direct democracy, and, finally, of the liberal Rechtsstaat striving to create a balancing of powers and to retain in a politically influential state president the residue of the constitutional monarchy. With varying strength at different times, *all* these tendencies could become valid politically and allow the literal meaning of the Constitution to appear in an entirely new light without a change in the constitutional text. One cannot speak at all of a change in meaning, because the many different [348] meanings, depending on the circumstances, are contained in the constitutional regime from the beginning. There is no constitutional rule of any earthly constitution that on the basis of norms could regulate the issue of political leadership and administration with the completeness of a trial procedure. The previous overview showed the different possibilities that could reside in the same words such as "responsibility" or "confidence." Such questions permit solution neither in the form of command nor in that of a trial. It would also be foolish to appeal here to a court of law, in order to handle the question of political leadership in a judicially formal way and to determine the guiding principles of policy according to judicial forms.

3. *The cabinet system.* The previous discussions are necessary for the constitutional evaluation of the parliamentary system of the Weimar Constitution, because the present practice of the coalition governments has apparently eliminated the prime minister system. Today, the government does not form itself such that a party leader with a firm program finds a majority for this program and then directs the policy of the Reich. Rather, the government program rests on an agreement of the factions, which commit themselves to participate in the government and pose conditions for their cooperation. "The guiding principles of policy" are the result of such agreements among factions. The "guiding principles of the future government" resulted during the formation of the government in January 1927. A program that was complete and fully transcribed, and which contained the exact provisions on foreign and social policy, etc., was agreed upon by Chancellor Marx of the Center faction, and the other coalition parties, in particular the German National Party, on 24, 25, and 26 January. In this way, the guiding principles of policy are determined before the appointment of the Chancellor and, at his suggestion, of the other Reich ministers. The Chancellor is bound to these guiding principles if he wants to stay in office. A deviation from the guiding principles requires the consent of the coalition parties. A uniting of the government factions comes about in the form of a cabinet vote. Thus, the opinion could be held that Art. 56 and the premier system has been eliminated in practice and that the cabinet as such, in contrast to the Chancellor, has become a higher organ in regard to the guiding principles of policy (Glum, *Die staatsrechtliche Stellung* [349] *der Reichsregierung sowie des Reichskanzlers und des Reichsfinanzministers in der Reichsregierung*, Berlin 1925).

This opinion errs above all because it fails to recognize the degree to which the constitutional regime of the Weimar Constitution facilitates and leaves open all four subsystems of the parliamentary system. The fact that the current practice of the coalition governments corresponds to the cabinet system may be correct, but that in no way signifies an infringement of any constitutional provisions. However, it would be unconstitutional to the same limited degree if a Chancellor were appointed with a firm program that came about without prior negotiation and agreements among the factions. It would also be unconstitutional if this Chancellor first sought a Reichstag majority for his program after his appointment and if the President, in the event that this majority did not come about, dissolved the Reichstag. The prime minister system, together with the other systems, retains its significance, and the constitutional provisions of the Weimar Constitution have no other positive content than that of facilitating an unstable balancing of these four subsystems. There are many different uses of the various applications that all remain in the broad discretion of the constitutional regime, and it is not unconstitutional and not a constitutional change if instead of one possibility another realizes itself. Today, one can only establish that the premier system, which the creators of the Weimar Constitution thought of as ideal, has in the event not come into its own. However, it is not ordained as a constitutional demand (for one cannot command that there be political leaders). The premier system, rather, is *facilitated* as one element of the parliamentary system alongside others. In December 1924, a committed government could have been able to dissolve the Reichstag a second time in order to create a majority capable of partisan government. That would have been fully constitutional. A political leader would have been able to validate the premier system. When that did not happen, it was not unconstitutional. Many a party politician, whom the mechanism of party organization and of agreements among factions has put in the position of the Chancellor, may have no interest at all in leading politically. He wants to protect his party from political tremors and does not think of assuming the risk of political activity, which remains constantly [350] linked with true leadership. Instead of the premier system, other possibilities of the parliamentary systems come into play.

4. *The presidential system.* The position of the President is based on the monarchical element, which in a modern Rechtsstaat constitution is used for the construction of a counterpoise between the legislative and executive branches (above p. 290). Together with the Rechtsstaat construction of a balance, there were also ideas of a direct democracy at work in the introduction of the presidential system. The President is elected by the entire German people. His legal authority to dissolve the Reichstag (Art. 25) or, in opposition to the Reichstag's statutory decision, to order a referendum (Art. 73), provides him the opportunity to direct an "appeal to the people" and to produce a direct connection with the enfranchised state citizens

against the parliament. The "people" is the higher, decisive third party, both in regard to the parliament as well as to the government, and the President has a direct connection with the people. Ideally, he is thought of as a man who beyond the limits and the framework of party organizations and party bureaucracy unites in himself the trust of the entire people, not as a party man, but as trustee of the *entire* people. A presidential election, which really does justice to this sense of the constitutional provision, would be more significant than any of the many elections in a democratic state. It would be a marvelous acclamation of the German people and would have the full irresistibility that accrues to such acclamations in a democracy. But what sense and purpose could such a justified position of the President have other than that of political leadership? If the confidence of the entire people genuinely unifies itself in an individual man, then he certainly cannot remain insignificant politically, hold celebratory speeches, and set his name under foreign decisions. It is a small step, therefore, and corresponds thoroughly to the basic ideas of Art. 41, to say that the President is a political leader. Even if their exercise remains tied to the countersignature of a minister, the important government powers that he receives under the constitution, high command of the army, issuing measures during the state of exception, right of pardon, etc., also prove that a nonpolitical office is not [351] at issue here. The consequence is that under the Weimar Constitution *two* political leaders come into play, the Chancellor and the President. The former defines the guiding principles of policy, but only because he holds the confidence of the Reichstag, in other words, of a shifting and unreliable coalition. The President, by contrast, has the confidence of the entire people not mediated by the medium of a parliament splintered into parties. This confidence, rather, is directly united in his person. The fact that a people should have two political leaders in such manner can lead to dangerous political conflicts, if both are genuinely political leaders and do not have the same political orientation. That would be a dualism that could have worse consequences than the dualism of the constitutional monarchy. One cannot just let the conflicts that can then result be decided simply by the people, because that would lead in effect to an ongoing practice of plebiscites, which is just as undemocratic as it is impossible. For the people elects its leaders so that they lead, not to continuously resolve the problems of and differences of opinion among the leaders themselves.

If, however, the President is not the leader, but instead the "objective" man as a nonpartisan, neutral arbiter, then he is this as bearer of a neutral authority, of a *pouvoir neutre*, a mediating organ, a pouvoir modérateur, a referee, who does not decide. He brings the parties together, and through the prestige and confidence he finds among the parties, he creates an atmosphere of understanding. President Ebert, who still was not elected by the entire German people, fulfilled this task in important cases, certainly most clearly in the summer of 1922 during the conflict between Bavaria and the Reich. Otherwise, according to its nature, this activity has something unnoticeable and even invisible about it and presupposes that the President is able to free himself from the claims of a party. A monarch who assumes his position by way of hereditary succession as a member of an old, securely held dynasty can in general easily hold a neutral position without it degenerating into political insignificance. An elected president, by contrast, is really elected by the entire people. Because the entire people are necessarily a political entity, he will be a politician in an especially decisive and intensive sense, [352] a political leader and not merely the neutral third. The other possibility is he is elected by a party coalition on the basis of party agreements. Then he cannot easily exercise the special function of the neutral organ. For the party organizations will make the President either a reliable party follower or a harmless person, who does not stand in the way. The neutral, mediating, refereeing activity he exercises loses its value and its effect. In this instance, he has neither the power of political decision nor a genuine neutral authority; he is, rather, still only an annex of the parliament or of the government. If that in fact occurs, one cannot also term it unconstitutional, for even this possibility remains completely open under the constitutional regime of the Weimar Constitution. The example of the present President Hindenburg in no way proves that a President elected by the people necessarily evades the consequences of the partisan organization of the electorate. For the prestige and the confidence President Hindenburg finds among the largest part of the German people beyond party boundaries still stems from traditions and impressions formed *prior* to the present constitutional condition. This prestige and confidence arose in the war and during the collapse. In times of normal parliamentary party politics, by contrast, each person engaged in the public sphere of politics is committed very quickly in partisan terms.

Under the Weimar Constitution, the President can exercise his grants of authority only with the cooperation of the government, because he is bound to the countersignature of the Chancellor or of the ministers (Art. 50). When the President and the government agree, the dualism of the executive is eliminated, and a strong government stands opposite the Reichstag. This is still the case whether the President adapts himself to the government, the government allows itself to be led by the President, or, ultimately, a common action based on shared understandings occurs. In a conflict between the President and the Reichstag, there remain various opportunities for an "appeal to the people," such as dissolving the Reichstag, ordering a referendum, and petitioning the Reichstag for removal of the President. These possibilities for a popular appeal [353] provide genuine content to all constitutional provisions concerning the government and its relationship to the parliament, so these provisions may only be considered in the context of the entire system, not in isolation from it. Today, the dissolution authority and the type of its practical use is decisive both for the parliamentary system in general as well as for whichever subsystem of the system gains validity in the reality of the political life.

28

Dissolution of Parliament

The fulcrum of the current parliamentary system is the dissolution authority. This is the case generally and for the regime of the Weimar Constitution in particular.

I. *Types of dissolution.* The dissolution of parliament has various meanings in different constitutional systems.

1. *The Monarch's dissolution authority.* In a nonparliamentary monarchy, the dissolution of the parliament mostly serves the purpose of preserving the advantage of the monarchical government against the popular assembly, rendering the dissolution authority into a weapon directed against the parliament. The exercise of the dissolution authority usually presupposes a conflict. But the dissolution is not an appeal to the people, and the new election is not a conclusive decision, because the king can often arbitrarily repeat the dissolution. The history of the Prussian conflict between the royal government and Prussian Land parliament between 1862 and 1866, with its multiple dissolutions of the Prussian Land parliament, contains the most famous example of this monarchical dissolution authority. The impression made by this process was very strong. Its aftereffect is still discernible in the Weimar National Assembly. This is evident in the explicit addition to Art. 25 that stipulates that the President's dissolution authority can, "however, only be exercised once for the same reason." "The sense of the provision (for the same reason)," according to Hugo Preuß, "is certainly clear. The President and the government should not have the opportunity to attempt, by repeated dissolution for the same reason—*I remember the period of conflict*—to gradually wear down the Reichstag and the electorate" [354] (*Protocol*, p. 233). Obviously with this "conflict" in mind, Preuß takes as his point of departure the fact that the dissolution of the Reichstag always means a conflict and, consequently, is something abnormal, indeed, something dubious and reminiscent of a coup d'état. That may apply to the German-style constitutional monarchy, but it does not in any case apply to the parliamentary system of a democratic republic.

2. *The presidential dissolution authority.* According to Art. 25, "The President can dissolve the Reichstag."

In this context, the dissolution authority is a necessary and normal means of achieving balance and of bringing about the democratic appeal to the people. The Art. 25 requirement that the President may dissolve the Reichstag "only once for the same reason" only applies when the dissolution stems from a genuine conflict, rests on the clear opposition of two different opinions, and the people approves either the standpoint of the Reichstag or that of the government (with the President), thereby deciding the conflict. The appeal to the people is conclusive, and it is self-evident that it cannot be repeated for the same reason, because of the same difference of opinion, in other words. That presupposes, however, that there is a genuine conflict.

The dissolution authority of the president under the French Republic rests on Art. 5 of the Constitutional Law of 25 February 1875, according to which the president of the Republic, in agreement with the Senate, can dissolve the Chamber of Deputies before the expiration of the electoral period. Although since 1877 the dissolution authority became impractical (above p. 29), this example of the presidential dissolution authority is especially instructive for the substantive content of constitutional theory. It stems from Prévost-Paradol's typically liberal Rechtsstaat ideas and constructions and is understandable only in the context of these ideas about the mixing and rendering relative of political form elements that prompted the renewal of monarchical organizational forms (above p. 291).

3. *The ministerial dissolution authority.* The essence of the ministerial dissolution authority is that a parliamentary government, whether it is the prime minister or the cabinet, can order an "appeal to the people" when the majority in parliament no longer agrees with it. Through the dissolution of parliament and the calling of new elections, it can attempt to achieve a new majority. A conflict between parliamentary majority and minister is presupposed, a conflict that the people [355] can resolve conclusively through the new election. The result is the dissolution may not be repeated because of the same conflict. The new election decides the issue. This ministerial dissolution developed as a special case especially clearly in the English parliamentary practice, although the ministry as such does not have its own formal dissolution authority. Instead, the dissolution occurs formally through an order of the head of state, which in England requires a royal decree.

4. *Self-dissolution of parliament.* Self-dissolution developed as an additional case of parliamentary dissolution, which today is recognized above all in the Land constitutions (for example, Art. 14 of the Prussian constitution of 1920 and §31 of the Bavarian constitution of 1919). In this case, the limitation regarding the one-time nature and the occasion for calling for a dissolution is senseless, for any parliament can obviously dissolve itself only once.

5. *Dissolution due to popular initiative.* A final form of dissolution of parliament, that stemming from a popular initiative, is also recognized today in the German Land constitutions (for example, Art. 14 of the Prussian constitution and § 30 of the Bavarian constitution), but it does not come into consideration for the Reich Constitution.

6. Peculiar cases are the consent of a senate (above p. 300) and dissolution by special "committee" (Art. 14 of the Prussian constitution), among others.

II. *The President's dissolution authority.*

1. The Weimar Constitution does not recognize a form of Reichstag dissolution other than one ordered by the President (Art. 25). In fact, however, the exercise of this formal dissolution authority of the President can serve different types of parliamentary dissolution. Normally, a Reichstag dissolution ordered by the President is a presidential dissolution not only in terms of form, but it is also presidential in terms of the circumstance under which it occurs. For it serves the goal of protecting the President's independent position vis-à-vis the Reichstag and, above all, of resolving a pending conflict between a Reichstag majority and the President by means of an appeal to the people. At the same time, however, a Reichstag dissolution that is formally presidential, and yet that is also ministerial according to circumstances, is especially important. In this case, the dissolution ordered by the President bolsters the government's independence and constitutes a limitation of the principle that the government is dependent on the transitory Reichstag majority. A self-dissolution [356] of the Reichstag could even occur in the form of a presidential dissolution, if the Reichstag itself desires the dissolution. Ultimately, it would still be conceivable that by dissolving the Reichstag, the President is conforming to the will of a minority and that something which under the circumstances would be the dissolution of parliament by popular initiative also assumes the form of the presidential dissolution. The distinction of the different types of dissolution remains of great significance, even if nothing other than the form of the presidential dissolution is an option and the President cannot be compelled to order the dissolution against his will.

2. The fact that the President requires the countersignature of the Chancellor or of the responsible minister for all his official actions, even the dissolution of the Reichstag according to Art. 50, raises another question regarding the manner in which both types of dissolution that are most important in practical terms, the presidential and ministerial forms, regulate themselves. For only the President can order the dissolution of the Reichstag, and he can do so only with the countersignature of the Chancellor. This means that the two independent and distinct types of dissolution are inseparably linked with one another. And if the President is unable to obtain a ministerial dissolution or the Chancellor cannot gain a presidential dissolution, then neither type of dissolution can become effective.

Previous cases: The presidential decree of 13 March 1924 (*Reichgesetzesblatt* I, p. 173), which dissolved the Reichstag "after the government determined that the demand, issued on the basis of the Enabling Acts of 13 October and 8 December 1923 allowing the decrees it designated as a matter of life and death at the time to stand, did not receive the consent of the Reichstag." Furthermore, the President's decree of 20 October 1924: "Parliamentary difficulties," it reads, "render impossible the retention of the present government and, at the same time, make impossible the formation of a new government on the basis of the previously pursued domestic and foreign policy."

Both types of dissolution are part of the parliamentary system under the Weimar Constitution. Difficulties can arise that are resolvable only by recognizing in proper significance the dependence on the confidence of the Reichstag. The government requires the confidence of the Reichstag in the conduct of its office (Art. 54), but the Chancellor and, at his suggestion, the ministers are named by the President (Art. 53). It was shown above that Art. 54 obtained its actual content [357] from the fact that the explicit vote of no confidence represents the fall of the cabinet. Consequently, there can be a government that conducts its office without having the confidence of the majority of the Reichstag. Every minority government is in this position. Now, if the President names a Chancellor and orders the dissolution of the Reichstag under the Chancellor's countersignature, there is no violation of Art. 54, because otherwise every minority government would also represent such a violation. That ought to be indisputable given the practice of government formation in the German Reich up to now.

The more difficult question is this: if there is an express vote of no confidence by the Reichstag, the duty to resign according to the text of Art. 54.2 is undoubtedly justified. In this case, the *presidential* dissolution occurs such that the previous cabinet steps down, the President appoints a new cabinet, and dissolves the Reichstag with the cabinet's countersignature, before an explicit, new no-confidence vote can be achieved. The *ministerial* dissolution, by contrast, seems in this case to be entirely precluded, although it comes especially into consideration precisely for this case. Given the formalistic biases of German constitutional law, one will probably insist on the text of Art. 54 and deny the government the possibility of appealing to the people in regard to an explicit no-confidence vote. However, one must at least distinguish the type of majority that withholds its trust through a no-confidence vote on the government. If it is a firm majority, which is ready to form the government with recognizable political guidelines itself, it would certainly not be unreasonable, even if in no way pressing, to reject the ministerial dissolution, although the ministerial right of dissolution conforms most closely to precisely this case. If, however, the majority that formulated the vote of no confidence is not a unified majority and the political motives of the vote are recognizably contradictory, as with a no-confidence vote carried by the votes of the reactionary nationalists, the communists, and the German People's Party, for example, it would be nonsensical to declare the ministerial dissolution impermissible and to demand that the President first not dissolve the Reichstag before he formed a [358] new government, in other words, to actually demand that the Reichstag's inability or unwillingness to govern be treated as a type of constitutionally protected legal entitlement.

3. In interpreting the constitutional provisions on the parliamentary system of the current German Reich as well as in evaluating the legal authority for dissolution under the Weimar Constitution, the connection of both institutions must be taken into account, and the different constitutional provisions must not be isolated from one another and then emphasized in an excessive and exclusive manner. All these provisions extend themselves, more precisely, into a pliable system that holds open the most diverse possibilities. The President's dissolution authority stands at the center of this system as a normal institution that supports the entire system and modifies all other constitutional provisions, an institution with the goal of permitting the will of the people to decide in opposition to a parliamentary majority. In its decision of 21 April 1925 (*Archiv des öffentlichen Rechts*, vol. 9, 1925, p. 224ff.), the Staatsgerichtshof of Oldenburg considered the case of a dissolution of the Land parliament after the rejection of a confidence declaration and emphasized this democratic perspective that "precisely through the dissolution the people come into the position of validating their will in the conflict." The reporter in the Constitutional Committee of the Weimar National Assembly, Dr. Ablaß, recognized and expressed the same thought very clearly (*Protocol*, p. 233). "This right," he argued, "(in particular, the President's dissolution authority) undoubtedly extends very far, but under all circumstances we must approve it. When the President proceeds with the well-founded conviction that the Reichstag is on the wrong path with its decisions or contradicts the people's sensibilities, he must have the opportunity of appealing to the people against the Reichstag. That is democratic, and a good democrat has no defense against the appeal to the people." In terms of the spirit of the provision, the same holds for the politically especially important case of a dissolution instituted by the President, yet one that is a ministerial dissolution in substantive terms. For then the dissolution has precisely the purpose of giving to a government that has lost the majority in parliament the possibility of bringing about the decision of the voters through a new election and thus allowing the majority of the enfranchised voters to decide, [359] in contrast to a mere parliamentary majority with its accidental and shifting factional groupings. The political and public law purpose of the ministerial dissolution, which is nevertheless part of the system of the Weimar Constitution, would diminish if one intended to interpret Art. 54 without regard to Art. 25 and would insist that the current government is nothing more than the automatically changing component of factional groupings that shift daily. I would therefore assume that a government deprived of confidence through the explicit no-confidence vote by the Reichstag can even countersign the order of the President through

which this Reichstag is being dissolved. There is, of course, the duty to resign grounded in Art. 54. In that type of case, however, one must await the decision of the people on the composition of the Reichstag. The duty to resign then occurs when the new election has not provided a Reichstag majority for the government and the newly constituted Reichstag withdraws its confidence from the government. [360]

PART IV
CONSTITUTIONAL THEORY OF THE FEDERATION

§ 29.

Fundamental Concepts of a Constitutional Theory of the Federation

I. [363] *Overview of the types of interstate relations and connections.*

1. There are relations between states wherever political unities exist alongside one another peacefully or hostilely. International law is the sum of customary or conventionally recognized rules for these relations of mere coexistence. The compatibility of states sharing only international legal relations still does not establish a *connection* between these states. When speaking of "the" international law as a preponderance of rules that in fact varies from case to case and from relation to relation, and yet that establishes an "international legal community" or a "family of nations," one is designating only the logical cognate of these relations of coexistence. If one also speaks of an "international legal order," one may understand the concept of order not as a closed system of norms, but rather as something that is present existentially. This international legal community is not a contract, nor is it based on a contract. It is also not an alliance and still less a federation. It does not have a constitution in the distinctive sense. It is, instead, the reflex of the politically plural universe, which expresses itself in individual, generally recognized rules and considerations. In other words, it is a pluralistic universe understood as a multitude of political unities that exist alongside one another.

One can portray general and abstract norms as the "constitution" of the international legal community to the same limited degree that one can find the "constitution" of a family in general norms such as that "you should honor your father and mother" or "love thy neighbor." In particular, it is a fruitless endeavor to portray general principles like "right before might" or the sanctity of contracts as the constitution of the international legal community and to falsely ascribe the character of a genuine federation to the general "international legal community." The principle *pacta sunt servanda*, which A. Verdroß presented as the "constitution" of the international legal community, is the least appropriate of all principles for constituting a community and order that extends beyond mere relations of coexistence. In terms of international law, the contract concluded by the states is valid, but not the more abstract second principle [364] that contracts are valid, a principle that extends beyond the concrete content of the contract. That would be a fictional doubling of norms, which is logically false and without practical value. For further critique of this principle, cf. above p. 69.

A large part of the misunderstandings and errors that dominate the fundamental deliberations of international law today are explained by the fact that the word "international" is ambiguous and can designate relations that are opposed politically to one another. The German manner of expression makes possible a clear distinction between *interstate* and *international*, and intellectual integrity requires that this distinction be honored. In contrast to "international," "interstate" means that states as political unities marked off from the outside by firm boundaries, impenetrable, "impermeable," stand opposed to one another and alone bear the decision over the question of its own existence ("sovereign" means precisely that a foreigner does not decide the question of political existence). "International," by contrast, designates (in the proper German manner of expression) the simultaneous elimination and subsumption of national distinctions, a penetration and connection that extends beyond state boundaries. The Roman Catholic Church is an international, not an interstate organization; international unions, international cartels, etc., are international in the same degree that they are not interstate.

This distinction, which is self-evident and has been widely recognized for a long time (cf. for example, G. Jellinek, *Allgemeine Staatslehre*, p. 116, inter alia), is often overlooked even in the legal scholarship on the League of Nations. The League of Nations is an interstate organization, while pacifism is an international movement. When one continues to confuse pacifism with a federation of peoples (in the vague sense of peace and understanding among peoples), on the one hand, and federation of peoples with the Geneva "Société des Nations," on the other, one can easily draw imaginary consequences. The essay by Arthur Wegner, "Kriminelles Unrecht, Staatsunrecht und Völkerrecht" (*Hamburgische Schriften zur gesamten Strafrechtswissenschaft*, Hamburg 1925, pp. 11, 78), considers the question of whether a report to a foreign government stipulating that behavior of one's own government or state officials is contrary to international law is a criminal offense, such as treason against one's land. "Certainly," Wegner argues, "each has the right to resist governmental injustice. But according to our cultural understanding, the means of this resistance is not the appeal abroad, but rather the appeal to one's own people." On p. 11, he writes that in terms of criminal law, a state secret contrary to international law could exist (that may not be "betrayed"), much like the employer may not communicate a business secret to the competitor. This discussion (in which the state as the political unity of one's own people is reduced to a "trade organization") concludes with the statement: "But if, for example (literally: for example), the federation of peoples has been notified, the decision is still more difficult." More precisely, this is the case because today thousands oscillate between "federation of peoples and fatherland." This German criminal law expert apparently considers Geneva an analogue of Moscow and makes an "international" organization out of an interstate one.

2. Among the contractually regulated *individual relationships* for the advancement of individual goals of the state, there are numerous different types of international law contracts, such as trade and delivery contracts, contractual connections for the ongoing regulation of such individual goals, unions such as postal association contracts, customs and trade unions, etc. This type of contractual relation or connection is characterized by the fact that it establishes obligatory commitments with a definable content, which are often very important, but it does not directly entail the political existence of the state as such in its totality. [365] It is never a connection that is a matter of life and death.

It can be that economic or other connections become significant, but they are first decisive when they involve the political existence of the state. That economic connections still do not by themselves constitute a community of political existence is evident in the example of coin and currency unions. Such a "union" cannot prevent the currency of the individual member Lands and states of the union from developing differently, as the fate of the Latin union of 23 December 1865 and the Scandinavian coin union of 27 May 1873 and 16 October 1875 proves. If an economic connection like that of a customs union would result in a political community, the political element would simply become decisive and an additional connection involving the existence of the state would occur in lieu of the contractually regulated individual relations.

3. *Confederation* (alliance) is a contractual relation that obligates a state to go to *war* in a particular instance. Because the war takes hold of the state as a whole in its political existence and is the last and decisive expression of the distinctively political element, that is to say of the friend/enemy grouping, this obligation has a special character and distinguishes itself from any other obligation, however valuable and important the contractual regulations or connections are. Nevertheless, the political status of a state and its constitution is otherwise not changed through the conclusion of this confederation. The decision on the *jus belli* is contractually bound with respect to a particular case, but the *jus belli* itself is not given up and turned over to a third party. Through the confederation contract, the exercise and use of this right is contractually determined. It is part of the political existence of a state that it decides itself the question of its political existence. A state that renounces conclusively its right to self-defense or transfers this right to another state or to another organ does not have its own political existence. The issue is not how one designates the different "half-sovereign" intermediary formations and whether because of diverse considerations one still typically speaks of the state in this instance. In any case, it inheres in the political existence of a state that it retains the possibility of its own decision about the defense of its own existence. Consequently, the conclusion of a confederation signifies a foreign political act, of which only a politically existing state is capable. Yet it does not signify a constitutional change, but rather only the exercise of an authority presupposed explicitly or implicitly in each state constitution. [366]

It can be ordained constitutionally that the conclusion of confederations is prohibited or is submitted to a particular procedure. The Weimar Constitution provides in Art. 45, 3: "Confederations . . . require the consent of the Reichstag." This means that the concrete individual confederation contract is not a constitutional change. It is, rather, only the realization of a constitutionally provided possibility and the result of external political independence. The form of the confederation, however, can be used for the purpose of changing the status of a state concluding the contract and of forcing upon it a permanent renunciation of the independent decision on its ius belli. The form of the confederation contract in fact facilitates the establishment of a protectorate relationship (above § 7, p. 73).

4. The *federation* is a permanent association that rests on a free agreement and that serves the common goal of the political self-preservation of

all federation members, through which the comprehensive status of each individual federation member in political terms is changed in regard to the common goal.

The distinguishing marks and consequences of this federation concept should be developed without regard to the distinction of a state federation and federal state. The theoretical treatment of the federation problem given until now in Germany has suffered from the fact that it is dominated entirely by the interest in a juxtaposition of a federation of states (put concretely, the German Federation of 1815) with the federal state (in particular the German Reich of 1871) and searches now for the simplest possible antithesis for this distinction. The German public law textbooks of Laband and Meyer-Anschütz are typical of this tendency. They present seemingly clear and striking alternatives, yet ones that are in fact logically peculiar or impossible. The federation of states should be a pure international law relationship, in contrast to a federal state, which is an unadulterated public law subject. The one rests on an international law *contract*, the other has a public law *constitution*; the one is a legal relationship, the other a legal subject, etc. With such schematic and convenient formulas, the common fundamental concept of the entire problem is left out of account and some detail that is interesting for the political situation is raised to the status of a distinguishing conceptual marker. It is understandable and explicable historically that after the year 1871 the public law theory of the German Reich rendered the distinction of this Reich in regard to the earlier German Federation of 1815 in such simplistic slogans and with that the general federal problem seemed resolved. Today, this simple method is no longer possible.

The aftereffect of this epoch is still very strong. The entrance of Germany into the League of Nations and the public law questions that result from this for the interpretation of Art. 45 were never able to awaken scholarly interest in the concept of the "federation." Characteristic of this tendency is the essay by F. Schiller, *Archiv des öffentlichen Rechts*, new series, vol. 11, 1926, p. 41ff., which wants to treat the question of the entrance of Germany into the League of Nations as a pure "legal question" and ignores the concept "federation." In this essay, he dismisses my attempt at a discussion of the issue ("Die Kernfrage des Völkerbundes," Berlin 1926) with the linguistic sleight of hand that it involves a "nonpolitical" investigation. Scholars are not at all aware of the fundamental question in constitutional theory terms (for a genuine federation contract is an act of the constitution-making power).

The federation establishes a new *status* for each member. The entry into a federation signifies a change of the new member's *constitution*. Even if the wording of not a single [367] constitutional provision is changed, it is far more important that the constitution in the positive sense, in other words, the concrete content of the fundamental political decisions on the entire manner of existence of the state, is nevertheless essentially changed. The federation contract, therefore, is an agreement of a special type. It is a free contract insofar as it is dependent on the will of the member to enter the federation. This means it is free in regard to its conclusion. Yet it is *not a* free contract in the sense of one that is freely promulgated and that only regulates definable individual relations. More precisely, by belonging to the federation, a state is integrated into a politically comprehensive system. The federation agreement is an interstate status contract.

II. Consequences of the conceptual definition of the federation.

1. The federation comprises every member state in its total existence as a political unity and incorporates it as an entirety into a politically existing connection. This means that not only individual linkages stem from the federation agreement. When in the federal constitution the "competence" of the federation is limited and the federation should be competent only for matters that are expressly enumerated (for example, § 5 of the Frankfurt constitution of 1849), that involves the one technical question of the jurisdictional presumption and regulates the organizational execution of the division of jurisdiction inside the existing federation. It does not involve the entirely different question of the fundamental *presuppositions* of the federation and the problem of sovereignty. On this problem, see III below.

2. The federation contract aims to establish a *permanent order*, not just a provisional regulation. That also follows from the concept of *status* because a merely provisional individual regulation that can be promulgated and defined cannot establish status. So every federation is an "eternal" one, in other words, a federation counted on for the *long term*.

The historical examples of federation contracts, therefore, always speak of this duration in any of their formulations. The German Federation Acts of 1815 state that the members "unite" themselves into a "continuing federation." The Vienna Concluding Acts of 1820 should "render indissoluble the bond that commits the entirety of Germany in solidarity and peace," and Art. V of this concluding act provides that "the federation is founded as an indissoluble association, and hence no member is free to leave it." The introduction of the constitution of the North German Federation of 26 July 1867 speaks of an "eternal federation," just as the constitution of the German Reich of 16 April 1871 says that the king of Prussia, in the name of the North German Federation, and the rulers of the southern German states are consummating an "eternal federation.".

Even in the doctrine of the great state theorists, duration is emphasized as an essential characteristic of the federation. This is best of all clear in Pufendorf, *De Iure Naturae et Gentium*, VII, c. 5, § 18. [368]

3. The federation agreement is a contract of a particular type, a constitutional contract specifically. Its conclusion is an act of the constitution-making power. Its content is simultaneously the content of the federation constitution (above p. 62f.) and a *component of the constitution of each member state.*

For this reason, numerous states of the German Federation of 1815 placed at the forefront of their constitution the clause that they form a component of the federation. Take, for example, the Grand Duchy of Baden (constitution of 22 August 1818, §1), which provides that "the Grand Duchy forms a component of the German Federation." It is exactly the same with the Grand Duchy of Hesse, constitution of 17 December 1820, § 1; the Kingdom of Saxony, constitution of 4 September 1831, § 1; and especially extensively and pointedly the Kingdom of Württemberg, constitution of 25 September 1819, § 3, which states that "the Kingdom of Württemberg is part of the German Federation, so all organic decisions of the Federation Assembly that involve the constitutional relations of Germany or the general relations of German state citizens also have binding force for Württemberg." "However," it continues, "in regard to the means for fulfillment of the commitments hereby established, the constitution provides for the participation of the estates." When there are such clauses in Land constitutions of the contemporary German Reich under the Weimar Constitution (for example, Art. 1 of the Prussian constitution of 30 November 1920, which provides that Prussia is a republic and member of the German Reich), that does not have the same significance in this context, because the current German Reich is no longer a federation. On this, compare below p. 388f.

4. The federation aims at the preservation of the political existence of all members in the framework of the federation. The consequence is that the federation constitution unconditionally contains a *guarantee* of the political existence of every federation member, even if it does not explicitly speak of it. More specifically, existence is guaranteed to each individual member in regard to all others, and of all members in regard to every individual member and all together. *Within* the federation the political *status quo* in the sense of political existence must also be guaranteed. Normally, the guarantee of territorial integrity is part of this. No federation member may have a part of its area taken without its consent, much less can its political existence be at all eliminated. That is not to say that every guarantee of political existence or of territorial integrity already signifies a federation agreement. But conversely, this guarantee of existence and territorial integrity certainly inheres in every federation. The guarantee stems from both the goal of self-preservation and the concept of duration that is essential to the federation.

5. *Externally*, the federation protects its members against the danger of war and against every attack. *Internally*, the federation necessarily signifies [369] enduring *pacification*, as the traditional federation agreements already state since the eleventh century, a "civil peace." The "unconditional duty of the individual states is to resolve each and every state dispute only by legal means that are established or permitted (in the federal constitution specifically)." This principle of Haenel regarding Art. 76, para. 1, of Bismarck's Reich Constitution (Staatsrecht, p. 577) is valid within every federation without regard to the distinction between state federation and federal state and is a product of the peace inside the federation that is essential to the federation.

The result is that the essential change of the total status of the federation members affects their *jus belli*. Through the federation agreement, the exercise of this ius belli is not contractually determined for a particular case, for the casus foederis, as in a confederation agreement. Rather, within the federation self-help is renounced on an enduring basis. War may no longer take place within the federation and between federation members. Within the federation, as long as the federation exists, only a federation *enforcement action* of the entire federation against a member is possible. If there is war, then the federation no longer exists in the same form.

The German Federation of 1815 was dissolved in 1866 by the war between Prussia and Austria. On 28 May 1866, the Austrian government broke off negotiations with Prussia, and Prussian troops under Manteuffel marched into Holstein on 10 June 1866. Austria requested the *mobilization* of federation troops (except for the Prussian corps) in the Bundestag on 11 June, a petition that Prussia declared contrary to the federation, but that was nonetheless accepted on 14 June 1866. Regardless of one's view on the "question of guilt," the Prussian declaration of 14 June 1866, which was issued after the acceptance of the Austrian petition (printed in Nouveau Recueil général de traités, XVIII, p. 310ff., and Strupp, Documents, I, p. 324ff.) contains an interesting discussion of the question as to what a mobilization and a war inside a federation means:

> In regard to federation members, federation law recognizes only an enforcement procedure, for which particular forms and prerequisites are prescribed. The establishment of a federation army against a federation member on the basis of the federation war constitution is just as foreign to this constitution as any intervention of the federation assembly against a federation government outside of the norms of the enforcement procedure. After Prussia's confidence in the protection that the federation had ensured to each of its members had been deeply shaken by the circumstance that the most powerful member of the federation had armed for the purpose of self-help against Prussia, the royal government must recognize that external and internal security, which is the primary goal of the federation according to Article II of the Federation Acts, is already endangered to the highest degree.
>
> Because of *the declaration of war against a federation member, which is precluded under federation law*, the royal cabinet looks upon the rupture of the federation as complete.

The critique that Haenel, "Vertragsmäßige Elemente der Reichsverfassung," *Studien I*, 1873, applied to the Prussian interpretation (it is "nullo jure justificabilis") overlooks the fundamental problem of every federation. [370]

If the federation is not dissolved even though there is war, then that is only possible when one of the disputing parties succeeds in portraying its war as a mere federation enforcement action, as the outcome of the United States war of secession of 1861–1865 enabled the Northern states to do in regard to the Southern states, and as Austria would have done in 1866 if Prussia had suffered a defeat. For the argument that a war between federation members ends the federation, see Pufendorff, *De Iure Naturae et Gentium*, VII, c. 5, § 21.

6. There is no *federation without involvement of the federation* in the affairs of the member states. Because the federation has a political existence, it must have a *right of supervision*. It must also be able to decide on the means for the maintenance, preservation, and security of the federation and, if necessary, to intervene.

7. Every federation can wage war as such and has a *jus belli*. There is *no federation without the possibility of a federation war*. Nevertheless, it is

another question in itself whether the federation has an *exclusive* ius belli *externally*, that is, in regard to nonmembers. The federation protects its members against attacks from abroad. But individual members need not be deprived of the possibility of conducting war against nonmembers. As a factual and practical matter, the war of a member against a nonmember can easily threaten the federation. Nonetheless, the renunciation of the ius belli in regard to a nonmember does not at all follow from the nature of the federation. Conversely, it follows from the nature of the political existence of the individual members that a right to self-help and to war is only being given up insofar as it is conditioned by membership in the federation.

III. The legal and political *antimonies of the federation* and their elimination through the requirement of *homogeneity*.

1. *The antimonies.* The first antimony is (a) the federation aims at self-preservation, in particular the maintenance of the political independence of every member. On the other hand, the membership in the federation entails a lessening of this independence, for it leads to a renunciation of the ius belli, the essential means of self-preservation, and to the *renunciation of self-help.* This antimony involves the *right of self-preservation* of each federation member.

The second antimony is (b) the federation member seeks to preserve its political independence through the federation and to guarantee its self-determination. *On the other hand*, in the interest of the security of the federation, a federation cannot ignore the domestic affairs of its members. Every federation leads to *interventions*. [371] Any genuine federation enforcement action is interference in domestic affairs, which subsumes the fully independent self-determination of the affected state to the federation and which eliminates its enclosed character and external impenetrability, its "impermeability." This antimony involves the *right of self-determination* of every single federation member.

The third (most general) antimony is (c) every federation, independent of the distinction between a state federation or federal state, has a collective will and political existence. In this way, it distinguishes itself from an alliance. Consequently, existing alongside one another in every federation are two types of political existence: the collective existence of the federation and the individual existence of the federation members. Both types of political existence must continue to coexist as long as a federation is to remain in place. The collective existence of the federation must not subsume the individual existence of the member states, nor can the existence of the member states subsume that of the federation. The member states are not simply subordinated, subjects of the federation, nor is the federation subordinated and subject to them. The federation exists only in this existential connection and in this balance. From both directions, various levels of association are possible, the most extreme case of which always leads to the fact that either the federation dissolves itself and only individual states still exist or the individual states cease to exist, and there remains only a single state. The essence of the federation resides in a dualism of political existence, in a connection between federalist togetherness and political unity, on the one hand, and the persistence of a majority, a pluralism of individual political unities, on the other. Such an intermediary condition necessarily leads to many conflicts, which must be decided.

The question of sovereignty, however, is the decision on an existential conflict. There are several methods for the peaceful resolution and mediation of disputes, but if the circumstances of the case demand a *decision*, and only this case is at issue here, the political conflict cannot be resolved in a judicial procedure. For this does not involve normative elements and statutory interpretations. As soon as the case is regulated by a conclusive, recognized norm, it does not simply lead to a genuine conflict. But if that type of regulation is not present, the procedure does not, in fact, take a judicial form. And a court, [372] which in lieu of stable, preexisting, general norms decides a political conflict according to its own discretion, only appears to be a court. Such an organ is either an office of the federation or of one or of several member states; it is always a party. A "mixed office" would also be inconceivable in regard to a genuine political conflict. If it should be composed with parity between the components, the number of the members that are named by each party and that, in the absence of a bond to a statute, are dependent and instructed by the party must be the same. For a decision can only succeed when one or several of the appointed members fail to fulfill the presuppositions of their appointment. Otherwise, this office would stand *above* the parties, not by virtue of the dependence on the statute, which in fact alone establishes such independence, nor because of a norm that is valid in the same way for both parties. It does so, rather, because of its *existence*. This office itself would be sovereign. It would no longer be a court, but rather an existing political power, which, consequently, also strives for its self-preservation. Many disputes, differences of opinion, and disagreements could be mediated by astute and just persons in good conscience. An existential conflict is not eliminated in this way. In every instance of a politically existing people, they necessarily decide the questions of their political existence themselves and on their own responsibility. The people can only decide as long as they exist politically. This is the case even for determining whether an existential question is at issue.

This existential conflict is always possible in any independent entities existing politically, and the question of sovereignty, in other words, of the last existential decision, consequently always remains open. It can only confuse the situation and is not a solution of the difficult question, if one intends to make use of, first, a distinction between sovereign and non-sovereign states and, second, that between state federation and federal state and say with the dominant theory of German public law (Laband, I, p. 91ff., Haenel, I, p. 221, cf. Meyer-Anschütz, p. 48) that in a state federation the individual states are *sovereign*, while in a federal state the state collective as such is *sovereign*. That is not at all an answer under the proper understanding of the significance of an existential conflict and of the essence of the sovereign decision. For it only says that the state federation dissolves itself in the case of conflict, but that the federal state [373] does not. In this way, the collective will in a political sense is taken from the state federation. The state federation is still only an interstate "relation" (which oddly enough, however, like the German Federation, can wage war as such like the German Federation!). The federal state, by contrast, becomes a sovereign state and loses its federal character because the independent decision on its political existence is taken from the states, and they are allowed only an "autonomous legal authority for legislation." It is part of the essence of the federation, however, that the question of sovereignty between federation and member states always remains open as long as the federation as such exists alongside the member states as such. If one speaks of a federation in which the federation as such, not the member states, is sovereign; and if one speaks of a construct in which only the "federation," that is the collective as such, has political existence; then that is, in fact, a sovereign unified state. By this means, the actual problem of the federation is simply evaded.

The basis of this third, most general antimony is ultimately the fact that every assemblage of independent political unities must appear as a contradiction in the context of a collective unity that also exists politically. Max von Seydel cites with lively affirmation the statement of a Frenchmen: "Il ne peut y avoir deux unités, car l'essence de l'unité c'est d'être une," which translates as there cannot be two unities, for the essence of the unity exists precisely in being a unity (statement of Léon, *Abhandlungen*, p. 19). That is correct for the case of conflict, despite the subtle distinctions of sovereign and nonsovereign "states." The contradiction is evident in all essential conflicts inside the federation and in all famous, disputed questions of federation law, so long as a political decision has not yet eliminated the genuine federation balance. Thus, for the constitution of the United States of America, the actual fundamental questions had been discussed *before* the war of secession. At that time, John C. Calhoun presented his famous theses (his collected essays appeared in 1851), to which Max von Seydel explicitly appeals (Zur "Lehre von den Staatenverbindungen," 1872, *Abhandlungen*, p. 15). Its theoretical significance for the concepts of a constitutional theory of the federation is even today still great and in no way settled by the fact that in the war of secession the Southern states were defeated and that in the German Reich under Bismarck's constitution, the dominant theory [374] was content with a few antitheses and sham distinctions of state and sovereignty, on the one hand, and state federation and federal state, on the other. The theories of Calhoun and Seydel involve essential concepts of constitutional theory for a federation, with the aid of which one should recognize the distinctiveness of certain political formations, and the scholarly value of which persists even if their creators stood on the defeated side. Proving that the United States of America in its current political form or the German Reich with its contemporary constitution are definitely "federations" is not the point. On the contrary, it is to ask, without preconceived concepts and expressions, whether even today a federation or only just the remnants of an earlier federation is at issue, remnants that had been used as organizational elements in a state construction, or that transformed themselves gradually out of genuine federal elements into such organizational aids.

Calhoun's most important theses involve the theory of the independent sovereign rights of the states, *state rights*. According to Calhoun, these rights are only limited insofar as this is explicitly provided in the constitution, while the supposition of the unlimited character of these rights speaks in favor of the member states. The supposition of limitlessness, the "plenitude of state authority," does not serve as a rule of interpretation for a particular statute. Instead, much like in the question of the monarchical principle, it serves as a logical formula for sovereignty. This theory, therefore, is incorrect, because it presents the member states as sovereign, not the federation, which is just as unfair to the distinctiveness of the federation as the opposite claim. Additionally, however, Calhoun grants the member states a right to *nullification* of federation statutes and actions. According to the nullification doctrine, an individual member state itself decides to deny a federation action recognition and execution, if in the understanding of the member state the federation's constitutional powers are exceeded. In this case, the popular assembly of the member state provisionally decides until a three-fourths majority of the chamber of states of the federation recognizes the constitutionality of the federal act. But even a constitution-amending majority cannot eliminate the contractual foundations of the federation. If a member state perceives its security and existence endangered and threatened and, according to its sovereign decision, [375] the federation powers are being misused, it has a right to nullify the federation contract. This is the right to *secession*. These theses of *Calhoun* formed the theoretical justification for the secession of the southern states, which led to the war of secession of 1861–1865. Since the war ended with the defeat of the southern states, the theory is settled for the United States of America. "Henceforth," N. Murray Butler argues, "the attempt to evade the predominance of the national (that is, federation) government is looked upon as rebellion, and for this reason neither nullification by any given state nor succession of a state is permissible under the political system of the United States . . . From now on, the highest court of law decides . . . So quickly did the war resolve all the difficult questions that had exercised the legislative bodies, the courts, and not least the people itself through two generations (N. Murray Butler, *Der Aufbau des amerikanischen Staates*, p. 219). This "solution" of the question through war, however, only means that the constitution changed its character and the federation as such ceased to be something determined by war. The possibility of an existential conflict between the union and an individual or several member states is now precluded. The federal elements of the constitution no longer involve the question of the independent political existence of the states. Federalism, rather, only views the states as organizational components of extensive legislative autonomy and self-government. In the question of secession, this fundamental problem of the federation comes clearly into view. If the essence of the federation is that it should be ongoing, the entry into the federation must mean the continual renunciation of the right to secession. If, however, the federation should simultaneously be a contract and the states of the federation should not lose their independent political existence, then the federation members must remain in the position of deciding for themselves the question of the current impossibility, applicability, and annullability of this "contract." And that is precisely a right to secession. They must opt either for the perpetuation of the federation, in other words, for neither secession nor nullification, or for the independent political existence of the member states, specifically, for nullification and secession, even if only in the most extreme case. But the concept of a political unity composed of states that is enduring and that, nevertheless, does not abandon its contractual foundation appears as something contradictory in the highest degree.

2. *The resolution of the antimonies of the federation* is that every federation rests on an essential presupposition, specifically [376] of the *homogeneity of all federation members*, in particular on a substantial similarity that justifies a concrete, existential agreement of member states and ensures that the extreme case of conflict does not emerge within the federation. As with democratic homogeneity (above p. 228), substance in this context can also be part of different areas of human life. There can be a national, religious, cultural, social, class, or another type of homogeneity. Apart from the case of the Federation of Soviet Socialist Republics, substance resides mostly today in a national similarity of the population. Nevertheless, the similarity of the political principle (monarchy, aristocracy, or democracy) is still added to the homogeneity of the population as a further element of

homogeneity. Deviations and differences in fundamental questions, such as the difference in the evaluation of slavery in the Northern and Southern states of the American union, must come to a resolution if they are not to endanger homogeneity.

Montesquieu proved the value of his state theory insight when he expressed this essential presupposition of the federation. A federal constitution must be composed of states with the same nature, above all, of republican states. "Que la constitution federative," he argues, "doit être composée d'états de même nature, surtout d'états républicains." *Esprit des lois*, IX, 2. For the spirit (esprit) of the monarchy is warlike and inclines toward expansion; the spirit of the republic is peaceful and moderate (Montesquieu is thinking here of the aristocratic republic, whose principle, according to him, is moderation). Be that as it may, opposing types of state principles and political outlook cannot exist together in a federalist construct.

For that reason, most federal constitutions contain explicit *guarantees of homogeneity*. The actual substance of homogeneity is for the most part tacitly presupposed. The explicit guarantee usually involves the state form. Thus Art. 4, section 4, of the American federal constitution of 1787 contains a guarantee of the republican state form. The *German Federation* of 1815 contains a guarantee already in Art. 13 of the Vienna Federation Acts, which provided for Land-level estate constitutions of the member states. In Art. 57 of the Vienna Concluding Acts of 1820, the monarchical principle was expressly proclaimed as the state form for all members on an equal basis (the minor exception of the free cities comes into consideration in this context to the same limited degree as in the North German Federation of 1867 and in the German Reich of 1871). Especially interesting in regard to this Art. 13 is a letter from Gentz of 16 February 1818 or 1817 (Wittichen III, pp. 384–85), which states that if Land-level estate systems inside the federation exist alongside pure representative systems, then confusion and discord would emerge. "Such a circumstance," he argues, "had certainly neither been intended nor desired during the drafting of the federal acts, nor even only accepted as possible, and it stands in unmistakable contradiction with the concept of unity, of order, and of peace in Germany." The Frankfurt constitution of 1848/49 provided in Art. XII the comparability of the basic rights on the foundation of [377] limited constitutions with certain minimal rights of the popular assembly. According to § 195, every change in form of government in an individual state is dependent on the consent of the Reich authority. In § 130, the basic rights are presented as a norm for all constitutions of the individual states.

The German Reich under the 1871 constitution contains no explicit guarantee of that type, but it is not based to a lesser degree on the fact that it was a federation of monarchical states. On the resulting difficulty for the problem of a parliamentary government in the Reich, see above § 25, pp. 333/34.

Art. 6 of the Swiss federal constitution of 29 May 1874 provides that "the cantons are obligated to petition for the federation's guarantee for their constitutions.

The federation takes up this guarantee insofar as:

(a) these cantonal constitutions contain nothing contrary to the provisions of the federal constitution;

(b) they guarantee the exercise of political rights according to republican (representative or democratic) forms;

(c) they have been accepted by the people and can be revised, if the absolute majority of the citizens demands it."

The *Weimar Constitution* guarantees homogeneity on the foundation of a constitutional democracy with a parliamentary government and thereby excludes both the monarchy as well as a proletarian council system. Art. 17 stipulates that "every Land must have the constitution of a free state. The popular assembly must be elected by all men and women of the German Reich according to proportional representation in an election that is general, equal, direct, and secret. The Land government requires the confidence of the popular assembly." On the fact that the German Reich today is no longer a federation, see p. 388f.

(a) The solution of the first antinomy is that a state inside of a homogeneous community of states can forgo the ius belli and every form of self-help without denying or diminishing its will to self-preservation. For a war receives meaning from being conducted in the interest of self-preservation against a genuine enemy. In conceptual terms, the enemy is something existentially other and foreign, the most extreme escalation of the otherness, which in the case of conflict leads to the denial of its own type of political existence. An enduring and conclusive renunciation of war is only possible and meaningful in regard to such states for which the possibility of the enmity is continuously and conclusively excluded. But that does not depend simply on the good will of men. The best will is impotent in regard to the concrete reality of different types of peoples and colliding interests and convictions. The existential distinctiveness of these peoples, interests, and convictions find their political form in the state. Only if there is a substantial comparability, an existential relationship, as can be the case, for example, in states with a nationally comparable and similarly disposed population, is it reasonably conceivable to consider hostility permanently precluded even as a possibility. [378] Only in such a case can one forgo the ius belli permanently without this act of forbearance at the same time constituting a renunciation of state independence as well as of the right to the preservation and to the security of the state's own political existence. If each member state also forgoes the *jus belli* against nonmembers and ascribes this right exclusively to the federation, then it is presupposed that every member state can have no enemy that is not simultaneously the enemy of all other member states and of the entire federation. However, the federation cannot have an enemy that would not at the same time be an enemy of every member state.

(b) The solution of the second antinomy is that the will to self-determination, which belongs to anything that exists politically, is nullified or endangered only through interference that is *foreign* in existential terms. Interventions of the federation in the affairs of its members are not a foreign interference, and they are politically and legally possible and bearable because the federation rests on an existentially substantial similarity of the members. For a monarchical, individual state of the 1871 German Reich, for example, this did not signify a diminishment; that it could not transform itself into a democratic republic was a guarantee of its constitution-making power.

(c) The solution of the third antinomy is that the instance of conflict that is decisive in existential terms is precluded in a substantial homogeneity of the federation members. Sovereignty is also not absent in a federation. But because the question of political existence can emerge differently in various areas, especially in terms of foreign and domestic politics, it is possible that the decision concerning a particular type of such question, for example, questions of external political existence, lies with the federation. By contrast, the decision concerning other such questions—for example, the preservation of public security and order inside of a member state—remains with the member state. That is not a division of sovereignty. It follows from the coexistence of the federation with the federation members. There is not a division because the instance of conflict that determines the question of sovereignty involves political existence as such and the decision in the individual case is always *entirely* attributed to the one or the other. The simple either/or that is part of sovereignty and does not permit a division in substantive terms, or a limitation and halving, remains preserved therefore, [379] and the authors who stress the indivisibility of sovereignty in this problem, as does Max von Seydel, are completely right. But because of this substantial homogeneity, the deciding case of conflict *between the federation and member states* cannot emerge, so that neither the federation in regard to the member states nor the member state in regard to the federation plays the sovereign. The existence of the federation rests fully on the fact that this case of conflict is existentially excluded. That can certainly not be brought about through just any agreements, wishes, and urgent, persistent requests. That sort of thing would be empty and falsely conceived, if not deceptive, as long as the existential similarity and relationship is absent. However, where there is homogeneity, a federation is legally and politically possible, and the substantial homogeneity inheres in every single constitutional provision as an essential presupposition. Where the substantial homogeneity is absent, the agreement on a "federation" is an insubstantial and misleading sham enterprise.

Consequences of the Fundamental Concepts of the
Constitutional Theory of the Federation

I. *Political existence of the federation.* Every federation has as such a political existence with an independent *jus belli.* The federation, on the other hand, does not have its own constitution-making authority, because it rests on a contract. Conditional jurisdiction for revisions of the federation order is not constitution-making authority. On this issue, see below IV, 4a.

II. *Federation as subject.* Every federation as such is a subject in terms of international as well as public law.

1. The capacity of an independent *international* law subject is already ascribed to every federation because it necessarily assumes a ius belli and the federation members, either entirely or in part, renounce their ius belli in favor of the federation. The renunciation by the federation members of their ius belli is not a renunciation extending into nothingness, but one in favor of the federation.

What further consequences can be drawn from the federation's international legal capacity for action is an organizational question.

It can be that the federation has an independent *right of embassy* like the German federation of 1815, and that as such it proclaims the international *recognition* of foreign governments (for example, the decision of the [380] German Federation of 23 September 1830 on the recognition of the ascension to the throne of King Louis-Philippe, or of 4 October 1832 on the recognition of Prince Otto of Bavaria as king of Greece). That a distinct and independent recognition of foreign governments by the individual member states is impossible is also accepted for the British global empire. Compare Heck, *Der Aufbau des Britischen Reiches,* 1927, p. 35, on the recognition of the Russian Soviet government through the English government and the validity of this recognition for all dominions. On the fact that a declaration of war by Great Britain or against it places the entire Reich territory into a state of war, see B. Mückenberger, *Die britische Reichskonferenz und das Verfassungsproblem,* Leipzig 1927, pp. 73 and 94.

If the League of Nations were a genuine federation, it would have as such an ius belli. Even here it is evident that the question regarding the distinguishing characteristics of the federation is the core question of the "federation" of peoples. Without a clarification of this federation problem, all discussions move in a vicious circle as soon as they impinge on the essential points. Characteristic of this is the statement by Schücking and Wehberg in their commentary on the League of Nations' by-laws, 2nd ed. 1924, p. 118, where they argue that "as a legal subject of international law, the federation undoubtedly also has the right to declare war and to conclude peace." In fact, the opposite is the case. If the League of Nations has a *jus belli,* it is a subject of international law in the full sense, and it can only have a *jus belli* if it is a genuine federation.

2. The federation exists as *public law* subject because it is the bearer of its own public law powers in regard to the federation members, and the relations between the federation and member states have a public law character. The status of every federation member state is qualified through membership in a special way not only externally, and membership in the federation, consequently, has direct public law effects. There is no federation that is nothing more than an external relation among members with a public law character. It suffices to refer to two institutions essential to every federation in order to make clear its capacity as a public law subject. These are a federal enforcement action and a federal intervention.

(a) During the *federal enforcement action*, the authority for which is necessarily accorded to the federation as such, the federation approaches, as a public law organ, the member state against which the enforcement action is directed and issues commands directly to the member state officials, even if otherwise the federation organization carefully attempts to avoid a direct legal authority for commands. That the federal enforcement action is a public law, not an international law act, is essentially part of the federation character, because the enforcement action otherwise would be a war, which would contradict the essence of the federation and dissolve it. The concept of federal enforcement action, therefore, requires a public law connection.

(b) The federation's right of intervention also leads to such directly public procedures and actions. Even if the intervention directs itself only to the state as a whole, [381] it nevertheless directly involves domestic affairs and has no international law character within the federation. When the question of the abolition of slavery was raised in the federation of the United States of America, the Southern states were not permitted, if the federation should continue to exist in fact, to reject the discussion of these questions simply with the justification that it involved "internal state affairs," "household" matters, "domestic affairs" [Schmitt's English]. However, they could make good on their right of secession and declare the federal contract a nullity, as they even attempted to do. Whether they did so rightly or wrongly is another question. Yet as long as the federation existed, they were not permitted to reject an act of interference by the federation in the same way as under general international law principles a state rejects the intervention of a foreign state. In terms of international law, at least still today, the independent states stand opposite one another as formations closed to the outside, impenetrable, impermeable, or (according to the somewhat banal American expression) "waterproof." Internally, a federation cannot be closed off and impermeable.

3. This public law character of every federation leads logically to *federation law* always having *precedence over Land law* to the degree that the

federation uses its authority to oppose the members, whether or not such opposition only occurs in a very restricted field. If we leave aside the fact that the German Reich is today no longer a federation (p. 388) and that in the framework of the Weimar Constitution Art. 13 gains its special meaning through section 2 (resolution of differences of opinion), then the provision of Art. 13, 1, stipulating that "Reich law trumps Land law" conveys something self-evident in terms of federation public law. German legal history explains the remarkable formulation of Art. 13. There is a legal saying that formulated the relationship of local and territorial law to the common law. It was then applied to the public law relationship of federation and members, formed on an entirely different basis, and was used as a slogan-like turn of phrase in order to express something essentially different. More specifically, with their entry into force, federation statutes that are valid for the officials and subjects of the member state are to be applied and obeyed immediately as statutes even inside the member states without a special act of adaptation. The federal law significance of the clause is that it [382] answers the question of whether directly applicable federal statutes are issued for all officials and subjects of the individual state or whether it requires the formality of a special adaptation. According to Art. 13, it should not require such a special adaptation. But even if such were required, and presupposing the procedurally correct issuance of statutes, there would naturally still be the unconditional constitutional duty of adaptation. However, the legal nature of this adaptation within the alliance is something other than a "transformation" in public law actions, which emerges on the basis of an individual international law contract, is undertaken in fulfillment of an international law obligation, and is necessary for the internal state execution of the international law bond. The adaptation within the federation is only one of the different types and cases of adaptation for the purpose of execution. Even within a state, instructions to autonomous bodies, such as to a religious society, for example, can be issued, necessitating adaptations for the legal relationships among persons within the instructed body. Seen from the technical necessities of every large administrative apparatus, adaptations could become necessary on an ongoing basis, if, for organizational reasons, a directive is not issued directly to the last administrative official, but rather via the superiors through official channels. Often, the public law situation is such that what can be demanded is not that an order be actually carried out, but instead only that there be one. Similarly, what can be demanded is that there is only the possibility of suspension, not that something be suspended, as would be the case, for example, with the measures issued by the President under Art. 48, 3, p. 2, that are to be suspended by order of the Reichstag. The presidential order that such a demand suspends is also an adaptation. The international law adaptation is now actually a "transformation," for it contains a qualitative change of the legal nature of the affected instrument. An international law obligation of one state to another state becomes the motive for the obligated state to undertake domestic actions or to justify domestic obligations, etc. One can speak here of an "adaptation" only imprecisely because what is absent is an identity of and continuity between international law duty and domestic execution in general. The "transformation" does not change an international [383] law obligation into public law relations. Rather, it produces a new legal foundation and inserts it between international and public law. As presented in H. Triepel's fundamental work on international law and Land law from 1899, it provides a new source of law through which something qualitatively new and different arises without legal continuity.

The "adaptations" within the federation, by contrast, arise from a *constitutional* duty of the federation members, hence directly from its *public law* status. Moreover, they do not involve the relations of states, which stand opposite one another in isolated impermeability, and which are not only allied with one another but are also "bound" to one another. Consequently, they do not signify a qualitative renewal and not an elimination of identity for the "transformed" legal relations. The command issued in the fulfillment of a federation duty, which issues from the central offices of the member state to the subordinate officials or to the state subjects of the member state, is the same command as that which issues from the federation to the competent central offices of the member state. There is not a qualitative difference here, but instead a thoroughgoing continuity.

III. Every federation has a *federation territory*. There is always a territorial demarcation of the federation as such against other, territorially demarcated political unities. The federation territory consists of the territories of the federation, the member states. A territory dominated by the federation as such (for example, federation colony) can be added to this. This last type of territory, however, is "federation territory" in an entirely different sense than the territory of the member states of the federation. A federation territory is necessarily part of the federation only in the sense of the state territory of the member states, while the federation territory in the sense of a territory governed by the federation (federation Land, Reich Land, federation colony) does not necessarily belong to the federation. If several states govern a territory in common, they still do not become a federation by virtue of this, and the governed territory is also not a "federation territory." Otherwise, every condominium would establish a federation, which is undoubtedly not the case.

The Generality Lands of the United Netherlands until the unification into a state (1579–1795) and the confederation of American states 1778–1787 until the founding of the territories governed by the Union, are examples of federation territories in the second sense of the word developed here. In the framework of the German Reich 1871–1918, the Reich Land Alsace-Lorraine is not an example of a territory merely governed by the federation. Rather, it was part of the federation territory in the actual sense of the word, as even its population had state membership inside the federation. Nevertheless, this form of a Reich Land signifies an unclear intermediary form.[384]

The League of Nations is not a federation. The territories of the member states are not the territory of the League of Nations in the sense of the territorial government or federation authority. The League of Nations, however, also does not govern a federation territory in the second sense of the word. On grounds of the Versailles Treaty, the Saar *territory* is subjected to a provisional regime until the conclusive determination of its political destiny. In the execution of this regime, interstate conferences and institutions become active as the federal council of peoples. That is not a sovereignty of the League of Nations. And the Saar territory is the territory of the League to the same limited degree that the population of the Saar territory attains state membership in the League of Nations. The mandate territories (according to Art. 22 of the League's by-laws) are not governed by the League as such. They are, instead, partly protectorates, partly colonies under the rule of the mandate states (above § 7, p. 71). At least, it should be said that the League is "sovereign." The League of Nations is an interstate relationship, not a federation. So it can also not be the subject and bearer of a sovereignty, whether or not one would also like to transfer a series of interstate functions and authorities to the institutions and conferences of an interstate organization. H. Wehberg attempted to make the mandate territories into territories, in which a territorial government of the League is exercised, in order in this way to construe a distinct federation territory and with it a distinguishing conceptual feature of state existence. ("Besitz der Völkerbund ein eigenes Territorium?" in the journal "Völkerbundfragen," 1 June 1926, pp. 92/94). He refers to the examples noted above to show that a state federation possesses territories "for collective use" and intends to constitute the mandate territories according to the analogy of the previously mentioned "Generality Lands." The circle in which the mode of thought moves is entirely obvious. Naturally, if the League were a genuine federation, it could also as such govern areas (whereby, moreover, the distinction, discussed above, of different types of "federation area" were still observed), but the question is simply whether the League of Nations is a federation. If it is a federation, the League's supervision of the governance of the mandate states in the mandate territories (which, again, is in itself very problematical) is not constituted as the federation's territorial authority. The question regarding the characteristics of the genuine federation also proves itself to be the core question of the League of Nations.

IV. *Federation representation, institutions and officials, federal jurisdiction.*

1. The federation must be represented as a political unity. Naturally, the representative of the federation is the federal assembly as the assembly of representatives of the political entities that form the federation. If a more select collegium has a representative property, that already signifies a transition to the unified state.

The organization of the federation authorities and competencies corresponds in general to a simple scheme: collective assembly of all member states, moreover, a more select (executive or even representative) collegium as a "council" or "committee" and a bureau or office for the administrative-technical preparation and execution of the federation decisions.

As long as the federation exists, the will of the federation is directly the [385] will of every member state. It is so, in other words, without transformation in the actual sense of the word. Even if the federation decisions come about through unanimous decision of all members—not just by all of the members present at the vote—and no one can be outvoted, there is still an essential difference between a federation decision and the unanimous decision of an international law conference, because the federation decision needs no special ratification through the individual states. More precisely, every member state is constitutionally (because the federal constitution is a component of its own constitution) bound directly and in public law terms by the federation decision.

The League of Nation's official decisions with a public law character apply without special ratification directly to all member states. In this regard, the League of Nations contains an element of a genuine federation organization, while otherwise it is not a genuine federation. A confusion results from this combination that cannot be overlooked. On these decisions of the League of Nations, see H. Jahrreiß, *Völkerbundsmitgliedschaft und Reichsverfassung*, 1926, whose expositions provide the service of correctly recognizing the public law side of every federation, and D. Schindler, *Die Verbindlichkeit der Beschlüsse des Völkerbundes*, Zürich 1927. The essentially contradictory organization of the League of Nations institutions and thus the necessity of a clarification of the federation concept become even more evident.

2. One must distinguish between the question of the direct command authority of the federation in regard to officials and state subjects of the member states and the question of the direct constitutional, specifically, public law obligation, of the member state. This question involves only the type of adaptation within the federation, whether or not a direct power of instruction of the federation authorities in regard to officials of member states is being introduced. Even if there is no direct power of instruction, the necessary adaptation is not one from international law to the public law of the member state. It is, by contrast, a public law process occurring within the federation. On this, cf. above p. 381f.

3. The federation always has certain essential powers: an independent *jus belli* externally, federal oversight (with the possibility of a federation enforcement action and of an intervention by the federation) internally. The additional competencies result from the constitutional legislation of the federation ordinances, which is always a component of the member state constitution. The question as to whether in this instance a supposition speaks for or against the jurisdiction of the federation or for or against the

jurisdiction of the member states also belongs in the [386] constitutional legislation of the federal constitution and is a question of the organization of the concrete, individual federation.

It is often designated as a general principle of federal constitutional law that the federation only has the competencies expressly delegated to it, while all other competencies remain with the member states (cf. H. Kelsen, *Kommentar zur öster-reichischen Bundesverfassung*, Art. 15, 1, p. 80). This does not apply at this level of generality. "The supposition of the unlimited powers" has a double meaning and can have different functions: first of deciding the question of sovereignty (on this, see below under 4); second, however, of achieving a principle of interpretation *in the framework of the constitutional legislation*, therefore, not for the sovereignty, but for genuine, that is, unlimited competencies. In the latter case, it is a matter of the constitutional legislation of the federal constitution. Initially, the additional question for this case is whether the express attribution of enumerated competencies is to be interpreted restrictively (because every enumeration entails a limitation, according to the principle *enumeratio ergo limitatio*), or whether additional competencies could, more accurately, evolve *implicite* from the attributed competencies (on this, see *H. Triepel*, "Die Kompetenzen des Bundesstaates und die geschriebene Verfassung," in *Festgabe für Laband*, 1908, II, p. 249, and R. Grau, "Vom Vorrang der Bundeskompetenzen im Bundesstaat," *Festschrift für E. Heinitz*, 1926, p. 362). If Triepel (*Kompetenzen*, p. 335) states "there are competencies in the federal state indeed outside of the written constitution, but never outside of the federation," it is evident how much a general constitutional theory of the federation needs the distinction between constitution and constitutional laws. The federal constitution is self-evidently the foundation of all further discussions of the delimitation of powers of the federation and of the member states, and there are no rights outside of the federal constitution, but "written constitution" is meant here by Triepel certainly only in the relative sense of a constitutional *law*. In the public law literature on Bismarck's constitution, this opposition is recognizable throughout all the controversies (on the contractual foundations and elements of the constitution, on a unitary state, and federalism). When R. Smend understands "contractual loyalty and federalist outlook" of the member states as a legal principle of the *unwritten* federation law (in the essay, "Ungeschriebenes Verfassungsrecht im monarchischen Bundesstaat," *Festgabe für Otto Mayer*, Tübingen 1916, p. 260ff.), his reasoning places the constitution prior to the constitutional law. The entire controversy (cf. the exposition of Karl Bilfinger, *Der Einfluß der Einzelstaaten auf die Bildung des Reichswillens*, 1923, p. 52ff.) can only be explained and advanced through a proper constitutional concept. It is not a matter so much of the recognition that Bismarck's "constitution" was "complete" and "gapless" as it is of the awareness that in fact the opposition between the constitution (in the positive sense) and constitutional law was the foundation of the distinction between "written and unwritten constitution."

4. The term the "competence-competence" of the federation can be intended in different ways.

(a) It can mean the *constitutional jurisdiction* for constitutional amendments or, more precisely, for the revision of constitutional provisions. This competence is not boundless and finds its limits in the constitution (above p. 102f.). It is possible that in the course of the historical development and through exploitation of the possibility of constitutional revisions, [387] the competencies of the federation are extended so far that the member states no longer have significant powers and lose their political existence. The federation, therefore, makes a transition into a unified state. By contrast, it would doubtless be an offence against the federal constitution if this competence for competencies, in other words, jurisdiction for constitutional revisions, were to be used methodically for the elimination of the political independence of the member states.

(b) Or it can be a mere *accessory* to a competence, in particular, the authority of every competent official, which is general and assumed in doubtful cases, to decide on the question of whether the prerequisites of their jurisdiction are satisfied. Then, a court can have a competence for competencies in the sense that it itself decides whether the access to courts is permitted, whether the matter belongs before this court, etc. In Article 36, 5, of the governing statute of the permanent international court of justice in The Hague, for example, it states: "If the jurisdiction of the permanent international court of justice is challenged, the court decides itself." Such a competence for the determination of its own competence can become very important and significant in practical terms (as in the aforementioned case of the permanent international court of justice), but it only facilitates the competence, to which it is added as a mere accessory.

(c) Another sense is an unbounded authority for all types of *sovereign acts*. German public law theory of the Reich period understood the word in this meaning (cf. Meyer-Anschütz, p. 692; Haenel, *Studien* I, p. 111; *Staatsrecht*, p. 771ff.) and confused it with the competence for revision under Art. 78 of Bismarck's constitution. When taken to mean "sovereignty," however, the concept "competence for competencies" is intrinsically contradictory. Sovereignty is not a competence, not even a competence for competencies. There is no boundless competence, if the word is to retain its sense, and if a jurisdiction should be provided that is regulated in advance through norms, factually circumscribed, and, consequently, bounded. The term "competence for competencies" designates either a genuine competence, which then means it has nothing to do with sovereignty and cannot even be used as a formula for sovereignty, or it is a general slogan for a sovereign power, which means it is not clear why one speaks here of "competence."

V. *Treasonous undertakings* against the federation as such are to be treated as high treason in every member state. The same is true for treason against a Land and similar affairs. [388]

The previously discussed decision of the German Federation of 8 August 1836 concerning high treason in the German Federation is especially clear and logically consistent in this regard. Because it extends far beyond its historical occasion and concrete political goal, it is of general significance for the constitutional theory of the federation. According to Art. I (printed in G. von Struve, *Das öffentliche Recht des Deutschen Bundes* I, 1856, p. 247), "Since the purpose of the German Federation consists not only in the preservation of the independence and inviolability of the German states as well as in the preservation of the external and internal peace and security of Germany; but rather also because the federal constitution, on account of its essential connection with the constitutions of the individual federation states, is to be viewed as an essential component of the latter; an attack directed against the federation or its constitution necessarily entails an attack against each individual member state. Thus, *every enterprise against the existence, integrity, security, or constitution of the German Federation, undertaken in the individual states*, is to be judged and punished according to the standard of the most recently existing statutes or those which come into effect in the future, statutes under which an action committed against the individual federal state were to be judged equally *as high treason, treason against the land*, or under some other designation."

VI. *Democracy and federalism.*

1. Both democracy and the federation rest on the assumption of homogeneity. On the place of this assumption in democracy, cf. above § 17, p. 228; for the federation, cf. § 29, p. 376. If, however, a federation of democratic states forms, the necessary consequence is that democratic homogeneity converges with the federation-homogeneity. Therefore, it is part of the natural development of democracy that the homogeneous unity of the people extends beyond the political boundaries of member states and eliminates the transitional condition of the coexistence of the federation and the politically independent member states, and replaces it with a complete unity.

This explains the development of most federal states of the nineteenth and twentieth centuries, especially of the United States of America and of the German Reich. To the same degree that democracy advanced, the political independence of the member states also decreased. In the United States of America, this development already begins with the consent of the people in the individual states (in contrast to these states themselves) to the federal constitution (on this procedure, see above p. 86). The preamble of the federal constitution, "We the people of the United States," caused Calhoun exceptional difficulties (*Works* I, p. 132ff.). The war of secession settled conclusively the controversy over this development. In the German Reich, it was the democratization of the year 1918/1919 that had a similar effect and transformed the member states of the federation of the German Reich into "Lands." The federal state theories of Calhoun (for the United States of America) and Max von Seydel (for the German Reich) are thereby superseded, but not because, considered in view of the proper concepts of federal law, they were wrong about everything. Instead, it was because the democratic development and in particular the democratic consequence of the image of a united and undivided people within a nationally homogeneous federation must lead to state unity. As soon as that is recognized, the remaining correct portion in the aforementioned federation theories can also be unconditionally appreciated and used for constitutional theory.[389]

2. The connection of democracy and federal state organization leads to a distinctive, independent type of state organization, to the *federal state without an alliance foundation*. It is falsely assumed that that is a contradic-

tory concept. However, the federal state character concerns a constitutional component in which elements from an earlier federalist organization are incorporated into the new state form. Political formations like the United States of America or the German Reich of the Weimar Constitution are no longer a federation. If they are nevertheless designated federal states, then on the basis of their constitution, by virtue of the positive decision concerning the type of political existence (Art. 2 RV), such formations *intend* to guarantee the federal state character.

Through the democratic concept of the constitution-making power of the entire people, the alliance foundation and with it the federation character is eliminated. The federal state organization, which nevertheless can still be retained, is then a part of the constitutional organization of the entire state and establishes a special type of state. They usually bind themselves with organizational principles of the Rechtsstaat and facilitate a complicated system of separation of powers and decentralization. The constitution of the United States already has consciously intended that. The Federalist (no. 49, 1788) states that the American federal constitution is neither an entirely unified state nor a fully federalist one. In this regard, the independence of the states is used to give new security and guarantees to the organizational principle of the bourgeois Rechtsstaat.

3. In the federal state without an alliance foundation, there is only a single people. The state character of the prior member states is, therefore, eliminated. For the state is the political unity of a people, and in a state, whose type and form of political existence rests on the constitution-making will of the entire people, there can be no more than *one* political unity. Distinctively political decisions, such as the determination of friend and enemy from its own political existence, can only lie in the entirety of this political existence, just as is the case with the decision concerning other existential concepts like public order and security. There is, consequently, only *one* political unity, while in every genuine federation—federation of states as well as federal state—a multitude of political unities continue to exist alongside the federation. The question of whether in the German Reich today there is a people in the political sense besides a Prussian, Bavarian, Hamburgian, etc., people is answered in the negative. The preamble of the Weimar Constitution rightly uses the apt turn of phrase "the German people united in its origins." It does not speak of a unification or unity of the German *peoples*. [390]

The consequence of this type of federal state organization of a single people is that the earlier states are no longer units that are impenetrable and closed off to one another. Not only is there a common jurisdiction, as under Art. 3a of Bismarck's constitution and under the even more extensive Art. 110 of the Weimar Constitution, but it also becomes possible to distinguish the population of the member states and even parts of this population from the member state as such. This distinction would be impermissible if the member state still had its own political existence, which, from the democratic standpoint, would, indeed, be contradictory. This is because in a democratic state, that is, one ordered according to the principle of identity, the will of the state is comparable with the will of the population and both may not be distinguished from one another.

4. Art. 18 regulates the procedure for a territorial rearrangement of the Lands within the German Reich. Insofar as through these articles the will of the population, whether it is of an entire Land or of an individual part of the Land, contains public law meaning and is distinguished from the will of the Land as such, the provisions of Art. 18 rest on the unitary logic of democracy. Nevertheless, one cannot look upon it simply as a sign of the unitary character of the current German Reich and see in it evidence for the fact that one may not speak anymore at all of federal state organization. "In which arsenal Art. 18 belongs, whether actually in the unitary and not, more precisely, in the federalist," is, as Anschütz (*Veröffentlichungen der Vereinigung der deutschen Staatsrechtslehrer*, vol. I, 1925, p. 19) correctly states, in fact still very questionable. For it was precisely federalist views and tendencies that led to the currently valid provisions and their wording. On the one hand, the article should make it possible to dissolve Prussia, because it appears too *large* owing to its disproportionate and overwhelming territory, and, on the other hand, to eliminate the unviable dwarf lands and irregular territories, because they are too small. Thus, it should lead to the formation of viable lands of approximately equal size. This regulation would correspond to the idea of a so-called genuine (more accurately, balanced) federalism (K. Frantz) in contrast to the "hegemonial" federalism considered and defended by K. Bilfinger (*Veröffentlichungen der Vereinigung der deutschen Staatsrechtslehrer*, p. 38). Apart from the different practical opportunities for application of Art. 18, which [391] could lead to unexpected results, the following is authoritatively established as constitutional content of this provision:

(a) Art. 18 regulates the procedure for the reconfiguration and new construction of the German Lands and provides the Reich wide-ranging opportunities for the exercise of power, but not the authority to eliminate *the Lands altogether* and to transform the German Reich into a unitary state, whether it is with the help of Art. 18 or via Art. 76.

(b) The question of whether through a "constitutionally amending" statute a *specific* individual Land can be eliminated against its will is to be affirmed, but only under the presupposition that the elimination serves the territorial regrouping of the Lands and not a unitary elimination of the federal state organization. Section 4 of the law on the provisional Reich authority of 10 February 1919 stated that the territorial circumstance of the free states (of the Lands) could only be changed with their consent. This provision is meaningless today, not only because this statute is eliminated without reservation, but also above all, therefore, because in truth it signifies only a type of bylaw that the constitution-making national assembly provided itself, and through which a constitutional guarantee of a territorial *status quo* could not be justified at all. The Weimar Constitution contains neither a guarantee of the territorial *status quo* of the Lands as it was in the year 1919 nor a guarantee of the existence of every individual Land existing in 1919. An individual Land cannot be divided or incorporated into another one against its will, whether on the basis of the will of the population (in the event it should be possible that in a democratic Land a difference exists between "will of the population" and "will of the Land"), or whether it is through "constitution-amending Reich statute" by-way-of of Art. 76.

(c) By contrast, it would be unconstitutional to use Art. 18, which serves a rational regrouping and, with it, the interest of the preservation of the lands, to eliminate the federal state component of the Weimar Constitution. An act of the constitution-making power of the German people is part of such a transformation of the contemporary German Reich into a unified state.

Appendix:
The Weimar Constitution

First Principal Part: Development and Responsibilities of the Reich

SECTION 1: Reich and Lands

Article 1

The German Reich is a republic.[1] State authority derives from the people.

Article 2

The Reich territory consists of the areas of the German Lands. Other areas can be incorporated into the Reich via statute, if the population of these areas desires it by virtue of the right of self-determination.

Article 3

The Reich colors are black-red-gold. The flag of the merchant marine is black-white-red with the Reich colors in the upper inside corner.

Article 4

The generally recognized rules of international law are valid as binding components of law at the Reich level.

Article 5

State power is exercised in Reich affairs by the organs of the Reich on the basis of the Reich Constitution. In Land affairs, it is exercised by the organs of the Lands on the basis of the Land constitutions.

Article 6

The Reich has exclusive legislative authority over:

    1. foreign relations;
    2. the colonial system;
    3. citizenship, free movement; immigration, emigration, and deportation;
    4. defense;
    5. coinage;
    6. customs' system as well as the unity of the customs and trade areas and the free movement of goods;
    7. the postal and telegraph systems including the telephone system.

Article 7

The Reich has concurrent legislative authority over:

    1. private law;
    2. criminal law;

3. the judicial process including application of penalties as well as official aid among authorities;

4. passport system and police authority over foreigners;

5. system of poverty relief and assistance for transients;

6. the press, associations, and assemblies;

7. population policy, care for mothers, infants, children, and the youth;

8. system of health care, of veterinary medicine, and the protection of plants against disease and destructive elements;

9. labor law, insurance for and protection of workers, employees, and proof of employment;

10. institution of professional representatives for the Reich territory;

11. care for war veterans and their dependents;

12. law of expropriation;

13. the socialization of natural treasures and economic enterprises as well as the cultivation, production, distribution, and pricing of economic goods for the public economy;

14. trade, the system of weights and measures, the issuance of paper money, the banking and exchange systems;

15. traffic in basic food stuffs and luxury foods as well as in the articles of daily need;

16. business and mining;

17. the insurance system;

18. shipping on the high seas, fishing on the high seas and along the coasts;

19. the railroads, travel by ship in the interior, traffic with powered vehicles on land, in water, and in the air as well as the construction of roads, insofar as it involves general traffic and the defense of the land;

20. theater and movie systems.

Article 8

The Reich has additional legislative authority over rents and other income, insofar as these sources of revenue can be claimed, in whole or in part, for its purposes. If the Reich claims rents or other income that previously were the jurisdiction of the Lands, then the Reich must take into account the preservation of the viability of the Lands.

Article 9

To the extent that there is a need for the issuance of unified provisions, the Reich has legislative authority over:

1. provision for public welfare;

2. protection of the public order and security.

Article 10

Via legislation, the Reich can establish principles for:

1. the rights and duties of religious societies;

2. the school system including universities and scholarly bookstores;

3. the law for civil servants of all public bodies;

4. the law of landed property, distribution of land, system of settlements and limited use property holdings, the obligations of landed property, the system of living quarters, and the distribution of the population;

5. the burial system.

Article 11

Via legislation, the Reich can establish principles on the permissibility of Land taxes and on the means of their generation, insofar as these principles are necessary, in order either to exclude or to protect important societal interests, such as the following:

1. harm to the income or trade relations of the Reich;

2. double taxation;

3. excessive charges or those that hinder traffic for the use of traffic routes and institutions;

4. tax disadvantages for wares introduced into a Land compared to its own products in traffic between individual Lands and parts of the Land or

5. export premiums to protect exclusive or important social interests.

Article 12

So long and insofar as the Reich makes no use of its legislative authority, the Lands retain legislative authority. This provision does not apply to the Reich's exclusive legislative authority.

The Reich government has the right to challenge Land statutes passed in reference to the matters set forth in Art. 7, 13, insofar as the collective welfare is affected.

Article 13

If there are doubts or differences of opinion over whether a provision of Land law is compatible with Reich law, then the competent, central Reich or Land officials may petition the opinion of a Reich high court, as specified by a Reich statute.

Article 14

Reich laws are executed by the officials of the individual German Lands to the extent that Reich statutes do not provide for something else.

Article 15

The Reich government exercises supervisory authority in those matters in which the Reich has legislative jurisdiction.

To the extent that Reich statutes are executed by Land authorities, the Reich government can issue general instructions. The Reich government is authorized to send commissioners for the supervision of the execution of Reich statutes to central Land officials and, with the latter's consent, to the lower officials as well.

At the formal request of the Reich government, Land governments are obligated to eliminate deficiencies in the execution of Reich statutes. When there is a difference of opinion, both the Reich and Land governments can petition for an opinion of the Staatsgerichtshof to the extent that another court is not specified by Reich statute.

Article 16
Civil servants entrusted with the direct administration of Reich matters in the Lands should typically be citizens of the Land. The civil servants, employees, and workers of the Reich administration are to be used in their home areas, if they wish, insofar as this is possible and does not conflict with concerns for the training or requirements of the position.

Article 17
Every Land must have the constitution of a free state. The popular assembly must be elected in an election by all men and women of the German Reich according to proportional representation, an election that is general, equal, direct, and secret. The Land government needs the confidence of the popular assembly.

Article 18
Taking into account the greatest possible regard for the will of the participating population, the formation of the Reich into Lands aims to facilitate the highest economic and cultural achievement of the people. The alteration of the territory of Lands and the new formation of Lands within the Reich take place through a constitution-amending Reich statute.

If the directly participating Lands consent, such a change only requires a simple Reich statute.

A simple Reich statute is also sufficient, moreover, when one of the participating Lands does not consent, but when at the same time the territorial change or rearrangement is demanded by the will of the population and is necessary for an overriding Reich interest.

The will of the population is determined by a vote. The Reich government institutes the vote when it is demanded by one-third of the inhabitants of the area to be divided who are eligible to vote for the Reichstag.

Three-fifths of the votes cast, but at least a majority of those entitled to vote, is required for the conclusion of a territorial change or rearrangement. Even if it is only a question of dividing a portion of a Prussian governmental district, of a Bavarian district, or a corresponding administrative district in another Land, the will of the population of the entire district under consideration must be determined. When there is no spatial connection between the area to be divided and the entire district, a special Reich statute can declare the will of the affected area's population to be sufficient.

After the determination of the consent of the population, the Reich government must present to the Reichstag a corresponding statute for final approval.

If in regard to the unification or division there is a dispute over wealth issues, then, on petition by one of the parties, the Staatsgerichtshof of the Reich decides the question.

Article 19

In response to a petition from one of the parties, the Staatsgerichtshof for the German Reich decides constitutional disputes inside a Land, for which no court exists to settle it, as well as disputes of a non–private law nature between different Lands or between the Reich and a Land, to the extent that another court does not have jurisdiction.

The Reich President enforces the judgment of the Staatsgerichtshof.

SECTION 2: The Reichstag

Article 20

The Reichstag is composed of deputies of the German people.

Article 21

Deputies are representatives of the entire people. They are subject only to their own conscience and are not bound by instructions.

Article 22

Deputies are elected in general, direct, equal, and secret elections by men and women over twenty years of age according to the principles of proportional election. Election day must be a Sunday or a public holiday.

Details are determined by the Reich Election Law.

Article 23

The Reichstag is elected every four years. A new election must take place at the latest on the seventeenth day after the expiration of the Reichstag's term of office.

At the latest, the Reichstag convenes for the first time on the thirteenth day after the election.

Article 24

The Reichstag assembles every year on the first Wednesday of November at the seat of the Reich government. The president of the Reichstag must convene it earlier if the Reich President or at least a third of the members of the Reichstag demands it.

The Reichstag determines the conclusion of the session and the day of its reconvening.

Article 25

The Reich President can dissolve the Reichstag, but only once for the same reason.

The new election takes place on the seventeenth day after the dissolution.

Article 26

The Reichstag elects its president, his deputy, and its secretaries. It determines its own order of business.

Article 27

Between two sessions or electoral periods, the president and his deputy continue their business from the last session.

Article 28

The president enforces house rules and exercises police authority within the Reichstag building. The house administration is subject to his authority; he orders income and expenditures of the Reichstag according to the standards of the Reich budget, and he represents the Reich in all legal business and legal disputes involving its administration.

Article 29

The Reichstag conducts its business publicly. On petition of fifty members, the public can be excluded by a two-thirds majority vote.

Article 30

Accurate reports on deliberations in public sessions of the Reichstag, of a Land parliament, or its committees remain free of any accountability.

Article 31

In the Reichstag, an electoral review commission is formed. It also decides the question, whether a deputy lost member status.

The Electoral Review Commission is composed of members of the Reichstag, which selects them for the election period, and of members of the Reich administrative court, which the President orders on suggestion of the presidium of this court.

The Electoral Review Commission conducts business on the basis of public, oral deliberation by three members of the Reichstag and two judicial members.

Beyond the deliberations before the Electoral Review Commission, the procedure will be led by a Reich commissioner, whom the Reich President names. Otherwise, the procedure is regulated by the Electoral Review Commission.

Article 32

A simple majority vote is required for a decision of the Reichstag, insofar as the Constitution does not prescribe another proportion of the vote. The order of business can permit exceptions to votes undertaken by the Reichstag.

The order of business will regulate the requirements for a valid decision.

Article 33

The Reichstag and its committees can demand the presence of the Chancellor and any minister.

The Chancellor, the ministers, and deputies commissioned by the Chancellor have access to the meetings of the Reichstag and its committees. Lands are authorized to send to these meetings representatives empowered to act on their behalf, and they present the Land government's viewpoint on the matter in question.

If the Reich government insists, the government representatives must be heard during deliberations, even if they are not part of the day's agenda.

These representatives submit to the authority of the chair of the session.

Article 34

The Reichstag has the right and, on petition of one-fifth of its members, the duty to initiate investigative committees. In public proceedings, these committees raise the evidence that they or the petitioners deem necessary. A two-thirds majority vote can exclude the public from the investigative committees. The order of business governs the committees' procedure and determines the number of its members.

The courts and administrative officials are obligated to respond to the committees' request for evidence; official documents are to be presented to the committees if they request them.

The provisions of the law of criminal procedure are appropriately applied to the investigations of the committees and the officials investigated by them, but the secrecy of letters, packages, telegraph, and telephone is unaffected.

Article 35

The Reichstag establishes a standing committee for foreign affairs, which can meet even when the Reichstag is not in session and after the end of the election period or after the dissolution of the Reichstag until the convening of the new Reichstag. The meetings of this committee are not public, unless the committee decides otherwise with a two-thirds vote.

The Reichstag also establishes a standing committee for the preservation of the rights of the popular assembly in regard to the Reich government during the period outside the legislative session and after the end of the electoral period.[2]

These committees have the authority of investigative committees.

Article 36

No member of the Reichstag or of an individual Land parliament may be prosecuted judicially or internally at any time because of their vote or because of statements made in the exercise of their duty or otherwise be made accountable outside of the assembly.

Article 37

No member of the Reichstag or of an individual Land parliament, without approval of the house to which they belong, may be investigated or arrested during the session because of an action subject to criminal sanction, whether or not the member is apprehended in the act or at the latest during the following day.

The same approval is necessary for any other limitation of personal freedom that impinges on the exercise of the deputy's duty.

Every criminal trial against a member of the Reichstag or of an individual Land parliament and every arrest or other limitation of his personal freedom is abrogated on demand of the house to which he belongs for the duration of the legislative session.

Article 38

The members of the Reichstag and of the Land parliaments have the right to refuse to provide testimony concerning persons who have confided in them in their capacity as deputies or to whom they have confided in their capacity as deputies, insofar as this testimony involves these matters in particular. Even in regard to the confiscation of official papers, deputies are in the same position as persons who have a statutory right to confidentiality.

A search or confiscation may only be undertaken in the rooms of the Reichstag with the consent of the president of the Reichstag.

Article 39
Civil servants and members of the armed forces do not require vacation time to exercise their office as members of the Reichstag or of a Land parliament.

Article 40
Reichstag members receive the right to free passage on all German railroads as well as compensation for expenses according to the dictates of a Reich statute.[3]

SECTION 3: The President and the Reich Government

Article 41
The President is elected by the entire German people.

Any German over the age of thirty-five is eligible for election.

Article 42
The President takes the following oath before the Reichstag on assuming his office:

I swear that I will dedicate my strength to the well-being of the German people, multiplying their advantages, protecting them from harm, protecting the Constitution and the laws of the Reich, fulfilling my duties conscientiously, and extending justice toward all.

The addition of a profession of religious faith is permitted.

Article 43
The President's term of office is seven years. Reelection is permitted.

Before the expiration of the term, the President can be removed by popular vote at the instigation of the Reichstag. The Reichstag vote requires a two-thirds majority. By this decision, the President is prevented from further exercise of the office. The rejection of the removal by the popular vote counts as a new election and results in the dissolution of the Reichstag.

The President cannot be prosecuted under criminal law without consent of the Reichstag.

Article 44
The President cannot simultaneously be a member of the Reichstag.

Article 45
The President represents the Reich in terms of international law. In the name of the Reich, he concludes alliances and treaties with foreign powers. He confirms and receives ambassadors.

Declaration of war and conclusion of peace require a Reich statute.

Alliances and treaties with foreign states, which involve objects of Reich legislation, require the consent of the Reichstag.

Article 46

The President names and dismisses civil servants and officers, insofar as something else is not provided by law. He may allow other officials to exercise the authority of appointment and dismissal.

Article 47

The President has high command of the entire armed forces of the Reich.

Article 48

If a Land does not fulfill its duties according to the Reich Constitution or Reich statutes, the President can compel it to do so with the aid of armed force.

If in the German Reich the public security and order are significantly disturbed or endangered, the President can utilize the necessary measures to restore public security and order, if necessary with the aid of armed force. For this purpose, he may provisionally suspend, in whole or in part, the basic rights established in Articles 114, 115, 117, 118, 124, 153.

The President must inform the Reichstag without delay of all the measures instituted according to paragraph 1 or paragraph 2 of this article. The measures must be set aside at the request of the Reichstag.

In the case of immediate danger, the Land government can institute for its territory the type of measures designated in paragraph 2 on an interim basis. The measures are to be set aside at the demand of the President or the Reichstag.

A Reich statute determines the details of these provisions.

Article 49

The President exercises the right of pardon for the Reich.

Reich amnesties require a Reich statute.

Article 50

In order to be valid, all orders and legal instruments of the President, even those involving the defense forces, require the countersignature by the Chancellor or the minister with jurisdiction. With the countersignature, responsibility is assumed.

Article 51

In case of incapacitation, the Chancellor will initially substitute for the President.[4]

The same applies for the case of an early end to a presidency until a new election is carried out.

Article 52

The Reich government consists of the Chancellor and the ministers.

Article 53

The Chancellor and, at his suggestion, the ministers are appointed and dismissed by the President.

Article 54

The Chancellor and ministers require the confidence of the Reichstag for the execution of their office. Each of them must resign if the Reichstag withdraws its confidence through an explicit decision.

Article 55

The Chancellor chairs the Reich government and guides its business according to the rules of procedure determined by the Reich government and approved by the President.

Article 56

The Chancellor determines the guiding principles of policy and bears responsibility for this policy before the Reichstag. Within these guiding principles, every Reich minister administers his assigned portfolio independently and under his own responsibility before the Reichstag.

Article 57

The ministers must submit to the Reich government for debate and decision all statutory drafts. Moreover, they must also do so when the Constitution or statute requires debate and decision, as well as for differences of opinion over questions that involve the portfolios of several ministers.

Article 58

The Reich government reaches decisions by majority vote. Ties are broken by the vote of the chair.

Article 59

The Reichstag is authorized to raise charges against the President, the Chancellor, and ministers before the Staatsgerichthof for the German Reich, claiming that they have intentionally violated the Reich Constitution or a Reich statute. The petition for the lodging of the indictment must be signed by at least one hundred members of the Reichstag and requires the consent of the majority prescribed for constitutional amendments.

SECTION 4: The Reichsrat

Article 60

A Reichsrat is formed for the representation of the German Lands in the areas of legislation and administration of the Reich.

Article 61

Every Land has at least one vote in the Reichsrat. The larger Lands receive one vote for every one million inhabitants. Any inhabitant surplus beyond an even million or even several millions that matches the inhabitant count of the smallest Land shall be rounded off to the next million.[5] No Land may be represented by more than two-fifths of all votes.

After its incorporation into the German Reich, the German portion of Austria has the right of participation in the Reichsrat with a number of votes corresponding to its population. Until that time, the German portion of Austria may participate in debates.[6]

The number of votes is reset by the Reichsrat after every general census.

Article 62

In the committees that the Reichsrat forms from its membership, no Land has more than one vote.

Article 63

The Lands are represented in the Reichsrat by the members of their governments. However, according to the dictates of a Land statute, half of the Prussian votes are provided by the Prussian provincial administration.

The Lands are authorized to send as many representatives to the Reichsrat as they have votes.

Article 64

The Reich government must convene the Reichsrat when a third of the Reich government's members demand it.

Article 65

A member of the Reich government holds the chair in the Reichsrat and its committees. The members of the Reich government have the right and, on demand, the obligation to participate in the proceedings of the Reichsrat and its committees. Whenever they request it, they must be heard during debate.

Article 66

The Reich government as well as every member of the Reichsrat is authorized to initiate petitions in the Reichsrat.

The Reichsrat regulates its proceedings through rules of procedure.

The plenary sessions of the Reichsrat are public. According to the dictates of the rules of procedure, the public can be excluded in the case of individual matters of debate.

Article 67

The Reichsrat is to be kept informed by the Reich ministers about the conduct of Reich business. The Reich ministers should inform the competent committees of the Reichsrat about debates on important matters.

SECTION 5: Reich Legislation

Article 68

Proposed statutes are introduced by the Reich government or by the membership of the Reichstag.

Reich statutes are passed by the Reichstag.

Article 69

The introduction of proposed statutes of the Reich government requires the consent of the Reichsrat. If an agreement between the Reich government and the

Reichsrat does not come about, the Reich government can nevertheless introduce the proposal, but it must also present the Reichsrat's conflicting view.

If the Reichsrat passes a proposed statute, to which the Reich government does not consent, then the Reich government must introduce the proposal into the Reichstag for consideration of the Reichsrat's position.

Article 70

The President has to process statutes arising in a constitutional manner and promulgate them in the Reich Legal Gazette within the legally required one-month period.

Article 71

Reich statutes enter into force fourteen days after the Reich Legal Gazette is distributed in the capital, so long as nothing else has been provided.

Article 72

The promulgation of a Reich statute is postponed for two months when a third of the Reichstag demands it. The President can promulgate statutes that the Reichstag and the Reichsrat declare pressing, regardless of this demand.

Article 73

A statute concluded by the Reichstag is brought to a referendum before its promulgation if the President so decides within a month of its passage.

A statute whose promulgation is requested by petition of at least a third of the Reichstag is submitted to a referendum if one-twentieth of those entitled to vote demand it.

Additionally, a popular vote should be held if a tenth of those entitled to vote present the demand for the submission of a draft statute. A completed draft statute must be the foundation of the initiative. It must be presented to the Reichstag by the Reich government with its recommendations. The referendum does not take place if the desired draft statute has been accepted unchanged by the Reichstag.

Only the President can institute a referendum on the budget, expenditures, and compensation systems.

A Reich statute regulates the procedure during the referendum and during the initiative.

Article 74

The Reichsrat may object to a statute concluded by the Reichstag.

The objection must be introduced by the Reich government within two weeks after the final vote in the Reichstag and must be supplied with reasons within an additional two weeks.

In cases of objection, the statute is presented to the Reichstag for an additional vote. If no agreement between the Reichstag and the Reichsrat is reached in this way, the President can order a referendum on the matter of dispute within the following three months. If the President makes no use of this authority, then the statute counts as not having come about. If the Reichstag votes with a two-thirds majority against the objection of the Reichsrat, the President must promulgate the statute in the form concluded by the Reichstag or call for a referendum.

Article 75

A decision of the Reichstag can be suspended by referendum only when the majority of enfranchised voters participate in the vote.

Article 76

The Constitution can be amended via legislation. However, a decision of the Reichstag regarding the amendment of the Constitution only takes effect when two-thirds of those present consent. Decisions of the Reichsrat regarding amendment of the Constitution also require a two-thirds majority of the votes cast. If a constitutional amendment is concluded by initiative in response to a referendum, then the consent of the majority of enfranchised voters is required.

If the Reichstag passes a constitutional change against the objection of the Reichsrat, the President is not permitted to promulgate this statute if the Reichsrat demands a referendum within two weeks.

Article 77

To the extent the law does not provide otherwise, the Reich government issues the necessary general administrative provisions for the enforcement of Reich statutes. The Reich government requires the consent of the Reichsrat when Land officials are authorized to execute Reich statutes.

SECTION 6: Reich Administration

Article 78

The cultivation of relations with foreign states is exclusively a matter for the Reich.

Lands can conclude agreements with foreign states in matters for which they have legislative jurisdiction; the agreements require the consent of the Reich.

Agreements with foreign states on the alteration of Reich boundaries are finalized by the Reich after the consent of the affected Land. The boundary changes occur only on the basis of a Reich statute to the extent that it is not a mere correction of the boundaries of an uninhabited area.

In order to ensure the representation of interests of individual Lands that arise from their special economic relationships or from their position as neighbors of foreign states, the Reich will provide the necessary institutions and measures in agreement with the affected Lands.

Article 79

The defense of the Reich is a matter for the Reich. The German people's defense system is regulated by a Reich statute in a unified manner with a view to the special circumstances of the people of individual Lands.

Article 80

The colonial system is exclusively a Reich concern.

Article 81

All German merchant ships form a unified trade fleet.

Article 82

Germany forms a customs and trade area, surrounded by a common customs boundary.

The customs boundary coincides with the boundary to foreign territory. At sea, the coast of the dry land and the islands belonging to the Reich form the customs boundary. Deviations from the customs boundary can be provided for those portions of it along the sea and along other bodies of water.

Foreign state areas or portions of territory can be added to the customs zone by state treaties or agreements.

According to special need, portions of the customs zone can be excluded from it. For free harbors, these exceptions can only be eliminated through a constitutional amendment.

Customs exceptions can be added to a foreign customs zone by state treaties or agreements. All products of nature as well as works of art and objects of commerce that move in the free traffic of the Reich can be brought into, out of, or through the boundaries of the Lands and communities. Exceptions are permissible on the basis of a Reich statute.

Article 83

Tariffs and excise taxes are administered by Reich officials.

In the administration of Reich taxes by Reich officials, there is provision for institutions that make possible the preservation for the Lands of special Land interests in the areas of agriculture, trade, acquisition, and industry.

Article 84

The Reich establishes provisions for:

1. the institution of tax administration of the Lands, insofar as it requires the uniform and equal execution of Reich tax laws;

2. the establishment and powers of the officials entrusted with the supervision of the execution of Reich tax laws;

3. settling accounts with the Lands;

4. compensation for the administrative costs resulting from the execution of Reich tax laws.

Article 85

All income and expenditures of the Reich must be printed and placed in the budgetary plan.[7]

The budgetary plan is established by statute before the beginning of the budgetary year.

As a rule, the expenditures are approved for a year; in special cases, they can also be approved for a longer period. Otherwise, provisions that extend beyond the financial year or do not make reference to the income and expenditures of the Reich or its administration are impermissible in the Reich budget statute.

In the draft budgetary plan, the Reichstag cannot raise or reset expenditures without the approval of the Reichsrat.

Article 86

The Reich finance minister makes a report to the Reichsrat and Reichstag that confirms the probity of the Reich government in the use of all Reich income. This accounting report is regulated by Reich statute.

Article 87

Funds in the form of credits may be established only in cases of dire need and, as a rule, only for expenditures for recruitment purposes. Such an establishment as well as assumption of a security service by the Reich may only be pursued on the basis of a Reich statute.

Article 88

The postal and telegraph systems, including the telephone system, are exclusively a Reich concern.

The denomination of postage stamps is uniform for the entire Reich.

With the consent of the Reichsrat, the Reich government issues the decrees that set the principles and fees for the use of traffic facilities. It can delegate this authority to the Reich postal minister with the consent of the Reichsrat. Also with the consent of the Reichsrat, the Reich government can establish a council with powers of deliberative consultation in matters of tariffs and of postal, telegraphic, and telephone traffic.[8]

The Reich alone consummates treaties on traffic abroad.

Article 89

It is the duty of the Reich to assume ownership of trains that serve general traffic and to administer them as a unified means of traffic.

The right of the Lands to acquire private railroads is transferred to the Reich on its demand.

Article 90

With the takeover of the railroads, the Reich assumes the power of expropriation and the state right of supremacy in regard to the railroad system. In case of dispute, the Staatsgerichtshof decides on the scope of these rights.

Article 91

With the consent of the Reichsrat, the Reich government issues decrees that regulate the construction and operation of railroads as well as traffic on them. It can delegate this authority to the competent minister with the consent of the Reichsrat.

Article 92

Without regard to the inclusion of their budget and their accounts into the general budget and the general accounts of the Reich, the Reich railroads are to be administered as an independent, economic enterprise meant to fulfill its obligations itself, including paying interest and retiring railroad debt, and to collect the railroad reserve funds. The level of interest and reserve funds as well as the purposes of the reserve funds are regulated by special statute.

Article 93
With the consent of the Reichsrat, the Reich government establishes on behalf of the Reich railroads advisory boards for expert consultation in the matters of railroad traffic and tariffs.

Article 94
If the Reich has taken over the railroads of a certain area that serve general transportation, then new railroads that serve general transportation may be built within this area only by the Reich or with its consent. If the construction of new railroad facilities or the alteration of existing ones has an impact on the Land police, the Reich railroad administration must hear the case of the Land officials before coming to a conclusion about the matter.

Where the Reich has not yet incorporated the railroads into its administrative system, the Reich by statute can include them in its accounts when it deems this necessary for general traffic or for the defense of the Land, even against the objection of the Lands, whose territory is traversed, but without prejudice to the Land's rights of supreme authority. Under the same conditions, it can assign another organization the task of their construction, when necessary conferring on it the authority of expropriation.

Any railroad administration must assume the costs of any annexation of other railroads.

Article 95
Railroads for general transportation not administered by the Reich are subject to Reich supervision. The railroads subject to Reich supervision are bound equally by the principles established by the Reich and are to be outfitted in accord with these principles. They are to be maintained in a secure operating position and to be expanded in accord with the demands of transportation. Transportation of goods and persons is facilitated and developed in accord with need.

In the supervision of the tariff system, effort must be made to achieve equal and low railroad tariffs.

Article 96
At the demand of the Reich, all railroads, even those that do not serve general transportation, must submit to use for the purpose of Land defense.

Article 97
It is the duty of the Reich to assume ownership of the waterways that serve general transportation and to administer them itself.

After the takeover, the waterways that serve general transportation can be put to use or expanded only by the Reich or with its consent.

Regarding the administration, expansion, or new construction of waterways, the needs of the Land culture and of the waterway economy must be preserved in agreement with the Lands.

Any waterway administration is permitted to incorporate other internal waterways at the cost of the entrepreneurs. The same obligation exists for the establishment of a connection between internal waterways and railroads.

As the transfer of the waterways is undertaken, the Reich retains the power of expropriation, authority over tariffs, as well as police authority over the current and ship movements.

The duties of the current building associations regarding the expansion of natural waterways in the Rhein, Weser, and Elbe areas are to be assumed by the Reich.

Article 98

The Reich government, with the consent of the Reichsrat and according to its more detailed order, can establish advisory bodies for consultation on affairs of the waterways.

Article 99

Taxes may be raised for such works, institutions, and other facilities on the natural waterways that are provided for the easing of traffic. In regard to state and community facilities, these taxes may not exceed the costs necessary for their manufacture and maintenance. The production and maintenance costs for facilities that are not exclusively for the easing of traffic but rather are established for the promotion of other purposes may be met only through a proportional share of shipping taxes. Interest and debt retirement payments for the means used count as production costs.

The provisions of the previous sections are applicable to taxes that are raised for the artificial waterways as well as for the facilities in such waterways and in ports.

In the realm of domestic shipping, the total costs of a waterway, of a river basin, or of a waterway network may provide the basis for setting the shipping tax.

These determinations are valid for all manner of conveyance on navigable waterways.

Only the Reich may place other or higher taxes on foreign ships and their cargoes. For the creation of means for the maintenance and the expansion of German waterways, the Reich can by statute even induce those participating in shipping to contribute in another way.

Article 100

In regard to the costs of maintenance and construction of interior waterways, a Reich statute can even determine who makes use of the construction of dams in ways other than travel, insofar as several Lands participate or to the extent the Reich assumes the costs.

Article 101

It is the duty of the Reich to expropriate and administer all seacoasts, especially lighthouses, fire boats, buoys, docks, and markers. After the assumption of control, maritime designations can still only be produced or expanded by the Reich or with its consent.

SECTION 7: The Administration of Justice

Article 102

Judges are independent and subject only to the law.

Article 103

Ordinary adjudication is exercised by the Reichsgericht and by the Land courts.

Article 104

Judges of ordinary judicial claims are appointed for life. They can be deprived of their office against their will, either permanently or temporarily, or be placed in another position or put in retirement only as a result of a judicial decision and only for reasons and under the forms that are set by law. Legislation can establish age limitations when judges can enter retirement.

Temporary release from duty, which is introduced by virtue of law, is not hereby affected.

In the course of introducing changes in the institution of the courts or of their districts, the Land judicial administration can make involuntary transfers to another court or removals from office, but only with continuation of full pay.

These provisions do not apply to trade judges, lay judges, and juries.

Article 105

Exceptional courts are not permitted. No one may be removed from the jurisdiction of a judge established by law. The statutory provisions on wartime courts and status courts are not hereby affected. The military honor courts are eliminated.

Article 106

Military justice is to be eliminated except for times of war and on board warships. A Reich statute regulates the details.

Article 107

In the Reich and the Lands, there must be administrative courts that operate according to the standards of the law for the protection of the individual against the orders and legal instruments of administrative officials.

Article 108

A Staatsgerichtshof for the German Reich is established according to the standards of Reich law.

Second Principal Part: Basic Rights and Duties of Germans

SECTION 1: The Individual

Article 109

All Germans are equal before the law. Men and women in principle have the same state civil rights and duties.

Privileges or disadvantages of birth or of status that are based in public law are to be eliminated. Signs of nobility are valid only as part of the name and may no longer be conferred.

Titles may only be conferred when they designate an office or a profession; academic degrees are not affected.

Orders and honorary titles may not be awarded by the state.

No German may accept a title or order from a foreign government.

Article 110

State affiliation in the Reich and the Lands is attained and lost according to provisions of a Reich statute. Every member of a Land is simultaneously a member of the Reich.

Every German has the same rights and duties in any Land as the members of the Land themselves.

Article 111

All Germans enjoy free movement in the entire Reich. Every German has the right to stop in and to remain in any given place in the Reich. They may acquire pieces of property and obtain means of sustenance. A Reich statute permits limitations.

Article 112

Every German has the right to emigrate to non-German countries. Emigration may only be restricted by statute.

All state members have a claim to the protection of the Reich both inside and outside Reich territory.

No German may be delivered to a foreign government for the purposes of prosecution or punishment.

Article 113

The population segments in the Reich speaking a foreign language cannot be hindered, by legislation and administrative means, in their development as a people, particularly not in the use of their mother tongue in school as well as in the domestic administration and legal process.

Article 114

The freedom of the person is inviolable. An infringement on or deprivation of personal freedom by the public authority is permissible only on the basis of statutes.

Persons deprived of freedom are to be informed by the next day at the latest by which officials and for what reasons the deprivation of freedom has been ordered; without delay, the opportunity should be given them to present objections against the deprivation of their freedom.

Article 115
The living quarters of every German is for him a sanctuary and is inviolable. Exceptions are permissible only on the basis of statutes.

Article 116
An action can only be punished when its punishable character was defined by statute before the action occurred.

Article 117
The privacy of letters as well as of the mail, telegraphs, and telephone calls is inviolable. Exceptions can be established only by Reich statute.

Article 118
Every German has the right, within the limits of the general laws, to freely express his opinion through word, writing, print, image, or in other manner. No work or professional relationship may hinder him in this right, and no one may disadvantage him if he makes use of this right.

Censorship is not permitted. However, exceptions may be established by statute for film. Also, statutory measures are permitted for preventing the display and sale of defamatory and pornographic literature as well as for the protection of youth.

SECTION 2: Communal Life

Article 119
As the foundation of family life and the preservation and the growth of the nation, marriage stands under the special protection of the Constitution. It rests on the equal rights of both sexes.

To preserve the purity, health, and social advancement of the family is the duty of the state and of the community. Families with many children have a claim to compensating care.

Motherhood has a claim to the protection and care of the state.

Article 120
The rearing of offspring to achieve physical, spiritual, and social capacity is the highest duty and natural right of parents, whose activity the state community supervises.

Article 121
Legitimate and illegitimate children are to have the same statutory conditions for their physical, spiritual, and social development.

Article 122
Young people are to be protected against exploitation as well as moral, spiritual, or physical neglect. State and community authorities are required to provide the necessary institutions.

Compulsory provision of welfare services can only be ordered by statute.

Article 123

All Germans have the right to assemble peaceably and unarmed without prior notice or special permission.

A Reich statute may stipulate that open-air assemblies require prior notification and that they can be prohibited in cases of direct danger to public security.

Article 124

All Germans have the right to form associations or societies for purposes that do not run counter to the criminal laws. This right cannot be limited through preventative rules. The same provisions are valid for religious associations and societies.

The acquisition of legal capacity is open to every association according to the prescriptions of the civil law. Legal capacity cannot be denied for the reason that the association pursues a political, social-political, or religious aim.

Article 125

Electoral freedom and secrecy are ensured. Electoral statutes provide the details.

Article 126

Every German has the right to address in writing the competent officials or the popular assembly with requests or complaints. This right can be exercised both by individuals as well as by several working in common.

Article 127

Local communities and associations of the local communities have the right of self-government within the limitations of statutes.

Article 128

All state citizens without distinction qualify for public offices according to the standards of law and corresponding to their capacity and accomplishments.

All exceptional provisions against female civil servants are eliminated.

The foundations of civil servant standards are regulated by Reich statute.

Article 129

Employment of the civil servant is for life, so far as a statute does not provide otherwise. Retirement pay and care for dependents are regulated statutorily. The vested rights of civil servants are inviolable. Legal redress is available for the monetary claims of the civil servant.

Civil servants can be removed from office temporarily, placed in retirement for a time or permanently, or transferred to another office with less pay only under statutorily determined presuppositions and forms.

There must be a complaint procedure and a procedure for possible reinstatement for any criminal judgment involving official actions. Regarding evidence on the personal characteristics of the civil servant, written documentation of the facts unfavorable to him is to be first undertaken, when the civil servant was given the opportunity to express himself in regard to them. The civil servant is guaranteed the secrecy of his personal documents.

The inviolable character of the vested rights and the holding open of the legal process for monetary claims are also guaranteed to professional soldiers in particular. Otherwise, their legal position is regulated by Reich statute.

Article 130

Public officials are servants of the collective, not of a party.

All civil servants are guaranteed the liberty of their political conscience and the freedom of association.

Civil servants receive special civil servant representation according to more specific Reich statutory provisions.

Article 131

If a civil servant, in the exercise of public authority entrusted to him, injures a third party, then the responsibility rests with the state or the body in whose service the civil servant stands. Redress against the civil servant is reserved. Ordinary legal channels may not be excluded.

The competent legislature is obligated to provide more detailed regulation.

Article 132

According to law, every German has the obligation to undertake voluntary activity.

Article 133

All state citizens are obligated, according to law, to provide personal services for the state and the localities.

Mandatory military service complies with the provisions of the Reich Defense Law. This statute also provides the extent to which individual fundamental rights may be limited for the members of the defense forces in the fulfillment of their tasks and for the maintenance of discipline.

Article 134

All state citizens without distinction contribute to all public burdens in proportion to their means in accordance with statutes.

SECTION 3: Religion and Religious Societies

Article 135

All inhabitants of the Reich enjoy full freedom of belief and conscience. Undisturbed religious exercise is guaranteed by the Constitution and stands under state protection. The general state statutes remain unaffected.

Article 136

Civil and political rights and duties are neither dependent on nor limited by the exercise of religious liberty.

Enjoyment of civil and political rights and the eligibility for public office is independent of religious affiliation.

No one may be required to disclose his religious beliefs. Officials have the right to inquire into a person's membership in a religious body only insofar as rights or duties depend on it or to the degree that a legally mandated statistical survey requires it.

No one may be compelled to perform any religious act or ceremony, to take part in religious exercises, or to take an oath of a religious form.

Article 137

There is no state church.

The freedom of association to form religious societies is guaranteed. There are no restrictions on the union of religious bodies in the Reich territory.

Every religious body must regulate and administer its affairs independently within the limits of the generally applicable law. It confers its offices without the participation of the state or of the civil community.

Religious bodies obtain legal capacity in line with the general provisions of civil law.

Religious bodies shall remain corporate bodies under public law to the same degree as they have in the past. Other religious bodies shall be granted the same rights upon application, if their constitution and the number of their members offer assurance of their permanence. If two or more religious bodies established under public law unite into a single organization, this organization will also be a corporate body under public law.

Religious bodies that are corporate bodies under public law are entitled to levy taxes in line with Land law on the basis of the civil tax lists.

Associations whose purpose is the common cultivation of a worldview have the same status as religious bodies.

Further regulation required for the implementation of these provisions is a matter for Land legislation.

Article 138

State services for religious societies based on statute, contract, or special legal title will be discontinued through Land legislation. The guiding principles for this transfer of authority are established by the Reich.

Article 139

Sunday and public holidays that are recognized by the state are legally protected as days of rest from work and for spiritual growth.

Article 140

The members of the armed forces must be guaranteed the free time necessary for the fulfillment of their religious duties.

Article 141

Religious bodies are permitted to provide religious services and spiritual care in the army, in hospitals, in prisons, or in other public institutions to the extent that there is a need. There is no compulsion in the provision of these services.

Article 142

There is freedom of art, scholarship, and its teachings. The state ensures their protection and participates in their cultivation.

Article 143

Care for the education of youth is provided through public institutions. The Reich, Lands, and local communities work together in their establishment.

Article 144

The entire school system stands under the supervision of the state; local communities can participate in it. School supervision is exercised by expertly trained civil servants acting in an official capacity.

Teachers in public schools have the rights and duties of civil servants.

Article 145

There is a general obligation to attend school. The primary schools with a minimum of eight years of instruction and the affiliated continuing education schools until the age of eighteen primarily fulfill this obligation. The instruction in the elementary and continuing education schools is free.

Article 146

The public school system is composed organically. The intermediate and higher school system is built on top of the basic education school, which is common for all. The diversity of life professions is determinative of the composition of this system. The capacity and inclination of the child, not the economic and social position or the religious faith of the parents, determines whether a child is included in a particular school.

Inside local communities, however, the legally competent elementary schools with a particular religious orientation or secular worldview may apply to establish the extent to which a compulsory subject even in terms of paragraph 1 is not being infringed. The will of those legally competent in educational matters is to be taken into consideration to the greatest possible degree. Land legislation in accordance with the basic principles of a Reich statute determines the details of this stipulation.

The Reich, the Lands, and local communities must make available the public means facilitating access to the middle and higher schools for those with limited financial resources, especially child-rearing assistance for the parents of children who are considered capable of being educated in the middle and upper schools, until the conclusion of their education.

Article 147

Private schools as a substitute for public schools require the approval of the state and are subject to Land laws. The approval is granted when the private schools are not inferior to the public schools in terms of learning goals and institutional means as well as in the scholarly training of their teaching staff. Additionally, categorization of students by their relative property holdings cannot be required. Approval is denied when the economic and legal position of the teaching staff is not sufficiently guaranteed.

Private schools are only permitted when the local community does not have a public elementary school of the religious faith or worldview of those entitled legally to raise children, whose will must be taken into account according to Article 146, 2. Such a school is also permitted when the instructional administration recognizes a special pedagogical interest.

Private preparatory schools are eliminated.

Private schools that do not serve as a substitute for public schools remain under the applicable law.

Article 148

In all schools, the aim is moral education, a disposition toward state citizenship, personal and professional capability in the spirit of the distinctive nature of the German people and of fellowship among peoples.

In the course of public school instruction, an effort is made not to injure the sensibilities of those who think differently.

Knowledge about state citizenship and labor instruction are subjects in the schools. Every student receives a copy of the Constitution at the conclusion of their obligatory schooling.

The Reich, Lands, and local communities all work to advance the popular education system, including the colleges for working persons.

Article 149

Religious education is a proper subject in schools with the exception of those that are unaffiliated with a religious faith (secular schools). The provision of religious instruction is regulated within the framework of school legislation. Religious instruction is to be offered in agreement with the basic principles of the religious society that is involved, but without adversely affecting the state's right to supervise schools.

The provision of religious instruction and the carrying out of church obligations remain subject to the declaration of intent of teachers. Participation in religious courses of instruction and in religious ceremonies or actions is submitted to the declaration of intent of those responsible for the religious upbringing of the child.

The theological faculties in universities are to be preserved.

Article 150

Commemorative objects of art, history, and nature as well as the landscape enjoy the protection and care of the state.

The Reich is charged with preventing the removal of German art holdings abroad.

Article 151

The regulation of economic life must correspond to the principles of justice, with the aim of guaranteeing to all a humane existence. Individual economic freedom is secured under these limitations.

Legal compulsion is only permissible for the achievement of endangered rights or in the service of superior claims of the common good.

The freedom of trade and occupation is ensured according to Reich statutes.

Article 152

Contractual freedom as defined by statute is valid during economic transactions.

Usury is forbidden. Legal transactions in conflict with proper morals are null and void.

Article 153

Property is guaranteed by the Constitution. Its content and its limits are derived from statute.

An expropriation can be undertaken only for the general good and on a statutory basis. It proceeds against appropriate compensation, so far as a Reich statute does not provide otherwise. Regarding the extent of compensation, the legal process in the ordinary courts remains open in disputed cases, so far as Reich statutes do not determine otherwise. Expropriation by the Reich against Lands, localities, or common-use associations can only proceed with compensation.

Property creates obligations. Its use should at the same time serve the general good.

Article 154

The right of inheritance is guaranteed in terms defined by civil law. The share of the state in the estate of the deceased is defined by statute.

Article 155

The distribution and use of land is supervised by the state to prevent misuse and with the aim of securing for every German a healthy dwelling place and for all German families, especially those with many children, a place of work and residence that corresponds to their needs. War veterans are to enjoy special treatment in the right of abode that is to be created.

Landed property whose acquisition is necessary for the satisfaction of housing requirements, for the promotion of settlement, or for the clearance or improvement of agricultural land, can be expropriated. Entailment is to be eliminated.

The cultivation and use of land is a duty of the landowner toward the community. The increase of land values that arises without the application of labor or capital is to be placed at the disposal of the collectivity.

The wealth of all land and all economically utilizable natural forces are placed under state supervision. Private domains are transferable to the state via legislation.

Article 156

By statute, the Reich can transfer expropriated private economic enterprises into common property, without needing to pay compensation for socialization during the application of the valid provisions for expropriation, broadly understood. It can take part itself in the administration of economic enterprises and associations, as can Lands or local authorities, or it can secure a defining influence for itself in another way.

Additionally, in instances of pressing need and for the benefit of the community economy, the Reich can legally consolidate economic undertakings and associations on grounds of self-government, in order to secure the participation of all working sections of the population, to involve employer and employee in administration, and to regulate production, manufacture, distribution, use, and pricing as well as the import and export of economic goods in accordance with the principles of the community economy.

Cooperative societies and economic associations are to be integrated into the community economy at their request, while respecting their constitution and distinctive nature.

Article 157

Labor power enjoys the special protection of the Reich. The Reich establishes a unified body of labor law.

Article 158

Intellectual work, the rights of authors, inventors, and artists, all enjoy the Reich's protection and care.

The creations of German science, art, and technology are to be given validity and protection even abroad by international agreement.

Article 159

Freedom of association for the preservation and promotion of conditions of labor and in the economy is guaranteed for everyone and for all occupations. All agreements and measures that limit this freedom or seek to hinder it are unlawful.

Article 160

Whoever stands in a relation of service or work as an employee or worker has the right to protection by the relevant civil laws and has the right to the free time required for the fulfillment of honorary offices conferred upon them, insofar as the enterprise is not materially harmed by this activity.

Article 161

In close collaboration with the insured, the Reich establishes a comprehensive scheme of insurance that secures their health and ability to work, protects motherhood, and provides for the economic consequences of old age, infirmities, and uncertainties of life.

Article 162

The Reich advocates an interstate regulation of the legal circumstances of workers that is aimed at a general minimum of social rights for the entire working class of mankind.

Article 163

Without detriment to his personal freedom, every German has the moral duty to activate his spiritual and bodily forces such that it advances the well-being of the whole society. Every German should be granted the opportunity to earn his living through productive labor. To the extent that an appropriate opportunity for work cannot be found for him, his necessary living needs will be provided for. Details are determined through special Reich statutes.

Article 164

The independent middle class in agriculture, commerce, and trade is promoted by legislation and administration and is protected against exceptional burdens and assimilation.

Article 165

Workers and employees are entitled to determine in common with entrepreneurs and as their equals in the regulation of wages and working conditions as well as in the entire economic development of productive forces. The reciprocal organizations and their agreements are recognized.

Workers and employees must be legally represented in the enterprises' labor councils as well as in district labor councils and in a Reich workers' council in order to protect their social and economic interests.

In conjunction with representative employers' organizations and other related popular participant associations, the district and Reich councils cooperate in the fulfillment of comprehensive economic tasks and in the joint execution of socialization statutes. The Reich and district councils are composed such that all significant occupational groups are represented commensurate with their economic and social importance.

The Reich government should submit fundamentally significant draft statutes on social and economic policy to the Reich Economic Council for its advice before their introduction to the Reichstag. The Reich Economic Council itself has the right to submit such draft statutes. If the Reich government is not in agreement with such submissions, it must nevertheless present them to the Reichstag together with an account of its view of the issue. The Reich Economic Council has the authority to appoint one of its members to represent its submissions to the Reichstag.

Workers' and economic councils may assume powers of supervision and administration in the areas of activity accorded them.

It is a matter of exclusive Reich authority to regulate the composition and tasks of workers' and economic councils as well as their relation to other self-administrating bodies.

Transitional and Concluding Provisions

Article 166

Until the establishment of the Reich Administrative Court, the Reichsgericht takes its place in terms of forming the Electoral Review Commission.

Article 167

The provisions of paragraphs 3 to 6 of Article 18 first enter into force two years after the promulgation of the Constitution.[9]

Article 168

Until the issuance of the Land statute envisioned in Article 63, but at the most for one additional year, the collective Prussian votes in the Reichsrat may be cast by the members of the government.[10]

Article 169

The Reich government determines the time for the entry into force of Article 83, 1.

The raising and administration of customs and excise taxes may be left to the Lands at their request for an appropriate transition period.

Article 170

The postal and telegraph administrations in Bavaria and Württemberg are to be taken over by the Reich by 1 April 1921 at the latest.

The Staatsgerichtshof decides the issue when there is no agreement on the conditions of the transfer of authority by 1 October 1920.

Until the transfer of authority, the present rights and duties of Bavaria and Württemberg remain in force. The Reich, however, exclusively regulates the postal and telegraph traffic with the neighboring foreign states.

Article 171

The Reich assumes control of state railroads, waterways, and seacoasts on 1 April 1921 at the latest.

If by 1 October 1920 no agreement has been achieved on the conditions for the transfer of authority, the Staatsgerichtshof will decide the matter.

Article 172

Until the Reich statute on the Staatsgerichtshof comes into force, a seven-member senate exercises its authority, of which the Reichstag contributes four. The Reichsgericht selects three of its members for the court. The Staatsgerichtshof's regulates its own procedure.

Article 173

Until the issuance of a Reich statute according to Article 138, religious societies retain state services that were previously based on statute, contract, or special legal title.

Article 174

Until the issuance of the Reich statute anticipated by Article 146, 2, the existing legal circumstance remains in place. The statute must in particular take into account areas of the Reich in which there are schools that legally do not distinguish on the basis of religious faith.

Article 175

The provision of Article 109 does not apply to orders and honorary awards that are to be conferred for service during wartime from 1914 to 1919.

Article 176

All public civil servants and members of the defense forces must take an oath of allegiance to the Constitution. Details are determined by a decree of the President.

Article 177

Where existing statutes provide for the use of a religious form of oath in swearing a vow, the act of taking an oath may also be legally valid when it is executed without the religious form "I swear." Otherwise, the content of the vow as it is provided in statutes remains unaffected.

Article 178

The Constitution of the German Reich of 16 April 1871 and the statute on the provisional Reich authority of 10 February 1919 are superseded.

Other statutes and decrees of the Reich remain in force to the extent that this Constitution is not in conflict with them. The provisions of the peace treaty signed at Versailles on 28 June 1919 are not affected by the Constitution.[11]

Official orders that were issued in a legal manner on the basis of previous statutes retain their validity up until their supersession by way of additional orders or legislation.

Article 179

To the extent that statutes or decrees refer to provisions or institutions that are eliminated by this constitution, the corresponding provisions and institutions of this constitution take their place. In particular, the Reichstag takes the place of the National Assembly, the Reichsrat substitutes for the Committee of States, and the President elected on the basis of this constitution replaces the President elected on the basis of the statute on the provisional Reich authority.

The authority to issue decrees that was granted to the Committee of States by previous provisions is transferred to the Reich government, which requires the consent of the Reichsrat according to the standards of this constitution in order to issue decrees.

Article 180

The National Assembly serves as Reichstag until the convening of the first Reichstag. Until the first President assumes his office, the President elected on the basis of the statute on the provisional Reich authority executes the office of the President.[12]

Article 181

The German people has drafted and passed this constitution through its National Assembly. It enters into force on the day of its promulgation.

Notes

1. [11 August 1919 (*Reichgesetzblatt* I, p. 1383). Entered into force on 14 August 1919. Trans.]

2. [Law of 15 December 1923 (*Reichgesetzblatt* I, p. 1185) added: "or the dissolution of the Reichstag until the convening of the new Reichstag." Trans.]

3. [Law of 22 May 1926 (*Reichgesetzblatt* I, p. 243), added Article 40a, which reads:

"The provisions of Articles 36, 37, 38, 1, and 39, 1, are valid for the president of the Reichstag, his deputies, and the members of the committees established in Article 35, both permanent and primary deputy members, even during the time between sessions (meeting periods) or election periods.

The same is valid for the president of a Land parliament, his deputies, and permanent and primary deputy members of Land parliament committees, when they can be active outside of the session (meeting period) or electoral period according to the Land constitution.

To the extent that Article 37 provides for consent of the Reichstag or of a Land parliament, the committee for the protection of the rights of the popular assembly takes the place of the Reichstag and, in case committees of the Land parliament continue to exist, the committee established by the Land parliament for this purpose takes the place of the Land parliament.

The persons designated in paragraph 1 have the rights indicated in Article 40 between election periods." Trans.]

4. [Law of 17 December 1932 (*Reichgesetzblatt* I, p. 547), replaced "Chancellor" with "President of the Reichsgericht." Trans.]

5. [Law of 24 March 1921 (*Reichgesetzblatt* I, p. 440) replaced the number "one million" in the second sentence with the number "700,000," and the words "an even million or even several millions, which matches the inhabitant count of the smallest Land, shall be rounded off to the next million," by "of at least 350,000 becomes 700,000." Trans.]

6. [Versailles Treaty and a special protocol of 22 September 1919 invalidated this provision. Trans.]

7. [Section 15, 2, of the Reich Postal Finance Law of 18 March 1924 (*Reichgesetzblatt* I, p. 287) stipulates that "the provisions of Articles 85 to 87 of the Constitution are valid from the same date (1 April 1924) with the directive that the administrative council takes the place of the Reichsrat and Reichstag, and that a Reich statute is not required for the assumption of credits and adoption of guarantees." Trans.]

8. [Section 15 of the Reich Postal Finance Law of 18 March 1924 (*Reichgesetzblatt* I, p. 287) invalidated paragraphs 3 and 4 of this article. Trans.]

9. [Law of 27 November 1920 (*Reichgesetzblatt* I, p. 1987) added paragraphs 2 and 3:

"In the Prussian province of upper Silesia, within months after German authorities reassume administration of the area currently occupied, a vote will take place according to Article 18, 1 and 5, deciding the question of whether a Land of Upper Silesia will be formed.

If the question is answered affirmatively, then the Land will be formed without delay. This establishment does not require a Reich statute. The following provisions apply:

1. There is to be the election of a Land assembly, which, within three months of the official determination of the vote results, must be convened to form a Land government and to produce a Land constitution. The President issues the call for the election and determines the election day.

2. The President, in cooperation with the Land assembly, determines when the Land counts as established.

3. Upper Silesia's acquisition of state affiliation requires that
(a) those of majority age affiliated with the Reich, who, on the day of the establishment of the Land of Upper Silesia (section 2), have their abode or continuous residence in its territory;
(b) other persons of majority age affiliated with the Prussian state who were born in the territory of the province of Upper Silesia and who, within a year of the establishment of the Land (paragraph 2), declare to the Land government that they want to acquire state affiliation in Upper Silesia on the day of submission of this declaration;
(c) all persons affiliated with the Reich who obtained state affiliation through birth, naturalization, or marriage, to whom sections a and b apply." Trans.]

10. [Law of 6 August 1920 (*Reichsgesetzblatt* I, p. 1565) replaced "after the period of a year" with "up until 1 July 1921." Trans.]

11. [A law of 6 August 1920 (*Reichsgesetzblatt* I, p. 1566) added a third sentence: "With regard to the negotiations over the acquisition of the island Helgoland, a rule that deviates from that in Article 17, 2, may be adopted for the benefit of the inhabitants. Trans.]

12. [A law of 27 Octobner 1922 (*Reichsgesetzblatt* I, p. 801) replaced the second sentence with the following one: "The President selected by the National Assembly holds office until 30 June 1925." Trans.]

Notes

Introduction

1. The Schmitt literature is so vast it defies citation. Some of the major works in German are Jürgen Fijalkowski, *Die Wendung zum Führerstaat: Ideologische Komponenten in der politischen Philosophie Carl Schmitts* (Cologne: Westdeutscher Verlag, 1958); Christian Graf von Krockow, *Die Entscheidung: Eine Untersuchung über Ernst Jünger, Carl Schmitt, Martin Heidegger* (Stuttgart: F. Enke, 1958); Hasso Hofmann, *Legitimität gegen Legalität: Der Weg der politischen Philosophie Carl Schmitts* (Berlin: Duncker und Humblot, [1964] 1992); Ingeborg Maus, *Bürgerliche Rechtstheorie und Fascismus: Zur sozialen Funktion und aktuellen Wirkung der Theorie Carl Schmitts* (Munich: Wilhelm Fink Verlag, [1976] 1980); Christian Meier, *Carl Schmitt, Leo Strauss und "Der Begriff des Politischen": Zu einem Dialog unter Abwesenden* (Stuttgart: J. B. Metzlersche Verlagsbuchhandlung, 1988); and Reinhard Mehring, *Pathetisches Denken: Carl Schmitts Denkweg am Leitfaden Hegels* (Berlin: Duncker und Humblot, 1989). The first major work in English was George Schwab, *The Challenge of the Exception: An Introduction to the Political Ideas of Carl Schmitt between 1921 and 1936* (Westport, Conn.: Greenwood Press, [1970] 1989). For a more recent overview, see John P. McCormick, *Carl Schmitt's Critique of Liberalism: Against Politics as Technology* (Cambridge: Cambridge University Press, 1997). Some recent works in English focusing on Schmitt's legal theory are William Scheuerman, *Between the Norm and the Exception: The Frankfurt School and the Rule of Law* (Cambridge, Mass.: MIT Press, 1994); Peter Caldwell, *Popular Sovereignty and the Crisis of German Constitutional Law: The Theory and Practice of Weimar Constitutionalism* (Durham: Duke University Press, 1997); David Dyzenhaus, *Legality and Legitimacy: Carl Schmitt, Hans Kelsen and Hermann Heller in Weimar* (Oxford: Oxford University Press, 1997); Jeffrey Seitzer, *Comparative History and Legal Theory: Carl Schmitt in the First German Democracy* (Westport, Conn.: Greenwood Press, 2001); and Ellen Kennedy, *Constitutional Failure: Carl Schmitt in Weimar* (Durham: Duke University Press, 2004).

2. Jan-Werner Muller, *A Dangerous Mind: Carl Schmitt in Postwar European Thought* (New Haven: Yale University Press, 2003).

3. Bernard Schlink, "Why Carl Schmitt?" *Rechtshistorisches Journal* 10 (1991): 160–76, addresses the continuing interest in Schmitt in Germany, while Jürgen Habermas, "Die Schrecken der Autonomie: Carl Schmitt auf englisch," in *Eine Art Schadenabwicklung* (Frankfurt a. M.: Suhrkamp, 1987), considers Schmitt's appeal to an English-speaking audience.

4. Joseph W. Bendersky, *Carl Schmitt: Theorist for the Reich* (Princeton: Princeton University Press, 1983), 107–91. See also Paul Noack, *Carl Schmitt: Eine Biographie* (Berlin: Propyläen, 1993).

5. On Schmitt in the Nazi period, cf. Bendersky, *Theorist for the Reich*, 195–273; and Bernd Rüthers, *Carl Schmitt im Dritten Reich: Wissenschaft als Zeitgeist-Verstärkung?* (Munich: Verlag C. H. Beck, 1990).

6. Dirk van Laak, *Gespräche in der Sicherheit des Schweigens: Carl Schmitt in der politischen Geistesgeschichte der frühen Bundesrepublik* (Berlin: Akademie Verlag, 1993).

7. On Schmitt's influence as a legal theorist in the Federal Republic, see Hans Lietzmann, "Vater der Verfassungsväter—Carl Schmitt und die Verfassungsgründung in der Bundesrepublik Deutschland," in *Carl Schmitt und die Liberalismuskritik*, ed. Klaus Hansen and Hans Lietzmann (Opladen: Leske und Budrich, 1988); and Reinhard Mehring, "Carl Schmitt und die Verfassungslehre unserer Tage," *Archiv des öffentlichen Rechts* 120 (1995): 177–204. See also the individual country reports in Helmut Quaritsch, ed., *Complexio Oppositorium: Über Carl Schmitt* (Berlin: Duncker und Humblot, 1988).

8. For contrasting views on the question of continuity in Schmitt's work, cf. Ingeborg Maus, "Zur Zäsur von 1933 in der Theorie Carl Schmitts," *Kritische Justiz* 2 (1969): 113–24; and Lutz Berthold, *Carl Schmitt und der Staatsnotstandsplan am Ende der Weimar Republik* (Berlin: Dunker und Humblot, 1999). More recently, Joseph Bendersky argues that Schmitt's "concept of concrete orders, with its emphasis on traditional institutions, community, and cultural foundations, reconfirms that Schmitt remained primarily a traditional conservative thinker" even in the Nazi period. See "Introduction: The Three Types of Juristic Thought in German Historical and Intellectual Context," in Carl Schmitt, *On the Three Types of Juristic Thought*, trans. Joseph W. Bendersky (Westport, Conn.: Praeger, 2004), 2.

9. For a recent, full-length treatment of Schmitt's apparent rapprochement with liberalism, see Renato Cristi, *Carl Schmitt and Authoritarian Liberalism: Strong State, Free Economy* (Cardiff: University of Wales Press, 1998).

10. In the main text, the term *Rechtsstaat* is left in the original German. To remain consistent, we have not translated it in our introduction as well.

11. See Claudius Müller, *Die Rechtsphilosophie des Marburger Neukantianismus: Naturrecht und Rechtspositivismus in der Auseinandersetzung zwischen Hermann Cohen, Rudolf Stammler und Paul Natorp* (Tübingen: J. C. B. Mohr, 1994), 8–15.

12. See Hermann Cohen, *System der Philosophie, Zweiter Theil: Ethik des reinen Willens* (Berlin: Bruno Cassirer, 1904), 309.

13. Ibid., 74.

14. See Emil Lask, "Rechtsphilosophie," in *Die Philosophie im Beginn des zwanzigsten Jahrhunderts: Festschrift für Kuno Fischer*, ed. Wilhelm Windelband (Heidelberg: Carl Winter, 1907), 269–320; 271; also Heinrich Rickert, *Die Grenzen der naturwissenschaftlichen Begriffsbildung: Eine logische Einleitung in die historischen Wissenschaften* (Tübingen: J. C. B. Mohr, 1902), 702.

15. Cohen, *Ethik des reinen Willens*, 304. See also Rudolf Stammler, *Sozialismus und Christentum: Erörterungen zu den Grundbegriffen und den Grundsätzen der Sozialwissenschaft* (Leipzig: Felix Meiner, 1920), 69.

16. Hans Kelsen, *Das Problem der Souveränität und die Theorie des Völkerrechts: Beitrag zu euiner reinen Rechtslehre* (Tübingen: J. C. B. Mohr, 1920), 72.

17. Hans Kelsen, *Der soziologische und der juristische Staatsbegriff: Kritische Untersuchung des Verhältnisses von Staat und Recht* (Tübingen: J. C. B. Mohr, 1922), 2.

18. Hans Kelsen, *Reine Rechtslehre* (Leipzig/Vienna: Deuticke, 1934), 9.

19. Hans Kelsen, *Allgemeine Staatslehre* (Berlin: Julius Springer, 1925), 278.

20. Ibid., 76.

21. Kelsen, *Das Problem der Souveränität*, 227.

22. Hence the express antilegalism in Heidegger's interpretation of Kant. See Martin Heidegger, *Kant und das Problem der Metaphysik*, in: *Gesamtausgabe*, vol. 3, ed. Fr. W. von Hermann (Frankfurt a. M.: Klostermann, 1990), 158.

23. Max Scheler, *Der Formalismus in der Ethik und die materiale Wertethik: Neuer Versuch der Grundlegung eines ethischen Personalismus*, 2nd ed. (Halle: Niemeyer, 1921) 104–7, 544.

24. Karl Jaspers, *Psychologie der Weltanschauungen* (Munich: Piper, 1919), 221, 226.

25. Paul Natorp, *Der Deutsche und sein Staat* (Erlangen: Verlag der Philosophischen Akademie, 1924), 88.

26. See Eugen Ehrlich, "Freie Rechtsfindung und freie Rechtswissenschaft," in *Recht und Leben: Gesammelte Schriften zur Rechtstatsachenforschung und zur Freirechtslehre* ed. M. Rehbinder (Berlin: Duncker und Humblot, 1967), 170–202 esp. 192, 184; Gnaeus Flavius [Hermann Kantorowicz], *Der Kampf um die Rechtswissenschaft* (Heidelberg: Carl Winter, 1906), 35; and Hermann Kantorowicz, *Zur Lehre vom richtigen Recht* (Berlin: Walter Rothschild, 1909), 37; also Gustav Radbruch, "Rechtswissenschaft als Rechtsschöpfung: Ein Beitrag zum juristischen Methodenstreit," in *Archiv für Sozialwissenschaft und Sozialpolitik* 22 (1906), 355–370, esp. 365.

27. Erich Kaufmann, *Kritik der neukantischen Rechtsphilosophie: Eine Betrachtung über die Beziehungen zwischen Philosophie und Rechtswissenschaft* (Tübingen: J. C. B. Mohr, 1921), vi.

28. Julius Binder, *Rechtsbegriff und Rechtsidee: Bemerkungen zur Rechtsphilosophie Rudolf Stammlers* (Leipzig: Deichert, 1915), 72.

29. See especially Hugo Sinzheimer, *Ein Arbeitstarifgesetz: Die Idee der sozialen Selbstbestimmmung im Recht* (Munich: Duncker und Humblot, 1916).

30. For the classic account of integration theory, see Rudolf Smend, "Verfassung und Verfassungsrecht," *Staatsrechtliche Abhandlungen und andere Aufsätze*, 2nd ed. (Berlin: Duncker und Humblot, 1955), 119–276, esp. 260. Hermann Heller, Schmitt's other great theoretical rival of the 1920s, was surely not resolutely opposed to all aspects of neo-Kantian thinking; he clearly shared the Kantian assumption that the formation and exercise of power is always restricted by law. However, he also accommodated an organic theory of legal integration, which imputes central importance to social organizations as the basic units of political will formation and political integration in the modern political order, and which thus moves him away from purely Kantian constitutional analysis. See Hermann Heller, *Staatslehre*, in *Gesammelte Schriften*, 3 vols., ed. G. Niemeyer (Tübingen: Mohr, 1992), 3:81–397, esp. 348.

31. A particularly important element in Schmitt's intellectual background can be found in nineteenth-century historiographical reflection. Indeed, while positivism constituted the major orthodoxy in legal-political thought in later Imperial Germany, the underlying ideas of national-political thought at this time were to a large extent defined by *historicism*. Historicism was an intellectual outlook that rejected the rational-metaphysical, universalist and ius-natural traditions of social analysis derived from the Kantian Enlightenment, and it argued that each nation has its own

distinctive history, its own distinctive laws, and its own very distinctive ideas about legitimacy and necessary order. In consequence, historicism argued for highly relativizing definitions of political legitimacy and cultural integrity, and it positioned itself against all formalist models of legal order.

In the earlier part of the nineteenth century, this outlook tended to be flanked by national-liberal political perspectives, which saw the historicist emphasis on historical particularity as serving an emancipative interest in national freedom. For instance, one of the greatest of all historicists, Johann Gustav Droysen, was a liberal delegate in the Frankfurt Parliament of 1848–49. By the later nineteenth century, however, historicism was gradually falling under the influence of more dogmatically nationalist historians, such as Heinrich von Treitschke, who, though broadly still inside the national-liberal camp, saw the abandonment of universal ethical concerns in the definition of historical culture as the foundation for a creed of strong-state nationalism. Notable exceptions to this tendency, such as the great liberal historian Friedrich Meinecke remained influential into the twentieth century. Generally, however, by the early twentieth century historicism provided the general foundation for most conservative political ideologies in Germany.

The Weimar era saw a fundamental radicalization of the political ideas characteristic of historicism, and these paved the way for the emergence of still more reactionary historicist views in the 1930s. The main lines of radical-conservative and *völkisch* ideology that prevailed at the end of the Weimar Republic can be seen to arise from a polemical intensification of earlier historicist arguments about the particularity of culture, the relativity of right and law, and the contingency of valid law on a uniform political will and an exclusive political culture.

The essential theoretical residue of historicism is that human life is most authentically human where it is historically free from all external determinacy, and independent both of causal regulation and of perennial or rationalized values and ethics. This condition of historical freedom, for the historicists, is also the fundamental precondition of true politics, and of true legitimacy in politics: politics is the highest expression of human historical being, and so also the highest expression of humanity itself. It is not always easy to align Schmitt to the more humanist arguments evolving from historicism. Nonetheless, he clearly concurs with the fundamental humanist claim of the historicists, articulated initially by Dilthey: that politics, in a historically specific location, is the most genuine determinant of human life, and that the legitimate political apparatus is one that is founded in and that re-presents this political-historical quality of the people. In fact, we can see how at the very heart of Schmitt's work the historicist claim that humanity is constituted by its shared historical experiences is transformed into an existential or anthropological argument that sees authentic human existence as constituted by its shared possession of a uniform political will. This perspective views such politicality as the defining resource of human life, and as the resource that the legitimate state must both represent and protect from all formal, material, positivist, or nonpolitical violation.

32. Anton F. J. Thibaut, *System des Pandekten-Rechts*, 2. vols (Jena: Johann Michael Manke, 1803), 1: 35.

33. G. F. Puchta, *Cursus der Institutionen*, 3 vols. (Leipzig: Breitkopf und Härtel, 1841), 1:100; Rudolph Jhering, *Geist des römischen Rechts auf den verschiedenen*

Stufen seiner Entwicklung, 3 vols. (Leipzig: Breitkopf und Härtel, 1852), 1:12; Carl Friedrich von Gerber, *System des deutschen Privatrechts*, 6th ed.(Jena: Friedrich Mauke, 1858), 19. It should be noted, however, that Gerber also expressed a measured sympathy for historical-organic and associational theories of law and state (10–11), and he was in certain respects a mediator between positivist and organic theories of law.

34. Bernhard Windscheid, "Die Aufgaben der Rechtswissenschaft," in *Gesammelte Reden und Aufsätze* (Leipzig: Duncker und Humblot, 1904), 100–16; 112.

35. Paul Laband, *Das Staatsrecht des deutschen Reiches*, 4 vols., 4th ed. (Tübingen/Leipzig: J. C. B. Mohr, 1901), 1:89–90.

36. For an early version of this view, see Georg Beseler, *Volksrecht und Juristenrecht* (Leipzig: Weidmannsche Buchhandlung, 1843), 69–70, 84; for a later version, see Johann Caspar Bluntschli, "Der Rechtsbegriff," in *Vorträge gehalten zu München im Winter 1858* (Braunschweig: Friedrich Vieweg und Sohn, 1858), 143–83, for the classic articulation of this perspective, see Otto Gierke, *Das deutsche Genossenschaftsrecht*, vol. II: *Geschichte des deutschen Körperschaftsbegriffs* (Berlin: Weidmann, 1873), 37.

37. Georg Jellinek, *Allgemeine Staatslehre* (Berlin: Häring, 1900), 308.

38. Charles Maier, *Recasting Bourgeois Europe: Stabilization in France, Germany, and Italy in the Decade after World War I*, with a new preface (Princeton: Princeton University Press, [1975] 1988), 136–53.

39. Ibid., 249–72, 356–87, esp. 364–87.

40. Werner Conze, "Die Krise des Parteienstaates in Deutschland, 1929/30," in *Von Weimar zu Hitler, 1930–1933*, ed. Gotthard Jasper (Cologne: Kiepenheuer und Witsch, 1968); Larry Eugene Jones, *German Liberalism and the Dissolution of the Weimar Party System, 1918–1933* (Ann Arbor: University of Michigan Press, [1988] 1998); Michael Stürmer, *Koalition und Opposition in der Weimarer Republik, 1924–1928* (Düsseldorf: Droste, 1967), 265–73.

41. M. Rainer Lepsius, "Parteisystem und Sozialstruktur: Zum Problem der Demokratisierung der deutschen Gesellschaft," in *Demokratie in Deutschland: Soziologisch-historische Konstellationsanalysen* (Göttingen: Vandenhoeck und Ruprecht, 1993), 81–38; also Detlev J. K. Peukert, *The Weimar Republic: The Crisis of Classical Modernity*, trans. Richard Deveson (London: Penguin, [1987] 1991), 38.

42. For an exhaustive study of parliamentary elections in the Weimar Republic, see Richard F. Hamilton, *Who Voted for Hitler?* (Princeton: Princeton University Press, 1982). Appendix A contains a summary analysis of Reichstag elections. See also Peukert, *Weimar*, 38.

43. There is a long-standing controversy about how much political room for maneuver the parties supporting the Republic had. Knut Borchardt, *Wachstum, Krisen und Handlungsspielraum der Wirtschaftspolitik: Studien zur Wirtschaftsgeschichte des 19. und 20 Jahrhunderts* (Göttingen: Vandenhoeck und Ruprecht, 1982), 162–82 and 183–205, sparked a debate over the limited range of options available to the German government in responding to the economic crisis in the final years of the Republic, which, in turn, rendered effective parliamentary government increasingly difficult, if not impossible. For reactions to the so-called Borchardt thesis, see Carl-Ludwig Holtfrerich, "Zu hohen Löhnen in der Weimarer Republik? Bemerkungen zur Borchardt-These," *Geschichte und Gesellschaft* 10 (1984): 122–41; Jürgen von

Kruedener, "Die Überforderung der Weimarer Republik als Sozialstaat," *Geschichte und Gesellschaft* 11, 3 (1985): 358–76, and Kruedener, ed., *Economic Crisis and Political Collapse: The Weimar Republik, 1924–1933* (New York: Berg, 1990); Charles Maier, "Die Nicht-Determiniertheit ökonomischer Modelle: Überlegungen zu Knut Borchardts These von der 'kranken Wirtschaft' der Weimarer Republik," *Geschichte und Gesellschaft* 11 (1985): 275–94; and Jans-Joachim Voth, "Wages, Investment, and the Fate of the Weimar Republik: A Long-Term Perspective," *German History* 11, 3 (1993): 265–92. In a recent reassessment of Brüning's role in the Weimar Republic, William J. Patch Jr., *Heinrich Brüning and the Dissolution of the Weimar Republic* (Cambridge: Cambridge University Press, 1998), 94–95, argues that the collapse of the coalition government in 1930, leading to the first big electoral breakthrough for the Nazis, was "probably inevitable" because bourgeois parties risked further loss of votes through cooperation with the SPD. Sheri Berman, *The Social Democratic Moment: Ideas and Politics in the Making of Interwar Europe* (Cambridge, Mass.: Harvard University Press, 1998), by contrast, argues that the SPD might have broadened its base if it had been willing to give up certain firmly held beliefs.

44. David Abraham, *The Collapse of the Weimar Republic: Political Economy and Crisis*, 2nd ed. (New York: Holmes and Meier, [1981] 1986), 1–41, 229–318.

45. Dietmar Petzina and Werner Abelshauser, "Zum Problem der relativen Stagnation der deutschen Wirtschaft in den zwanziger Jahren," in *Industrielles System und politische Entwicklung in der Weimarer Republik*, ed. Hans Mommsen et al. (Düsseldorf: Droste Verlag, 1974); and Peukert, *Weimar*, 118–24.

46. Because they were passed with a two-thirds majority of the Reichstag, enabling acts (*Ermächtigunggesetze*) met the requirements for passage of a constitutional amendment. They granted certain organs, typically the Reich government or the President, the power to issue decrees with the force of law (*Rechtsverordnungen*), which, in some cases, could deviate from express constitutional provisions (*Verfassungsdurchbrechungen*). This decree power was subject to time limitations as well as restrictions on the content and object of the decrees issued. See Ludwig Richter, "Das präsidiale Notverordnungsrecht in den ersten Jahren der Weimarer Republik: Friedrich Ebert und die Anwendung des Artikels 48 der Weimarer Reichsverfassung," in *Friedrich Ebert als Reichspräsident: Amtsführung und Amtsverständnis*, ed. Eberhard Kolb (Munich: Oldenburg, 1997), 248–53; and Hans Rein, *Weimar, rechtsgeschichtlich dokumentiert* (Stuttgart: Richard Boorberg, 1991), 127–29.

47. Bismarck's Reich Constitution forged a national government from numerous independent states by permitting the Lands to retain a good deal of their former sovereignty. After the collapse of the Reich system, there was substantial support for a fundamental reform of the federal system. In the end, however, the Weimar Constitution preserved the traditional system with some modifications. Reich authority increased significantly, particularly in regard to taxation, but the Lands were still relatively autonomous governing units, with their own parliaments and court systems. Moreover, as under the traditional system, the Lands retained control over much of the administrative apparatus needed to enforce Reich laws. Finally, though the Land governments had a high degree of autonomy from the Reich, they could exert considerable influence at the Reich level. For example, they could hinder the full implementation of Reich laws through opposition in the Reichsrat or through half-hearted administration at the regional or local levels. Also, because

parties with a narrowly local or regional orientation could gain representation in the closely divided Reichstag, more parochial interests could force concessions from hard-pressed parliamentary majorities that were detrimental to the national interest. Hence, the problem of political pluralism so destructive at the Reich level, in Schmitt's view, was duplicated at the regional and local levels, complicating greatly the already difficult task of governing. See *Hüter der Verfassung* (Berlin: Duncker und Humblot, [1931] 1985), 72, 92–93.

On the failed efforts to reform the federal system, see Ernst Rudolf Huber, *Deutsche Verfassungsgeschichte seit 1789* (Stuttgart: W. Kohlhammer, 1984), 7:668–79; and Gerhard Schulz, *Zwischen Demokratie und Diktatur: Verfassungspolitik und Reichsreform in der Weimarer Republik* (Berlin: Walter de Gruyter, 1963), 3:486–515, 564–612. On the complex changes in the tax system, see Huber, *Verfassungsgeschichte*, 6:486–504; and Mabel Newcomer, *Central and Local Finance in Germany and England* (New York: Columbia University Press, 1937), 42–97. The impact of local and regional parties and interests on the Reich level is discussed in Huber, *Verfassungsgeschichte*, 6:498–99; and Patch, *Brüning*, 94–95. Jeffrey Seitzer, *Comparative History and Legal Theory: Carl Schmitt in the First German Democracy* (Westport, Conn.: Greenwood Press, 2001), 41–71, examines Schmitt's critique of German federalism.

48. Schmitt's first major work on constitutional dictatorship, *Die Diktatur: Von den Anfängen des modernen Souveränitätsgedankens bis zum proletarischen Klassenkampf* (Berlin: Duncker und Humblot, [1922] 1989), was not written in explicit reference to Art. 48. Schmitt distinguishes between two forms of dictatorship, sovereign and commissarial. The Roman dictator was of the commissarial type in that he was not empowered to make permanent changes in the Roman constitution. Rather, the dictator's sole purpose was to restore the Roman constitution, even though some actions in pursuit of this goal violated particular aspects of the constitutional order, such as the rights of particular citizens. A sovereign dictator, by contrast, brings about a fundamental change in the existing order or establishes a new order under his own authority.

A 1924 essay, "Die Diktatur des Reichspräsidenten," later included as an appendix to *Die Diktatur*, is arguably Schmitt's most important explication of the legal basis of presidential government under Art. 48. The first principal question, Schmitt argues, is the relation to one another of the first two sections of Art. 48. Schmitt argues that until the passage of supplementary legislation under Section 5 (which never occurred), Section 1 is an independent grant of authority to the President to issue measures with the force of law, which is subject to only two limitations. First, the President cannot issue measures that involve permanent, general, and fundamental changes in the established constitutional order. In other words, his authority is commissarial, not sovereign. The National Assembly that promulgated the Weimar Constitution exercised a sovereign dictatorship, but this lasted only until the constitution took effect. Second, the Reichstag retains the right to demand the suspension or abrogation of any presidential action taken under Section 1. Section 2's enumeration of the Basic Rights that the President can suspend during an emergency, by contrast, is not a limitation on the general authority of Section 1, according to Schmitt. This listing of the Basic Rights does not indicate that these are the only provisions of the Weimar Constitution that the President can suspend during a state of emergency. The drafting history of the article indicates that if anything, Section 2 was intended to reinforce the authority granted under the first section. Moreover, Schmitt continues, the widely accepted practice of the exercise of presidential emergency powers under Art. 48 indicates that the President's authority extends to all provisions of the Weimar Constitution, so long as it does not violate the previously mentioned limitations.

On presidential emergency decrees in Weimar generally, see Frederick Watkins, *The Failure of Constitutional Emergency Powers under the German Republic* (Cambridge, Mass.: Harvard University Press, 1939); Clinton L. Rossiter, *Constitutional Dictatorship: Crisis Government in Modern Democracies* (Princeton: Princeton University Press, 1948), 31–73; Ulrich Scheuner, "Die Anwendung des Art. 48 der Weimarer Reichsverfassung unter den Reichspräsidentschaften von Ebert und Hindenburg," in *Staat, Wirkschaft und Politik in der Weimarer Republik: Festschrift für Heinrich Brüning*, ed. Ferdinand A. Hermens and Theodor Schieder (Berlin: Duncker und Humblot, 1967), 249–86; Heinrich Oberreuter, *Notstand und Demokratie* (Munich: Vögel, 1978), esp. 43–71; Ernst Rudolf Huber, *Deutsche Verfassungsgeschichte seit 1789* (Stuttgart: W. Kohlhammer, 1981), 6:434–50; Hans Boldt, "Der Artikel 48 der Weimarer Reichsverfassung: Sein historischer Hintergrund und seine politische Funktion," in *Die Weimarer Republik: Belagerte Civitas*, ed. Michael Stürmer (Königstein: Verlagsgruppe Athenäum, Hain, Scriptor, Hanstein, 1980), 288–309; Michael Frehse, *Ermächtigunggesetzgebung im deutschen Reich, 1914–1933* (Pfaffenweiler: Centaurus-Verlagsgesellschaft, 1985); John E. Finn, *Constitutions in Crisis: Political Violence and the Rule of Law* (New York: Oxford University Press, 1991), 139–78; and Peter Blomeyer, *Der Notstand in den letzten Jahren von Weimar* (Berlin: Duncker und Humblot, 1999).

For a critical evaluation of the use of emergency powers by the Republic's two Presidents, Friedrich Ebert and Paul von Hindenburg, see Gotthard Jasper, "Die verfassungs- und machtpolitische Problematik des Reichspräsidents in der Weimarer Republik: Die Praxis der Reichspräsidenten Ebert und Hindenburg im Vergleich," in *Friedrich Ebert und seine Zeit: Bilanz und Perspektiven der Forschung*, ed. Rudolf König et al. (Munich: R. Oldenburg, 1997).

On Schmitt's understanding of emergency powers and his role in late Weimar, compare Schwab, *Challenge of the Exception*, 80–89; Bendersky, *Carl Schmitt*, 107–91; and Lutz Berthold, *Carl Schmitt und der Staatsnotstandsplan am Ende der Weimar Republik* (Berlin: Duncker und Humblot, 1999), 32–77, on the one hand; with John McCormick, *Carl Schmitt's Critique of Liberalism: Against Politics as Technology* (Cambridge: Cambridge University Press, 1997), 121–56; and Dyzenhaus, *Legality and Legitimacy*, 70–85, on the other.

49. For Schmitt, the mere fact that a coalition of parties can muster a majority on a particular issue does not justify permitting it to bring down the current government. If a majority is composed of parties with diametrically opposed positions, and if this temporary majority supports a vote of no confidence under Art. 54 merely as a means of obstruction, rather than as a way of furthering a positive government program, then there is no duty of the government to step down, particularly when the President has already ordered the dissolution of the Reichstag. *Constitutional Theory*, 345.

Unless otherwise indicated, all page references in this introduction are to

Schmitt's 1928 edition, the page numbers of which are included in brackets in the translated text.

Schmitt's concern about negative majorities was widely shared during the Weimar era. See, for example, Heinrich Herrfahrdt, *Die Kabinettsbildung nach der Weimarer Verfassung unter dem Einfluss der politischen Praxis* (Berlin: O. Liebmann, 1927), the most likely inspiration for Art. 67 of the Basic Law (the current German constitution), which provides for a "constructive vote of no confidence." Under the postwar provision, a vote of no confidence is only permissible when a majority opposed to the current government can itself agree on a successor government.

50. This is the central argument of *Hüter der Verfassung*.

51. Four members of Schmitt's family served as priests and were engaged on the Catholic side in the religious and political controversies of the early 1870s known as the *Kulturkampf*, in which Bismarck's government introduced a series of aggressively discriminatory anticlerical laws. Schmitt was quite proud of the Catholic resistance to the German state, and he would remain loyal to the Catholic cause well into the Weimar Republic. Though Schmitt never joined a political party during the Weimar Republic, he was closely associated with the authoritarian wing of the Catholic Center Party, which stressed the enforcement of natural law over individual liberties as a guiding principle and was thus opposed to the form of interest group politics associated with modern democracy that is either pluralist or concerned with social welfare. Schmitt's early scholarly work reflected this Catholic outlook. The state had a special mission upholding moral principles, he argued, and this mission had priority over the enforcement of individual liberties. Moreover, the Catholic Church could mediate cases of conflict over the nature of these moral principles or how they should be realized. Bendersky, *Theorist for the Reich*, 3–7. See generally G. L. Ulmen, "Introduction" to Carl Schmitt, *Roman Catholicism and Political Form* (Westport, Conn.: Greenwood Press, 1996).

52. These rights are Art. 114 (personal liberty), Art. 115 (inviolability of the home), Art. 117 (confidentiality of communications), Art. 118 (freedom of expression), Art. 123 (freedom of assembly), Art. 124 (freedom of association), and Art. 153 (right to property).

53. On the exercise of emergency powers during Weimar, see Rossiter, *Constitutional Dictatorship*, 31–73; Finn, *Constitutions in Crisis*, 139–78, esp. 175–77; and Watkins, *Failure of Constitutional Emergency Powers* .

54. This is a principal theme of Schmitt, *Legality and Legitimacy*, trans. and ed. Jeffrey Seitzer (Durham: Duke University Press, 2004). See also Finn, *Constitutions in Crisis*, 145.

55. Gerhard Anschütz, *Die Verfassung des deutschen Reiches vom 11. August 1919: Ein Kommentar für Wissenschaft und Praxis* (Berlin: Verlag von Georg Stilte, 1930), 1–28.

56. Ibid., 3–15.

57. Richard Thoma, "On the Ideology of Parliamentarism (1925)," in Carl Schmitt, *The Crisis of Parliamentary Democracy*, trans. Ellen Kennedy (Cambridge, Mass.: MIT Press, 1985), 79–80.

58. See also *Hüter der Verfassung*, 89.

59. Reinhard Mehring, "Carl Schmitts Lehre von der Auflösung des Liberalismus:

Das Sinnegefüge der 'Constitutional Theory' als historisches Urteil," *Zeitschrift der Politik* 38 (1991); 200–216; and Scheuerman, "Is Parliamentarism in Crisis?" 142.

60. Max Weber, "Parliament and Government in a Reconstructed Germany: A Contribution to the Political Critique of Officialdom and Party Politics," in *Economy and Society: An Outline of Interpretive Sociology*, ed. Guenter Roth and Claus Wittich (Berkeley: University of California Press, [1918] 1978), esp. preface and 1449–59).

61. Ibid., 1451–59. Guenther Roth and Wolfgang Schluchter, *Max Weber's Vision of History: Ethics and Methods* (Berkeley: University of California Press, 1979), 195–206, offer a good discussion of Weber's approach to history in his political writings. For an attempt to apply Weber's theory of ideal types to the issue of institutional borrowing between systems, see J. W. B. Allison, *A Continental Distinction in the Common Law: A Historical and Comparative Perspective on English Public Law* (Oxford: Clarendon Press, 1996).

62. Max Weber, *The Methodology of the Social Sciences*, trans. and ed. Edward S. Shils and Henry A. Finch (Glencoe, Ill.: Free Press, 1949), 104.

63. Ibid. Weber is referring to Constant's famous essay "The Liberty of the Ancients Compared with That of the Moderns," in *Benjamin Constant: Political Writings*, trans. and ed. Biancamaria Fontana (Cambridge: Cambridge University Press, 1988), 307–28.

64. Weber, *Methodology*, 98.

65. On Schmitt's relation to Weber, see Reinhard Mehring, "Politische Ethik in Max Webers 'Politik als Beruf' and Carl Schmitts 'Der Begriff des Politischen,'" *Politische Vierteljahresschrift*, 31, 4 (1990): 608–26, and "Schmitts Lehre"; Wolfgang Mommsen, *Max Weber and German Politics, 1890–1920*, trans. Michael S. Steinberg (Chicago: University of Chicago Press, [1959] 1984), 381–89; Seitzer, *Comparative History and Legal Theory*, 22–35; Rune Slagstad, "Liberal Constitutionalism and Its Critics: Carl Schmitt and Max Weber, in *Constitutionalism and Democracy*, ed. Jon Elster and Rune Slagstad (Cambridge: Cambridge University Press, 1988); and G. L. Ulmen, "The Sociology of the State: Carl Schmitt and Max Weber," *State, Culture, Society* 1 (1985): 3–57, and *Politische Mehrwert: Eine Studie über Max Weber and Carl Schmitt* (Weinheim: VCH Acta humaniora, 1991).

66. See, for example, Reinhard Bendix, *Nation-Building and Citizenship: Studies of Our Changing Social Order* (Berkeley: University of California Press, [1964] 1977).

67. Schmitt, *Hüter der Verfassung*, 71–108.

68. Ibid., 71–72. On this section of *Guardian*, see Seitzer, *Comparative History and Legal Theory*, 41–71.

69. Alexis de Tocqueville, *The Old Regime and the French Revolution*, trans. Stuart Gilbert (Garden City, N.Y.: Doubleday, 1955), 32–41, 57–60, esp. 72–77; and Tocqueville, *Democracy in America*, trans. George Lawrence and ed. J. P. Mayer (New York: Harper and Row, 1969), 61–98, esp. 87–98.

70. Mary K. Geiter and W. A. Speck, "Anticipating America: American Mentality before the Revolution," in *Britain and America: Studies in Comparative History, 1760–1970*, ed. David Englander (New Haven: Yale University Press, 1997), 26–50.

71. Gail Bossenga, "City and State: An Urban Perspective on the Origins of the French Revolution," in *The French Revolution and the Creation of Modern Political*

Culture, ed. Keith Baker (Oxford: Pergamon Press, 1987), 1:115–40, esp. 131–34; also P. M. Jones, *Reform and Revolution in France: the Politics of Transition, 1774–1791* (Cambridge: Cambridge University Press, 1995), 176–214.

72. On the complex and ever changing relationships among theory and practice in the American Revolution, see Gordon S. Wood, *The Creation of the American Republic, 1776–1787* (New York: W. W. Norton, [1969] 1972).

73. Weber, *Methodology*, 97.

74. Seitzer, *Comparative History and Legal Theory*, 1–40.

75. Werner Weber, "Der Einbruch politischer Stände in die Demokratie," in Weber, *Spannungen und Kräfte im westdeutschen Verfassungssystem* (Stuttgart: Vorwerk, 1951), 39–64; Ernst Forsthoff, "Verfassungsprobleme des Sozialstaats," in *Rechtsstaatlichkeit und Sozialstaatlichkeit*, ed. Ernst Forsthoff (Darmstadt: Wissenschaftliche Buchgesellschaft, 1968), 145–64.

76. Otto Kirchheimer, "Verfassungswirklichkeit und politische Zukunft der Arbeiterbewegung," in Kirchheimer, *Von der Weimarer Republik zum Faschismus: Die Auflösung der demokratischen Rechtsordnung*, ed. Wolfgang Luthardt (Frankfurt a. M.: Suhrkamp, 1976), 69–76, esp. 73.

77. Otto Kirchheimer, "Weimar—und was dann? Analyse einer Verfassung," in Kirchheimer, *Politik und Verfassung* (Frankfurt a. M.: Suhrkamp, 1964), 9–56, esp. 54.

78. See Franz Neumnn, "The Concept of Political Freedom," *Columbia Law Review* 53, 7 (1953): 901–35.

79. Jürgen Habermas, *Strukturwandel der Öffentlichkeit: Untersuchungen zu einer Kategorie der bürgerlichen Gesellschaft*, with an introduction for the new edition (Frankfurt a. M.: Suhrkamp, 1990), 294.

80. Ibid., 273.

81. Jürgen Habermas, *Legitimationsprobleme im Spätkapitalismus* (Frankfurt a. M.: Suhrkamp, 1973), 68–69.

82. See Ulrich K. Preuß, *Legalität und Pluralismus: Beiträge zum Verfassungsrecht der Bundesrepublik Deutschland* (Frankfurt a. M.: Suhrkamp, 1973), 63.

83. Ulrich K. Preuß, "Zum Begriff der Verfassung," in *Zum Begriff der Verfassung: Die Ordnung des Politischen*, ed. Ulrich K. Preuß (Frankfurt a. M.: Fischer, 1994), 7–33.

84. In a slightly earlier work, Schmitt observes that "the people are precisely those who do not have official functions, who do not govern" (Carl Schmitt, *Volksentscheid und Volksbegehren: Ein Beitrag zur Auslegung der Weimarer Verfassung und zur Lehre von der unmittelbaren Demokratie* (Berlin: Walter de Gruyter, 1927), 33.

85. Elsewhere he states that "acclamation" is the "most genuine activity, capacity, and function of the people." He concludes here by claiming that there is "no state without a people, no people without acclamation." Ibid., 34.

86. Ibid., 36.

87. Ibid., 35.

88. Gerhard Leibholz, "Der Strukturwandel der modernen Demokratie," in *Strukturprobleme der modernen Demokratie* (Karlsruhe: C. F. Müller, 1967), 78–131.

89. Neumann, "The Concept of Political Freedom," esp. 928.

90. Cristi, *Carl Schmitt and Authoritarian Liberalism*, 33.

91. For examples of this technocratic antihumanism, see Hans Freyer, *Theorie des gegenwärtigen Zeitalters* (Stuttgart: Deutsche Verlags-Anstalt, 1955), 97; also Helmut Schelsky, "Der Mensch in der wissenschaftlichen Zivilisation," in Schelsky, *Auf der Suche nach der Wirklichkeit: Gesammelte Aufsätze* (Düsseldorf: Eugen Diederich, 1965), 439–80.

92. Arnold Gehlen, "Soziologische Voraussetzungen im gegenwärtigen Staat," in Forsthoff, *Rechtsstaatlichkeit und Sozialstaatlichkeit*, 320–39; 337–38.

93. Ernst Forsthoff, "Zur heutigen Situation einer Verfassungslehre," in *Epirrhosis: Festgabe für Carl Schmitt*, ed. Hans Barion (Berlin: Duncker und Humblot, 1968), 185–211.

94. See Michael King and Chris Thornhill, *Niklas Luhmann's Theory of Politics and Law* (Basingstoke, U.K.: Palgrave, 2003), 76.

95. Niklas Luhmann, *Die Wirtschaft der Gesellschaft* (Frankfurt a. M.: Suhrkamp, 1988), 142.

96. See Otto Koellreutter, *Grundfragen des völkischen und staatlichen Lebens im deutschen Volksstaate* (Berlin: Pan-Verlagsgesellschaft, 1935).

97. On the critical and covertly anti-Nazi intentions underlying Schmitt's analyses of politics and the state in the late 1930s, see George Schwab, introduction to Carl Schmitt, *The Leviathan in the State Theory of Thomas Hobbes: Meaning and Failure of a Political Symbol*, trans. George Schwab and Erna Hilfstein, Contributions in Political Science, Nr. 374 (Westport, Conn.: Greenwood Press, 1996), ix–xxxii, esp. x.

98. As an example of this, consider John Rawls, who expressly defines his liberalism as political liberalism but still only sees the political content of his liberalism as residing in its insistence that power should be based in the residual overlapping consensus between reasonable social groups in a pluralized society. John Rawls, *Political Liberalism* (New York: Columbia University Press, 1996), 192. For a good recent critique of the depoliticizing tendencies in contemporary liberalism, see Glenn Newey, *After Politics: The Rejection of Politics in Contemporary Liberal Philosophy* (London: Palgrave, 2001).

Schmitt's Preface

1. [In the Weimar context, the term *Staatsrecht* refers to the organization and operation of state organs. There is some overlap, therefore, with contemporary constitutional law (*Verfassungsrecht*). However, because Staatsrecht in the Weimar period did not involve constitutional rights, it would be misleading to see it as equivalent to constitutional law, as suggested by Carl Crefield et al., eds., *Rechtswörterbuch* (Munich: C. H. Beck, 2000), 1231. The largely unfamiliar literal rendering "state law" might obscure the limited range of the concept's meaning. I have opted for "public law," though with an important caveat. Germans have a specific term for public law, *öffentliches Recht*, which includes constitutional and state law as well as administrative law (*Verwaltungsrecht*). The reader should keep in mind that unless otherwise indicated, "public law" is a rendering of "Staatsrecht," not "öffentliches Recht." For a history of Staatsrecht that indicates the range of meanings of the term, see Gerhard

Anschütz and Richard Thoma, eds. *Handbuch des deutschen Staatsrecht* (Tübingen: J. C. B. Mohr (Paul Siebeck), 1930–32), 1:1–95. Trans.]

2. [*Allgemeine Staatslehre* sought to consider fully the "'timeless' foundations of the state," rather than merely the characteristics and scope of currently valid law. Michael Stolleis, *Geschichte des öffentlichen Rechts in Deutschland* (Munich: C. H. Beck, 1992), 2:423. It arguably reached its apex in Georg Jellinek's monumental *General Theory of the State* (Berlin: Verlag von Julius Springer, [1900] 1922). Jellinek examines the state from every conceivable angle. Among the many issues considered are the purpose of state theory (ibid., 3–24), the history of state theory (53–70), and even "the name of the state" (129–35). Throughout this comprehensive treatment, Jellinek insists on distinguishing clearly between empirical and normative dimensions of his subject. The work is divided, for example, into sections treating either an empirical or a normative issue. And in an extensive methodological discussion early in the work (25–52), Jellinek emphasizes the need to achieve methodological clarity about the nature of concepts in state theory (34–42). Trans.]

3. [Schmitt discusses many features of the German constitutional system in detail. We have also touched on some aspects of it in the introduction to this work, and other aspects will be addressed in subsequent explanatory notes. Nonetheless, a brief overview of the institutional changes introduced by the Weimar Constitution will aid the reader in evaluating Schmitt's argument.

The unification of Germany under Bismarck's Reich Constitution in 1871 was achieved by combining elements of the traditional German state and democratic reforms. The new national parliament, the Reichstag, was elected by universal manhood suffrage. As the lower house of parliament, the Reichstag could introduce legislation, and proposed legislation, including the annual budget, required its approval. Nonetheless, it did not mark the advent of a unified, fully democratic German polity, for the true center of authority remained the executive branch, particularly the plural executive in the upper house of parliament, the Bundesrat.

Composed of delegations of the various state governments, the Bundesrat voted on proposed statutes, including constitutional amendments, and supervised the administration of Reich statutes. In fact, the Bundesrat, not the Kaiser, had the veto power over legislation passed by the Reichstag. The Kaiser, however, appointed the Chancellor, who chaired the Bundesrat, and the Chancellor was responsible to the Kaiser, not the Reichstag. With the consent of the Bundesrat, the Kaiser could declare war; he was commander of the armed forces and opened and closed the sessions of both houses of parliament.

The rise of mass political parties at the end of the nineteenth century, particularly the Social Democrats, and the corresponding political decline of the bourgeoisie did not bring about fundamental changes in the system. Because only fourteen votes were required to block a constitutional amendment in the Bundesrat, Prussia was able to prevent any significant change in the system. And, until the Weimar Republic, conservatives controlled the Prussian delegation because of the Prussian three-tiered electoral system weighted heavily in favor of the wealthy, providing conservatives disproportionate political influence in the system overall.

This basic dualistic structure took on a new form with the collapse of the monarchy after World War I. Under the Weimar Constitution, the upper house, now the Reichsrat, had a much less important position. It remained composed of Land delegations, with an undivided Prussia still the largest by far. However, the Prussian provinces were not empowered to select some of the Prussian delegation, reducing the power of the Prussian government, and the Prussian tripartite electoral system was eliminated, lessening the hold of conservatives on the Land government. More important, the Reichsrat no longer had a role in adjudicating constitutional disputes among Lands, this role having been shifted to the new Staatsgerichtshof and the existing Reichsgericht. Also, the Reichsrat could only object to Reichstag legislation by exercising a suspensive veto that could be overridden by a two-thirds majority or by a referendum. The Reichsrat was reduced to advising the Reich government on proposed legislation and supervising administration that affected Land affairs.

Rather than concentrating all authority in the Reichstag, the Weimar Constitution divided authority between the Reichstag, on the one hand, and the President and the Reich government, on the other. The Reichstag, elected by universal suffrage in a system of proportional representation, had the power of initiative for both ordinary legislation and constitutional amendments, could pass a vote of no confidence in the Reich government, and demand the presence of its ministers to answer questions about the exercise of their lawful authority. The Reichstag could also demand a recall vote for the President, order the suspension of presidential action taken under Art. 48, and, by petition of 100 members, compel the President to appear before the Staatsgerichtshof regarding an alleged violation of law on his part, a power the Reichstag did not have in regard to the Kaiser.

In formal terms, the Reichstag had the authority to enforce its will against the President and the Reich government. The President's powers, however, were considerable and well adapted to use in times of political instability and parliamentary paralysis. Besides appointing the Chancellor, the President was commander in chief of the armed forces, which, under Art. 48, he could use to enforce Reich law against the Lands and keep domestic peace and restore order. The President could also dissolve parliament and call for new elections, though not twice for the same reason. The authority to dissolve parliament at key points proved an effective means of countering parliamentary efforts to control the exercise of presidential emergency powers.

On the German concept of the state, see Rupert Emerson, *State and Sovereignty in Modern Germany* (Westport, Conn.: Hyperion Press, [1928] 1979); and Leonard Krieger, *The German Idea of Freedom: History of a Political Tradition* (Boston: Beacon Press, 1957). Ernst-Wolfgang Böckenförde, "Die Bedeutung der Unterscheidung von Staat und Gesellschaft im demokratischen Sozialstaat der Gegenwart," in *Recht, Staat, Freiheit: Studien zu Rechtsphilosophie, Staatstheorie and Verfassungsgeschichte* (Frankfurt a. M.: Suhrkamp, 1991), provides a history of the state/society distinction. On the German political system in the Reich and Weimar periods, see Peter C. Caldwell, *Popular Sovereignty and the Crisis of German Constitutional Law: The Theory and Practice of Weimar Constitutionalism* (Durham: Duke University Press, 1997), 23, 27, 68, and 70. Trans.]

4. [Both *Gesetz* and *Recht* can be translated simply as "law." Doing so, however, would obscure the rich texture of German legal terminology. Moreover, since part of Schmitt's purpose is to redraw some of the boundaries among traditional legal

concepts, it is necessary to distinguish among types of law and administrative instruments to the extent possible without violating accepted English usage.

Law in the formal sense (*Gesetz im formellen Sinn*) refers to statutes produced by legislatures through formal lawmaking procedures. Law in the substantive sense (*Gesetz im materiellen Sinn*) refers to forms of law containing legal rules. The latter form of Gesetz can include customary law (*Gewohnheitsrecht*), which is not written law, as well as some administrative instruments that have the force of law (e.g., *Rechtsverordnungen*). Recht, by contrast, refers to laws generally, whether written or unwritten, formal or substantive, but it can also mean justice. For a brief overview of the sources of the law in Germany, see Nigel Foster, *German Legal System and Laws* (London: Blackstone Press, 1996), 51–53.

Often, Schmitt does not make explicit reference to the classic formulations of law in the formal or substantive sense. It is necessary to discern from the context whether he is referring to statutes in the narrow formal sense or legal instruments containing a legal rule that are not the product of the formal lawmaking procedures of parliament. Even in these instances, however, a clear distinction is often not available. Schmitt is calling attention to what he considers a fundamental, and detrimental, change in the understanding of statutes under the Weimar Constitution. A statute, in Schmitt's view, should not merely be a product of the formal lawmaking procedures of parliament, in this case the Reichstag. It should also meet certain other criteria, most notably the generality requirement. In other words, a statute should not apply to individuals or to a particular instance, as would typically be the case with an administrative law instrument. Rather, it should be applicable generally and beyond the immediate instance. Schmitt's preferred understanding of a statute, therefore, combines the formal and substantive concepts outlined above.

Schmitt's argument also involves myriad administrative law terms. *Maßnahmen*, or measures, is a general term that can refer to any one of several administrative law instruments, such as decrees (*Verordnungen*) and orders (*Anordnungen*). Art. 48, for example, which empowers the President to take extraordinary action under certain conditions, refers to Maßnahmen, even though presidential action under Art. 48 typically took the form of decrees (Verordnungen) and, less frequently, orders (Anordnungen). Mostly, however, the term *measures* (Maßnahmen) is meant to refer to administrative law instruments that do not apply beyond the particular case. As noted, decrees under certain conditions can have the force of law in that they contain a legal rule that applies beyond the particular case (*Rechtsverordnungen*). Keeping in mind that there is no hard-and-fast rule, one can set up a hierarchy of administrative law instruments, proceeding from the highest potential level of generality to the lowest: decrees with the force of law (Rechtsverordnungen); simple decrees (Verordnungen), which may or may not have the force of law; orders (Anordnungen) and rulings or judgments (*Verfügungen*), which tend to apply to a particular instance, though these might have more lasting consequences; and instructions (*Anweisungen*), which are usually merely internal administrative directives. Trans.]

5. [The Reichsgericht was the only national court during the Reich period. Established in 1877, it had appellate jurisdiction in civil and criminal cases. The Reichsgericht was retained under the Weimar Constitution, though it took a decidedly

different posture. Reflecting the German tradition of a judiciary deferential toward state authority, the Reichsgericht did not question the constitutionality of Reich laws prior to the Weimar Republic. In the post–World War I era, the Reichsgericht, along with the other newly established high courts, the *Reichsfinanzgericht* (Federal Tax Court) and the *Reichsarbeitsgericht* (Federal Labor Court), claimed the power of judicial review. Art. 13 of the Weimar Constitution permitted high courts to review cases of conflict between Reich and Land laws. As was the case in the United States, such issues of federal supremacy provided courts the opportunity to consider the constitutionality of laws, but this did not constitute an explicit grant of the authority of judicial review. Nonetheless, the President of the Reichsgericht from 1922 to 1929, Walter Simons, advocated a role for the Reichsgericht in German politics comparable to that exercised by the U.S. Supreme Court. The Reichsgericht did find a number of laws in violation of the Constitution. Despite this newfound judicial assertiveness, however, the Reichsgericht never attained the position in German politics envisioned by Simons, remaining most of the time quite careful not to challenge state authority directly.

On the history and institutional features of the Reichsgericht prior to Weimar, see Kai Müller, *Der Hüter des Rechts: Die Stellung des Reichsgerichts im deutschen Kaiserreich, 1879–1918* (Baden-Baden: Nomos, 1997). The personnel and institutional features of the Reichsgericht in the Weimar period are covered extensively in Adolf Lobe, ed., *Fünzig Jahre Reichsgericht* (Berlin: Walter de Gruyter, 1929). On judicial review during the Weimar period, see Knut Wolfgang Nörr, *Richter zwischen Gesetz und Wirklichkeit: Die Reaktion des Reichsgerichts auf die Krisen von Weltkrieg und Inflation, und die Entfaltung eines neues richterlichen Selbstverständnis* (Heidelberg: C. F. Müller, 1996); Gertrude Lübbe-Wolff, "Safeguards of Civil and Constitutional Rights—the Debate on the Role of the Reichsgericht," in *German and American Constitutional Thought: Contexts, Interaction and Historical Realities*, ed. Hermann Wellenreuter (New York: Berg, 1990); and Caldwell, *Popular Sovereignty and Crisis*, 145–70. Johannes Mattern, *Principles of the Constitutional Jurisprudence of the German National Republic* (Baltimore: Johns Hopkins Press, 1928), 249–56, examines the jurisdictional grant of Art. 13 and the decisions reached on the basis of it. Trans.]

6. [Like the Anglo-American idea of the rule of law, the Rechtsstaat entails legal limitations on the conduct of government. An important difference is that the rule of law involves the consent of the governed in some form, whether expressed in terms of democratic control of the state or more implicitly, such as in tacit acceptance of common-law principles. The Rechtsstaat concept, by contrast, did not always necessarily entail consent of the governed. Limitations on the conduct of state action in early nineteenth-century Germany, for example, were conceived as acts of grace by monarchs and their governments. Though the monarchs need not have granted political and civil rights, once conferred on the citizenry these legal limitations were genuine restraints on state action. Over the course of the nineteenth century, Germans received significant degrees of legal protection from arbitrary state action, even though they often did not have full rights of political participation in a democratic government. Because the state could define itself only through law, it expanded the sphere of law as it extended the reach of its own authority, perfecting the Rechtsstaat idea without ever becoming fully democratic.

Notes to Schmitt's Preface

For leading nineteenth-century understandings of the concept, see Robert von Mohl, *Das Staatsrecht des Königreich Württemberg* (Tübingen, 1829), 1:8; and Friedrich Julius Stahl, *Die Philosophie des Rechts* (1837), vol. 2, sec. 36. Konrad Hesse, "Der Rechtsstaat im Verfassungssystem des Grundgesetzes," in *Staatsverfassung und Kirchenordnung: Festgabe für Rudolf Smend zum 80 Geburtstag am 15 Januar 1962*, ed. Konrad Hesse, Siegfried Reicke, and Ulrich Scheuner (Tübingen: J. C. B. Mohr [Paul Siebeck], 1962), is an influential contemporary account of the more directly legal aspects of the Rechtsstaat. On its history, see Böckenförde, "Entstehung und Wandel des Rechtsstaatsbegriffs," in *Recht, Staat, Freiheit*; and Ingeborg Maus, "Entwicklung und Funktionswandel der Theorie des bürgerlichen Rechtsstaats," in *Rechtstheorie und politische Theorie im Industriekapitalismus* (Munich: Wilhelm Fink, 1986). Trans.]

7. [Unless otherwise indicated, all page references will be to the original German edition. Trans.]

1. Absolute Concept of the Constitution

1. [The legislative-reservation clauses (*Gesetzesvorbehalte*) reflect the German understanding of the role of the legislature in rights protection prior to the Federal Republic. Under absolutist monarchies of the seventeenth and eighteenth centuries, the German state was understood as an impersonal entity with a purpose independent of the strivings of the individuals and groups that constituted society. The concept of the independent state remained vibrant into the Weimar Republic, though in modified form, and was particularly important to Schmitt. The important change concerned the institutional connections between state and society. Specifically, the liberal reforms of the nineteenth century in many parts of Germany instituted what is commonly termed "constitutional dualism," under which the state and its executive retained a considerable degree of independence from society. However, for certain actions, in particular, those that interfered with the freedom and property of citizens, the state required the consent of society represented in the legislature. In contrast to Americans, therefore, who viewed both the executive and legislature as potential threats to citizens' rights, nineteenth-century Germans looked to the legislature as the primary guarantor of rights against an overbearing executive. The people's representatives in parliament, it was thought, would not infringe on their own liberties, so German rights provisions typically proclaimed that a right could not be infringed "unless by law." Such provisions are explicit grants to parliament to enact restrictions on rights. Article 118 of the Weimar Constitution, for example, permits statutory exceptions to the right of freedom of opinion. See Ernst-Wolfgang Böckenförde, *Gesetz und gesetzgebende Gewalt: Von den Anfänger der deutschen Staatsrechtslehre bis zur Höhe des staatsrechtlichen Positivismus* (Berlin: Duncker und Humblot, 1981), esp. 271–80; and Michael Stolleis, *Geschichte des öffentlichen Rechts in Deutschland* (Munich: C. H. Beck, 1992), 2:111. Trans.]

2. On the opposition of Power (Macht) (potestas) and Auctoritas, cf. the remarks to § 8, p. 75.

4. Ideal Concept of the Constitution

1. [Schmitt includes the English translation of "freie Regierung" in quotation marks, which would be redundant here. Trans.]

2. [*Unterscheidung* and *Trennung* are typically rendered "distinction" and "separation," respectively. However, speaking of a "distinction of powers" would be confusing to an English reader in this context. So I have used the more conventional "separation of powers" for *Gewaltenunterscheidung* and *Unterscheidung der Gewalten*, while Trennung retains its standard meaning of "separation." *Teilung* is usually rendered "division." I have adhered to this except where it might again be confusing to English readers. In such cases, I have used "separation of powers" as well. Trans.]

5. Meanings of the Term "Basic Law"

1. [The term used here, the past tense of *durchbrechen,* refers to a debate during the Weimar Republic on the legitimacy of a *Verfassungsdurchbrechung.* In other words, can a qualified Reichstag majority (i.e. a two-thirds majority capable of formally amending the constitution) pass a statute that directly violates a constitutional provision without making a formal change in the constitutional text. Horst Ehmke provides an excellent review of the origins of the disputed concept and the response to the problem in the early Federal Republic. See "Verfassungsänderung und Verfassungsdurchbrechung," in *Beiträge zur Verfassungstheorie und Verfassungspolitik,* ed. Peter Häberle (Königstein: Athenäum Verlag, 1981).

There is no direct English equivalent for this term, so any rendering will be somewhat awkward. I have used either "rupture" or "violate" depending on the stylistic demands of the particular passage. Trans.]

6. Origin of the Constitution

1. According to G. Jellinek, *Allgemeine Staatslehre,* p. 465, the public law of the German Reich includes the concept of the basic law (lex fundamentalis) since the Peace of Westphalia. Nevertheless, the word occurs earlier in the public law literature and designates the Golden Bull of 1356, the electoral concessions of the electors with the Kaiser and the written results of the Reichstag. See, for example, Arumaeus, *Discursus academici de iure publico,* Jena 1616, p. 65, 1007, disc. XXXIII.

8. The Constitution-Making Power

1. The distinction of power and authority need not be further elaborated for the continuing exposition of this constitutional theory. Nevertheless, it is briefly outlined here because of its great significance for the general theory of the state. Concepts such as sovereignty and majesty by necessity always correspond only to

effective power. Authority, by contrast, denotes a profile that rests essentially on the element of *continuity* and refers to tradition and duration. Both power and authority are, combined with one another, effective and vital in every state. The classic juxtaposition is also found in Roman public law. The *senate* had *auctoritas*; *potestas* and *imperium*, by contrast, are derived from the *people*. According to Mommsen, *Römisches Staatsrecht*, III, p. 1033, auctoritas is a "word that defies any strict definition." According to Victor Ehrenberg, "Monumentum Antiochenum," *Klio*, vol. XIX, 1924, pp. 202/3, the word denotes something "ethical-social," a "position oddly mixed together from political power and social prestige" that "rests on supplements and social validity." Cf. further v. Premerstein in the journal *Hermes*, vol. 59, 1924, p. 104. Also R. Heinze, *Hermes*, vol. 60, 1925, p. 345, and Richard Schmidt, *Verfassungsaufbau und Weltreichsbildung*, Leipzig 1926, p. 38. Despite its subsequent powerlessness, the Senate retained its authority, and, in the imperial period, it ultimately became the sole organ still able to confer something like "legitimacy" after the power of the Roman people perished in the Empire. In reference to the emperor, the roman *pope* also claimed for himself auctoritas (not potestas) in the special sense, while the emperor had potestas. The manner of expression in St. Gelasius I's letter to the emperor Anastasius from the year 494 is especially apt in this regard and, as an often cited document dominating the great polemic of the tenth and eleventh centuries, is especially meaningful: "Duo sunt quibus principaliter mundus hic regitur: *auctoritas sacra pontificum et regalis potestas*" (Migne, *Patr. Lat.* 59, p. 42 A; Carl Mirbt, *Quellen zur Geschichte des Papstums*, 3d ed., pp. 67, 122, 123).

Perhaps the distinction is of interest also for the clarification of currently relevant questions. One could raise the question whether the League of Nations has a potestas or auctoritas that is different from the potestas or auctoritas of the states directing it. Previously, the League of Nations was permitted to have neither [76] independent potestas nor its own auctoritas. On the contrary, one can certainly say that the standing International Court of Justice in The Hague has authority. It naturally has no potestas. Nevertheless, the authority of a court of justice, because of the bond of the judge to the valid law, is again a special case of authority and is not actually *political* because due to this normative bond it does not have its own political existence, and its pouvoir, after the expression of Montesquieu, is "en quelque façon nul" (cf. p. 185). The question of the extent to which both concepts, power and authority, correspond to the principles of political form, identity, and representation presented below (p. 204), would be developed most optimally in a general *theory of the state*.

2. [William Barclay (1546–1608), who introduced the term in the title of a work published in 1600, intended to emphasize hostility toward the emerging absolute monarchs. Subsequent writers associated with the term, such as Theodor Beza (1519–1605) and François Hotman (1524–90), did not reject kingship. They were concerned, rather, with restoring the traditional rights of the estates vis-à-vis monarchs. See Jürgen Dennert, comp., *Beza, Brutus, Hotman: Calvinistische Monarchomachen*, trans. Hans Klingelhöfer (Cologne: Westdeutscher Verlag, 1968). Trans.]

11. The Concept of the Constitution

1. [*Kompetenz-Kompetenz* refers to the nineteenth-century theory that the Reich had an unlimited authority to define the extent of its own authority. Michael Stolleis, *Geschichte des öffentlichen Rechts in Deutschland*, vol. 2: *Staatsrechtslehre un Verwaltungswissenschaft 1800–1914* (Munich: Verlag C. H. Beck, 1992), 2:358, 367. Trans.]

2. [The asterisks at several points in this paragraph referred to a number 8 at the bottom of the original p. 115. Trans.]

3. [The Staatsgerichtshof differed from the other high courts in the Weimar Republic in that it was only convened on occasion to address particular questions brought to it by governmental officials, with its composition varying according to the issue at hand. Moreover, the fact that Art. 19 constituted an explicit grant of authority to consider a range of constitutional questions in the area of federalism, while Art. 59 established a complaint procedure allowing the Reichstag to challenge actions by the President, the Reich government, and its ministers, together suggest that the Staatsgerichtshof was meant to function like a constitutional court. Though the Staatsgerichtshof decided a number of very important cases, it never exercised significant control over governmental action, rarely challenging state action, particularly that taken under Art. 48. For an analysis of the Staatsgerichtshof's jurisdiction and a review of its decisions, see Johannes Mattern, *Principles of the Constitutional Jurisprudence of the German National Republic* (Baltimore: Johns Hopkins University Press, 1928), 266–304. Trans.]

12. The Bourgeois Rechtsstaat

1. [Article 31 of the Weimar Constitution established an Electoral Review Commission (*Wahlprüfungsgericht*) to settle electoral disputes. It was to function procedurally somewhat like an administrative court, though it was to be composed of an unspecified number of the members of the Reichstag, who were chosen for the duration of the current session and of the members of the anticipated National Administrative Court (*Reichsverwaltungsgericht*), which was never established. Instead, judges were selected from the Reichsgericht. Three members from the Reichstag and two from the Reichsgericht formed a quorum necessary for judgment, which could be rendered only after a public hearing. When the commission was not conducting a hearing prior to a judgment, a national commissioner appointed by the President led its proceedings. For an overview of the commission's history, composition, jurisdiction, and procedure, see Georg Kaisenberg, "Die Wahlprüfung," in *Handbuch des deutschen Staatsrechts*, ed. Gerhart Anschütz and Richard Thoma (Tübingen: J. C. B. Mohr, 1930–32); and Johannes Mattern, *Principles of the Constitutional Jurisprudence of the German National Republic* (Baltimore: Johns Hopkins Press, 1928), 428–29.

"Electoral Review Court" would be a more literal rendering. The term *commission*, however, better captures the combination of adjudication and administration characteristic of the administrative state in the United States. Trans.]

13. The Rechtsstaat Concept of Law

1. [Schmitt includes this phrase in English. I have deleted it to avoid repetition. Trans.].

2. In the overview by G. Jellinek, *Gesetz und Verordnung*, p. 113ff., numerous notes are found on the concept of statute. Nevertheless, Jellinek's quotations are extraordinarily prone to misunderstanding and are even incorrect. On p. 113, for example, he introduces an expression of Pfister that directly shows how much the character of the *generality* of the statute had been retained. The misunderstandings of Jellinek go so far that on p. 30 he translates the turn of phrase "without a rule" as "without special (!) provision," while the essential element consists precisely in the fact that it means "without general rule." "Rule" and "will" are confused with one another without distinction (p. 35), and the most astounding thing is Hobbes (p. 45) appears as a proponent of the Aristotelian concept of law.

14. The Basic Rights

1. [Prior to World War I, the Reich government was not the primary institutional locus for regulation of the economy and the provision of welfare services. Municipalities operating under the law of "local self-government" (Selbstverwaltung), which stemmed from the Prussian reforms of the early nineteenth century and became quite common throughout Germany in the nineteenth and early twentieth centuries, were primarily responsible for these governmental functions. The law of local self-government provided local communities considerable autonomy from central (then Land, later Land and Reich) control because, it was thought, local government was merely "society" managing the "technical" details of everyday life that did not impinge on "political" affairs, such as the underlying purpose of the state itself. Under this system, cities operated businesses, regulated industry and commerce, and provided extensive social welfare services, anticipating the welfare and administrative state in the twentieth century.

During World War I, the Reich government became ever more actively involved in regulating the economy and engaging in economic activities. On the basis of an enabling act, the Bundesrat issued hundreds of decrees covering almost every conceivable area of productive activity and economic exchange. The wartime government by decree clearly violated prewar understandings of the priority of the statute and enabled the Reich to attain a level of authority not possible in peacetime, more or less circumventing the complex constitutional arrangements under Bismarck's Reich Constitution. But the general sense was that such actions were temporary deviations from accepted practice necessitated by the war effort.

On local self-government in the German state, see Hans Herzfeld, *Demokratie und Selbstverwaltung in der Weimarer Epoche* (Berlin: Kohlhammer, 1957). For Schmitt's critique of local self-government's role in the tendency toward the quantitative total state, see *Hüter der Verfassung* (Berlin: Duncker und Humblot, [1931] 1985), 92–93. Seitzer, *Comparative History and Legal Theory: Carl Schmitt in the First German Democracy* (Westport, Conn.: Greenwood Press, 2001), 41–71, argues that Schmitt's position on local self-government misunderstands the nature of the independent state in the Reich period. On the issue of the changing role of law in the emerging welfare and administrative state in interwar Germany, see William E. Scheuerman, *Between the Norm and the Exception: The Frankfurt School and the Rule of Law* (Cambridge, Mass.: MIT Press, 1994). For a survey of the administrative measures during World War I and the reaction to them, see Michael Stolleis, *Geschichte des öffentlichen Rechts in Deutschland* (Munich: C. H. Beck, 1999), 3:67–71. Trans.]

15. The Separation of Powers

1. [*Unterscheidung* and *Trennung* are typically rendered "distinction" and "separation," respectively. However, speaking of a "distinction of powers" would be confusing to an English reader in this context. So I have used the more conventional "separation of powers" for *Gewaltenunterscheidung* and *Unterscheidung der Gewalten*, while Trennung retains its standard meaning of "separation." *Teilung* is usually rendered "division." I have adhered to this except where it might again be confusing to English readers. In such cases, I have used "separation of powers" as well. Trans.]

2. On the meaning of this expression, cf. *Die Diktatur*, p. 109. Perhaps the position signifies that the judicial power as such does not have its own political existence, because it is entirely subsumed under the normative element. Montesquieu's profundity is concealed through his apparently aphoristic style and, therefore, escapes notice.

3. [Actually, such an override vote requires a two-thirds majority vote of both houses of Congress. Trans.]

4. [This should read "both houses of Congress." Trans.]

17. The Theory of Democracy

1. Total number of the inhabitants of the English global empire: 453 million

Europe	47 million
Australia	7 million
America	11 million
	65 million overwhelmingly white population
Africa	54 million
Mandates	8 million
Asia	324 million

Total number of the inhabitants of the French area of dominance:

Europe	39 million
Colonies	60 million
Mandates	14 million
	113 million

2. Clause 1 of this much disputed Art. 27 declares property rights over ground and mineral stores inside the borders of the Mexican state to be property of the nation, which is transferred to the individual as private property. Section VIII stipulates that the possibility of obtaining property in land or waterways is guided by the following requirements: 1. only Mexicans, by birth or through naturalization, or Mexican companies have a right to obtain such property or concessions for the exploitation of mines, water works, or valuable minerals. The state can guarantee the same right to foreigners provided that they declare their consent to the Mexican Foreign Office that their private property obtained in this way remains Mexican national property and that they do not call for the protection of their government for the benefit of this private property. If they infringe on this provision, they lose their rights in favor of the Mexican nation. In a zone of 100 kilometers from the coast, a foreigner can under no conditions obtain this direct property over land or water.

25. Development of the Parliamentary System

1. On the "false portrayal" of the voters' will through the individual vote system, see K. Loewenstein, "Minderheitsregierung in Grossbritannien," *Annalen des Deutschen Reiches*, 1925, pp. 61, 52ff. The figures are:

	1924	1923
Total number of the enfranchised	19,949,000	19,174,000
Votes cast	16,120,735	14,186,000
Conservatives	7,385,139	5,360,000
Labour	5,487,620	4,348,000
Liberals	2,982,563	4,252,000

Mandates		
Conservatives	413	258
Labour	151	193
Liberals	40	158
Others	−5	6

The Association for the Proportional System of Representation (Proportional Representation Society [Schmitt's English]) calculates (Loewenstein, p. 54) that among the Conservatives a mandate required 20,000 votes; among Labour 39,000; among the Liberals, by contrast, 90,000. In Scotland, Labour has more votes than Conservatives, but, nevertheless, ten fewer mandates, etc.

26. Formation of the Parliamentary System

1. [Schmitt's play on words involving *Fall*, which might variously be rendered "instance" or "collapse," does not work in English when, as here, it is used in reference to the term for "war," *Krieg*. Trans.]

CARL SCHMITT (1888–1985) was a leading political and legal theorist of the twentieth century. His translated works include *Political Theology: Four Chapters on the Concept of Sovereignty* (1985); *The Crisis of Parliamentary Democracy* (1985); and *The Concept of the Political* (1976).

JEFFREY SEITZER teaches at Roosevelt University. He is the author of *Comparative History and Legal Theory: Carl Schmitt and the First German Democracy* (2001) and editor and translator of Carl Schmitt's *Legality and Legitimacy* (Duke, 2004).

ELLEN KENNEDY is a professor of political science at the University of Pennsylvania. Her books include *Constitutional Failure: Carl Schmitt in Weimar* (Duke, 2004); *The Bundesbank* (1997); and *Freedom and the Open Society: Henri Bergson's Contribution to Political Philosophy* (1987).

CHRISTOPHER THORNHILL is a professor of politics at the University of Glasgow. His books include *German Political Philosophy: The Metaphysics of Law* (2006) and *Political Theory in Modern Germany: An Introduction* (2000).

Index